Experimental
Psychology second edition

Series in Psychology

Experimental

John Wiley & Sons, Inc.

New York • London • Sydney • Toronto

Psychology second edition

Burton G. Andreas

Professor of Psychology

State University of New York

College at Brockport

Library of Congress Catalogue Card Number: 78–171910

ISBN 0–471–02905–X

Printed in the United States of America

10 9 8 7 6 5 4 3 2 1

To Jan

Preface

Continuing advances in experimental psychology demonstrate the vigor of its contribution to our understanding of numerous behavioral processes. Empirical findings from the laboratory proliferate with accelerating pace. More significant for the maturing of psychological science, theoretical constructs are refined, investigative methods are improved, and productive new procedures are invented. These trends point to an ever-increasing quality of research to match its growth in quantity.

This textbook is designed to help students to deepen and expand their knowledge of psychological principles and to sharpen their skills in the laboratory approach to the study of behavior. While Part I introduces many basic concepts and concerns of the experimentalist and elucidates some of his general methods, Part II explores several topical areas with illustrative studies. With additional guidance from their instructors and with their own experiences as generous contributors to learning, students will find that this dual approach yields a broad comprehension of psychological science as it is actively pursued in many laboratories. I feel that drawing on the research literature for examples as well as expounding on methodological matters brings extra strength to instruction. This is the position I took in two symposia on the teaching of experimental psychology that were part of annual programs of the American Psychological Association.

Although I have retained the two-part format and the focus on human behavior studies that characterized the first edition, I felt that a second edition was required in order to represent the new methods and findings that mark the progress of experimental psychology. The material has been broadened to reflect, for example, an intensified interest in the personal attitudes and perceptions of the individuals who serve as subjects in a laboratory study. A new Chapter 14, on *Motivation*, has been added. The inclusion of this major topic with its key concepts of activation, incentive, and reinforcement will help to round out the coverage of human behavior science. Selected areas of investigation that have been retained from the first edition include sensory and perceptual processes; verbal behavior; perceptual-motor performance; memory and transfer; and problem solving and social processes. Studies that offer new illumination of research on these topics are cited. To allow for this updating and for the new chapter, the treatment of statistics was eliminated. The student will usually cover this material in another course or with guidance from other sources.

Work in a laboratory science has long been a valued part of a liberal education. In this regard the study of experimental psychology offers much to any college student, I believe, no matter what his professional or vocational goal. For the student pursuing graduate study in psychology a broad and intensive grounding in research fundamentals is invaluable. Students having either sort of educational aim will profit from this text.

BURTON G. ANDREAS

Brockport, 1971

Acknowledgments

After a three-year effort in educational research and development I returned to experimental psychology in 1970. First, I thank my new colleagues at Brockport who have made me feel very welcome as I joined them in the classroom and the laboratory. Their own studies, ranging broadly over problems in both animal and human behavior, have been a continuing inspiration as I labored over these chapters.

Like the first edition, this text reflects the investigative accomplishments and the methodological and theoretical innovations of scores of scholars. This is evident in the numerous citations of original publications. I am indebted to these psychologists for the information and insights they have shared in their articles and research reports. Students who explore these primary sources will gain a special dividend in their understanding of psychological science.

My deepest appreciation goes to my wife, Jan, to whom this textbook is dedicated. Once again she typed every page of a massive manuscript. And again she assisted with the demanding tasks of proofreading and indexing —all this in addition to enduring my mercurial manifestations of the syndrome designated as authorship.

For permission to quote and to use graphic and tabular material from other sources, I am grateful to numerous individuals, organizations, and publishers: Academic Press; Acoustical Society of America; *The American Journal of Psychology*; American Psychological Association; Professor

R. F. Bales; Professor I. McD. Bilodeau; Professor Charles Haig; Holt, Rinehart and Winston; The Journal Press; Dr. Nathan Kogan, McGraw-Hill Book Company; National Research Council of the National Academy of Sciences; *Psychometrika*; *Psychonomic Science*; Dr. D. H. Raab; The Rockefeller Institute Press; Dr. R. Rosenthal; Southern Universities Press; Dr. M. A. Wallach; and John Wiley & Sons.

Finally, I thank numerous kind people who have helped me in many ways to complete this effort. I am indebted to colleagues, former professors, secretaries, and students for their assistance and encouragement at different times in my exhilarating encounter with experimental psychology. My roles as investigator, as report writer, as textbook author, and even as experimental subject have all yielded satisfaction in sharing in this science of behavior.

B. G. A.

Contents

part 1
Introduction
and
General Methods

chapter 1
Psychology
as the Science
of Behavior

Science is an enterprise of great complexity. It is deeply rooted in history and in prehistorical human curiosity; yet its rapid growth and proliferation are salient characteristics of modern society. Indeed science and society have been strongly interactive in recent centuries. Social and psychological forces have influenced the development of science. Conversely, science has become a major force in social evolution—both through the technological processes and products it has engendered and through its impact on philosophical and political thought.

In spite of the diversity of activities and outlooks of scientists of every stripe, there are some unifying themes in scientists' efforts. In science—an abstract concept that encompasses their endeavors—they cooperate in an inquiry of grand proportions. They seek to observe, to describe, to explain a seemingly infinite number of natural processes and events. In classical antiquity and in more recent times the realm of behavior and experience has captured the attention of some inquirers. Psychology has emerged as a major discipline of science to sustain and refine this line of inquiry.

As a scientific specialty (with numerous special areas of its own), psychology remains a part of science in general. At the same time it has progressed notably in devising its own methods of investigation, using them to search out the regularities of interaction between behavioral and environmental events. In this book we examine, particularly, experimental methods and some of the research findings that focus on human behavior. Studies of animals comprise another domain of inquiry yielding rich information and insights; but experimentation employing human subjects is itself a topic of sufficient scope for a single volume.

The Aim of Psychological Science

Science has a general goal of discovering the regular relationships linking different events and processes in nature. It seeks to express these as an interlocking set of natural laws describing these regularities. This formal statement of the aim of science is of course an abstraction. It is by no means an account of the specific striving of an individual scientist at any given time. He may be working out a way to measure some reaction. He may be analyzing some data he has collected. He may be trying to figure out what went wrong in his latest experiment. He may be trying to develop a hunch into a plan for his next research effort. In the abstract, however, he may be said to be contributing to the general advance of scientific inquiry.

Psychology seeks to find and formulate the laws of behavior. It makes the fundamental assumption that all aspects of behavior, like other natural phenomena, are dependent on the conditions under which the reactions occur. Just as a biologist assumes that a green plant's production of carbohydrates depends on genetic and environmental factors, a psychologist assumes, for example, that a person's learning of verbal material depends on his intellectual endowment and on the conditions surrounding his study of the verbal items. Psychology is aimed at describing such dependence of the activities of people on their environments and their states of being. Psychology's place in the unity of science is delineated by this particular goal and the special methods developed for working toward it. Later as we consider particular aims and techniques of psychological research, we should see them as concrete examples of the broader endeavor of science.

Behavior Laws and Hypotheses

We continue our analysis of experimental psychology by considering the roles played by laws and hypotheses in developing a science of behavior. Psychology shares the assumption common to all of science that the phenomena it studies are lawful. Although it sometimes makes investigators uneasy to have their work so abstractly and formally described, it is a fact that numerous research efforts have led to the discovery and refinement of a great number of psychological principles. Some of these findings apply to broad segments of human activity while others deal with specific reactions in more narrowly defined situations. The scope of accomplishment is indicated in a compendium of research results compiled by Berelson and Steiner (1964). The experimental outcomes they listed range from research in child development to studies of group processes. Here are a few paraphrased examples dealing with sensory functioning, perception, learning, problem solving, and motivation:

1. Visual sensitivity to light increases during time spent in darkness.

2. When a visual display of multiple elements is scanned, perceptual grouping based on physical proximity occurs.

(A simple demonstration: ... ...)

3. Attention is captured by stimuli which contrast sharply with the background.

(This law of perception is exemplified if THIS especially catches your eye).

4. Meaningful verbal material is more readily learned than is material which is relatively devoid of meaning.

5. Using a familiar object in a normal way reduces the probability of then using it in a novel way to solve a problem.

6. A moderately high level of motivation is most beneficial in many learning and problem-solving activities.

These varied examples bear out the assumption that behavior is related in regular ways to environmental stimulation and to the state of the reacting individual.

Before continuing this analysis of psychological science it must be emphasized once more that we are not describing the actual course of activity and thinking in which an investigator is engaged as he pursues his research on a day-to-day basis. This abstract treatment has a different purpose. We are preparing in this discussion to deal later on with the complex interplay between research and theory construction. For this reason we describe the work of the experimenter in a way which may be foreign to his own perceptions of how he proceeds from study to study. He may insist that he is collecting data in his laboratory only to answer some insistent question or to solve some knotty problem. We may say, more formally, that he is testing some hypothesis—one which he may never have stated in the precise terms of the theorist. The results of his experimentation, in any case, should render some hypotheses about behavior more tenable while possibly disconfirming certain other formulations.

Law and Hypothesis

Although psychology seeks ultimately to express numerous behavior laws in a systematic fashion, much research activity centers around the testing of hypotheses. As we shall employ the terms, a hypothesis and a law differ only in the extent of scientific confirmation which has been accomplished. A hypothesis is a tentative law awaiting initial test or requiring further checking before it can be regarded as a law. A law is a hypothesis which has received a relatively high degree of confirmation. Both are conditional statements in their format, stating that *if* certain conditions are established, *then* particular behavioral consequences will follow.

A scientist may hypothesize that "if a line segment is presented in vertical orientation, then it will be judged longer than when it is presented horizontally." If several experiments are performed and it is consistently found that the line-judging behavior of a number of people conforms to his formulation, then his hypothesis may be regarded as a law of perception. The law might be stated in exactly the same words that the hypothesis was. The close correspondence between hypothesis and law, in phrasing as well as in form, thus bears out our definition of a hypothesis as a tentative statement of a law.

Strictly speaking, an experiment does not lead to the absolute confirmation of a hypothesis but only to a considerable increase of confidence in its tenability (assuming it is not rejected on the basis of the experimental observations). The laws of science may be considered, then, as hypotheses in which great confidence has been placed as a result of repeated observations and testing. Research leads from hypothesis to law by increasing the confidence that anyone may have that the stated formulation is indeed tenable. Alternatively, the outcome of research may force the scientist to reformulate the hypothesis so that it is still in agreement with his observations and then to retest it.

A Model for the Form of a Law or Hypothesis

Despite the diversity of ways in which they were stated, all the examples of behavior laws we cited may be paraphrased to correspond to a single form, represented by the model: if A, then B. This model or paradigm helps demonstrate what is meant by a behavior law or hypothesis. As a matter of fact, this paradigm, if A, then B, can be considered as a model for a law formulated in any discipline of science. Let us concentrate here on how we reformulate and amplify some of our psychological laws to conform to it.

Visual sensitivity to light increases over time spent in darkness.

becomes

If the eye is kept in darkness for time t, then its sensitivity to light will reach a level capable of detecting a retinal illuminance value, E.

Similarly,

Meaningful verbal material is more readily learned than material which is relatively devoid of meaning.

becomes

If material studied is meaningful, *then* learning is facilitated.

You will find that you can convert the other examples to the format, if A, then B. Further, you may think of other laws of behavior which may be expressible in the form of this simple if-then model.

Since a hypothesis, like a law, is a conditional statement of the dependence of an event upon preceding and surrounding conditions, it may also be structured like our model: if A, then B. The model serves as a guide as we formulate hypotheses for experimental testing. The "if" clause demands that we specify the conditions surrounding the behavior; the "then" clause requires us to state what effect on behavior is expected or to indicate the response measurements we shall take to see if there has been an effect.

Expansion of the model

A little reflection will convince us that scientific laws often contain numerous factors in their conditional clauses. There are several things besides meaningfulness, for example, that contribute to the memorizing of verbal material. "If A, then B" becomes "if A_1 and if A_2 and if A_3 ... and if A_n, then B." One aim of behavioral science is to discover numerous factors that govern a particular activity. We try to determine how these different factors interact in their effects on the behavior. This searching out of multiple relationships should permit the formulation of various laws that cover most cases of the phenomenon under investigation. The limitation to "most cases" does not mean that the formulations are now and then invalid, but rather that they are incomplete in identifying all the forces or variables which may be interacting in certain instances.

The model in quantitative expression

The different disciplines of science strive to arrive at precise quantitative laws describing phenomena or processes. Our first example of a law, dealing with the course of visual sensitivity change over time in the dark, has been quantified in a number of investigations. Such a quantitative relationship may be cast as a series of if-then relationships. If the eye (under certain experimental conditions) is kept in darkness for 1 minute, then its sensitivity to light will reach a level capable of detecting a retinal illuminance value of 1.0 troland (a standard unit of light intensity measurement). If kept in darkness for 8 min, then it becomes capable of detecting 0.01 troland. If 16 min, then 0.001 troland. The successive pairs of values, determined through laboratory research, have expanded the verbally phrased if-then law into a quantitative relationship that is expressible as a mathematical function. A law in this form would be termed a *functional relationship*. A quantified expression adds precision to a law. This precision is gained only through complete and accurate description of the "certain experimental conditions" under which the data were collected. When the experimental conditions are systematically varied a whole family of functional relationships often emerges. The verbal form for stating the law gives a general description of the numerous functional relationships that might be found as different experimental factors were varied.

The functional relationship as an alternate model

Many attempts to state behavioral laws suggest functional relationships. The experimental approach to quantifying a behavioral law is to vary any factors considered relevant and to look for covariation in some measure of the behavior. If it is observed, this covariation may be expressed as a mathematical equation or functional relationship. When this is done, the paradigm for the law may be changed from "if A, then B" to "$B = f(A)$." This may be read "B is a function of A" or "B is quantitatively dependent upon A." Besides being expressible as a mathematical equation, a functional relationship lends itself readily to graphic portrayal. The illustrative data indicating dark adaptation as a functional relationship are based on one of the curves presented in Chapter 7, Figure 7.2, p. 217. Such a family of curves clearly portrays the course taken by the sensory process and emphasizes the additional effects of different experimental conditions. In Figure 7.2, dark adaptation (sensitivity to lower levels of illuminance as time in the dark increases) is plotted as three different curves to show the influence of three different luminous intensities to which the eye was exposed just before dark adaptation began. The range of visual sensitivities found in this process is so great that a logarithmic scale is used to compress the ordinate of such graphic plots. While we cited values in trolands, the original graph presented the detectable luminous intensities in log microtrolands, as reflected in Figure 7.2.

Dependent and Independent Variables

When a psychologist gathers data to use in formulating a behavioral law, especially in the form of a functional relationship, the measurements of behavior that he makes are generally regarded as *depending* on values of the conditions under which the behavior has occurred. Any behavior measure is therefore termed the *dependent variable* in the formula, $B = f(A)$. The functional relationship is a mathematical expression of the dependence of the behavioral data, B, upon the values of the antecedent conditions, A. With B representing behavior and A standing for antecedent conditions, you can see that B is also the dependent variable in our first paradigm: if A, then B. Antecedent conditions are called *independent variables* in formulations of behavioral laws. In seeking to formulate behavioral laws we can often assign numerical values to these factors or variables. Sometimes we assign them by measuring some given aspect of the environment or some state of the organism; at other times we may experimentally manipulate an environmental factor or a state of the subject to achieve desired values. In either case, the data on these factors are regarded as independent of the behavior that occurs, thus accounting for the term, independent variables. Our models or paradigms for be-havior laws, "if *A*, then *B*" or "$B = f(A)$," are seen to contain terms for both the dependent variable, *B*, which is the measurement of behavior that is taken, and the independent variables, *A*, which are the data de-scribing the antecedent conditions.

Antecedent Conditions as Determinants of Behavior

The domain of natural events that we call "behavior" is extremely broad, ranging from the blink of an eye to the spirited cheering of the crowd at a game. Accounting for the determinants of behavioral phenomena is a monumental undertaking. Behavioral scientists appreciate the enormity of the task and the impossibility of its completion. But they realize, too, that the essence of science is the working toward the goal rather than the attainment of it. No matter how remote ultimate success may be, we know that the stuff of which science is being made is the descriptive formulation of relationships among dependent and independent vari-ables. *In behavior science, it is in specifiable antecedent conditions that we seek to account for the aspects of behavior that we consider as the dependent variables.* Considering the tremendous diversity of factors which might affect behavior, we can see that the expression "antecedent conditions" must be very broadly interpreted if it is to include every-thing that would be a possible determinant of the actions of an individual.

Theory

Empirical laws stem from past research and hypotheses guide future re-search. An interrelated set of laws and hypotheses pertaining to a particular realm of investigation may be termed a *theory*. In considering both hypotheses and empirical laws to be a part of theory we recognize that these are essentially one sort of relationship, differing in the degree to which they have been supported by observations. Many things consid-ered later in this chapter should help to delineate the nature of theory. Initial orientation may stem from an attempt at verbal definition, offered in an effort to insure a proper framework for the remainder of our discussion. One way of defining theory is as follows:

Theory is an ever-changing structure of Interrelationships—hypotheses and laws—among abstract concepts which are founded on observations.

Among the elements included in this definition are indications that theory is (1) dynamically complex, (2) heterogeneous in composition, (3) symbolic, and (4) related to the empirical aspects of science. These different facets of theory will all receive attention in our continuing discussion.

It is commonplace to use phrases like "Hull's theory" or "according to the theory" in referring to particular sets of hypotheses. Our use of the word theory has a broader connotation, indicating *all* of the laws and hypotheses pertaining to a realm of investigation. Specific formulations offered by different theorists are all included in our usage. As we shall employ it the term will also cover stated relationships observed by research workers who profess no interest—even protest their disinterest—in theorizing. These researchers work vigorously and productively at extending empirical findings. Our formal analysis of science encompasses the activities in which they informally engage.

Adopting a broad definition of theory means that we are dealing with an entity of numerous facets or dimensions. In subsequent discussion we shall try to indicate some of these. We are dealing also with a dynamic entity. Theory changes every time a hypothesis is formulated, and every time an experimental outcome leads to the acceptance or rejection of a postulated relationship. Theory is unfinished business. It demands extension into areas not already covered and revision in places previously explored.

The Construction of Theory

What is the form taken by this complicated thing we are calling theory, which changes a little bit every time an experiment is performed? Despite its essential modifiability we shall find that theory is constructed in a fashion which will permit us to discuss it systematically. A more extensive treatment of theory construction has been presented by Marx (1963). His introductory chapter is followed by chapters on special aspects of theoretical psychology as viewed by numerous experts.

Operational definition

The terms which a scientist uses in describing his work are given essential meaning by the operations involved in the research he conducts. Such operational definitions take precedence over any verbal definitions in our understanding of the nature of theory. Suppose two investigators measure the memory for verbal material which subjects learned 48 hours earlier. Suppose further that each experimenter used identical procedures to measure the retention of the verbal items. The complete description of the experimental procedures and the data collection is the valid representation of "memory" which places the research findings in scientific theory. The concept is delineated by such an operational definition rather than by any verbal definition of a term. One investigator might write, "Memory is the encoding, storage, and retrieval of information in human cognitive activity." The other might state that "Memory is active assimilation, transformation, comparison, and discrimination of neural representations of symbols which have been perceptually processed." While these assertions may play a role in scholarly exposition of a theoretical viewpoint, they do not affect the functional relations of retention data to the quantified experimental conditions and states of the learners. These relations among independent and dependent variables reflect the operational definitions of the constructs involved. Further, the operational definitions of scientific constructs are the valid guides to further testing of hypotheses in continuing research.

Our imagined studies by two psychologists who employ identical experimental procedures is but a fantasy. Far more common in behavioral science is a sharing of identical terms and a disparity in investigative procedures—resulting in different operational definitions. Research reports and theoretical articles do attempt, however, to reflect different laboratory approaches to a general concept by using modifiers in terminology. It may be found, for example, that a research worker or a theorist may refer to "recognition memory" or "free recall" in an effort to reflect different defining operations for the general phenomenon they are treating.

Operational definitions which link any concept to the observations of the scientist may vary in directness or complexity. Strength of a subject's grip, which might need to be measured (that is, defined) for a study of motor performance, could be ascertained by a simple test with a hand dynamometer. The observation defining strength of grip would be the investigator's reading of the kilogram scale under a few specified conditions. Contrastingly, if an experiment required that the IQ of subjects be known, it would be necessary to administer some standardized intelligence test. The IQ determined for each subject would thus be very abstractly defined, depending not only on the numerous steps in giving the test but on the earlier steps which had been taken in standardizing the test so that scores would be meaningful with respect to some particular population. The observations of those who devised the test are thus pooled with the experiences of the administrator in providing the measurement of intelligence, an abstract concept indeed.

In actual practice we do not find it necessary to state a full operational definition for every term used in a theoretical formulation or in a report of an experiment. Many constructs at the abstract level have standard operational definitions. We tacitly rely on these in scientific communication. For example, if we say that strength of grip was measured in kilograms using a hand dynamometer, it is generally not necessary to say any more about the unit of measurement or the instrument used. We may need to enlarge our operational definition by telling about the number and spacing of trials used in taking the measurements. In other words, we need to give special attention to showing just how our operational definitions have been built up from standard operations plus our own special techniques of observation or measurement. Whenever we employ techniques or formulations that are novel to a considerable extent, we must present our operational definitions quite fully. From our descriptions of the steps taken, another investigator should be able to duplicate our work.

Coordinating linkages

Two constructs may have been built up through different operational definitions and still may possess an essential equivalence in the way they relate to other constructs. A statement of this functional equivalence may be termed a *coordinating linkage*. An example would be a statement that IQ as determined with the Stanford-Binet test might be assumed, for certain practical purposes of theory construction, to be the same as IQ obtained with one of the Wechsler Intelligence Scales. By using such a linkage a theorist might bring into conjunction two different sets of research findings which had been based on two different measuring instruments. A coordinating linkage does not assert the identity of the constructs involved. Their different operational definitions actually give them different identities. The linkage simply asserts a working equivalence. With respect to our IQ example, a coordinating linkage might permit us to state that IQ_{SB} was related to certain other specified constructs in the same way that IQ_W had been found to relate to them. Such a statement is actually an hypothesis for potential testing. The tentative assumption based on the coordinating linking helps to give a temporary filling-in of the theoretical picture.

Scientific significance

We have seen that a construct must have an unambiguous operational definition if it is to be a useful part of science. Even a complete and precise operational definition, however, does not guarantee much utility for a construct. To be useful in theory construction a construct should also have *scientific significance*. This may be described as empirically determinable relationships to *other* constructs. In other words, a significant construct is one which enters into the formulation of hypotheses and laws. (As the expression is used here, scientific significance is quite different from statistical significance and only indirectly related to it.)

The futility of complete operational definition without any scientific significance is aptly demonstrated by Professor Bergmann of the University of Iowa. His students are asked to copy from the chalkboard the formula for the Bergmann Index, one of its forms being

$$B = \frac{W_B - L_T}{N_H}$$

where B = the Bergmann Index for any person,
$\quad\;\; W_B$ = his body weight, in kilograms,
$\quad\;\;\; L_T$ = the length of his great toe, in centimeters,
$\quad\;\; N_H$ = the numbers of hairs on his head.

Students are most impressed when they see the formula in its symbolic form. As they hear each term described they must admit that the definition is operational. By following the formula we can compute the value of the index for any individual, a somewhat laborious task when we encounter the denominator, N_H. Despite its beautiful operational definition, the Bergmann Index is a construct which has found no place in biological or social science. It lacks scientific significance—any relationship to other constructs. It is found in no behavior laws in psychology, nor even in the multitude of hypotheses which candidates for advance degrees have formulated in great profusion. The obviously patient care with which Professor Bergmann constructed his index goes for naught, if naught be found to correlate with it or to depend mathematically upon it. At this point, many students helpfully suggest that the index *might* correlate with something after all. Perhaps the index increases with chronological age.

Devised merely for pedagogical purposes, this construct may turn up in an M.A. thesis yet!

There is a dilemma in the requirement that a construct must have both operational definition and scientific significance in order to be of use in theory construction. How much effort can we expend in devising a complete operational definition when we risk the discovery that the construct is not related to others as we might have hypothesized? On the other hand, if no relationship is empirically found between two constructs, to what extent might this be due to a failure to invest heavily enough in an operational definition which demanded elaborate control over conditions? Might a lack of relationship be attributable to narrowly missing the necessary operational definition of one of the constructs involved? These questions indicate the close interdependence of operational definition and scientific significance.

The solution to the dilemma seems to lie in a stepwise approach to theory construction. Constructs are given operational definitions which are judged sound enough to reveal any relationships which may exist among these constructs or among any constructs which might be defined by similar operations. If no hint of relationship is found, the definitions of one or more constructs may be changed quite drastically, or some concepts may be abandoned. If some degree of relationship is found empirically, the scientist may attempt to refine this part of theory by making moderate changes in one or more constructs or by adding more relevant constructs to the hypothesis before testing it again. Operational definition, formulating hypotheses, and empirical testing thus succeed each other in an endless spiral which is a basic process in theory construction. When an operational definition is achieved which reveals considerable scientific significance for a particular construct, that definition may be maintained for some time as more extensive relationships are sought for that construct. Such an interplay of research and refinement of theory is illustrated in a book by Lawson (1965). In a treatise and collection of papers on the topic of frustration, he has traced the development of this concept over a period of years. The effort involved numerous experimenters and theorists in controversy as well as cooperation.

Dimensions of Theory

A scientific theory is a multidimensional structure. Some of its more prominent aspects have already been revealed in our prior discussion. We shall now consider several dimensions of theory, or of particular theories. Our list may serve as a set of categories for the examination of the offerings of particular theorists in behavior science whose formulations we may encounter in reading the psychological literature.

Degree of confirmation of relationships

Hypotheses and laws have been repeatedly mentioned as two major types of relationship existing among constructs in theory. Let us emphasize that these are not distinct kinds of relationship. The two terms are employed to highlight different degrees of confirmation. When a relationship between constructs has been merely postulated, prior to any experimental testing, we term it an hypothesis. Repeated validation in research may establish it as a law. A single validation of an hypothesis may strengthen its tenability without warranting our calling it a law.

A convenient way to think of degree of confirmation is in terms of probability. A relationship is a law if there is very high probability that it will prove sound in further direct testing or if there is a high probability that propositions carefully derived from it will be found to be valid. A relationship is only an hypothesis if only low or moderate probability exists for its continued validation. The concept of probability offers a quantified approach to thinking of the continuum of tenability of the many postulated relationships which go to make up a theory.

Scope

When we speak of theory construction as a unified enterprise in which all the scientific disciplines contribute to a picture of the nature of the universe and its inhabitants, we are dealing with an effort of practically limitless scope. The dimension of scope, or inclusiveness, becomes meaningful only as we examine particular theories or sets of hypotheses and laws which cohesively form a limited system. Various systems which different theorists in psychology have offered are characterized by great differences in the breadth of phenomena for which the system attempts to account. A few theories tried in the past to achieve a general accounting for behavior, utilizing principles of wide applicability to animal and human activity. Such formulations necessarily included many areas which would require filling in with details. Other theories are *miniature systems* which deal with a very circumscribed aspect of behavior such as memory or the changing of attitudes through persuasive communication. These more modest attempts to treat a part of the vast realm of behavior are usually characterized by a more detailed set of hypotheses.

In working with any theoretical system it is advisable to be aware of the scope of coverage intended by the theorist. It is particularly important to respect the limits which may have been set for the application of the theory, avoiding any testing in areas where the formulation is not intended to apply. This does not preclude attempts to extend a theory, but it suggests that these efforts be clearly identified as such. If an attempted extension should fail, this does not necessarily weaken the system in its area of intended applicability.

Degree of formalization

We have suggested that research workers are continually modifying theory as they formulate hypotheses and test them. Such changes frequently do not constitute theory construction as a deliberate undertaking. When we turn to the work of those who have consciously tried to treat some area of behavior in a systematic fashion, we find wide divergence in the degree of formalization of statements defining constructs and hypothesizing relationships. Theorists have also differed in the extent to which they have arrived at hypotheses by applying logic as opposed to using a more intuitive approach.

The merit of a formally stated system does not lie in verbal elegance but in the precision with which terms are used and hypotheses are stated. Such precision generally lends itself to experimental testing of the formulations. Less formally stated hypotheses are sometimes characterized by a vagueness which discourages rigorous attempts at validation. A clearly stated hypothesis should point the path to its disconfirmation through research as well as inviting a confirmatory experiment.

We must remember, of course, that even the most formal of verbal definitions must be in agreement with the operational definitions of the research supporting a theory if the formal statements are to be given due weight. Another caution regarding formalization is that it may be carried further in the direction of making specific, quantitative predictions than is warranted by the status of the system. Degree of formalization, like degree of confirmation of relationships, is a dimension of theory which should be expected to develop as theory construction proceeds. The pace of theory building depends heavily on success in identifying potential relationships among variables and testing them experimentally.

Size of units of description

In choosing the constructs to be used in formulating hypotheses, a theorist generally makes a choice among possible units of description for the events to be studied. Psychologists have employed descriptive units in great variety, with size of unit forming a sort of dimension. Depending on research purposes, an investigator might report that a subject scored in the upper quartile in problem solving, that he solved 10 out of 12 problems of a specific test battery, or that he made 3 errors in solving Problem No. 11. The nature of Problem No. 11 would have to be part of the operational definition of some particular construct before such detailed attention to its solution would be warranted. In a relative sense, different size units of description are termed *molar* or *molecular*. Molar usually refers to the activity of the entire organism during a fairly protracted period of time. Molecular generally indicates a more restricted segment of behavior covering a brief time span and sometimes involving responses that represent only a fraction of ongoing behavior. The molar-molecular continuum is always present in behavior. A particular choice of size of unit for describing behavior represents a strategic decision in research and theory construction. Although the terms molar and molecular have been employed with other meanings than these, the foregoing viewpoint seems to be the most useful for us to adopt.

Reductionism

In theory construction *reductionism* refers to the use of constructs and laws from one scientific discipline to explain the relationships found in another realm of investigation. In psychology a theory may be considered reductionistic if, in addition to describing behavioral events, it employs constructs from physiology. For example, a theorist might wish to go beyond the delineating of empirical laws surrounding a motor performance like repetitive tapping. Having quantified rate of tapping and its decline with continued performance, he might seek to describe the neural, the muscular, and the metabolic events which constitute different aspects of the behavior. These relatively more molecular events would naturally have to be approached by quite different techniques or operational definitions. Laws from both the behavioral and the physiological levels of inquiry would all be part of the theory, all being descriptive of regular relationships existing in nature under specified conditions. The description of intramuscular events, however, might be considered as explanatory of the events of overt motor performance. *Explanation* can be seen here to consist of *description* at a more molecular level.

Many psychological theorists do not employ reductionism in expanding their theories. They accomplish a more complete understanding of behavioral events by formulating and verifying more and more hypotheses at the behavioral level. The structure of theory is strengthened by increasing the number of constructs and interrelationships among them which are taken into account. By using operational definition properly, these theorists provide just as strong a foundation at the observational level for their constructs as may be obtained for physiological constructs. Thus theoretical advances in the behavioral sciences can be made without reductionism. On the other hand, since the boundaries between levels of inquiry represent mere classificatory conveniences, the complete development of theory in unified science must involve the use of investigative techniques of all disciplines. Laws which describe natural events of all kinds must ultimately be tied together with reductionism necessarily involved. In this joining of different realms of theory, coordinating linkages will be needed to identify equivalent constructs which have been established by different operational definitions. Opposing viewpoints on the role of physiological reduction in advancing psychological science have been set forth by Silverstein (1966) who argues against reductionism and Reid (1967) who stresses its utility.

Theoretical Models

In formulating new hypotheses a theorist may sometimes be guided by a *model*—a set of interrelationships borrowed from somewhere besides the realm of natural events which he is investigating. Models of various sorts have been employed in behavioral theory development. They are adopted as guides to the creative thinking of the theorists when some aspects of the model appear to be congruent with certain aspects of the psychological events. Having noted these parallel interrelationships, the theorist borrows further relationships from the known model. These may then be used as predictions of relationships which will be sought among the constructs with which he is working. Another use of a model may be to guide the operational definition of a new construct which appears necessary in the theory to complete its resemblance to the model.

In our discussion of theory building prior to this point, we did not find it necessary to consider the use of a model. In our brief treatment of how models are used we have just seen that they are guides to thinking. They are analogies or analogues of the interrelated events which a theory describes. Thinking by means of an analogy can be a creative process, suggesting good hypotheses for testing. It can be misleading as well, indicating relationships that do not prove to be verifiable. However, this latter aspect can do little harm as long as experimental checks continue to be applied as a theory develops. The danger in using models is that the laws observed in the models will be considered to indicate laws in the theory itself when this is not justified. A further restriction on the employment of a model is that it may prove deceptively simple, having variables enough to resemble some aspects of the events under study but not reflecting their total complexity.

Almost all theorists who attempt to formulate quantified relationships make some use of limited mathematical models. When an experimental outcome yields data to which a curve is fitted, the mathematical form of the fitted function is used as a model for the relationship which is postulated as part of the theory. It remains for further empirical research to determine whether the function selected and the parameters determined by curve-fitting can be retained as descriptive of the relationship holding among the constructs of the theory. New data may require finding a new function as the model for the relationship. This limited use of mathematics is usually not considered as an employment of a model. A model generally involves a more complex set of interrelationships borrowed from mathematics, engineering, technology, or elsewhere. In the book edited by Marx may be found three stimulating papers on the uses of models by Lachman (1963), Simon and Newell (1963), and Chapanis (1963).

Research

Discussion of research is found in all chapters of this book, with varied emphases ranging from the general design of experiments to details of specific methods and illustrative experimental findings. Here we shall consider in general the aims of research and the various types of investigative endeavor which are found in the science of behavior.

Aim of Research: Modification of Theory

We have suggested that the formulating and testing of hypotheses are the aim of experimentation. We need not abandon that position at this juncture, but we can strengthen it by using our discussion of theory as an anchor point. We have seen that theory is a structure composed of hypotheses in varied degrees of confirmation which interrelate constructs that have been operationally defined. If research is the formulating and testing of hypotheses, as we have said, then it is a most essential part of theory construction. Research activity begins with the operational defining of constructs involved in theorizing. It is the enterprise which places the different constructs in their positions in the theoretical structure and strengthens these placements by empirical validation. Besides strengthening existing parts of theory, research extends theory by providing new constructs to fill in gaps.

Research may weaken as well as strengthen and extend parts of theory. It may reveal certain hypotheses to be untenable in the light of experimental results. Besides leading to the rejection of specific hypotheses, negative outcomes of studies may cast doubt on the general scientific significance of particular constructs. In this way research forces the theorist to modify operational definitions or to define new constructs. Our abstract discussion may make it appear that every research worker has at his elbow a volume filled with theory which he scans to pick out the next problem to investigate. The usual situation, of course, is far less formally structured than this. Most hypotheses are selected for testing even as prior research is reported. This intimate serial linking of research efforts is a systematic interaction between theory and research. The findings of previous research are exactly what we mean by theory as it influences further investigation. The fact that some investigators do not label their findings as theory does not invalidate our analysis of how the description of scientists' observations—their contribution to theory—and their laboratory activities are mutually supporting as the scientific enterprise moves forward.

Individual Differences

We noted earlier that the behavior we observe in a psychological experiment may be considered to depend on environmental factors (the experimental treatments which incorporate particular values of independent variables) and on the states of the reacting subjects. This dependence of experimental outcome on the characteristics of the individuals in the study poses special problems for behavioral research. People do differ! The variation which individual subjects contribute to the array of dependent variable values would seem to be a real obstacle to a search for general behavior laws. Differences in verbal fluency or visual acuity may make it difficult to determine how environmental variations affect performances in verbal learning or visual perception. Research psychologists have worked out a number of ways to deal with this broad problem.

Using a substantial number of subjects for each experimental treatment has been the common solution to the problem. Combining individual scores or response measures yields a group statistic—a mean or median—which is taken to reflect the general reaction tendency under the treatment administered. If subjects have been assigned randomly to the experimental conditions, the mean or median scores may be used to test for differential effects on behavior of the treatments administered. Particular aspects of planning, conducting, and interpreting multiple-subject investigations will be discussed in subsequent chapters. Before going on to another approach to working with individual differences, a fact contrary to usual research practice should be noted. Dukes (1965) has documented a substantial number of psychological inquiries conducted with just one human or animal subject. Ranging across many topics, these studies include some salient contributions to our understanding of behavior and experience. They fall outside the scope of our concern with multiple-subject laboratory experiments, however.

Returning to the fact of differences within any subject group, we may note that individual differences can be turned to the advantage of the investigator. Cronbach (1957) urged that behavioral research be advanced by combining the strengths of psychometrics and of experimental psychology. By testing subjects and thus delineating important individual differences, it is possible to obtain a more systematic analysis of behavior. It can be determined how the individuals' abilities interact with the experimental treatments in the determination of their performances. An experiment performed by Spielberger and Denny (1963) exemplified this approach. They built upon the earlier established fact that the flash recognition of words depended on an independent variable, the frequency of usage of the test words. To explore how individual differences might interact with this finding, they selected different groups of subjects using a language test. College students scoring at either a very high level or a very low level on this test were assigned to different groups for data analysis. Their perception scores for rapidly flashed words were examined for words of high, moderate, or low frequency. The outstanding interaction observed was that subjects of a high level of language aptitude were significantly better in recognizing the words of low frequency of usage. This finding, added to the main effect of word frequency, shows the advantage of selecting an individual difference score as an additional independent variable.*

In a follow-up of Cronbach's article, Owens (1968) has urged the use of biographical data as a special psychometric technique to establish subgroups of subjects to be run in psychological experiments. This might lead to families of curves linking the dependent and independent variables. Functional relations of this sort can reveal how behavioral laws reflect individual difference variables. Vale and Vale (1969) explored broadly this role of individual differences in a search for general behavioral laws, They suggest certain research strategies designed to bring out organism-environment interactions as behavior laws are refined. These considerations concern us further in Chapter 2 as we deal with the designing of experiments.

Subject, Experimenter, and Situation

The natural and social complexity of the individual as a human being poses some difficult problems for psychological research on human behavior. The problems are particularly acute when studies are directed at examining attitudes, aspects of personality, and social processes. However, since almost any experiment which involves human subjects is itself a special social situation, concerns over the personal actions and reactions of both subject and experimenter are proper topics in research methodology. Fortunately those who have examined threats to experimental validity have been constructive in pointing out new ways to continue progress in psychological research. Only occasionally have investigators been advised to abandon the laboratory approach and turn to naturalistic field studies, themselves posing numerous methodological problems.

Subject

Reviewing the roles which human subjects have played in psychological inquiry, Schultz (1969) has identified three historical phases. Once the subject was a trained introspectionist. Then he was regarded too simplistically as a kind of mechanism responding to stimuli. Today his personal

---

*This experiment is offered in Chapter 2 as an example of a treatment-by-levels design, p. 60. It is also summarized in Chapter 7 (pp. 252–254) with its results portrayed in Figure 7.13.

characteristics as a human being are recognized more widely. His perceptions of the experiment are being sought along with his responses to the experimental stimuli.

The widespread use of college students as subjects in psychological research has raised a host of questions about the validity of accepting findings at face value. Schultz points out that college students are emphatically not representative of any general population. They are special in age bracket, intelligence, and often social class. Orne (1969) suggested that student subjects may try to discern the purpose of the experiment. Reacting to is *demand characteristics*, they may try to give the experimenter the sort of performance he expects of them. Argyris (1968) indicated a different subject strategy. Resentful of having to "volunteer" as a subject and suspicious that the true purpose of the study is hidden from them, students may try to react in such a way as to contribute data which will render the experiment ineffective. Rosenberg (1969) has pointed to still another psychodynamic process which he has demonstrated to operate in some research. Having a natural "evaluation apprehension" in any situation which resembles psychological testing, subjects tend to react in ways which will make them look good instead of responding more naturally by accepting the situation as presented to them. These various tendencies of human subjects—especially sophisticated students—pose a challenge to ingenuity in devising research. At the same time, the postulated perceptions and processes represent new topics for experimental inquiry.

Experimenter

Most experimenters think of themselves as objective and rigorous in conducting their investigations. They often go to great lengths to control their experiments and to insure the valid collection of data. However, the complexity of human beings—both experimenter and subject—and the laboratory as a miniature social situation pose problems for behavioral research. Rosenthal (1967) has stressed that there is a two-way communication link between subject and experimenter. While they communicate overtly in carrying out the experiment, he points out that covert communication may also take place through an experimenter's unintentional gestures or vocal intonations. Rosenthal cites observations which also show that the amount of experience in running subjects and even the sex of the experimenter can affect the data collection and possibly introduce bias into the outcome.

Situation

Rosenthal further reports on subjects' reactions to experimenters who met them in laboratory rooms which presented various appearances as research environments. It was found also that graduate students enlisted from disciplines outside psychology were inclined to take their duties as experimenters more seriously if assigned to a room that was sparsely furnished or was cluttered to correspond to a certain stereotype of the scientific laboratory. Other approaches to the experimental environment also suggest its importance as an influence in behavioral studies.

Ethics of Psychological Research

Like numerous other professional and scientific groups, psychologists have been involved for a long time in establishing and maintaining ethical standards. This activity is a special concern of the American Psychological Association, working through committees, conferences, and membership surveys. From time to time the work is reported in the organization's official journal, *American Psychologist*. With respect to psychological inquiry, the topics of testing and of experimentation using human subjects have been given some emphasis. The responsibilities of the psychologist to society as a whole and to the individual persons from whom he gathers information and data are both stressed in many articles. After briefly indicating the more general considerations, we shall look more closely at three problems pertinent to experimentation.

Strong contributions to the ethics of psychological investigation were made in *American Psychologist* (1965, 1968). The November 1965 issue was a special one, devoted to broad examination of testing and public policy. In May 1968 the journal published "Ethical Standards of Psychologists" with several sections of Principle 16 dealing with the obligations of the experimenter toward his subjects, both animal and human. Minimizing any stress or possibility of harm is the emphasis of this principle.

A call to social responsibility on the part of experimental psychologists was issued by Walker (1969) in his presidential address to the Midwestern Psychological Association. In an article on the shaping of psychological science F.B. Tyler (1970) has urged that psychologists be vitally interested in the interactions of their discipline with various needs and forces in modern society. Finally we note a forceful presidential address to the American Psychological Association by G.A. Miller

(1969). He advocates that scientific psychology be "given away" to people striving in many settings to promote human welfare.

Turning more specifically to research employing human subjects, we may identify three ethical issues: possible invasion of privacy, stress and potential harm, and deception required in certain areas investigated. These problems have evoked concern among psychologists and several persons have formulated solutions to eliminate or to minimize the possible negative aspects of some experiments. On the matter of possible invasion of privacy some positive protective guidelines have been developed to guide the investigator. Where research requires that personal information or data be collected, the confidential nature of this material is to be conscientiously respected. In fact, research data may often be collected so as to assure anonymity to any participant. In either case, the right to privacy is the principle which governs the procedures. In the matter of psychological or even physical stress, ethical standards call for it to be carefully controlled if it cannot be avoided. All precautions possible must be taken to protect subjects. Safeguarding human subjects cannot stop with the publication of professional guidelines; local committees have been established in many research institutions to examine all proposals for studies which might entail risk and to act wherever any undue possibility of harm is seen. Deception is required if individuals are to be studied appropriately for examining certain hypotheses about personality or social processes. In a discussion of this serious topic. Kelman (1967) arrived at a number of constructive suggestions. He urged an active awareness of the problem and an effort by research workers to take alternative approaches in planning their studies. He also urged careful and effective use of postexperimental feedback, or debriefing, given to subjects after the data have been collected. This practice is widely used where a topic of investigation has made it necessary to misinform subjects about some aspect of the inquiry.

Although psychologists are rightly concerned about ethical matters as behavioral research is pursued, it should be noted that a great number of hypotheses of many kinds are probed with practically no threat of any sort to participating individuals. As will be seen in the numerous illustrative studies cited in Part 2 of this book, experimenters often ask subjects to perform tasks of motor skill, sensory judgment, verbal fluency, or intelligent problem solving which pose no ethical problem. By their cooperation in such inquiries, subjects are contributing to the advance of psychological science and to its creative interaction with society.

Types of Research

There is no homogeneity of appearance in the activities which are all a legitimate part of scientific research. Despite the general aim which we have claimed for it all, specific investigators give different directions and degrees of impetus to their studies. We shall try to improve our orientation in behavioral research by noting a few major types of experimentation.

Basic and applied studies

If an investigator seeks facts or relationships which he may apply in the solution of some practical problem, his studies are often labeled applied science. If relationships are sought by testing hypotheses without regard for their applicability, the investigations are often termed a part of basic or pure research. A prime quality of some basic research is the generation of new constructs. These may open vast territories of the theoretical domain for future exploration. Often the constructs involved in basic science may be operationally defined at a higher level of abstraction than those which figure in applied research. Despite this distinction and others which may be made with a modicum of validity, it is rightly pointed out that so-called basic and applied research have fundamental similarity which results in an overlap of their consequences. This is illustrated by the fact that applied research cannot help but explore relationships which can be profitably strengthened in the theoretical structure. A more dramatic illustration is found when basic research, undertaken as a pure exploration of natural phenomena, proves to have practical applicability of great importance.

Abstract and representative experiments

Another dimension along which behavioral studies may vary is the degree to which they resemble real life situations. Some investigators prefer to manipulate independent variables over ranges which reflect the quantitative values which a person might encounter in actuality. It might be further desired to utilize sets of these variables in combinations which similarly mirrored real experience. These are among the aspects of *representative experiments,* designed to explore behavior as it actually occurs. The utility of this approach in applied research is fairly apparent since it should yield useful findings. It is maintained by some behavior scientists that these realistic guidelines for experimental design should be followed even in basic research.

Abstract experiments, or *systematic studies,* have more typically been employed in laboratory experimentation. This approach to discovering relationships among constructs is typified in much of the research which we encounter in this book. It sometimes involves using an isolated, controlled situation in which just one variable is permitted to vary so that its effect on behavior may be noted. This effect is a real one even though it could not be observed outside the restricted situation established in the study. Such a univariate design is replaced in much recent research by multivariate studies; these still represent severe abstraction from everyday behavioral situations. Such systematic research reveals interactions or interdependencies among variables which might be obscured in the complexity of an experiment which represented real life more accurately.

"Crucial" and functional experiments

Occasionally an experimenter attempts a "crucial" test of some theoretical formulation, perhaps some hypothesis that is a part of a miniature system. A plan for such an experiment is often an ingenious creation, designed to reveal once and for all if the hypothesis is tenable. Unfortunately, the study rarely seems so decisive when the data have been collected. Even if the one hypothesis be rejected, a substitute takes its place, slightly different but tenable even in view of the new findings. Then it is time for another "crucial" experiment. Not infrequently, a theorist may debate the right of an experimenter to reach a particular negative conclusion in a research report on the grounds that the research worker did not adhere to certain requirements of the theoretical system as he set up the experimental operations.

As an alternative to the usually futile attempts at "crucial" experimentation, we may note the merit of the more systematic search for functional relationships. There is value in strengthening a miniature system by adding to the scientific significance of its constructs. It may be useful also to revise some of its operational definitions. These positive attempts to improve one theoretical system are the best way to insure its competition with other systems.

Methodological research

Some experimentation in psychology is directed at devising and refining techniques, especially methods of quantifying behavior. The outcome of such efforts is perhaps most broadly portrayed in the psychophysical methods and the techniques for psychological scaling. Individual psychological tests of many kinds also represent instruments of considerable potential in the future search for behavior laws. The proper development of such tests is a research effort of great magnitude. Another type of methodological research which may be cited is the delineation of various aspects of stimulus materials, ranging from the meaning of words to the mathematical properties of various polygons and other stimulus forms useful in perceptual research.

Although methodological research is preliminary to investigations aimed more directly at theory construction, it is to be hoped that it will prosper. Sound methods, once devised, can be incorporated in operational definitions so as to provide a good foundation for constructs at higher levels of abstraction. Too often in psychology experimenters have adopted makeshift methods, resulting in unique operational definitions. Standardized techniques can provide standard definitions of terms with the result that theory should mature more rapidly due to a greater interlocking of empirical findings. Advocating standardization in research procedures is often misunderstood as a restrictive demand which imposes narrow limits on investigation. On the contrary, the desired uniformity is actually intended as a liberating step. It should lead to speedier progress. No limitation on creative invention of new methods is intended.

Programmatic research

A research worker, or a team of investigators, will often carry out a consecutive program of studies which has certain advantages over conducting individual experiments unrelated to each other. The familiarity that arises from repeated excursions into some problem realm is a primary benefit. Another advantage is found when a preliminary strategy is mapped out for a series of studies. In planning the sequence it is possible to insure progression from one relevant variable to another instead of frantically trying to cram everything into one experiment which might be grandiose in design but minimal in yield. Serially conducted studies typically contain an element of repetition which may add confirmation to earlier results when later findings are examined. Programmatic research repeats the use of particular operational definitions and therefore leads to networks of relationships instead of isolated outcomes.

The preplanning of a group of experiments should not prevent investigators from turning aside to pursue some unexpected aspect of behavior which may occur. The pursuit of such fortuitous leads represents some of the most exciting and rewarding moments in the history of science. By executing a succession of studies in the same problem area we increase our chances of recognizing anything unusual. We should keep our planning flexible enough to exploit such an opportunity.

Opportunities in Psychological Research

Psychology is a discipline that should be particularly attractive to beginners in research. Although many studies require complicated techniques and elaborate instrumentation, there are some equally fascinating problems that may be attacked with far simpler methods. Simple procedures, however, must be supported by just as rigorous experimental design as more complex investigations require. Simple techniques must be very carefully administered, too, if they are to test adequately the desired hypothesis. When the research is conscientiously conducted, experiments performed by graduate students and by undergraduates have made important contributions to our knowledge of behavioral processes.

Summary

Psychology shares the general assumption and aim of science as it seeks to formulate laws which represent behavioral phenomena. The paradigm, if A then B, serves as a model for any conditional statement which indicates the dependence of behavior, B, on antecedent conditions, A. The paradigm must be expanded to provide for multiple determinants and quantitative expression. The functional relationship may serve as an alternate model in many cases.

As the independent variables in hypotheses or laws about behavior, antecedent conditions may be classified as environmental factors or as states of the person whose responses are being studied. Variables in both of these classes may affect behavior. The two-part classification is not a rigid one; many experimental operations can be considered as manipulating either an environmental factor or a state of the person.

Theory is a dynamically interrelated set of laws and hypotheses related to observations made in some area of investigation. Operational definition was described as a basic process in theory construction. It was seen to give meaning to the concepts employed, spanning the gap between raw observation and the theory language of science. Since constructs may be defined by operations of varying degrees of complexity, we found that theory is a structure with several levels of abstraction representing these different degrees of construction upward from simple observations. Besides the constructs, which are the stuff of which theory is made, we noted structural members in the form of coordinating linkages, hypotheses, and laws. We saw that in these relationships to other parts of the theoretical system a construct takes on scientific significance. We considered the dilemma which faces a scientist who tries to attain a good operational definition for a construct while at the same time trying to see if the construct actually relates to anything. The Bergmann Index was used to show that operational definition does not guarantee scientific significance.

Our general appreciation of how theory arises formed a background for our looking at several of its dimensions. We noted that different parts of theory may differ in the degree of confirmation of the relationships they involve. Different theories vary in scope, some very general in their nature and others being miniature systems. Another theoretical dimension is degree of formalization. Next on our list was a consideration of units of description, whether molar or molecular. We then dealt with the extent to which particular theories involve reductionism and the use they may make of theoretical models.

Turning to research, we saw the modification of theory as one way to describe its primary aim. Individual differences were seen as a special problem in behavioral research, a challenge for investigative ingenuity. Subjects and their different response tendencies must be carefully considered in research planning; the experimenter and the laboratory itself represent other sources of influence on behavior. In addition to the demand for great care in dealing with these complexities, the research psychologist also is concerned with certain ethical questions as he works with human subjects. This responsibility was reviewed as we noted the safeguards which have been established for the persons who participate in psychological experiments.

We devoted our attention to several different kinds of research, beginning with a view of its basic and applied aspects. We then gave a discussion of abstract and representative experiments, followed by a comparison of "crucial" and functional studies. We concluded our survey with a consideration of the utility of methodological and programmatic research. Many opportunities exist in psychological research for those who will make the effort to master fundamentals. Even the simplest of techniques must be carefully administered in combination with good research design if valid conclusions are to be reached.

References

American Psychological Association. *American Psychologist*, 1965, **20**, 857–1005.

American Psychological Association. Ethical standards of psychologists. *American Psychologist*, 1968, **23**, 357–361.

Argyris, C. Some unintended consequences of rigorous research. *Psychological Bulletin*, 1968, **70**, 185–197.

Berelson, B., & Steiner, G. A. *Human behavior: An inventory of scientific findings.* New York: Harcourt, Brace & World, 1964.

Chapanis, A. Men, machines, and models. In M. H. Marx (Ed.), *Theories in contemporary psychology.* New York: Macmillan, 1963. Pp. 104–129.

Cronbach, L. J. The two disciplines of scientific psychology. *American Psychologist*, 1957, **12**, 671–684.

Dukes, W. F. $N = 1$. *Psychological Bulletin*, 1965, **64**, 74–79.

Kelman, H. C. Human use of human subjects: The problem of deception in social psychological experiments. *Psychological Bulletin*, 1967, **67**, 1–11.

Lachman, R. The model in theory construction. In M. H. Marx (Ed.), *Theories in contemporary psychology.* New York: Macmillan, 1963. Pp. 78–89.

Lawson, R. *Frustration: The development of a scientific concept.* New York: Macmillan, 1965.

Marx, M. H. The general nature of theory construction. In M. H. Marx (Ed.), *Theories in contemporary psychology.* New York: Macmillan, 1963. Pp. 4–46.

Miller, G. A. Psychology as a means of promoting human welfare. *American Psychologist*, 1969, **24**, 1063–1075.

Orne, M. T. Demand characteristics and the concept of quasi-controls. In R. Rosenthal & R. L. Rosnow (Eds.), *Artifact in behavioral research.* New York: Academic Press, 1969. Pp. 143–179.

Owens, W. A. Toward one discipline of scientific psychology. *American Psychologist*, 1968, **23**, 782–785.

Reid, L. Comment on "grubo" psychology. *Psychological Bulletin*, 1967, **67**, 226.

Rosenberg, M. J. The conditions and consequences of evaluation apprehension. In R. Rosenthal & R. L. Rosnow (Eds.), *Artifact in behavioral research.* New York: Academic Press, 1969. Pp. 279–349.

Rosenthal, R. Covert communication in the psychological experiment. *Psychological Bulletin*, 1967, **67**, 356–367.

Schultz, D. P. The human subject in psychological research. *Psychological Bulletin*, 1969, **72**, 214–228.

Silverstein, A. The "grubo" psychology: Or can a science over 95 be happy without reductionism? *Psychological Bulletin*, 1966, **66**, 207–210.

Simon, H. A., & Newell, A. The uses and limitations of models. In M. H. Marx (Ed.), *Theories in contemporary psychology*. New York: Macmillan, 1963. Pp. 89–104.

Spielberger, C. D., & Denny, J. P. Visual recognition thresholds as a function of verbal ability and word frequency. *Journal of Experimental Psychology*, 1963, **65**, 597–602.

Tyler, F. B. Shaping of the science. *American Psychologist*, 1970, **25**, 219–226.

Vale, J. R., & Vale, C. A. Individual differences and general laws in psychology: A reconcilation. *American Psychologist*, 1969, **24**, 1093–1108.

Walker, E. L. Experimental psychology and social responsibility. *American Psychologist*, 1969, **24**, 862–868.

chapter 2
Designing Behavioral Experiments

To design an experiment is to create a plan to be followed in conducting a scientific investigation. Such a plan is a way of testing a hypothesis or of framing a question to be put to nature. In psychological research it is a blueprint to be followed in establishing experimental conditions or treatments; administering them to subjects; and collecting, analyzing, and interpreting behavioral data. Both logic and empirical facts serve to guide the designing of experiments. And practical considerations are also influential. All in all, the planning of research is a challenge to creative problem solving.

A brief review of some topics introduced in Chapter 1 may provide us with a foundation for our dealing with the design of investigations. Of paramount importance is the assumption that behavior is lawfully influenced by environmental conditions and by states of the individual. The fact of such multiple influences or determinants is a principal reason for the need to arrange conditions very carefully to test any hypothesis. Due care must be taken to be sure that the test is a valid one, that the logic embodied in the design permits the investigator to reject the hypothesis or to consider it tenable with some degree of confidence. Testing a hypothesis generally involves the systematic varying of selected independent variables and the measuring of selected dependent variables.

A sound experimental design assures us that the data collection will contribute to an advance in theory and not be a mere exercise without scientific value.

Multiple Determinants of Behavior

Using an example which illustrates the multiple determination of behavior will provide a referent for some of the points to be made concerning the design of research. Consider the simple task of solving an anagram—unscrambling a group of mixed letters to form a word or perceiving a word in a set of letters formed by resequencing its letters. To get a feel for this, try to form a word from NIDSEG. Your attentive reading of these paragraphs might have prepared you for solving this problem quite readily. As a special case of problem solving, and one which lends itself to psychological study under easily managed circumstances, the anagram task has been the focus of numerous experiments. A study by Ekstrand and Dominowski (1968) is summarized briefly in Chapter 13, pp. 495–496.

Anagram research has been reviewed by Johnson (1966). The survey of studies and their results indicates that success in solving anagrams has multiple determinants. With either average solution time or percent of subjects attaining a solution in a limited time as the dependent variable, the list of effective independent variables includes:

1. Order of letters in the anagram.

2. Frequency of occurrence in English of the solution word.

3. Cognitive or perceptual set established by instructions or training.

4. Verbal ability levels of subjects.

Although not given special attention in the research reviewed, there is another simple variable which may be listed as a likely determinant of anagram solution:

5. Length of words to be unscrambled.

Environmental Factors and States of the Person

As we examine illustrative experiments dealing with numerous areas of psychology in Part 2, we shall find that many kinds of sensory, cognitive, and perceptual-motor behaviors and a number of motivational and social processes have multiple determinants. It is generally possible to divide such influences into environmental factors and states of the individual. In the case of our five listed variables influencing anagram solution, Nos. 1, 2, and 5 pertain to the stimulus items presented to experimental subjects and so might be classed as environmental. Nos. 3 and 4 refer to states of the individuals, No. 4 reflecting long-term development and education and No. 3 established through experimental treatment. Any classification of relevant variables has a somewhat arbitrary nature. This is indicated when we realize that No. 2 is important for anagram solution only insofar as it reflects our subjects' familiarity with the solution words (as it generally would). This means that No. 2 could be restated to emphasize its representing a quantifiable state of a person, his past experience with the words. Conversely, No. 3 might be restated to stress the environmental variables manipulated to affect anagram solutions differentially. The virtual impossibility of a single, rigid classification of independent variables alerts us to multiple interactive influences with which we must deal in planning research. We are alerted also to the alternative ways of incorporating certain of these variables into our investigations.

Manipulation of Variables

One essence of experimentation is the controlled manipulation of variables in testing hypotheses. We may explore this aspect of research in a preliminary fashion by considering how studies of anagram solving may be conducted. Our examples are merely illustrative although they resemble the investigative tactics described in the review by Johnson.

The designation of the task as "solving anagrams" suggests some possible dependent variables as measures of the behavior under study. The average time required to reach solutions and the percent of subjects solving within a time limit are two different measures of task performance. Their validity as indices of problem solving is probably quite acceptable and their operational definitions are easily established. The time limit to impose on subjects might be an investigator's most open decision. Its determination might be governed by practical considerations such as keeping total participation time reasonable for subjects. The time limit might also be set so as not to risk undue frustration of subjects (if too brief a time is allowed) or too great boredom or chagrin (if too long a time is spent on difficult anagrams). Since the time limit will be an operational determinant of the percent of solutions achieved, its value is actually a determinant of the sensitivity of the response measure to the experimental variables.

Our five listed factors give great latitude for selecting one or more independent variables to manipulate systematically. They also suggest the need for careful control of other variables. Making decisions as how to control for the influence of some variables while manipulating others is a fundamental aspect of research design. As an example we may consider how these decisions might be handled in a study of anagram solution as it depends on variable No. 1, the order of letters in the anagram.

Deferring possible approaches to this selected independent variable, we might first consider how to deal with the other factors listed on page 36. For No. 5, we might decide to hold the word length constant at 6 letters. This would reduce the varied influence on performance that would result from letting this range from, say, 3 to 10 letters. As to 2, we might confine the problems posed to anagrams which may be unscrambled into "common English words." This is not as precise an operational definition of word frequency as might be desired. Greater specificity might be obtained by reference to published word counts as mentioned in the article by Johnson. Relatively high frequency of occurrence and the restriction to 6-letter length would tend to define a series of relatively easy anagram problems. Variable No. 4 might be allowed to vary over the range represented in the abilities of our subject sample. If we used college students, of course, we would be limiting this variable to some generally high range, not readily specified. Greater control might be exerted by use of a verbal ability test and possible criterion scores to limit subject participation. For No. 3, it is likely that we would use general instructions and not attempt to induce any special set to respond. Our suggestions have been guided by the principle of holding most variables constant or within some specified range so that we may focus our investigation on the influence of the selected independent variable, No. 1 in our example.

Manipulating the order of letters comprising the problem anagrams permits several possible approaches. To some extent these test different hypotheses about how the structure of the anagram influences task performance. One point of departure for creating an anagram is the solution word itself. For example, Oléron (1961) scrambled just 6 of the letters of 9-letter words. The remaining 3 letters were retained in the anagram in the same ordinal positions they occupied in the original word, the first, middle, or terminal portion. It was found that preservation of either the first or the terminal letter sequences was more facilitative of problem solution than retaining the middle third of the word. A quite different guide to arranging letters in an anagram is the frequency with which different digrams (2-letter sequences) occur in words generally. Thus, HICAR is composed of more frequent digrams than is IHRCA. Evidence reviewed by Johnson suggests that an anagram structured with higher digram frequencies tends to resist solution more than a different sequence with less frequent digrams. Some divergence in findings suggests that this factor may be relatively weak in comparison with other influences on anagram solving. In view of these past findings with digram frequencies manipulated—the research summarized by Johnson (1966, pp. 374–375) —we might decide for our hypothetical experiment to define our anagram variable in a different way. Various rearrangements of our solution words might be given first to judges for psychological scaling. We might obtain association values (average number of responses elicited in a designated time) or ratings on "cohesiveness" or "word-like" character. In fact, these two different scalings of a set of anagrams might assist us in testing two different hypotheses about anagram solving. A Gestalt hypothesis indicates that a word or wordlike configuration presented as an anagram might resist solution because of its "good form." An associationistic hypothesis suggests that wordlike anagrams may lead to verbal associates which are distracting rather than facilitating in arriving at solutions. Johnson lists some research along this line.

If indeed we varied No. 1 of our determinants of anagram solving as suggested, its subtle influence would probably emerge only because we exerted some restriction or control over Nos. 2 through 5. This is a simple illustration of some profound principles of experimentation: Manipulate one or more independent variables in a regular (operationally defined) way; measure the related variation in the dependent variable; while so doing, eliminate any differential influence of other relevant variables by keeping them nonoperative, holding them constant, or making them equivalent across experimental treatments either through randomizing or matching. The meaning and technical management of these methods of research will require our attention as we deal further with the planning of experimental inquiry in behavior science.

Aspects of Design

As one of the creative activities of the scientist, the designing of a study can be much more exciting than actually conducting it. Professors have been known to invest their talents heavily in the planning of an investigation and then to let their graduate or undergraduate assistants work to carry it out. Their plan and their procedures may be seen as the testing of hypotheses. This is a formal way of viewing what may be quite informally accomplished, especially in the early stages of questioning, getting hunches, abandoning them for new ones, struggling with some dilemma of design alternatives, and finally deciding to go ahead with an experiment which is foreseen to raise more questions than it answers— often representing a sound contribution to scientific advance. As some experiments are conducted and reported, it might appear that there was no hypothesizing involved. The experimenter might merely have been exploring to see whether a particular independent variable would have an effect on a selected dependent variable. He is willing to bet his time and somebody's money that there will be an effect. In this sense, *all* experiments test hypotheses. We make this claim with full knowledge that there are vast differences in how formally the hypotheses are generated, how precisely they are stated, and how adequately they are tested. Also widely varied is the attention paid to alternative hypotheses as a study is planned. Stated or not, thoughtfully considered or not, hypotheses are important determiners of many parts of any experimental plan which may be devised.

Sources of Hypotheses

Where does an experimenter get his hunches and hypotheses? He has a multiplicity of sources, which overlap in their potential for stimulating his thinking. If he is an experienced investigator immersed in a continuing program of research, a strong source of ideas to be tested will be his earlier laboratory findings. As a specialist in some area of inquiry, he continues to pursue the leads which arise in his own experimentation— his successes and his failures. Research reported by other scientists may also activate his thinking. He probes deeper into the phenomena of interest, he broadens the search for behavior laws into related areas, or he explores the interactions between different independent variables which appear potentially important. Besides current research, past findings located in archival journals may inspire further pursuit and elaboration. Research reports are often introduced by citing a few, or many, earlier studies from which new questions arise for testing. A proliferation of investigations in psychology attests to its vigor in the scientific enterprise.

Models and theories which attempt to account for some realm of behavior are another rich source of hypotheses for the experimenter. If explicitly stated or presented, a model or a particular theoretical formulation should suggest research of several sorts. It might suggest hypotheses which need to be tested in new situations to broaden their relevance in explaining behavior. It might call for refinements in quantification to make its principles more precise. A good theory will also be clear enough to invite testing of some of its postulations in ways which could disconfirm them. Campbell (1969) has pointed out that the rejection of a hypothesis may carry a logical validity. In contrast, he notes, the confirming of a hypothesis through experimental testing may increase its tenability but cannot be considered as logical proof of its status as a natural law. This line of thinking suggests the utility of designing research with alternative hypotheses identified whenever possible. Results of a study may thus eliminate some formulations while others are retained for further examination.

Practical problems or field observations of situations beyond the psychology laboratory may be another source of hypotheses. Relatively unstructured observations of behavior may lead to a hunch as to what conditions are responsible for the actions seen. Then a more controlled situation, possibly an experiment, may be designed to check this out. Such investigations may yield data which contribute to basic understanding of psychological processes and to the solution of problems in some real setting as well. The complexities of actual problem situations will probably preclude any resolution being achieved with a single, simple experiment. A series of studies or a multivariate design may be required.

Testing Hypotheses

Recalling from Chapter 1 the general form for an hypothesis—if A, then B—we might see our testing task as simply to set up condition A and to see if behavioral event B occurred. However, Boring (1969) has reminded us that we must also test the hypothesis, if not-A, then not-B. This dual aspect of hypothesis testing is in accordance with John Stuart Mill's classical rules for reaching a valid inference. By applying both tests, as would be incorporated in a well-designed experiment, we would round out our establishment of the relationship of B to A. For example, if we wish to determine adequately the facilitation of anagram solving by the giving of instructions to establish a set, we must test subjects not given such instructions to compare with those who are so instructed. Such a control group provides comparison data of the sort, if not-*A*, then not-*B*.

Predicted outcomes

A prediction of the outcome of an experiment represents a variation on a positively affirmed hypothesis. Either format can vary greatly in specificity or precision. Some hypotheses are so broadly stated as to lead merely to the prediction that an independent variable will show an effect on the behavior as observed and quantified. The magnitude, or even the direction, of the effect may not be stated. For example, consider the hypothesis that background music affects studying. Some students claim it helps them to study; others maintain it hinders their concentration. A neutral investigator might test the hypothesis that some effect might be found through research, without adopting either of the conflicting views. More commonly an experimenter will predict at least the direction of the effect expected in the data collected and analyzed comparatively. His forecast may indicate that a particular behavior will be enhanced by an experimental treatment. The amount of such enhancement may not be incorporated in the hypothesis if available data are insufficient for such precision. If, however, there is a body of previous findings and maybe a well-developed theory, a research worker may develop a quantitative prediction for his experimental findings. He may even predict a quantified functional relationship linking the dependent variable to the controlled experimental treatment.

A salutary exercise in designing an experiment is to prepare a graphic sketch of the expected results, possibly a bar graph or a function plotted on rectangular coordinates. Suppose, for example, that a student experimenter postulates a rectilinear relationship of some behavior measure, *B*, to a particular independent variable, *A*. He might examine data obtained in the past and then sketch out the hypothetical function shown as a dashed line in Figure 2.1*A*. Choosing 10 and 20 as the values of *A* to be used, he conducts some experimentation and obtains mean values shown as the two data points in the figure. Although disappointed with the discrepancy from his predicted outcome, he now draws in the solid line connecting the data points. He feels that he has at least confirmed the hypothesis that *B* increases monotonically with changes in *A* and that their relationship is rectilinear as he had assumed.

Although the student may have had good reasons for positing a straight-line function and for holding to this view after obtaining his two

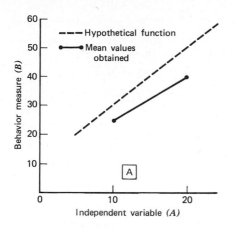
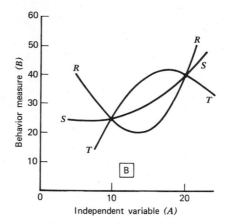

Fig. 2.1A. (*Left*) Postulated rectilinear relationship (dashed line) of behavior measure, *B,* to independent variable, *A,* and two data points obtained empirically. The student experimenter has drawn a straight-line function through these points in conformity with his hypothesis that *B* is dependent on *A* in a rectilinear fashion.

Fig. 2.1B. (*Right*) Three curvilinear functions which also pass through the data points in the illustrative student experiment discussed in the text as represented in Fig. 2.1A.

data points, he might have done more in designing his study to bear upon his hypothesis. The linear form of the relationship would be better explored by using several values of *A,* three at the least. A two value test really substantiates little more than the fact that *B* is influenced by *A.* The full nature of that influence is not illuminated. Three data points would begin to explore some alternative hypotheses in which a curvilinear relationship might link *B* to *A.* In Figure 2.1*B* we see that the two obtained data points can readily be fitted with several curvilinear functions, *RR, SS,* and *TT. RR* is a nonmonotonic relationship, as is *TT.* Their interpretations would differ greatly since *RR* is U-shaped and *TT* is an inverted *U.* SS is monotonic but is a positively accelerated increasing function vastly different from the linear relationship which the student experimenter still considers tenable. While he was thoughtful enough to sketch out the expected experimental result, he did not adequately consider some of the alternative hypotheses. If he had done so he might have elected to use more values of *A* in his study. If the new data points did show a straight-line relation of *B* to *A,* his hypothesis would rest on firmer grounds. If they revealed a curvilinear relationship, he would have some information on its form. Experiments designed with just two values of an independent variable, or comparison of just two treatments, have been quite common in psychology. If they reveal a significant difference in behavioral outcome, they contribute something to understanding the dependence of *B* on *A*. However, using more values of the experimental variable would offer greater potential for elucidating the relationship.

Practicality

It is possible for a formulation to be stated quite specifically yet in such a way as to defy empirical test for practical reasons. We are not likely to find such a statement in the experimental literature, so let us make one up: Eighty percent of psychotic patients would show improvement in three months if taken out of institutions and placed in private homes. Stated with reasonable specificity, this hypothesis is testable in principle but its testing in actual practice would encounter great difficulty. The statement may be rephrased, however, to permit practical experimentation without doing violent injustice to the original formulation: If placed in a homelike atmosphere, given extended satisfaction of affiliative needs and some of the experiences of family life, 80 percent of psychotic patients would show improvement in three months. Even though it contains a degree of compromise, this statement, if confirmed experimentally within the institutional setting, would offer support to the first hypothesis which we judged to be practically untestable.

Identification of the population

Some hypotheses about behavior are intended to apply to practically all living creatures. *Frustration leads to aggression* is a formulation that has been tested with both human and animal subjects. Within the human species its applicability is assumed, of course, for children and adults, for both sexes, for every IQ level, etc.

More common in psychology are hypotheses that apply only to a particular group—preschool children or white rats or college students. A total group identifiable by specified characteristics is often called a *population*. The population to be included in a formulation must be specified if the hypothesis is to be considered complete. Often the population to which an hypothesis refers is not specifically stated but is identified implicitly in the statement offered. If the hypothesis is a tentative law that concerns verbal behavior, for example, we may assume that human beings are considered to be the population although the legalistic among us might demand to know if talking birds were to be included or not. Hypotheses about verbal learning are usually offered without placing age limits on the intended population although obviously a principle that governs the memorizing of a 20-word list is not assumed to apply to a lisping two-year-old of very limited vocabulary.

One fault that sometimes has been noted in research is not very different in principle from the foregoing example. Investigators on the campus occasionally have seemed to assume that the college sophomore was an appropriate representative of the human race for purposes of psychological research. With no disparagement of sophomores intended, we may join those who gently suggest that this may not be so. The college student differs demonstrably from the general population in IQ, in sensory and motor abilities, and in patterns of motivation and attitude. Thus, hypotheses that purport to be generalizations about people in general are not adequately tested with college students as subjects. We must quickly add that there are numerous areas of research where information about the reaction of college students can be used to formulate principles whose wider applicability cannot be doubted.

Surveys of published psychological research conducted during the 1960s found that around three-fourths of the studies had used college students as subjects, with around half of these drawn from introductory psychology courses. After presenting these findings Rosenthal and Rosnow (1969) go on to examine the question of whether volunteer subjects had special characteristics as compared with individuals who did not volunteer to participate. In numerous studies of this issue, some straightforward relationships of personal characteristics to volunteering have emerged, some interactions among variables have been found, and some conflicting data have arisen from different investigations. Among the outcomes listed by these authors (pp. 97-98) are the following:

Volunteers tend to be higher in the need for approval than nonvolunteers (though the relationship may be curvilinear with least volunteering likely among those with average levels of need approval).

Volunteers, especially males, tend to score higher than nonvolunteers on tests of intelligence (though school grades seem not clearly related to volunteering).

Volunteers tend to be better adjusted than nonvolunteers when asked to answer personal questions, but more poorly adjusted when asked to participate in medical research. (In psychological experiments the relationship is equivocal.)

Volunteers tend to be more sociable than nonvolunteers.

Volunteers tend more often than nonvolunteers to be females when the task is standard and males when the task is unusual.

These observations add complexity to the complaint that subjects in psychological experiments are not representative of any broadly defined population. This does not mean that valid relationships among variables are not emerging from laboratory investigations. What it does mean is that the data collected on behavioral processes are only points on a few empirical curves. Whole families of such curves are needed to portray the psychological laws in which subject characteristics are significant modifying parameters.

Insistence on identification of the population to which a hypothesis applies is not a special condition imposed on the hypothesis from outside, as it were. The specifying of the population is an important part of the conditional clause of the hypothesis when it is stated in complete form. *If a 10-word list is memorized to the point of one perfect recitation, 4.8 words will be retained one week later* is stated somewhat more adequately when we expand the conditional clause to read . . . *memorized by college sophomores* . . . . Reports of research do not often include specific reference to the pertinent population in a formal statement but the population is implied in some way, even if only in the description of the group of subjects used in the study.

Operational definition of terms

Let us examine a hypothesis that might be offered for experimental testing by a college junior proposing an original research project in experimental psychology: *Environmental noise decreases hand steadiness.* Rephrased in *if-then* form, it becomes: *if there is noise in the environment, then subjects' hands will be less steady than under quiet conditions.* In proposing this hypothesis for test, the experimenter probably has something more specific in mind than he has revealed in stating the hypothesis At least we hope he has. There are many questions we would want to ask before approving his project. His answers need to be incorporated in a more specific framing of the hypothesis. Central in our questioning would be these two queries: What do you mean by noise? And what do you mean by hand steadiness?

In asking for a definition of the independent variable, noise, and the dependent variable, hand steadiness, we want more than mere verbal description. We want specifications of the operations we would have to perform to test this experimenter's hypothesis to his satisfaction. In other words, we want *operational definitions* of the key terms in the hypothesis. When we ask "What kind of noise?" we cannot be satisfied with the reply, "A loud noise." We want detailed instructions as to what sound source is to be used and what the loudness level and duration of the noise must be. Similarly, we want detailed guidance as to the operations to be performed in measuring the hand steadiness of the subjects. Is there some standard test for hand steadiness that can be administered according to prescribed procedures? Or will the student devise some special technique for assessing steadiness in this research? What, precisely, are the operations to be used in quantifying hand steadiness?

In reported psychological research it is common to find that the hypothesis purportedly being tested is stated in very general terms as in the example we have just been discussing. The experimenter relies on his description of the procedure employed to inform the reader of the report just what operational definition he gives to the terms he used in his statement of the problem. Thus the report of the study may involve two hypotheses—the one stated in very broad terms and the one tested with specific techniques. If the latter hypothesis is confirmed, the experimenter sometimes makes the mistake of discussing the outcome of the investigation as if the broadly stated relationship had been explored thoroughly and found to hold true. The conclusions reported should reflect the particular relationship tested, not the general relationship which the study sought to explore partially. Extrapolations or generalizations may be offered, but this should be done with a recognition of the need for further testing. To avoid the danger of overgeneralizing from specific tests, a good rule is to state the hypothesis specifically in the first place, defining each term operationally.

Additional assumptions

Earlier, we recognized that a behavioral event has many determinants. To state it differently, any measure of behavior is a function of many independent variables. When a simple hypothesis is proposed for experimental testing by the manipulation of a single variable, numerous assumptions are being made about the action of other variables which could affect performance. It should be recognized that these assumptions are being tested concurrently with the major hypothesis that was proposed for verification. For example, in testing the formulation that hand steadiness is affected by noise in the environment, we make the assumption, without stating it, that the level of illumination provided in the laboratory is adequate for the visually guided performance of the steadiness test.

Other assumptions, often unknowingly incorporated in an experimental design, may not be so harmless. In testing the effect of noise on steadiness, an experimenter might assume that it did not matter whether the subjects had been smoking just before the experiment. If expected results were not obtained, it might be due not to the untenability of the noise hypothesis but to the untenability of the assumption that smoking has no effect on hand steadiness.

Factors Dictated by the Hypothesis

If he has given much thought to the complete and precise formulating of his hypothesis, an experimenter will find he has actually moved a long way toward planning his experiment. In fact he finds that a precisely stated hypothesis, with operational definitions established for key terms, will actually serve to dictate what must be done in conducting the research.

Subjects

As we noted, investigators do not always trouble themselves to define a population to which their findings may logically be generalized. However, selecting subjects or obtaining volunteers constitutes an indirect identification of population characteristics. Ideally a completely formulated hypothesis dictates the subjects who must be sought if it is to be tested validly. In practice, the subjects used must be regarded as explicitly delimiting the broadly stated hypothesis as it is put to empirical test.

Independent variables

A hypothesis contains an identification of one or more independent variables which must be manipulated in conducting the experiment. The independent variables may be just a single dimension of stimulus material to be presented to the subject. For example, we might think of the hypothesis that if advertisements are colored, as opposed to black and white, they will be remembered better. A student experimenter is free to choose the size of advertisement used, even to using a variety of sizes, but he *must* use the colored and the black and white material as dictated by the hypothesis. Whatever decision he makes as to size becomes a part of the hypothesis that his experimental design is testing whether he consciously reformulates it or not.

Dependent variables

The statement of a hypothesis will usually indicate, at least in general terms, what the dependent variable in an experimental test will have to be. The experimenter may have considerable leeway, though, in deciding just what measures of performance to take and how they are to be taken. Consider the hypothesis that the level of room illumination affects typing speed. Try to decide what you would regard as an appropriate measure of "typing speed." You might, for example, decide on the number of words typed from standard copy in 3 min as a good index of typing speed. Would you impose a penalty for errors? Would a 10-min session be preferable to a 3-min test? What effect might this have on the results you obtained? The operational definition that we give to typing speed adds specificity to the formulation we are testing. We might even get negative results on the specific hypothesis under test, whereas the general hypothesis is still tenable if interpreted in a slightly different way. We must exercise great care in designing an experiment to avoid testing a generally phrased hypothesis inadequately because of our faulty translation of its terms into operational definitions.

Factors Decided by the Experimenter

Although a well-formulated hypothesis determines some basic aspects of any investigation, an experimenter still has numerous options in preparing to test it. Among them we shall examine just three, deferring consideration of some procedural details until Chapter 3. The grouping of subjects and the treatments administered to them comprises a central part of experimental design; decisions on how to deal with relevant variables are also important; finally, the duration of subjects' required performances can be an influence on findings.

Grouping of subjects and treatments

Consider the commonly encountered experiment where the effects on behavior of two different treatments, or two values of the independent variable, are to be compared. A key problem is whether to administer the two conditions to the same group of subjects or to separate groups. In the first case, the score that a person makes under one condition can be compared with his score under the other condition or treatment. The comparing of group average scores made under each condition is possible too, of course. Where all treatments or values of the experimental variable are given to the same subjects, the arrangement is often termed a *within-groups design*. In a second possible design, where an individual is given only one of the two treatments, the comparison of a person with himself is impossible, naturally, and the comparison of group averages constitutes the usual test of the hypothesis that the two treatments affected performance differentially. This is commonly termed a *between-groups design*. Although an experimenter is free to plan the administration of treatments either within-groups or between-groups, the design he selects may actually be reflected in the research outcome. Reviewing a number of studies of animal subjects and of humans Grice (1966) pointed out that the effects on behavior of certain variables were found to be different when within-subjects designs were employed as contrasted with a between-subjects plan for differential treatment. The essential point is that successive performances under different treatments introduce an experiential factor which shows up in within-group results. This extra aspect of influence on the behavior may indeed be of great interest to the investigator. However, the within-group differences attributable to the treatments themselves may be quite different from the between-group findings. Both sorts of findings are important for psychological science.

A third possibility for grouping the subjects for the different treatments is to give a preliminary test that is related to the performance under investigation and then to match persons in equivalent pairs on the basis of scores made. Then members of each pair are assigned, one to each treatment group, at random. Now, although each person receives just one of the two treatments, it is still possible to compare individual scores, within matched pairs, to find out more about the effect of the treatments, perhaps, than would be revealed by merely comparing group averages. We might discover, for example, that two treatments were more potent in separating the higher scoring subjects than in their effect on the low scorers. Such a finding would not have been possible had the subjects not been pretested and assigned to matched pairs.

Values of additional variables

Besides the experimental variable whose manipulation is largely dictated by the hypothesis under test, there are many other variables in an experimental situation that may take on particular values at the discretion of the experimenter. To illustrate the handling of additional variables let us consider a study of the hypothesis that geometrical grouping of dots makes their number more perceptible than random arrangement does under short-exposure viewing. The geometrically grouped dots and some randomly arranged dots might be located on different slides for projected presentation in brief exposures of about a twenty-fifth of a second to a classroom group of subjects. The measure of performance taken in such studies is often the percent of subjects correctly identifying the number of dots projected under each stimulus condition. While the grouping or random arrangement of the dots constitutes the independent variable in this investigation, there are several additional variables that are also dimensions of the stimulus presentation. These related variables include the number of dots chosen for the test, the brightness contrast at the projection screen, the portion of the visual field occupied by the stimulus material, and the exposure time. All these might possibly affect performance and the test of the hypothesis.

There are several possible ways of dealing with a variable that is not involved directly in the test of the hypothesis. Such a variable may be held constant, it may be assigned a series of particular values, or it may be allowed to vary at random. For example, in our illustrative experiment the number of dots placed on different slides might range in a series from about five to about twenty-five. The brightness contrast might be held constant at a fixed value. The visual field might be permitted to vary at random in accordance with the distance of each subject from the screen. The exposure time might be held at a particular value determined in preliminary research, or several values might be used as the slides were repeatedly employed in an increasing series of exposure times. An investigator must make choices from among many such procedural possibilities.

A variable in our illustrative experiment which might affect performance even though it is not closely associated with the independent variable would be room temperature. This might or might not be controllable by the experimenter, depending on the weather and the whims of the men in the boiler room. Over a considerable range, temperature would not be likely to affect perceptual performance. An uncomfortably warm room might make the subjects less motivated, however, thus reducing the number of correct perceptions they would achieve.

Number of trials or duration of treatments

Except for experiments on special problems like learning or fatigue, the statement of a problem will rarely dictate a procedural detail like how many trials should be given to the subjects. The decision about the number of trials or the duration of any continuous treatment needs to be made by the experimenter on the basis of what is known about the behavior under investigation. Some general principles should be kept in mind. First, the session should be long enough to permit the independent variable to have an effect on the dependent variable. Second, performance should be measured often enough or over a long enough period of time to obtain a reliable assessment. Third, a session should not be so long as to permit unwanted fatigue or boredom to affect performance.

How would these principles govern the design of an experiment to determine the effect of room illumination on performance on a test of finger dexterity where the subject has to place small pegs in the holes of a pegboard? Suppose we were to give one trial of 10 sec duration under each of three levels of illumination. Such a brief trial under the lowest illumination might not be long enough to develop the eyestrain that might be typical of more prolonged perceptual-motor effort. The results of the experiment might thus be negative merely because the conditions were operative too briefly. In addition to providing little opportunity for the independent variable to take effect, such a brief trial would permit an uncontrolled factor like a monetary distraction of the subject to play too great a role in determining the score. In a much longer trial uncontrolled factors tend to cancel each other; a momentary heightening of motivation might be balanced by a momentary lapse of attention. Longer trials thus yield a more reliable measure of the effect of the variables that are being tested. However, trials can obviously be made too long. If we tried to keep subjects at the task in this experiment for 30 min under each condition, we would encounter a rebellion that would be likely to invalidate the results completely. Even when subjects are not moved to protest openly, their performance is likely to suffer and to detract from the effectiveness of the experiment. A compromise is evidently needed between samples of performance that are too brief and sessions that are too long.

The duration of the measured or observed performance that is required of subjects is something that must be determined after a consideration of all that can be known about the behavior in question. No duration of trials can be suggested that will be appropriate for all investigations. A rule of some general applicability, however, is to divide the gathering of performance data into several trials instead of using just one. The intertrial rest periods will help to stave off the development of fatigue or boredom, and a trial-to-trial comparison of performance scores will help later to detect any change in performance that might have occurred during the session.

Guides to the Experimenter

Designing an experiment is a creative activity. The designing of a study is one of the points at which a sort of artistic endeavor is found in science. Perhaps it would be more correct to say that planning an experiment calls for inventive ingenuity. Artist or inventor, you will probably need all the help you can get when you face the problem of just how to go about testing a behavioral hypothesis in the laboratory. Let us consider, then, some of the guides that may help you and some of the practical considerations that may be a limiting influence as you carry out the design phase of an investigation.

Past research on the same problem

It sometimes happens that an investigator will wish to study further a problem which has already been studied before. In your reading in textbooks, handbooks, and psychology journals you will encounter many hypotheses which may have been partially confirmed by experimentation but which deserve further exploration. When an experimenter decides to test a generally stated hypothesis in a specific study he will usually find that there have been previous experiments testing the same broad hypothesis with techniques somewhat different than those he intends to use. These previous studies are a great help in the designing of his investigation.

Reports of any such prior studies should be read very carefully before undertaking the designing of an experiment. They will contain suggestions that are pertinent to many aspects of the design problem: sharpening the hypothesis, operationally defining the variables, planning administrative procedures, and measuring the responses. Special attention should be paid to any difficulties in conducting the study that may be mentioned. Avoiding the mistakes made in earlier research calls for inventive ingenuity. Our challenge is to design ever better experiments.

Determinants of the behavior being studied

In addition to past research which was aimed at testing very similar hypotheses, studies which identify some of the determinants of the behavior in question provide valuable guidance in designing an experiment. We have seen that there are many variables that may affect performance besides the ones that are designated as the independent variables in a study. How will these other variables affect the responses that the subjects make? Past studies where these responses were measured under a variety of experimental conditions should provide some answers.

Suppose we wanted to test the effect of high environmental temperature on the learning of a list of words. We may have decided that we ought to keep our volunteer subjects in the overheated experimental chamber for only about 5 min. Should we give them a 10-word list or a 100-word list to memorize? To answer the question we would hope to find a research report which would indicate the time taken to learn lists of different lengths with the same method of presenting the words as we propose to use. Such data would enable us to select a list of appropriate length for our purposes. As often as not, we do not find the precise information we are seeking in the research literature. We find experimental results that are of some relevance, however, and from these we deduce the answers we need.

Information on behavioral processes

When an experimenter provides for an experimental session of sufficient duration to yield reliable data on the behavior being studied, he must be aware that the measures he obtains may be affected by factors arising out of the performance itself. During a long session scores may improve due to learning or they may deteriorate due to fatigue. Of course, some kinds of performance are more susceptible to one factor, others to another. Repetitive tapping with a stylus on a metal plate, for example, would not be expected to benefit much from learning, but it would definitely show a drop in rate as fatigue set in. Solving a series of puzzles based on a similar principle might exhibit a learning effect but would probably not evidence much fatigue. Some tasks, like sorting numbered cards into a sorting tray, would be subject to both learning and fatigue effects operating concurrently, with one possibly outweighing the other.

Assuming that he does not want to study the learning or fatigue processes themselves, an experimenter must nevertheless consider what their effects on performance may be. Considering the problem of learning, he must formulate the hypothesis he is testing so as to indicate clearly whether it applies to subjects who have had little practice at the task or to highly skilled persons. One possible way of handling the problem of learning is to give all subjects enough preliminary practice so that they have reached their peak performance before the experiment proper is begun. In recognition of a possible fatigue problem, an experimenter must plan a work-and-rest schedule which will reveal and not obscure the influence of his independent variable. Procedures may be planned to minimize the development of fatigue by giving liberal rest intervals to the subjects.

Another common way of dealing with learning or fatigue is to take repeated measurements during a session so that the occurrence of these processes in the performance can be studied in the data along with the effects of the independent variable which was of primary interest in the investigation. The effects of this major variable may thus be studied at different stages of practice, a desirable feature of many well-designed experiments.

Statistical analysis of the data

The statistical analysis which he intends to apply to the data he collects is an important consideration for the experienced investigator when he is designating an experiment. To the novice the data are too often something to be considered only after the study is all over. At that point it is too late to amend the study to provide the data that are now seen to be necessary for an adequate test of the hypothesis. The experimenter should have carefully examined the research problem and the plan of the study while he was designing it, to see if the data he proposed to collect would bear on the hypothesis when they were statistically analyzed.

Practical considerations

As in all the affairs of this world, practical considerations loom large when we attempt to design an experiment. We need to realize that trying different solutions to the practical problems of an investigation actually changes the specific hypothesis which will be tested. We must be ingenious enough to get around practical procedural difficulties without jeopardizing the test of the hypothesis that is our goal.

Some Basic Experimental Designs

From our consideration of numerous aspects of planning even simple experiments it is evident that experimental design is a challenge to thoughtful problem solving. As more complex research problems are encountered, there is an even greater proliferation of approaches to inquiry which may be appropriate. In an overview of his book on experimental design Kirk (1968, p. 12) listed some 25 designs which might be used in behavioral studies. Just a few of the randomized designs may serve as illustrations of how an experiment may be structured. In sketching out these plans we cannot cover their numerous quantitative aspects which are dealt with in many statistics textbooks and other treatises. Our brief look at some common designs should serve as a foundation for thinking about research strategies, not as a substitute for thought. Each design will be presented here in a graphic form. Careful study of these figures should serve to clarify the elegant simplicity of these experimental arrangements which embody Mill's canons for the investigation of natural phenomena.

A randomized group design

One basic way to compare the effects of two treatments is to administer them to two different groups of subjects. To compare these treatment effects in the behavior data obtained from the two groups validly, we must be able to state that the two groups were essentially equivalent at the outset of the experiment. This assumption of separate group equivalence is warranted if the designer of the study has followed one of two basic procedures. He should have (1) selected subjects to comprise each group by drawing them at random from the same specified population, or (2) assigned all available subjects to the two treatments on a purely random basis. Failure to constitute the groups by one of these randomizing methods would leave open the question of their equivalence. Any difference observed in experimental task performance might be attributed to differences between the groups instead of differential effects of the treatments. Of course even with randomly established groups this interpretation remains possible, but its likelihood or probability as a chance occurrence may be evaluated statistically. Such a statistical analysis must rest on the assumption of randomization of the individual difference variables if it is to constitute a test of the hypothesis that the treatments led to the observed performance difference.

The randomized group design is portrayed in Figure 2.2 for two

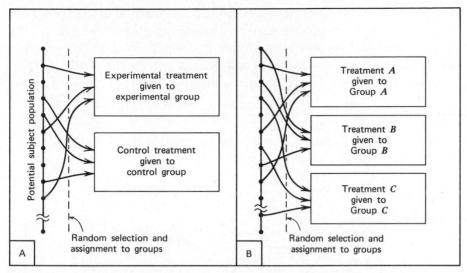

Fig. 2.2. Randomized group designs in which separate groups of subjects are randomly constituted to be run under the different treatments as required for testing the hypothesis.

common cases. Part *A* of the figure sketches a comparison of an experimental group with a control group. Part *B* suggests a three-group comparison of the effects of three different experimental treatments. In both instances, the randomized assignment of subjects to groups precedes the administration of the treatments. In the case of the three-group design, Treatment *C* given to Group *C* might be considered a control condition, if appropriate, or all treatments might represent different values of some experimental variable.

A matched group design

Instead of randomly assigning the available individuals, it is possible to establish groups which may be considered equivalent on another basis. We may obtain data on all the persons and then pair them off on their similarity on this measure which was selected for its relevance to the behavior under study. For example, we might match subjects on their vocabulary test scores before studying their performances in an anagram solving task. Constituting the groups by assigning one member of each matched pair randomly to the different groups, we reduce the possibility that individual differences might inadvertently offset or enhance the differential effects of treatments. A guiding principle in matching individuals is that the variable used for matching should be one which does correlate with the behavior under investigation. To match on the basis of an irrelevant variable is to achieve no refinement of the study at all. A matched group design is represented in Figure 2.3. For a three-

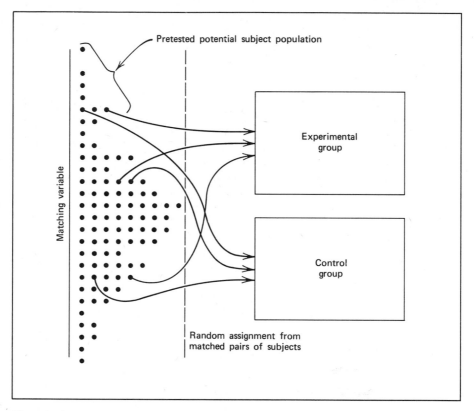

Fig. 2.3. Matched group design in which pairs of subjects are first matched on the basis of testing or other assessment and members of each pair are then assigned randomly to the required treatment groups.

treatment design, subjects would of course be assigned to treatments from triads of subjects who had been matched on the basis of similar assessment data.

Subjects serving as own controls

Still another way of arranging a two-treatment experiment is to administer each treatment in succession to all subjects. This within-subjects design may invite complications, as mentioned earlier in citing the review by Grice (p. 50) of alternative designs. Subjects' experience under one treatment may carry over to affect their performance under the other. A common attempt to equate such experiential effects is to have half the subjects given one sequence of the treatments or conditions and the other half given the reverse sequence. This counterbalancing of treatments may accomplish its intended effect, however, only if the transfer from Treatment A to B is the same as the effect from B to A. This is often a dubious assumption. As emphasized by Poulton and Freeman (1966) and by Dawes (1969) the asymmetrical transfer effects between two tasks encountered in different orders is a common enough possibility to suggest that we should avoid reliance on simple counterbalancing in most experiments. The approach might rarely be found acceptable, as in tasks where equivalent or zero transfer effects exist between two treatments. The design also has utility when an investigator purposely sets out to study transfer, of course.

A factorial design

Earlier we considered the varying of a single experimental variable while all other relevant factors were held constant or were randomized. In contrast to that single-variable search for behavior laws, multivariate research offers two special advantages. If we study the effects of two independent variables in a single investigation we gain an economy in research time and effort; second, we may determine how two relevant variables interact with one another in their effects upon the behavior. Such a search for interactions must be central in psychological science in view of our assumption and common finding that most behavioral phenomena have multiple determinants which act in concert to augment or offset one another. A multivariate experiment may take the form of a *factorial design* in which two or more independent variables each are used at two or more values as suggested in Figure 2.4 which represents the simple 2 x 2 design. Each of the two variables is used at just two values giving a 4-cell matrix of experimental conditions. A separate randomly constituted group of subjects is assigned to each of the four conditions in this design. Expansion of randomized factorial designs is obtained when more values of either treatment are used. For example, our 2 x 2 design might be expanded to 2 x 3, 3 x 3, or 4 x 6 if greater numbers of values of the two factors were employed. Greater complexity of factorial experiments occurs when more factors or treatments are added. Such designs might be designated 2 x 2 x 2 or 2 x 3 x 4 or 2 x 2 x 3 x 5

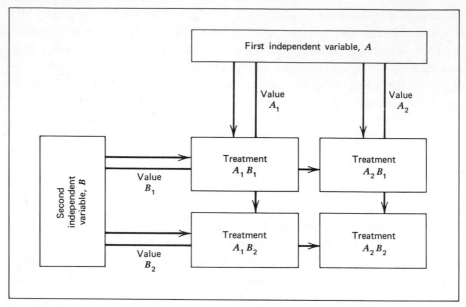

Fig. 2.4. Simple randomized 2 x 2 factorial design in which two factors, *A* and *B*, are each used at two values. The combinations create four experimental treatments to which subjects may be randomly assigned.

to indicate the number of factors simultaneously investigated and the number of values of each variable used in establishing the experimental conditions which are operative in the several cells of the design. A 2 x 3 x4 randomized factorial design would have, for example, 24 cells to accommodate all possible combinations of the three factors or treatments if one has two values of its variable, the second has three values, and the third takes on four values. We shall not pursue these more complex factorial designs further. Instead it may be useful to note that a factorial design may be used to combine two or more experimental variables or values as one factor and two or more levels of some subject characteristic as another factor. Such a design permits a search for any interaction between the effects of experimental treatments and the levels of the subjects' traits which differ over the groups employed. A design of this sort is often termed a treatments-by-levels design. An example of such an investigation was briefly described in Chapter 1, pp. 22–23. Spielberger and Denny selected college students of two contrasting levels of language aptitude and then administered experimental treatments in the form of words of high, moderate, and low frequency of usage to be recognized when very rapidly flashed. In addition to finding that word frequency made a significant difference in recognition performance, the investigators found an interaction between this treatment variable and the subjects' aptitude levels. Those with a high language aptitude were notably superior in recognizing flashed words of low frequency of usage, while this was not the case for words of moderate or high frequency. The uncovering of such interactions among variables is a primary purpose of factorially designed experiments, including those of a treatment-by-levels type. A fuller account of this experiment we have considered here is to be found in Chapter 7, pp. 252–254 which includes a graphic portrayal, Figure 7.13, of the aptitude-treatment interaction.

Having examined an interaction which was empirically uncovered in an actual experiment, it may be further instructive to consider some other interactions which might emerge when a factorial design is used. Suppose that we employ the 2 x 2 randomized factorial design portrayed in Figure 2.4 with a response measure, R, being averaged for each of the four groups of subjects. Among the possible outcomes of the experiment are several which are plotted in simple four-point graphs of Figure 2.5. These different hypothetical patterns of findings illustrate how a factorial design may reveal a main effect attributable to either factor or to both, as well as various kinds of interactions between the two factors or treatments in their combined effects on the behavior index, R. The potential discovery of some such interaction is the major advantage of the factorial experiment. This is true whether we are dealing with a treatments-by-levels design or one which combines two experimental treatment variables. Despite the complication in stating behavior laws which incorporate such interactive functioning of experimental variables, it is just such multiple-factor laws which represent important advances in theory construction. The interrelationships among independent variables are the keys to our explications of behavioral processes. Perhaps illustrative of this point is the careful examination of interactive learning processes in a volume edited by Marx (1970) entitled *Learning: Interactions.*

Other examples of interactions arising from factorial designs are found in later chapters of this book. A few may be mentioned to show the utility of this approach in psychological research. In Chapter 11, Memory, is a brief account of a study by Bower and Springston (1970) which included a factorial experiment combining two types of material to be

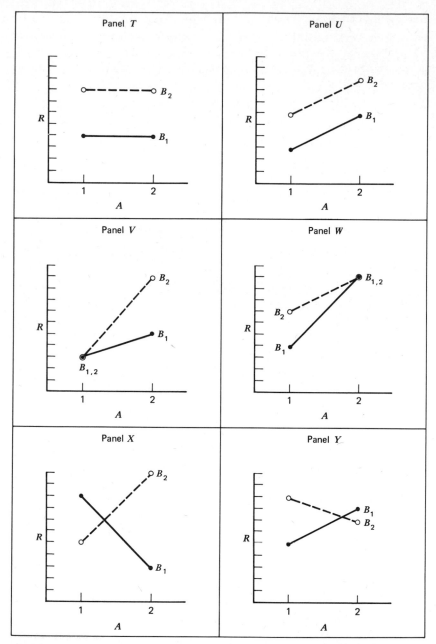

Fig. 2.5. Several illustrative hypothetical outcomes of a randomized 2 x 2 factorial experiment. Response measure, *R*, is plotted as a function of Factor *A* in each case, with Factor *B* used as the parameter which differentiates the two curves of each graph. The four plotted points are group averages, one from

each condition or cell of the 2 x 2 design. Panel T indicates only Factor B to be a significant independent variable. Panel U shows significant main effects due to Factor A and B, but no interaction between them. Panels V and W show two "weak" interactions in which Factor B has a significant effect on R only at one value of Factor A, even though both factors yield significant main effects. In Panel X, Factor B shows a main effect but Factor A does not when R values are combined; Factors A and B strongly interact, with A_2 elevating response when combined with B_2 and depressing it when combined with B_1. Panel Y shows another strong interaction which is significant even though the main effects of both Factor A and Factor B appear to be weak in their overall magnitudes.

memorized with two formats of presentation. The recall scores from this 2 x 2 design (p. 419) revealed an interaction of these variables. Chapter 13, Problem Solving, includes an experiment on response chaining conducted by Davis (1967). His experimental treatments, administered to 8 separate groups, included the number of switches to be pressed during the task as one variable. In addition to these required switches (2, 3, 4, or 5 in number), the other variable was the presence or absence of a distractor switch that was irrelevant to the problem solution. This 4 x 2 factorial design yielded group mean performance scores which demonstrated an interaction between these two classes of task variable. As shown in Figure 13.5, p. 500, the measure of behavior, Mean Switch Presses, increased somewhat more rapidly as a function of Number of Required Switches when there was a distractor switch than when there was not. This interaction, as well as the main effect of each variable, was statistically significant.

Retrospect and prospect

Experimental designs and their contributions to our research efforts have been treated quite abstractly in this section with a few illustrative experiments briefly cited. These might provide some illumination for an understanding of how research helps to expand and refine behavior theory. A firmer grasp on the relationship of experimental methods to the refining of hypotheses about behavior may result from our examination of how psychological experiments are carried out. This is our topic in Chapter 3. Further, the broad array of studies treated in Part 2 of this book will illustrate more convincingly how advance in behavior science depends on the designing and conducting of incisive investigations.

Summary

Designing an experiment means formulating a plan for adequately testing a hypothesis. A major reason for great care in experimental design is the fact that behavior has multiple determinants or influences. These need to be recognized as research is planned. An example of a study of the solving of anagrams illustrated this multivariate character of behavior and of its laboratory investigation. Manipulating some variables while holding others under control were shown to be prime aspects of well-designed experimentation.

Research begins with the formulation of hypotheses drawn from past research, field observations, or theory. Hypotheses may vary widely in their formality of statement and the specificity of predictions which they contain or imply. Great care should be exercised in stating a hypothesis for testing, so that it actually bears upon the problem we intend to investigate. We must pay close attention to operational definitions of terms, to the population involved, and to assumptions.

In the design of an experiment, the hypothesis to be tested will usually dictate the subjects to be used and the dependent and independent variables. Other details of the study are decided upon by the experimenter in the light of his experience and knowledge of earlier investigations. Among the points to be covered may be the grouping of subjects and treatments, values of variables, and duration of treatments. As he plans all these details of a study, an investigator may find useful guidance in past research, and in information about the behavior being examined. Practical considerations and the planned data analysis represent additional points to consider.

Some basic experimental designs were examined to see how simple strategies may insure that research really answers questions, confirming as tenable (or disconfirming) hypotheses under testing. Experimental plans that were reviewed included a randomized group design, a matched group design, and an arrangement under which subjects serve as their own controls. Some cautions regarding this third plan were offered. A factorial design was a final type we considered. Other parts of this book offer rich illustration of how behavioral experiments are designed to advance our knowledge of many psychological processes.

References

Boring, E. G. Perspective: Artifact and control. In R. Rosenthal & R. L. Rosnow (Eds.), *Artifact in behavioral research*. New York: Academic Press, 1969, Pp. 1–11.

Campbell, D. T. Prospective: Artifact and control. In R. Rosenthal & R. L. Rosnow (Eds.), *Artifact in behavioral research*. New York: Academic Press, 1969, Pp. 351–382.

Dawes, R. M. "Interaction effects" in the presence of asymmetrical transfer. *Psychological Bulletin*, 1969, **71**, 55–57.

Grice, G. R. Dependence of empirical laws upon the source of experimental variation. *Psychological Bulletin*, 1966, **66**, 488–498.

Johnson, D. M. Solution of anagrams. *Psychological Bulletin*, 1966, **66**, 371–384.

Kirk, R. E. *Experimental design: Procedures for the behavioral sciences.* Belmont, Cal.: Brooks/Cole, 1968.

Marx, M. H. (Ed.) *Learning: Interactions.* New York: Macmillan, 1970.

Oléron, P. Etude sur l'apprehension des mots. *Revue Psychologie Française*, 1961, **6**, 21–31.

Poulton, E. C., & Freeman, P. R. Unwanted asymmetrical transfer effects with balanced experimental designs. *Psychological Bulletin*, 1966, **66**, 1–8.

Rosenthal, R., & Rosnow, R. L. The volunteer subject. In R. Rosenthal & R. L. Rosnow (Eds.), *Artifact in behavioral research*. New York: Academic Press, 1969, Pp. 59–118.

Note: Statements concerning volunteer subjects on pages 45–46 are quoted from the chapter by Rosenthal and Rosnow with permission of the authors and publisher. Copyright 1969 by Academic Press.

chapter 3
Conducting
Behavioral
Experiments

We considered numerous aspects of psychological research in Chapter 2, and we shall keep these in mind as we proceed into the laboratory for the actual running of subjects. Conducting experiments includes a great variety of activities in which investigators and their assistants must engage. Among these are the preparation of stimulus materials, the devising of instructions for the subjects, the setting up and calibrating of any equipment needed, the presentation of the treatments to subjects according to the experimental design, and the collecting and tabulating of the response measures. Another research step is statistical analysis, which is not covered in this textbook. We shall, however, deal in Chapter 4 with the reporting of experimental findings.

No exposition can do justice to the multitude of ingenious ways in which psychological studies have been carried out. Our overview in this chapter will be limited to very general procedures which serve well in most investigations. Many special approaches in experimental psychology are exemplified in other chapters in both Part 1 and Part 2 of this book. Before we survey procedural approaches, we need to be alerted to possible experimenter effects as sources of influence or even distortion in our studies.

Experimenter Effects

The ideal of strict objectivity in research is sometimes difficult to attain in psychological science. In most behavioral experiments which involve human subjects the experimenter and the subjects meet in a face-to-face interaction. In Chapters 1 and 2 we referred to some of the characteristics of subjects as they participate. Now we must also examine the roles of experimenters. We shall see how their actions may intrude to contribute unwanted effects. A number of studies have demonstrated measurable impact of experimenters on the behaviors of subjects. While this is fine for any purposeful study of experimenter effects, it is a cause for concern when we consider that psychological research is typically directed at exploring behavior as it depends on *other* kinds of factors. In the majority of experiments we want the investigator himself to be neutral, not a source of variability or systematic bias in the data. One help in this matter is an awareness of the several ways through which an experimenter's influence may inadvertently affect the outcome of a study.

It is important at the outset to distinguish carefully between two types of experimenter effect: (1) an effect due to personal attributes or behaviors of experimenters and (2) an effect due to experimenter expectancy as to the outcome of an experiment. As our discussion of each kind of effect will show, either of them may take several forms as they exert influence on the data. The two classes of effect will be considered in sequence.

Attributes and Actions of Experimenters

Our first class of experimenter effect must itself be subdivided for systematic consideration. We first deal with some ways in which an investigator in any discipline might intentionally or unintentionally influence the conclusions he reaches. Then, turning particularly to psychological research, we shall see how the attributes of the experimenter and his laboratory may affect the behavior of subjects under particular experimental treatments. The sequence of this topical coverage is derived from a chapter by Rosenthal (1969) who deals with these matters at greater length.

Errors of observation, interpretation, and misrepresentation

Insofar as he relies on his own hearing and vision to perceive and to process the responses of his subjects, an experimenter is naturally open to errors in observation and recording of data. Precautions should be taken to minimize and, whenever possible, to eliminate such errors. Fortunately, reasonable care does seem to maintain the validity of recording data. For example, Rosenthal cited four different experiments in which almost 17,000 responses were recorded by around 100 observers. The error rate was only around 1 percent. In examining a selected sample of studies for computational errors in processing the data, Rosenthal found that a majority of experimenters or research assistants had made such errors. He found further that errors in both recording and computation tended to favor the investigator's hypothesis although their magnitude was generally too small to exert a damaging effect on conclusions reached. Still another concern of Rosenthal is the problem of misinterpretation of data. He states that "more of us are wrong longer than we need to be because we hold our theories not quite lightly enough" (1969, p. 184). Distortion of data may occur when experimenters (often undergraduates in college science courses) "manage" to get the results they are led to expect for a laboratory exercise. Such deliberate falsifying of observations is quite inappropriate in an educational endeavor. It is absolutely antithetical to the spirit of scientific inquiry.

Personal characteristics

In the chapter cited above and in a review article (1967), Rosenthal indicated how a variety of attributes of experimenters had been found in different studies to affect the behaviors of experimental subjects. Note that we are dealing here with sources of influences of a social sort to be found in behavioral research; the error tendencies mentioned in the previous section may bias the outcome of studies in any branch of science. Influences on psychological research include the research experience of the investigator and such personal characteristics as age, race, sex, and personality. Although these variables may be less influential in some kinds of laboratory work than in certain studies of social processes, they need to be given due attention. Additional discussion of these matters has been offered by Kintz, Delprato, Mettee, Persons, and Schappe (1965).

In the case of experimenter experience, we can see that the gaining of skill may change an investigator's conducting of research and may affect the results he gets. He may become more sure of himself in delivering the instructions and eliciting cooperation from subjects. He may benefit from practice in handling stimulus materials or operating the necessary equipment. In the social situation of a psychology experiment these changes in experimenter performance may differentially affect the reactions of subjects run earlier or later in the course of investigation. It is advisable for an investigator to become well-practiced before collecting data which will be part of a test of an experimental hypothesis. It is wise also to be alert for such a trend in an experimenter's mode of operating if it should persist into the research period.

Personal traits may be quite influential as an experimenter deals with human subjects. For example, Sarason and Minard (1963) found that an experimenter's perceived hostility and prestige value were among the factors which interacted to affect subjects' performances in an operant task of forming sentences from pronouns and verbs. The student experimenters' hostility had been assessed psychometrically and their prestige status was manipulated in the study. Experimenters high in hostility were effective verbal reinforcers only when high prestige was suggested for them. Under the low prestige suggestion, only the experimenters who were low in hostility were successful in the verbal operant conditioning. No learning effects were observed in the subjects run under the other two combinations of hostility and prestige—high hostility and low prestige, or low hostility and high prestige. The sex of the experimenter may also be a determinant of the data obtained from subjects. In a study also employing students as experimenters, for example, Stevenson and Allen (1964) found that a simple sorting task was performed better when the experimenter was of the opposite sex from the subject. The eight men and eight women serving as experimenters ranged in age from 21 to 54 years with mean age in the early thirties for each group. In both groups some experimenters were more successful than others in encouraging their subjects to do well at the manual task over a seven-minute period. But the interaction, noted above, showed that male experimenters obtained better scores from the women students volunteering as subjects, while the female experimenters got better performances on the perceptual-motor task from the men students in the experiment.

Another aspect of experimenters' personal characteristics that has received attention is that of race. Sattler (1970) reviewed and discussed a number of investigations in which the race of the experimenter or interviewer was either Negro or white. Some of the studies were in the context of counselling and clinical work, but others dealt with more experimental approaches to topics such as attitudes, preferences, task performance, and physiological responsiveness. Findings in the several dozen studies which Sattler cited are too complex to be simply summarized here. The point to be made is that race of experimenter, like sex and other characteristics, must be recognized as another possible influence on behavioral data we collect. Sattler offered methodological comments on the research he surveyed and concluded that more careful and more extensive investigation should be accomplished. Despite certain inadequacies and inconsistencies in some of the research reviewed, he did identify a tentative conclusion. It appeared that Negro subjects responded better, with less inhibition, to Negro investigators than to white persons when studies of attitudes, preferences, personality, and psychotherapy were conducted. In intelligence testing and various task performances, no overall trend of experimenter-subject interaction emerged. Almost any effects observed can be seen to interact with many other variables in these areas of investigation.

Experimenter Expectancy

In the article (1967) and chapter (1969) cited earlier, Rosenthal sets forth an hypothesis that an experimenter's expectations as to the outcome of his investigation may actually influence the responses he observes in his subjects. Evidence for the tenability of this view is taken from research on animals as well as humans. In the case of influences on the task performances of humans—our special interest—Rosenthal cites experiments from a number of different laboratories as well as special studies of his own and his students, some not published. In a typical study college student subjects are asked to examine portrait photographs and to give judgmental ratings (from -10 to $+10$) indicating for each face in the series whether the person had been "experiencing failure" to some degree (negative values used) or "experiencing success" (positive scale values). The experimenters, also students, have been told to expect either positive (average: $+5$) or negative (around -5) ratings from the subjects they run. In those studies where the experimenter expectancy effect is observed, it is found that subjects' ratings are reflective of the experimenters' expectations, tending to average at positive, negative, or zero values on the scale, depending on which outcome the experimenter anticipated in reflection of what he himself had been told. It seems as if a student experimenter may communicate with his subjects in some subtle and presumably unintentional way to influence the responses they give.

How might this influence be exerted? It is the answers to this question which offer guidance to us as we consider the effective conducting of psychological experiments. Analyses of some of the studies on experimenter expectancy suggest certain mechanisms which may mediate an influence on subjects. After reviewing a variety of studies, Barber and Silver (1968a) gave a summary listing of three, which are paraphrased here.

1. An experimenter may transmit his bias or expectancy by cues in his tone of voice as he gives instructions for the task and describes the use of the rating scale, for example.

2. Bodily movements or facial expressions may transmit an experimenter's expectations to the subjects he runs in a face-to-face situation.

3. An experimenter may in some way reward his subjects when they give responses of the expected or desired sort.

These several possibilities should warn us to use great caution in running human subjects in most studies. We want their behavior to reflect the operation of experimental variables and not the inadvertent cues which they may pick up from the experimenter. Fortunately, due care may be expected to rule out inappropriate experimenter effects in most psychological research. But some effort must be made to exert careful control; bias or carelessness can creep into research all too easily.

In their review and analysis of research on the experimenter bias effect Barber and Silver (1968a) were quite critical of some of the studies which purport to demonstrate experimenter influence. They examined 19 pertinent studies which they argue did not convincingly show this effect and 12 in which it evidently was operative. Their objections to a number of conclusions drawn by Rosenthal and others were based on criticisms of methodology and data analysis which cannot be reviewed here. Rosenthal (1968) offered a rebuttal to their arguments and Barber and Silver (1968b) in turn replied. As indicated above they did acknowledge some evidence for the effect of experimenter expectancy and did find some results which revealed some of its mechanisms of operation. The upshot of the controversy seems to be that such experimenter effects do take place in certain ways; precautions are in order as we run human subjects in any experiment. On the other hand, these effects may not be as pervasive or powerful as the large number of studies searching for them might seem to indicate.

Some Procedural Details

From the traditions of scientific investigation and also from common approaches developed in psychological research, we may examine a few practices which have general utility. The limited treatment of selected topics here is supplemented in other chapters which provide illustrations of numerous experimental methods. Reports in research journals offer another means for any student to educate himself in matters of methodology. Good general guidance in many aspects of psychological experimentation may be found in books by Scott and Wertheimer (1962) and Sidowski (1966).

The Experimenter's Notebook

An investigator's ongoing research efforts may benefit from a habit of jotting down ideas as they occur to him and from recording the day-to-day steps he takes in his laboratory pursuits. Insights are often elusive. Getting them down in a research diary will hold them so that they may be joined with other hunches and observations. In this way a theoretical viewpoint may be shaped, hypotheses may be refined, research findings may be interpreted, or a new line of investigation may be seen as profitable to pursue. The record of today's thinking may become the stimulus for tomorrow's inductive leap to a novel creative concept. More prosaically, the entries in a laboratory log may help in the interpretation of some unexpected outcome in an experiment. Notes on how the apparatus or the subjects were behaving on a particular day may help to account for some zig or zag in the cumulative record of performance.

Pilot Experiments

Before launching any major investigation with its great demands on time and effort, an experimenter is well advised to conduct some preliminary experimentation. Such pilot studies may vary greatly in their complexity or extent. They may be limited to simple tryout of research elements such as apparatus, instructions, or experimental task. They may include an experiment to examine the functioning of variables which may enter into the designing of the full-fledged research. Even though pilot work cannot be generally described since it varies so widely, the utility of various tests of procedural elements cannot be doubted. They promise great economies in achieving real advance in unraveling any problem area. Tryouts of stimulus presentation procedures, tests of particular ranges of independent variable values, examination of response measurement techniques—all of these elements of experimentation and numerous others should be pretested if past experience does not offer full assurance of their adequacy and appropriateness. Conducted with due care, pilot experimentation may accomplish even more than a validation of research elements. It may reveal a major flaw in framing the principal hypothesis. It might uncover an exciting new possibility to be probed in a subsequent effort. A continuous line of pilot studies, succeeded periodically by full-scale experiments, is apt to characterize the work of many productive scientists. But even the simplest research proposal of a student experimenter should include some planning for useful pilot investigation.

Manipulating Experimental Variables

If experimentation is seen as a search for relationships among variables, then the central core of any laboratory experiment is the control of conditions. A planned combination of variables must impinge on the subjects. In psychological research we may vary such things as intensity of auditory or visual stimuli, physical work load demanded of subjects, time permitted for performance, length of word lists to be studied, or complexity of problems to be solved. Due thought must be given to selecting values for such independent variables and to arranging conditions so as to present the experimental treatments properly.

Adequate separation

We select an independent variable for study because we believe it is one of the determinants of behavior. We test different values of it because we think they will affect performance differentially. If we expect that such a difference will appear in the measures of the dependent variable, we need to select values for the independent variable that are themselves different enough to produce a demonstrable behavioral difference. How brave is the student experimenter who predicts that the length of word list is a determinant of the time needed for rote memorization and then proceeds to look for the effect with lists of sixteen words compared with lists of eighteen words! Despite the plausibility of his hypothesis, he is unlikely to find statistical support for it with values of the independent variable so near to each other. Fortunately, few students are as brave, and as naively hopeful, as this. We can take this fictitious experimenter, however, as a horrible example to remind us to use values of our independent variables that are different enough to produce a significant effect.

Avoidance of Extremes

While separating the values of the independent variable to demonstrate their effect on performance, we do not want to go to such an extreme that we complicate the relationship we are studying. For example, if we were seeking to measure the improvement that occurs in typing as illumination is increased, we would not want to include in our choice of values a luminance so intense that it would cause glare in reflections from many surfaces and half-blind subjects. The introduction of glare would be an unwanted complication for the aims of our study. Of course, if our hypothesis demanded a study of typing under such extremely strong illumination, then such a high luminance value would be appropriate.

Seeking a functional relationship

As in many aspects of the planning of research, our best guide to setting values for the independent variable in a study may come from past investigations of the same behavioral phenomenon. A number of values of the experimental variable may already have been employed in different experiments. If we are altering some condition, but are otherwise repeating an earlier study, we may want to choose the same values that the previous experimenter used so that our results will be directly comparable with his. If we are seeking to establish a functional relationship between independent and dependent variables, however, we may choose values intermediate to those employed earlier in order to delineate better the mathematical function over this range of values. Quite possibly we may wish to extend the functional relationship by using greater values of the independent variable than have been used before.

Relating to Past Findings

In attempting to relate our research to past findings we may encounter an obstacle that has frequently been noted in psychological science. In many areas of investigation there have been such a variety of approaches, such a heterogeneity of variables introduced, that it is very hard to conduct new studies which are able to be compared and blended with the earlier efforts. Dominowski (1965), for example, has pointed up this difficulty at the end of a review of research on concept learning. Like others who have wrestled with the same problem, he points out that we need some systematization of efforts to explore any domain experimentally. We need standardized tasks which can serve us just as measuring instruments serve the physical scientist. In joining this call for comparability of investigations from one laboratory to another, we are not advocating any rigid restriction directed at preventing a research worker from devising an insightful new experimental method. We do, however, want the creative pioneer to be followed by the constructive work made possible by comparability of experimental techniques and behavioral measures.

Practical applications

Suppose we are undertaking a study of the effect of page format or layout on the retention of prose material. We need to specify certain dimensions of the task such as the length of the prose passages to be employed and their difficulty level. We would be guided in part by technical considerations like the need for reliable and discriminating performance measures, which might set a minimal length for the material to be studied. In planning such research there is no harm in selecting values that approximate those encountered in real situations—provided, of course, that such selections are congruent with the test of the hypothesis. Thus, we might use a passage that would be the length of a normal study unit and of a usual difficulty level for the scholastic group serving as subjects. Basic research may thus have an applied feature which need not invalidate its contribution to behavioral science.

Method of stimulus presentation

Several kinds of psychological research call for particular kinds of stimulus material, like words or geometric designs, but do not dictate any particular way in which these have to be presented to the subjects. This is left to the discretion of the experimenter. The stimuli may be projected on the screen or may be printed in booklets, to be studied by an entire group of subjects at once. Or the subjects may be run individually with the stimuli presented on cards or by means of special exposure devices. It might seem that the techniques to deliver the stimulation to subjects should be chosen merely on the basis of practical considerations. These, of course, are important. Emphasizing the purpose of the experiment, however, we need to point out that the technical means selected for stimulus presentation must be scrutinized for any effect it may have on the subjects' performance.

Materials to be used

The statement of a hypothesis may dictate the selection of stimulus material with respect to one of its dimensions. This specification may still permit the experimenter a wide choice of particular materials to be employed in a study. In making that choice he must consider other dimensions of the stimulus materials as they may affect performance. As an example we may take the hypothesis that nouns, since they often represent objects which may be visualized, are more easily memorized than are verbs. It might seem that the experimenter merely has to draw up a list of twenty nouns and a list of twenty verbs in order to prepare to test this hypothesis. We must realize, however, that words have other dimensions besides their part of speech, like noun or verb. Words differ in length, in familiarity or frequency of usage, in meaningfulness, and in the concreteness of imagery which they evoke. For this experiment we need a list of nouns and a list of verbs that are equivalent on these dimensions, which also affect ease of learning.

Psychologists need large pools of quantified stimuli from which they can draw representative samples for research of many sorts. Exemplifying efforts to fill such a need is an article by Brown and Owen (1967). The stimuli which concern them are randomly constructed polygons. These irregular shapes are useful in studies of visual perception of form and other investigations such as concept formation and stimulus generalization or discrimination. According to the discussion presented, investigators need to know how a sample of irregular polygons may relate to an entire defined population of such forms. An assessment of the representativeness of such stimuli requires in turn that a quantitative analysis be accomplished to identify the dimensional characteristics of the forms as they are created according to rules. Brown and Owen constructed such forms, building on the work of earlier contributors to research on form perception. Quantifying the forms on numerous physical dimensions such as angles and areas, they obtained the intercorrelations of these physical measures. Then the matrix of intercorrelations was subjected to factor analysis. Emerging from this were factors such as compactness, jaggedness, and area skewness. These procedures were followed for randomly constructed polygons ranging in number of sides from four to twenty. The analysis of the dimensionality of such stimuli offers promise of refinements in research. Experimenters may create samples of stimulus forms with much more assurance that they are representative of a much larger domain of irregular polygons. As will be seen in Part 2, similar gains have been posted in the study of verbal stimulus items that may be used in experiments on learning and memory.

Instructions to Subjects

Human beings are more complex than the molecules studied by physical scientists. In psychological research we usually begin by asking the cooperation of the subject and then instructing him as to what he is required to do. We cannot ignore the fact that among the determinants of what he will do or how he will perform are the very instructions given him. We need to give thought to the phrasing and delivery of the instructions so that they will have the desired effect.

Motivation

Subjects in psychological research sometimes arrive at the experimental session with no strong interest in participating. They may be members of a class group whose participation has been requested by the instructor. As you well know, this is no guarantee of individual interest. A student may volunteer to serve as subject for a fraternity brother. Again, personal motivation may not be high. It must be aroused by the instructions. One way to arouse interest is to state as much about the purpose of the study as may be revealed. Most people will take seriously a task that they can regard as a contribution to a scientific investigation. Sometimes it may be particularly appealing if we can indicate possible practical application of the results.

It may be possible to arouse the competitive aspects of motivation in college students if we can tell them that students at another institution have performed very well on the task we are assigning. Or we may create a competitive spirit within the group we are employing, perhaps by indicating that scores will be posted. However, we need to ask ourselves if such a technique will actually motivate *all* the subjects. Even if we can successfully increase motivation, we must be aware that the level of this factor may interact with some independent variable in our study.

Directive clarity

Subjects must perform in the manner we intend them to if the data are to reward our research effort. We may have been thinking about so many details of an experiment that when it is time to write the instructions we may write from the point of view of one who knows all about the study instead of from the viewpoint of the subject, who may not have the slightest idea of what he is to do. To be sure that instructions indicate clearly what subjects are to do, it is well to pretest their wording on a preliminary group. Without pretesting we run the risk of having to discard data because 10 or 20 percent of the subjects obviously did not understand the instructions. We may be even worse off when their mis-understanding is not detectable and yet is a factor that influenced the experimental results. It is common practice to ask if there are any questions after we read instructions to subjects, but it must be remembered that people are often reluctant to reveal that they did not understand. They may remain silent, hoping to grasp what is expected of them after the experiment gets under way. It is obviously desirable to avoid this by making instructions clear in the first place.

Besides being clear, instructions for some experiments may have to be particularly convincing. Subjects may need to be persuaded of the intent of the study so that they will perform the required task within the proper framework of attitudes, perceptions, and response sets. Orne (1969) has emphasized that human subjects are likely to develop their own views of the *demand characteristics* of any experiment in which they participate. Their ideas of what the experiment is all about, whether valid or not, are likely to affect their behavior. In examining certain phenomena in the psychology laboratory, Orne indicates, we may have to devise special controls or procedures to assess the impact on responses of the subjects' perceptions that they are participating in an experiment which has some particular purpose. Orne also points out that we need be much less concerned about subjects' perceptions of the demand characteristics in the many psychological experiments which call for them to do their best at some task administered under particular environmental conditions.

Repetition for emphasis

We know enough about the principles of human behavior to realize that some points in our instructions will have to be emphasized if we expect subjects to comply. This applies particularly to the parts of the instructions that call for a way of performing that might be antagonistic to established habits. For example, if our experiment requires that subjects leave no margins on the paper when performing a handwriting task, the warning to leave no margins ought to be repeated once or twice in the instructions since people will be inclined by training to leave space at the left and right of each line. It is well to repeat such a key part of the instructions just before the first trial begins.

Interprocedural instructions

Although instructions to subjects are often presented in their entirety before the experimental task begins, it is well to think of the value to be gained through delivering part of the instructions at a later point in the procedure. This may be useful to restore motivation when the subject's interest in the task may be flagging or when motivation needs to be brought to a peak just before the critical data are to be taken.

Sometimes it may help to alternate practice periods and additional instructions which may serve to extend the subject's knowledge of what is expected of him. A subject, for example, might be given some practice at reading as quickly as possible the adjectives that appeared on a screen. Then he might be given the additional instructions to read the adjective silently and to state aloud its opposite as quickly as possible. The preliminary reading of the words might have been used to establish baseline reaction times, to acquaint the subjects with the words being used, or merely to help them adjust to the experimental situation before the critical task of naming opposites was introduced.

Adjunctive instructional techniques

An experimenter need not rely solely on the verbal instructions given the subjects to motivate them and inform them of what they are expected to do. Some guidance may be provided by means of the material employed. The warning that appears in some test booklets, not to turn the page until told to do so, is a familiar example. Experimental apparatus may be constructed to flash a warning to a subject if he does something wrong. More simply, the experimenter may give such a warning if the plan of the study calls for it. Information as to how well he is doing may be given to a subject in some studies as a supplement to the instructions he was given. Such knowledge of results may be both motivational and informative, depending on what is presented and how it is related to the task being performed. Individual responses are sometimes identified for subjects as right or wrong through the use of appropriate cues. This type of adjunct to formal instructions may even include actual punishment, like a mild electric shock, for a wrong response.

Presentation of Treatments

The procedural heart of any behavioral experiment may be variously described as presenting the treatments to the subjects, administering the experimental conditions to them, or requiring the performance of the assigned task from them. All these are encompassed, too, in the vernacular phrase from psychological experimentation, "running the subjects." This aspect of conducting research is no less important than several others we have discussed. It is in the treatment of the subjects that we shall find the diversity of special methods that will occupy us in many subsequent chapters.

Instrumentation

Many kinds of apparatus or instruments may be found in the psychology laboratory. They may be used for stimulus presentation, for posing problem tasks, for recording responses, and for numerous other purposes. At the same time, many human behavior processes may be studied without any equipment beyond easily prepared stimulus materials or paper-and-pencil tests of various sorts.

Instrumentation is perhaps best studied in the context of particular experimental problems. Certain items of equipment such as audio oscillators, memory drums, and tachistoscopes are mentioned in the descriptions of experiments in this book. Real understanding of the utilities and limitations of such apparatus is gained, however, only through experience. For the guidance of students who wish to pursue the topic of instrumentation in different areas of investigation, two sources can be recommended. A volume edited by Sidowski (1966) covers instrumentation in several realms of inquiry in psychology. The following chapters may be noted as most appropriate for congruence with topics in this textbook:

Ch. 1. Some Preliminary Considerations in Research; by J.B. Sidowski and R.B. Lockard

Ch. 2. Basic Instrumentation; by J.B. Sidowski and M.J. Smith

Ch. 5. Psychophysics and Signal Detection; by J.P. Egan and F.R. Clarke

Ch. 6. Audition; by I.J. Hirsh

Ch. 7. Vision; by R.M. Boynton

Ch. 8. Perception and Recognition; by H.W. Hake and A.S. Rodwan

Ch. 12. Verbal Behavior; by W.N. Runquist

Ch. 13. Complex Processes; by L.E. Bourne, Jr. and W.F. Battig

Ch. 15. Social Psychology and Group Processes; by M.E. Shaw

Ch. 16. Motor Behavior; by H.P. Bahrick and M.E. Noble

Another useful source dealing with apparatus, equipment, and supplies useful in psychological laboratories is a special issue of *American Psychologist* (March 1969). It contains general articles and some which focus on particular experimental areas where special instrumentation is a necessity for research. A practical feature is a buyer's guide compiled by Sidowski which indexes commercial suppliers of various kinds of equipment.

Preliminary practice

The statement of a hypothesis may call for the collecting of data from subjects who are practiced at a task or at least quite familiar with it. The experiment may therefore be designed to give preliminary practice to the subjects. This may sometimes be done informally with the experimenter watching the subject's performance and perhaps offering suggestions that will aid performance. It is important to realize how this practice may affect the analysis of the formal part of the study, administered later. The assessment of any practice effect in the data of the latter portion of the experiment will not be very meaningful if subjects have been given different opportunities to benefit by practice in the preliminary part. It may be suggested, therefore, that everything about the preliminary part of a study, both treatment and performance, be made a matter of record so that it may be analyzed later if necessary.

Occluding extraneous stimuli

Shutting out unwanted stimulation is commonly required in psychological research since the aim of such studies is so often to determine the effect of particular stimuli on performance. The task of the experimenter is to see to it that these desired stimuli, and nothing but these stimuli, impinge upon the subjects. While this requirement is of paramount importance in most studies of sensory and perceptual processes, it is almost never absent from behavioral investigations. The laboratory or research room is generally situated and constructed to isolate the subjects from unwanted noise and visual distractions. Other solutions to the problem include blindfolding the subject when the study calls for no visual cues and delivering auditory stimuli through earphones when it is desired to minimize interference from noise in the room.

Measuring responses

Testing behavioral hypotheses requires that we measure responses as a key step in experimentation. Any behavior may have several measurable aspects. Typically we single out one of these to quantify—the dependent variable in the formulation we are examining. If the hypothesis states that response speed or reaction time will be affected by the experimental treatment, then this speed of reaction must be measured with appropriate accuracy. To take a different example, if we are investigating memory, then we might measure number of words recalled when a test follows the study and learning of a list of verbal items. Speed of response or recall score are just two indices which may serve as dependent variables in psychological science. We will encounter a great variety of operationally defined measures of behavior as we review research in many areas of investigation. For the present, our listing of types of response measures will indicate some of the indices taken by experimenters in illustrative studies cited in later chapters.

Response latency is a general term for the brief interval which separates a response from the stimulus which elicited it. *Reaction time*—as this interval may also be termed—is a common measure in studies of perceptual-motor behavior. In Chapter 10 is summarized an experiment by Moss (1969) who investigated how subjects' reaction time depended on their expectancies for the occurrence and timing of particular stimulus events. The speed of response may have utility in other kinds of studies as well. For example, the quickness of choosing one picture over another might be an indicant of strength of preference in a study of esthetic values.

Response duration is another temporal measure with widespread utility in research. Two examples should help illustrate this. In Chapter 7 we find that Krueger (1970) used the duration of visual search as his measure of subjects' information processing as they rapidly scanned a display to find a designated letter. In Chapter 13 the time taken to solve anagrams was the behavior measure used by Ekstrand and Dominowski (1968) as they studied the effects of different configurations of the problems posed.

Amplitude of response has often been used as an index of reflex response strength in experiments on eye blink, pupillary response, knee jerk, or salivation. It can also be used as a measure of motor reactions. Bilodeau and Levy (1964) measured the amplitude in degrees of a lever-positioning response. Their research sought to examine subjects' memory for such simple perceptual-motor responses; the study is reviewed in Chapter 11. *Amount* accomplished in a work task is another useful measure. It may help to reveal subjects' level of motivation, or their learning or fatigue. In Chapter 10 is summarized an experiment by Archer (1954). He used the mean number of alphabet letters printed during successive trials to plot the effects on performance of both learning and fatigue in different groups of college students. Another useful index of perceptual-motor proficiency may be the amount of *response error*. It is commonly used to gage the accuracy of positioning reactions. An example found in Chapter 10 is an experiment by Bilodeau, Bilodeau, and Schumsky (1959) who examined the precision with which subjects' could position a lever when knowledge of results of previous attempts was systematically varied.

Number of responses, or *response frequency,* is widely used in behavior research. Sometimes the responses are tallied within a unit of time to indicate *rate of response.* To suggest the variety of experiments in which the frequency of responding has proved a useful dependent variable, we may mention four contrasting examples to be found in different chapters of Part 2. In a study of locating sound sources, subjects' head movements were photographed and later counted by Thurlow, Mangels, and Runge (1967) as indicated in Chapter 8. In memory research the number of items recalled is a commonly used index of retention. This is exemplified in the Chapter 11 summary of an experiment by Postman, Stark, and Henschel (1969). In an investigation of syllogistic reasoning presented in Chapter 13 we find that Pezzoli and Frase (1968) tallied the number of errors made by college students to obtain a quantification of thinking processes under a variety of experimental conditions. Finally, the relative frequencies of certain matching responses made by children were counted and plotted by Montgomery and Parton (1970) in a study of self-reward as reinforcement, described in Chapter 14.

Complex response measures have been devised in great variety by research psychologists for investigative purposes. Special measurement methods are mentioned in many sections of this book. Often they are elaborations on some of the response indices listed here. Specialized measurement techniques are central concerns in two subsequent chapters—Chapter 5, *Psychophysical Methods* and Chapter 6, *Psychological Scaling.* The development of such widely useful measurement methods exemplifies the long-term vigor of psychology as the science of behavior and experience. Before we examine these additional approaches to conducting experiments, however, we shall consider in Chapter 4 another contributor to research progress, *Communication in Psychological Science.*

Summary

Laboratory studies in psychology have many facets to which any investigator must be attentive if his research is to produce findings of merit. The experimenter himself was noted as a primary source of influence on experimental outcomes. His attributes and actions and his expectancies may affect the behaviors of the subjects he is studying. Great caution in all phases of carrying out an experiment is necessary. Keeping a laboratory notebook and conducting pilot work were noted as two ways in which the quality of research may be kept high.

At the heart of psychological research is the manipulating of experimental variables. We select the values for independent variables with due attention to the behavior laws or practical applications we are seeking. All the details of conducting any study are similarly demanding of our concern—stimulus materials and their presentation, instructions to subjects, instrumentation, and the administering of the experimental treatments as demanded by our design.

Measuring behavior under carefully controlled conditions is the other requirement we face if our research is to be scientifically rigorous. We reviewed a number of common response measures that are to be illustrated further in the research we survey in Part 2. The list includes response latency or reaction time, response duration, amplitude or amount of behavior, error in responding, frequency or rate of response, and special complex indicants of behavior.

References

Bahrick, H. P., & Noble, M. E. Motor behavior. In J. B. Sidowski (Ed.), *Experimental methods and instrumentation in psychology.* New York: McGraw-Hill, 1966. Pp. 645–675.

Barber, T. X., & Silver, M. J. Fact, fiction, and the experimenter bias effect. *Psychological Bulletin Monograph*, 1968, **70**, No. 6, Part 2, 1–29. (a)

Barber, T. X., & Silver, M. J. Pitfalls in data analysis and interpretation: A reply to Rosenthal. *Psychological Bulletin Monograph*, 1968, **70**, No. 6, Part 2, 48–62. (b)

Boynton, R. M. Vision. In J. B. Sidowski (Ed.), *Experimental methods and instrumentation in psychology*. New York: McGraw-Hill, 1966. Pp. 273–330.

Bourne, L. E., Jr., & Battig, W. F. Complex processes. In J. B. Sidowski (Ed.), *Experimental methods and instrumentation in psychology*. New York: McGraw-Hill, 1966. Pp. 541–576.

Brown, D. R., & Owen, D. H. The metrics of visual form: Methodological dyspepsia. *Psychological Bulletin*, 1967, **68**, 243–259.

Dominowski, R. L. Role of memory in concept learning. *Psychological Bulletin*, 1965, **63**, 271–283.

Egan, J. P., & Clarke, F. R. Psychophysics and signal detection. In J. B. Sidowski (Ed.), *Experimental methods and instrumentation in psychology*. New York: McGraw-Hill, 1966. Pp. 211–246.

Hake, H. W., & Rodwan, A. S. Perception and recognition. In J. B. Sidowski (Ed.), *Experimental methods and instrumentation in psychology*. New York: McGraw-Hill, 1966. Pp. 331–381.

Hirsh, I. J. Audition. In J. B. Sidowski (Ed.), *Experimental methods and instrumentation in psychology*. New York: McGraw-Hill, 1966. Pp. 247–271.

Kintz, B. L., Delprato, D. J., Mettee, D. R., Persons, C. E., & Schappe, R. H. The experimenter effect. *Psychological Bulletin*, 1965, **63**, 223–232.

Orne, M. T. Demand characteristics and the concept of quasi-controls. In R. Rosenthal & R. L. Rosnow Eds.), *Artifact in behavioral research*. New York: Academic Press, 1969. Pp. 143–179.

Rosenthal, R. Covert communication in the psychological experiment. *Psychological Bulletin*, 1967, **67**, 356–367.

Rosenthal, R. Experimenter expectancy and the reassuring nature of the null hypothesis decision procedure. *Psychological Bulletin Monograph*, 1968, **70**, No. 6, Part 2, 30–47.

Rosenthal, R. Interpersonal expectations: Effects of the experimenter's hypothesis. In R. Rosenthal & R. L. Rosnow (Eds.), *Artifact in behavioral research*. New York: Academic Press, 1969. Pp. 181–277.

Runquist, W. N. Verbal behavior. In J. B. Sidowski (Ed.), *Experimental methods and instrumentation in psychology*. New York: McGraw-Hill, 1966. Pp. 487–540.

Sarason, I. G., & Minard, J. Interrelationships among subjects, experimenters, and situational variables. *Journal of Abnormal and Social Psychology*, 1963, **67**, 87–91.

Sattler, J. M. Racial "experimenter effects" in experimentation, testing, interviewing, and psychotherapy. *Psychological Bulletin*, 1970, **73**, 137–160.

Scott, W. A., & Wertheimer, M. *Introduction to psychological research.* New York: Wiley, 1962.

Shaw, M. E. Social psychology and group processes. In J. B. Sidowski (Ed.), *Experimental methods and instrumentation in psychology.* New York: McGraw-Hill, 1966. Pp. 607–643.

Sidowski, J. B. (Ed.) *Experimental methods and instrumentation in psychology.* New York: McGraw-Hill, 1966.

Sidowski, J. B., & Lockard, R. B. Some preliminary considerations in research. In J. B. Sidowski (Ed.), *Experimental methods and instrumentation in psychology.* New York: McGraw-Hill, 1966. Pp. 3–32.

Sidowski, J. B., & Smith, M. J. Basic instrumentation. In J. B. Sidowski (Ed.), *Experimental methods and instrumentation in psychology.* New York: McGraw-Hill, 1966. Pp. 33–114.

Stevenson, H. W., & Allen, S. Adult performance as a function of sex of experimenter and sex of subject. *Journal of Abnormal and Social Psychology,* 1964, **68**, 214–216.

chapter 4
Communication in Psychological Science

Scientific advance is a cumulative gain in empirical research findings and theory development. In psychology, as in other branches of science, progress is heavily dependent on an interchange of information among investigators. Several modes of communication serve different special functions but all contribute, at least potentially, to making a research psychologist aware of new insights, improved techniques, and experimental outcomes which relate to his areas of interest. Behavior scientists have worked to improve their channels of communication in recent years. The American Psychological Association has acted innovatively to contribute to this effort. Students of experimental psychology need to be generally aware of trends in the dissemination of research findings. More particularly, a student must refine his own skills of information retrieval and report writing in order to develop his scientific competence as fully as possible. In this chapter we first examine some aspects of information exchange and retrieval and then go on to concentrate on the important skill of preparing research reports.

Information Exchange and Retrieval

Psychologists pursuing research enjoy a variety of ways of exchanging ideas and sharing research results. Discussions with colleagues can be very helpful in sorting out alternative ways of approaching a problem, in designing a study, and in accounting for findings. Through exchanging letters and prepublication drafts of experimental reports, this mutually beneficial personal communication is broadened beyond the conversational circle. Interest groups, colloquia, seminars, and laboratory visits offer additional means of keeping up with current research activities. These relatively informal ways of gaining knowledge are augmented by official meetings and publication of journals. Psychologists have actively sought to make such channels more effective in advancing their investigative efforts.

Superabundance of Scientific Information

A flood of information threatens to inundate the scientist trying to keep himself informed in his field of specialization. Research findings pouring out of laboratories at an increasing rate have burdened the old ways of communication. The results of any experiment may meet with long delay before publication in the journals which formerly served as adequate outlets. Creating new journals may be of help in reducing publication lag but the reader still faces a formidable task in processing the flow of facts. In some "back-of-the-envelope" calculations Licklider (1966) emphasized the impossibility of the situation. He estimates that the information now on record for all of science and technology amounts to about ten trillion alphanumeric characters. Setting out to read one-thousandth of this, a specialist would require 13 hours a day, 365 days a year, for 12 years. However, on completion of this awesome task, he would find that during the 12 years an equal amount of new information in his area of interest would have been generated. The rate of output would have multiplied as well. No matter how we examine the dimensions of the problem, we can only conclude, with Licklider, that individual mastery of any scientific or technological field through reading has become impossible. A continuing advance in science must have cooperative group effort and interaction of the human mind and the computer as foundation stones for its information processing. Licklider has indicated current promising efforts by government, private companies, and professional societies to create the needed systems. In the cited article and other writings he has pointed to further developments which are necessary. A related projection of new modes of channeling scientific information was offered by Brown, Pierce, and Traub (1967). They propose that scientific journals, now in the form of bound periodicals, be replaced by a computerized service to subscribers. The system they outline would place in the hands of any individual scientist only those scientific articles which relate to his particular interests in research and theory. Those interests would be communicated to the system in a categorical request list. Changes in this topical request list might be made from time to time by the individual. A system of this type, now operative to expedite the flow of technical information in a company, is described in their article.

Information Flow in Psychology

Research psychologists working under the auspices of the American Psychological Association during the 1960's conducted a Project on Scientific Information Exchange in Psychology. Directors of the project for several years, Garvey and Griffith (1965, 1966) have described some of its findings and innovations. Their studies traced the typical dissemination of research findings through oral and written reports reaching both restricted and general audiences. A summary datum which they extracted from a number of investigations was an average of over thirty months from the initiation of research to its reporting in a psychological journal. Earlier public notice of completed work might occur through the listing of a paper to be presented at professional meetings. Of course an investigator might himself make his findings known to more restricted audiences in a variety of ways such as colloquium talks and distribution of preprint copies of a report. In an effort to reach a wider audience at an earlier time, the Project initiated and evaluated two departures in publication practices (Garvey and Griffith, 1966). One innovation was to have certain journals which are published by the American Psychological Association give a listing of manuscripts that have been accepted for publication. By giving the titles of articles together with the authors' names and addresses, the editors made it possible for interested scholars to contact the authors several months before their articles would actually be published. A second speed-up in the dissemination of research findings was the advance publication of the *Proceedings* of each annual convention of the American Psychological Association. In this way papers to be presented at these professional meetings could come to the attention of other psychologists several weeks before the sessions were actually convened. This has been found to increase the interchange of information between authors and those who share their research areas. Another advantage of publishing the *Proceedings* is that the papers are then abstracted in *Psychological Abstracts* through which they may reach the attention of scholars who use its topical index. Since they were evaluated as helpful in promoting the advance of psychological inquiry, both the convention *Proceedings* and the listing in journals of manuscripts accepted for publication were continued.

As the decade of the seventies began, the American Psychological Association undertook a developmental project known as the National Information System for Psychology (NISP). This study and the innovations which might stem from it have aroused interest from psychologists who are much concerned with communication in science. An examination of NISP was prepared by Clark (1971) who incorporated in his article several communications from other psychologists expressing various viewpoints. The project should benefit from this multifaceted examination and related discourse. In order that the activities of the Association be grounded in research about the processes of communication among scientists, its Board of Scientific Affairs requested the preparation of a paper published by Garvey and Griffith (1971). This overview examines publication and other avenues of information exchange in psychology in a number of different ways. Their data provide another input to those concerned with developing as effective a system of scientific communication as possible.

Surveying the Psychological Literature

Although investigators have devised ways to share their findings more expeditiously than through formal publications, the fact remains that periodicals or journals are the major archival repository for research reports and theoretical papers. An experimenter needs to know how to explore this literature to retrieve information that may guide his planning of a study. The knowledge gained through a literature search may help in formulating and refining a hypothesis to test, in suggesting experimental techniques, and in guiding decisions on the treatment variables to employ. If you should undertake an original experiment on some problem, you will want to look up anything pertinent that you can find. Where would you look? Some guidance may be helpful.

Books may be found which bring together a great deal of material on particular topics or areas of inquiry in psychology. As secondary sources, books aid in a speedy survey of past work but must generally be viewed as lagging somewhat behind the frontier advance of knowledge. Nevertheless you will find that handbooks of research, textbooks, and books on special subject matter are abundant and useful. Books of these sorts are listed at the end of some chapters in this text. Consulting them and the primary references which they cite will provide a background for your experimental efforts.

Review articles are found in the *Psychological Bulletin*. They bring together numerous references on a topic. Often the review author's analysis will help to guide you in shaping your own inquiry. In any case the cited research reports may be consulted as you pursue details of methods and findings. Again, the chapters of this book contain many references to illuminating review articles. Another sort of research review is to be found in the *Annual Review of Psychology*. Published annually in a single bound volume, this periodical is shown in reference lists with its individual chapters cited like journal articles with year, volume number, and inclusive pages given. In such chapters the authors cite and comment on recent publications pertinent to their broad topic, often mentioning books as well as research reports. The publishers of the *Annual Review of Psychology* have made it possible to purchase individual chapters to accommodate the special interests of students and research workers.

Psychological Abstracts is a likely source of help when you want to locate original articles on some particular topic. In this journal are printed brief abstracts of articles that appeared in previous issues of several hundred periodicals in psychology and related fields. The abstracting service covers numerous foreign language works published in all parts of the world. You may find *Abstracts* helpful also in locating review articles and bibliographies. For example, of the 18,068 entries in 1969, Volume 43, about 250 were books or reviews covering special problem areas.

It is not necessary to wade through several hundred entries in each volume of *Psychological Abstracts* to try to locate a few references that may be relevant to your needs. A cumulative index is issued every six months to augment the Table of Contents and Brief Subject Index in each monthly issue. This *Semiannual Index* contains a Subject Index with numerous headings and subheadings to help you locate any specific topic that interests you. Any entry provides one or more index numbers which you may look up in the issues covered. By reading the abstracts you have located you may be helped in deciding whether to seek out the original articles. You should note that the consecutive numbering of abstracts begins again with each new annual volume and that a different *Semiannual Index* covers each six months of issues. (In earlier years the cumulative index was compiled annually.)

Locating a comprehensive review article is a good way to cover several years of research with an economy of effort. "Reviews," "bibliographies," and "books" on all topics are brought together in the semiannual Subject Index of *Psychological Abstracts* with subheadings alphabetized according to the subject matter covered. Relying on review articles always entails the risk that the reviewer may have omitted some references that would be especially useful to you. You should estimate this risk as its relates to your scholarly needs. If it seems advisable, you may lessen the risk by extensive cross-checking of lists of references and by searching the *Abstracts* diligently yourself.

An Author Index also appears in the *Semiannual Index*. If you know that a scholar has been particularly active in an area of research that interests you, it might prove useful to look up his name in index volumes and review the abstracts of his published reports. This may help to locate articles relevant to your needs which might have been overlooked if you relied solely on finding their listing in the Subject Index.

In the 1960s certain changes were made in the operation of *Psychological Abstracts* to make it more effective in serving the scientific community. Siegmann and Griffith (1966) described the changes which have been instituted or contemplated. Briefly, the computerization of its printing process made it possible to consider *Abstracts* as a potential vehicle for studying and expediting the flow of information in addition to its published and indexed abstracts. Although *Psychological Abstracts* is recommended here for prime attention of the student of experimental psychology, it obviously is not the only such aid to information retrieval. Library research on many interdisciplinary topics may benefit greatly from consulting the abstracting services of other fields such as, for example, biology, engineering, or sociology.

Psychological Abstracts and *Psychological Bulletin* were mentioned as recommended starting points in a bibliographic search. For your general scholarship in psychology you may find it useful to study Table 4.1 which lists these and other journals published by the American Psy-

Table 4.1 Journals Published by the American Psychological Association

American Psychologist

Contemporary Psychology

Journal of Abnormal Psychology

Journal of Applied Psychology

Journal of Comparative and Physiological Psychology

Journal of Consulting Psychology

Journal of Counseling Psychology

Journal of Educational Psychology

Journal of Experimental Psychology

Journal of Personality and Social Psychology

Psychological Abstracts

Psychological Bulletin

Psychological Review

Note: As indicated in the text, articles and research reports appear in numerous psychological journals in addition to these which are published by APA.

chological Association. The APA publications are not the only scientific periodicals dealing with psychological research of course. Many fine journals are issued by other organizations and publishers. You will find these publications referenced in many sources, housed in many libraries, and abstracted in *Psychological Abstracts* and elsewhere. Your search of the literature of scientific psychology is likely to be wide-ranging if thoroughly conducted. If you continue such efforts for any length of time, you may need to develop a card filing system for storing and retrieving useful references.

Preparing Research Reports

A scientific research project may be considered to be complete only when it has been reported. By using scientific journals or widely circulated reports to describe his investigations, each scientist contributes to the success of further research efforts undertaken by others. Public dissemination of knowledge characterizes most modern science as a cooperative effort. It is our purpose to examine the conventional ways of reporting research. Conventions that are followed are often appropriate for student reports as well as for articles prepared for journal publication.

The observations that a scientist makes are essentially a part of his private experience. They become a part of scientific knowledge only as they are communicated to other scientists. Successful description of what the observations were and the conditions under which they were made puts research findings in their place in theory. A well-written research report also provides a basis for judging the findings and for conducting further experiments to verify them. Several different matters are treated in a single research report. One or more reasons are usually cited for undertaking the study. The findings may be interpreted, with implications drawn for the modification of theory or for the conducting of further investigations. The core of an experimental report, however, consists of information about how the research was carried out and what the results were. Details of procedure and the presentation of the data that were obtained are facts with which the reader of the report must reckon no matter what the author's interpretation of the study. It is the responsibility of the report writer to give these facts as clearly and completely as possible.

Purposes of the Reader

Our discussion of the writing of research reports will be aided if we first consider the aims of a reader of such a report. A description of an investigation that has been conducted may serve a number of purposes for different readers. By considering different aims that a reader may have in looking at a report, we may gain some insight into the criteria a report must meet to be judged satisfactory.

Repeat the study

One reason for getting the facts about a research effort is to guide a replication of the investigation. The repetition of a study may be undertaken as an instructive exercise, perhaps to become acquainted with a particular research method. Another reason for repeating a study may be to resolve any doubts that one might have about the outcome of the original investigation. Successful replication adds confirmatory strength to the tested hypothesis.

Devise new research

More common than the repetition of a study is the planning and conducting of new research that may be related to work that has been reported. Reports of earlier experiments can be helpful in numerous ways. They may suggest new hypotheses to be tested. They may report findings which require extension by means of using additional values of the independent variable or by combining new variables with those from the earlier work. Research reports may also describe experimental techniques which are applicable to other investigations of other problems, possibly quite different from those explored in the original research. A reported experiment that supports a particular theory may stimulate additional work that will relate the empirical results to the theory more completely. In contrast to this, a study that is supportive of one theoretical position may be the instigation for an experiment that offers countering strength to a rival theory.

Make practical applications

The reader of a research report may not have any scientific utilization in view. He may wish to incorporate the experimental findings in some practical application. For example, an educator might wish to employ findings on human learning as he formulates recommendations for curriculum reform. Like the person devising further research, he must be concerned not only with the data reported but also with the methods by which they were obtained. To ignore the procedural details of the experiment would be to risk misapplication of the results.

The Key Aim: to Inform

In the research report the writer's chief responsibility is to inform the reader completely and accurately about the conducting of the investigation and its outcome. The reader of a review or a theoretical article may have recourse to other papers to clarify his understanding of matters that are discussed, but a report of research often is the sole source of information about procedures that were followed or results that were obtained. If these are not presented clearly, much of the value of doing the study may be lost. The prime importance of giving the reader precise and complete information is a reflection of the aims of the reader in seeking out the research report. Whether he wants to repeat or extend the research, to use it in theory construction or practical application, he must be told without ambiguity or omission how the experiment was carried out and what observations or measurements were made.

Scientific reports are read by busy people. This suggests a need for brevity in writing. Brief research reports are desirable also on the basis of publication costs which are borne by the writers and readers of scientific articles. A number of conventions in report-writing have been adopted in the interests of saving time and money. Standard abbreviations, for example, conserve space on the printed page without any sacrifice of meaning. Since informing the reader is its cardinal goal, the writing of research reports calls for the economy of brevity only insofar as clarity of communication can be maintained. With the constraints of brevity on the one hand and clarity on the other, the writing of good reports of experiments is almost as much a challenge to skill in composition as is literary writing.

Conventions in Report Writing

With its informative purpose so paramount and with economy of time and money so pressing, it is easy to understand why certain conventions in the writing of research reports have evolved. The evolution of style and content of experimental reports in psychology is evident in the published journals of recent decades. In the interests of keeping the articles brief, the trend has been toward omitting many details of experiments that were formerly cataloged completely. Fortunately, other means of shortening reports with no loss of communication have been developed. These include abbreviations and brief phrases that are descriptive of commonly employed procedures. Some of these practices have been adopted informally and some have been made the subject of rules or suggestions adopted by the editors of psychology journals. A special way of keeping reports brief while making full information available is to file extensive tables or figures with the American Documentation Institute, Library of Congress.

Guides to writing conventions

A primary guide for the preparation of research reports in psychology is the *Publication Manual of the American Psychological Association: 1967 Revision*. This booklet contains much information about the publications and editorial policies of the association. It discusses the preparation of manuscripts in great detail, treating such topics as organization, headings, punctuation, abbreviations, tables, figures, and references. In preparing his first manuscript for publication, the research psychologist may find it troublesome to adhere to so many rules. Once the conventional ways of writing a report are learned, the job is actually expedited by using the methods that have been agreed upon. The real benefit for scientific communication comes from the combination of brevity and clarity that is achieved.

Although you will probably not be writing manuscripts for journal publication, you will want some guidance in the preparation of reports of the experiments you perform as part of your work in experimental psychology. Rather than setting up some arbitrary rules we shall follow the conventions set forth in the *Publication Manual* as we discuss the sections of the research report and present a model for your consideration.

A Sample Research Report

Your reports of experiments you perform are not likely to be as long as journal articles on research. Your introduction and your discussion of the results may be fairly brief. The design of a study which you carry out will probably be simpler than many that are reported in the journals, permitting a shorter description of the experimental method employed. To supplement your study of technical journals, then, you may wish to study a sample report. The one given below is a brief report of one of the author's studies. It is only intended as a guide, of course. Your instructor may have particular rules for you to follow in preparing certain reports, just as the editors impose certain requirements on those who submit articles to the psychology journals.

Indicants of Response Strength Hierarchies
in Continued Word Association

BURTON G. ANDREAS

One minute of continued word association was shown to yield both the Noble (1952) and Noble & Parker (1960) indicant of meaningfulness, m, and the Bilodeau & Howell (1965) indicant of probability of response occurrence. The probability values (proportion of Ss giving particular responses) were determined over the entire period of response production as well as for the initial group of three responses. The median ordinal position of response occurrence was also calculated. The probability values of the present study correlated positively with those obtained by Bilodeau & Howell. Over the restricted range studied, these p values did not correlate significantly with median ordinal position.

Noble (1952) and Noble & Parker (1960) allowed a full minute of continued word association to each verbal stimulus item. These studies were directed at determining a scale value of meaningfulness, m, for each stimulus word or paralog and did not report on the relative frequencies of occurrence of responses. Bilodeau & Howell (1965) required Ss to give three responses to each of several other stimulus words in their continuing word association technique for identifying response probability hierarchies. Their required termination of the response sequence naturally did not permit a determination of the m value for the stimulus word.

The present study employed most of the Bilodeau & Howell stimuli of five-letter length and CVCVC format, plus three words not on their list but scaled for m by Noble. The aim of the research was to see if Noble's technique could be used to obtain response probabilities comparable to those of Bilodeau & Howell as well as stimulus m values. In addition, the median ordinal position of the common responses was determined to provide additional evidence for the existence of associative response strength hierarchies in verbal behavior.

Method

Thirty-three army enlisted men and 35 summer session students from the University of Delaware served as Ss. The army men were volunteers for medical and psychological studies. The students were paid for participation in a series of experiments of which this was the first.

Each stimulus word, of five-letter CVCVC spelling, was arrayed in two double-spaced columns of ten repetitions each on a mimeographed page of a stapled test booklet.

Instructions to Ss were taken verbatim from Noble's (1952, p. 425) report. His procedure was modified by eliminating practice pages and the 15-sec inter-item interval. No rest period was required due to the brevity of the test administered. The test booklets were assembled with pages randomly ordered, except that stimulus words RIVER and WATER were placed in separate halves of the booklet.

Results

The results of the study are presented in Tables 1 and 2. The m value, defined as the mean number of responses (acceptable by Noble's criteria) given to the stimulus in 1 min, is shown with its SD in Table 1 for each

Table 1 Meaningfulness Value (*m*) and SD for Stimulus Words Given to Military and College Samples. Significant Differences in *m* Were Obtained ($p < .05$) for Each Word as *t* Ratios Indicate

Stimulus	33 Enlisted Men		35 College Students		
	m	SD	*m*	SD	*t*
COLOR	8.91	2.91	12.46	3.81	4.23
MUSIC	9.03	3.03	12.57	4.25	3.87
RIVER	9.85	3.21	12.20	4.01	2.61
WATER	11.12	3.13	14.37	3.68	3.87
WOMAN	8.33	2.98	10.20	3.14	2.47
LEMUR	3.61	3.27	8.03	4.20	4.75
MONEY	8.39	3.64	12.14	3.94	3.99
WAGON	7.73	2.09	10.09	2.85	3.81

stimulus word. The recorded scale values are based on data from the army men and the college students treated separately. This reporting of two *m* values is felt to be appropriate since the college students were significantly more productive of responses to every stimulus word than were the enlisted men as shown by the *t* ratios given in the table. This finding is similar to that of Noble & Parker (1960) who compared two such groups on total productivity over 96 stimulus items.

Response probability data are recorded in Table 2 for the responses found to have the most frequent occurrence as one of the first three responses given by *S*. Applying this criterion to the Bilodeau & Howell data and those of the present study separately required the tabulation of four responses in all common stimulus instances due to ties or inversions of probabilities obtained. The Bilodeau & Howell values were obtained from their compilation by summing across the probabilities they recorded for each ordinal position in the series of three responses they permitted. The adjacent column of probability values represents the proportion of *S*s in the present study who gave the response among the first three written. In the next column is the proportion of *S*s giving this response at any point in the 1-min period allowed. This *p* value is thus inclusive of the *p* value for response positions 1–3.

The final column of Table 2 contains the median ordinal position of each response tabled. The median is here considered more representative

Table 2 Probabilities of Occurrence and Median Ordinal Position of the Commonest Responses, $N = 68$

Stimulus	Response	B & H 1 – 3	Andreas 1 – 3	Andreas 1 – n	Median Ordinal Position
COLOR	red	.53	.47	.63	2.42
	blue	.51	.28	.60	3.80
	black	.20	.21	.41	3.50
	green	.20	.22	.51	4.13
MUSIC	song(s)	.23	.15	.21	1.50
	note(s)	.18	.16	.28	2.40
	sound(s)	.15	.09	.21	3.83
	dance	.07	.15	.40	4.38
RIVER	water	.56	.41	.62	2.20
	stream	.24	.24	.31	1.46
	lake	.17	.13	.18	2.50
	boat	.16	.16	.60	4.45
WATER	wet	.44	.15	.28	2.00
	drink	.41	.40	.65	2.30
	swim	.18	.12	.50	7.17
	river	.04	.22	.44	3.50
WOMAN	man	.47	.35	.44	1.39
	girl	.36	.25	.32	2.00
	wife	.25	.16	.28	3.20
	sex	.21	.32	.53	2.70
LEMUR	animal	—	.26	.26	2.00
	lemon	—	.22	.32	2.83
	French	—	.07	.12	2.17
MONEY	dollar(s)	—	.21	.34	2.25
	rich	—	.16	.31	3.40
	green	—	.12	.26	4.50
	coin	—	.12	.22	3.33
WAGON	wheel	—	.62	.76	1.37
	train	—	.32	.41	1.80
	covered	—	.25	.44	3.17

than the mean due to skewness of data distribution caused occasionally by the very late appearance of a common response in the production of one or two Ss.

Pearson product-moment correlation coefficients were computed as indicants of strength of agreement between several of the pairs of measures of response strength. Over the limited range of the high p values examined, the correlation of the probability of occurrence in the first three responses of the present study with the corresponding p values from Bilodeau & Howell (1965) was $r = +.724$ for the 20 responses of Table 2. When the present study's pairs of p values (for Positions 1–3 and 1–n) were correlated, r was found to be $+.782$. The correlation of p values for Positions 1–n in the present study and Bilodeau & Howell's p values was $+.424$. When p values for Positions 1–n were correlated with the median ordinal position for responses of this experiment, r was $+.098$, not significantly different from zero.

Discussion

The results tabulated in Tables 1 and 2 demonstrate the feasibility of using 1 min of continuing word association to obtain both the m value which describes the stimulus items' meaningfulness and the p values indicative of associative response strengths. This joint determination of descriptive values represents an economy over the separate approaches of prior investigations.

The correlation of present data with the p values of Bilodeau & Howell is sufficiently high, in the light of restricted range and possible subject population differences, to suggest that the present practice of allowing responses beyond the first three tabulated is acceptable. The Bilodeau and Howell interest in the first three responses can be satisfied even if subjects go on to give several more in the minute allowed.

The correlation between p values for Positions 1–3 and 1–n is not surprising in view of the fact that the latter set of responses contains the former. The lower correlation of the present p for Positions 1–n with Bilodeau & Howell's p values suggests that going on to permit additional responses uncovers different facets of response strengths than when responding is terminated with only three responses permitted.

The lack of significant correlation of median ordinal position with p values over the restricted range examined suggests that this separate index of response strength may be useful in describing response tendencies of subjects, apart from their propensity to give the same early responses. Over a greater range of responses given, we might expect this correlation to become significantly negative, with less frequent responses occurring later in the series. However, for the most common responses, the median ordinal position appears to yield a different sort of information from the *p* value. For example, the response *boat* to RIVER occurs a couple of response positions later than *water* even though given about as frequently when all *n* responses are tallied. To stimulus MUSIC, *dance* is given more frequently than other responses though it tends to be given somewhat later as Table 2 shows. This demonstrates the descriptive utility of adding median ordinal position of response to the *m* value and the *p* values when using continuing word association to explore response strength hierarchies.

In view of the demonstrated economy of multiple scaling of verbal stimuli and responses with the method employed here, it is felt that the approach should now be used to provide a larger pool of such scaled materials for use in verbal learning, memory, and perception experiments.

References

Bilodeau, E. A., & Howell, D. C. *Free association norms by discrete and continued methods.* Washington, D.C.: Office of Naval Research, 1965.

Noble, C. E. An analysis of meaning. *Psychological Review*, 1952, **59**, 421–430.

Noble, C. E., & Parker, G. V. C. The Montana scale of meaningfulness (*m*). *Psychological Reports*, 1960, **7**, 325–331.

Sections of the Research Report

Our sample report on the word association experiment has already illustrated the various sections of a research report and their organization. The format that we have suggested should be appropriate to any studies you may conduct and it conforms to the rules that govern publication in psychology journals. Another good way to get some help in preparing research reports is to browse through the psychology journals in which reports of investigations are given. Not all these journals adhere to the rules cited in the manual to which we have referred, because not all are published by the American Psychological Association. You will find, however, that the presentations of experimental studies are fairly similar in their broad outlines. Beyond acquainting you with some of the standard rules for the structure and content of reports, a survey of journal articles will familiarize you with some of the ways in which a writing style is slanted to achieve clarity of communication. You will see that a great deal of information about an experiment can be packed into a brief article. We now need to consider a research report section by section, sometimes commenting on the sample report and sometimes making points that are not covered in the sample.

Title

A comparison of the titles of psychological experiments and of popular novels will quickly convince you that there are vast differences, and for good reason. The titles of research reports might seem to be unnecessarily long and detailed, but the purpose underlying this is an important one for communication in science. When we search the literature for background material before we begin an experimental study we find that well-written titles in the cited references are a great aid to deciding which articles may be pertinent to our study and which probably are not.

With the major outline of the study revealed in its title, anyone searching the literature may establish his own criteria for looking up the report itself. If he is writing a critical review of studies in a certain problem area, he will go to more of the actual reports than if he is merely looking for a passing acquaintance with how research in that area is conducted. You may find it interesting to see how much you can guess about the way an experiment was carried out by merely reading its title.

To indicate both the phenomenon under investigation and the factors or conditions that were varied, many titles of research reports take one of two forms:

Y as a function of *X*
The effect of *X* upon *Y*

In both cases Y refers to the dependent variable or the behavior being studied and X refers to the independent variable(s) manipulated. Some authors introduce verbal variations within these formats and a few writers avoid such a standardized way of creating a title. Despite the stereotype they introduce into tables of contents in research journals, these forms are good guides to follow. If key words are fitted into them carefully, they insure a title that will convey as much information to a reader as may be expected.

Abstract

After the title and author of a report are indicated, an abstract is often the next section—as shown in the sample report's first paragraph. This abstract is a brief summary of the article, brought forward from the usual place at the end so that it can serve the reader better. He may scan the abstract quickly to learn the nature of the research. Then he may decide whether to read the report for details of the investigation. Written very concisely, an abstract should convey useful information about several aspects of the experiment. In published reports the printer sets off the abstract with special type or location on the page.

Introduction

The word "Introduction" did not appear as a heading in the sample report, but the section between the abstract and the Method section was precisely that. A heading is customarily omitted from this introductory part for reasons of appearance, considering that the abstract is already placed above the body of the report. The introductory section usually indicates the problem toward which the experiment was directed, so sometimes these paragraphs are considered as the "problem" part of the research article. Many introductions present background material first and then lead up to a statement of the problem or the hypothesis to be tested.

An introduction should answer the question "Why was this experiment carried out?" Very often an experiment is conducted to extend previous work. In such a case the prior studies are mentioned and cited as references and the relation of the current investigation to the past work is explained. Studies are often undertaken to test hypotheses that are derived from theory. The introductory portion of the report indicates the theoretical background and the derivation of the hypothesis, paving the way for the reader to understand how the study actually tests the hypothesis and, indirectly, the theory. Another reason for doing research is to obtain answers that may be applied in the solution of a practical problem. Here an appropriate introduction may be to outline this problem and then to indicate what information must be sought experimentally that may help in solving it.

Citation of references

You have probably seen references cited in technical books by footnotes. In a number of psychology journals a different convention is followed, as illustrated in the sample report. The dates of publication were used parenthetically in the citations together with the authors' names. Where citations are made of sources of some length, like a book, it is customary to add page numbers to the parenthetical citation to help the reader find the part cited. Where the citation refers to a major aspect of an experiment, the research report is usually mentioned without any page number. In many instances authors' names and publication dates are given parenthetically instead of in the text. This is done particularly when several references are cited together or when the writers of a report make reference to their own previous work. Example: "Recent experiments (Jones, 1968; Jones & Smith, 1969) have shown . . ." If material is quoted from any source, the parenthetical citation should include the author, year of publication, and the page number where the portion quoted may be found. The parenthesis initiating the citation data is placed right after the closing quotation mark.

Method

The Method section of a report is often divided into subsections. These may carry their own side headings such as *Subjects, Apparatus, Procedure.* As a major section heading, "Method" is often centered on the page in journal articles. In this section the writer must indicate the design of the experiment and must describe the treatments given to the subjects. In simpler experiments the design may be presented implicitly as the administering of the different conditions is described. In more complex research, the design may be outlined in its own subsection. As the running of subjects is described it is well to indicate key aspects of the instructions that were given to them. Sometimes these may be quoted verbatim in a *Procedure* subsection. A convention commonly found in publishing experimental reports is the use of the abbreviations, E for experimenter and S for subject (plural: Ss).

It is not easy to state categorically how detailed a description of the method of a study is needed. An experimenter should certainly describe every aspect of the investigation which is relevant to the hypothesis being tested or to the results that were obtained. If space permits, he may go further and give factual details that were only indirectly involved in the experimental test. Ideally, a research report should be complete enough to permit the study to be replicated in all its essential characteristics. In the technical journals, an economy is effected in describing experimental method if reference can be made to an earlier published description of the techniques used. Changes in procedure may be briefly described when these are variations in a standard method that has been described before. In student reports it is sometimes permissible to refer to a laboratory work sheet to indicate the procedures employed. If this is done, it is especially important to note in the Method section any departures from the techniques described in the guide to the laboratory work.

Results

Our major tasks in writing the Results section of an experimental report are (1) to present descriptive statistics on the outcome of the study and (2) to indicate the statistical tests that were applied in evaluating the data. The reader of a report can save time if the results are summarized in concise tables and figures. In order to tie them together in proper sequence they should never be presented without referring to them in the text of the report. This requirement is especially pertinent where complex experiments involve a number of measures of behavior which must be analyzed.

Tables

Organization and labeling of tables must be properly done if they are really to aid communication. A complete title is demanded because a reader may turn directly to a table without reading the textual material dealing with experimental results. The title should identify the statistics that are being presented, the response measures from which they were derived, and the conditions under which these measurements were taken. You can see how this has been done in the titles of tables in the sample report. Such information is included even though some of it is repeated in the headings of the rows and columns. Our sample titles include additional information concerning the data that have been collected and reduced to the statistics that are given. In many cases the N for different groups or conditions may be given in the body of the table; this is sometimes done as an adjunct to the title. Data on the statistical tests of significance are sometimes presented in tabular form, either together with descriptive statistics or separately. It will pay you to study numerous examples of tables in experimental journals to see how a well-planned table summarizes the results of an investigation. Tables are numbered consecutively through a research report.

Figures

The term *figure* is applied to a variety of graphic presentations which includes photographs and diagrams of apparatus, and graphs showing the results of a study. Figures are numbered through the report in a separate series of arabic numerals, so that the text of the report might state, for example, that "Figure 1 shows a schematic diagram of the apparatus . . ." and "Figure 2 presents the performance curves for the two groups . . ." We do not refer to "Diagram No. 1" or to "the first graph."

Figures that portray the results of an experiment may be of a number of different types: histograms or bar graphs, line graphs connecting plotted points, or smooth curves fitted by inspection or by mathematical methods to the plotted data. The type of graph to be employed should be determined by the information that is to be portrayed. For example, a bar graph seems most appropriate for representing separate statistics derived from discrete experimental conditions. If, however, we wished to picture a practice effect in some performance, we might use a line graph with straight line segments connecting the mean values for successive blocks of trials under a particular condition. The connecting of the segments would serve to portray the continuity of the process. Instead of connecting all the points we might choose a smooth curve which would pass among them, representing the abstract process underlying the empirical measurements that were taken.

A graph showing experimental results should be planned and executed with great care. The scale for the dependent variable generally ranges upward along the ordinate whereas the values of the independent variable, or the designations for the different conditions, are usually placed along the abscissa. The scale markings should be located along each coordinate so as to take advantage of the available space for the figure. To avoid compressing the performance measures unduly, the values plotted on the ordinate are often just those which will include the set of obtained values. The ordinate axis is then "broken" to indicate that the scale does not range upward from zero. The points and lines plotted in the graph are coded in different ways, with this coding indexed by a key that is located within the graph.

Below every figure is a figure number and a legend that aids in understanding the graphic portrayal and gives pertinent facts. These legends vary in length. Where several sentences are given, the first is usually a title for the graph with the others adding information about conditions under which the portrayed data were gathered. The values of N—the number of subjects in different groups or conditions—are sometimes included in the legend, sometimes in the key of a figure. Amplify your understanding of graphic presentations by studying carefully the figures in this textbook and in other sources of research reports.

Discussion

This section of the report is essentially a consideration of the results obtained in the experiment as they bear upon the problem which was stated in introducing the report. This discussion of the outcome of the study must be guided by the statistical analyses of the data that were reported in the Results section. The report writer states what conclusions have been reached as a result of the experiment, or indicates whether the hypothesis being tested is considered tenable or is rejected. Agreement or disagreement with previous findings is often mentioned. If the study was formulated to test some theoretical question, the implications of the results for the theory are discussed.

If unexpected results have been obtained, it is sometimes permissible in this part of the report to refer to the way in which the experiment was conducted and to suggest possible reasons for the outcome. This is a game that ought to be played with restraint. It should never be assumed that verbal explanations of an unwanted result automatically reverse the finding. Nor is fluency in listing the flaws in an experiment any substitute for carefully designing and executing the study in the first place. The value in discussing a result that was not anticipated lies in the suggestions it may generate for new ways of experimenting further with the problem.

References

When a report is being prepared, the entire list of references should be alphabetized by authors' names. The forms to be used in presenting two common types of reference, book and journal article, are illustrated in the sample report. You should study these very carefully so that you will be able to list references with complete accuracy of form. Pay close attention to what is included in each reference, the sequence of items, the capitalization, and the punctuation. Examine the references given in this book to obtain further information on matters like the capitalization of journal titles and the short version of names of publishers. The number which follows the year of journal publication is the volume number. It is important to include this because some journals are issued in more than one volume per year. You may wish to refer to a chapter that appears in an edited book. The form for such a reference is as follows: Bourne,

L.E., Jr., & Battig, W.F.   Complex processes.   In J.B. Sidowski (Ed.),
Experimental methods and instrumentation in psychology. New York:
McGraw-Hill, 1966.   Pp. 541–576.   The book and journal titles which
you are asked to underline would appear in italics in print; thus any
italicized parts of references that you see in books or journals should be
underlined when you prepare a report or a manuscript. In listing a
chapter which appears in an edited book the inclusive page numbers are
given; this is the only time that page numbers from a *book* should appear
in a listing of references. A specific page in a book may be cited parenthetically in the text of a report. Inclusive page numbers of *journal
articles* are always given in a list of references, and a particular page may
occasionally need to be cited in a report. A page citation must definitely
accompany quoted material.

Appendices

An appendix is never found in the usual journal report of an experiment, although one or more may be included with a monograph. However, in student reports there is often a definite need for appendices. If
a laboratory work sheet guided you in carrying out an experiment, it may
be advisable to use it as Appendix A to the report you write. Your instructor may permit you to refer to this Appendix A in writing the
Method section of your report. Even if this is not the case, the reader
of reports may be helped if work sheets are appended to them. A verbatim copy of the *Instructions to Subjects* is also a useful appendix.
Another appendix in your report might present the raw data of the experiment and the calculations you performed in treating the results. Part
of the data might have been collected on an individual subject whom
you have run. It is best if you submit the actual work sheet on which
you took down the response measures in the laboratory. This will tend
to show how carefully you have carried out the research and will avoid
errors that might occur in transcribing data.

Important General Considerations

We have considered the report of an experiment section by section, from
the title to the appendices. There remain a few points about report
writing that apply to the report generally rather than to any particular
part. These should provide guidance that will help you to write good
reports on your early attempts rather than by learning through the painful correction of your errors. Close examination of a publication like the

Journal of Experimental Psychology will teach you techniques of report writing that our space limitations would never permit us to treat. Some research reports are difficult to understand. The more of them that you read, the more comprehension you will gain for their further study.

Organization

A great deal of organization is imposed on a report when the different prescribed sections are used. You should be careful not to violate the intended structure by putting material into the wrong parts. You may find it a real challenge to your writing skill to say the right thing in the right place. It is all too easy to begin describing the experimental method while you are still writing the introduction. Sometimes it is actually difficult to avoid it. There may be great temptation, too, for you to begin discussing the results while you are still presenting them. And when you finally do get to the discussion section you may slip into repeating results unnecessarily. Discipline yourself to structure your writing with the conventional section headings as your blueprint.

Redundancy

While organization is something to be desired in reports, redundancy, or repetition, is something that should be avoided in the interest of brevity. Study the Method section of the sample report and note how various phrases are used to tell the story of the experiment. Without too much repetition, this is accomplished in eight sentences. If anything, this report may err in leaving out important details.

We did note a couple of places where redundancy in an experimental report is desirable. One is the titles of tables and the legends of figures where some indication of conditions under which the data were collected is given even though this information is contained in the body of the report. This is done as a convenience to a reader who wishes to peruse the results of the study quickly. Repetition is also needed, of course, in the abstract. We should repeat major points very briefly, avoiding the tendency to write the report all over again. Anyone who wishes details can read the appropriate parts of the report.

Even the style of writing research reports has been conventionalized to some degree. The demand for conciseness naturally rules out long, flowery phrasing. It is customary to write impersonally. Omitting personal pronouns leads to very common use of the passive voice. Instead of saying, "I presented the stimulus light," we say, "The stimulus light was presented." Again, you can learn about these conventions of style by reading some of the psychology journals.

The past tense is widely used in reporting studies since the experiments are completed at the time the report is read. Since the data have already been analyzed when the report is prepared, we refer to the outcome of the analysis in the past tense also. We do, however, use the present tense when we state that "means and SDs . . . are presented in Table 1" because here we are making a statement about the report, which is present, and not about the experiment or its analysis, which are past. If the problem of which tense to employ ever causes you concern, referring to the sample report may answer your questions.

Avoiding errors

Students writing their first reports of experiments are likely to make several sorts of errors. It is impossible to anticipate what difficulty you may encounter personally, but a general indication of some of the pitfalls might be of some assistance. Vague statements and factual errors sometimes creep into student reports. Omission of important details is a common error. Irrelevant discussion is occasionally introduced, as if in response to some nonexistent rule like: *Discuss, and discuss, but always discuss.* More serious from a scientific point of view is a tendency to overgeneralize from the results of a study. For example, the findings of the sample report would have been overgeneralized if the author had stated, "College students always give more responses in continued word association than are given by army enlisted men." Still more alarming to read is discussion by some experimenters of unexpected findings. Often they are explained away, so that the writer may go on to reach the conclusions which were his firm belief even before he conducted the experiment. In writing your first reports you will avoid making mistakes of some sort only if you edit your first draft very carefully. Report writing, of any kind, is work. It becomes relatively effortless only after considerable practice.

Summary

Scientific advance thrives on good communication among research workers and theorists. Psychologists have taken important steps to assure information exchange and retrieval in the face of a rising tide of reported research. Many of the new channels of communication have been designed to promote earlier dissemination of new findings. There is still a need, however, to delve into archival sources for results of past research. You have a vast literature at your disposal as you plan and report experiments in psychology. Textbooks and handbooks organize a great amount of information for you on particular problem areas. Review articles and bibliographies introduce you to reports from which you may select a few for further study. The *Annual Review of Psychology* helps to identify trends in research on a number of broad topics. The original research literature is open to you if you learn how to use *Psychological Abstracts* to find the information you need. Both a subject index and an author index are provided to aid you in locating the particular abstracts which may interest you. You may then go on to read the most promising of the references in their original sources.

Preparing your own research reports is a challenge to your developing skills in experimental psychology. Good reports provide the information needed to generate new research and to modify existing theory. The key aim of a scientific communication is to inform. Clarity and completeness of writing are therefore very much desired in research reports. A reader may wish to extend the test of the hypothesis to a wider set of values of the independent variable. Making practical application of findings may be another of his purposes. He must be told exactly what was done in an experiment and precisely what was found. While meeting these goals, the report writer must strive for brevity to avoid consuming his reader's time unduly. Clarity and brevity may be sought through consistently following the conventional rules that have been developed for reporting psychological investigations. The same rules established for reporting in psychology journals are excellent guides for the writing of student reports. A sample research report illustrates how they are applied.

Every section of the experimental report, from the title through the references, should give full and accurate information to the reader. He should be told exactly how the experiment was conducted and what results were obtained. The outcome of statistical analysis of the data should also be stated. Discussion should be guided by previous work cited in introducing the study and by the findings as analyzed statistically. Evaluation of a research effort should never wander far from the facts. In student reports, appendices provide a means of conveying additional details about the performing of the experiment.

Your efforts in writing reports will be rewarded if you strive for good organization and adopt a style that resembles the writing in psychology journals which report on experiments. You should avoid redundancy in your writing except where it is purposely introduced, as in titles of tables and legends of figures, to aid the reader to grasp the essentials of the research quickly. Good report writing is a useful skill that you may develop through careful attention to the guidance given you and, above all, through actual practice.

References

Andreas, B. G. Indicants of response strength hierarchies in continued word association. *Psychonomic Science,* 1966, **6,** 447–448.

American Psychological Association. *Publication manual of the American Psychological Association: 1967 revision.* Washington, D.C.: American Psychological Association, 1967.

Brown, W. S., Pierce, J. R., & Traub, J. F. The future of scientific journals. *Science,* 1967, **158,** 1153–1159.

Clark, K. E. A critical examination of the National Information System for Psychology. *American Psychologist,* 1971, **26,** 325–348.

Garvey, W. D., & Griffith, B. C. Scientific communication: The dissemination system in psychology and a theoretical framework for planning innovations. *American Psychologist,* 1965, **20,** 157–164.

Garvey, W. D., & Griffith, B. C. Studies of social innovations in scientific communication in psychology. *American Psychologist,* 1966, **21,** 1019–1036.

Garvey, W. D., & Griffith, B. C. Scientific communication: Its role in the conduct of research and creation of knowledge. *American Psychologist,* 1971, **26,** 349–362.

Licklider, J. C. R. A crux in scientific and technical communications. *American Psychologist,* 1966, **21,** 1044–1051.

Siegmann, P. J., & Griffith, B. C. The changing role of *Psychological Abstracts* in scientific communication. *American Psychologist,* 1966, **21,** 1037–1043.

Note: Sample report (pp. 99–104) is used with permission of *Psychonomic Science.*

chapter 5
Psychophysical Methods

Psychophysics deals with the dependence of psychological experience on the physical stimulus energies which reach our sense organs from the environment. Psychophysical methods have a century-old association with laboratory studies of sensation and perception. They have been used in determining hundreds of facts and relationships concerning how our senses operate. In addition to the classical psychophysical procedures some new approaches to quantifying reactions to stimuli have emerged in recent years. Our consideration of this domain of research methods must therefore be both historical and modern. We shall first treat the traditional methods which have been used extensively in delineating sensory and perceptual processes. Then we shall deal with some new concepts arising from the theory of signal detection. Finally, we shall examine the direct scaling methods used to quantify experiential magnitudes in audition, vision, and other receptor systems.

Oriented as they are toward quantification, the psychophysical methods involve the statistical treatment of the collected data. In fact, many of the central constructs in psychophysics are statistically defined. Accurate specification of such constructs naturally demands a foundation of reliable data, carefully treated mathematically to yield valid information. The basis, in turn, for the reliability of the data we obtain is to be found in taking enough repeated measurements while every safeguard against experimental error is exercised. The newer trends in psychophysics have extended the concern with quantification into such areas as rating one's confidence in detecting a faint stimulus and estimating the magnitude of one's sensations. The need for rigor in collecting and treating the data remains paramount.

Exploring Sensory Boundaries

The eye is sensitive only to a particular band of wavelengths of electromagnetic radiation, from about 400mμ to about 700mμ.* Hearing is limited to a frequency range between about 16 Hz and 16,000 Hz.† On the energy dimension, too, there are values of physical intensity for both auditory and visual stimuli that are at the limit of sensation. Weaker physical energies than these threshold values are not experienced. There are boundaries to these modalities of sensation, then, within the broad extent of physical stimuli for both the dimensions of energy level and of wavelength or frequency. An important application of the psychophysical methods is to survey these boundaries under varied conditions of testing.

The absolute threshold or limen

As we see how the methods are employed, we shall learn not only about the procedural techniques of psychophysics, but we shall become better acquainted with the historically established concept of *absolute threshold* or *limen* at the same time. An absolute threshold was conceptualized as a boundary point in sensation, separating sensory experience from no such experience when physical stimulus values reached a particular point. ("Limen" is the Latin word for the threshold of a door and it is generally used as a synonym for "threshold" in psychophysics. The often-used abbreviation for the absolute threshold is RL, taken from the German *Reiz Limen,* which means *stimulus threshold.*) Recent theorizing has placed renewed emphasis on the fact that a threshold determination is not dependent merely on a subject's sensory acuity. Certain attitudes and decision processes also govern his reporting of his subjective experiences. Long a concern of the methodologists who at-

*The abbreviation, mμ stands for millimicrons—units of wavelength measurement. Millimicrons are sometimes termed *nanometers*. Their length equals 10^{-9} meter.

†The abbreviation, Hz, stands for Herz—cycles per second of vibratory frequency. Herz is pronounced with a *t* sound, as in *hurts*. Another abbreviation used for this frequency unit is *cps*.

tempted certain procedural safeguards, these factors are now themselves quantified in many investigations of stimulus detection and sensory scaling. In view of this, the adjective "absolute" for such boundary thresholds is retained only as a reflection of historical usage.

The Method of Limits

Most psychophysical methods have been known by more than one name. The *method of limits,* for example, is also called the *method of minimal changes.* To locate the absolute threshold, the experimenter gives a series of trials in which stimulation is *minimally changed* in successive steps along some physical dimension until the boundary of sensation is passed. That is, a series of stimulations which begins above the sensory threshold is continued until a physical stimulus value is reached which arouses no reported sensation. Or, a series beginning somewhat below threshold is continued until a stimulus value is reached that arouses a reported sensation. In either case, the occurrence of a change in report on the part of the subject is an indication that the *limit* or sensory boundary has been reached. The series of trials is terminated whenever the subject's report of sensation changes from "Yes" to "No" or from "No" to "Yes." (In the tradition of the old psychophysics, we are ignoring the cognitive aspects of the task in these illustrative accounts.)

Determining the absolute threshold; an example

The method of limits is often used in audiometry—testing a person's hearing. The hearing specialist presents a series of tones that begins above threshold. Attenuation weakens the physical tone intensity with each stimulus presentation until it becomes so faint that it is not reported as heard. On other series of trials, the tone is initially below threshold and its intensity is increased in small steps until it can be heard. Several such series of trials, working down to and up to the limit of hearing, permit the calculation of an average threshold value. In audiometry, the threshold is obtained for each of several frequency values so that a threshold curve or audiogram may be plotted. Such a curve is drawn in a rectangular coordinate plot with threshold intensity levels related to tonal frequency. Besides being employed in clinical audiometry, the method of limits may be used as a research technique to determine hearing thresholds under special conditions like environmental masking noise.

Returning to our example, let us examine the procedural details of the method of limits as it might be used to test one subject in a normative study of hearing thresholds. Assume we are testing with a tone of 8000 cycles per second at this point in the experiment. With the tone presented monaurally, the absolute threshold, RL, may fall about 55 dB* below a reference pressure level of 1 dyne/cm² or −55. Some of our series of trials might begin above this value, say at −45 or −50, and descend in 1-dB steps until the subject could no longer hear the tone. These would be called *descending series*. Other series would begin below threshold, perhaps at −60 or −65, and be increased until reported as heard. These are termed *ascending series*. Most experimental work involves both descending and ascending series of trials with minimal changes being made in physical stimulus intensity until a limit of sensation is reached. We see that this psychophysical method employs *physical* changes in the physical stimulus to locate a boundary point on the *psychological* scale of sensation—a *psychophysical* procedure.

Our administration of the method of limits would be guided by a work sheet on which we would indicate the minimal change steps to be used and the starting points for the various descending and ascending series. Preliminary trials would have served to locate the threshold approximately. Table 5.1 shows a work sheet for determining the intensity threshold for the 8000-Hz tone with three descending and three ascending series of trials. Also included in the table are the symbols (Yes or No) which were used to tally the responses as the testing proceeded in this hypothetical study. Each column in the table represents one series of trials, either descending, *d*, or ascending, *a*. The scale at the left indicates the successive physical intensity values that made up a series. Each column indicates that a series was terminated as soon as the subject made a change in judgment from "Yes" to "No" or from "No" to "Yes" in response to some visual signal meaning, "Do you hear the tone?" For each series of trials an estimate of the threshold value was taken to be the value halfway between the intensity that elicited a change in judgment and the preceding intensity of the series. These threshold estimates are indicated at the bottom of each column of Table 5.1. An averaging of these series RL estimates over several series of trials completes the

---

*The abbreviation dB stands for decibels—units of sound pressure level relative to some specified or standard reference pressure.

Table 5.1 Completed Work Sheet for Determination of Absolute Threshold for an 8000-Hz Tone by the Method of Limits (the Testing of One Subject Is Represented)

*Stimulus Intensity	Type of Series					
	d	a	d	a	d	a
−44						
−45	†Yes					
−46	Yes				†Yes	
−47	Yes				Yes	
−48	Yes				Yes	
−49	Yes		†Yes		Yes	
−50	Yes		Yes		Yes	
−51	Yes		Yes		Yes	
−52	Yes		Yes		Yes	
−53	Yes		Yes		Yes	Yes
						—
−54	Yes	Yes	Yes		Yes	No
		—	—			
−55	Yes	No	No		Yes	No
	—					
−56	No	No		Yes	Yes	No
				—	—	
−57		No		No	No	No
−58		No		No		No
−59		No		No		No
−60		No		No		†No
−61		No		No		
−62		†No		No		
−63				No		
−64				No		
−65				†No		
Series *RL*:	−55.5	−54.5	−54.5	−56.5	−56.5	−53.5

*In decibels below 1 dyne/cm² reference pressure level.
†Predetermined starting point for this series.

operational definition of the threshold of hearing for this subject for an 8000-Hz tone. The liminal value, or RL, in our example is —55.17 dB below the reference level of 1 dyne/cm².

Procedural details

Several procedural details should be noted in our example of the method of limits. The steps used in each series of stimulus presentations are small ones, approximating minimal changes. Much larger steps would give only a coarse estimate of the threshold on each series of trials. Ascending and descending series of trials were both used, in this case alternately. The use of both types of series tends to guard against certain errors as our later discussion will show. Different series in either category are begun at different points on the scale. This prevents a subject from falling into a habit of changing his judgment after a fixed number of stimulus presentations. The threshold estimates from several series are averaged to give a more reliable value for the limen than one or two series would yield.

Research application

The method of limits was employed by Mote, Briggs, and Michels (1954) in taking successive visual threshold measurements to plot a curve of dark adaptation as a function of time. This experimental use of the method differed in several respects from the hypothetical example in audiometry which we discussed. Since they were measuring dark adaptation, the investigators could not risk destroying the adaptation by presenting a descending series of light stimuli that started well above threshold. Consequently, each estimate of the threshold was based on an ascending series of trials. The threshold value was approached from below in steps of 0.01 to 0.03 logarithmic units of intensity. Each ascending series was continued until the stimulus was reported as visible for two successive presentations of the same intensity value. In other words, whenever the limit of visibility was crossed to yield a positive report, that intensity of stimulus was repeated as a reliability check on the sensation reported. If the positive report were not repeated, the ascending series would continue. This experiment deviates in several procedural respects from the method of limits as we outlined it earlier. This serves only to show, however, that the psychophysical methods can be varied to suit different research purposes.

Another illustration of the point just made was the proposal by Cornsweet (1962) that a "staircase method" be used in locating sensory limits. He would reduce the length of ascending and descending series of trials, selecting steps of such size that just two to four stimulus changes would lead to a change in the subject's response. It is debatable whether this attempt at efficiency in a psychophysical procedure might unduly risk error in determining a threshold. Dallenbach (1966) argued strongly against this modification of the traditional method of limits.

Other Methods for Threshold Determination

We have cited examples of determining absolute thresholds by the the method of limits, also called the method of minimal changes. Various limens of sensation can also be determined by means of other psychophysical methods. We shall briefly indicate them here, while reserving a more complete discussion of these methods in another application, measuring discrimination.

The method of adjustment

Locating the limit of a sensation can also be achieved by the *method of adjustment*. In this psychophysical method, the subject himself adjusts the control that regulates stimulus intensity; hence the name, method of adjustment. The subject regulates the control until the stimulus can just barely be sensed, the subject having increased its intensity from below threshold. Or, starting above threshold, he reduces the stimulus intensity until the sensation just barely disappears. Thus the method permits both ascending and descending trials. The point from which the adjustment is originated is probably not too important in many cases since the subject is usually allowed to make adjustments back and forth when he gets to the boundary of sensation. Besides this active participation by the subject, it is the continuous change in stimulus that differentiates this method from the method of limits which employs small discrete steps in changing the stimulus. The liminal value, or RL, is determined in the method of adjustment by taking an average of a number of settings made by the subject.

The method of constant stimuli

Like the method of limits, the *method of constant stimuli* involves the presentation of discrete stimulus values. However, they are not presented in ascending or descending series but in a random or irregular order. The presentations are referred to as *constant stimuli* because they are not changed while being presented as they are in the method of adjustment.

If we do not present stimulus values in a regular series, how can we determine the boundary of sensation? In the method of constant stimuli the threshold value is computed somewhat more indirectly than in the other two methods. For each different stimulus value presented, we determine the percent of times that it was detected by the subject. A stimulus that is well above threshold will naturally be detected 100 percent of the time. Conversely, a stimulus that is quite far below threshold will never be sensed by the subject. Stimulus values that are near the threshold will be detected on varying percents of the trials. If each stimulus intensity is presented enough times, we should find that the percent of detection is an increasing function of the intensity value. The absolute threshold value, or RL, is defined as that stimulus intensity that is detected 50 percent of the time. If no stimulus value yields exactly 50 percent detection, interpolation may be used to calculate the limen. In view of modern critical concern over the concept of a threshold, it must be stressed that the definition of the RL is operational, beginning with instructions to the subject and possibly including some preliminary training. There is a danger here that too many investigators have arbitrarily defined too many different thresholds over the decades of psychophysical research.

Let us assume that our hypothetical experiment to determine the absolute threshold for an 8000-Hz tone had employed the method of constant stimuli. Nine different stimulus intensities might have been presented twenty times each, in random order. Table 5.2 indicates the data which might have been obtained. The more intense stimuli were detected a greater percent of the time. One stimulus, at —64 dB, was never sensed at all. What stimulus value was detected 50 percent of the time? None of the intensities yielded this exact percent of positive reports by the subject. The threshold apparently lies between —56 dB which was detected 45 percent of the time and —54 dB which was sensed on 60 percent of its presentations. Since 50 percent is one-third of the distance from 45 to 60 percent, we may use linear interpolation to fix the RL at a corresponding position on the stimulus intensity scale, —55.33 dB.

Measuring Discrimination

We have seen that the psychophysical methods can be used to determine absolute sensory thresholds. Next we shall find them used at

Table 5.2 Tabulation Sheet for Determination of Absolute
Threshold for an 8000-Hz Tone by the Method of Constant Stimuli

*Stimulus Intensity	Percent of Trials Detected
−48	95
−50	90
−52	75
−54	60
−56	45
−58	30
−60	15
−62	10
−64	0

*In decibels below 1 dyne/cm² reference pressure level.

stimulus values well above absolute threshold to find out how small a
stimulus difference can be reliably detected. The difference between
two stimuli that can just barely be differentiated from each other
is variously called the *differential threshold, difference threshold,* or *DL*
(for "difference limen"). We shall see that each one of the methods
we have already discussed can be employed in determining the DL. More
precisely, the concept of the DL is given a number of different operational definitions. The variations in these different sets of operations
are both procedural and statistical. Besides the DL for intensity differences in any sense modality, we may determine DLs for other stimulus
dimensions like the wavelength of chromatic visual stimuli or the frequency of tones.

The just noticeable difference
Before seeing how the various psychophysical methods are used in determining the DL, we should become acquainted with a construct closely
related to the DL, the *just noticeable difference* or *JND.** The JND is
the smallest difference between two stimuli which can be detected by an

*Often abbreviated j.n.d.

observer. Any stimulus, then, would have to be increased or decreased by one JND in order for the change to be detected. The determination of the magnitude of the JND is a key step in many of the methods for arriving at the DL. Often, in fact, the term JND is applied to instances where the calculation of the DL has actually been made.

Closely related to the JND is the *just unnoticeable difference,* or *JUD.* This is again a construct appearing in some methods for determining the DL. It may be defined as the largest difference in some physical stimulus dimension which cannot be detected by the observer. The magnitude of the JUD, then, is very slightly less than that of the JND for the same stimulus dimension. A DL is sometimes calculated, we shall see, by averaging JNDs and JUDs.

Weber's law

Among the early psychophysical investigations were studies of the tactual and kinesthetic senses conducted by Ernst Weber and others. They sought to determine, for example, the JND for lifted weights. By what amount do two weights have to differ to feel just noticeably different when lifted? As a matter of fact, it was found that there was no *absolute* difference that represented the JND. Rather, the JND was found to be a *relative* quantity, proportional to the weights being judged. The JND, they discovered, was a constant proportion, about 1/30, of the weights under comparison. If the standard weight were 30 grams, a 31-gram weight would seem just noticeably heavier, the JND being 1 gram. However, if the standard weight were 60 grams, it would take a 2-gram difference to be reliably detected. Similarly, a standard weight of 90 grams would require 93 grams in the comparison stimulus for dependable discrimination, a JND of 3 grams. This proportionality of the JND to the standard stimulus was noted by Weber and became known as *Weber's law.* The constant of proportionality, about 1/30 in the case of lifted weights, became known as *Weber's constant.* Attempts were made to determine the value of this constant for a great number of stimulus dimensions in all the sensory modalities. Evidence was gradually accumulated to show that there is no Weber's constant which holds over the entire range of stimulus values for any sensory dimension. Today, the determination of the JND or DL at any point on a stimulus continuum is regarded as an empirical problem rather than an attempt to verify or disprove Weber's law.

The Method of Adjustment or Average Error

One psychophysical approach to sensory or perceptual discrimination is the *method of adjustment,* sometimes referred to as the *method of average error* or the *method of reproduction.* All these names are descriptive of the procedure used in assessing the discriminatory abilities exhibited under the conditions of the experiment.

The procedure

Earlier we saw how the method of adjustment could be used to locate absolute thresholds by having subjects manipulate some stimulus dimension until the boundary of sensation was reached. For measuring discrimination a similar performance is required of the subject except that, in addition to the *variable stimulus* under his control, a *standard stimulus* is provided. Instead of adjusting the variable stimulus to the boundary of sensation, he must physically regulate its value until he judges it to be equal in sensory magnitude to the standard stimulus. In other words, the subject must manipulate the variable stimulus until he reproduces the sensation level of the standard stimulus—hence the designation, method of reproduction. When the two stimuli are measured in physical terms, it will be found that only on rare trials does the subject match the variable to the standard stimulus with perfect accuracy. The occurrence of some small error on most trials indicates a failure to discriminate very small stimulus differences. Various averages of these errors provide indices of discriminating ability. These treatments of the psychophysical data give us the name, method of average error.

Quantifying an illusion

The method of adjustment has found special utility in assessing the strength of certain visual illusions. A *constant error,* some directional tendency in making physical settings while adjusting a movable part of the stimulus figure, is an algebraic mean value which reveals the magnitude of the illusion. Data are typically taken from a number of subjects who are each given several adjustment trials. As an example, we shall briefly review an experiment by Novak (1966) which used different instructions to determine their effect on the Poggendorff illusion. This is represented in Figure 5.1 with a fixation cross used in this study but not normally included in the illusion. As the legend of the figure indicates, the solid lines represent a conventional configuration for this illus-

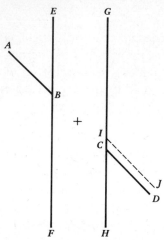

Fig. 5.1. The Poggendorff illusion figure (solid lines) with a special fixation cross added for experimental purposes. The dotted line *IJ* represents a typical setting by a subject. (After Novak, 1966.)

ion while the dotted line and fixation cross are related to particular aspects of the experiment.

Novak sought to determine the effect on the illusion of adding the fixation cross to the Poggendorff figure and requiring subjects to fix their gaze on this point while adjusting the movable portion of the configuration, the slanting line *CD* on the right. This adjustable portion of the visual display could be moved up and down in an effort to align it so as to make it appear to be a continuation of the left-hand slanting line segment, *AB*. Usually, a setting as suggested by dotted line *IJ* is seen to represent alignment, whereas *CD* in the figure is actually aligned with *AB* physically. Prior research had yielded conflicting results on the size of the constant error (the algebraic average of settings) when a fixation point or cross had been provided. This investigation was carefully designed and executed to determine the effect of the fixation cross under different instructions and angular variations of the illusion lines.

Eighteen female college students served as subjects under all of the experimental conditions. The three different viewing conditions are best understood through reading the instructions governing each of them:

Note: Figures 5.1 and 5.2 and instructions to subjects (p. 129) are reprinted with permission of author and publisher.

Condition *A* (Free inspection, no fixation cross).

> Inspect the Poggendorff figure freely and try not to fixate on any one point in the display. Scan the figure while you are adjusting the variable line segment.

Condition *B* (Free inspection, with fixation cross)

> Inspect the Poggendorff figure freely and try not to fixate on any one point in the display. Scan the figure while you are adjusting the variable line segment. Try to disregard the fixation cross and do not dwell on it while making your adjustment.

Condition *C* (Fixation, with fixation cross).

> Maintain a steady fixation on the small black cross in the Poggendorff figure. Do not interrupt this fixation from the time you start your adjustment until after you have completed your adjustment.

The other experimental variation was to use 4 different values for the size of angles *ABE* and *HCD* in the figure. These were fixed at 22.5, 45.0, 67.5, or 90.0 degrees, Earlier research had shown the magnitude of the illusion to be greater for the smaller transversal angles. Novak's report of his study gives numerous details of the apparatus construction, the dimensions of the Poggendorff figure, and its illumination and viewing conditions. Here we shall point out only that the 3 types of instructions and the 4 angles were used for different blocks of 8 trials in different sequences for different groups of subjects.

The results of the study are portrayed in Figure 5.2 which shows the mean constant error or average setting above ($+$) or below ($-$) the line of physical continuity (*CD* in Figure 5.1) as measured vertically in millimeters. The large positive constant errors for all the angles except 90° represent a strong illusory effect. (A 90° angle is actually a departure from a Poggendorff illusion figure.) Instructions to fixate the central cross greatly reduced the magnitude of the illusion as the curve for Condition C shows. This is attributable to the instructions and not merely to the inclusion of the cross in the figure since Condition B (cross included, but instructions to inspect the figure freely) did not show significantly different results from Condition A, with no fixation point.

Another instance of using the method of adjustment to assess the

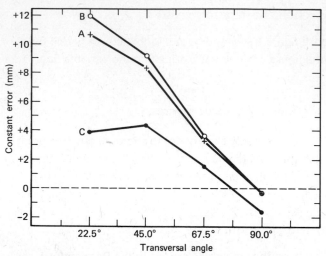

Fig. 5.2. Mean constant error in millimeters for each
transversal angle used in constructing the Poggendorff
illusion and for each viewing condition. (After Novak, 1966.)

potency of the Poggendorff illusion may be given. Liebowitz and Gwozdecki (1967) used this psychophysical method to test the illusion strength
in subjects ranging in age from 5 to 80 years. They found the illusion
to be significantly stronger in youngsters under 10 years of age. It did
not differ for the different age groups averaging from about 10.5 to 75.0
years. Data from males and females did not differ significantly.

Constant errors

In studies of geometric illusions like the one just summarized an algebraic average error which departs significantly from zero is attributable to the illusory effect and serves as an index of its magnitude. In
other psychophysical work such as estimates of sensory discrimination
through determining a DL value, certain constant errors may result from
particular parts of the psychophysical procedures. For example, inequalities in illumination might introduce a constant error if the adjustable
stimulus were always on one side of the visual display. Counterbalancing
this factor, left and right, should eliminate this constant error tendency
from a mean value obtained. An unbiased estimate of the DL would then
be based on variability of settings. Other sources of possible constant
error or bias may lie in the use of ascending and descending stimulus

values. We shall see later how using both is intended to offset this possibility in another psychophysical procedure.

The Method of Limits

Having seen earlier how the method of limits or method of minimal changes could be used to determine the absolute threshold, or RL, we may now consider its use in determining the DL. A standard stimulus is held at a constant value and a comparison stimulus is varied in minimal steps forming either an ascending or descending series of values.

An illustrative example

As a hypothetical study in psychophysics let us take the problem of finding the DL for loudness of an 8000-Hz tone at a standard level of 30 dB above threshold. You will note that we must state the standard tone intensity level since Weber's law suggests that the magnitude of the DL will depend upon it. Our procedure might be to present the standard tone on each trial together with a comparison tone, asking the subject to state whether the latter was louder or softer than the standard, or apparently equal to it. Later we shall see that the order and the timing of this pair of stimuli pose important problems for the determination of the DL. On a descending series of trials our comparison tones might start at intensities well above that of the standard so that the first few judgments would be "louder." Finally, the JND would give way to the JUD, and the subject would change his judgments to "equal." These judgments of equality would presumably continue to the point of physical equality of the two tones and slightly beyond. That is, the comparison tone would continue to be called "equal" to the standard even after it had become weaker in physical intensity. This series of judgments would prevail as long as a JUD or less was the difference between the two physical intensities. As the descending series continued, the JUD would finally be passed and the stimulus difference would be at least a JND in sensory magnitude. The change in judgment to "softer" would indicate that the limit of the series had been reached.

In the method of limits as we have described it, each series of trials yields two estimates of the DL. Our descending series first yielded an estimate of the upper DL when judgments changed from "louder" to "equal." This change might also be described as a change from a stimulus difference value of a JND or more to a value of a JUD or less. By taking a mean of these two difference values for the upper DL, we are taking a sort of average between an upper JND and an upper JUD. After the descending series has proceeded through the "equal" judgments, a lower DL is reached where the responses change to "softer." This may be calculated as the mean of the last two stimulus values in the series, one representing a lower JUD or less, the other a lower JND or more. In some psychophysical work, the upper and lower DLs will be separately calculated and cited. In other cases, the upper and lower DLs are averaged to obtain a single value for the defferential threshold.

Our determination of the DL for the loudness of an 8000-Hz tone might proceed as indicated in Table 5.3 which presents a completed work sheet from a hypothetical experiment. The intensity level of the standard tone is kept at 30 dB above absolute threshold and the comparison tone is varied in one-quarter dB steps. An estimate of an upper and a lower DL is obtained on each series of trials, either ascending or decending. The means for upper DL and lower DL are computed and a combined DL is calculated by taking the grand mean of all the upper and lower DLs, a value of 0.83 dB. This value of the DL is determined for one subject at one reference intensity, 30 dB above threshold, of the standard 8000-Hz tone. Most psychophysical studies involve taking many more data by utilizing more subjects and testing them with standard stimuli at varying intensity levels and, in the case of tonal stimuli, at different frequencies.

Errors of anticipation and habituation

Participating as a subject in a psychophysical experiment, with its demands for the making of difficult judgments, is a complex behavioral process. There is danger that other aspects of the situation besides the stimuli being presented may affect the subject's responses and hence the data. The method of limits is particularly subject to two classes of error called *error of anticipation* and *error of habituation*. Both these errors may stem from the repeated responses that a subject must make as a series of trials proceeds. We can describe these two types of error with reference to our hypothetical determination of the DL for the 8000-Hz tone.

As a descending series of trials begins in our illustrative study, the subject repeatedly responds "louder" as each different comparison tone is paired with the standard tone. He knows that the comparison tone is approaching the standard one in intensity and that he will be unable to distinguish the two loudnesses after a few trials. This knowledge, together

Table 5.3 Completed Work Sheet for Determination of the Differential Intensity Threshold for an 8000-Hz Tone at an Intensity Level 30 d*B* above Absolute Threshold (the Testing of One Subject is Represented)

Comparison Stimulus Intensity*	Type of Series					
	Descending	Ascending	Descending	Ascending	Descending	Ascending
32.25						
32.00					Louder	
31.75			Louder		Louder	
31.50	Louder		Louder		Louder	
31.25	Louder		Louder	Louder	Louder	
31.00	Louder		Louder	Equal	Louder	
30.75	Louder	Louder	Equal	Equal	Equal	Louder
30.50	Equal	Equal	Equal	Equal	Equal	Equal
30.25	Equal	Equal	Equal	Equal	Equal	Equal
30.00	Equal	Equal	Equal	Equal	Equal	Equal
29.75	Equal	Equal	Equal	Equal	Equal	Equal
29.50	Equal	Equal	Equal	Softer	Equal	Equal
29.25	Equal	Softer	Equal	Softer	Equal	Equal
29.00	Softer	Softer	Equal	Softer	Equal	Equal
28.75		Softer	Softer	Softer	Softer	Softer
28.50		Softer		Softer		Softer
28.25				Softer		Softer
Upper *DL*:	0.62	0.62	0.88	1.12	0.88	0.62
Lower *DL*:	0.88	0.62	1.12	0.38	1.12	1.12

Mean upper *DL* = 0.79   Mean lower *DL* = 0.87

Grand mean *DL* = 0.83

*In decibels above absolute threshold for 8000-Hz tone.

with his weariness at saying "louder" on every trial, may cause him to *anticipate* when the tones become indistinguishable in loudness. He may therefore begin saying "equal" when in fact he could still sense the comparison tone as louder, if he made the necessary effort. On a descending series of trials this error of anticipation will, of course, make the estimate of the upper DL somewhat larger than if the error were successfully avoided. In psychophysical experiments subjects must be instructed and trained to respond only on the basis of the stimuli presented to them on a given trial, ignoring their responses to stimuli earlier in the series.

What will be the effect of an error of anticipation if it occurs later in a descending series, when the subject has been responding "equal" to the paired stimuli on a number of trials? In our sample study, if he anticipates that the comparison tone is eventually going to be sensed as softer, the subject may change his report to "softer" when the two tones are in fact still indistinguishable to him in loudness. At this point in a descending series, the error of anticipation will cause an underestimate of the magnitude of the lower DL. This contrasts, you see, with the overestimate of the upper DL in a descending series due to anticipation.

In an *ascending* series, the error of anticipation will have opposite tendencies to affect the estimates of the lower DL and the upper DL. As we begin with a series of "softer" judgments, a premature response of "equal" will lead to an overestimated lower DL and an anticipation of the change to discriminably louder comparison tones will lead to an underestimation of the upper DL. These opposite effects in ascending series indicate one of the values of using both types of series in the method of limits. If a subject is prone to making errors of anticipation with some consistency, the effects of these on DL estimates will tend to cancel out, when the data for descending and ascending series are combined.

Some subjects may persevere in making one response as if by habit, so that this response may persist even beyond the point where their judgment would change if they were responding on the basis of their sensory discriminations alone. These errors of *habituation* have opposite effects from errors of anticipation in creating overestimates or underestimates of upper or lower DLs. In ascending and descending series of trials the data will be distorted by the error of habituation in opposite ways that tend to cancel out in combined data.

It would be unlikely that individual subjects would make either anticipation or habituation errors so consistently as to yield final estimates of upper and lower DLs that were free from distortion. We need to aid our subjects in avoiding errors of either sort. Besides our use of instructions and training we help to do this by alternating descending and ascending series and by varying the starting points of each type of series. This helps to prevent the development of anticipations and habituations in the subject's responding.

The Method of Constant Stimulus Differences

In discussing absolute thresholds we saw how the method of constant stimuli could be used to determine a physical intensity that would be detected by subjects on 50 percent of its presentations. A similar psychophysical technique can be used to determine the differential threshold or DL. The DL is computed with reference to some designated point on the stimulus continuum, of course, and so an application of this psychophysical method would begin by choosing such a value, termed the *standard stimulus*. With the standard having been selected, a series of *comparison stimuli* is chosen which ranges closely on either side of the standard value. The actual selection of the comparison values may be based on earlier psychophysical data or determined through preliminary work.

Each comparison stimulus is paired repeatedly with the standard stimulus, with the subject having to indicate on every trial which stimulus has the greater sensory value in his judgment. Since the fixed values of the comparison stimuli are selected to provide various fixed differences from the standard value, the technique is called the *method of constant stimulus differences*. How this method is employed to determine the DL will be illustrated with actual data from a study by Dinnerstein, Gerstein, and Michel (1967). Their research probed certain effects which influence the judging of lifted weights. Here, however, we shall use only the data from the control condition of one of their experiments. Using these real psychophysical data will enable us to calculate a DL as an example of the data treatment for such a purpose. Actually the aims of the experimenters were much more complex, requiring several experimental conditions to be run.

DL for weights in each hand

The problem as we are re-casting it for our illustrative purpose was to determine the DL for lifted weights when the standard stimulus is lifted by one hand while the comparison weight is simultaneously lifted by the other. The experimental procedure can be inferred to a considerable extent from the following paraphrasing of instructions given to subjects who were to perform the discrimination task while blindfolded.

Instructions to Subjects

We are doing an experiment in the judging of the weight of a number of objects. Two weights will be presented to you simultaneously, one for each hand, one from each turntable. When the bell rings you will grasp the objects, elbows remaining on the table, and lift with a wrist motion. When the bell rings a second time, replace the objects on the turntables in front of you. Please tell us whether the weight in your right hand is heavier or lighter than the weight in your left hand.

If you are not sure whether the weight in your right hand is heavier or lighter than the weight in your left hand, you have to say "guess heavier" or "guess lighter." You can give no "equal" or "uncertain" judgments. Therefore, you will have only four responses available to you: "heavier," "lighter," "guess heavier," and "guess lighter."

The standard stimulus weight was 80 g, always lifted with the non-dominant hand. The comparison or variable weight, lifted with the dominant hand, was one of 6 values: 50, 60, 70, 90, 100, or 110 g. (Instructions and presentation of weights were modified appropriately if a subject were left-handed.) The data which permit the DL to be estimated are the percents of trials on which the comparison weight is judged to be heavier. On the basis of 60 judgments per comparison weight by each of 30 college student subjects, our illustrative data are as follows:

Comparison Weight:	50	60	70	90	100	110
Percent "Heavier":	2	10	29	78	85	95

Both an upper and a lower DL may be estimated from these results. The upper DL is conventionally defined as the difference from the standard (80 g) which yields 75 percent "heavier" judgments. The lower DL is taken as the difference for which 25 percent "heavier" judgments would be given. To obtain these estimates we may conveniently use linear interpolation. This should be a satisfactory degree of precision for the example under consideration. Seventy-five percent lies 46/49 of the distance from 29 to 78 percent. Then, 46/49 of the 20 g corresponding to the interval from 70 to 90 g is equal to 18.8 g above the 70-g point or 8.8 g above the standard stimulus. This 8.8 g is our estimate of the upper DL, the point on the physical scale which elicits a hypothetical 75 percent "heavier" judgments. The lower DL is at a point 15/19 of the 10-g extent from 60 to 70 g, our data indicate. This is at 67.9 g on the weight dimension. The lower DL is thus indicated to be 12.1 g. This difference is hypothetically discriminable 75 percent of the time on the basis of the data used here. If we average the upper and lower DLs, we get 10.45 as our DL based on the upper and lower comparison weights. Although our treatment of the data was quite simple as we estimated a DL for weights as lifted in each hand, there are somewhat more elaborate treatments of psychophysical data which may be used if the experiment and its purpose warrant it. It should be noted that the DL for judging weights lifted successively by the same hand is somewhat less than the value calculated on the basis of using both hands, one for the standard and one for the comparison weight.

Signal Detection Methods

Several years ago psychophysical research was invigorated by an infusion of new concepts and methods of quantifying the reports of experimental subjects. The new approaches were based on a *theory of signal detectability* (TSD). The multiple roots of this theory and its rapid growth and proliferation need not concern us. Its contributions of ideas and techniques to psychophysics have been numerous, with resultant new information and insights, particularly in the investigation of audition and vision. We need to examine some basic notions from TSD and to become acquainted with methods of psychophysical data collection which they have engendered. These approaches differ markedly from some aspects of classical psychophysics; this fact will emerge as our treatment of the topic unfolds. The new theory and methods should be seen as valuable additions to psychophysical inquiry. They do not invalidate a vast array of facts about sensation and perception which have been revealed through investigations conducted with traditional techniques.

The term "signal detectability" may bring to mind the subject's problem of detecting a test stimulus in an experiment to determine an absolute threshold. TSD offers new ways of quantifying a subject's behavior in such a testing situation. In doing so, it raises some serious questions about the very concept of a threshold. Although we cannot examine the theoretical debates, we can explore the basic TSD analysis of a subject's performance as he is repeatedly tested with a very weak stimulus. A fundamental notion is that the reports given by the subject or observer depend upon decision processes as well as on sensory acuities. This key idea should become clear as we explore some of the foundation aspects of the theory.

Basic Concepts

Since TSD is a complex admixture of assumptions, empirical facts, hypothetical constructs, and quantitative transformations, an introductory exposition of its relevance to psychophysics must necessarily be greatly simplified. For more thorough treatment of the theory and its numerous applications, useful sources include Swets (1964), Egan and Clarke (1966), and Green and Swets (1966).

Let us begin our own acquaintance with concepts from TSD by imagining two subjects being tested in a psychophysical experiment in which a faint auditory stimulus is the signal to be detected on repeated trials. These trials are of two sorts: stimulus signal plus noise, or noise alone. We may consider the activity of a person's auditory system to vary from time to time as the stimulus or signal is presented with accompanying background noise. There is also varied activity in reaction to noise alone. (The term "noise" is here used very generally; it may include certain background stimulation but also neural activity which is continually varying). It is the task of a subject to distinguish, if he can, his auditory system's activity aroused by the stimulus plus noise (SN) from the activity initiated and experienced in the presence of noise alone (N). Since the two kinds of activity overlap considerably when a weak test stimulus is involved, this psychophysical task requires decision making in choice of an appropriate report of stimulus detection (as well as sensory acuity). TSD quantifies a subject's decision making as well as his sensitivity.

The hypothetical decision axis

Figure 5.3, Panel *A*, shows a *hypothetical decision axis* which represents one situation in our example. This single axis is conceptualized as functional in Subject *Q*'s deciding to report "Yes" or "No" in response to the experimental question, "Was a signal included in the stimulus

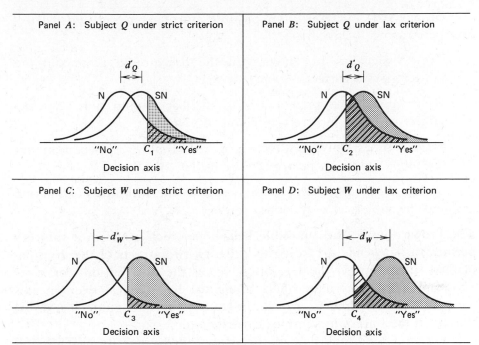

Fig. 5.3. Hypothetical decision axes of Subjects Q and W each operating under instructions to adopt either a strict criterion for "Yes" responses (Panels A and C) or a lax criterion (Panels B and D). Distribution N represents the sensory activity aroused in each subject by noise alone, while SN represents the signal plus noise. The TSD variables, d' and C, are treated in the text.

presentation you experienced?" Even though the stimulus situation is known to be multidimensional, this single axis is postulated to provide a theoretical basis for analysis of the psychophysical stimulus-response pattern. In Panel A it is assumed that the *criterion* adopted by Subject Q for giving a "Yes" response has been established at a fairly high value along his decision axis. He has set this cutoff point at C_1 in compliance with instructions to be strict in judging the presence of a signal in the stimulus presentations made to him. In Panel B Subject Q is shown to have adopted a lower cutoff, C_2, in accordance with instructions to assume a lax criterion in judging the stimulus presentations. In Panels C and D, Subject W is seen to have adopted somewhat different, but corresponding criteria, C_3 and C_4, under these same instructions.

On any trial, there are four possible outcomes in the signal detection performance of a subject:

Hit. A signal is presented with the background noise and the subject gives a correct response of "Yes."

Miss. A signal is presented with the background noise but the subject gives an incorrect response of "No."

False Alarm. Only noise occurs in the stimulus presentation but the subject gives an incorrect response of "Yes."

Correct Rejection. Only noise occurs in the stimulus presentation and the subject gives a correct response of "No."

The proportions of these possible behaviors which occur in a subject's performance depends, according to TSD, on two aspects of the decision-making situation: (1) the separation, d', of the distributions for noise (N) and signal plus noise (SN) along the hypothetical decision axis and (2) the criterion, C, which the subject uses to guide his verbal reports in the uncertain stimulus experience.

Figure 5.3 indicates how d', the symbol used generally in TSD, and C both contribute to the proportion of behaviors occurring in each possible contingency. In Panels A and B, d'_Q is fairly small as distributions N and SN overlap along the sensory decision axis. It may be noted that d'_Q does not change as Subject Q alters his criterion from C_1 to C_2 in the task of psychophysical judgment. This constancy of d' is both a theoretical assumption and an empirical finding in numerous studies. In Panels C and D the value of d'_W is also seen to remain the same as Subject W adopts his different criteria, C_3 and C_4, in response to the same instructions for strict or lax responding in the signal detection task. The two hypothetical distributions of sensory activity are seen to be separated by a greater amount in the auditory experience of this subject.

The stimulus-response matrix

In each panel of Figure 5.3, the stippled area under SN represents the proportion of hits attained, a subject reporting "Yes" since the stimulus situation is above his criterion along the hypothetical decision axis. The cross-hatched area represents the proportion of false alarms when the stimulus situation of noise alone is such as to elicit a "Yes" response. The two unshaded portions under the curves represent the correct rejections occurring when "No" is the response to noise alone and the misses occurring when "No" is reported after a signal actually has been included with the background noise. The numerical proportions of these four contingencies as represented in the panels of Figure 5.3 are given in the matrices of Part I of Table 5.4.

Table 5.4 Illustrative Signal Detection Data from Two Hypothetical Subjects Operating under Either a Strict or Lax Criterion in Decision Making as Represented in Figure 5.3

Part I. Proportion of trials yielding hits, misses, false alarms, and correct rejections by Subject Q and Subject W under strict and lax decision-making criteria.

Matrix A: Subject Q
Under Strict Criterion

	Response	
Stimulus	"Yes"	"No"
SN	.20	.30
N	.07	.43

Matrix B: Subject Q
Under Lax Criterion

	Response	
Stimulus	"Yes"	"No"
SN	.39	.11
N	.23	.27

Matrix C: Subject W
Under Strict Criterion

	Response	
Stimulus	"Yes"	"No"
SN	.35	.15
N	.04	.46

Matrix D: Subject W
Under Lax Criterion

	Response	
Stimulus	"Yes"	"No"
SN	.46	.04
N	.18	.32

Part II. Hit rates (HR) and false alarm rates (FAR) computed from the matrices of Part I.

From Matrix A:
  HR = .40
  FAR = .14

From Matrix B:
  HR = .78
  FAR = .46

From Matrix C:
  HR = .70
  FAR = .08

From Matrix D:
  HR = .92
  FAR = .36

The ROC curve

Our consideration of the signal detection situations represented in Figure 5.3 shows that TSD concerns itself with two aspects of a subject's performance of a psychophysical task. First, how effectively can the subject separate the signal-plus-noise distribution from the distribution of noise alone as he undertakes his decision making? This separation, of which d' is the indicant, is naturally dependent on the physical stimulation itself, the energy level of the test signal as compared with the noise level. But d' for any given signal is also reflective of the subject's ability to discriminate SN from N. Hence d' is considered in TSD to be an indicant of sensory or perceptual sensitivity. In the second place, the value of C is an index of how the subject approaches his decision making. Are his responses characterized by extreme caution so that he responds "Yes" relatively rarely? Or does he use the positive response quite liberally, increasing his proportion of hits and also of false alarms? The *criterion* which is characteristic of his responding, also termed a *cutoff*, is a cognitive aspect of psychophysical performance which is explicitly recognized in TSD together with sensitivity of reception of signals. As our illustrative example suggests, response criteria may be manipulated through instructions or other experimental techniques. We shall go on to see how both d' and various criteria of decision making, C, are represented in a plotted curve known as the *receiver operating characteristic* (ROC).

The ordinate of the ROC curve is scaled as the *hit rate* (proportion of hits obtained on all SN trials). The abscissa is scaled as the *false alarm rate* (proportion of false alarm responses occurring on N trials). From the data of Part I of Table 5.4, these derivative proportions have been computed and presented in Part II of the table. The formula for hit rate (HR) is:

$$\text{HR} = \frac{p_{\text{HIT}}}{p_{\text{HIT}} + p_{\text{MISS}}} \qquad \text{Formula 5.1}$$

For false alarm rate (FAR), the formula is:

$$\text{FAR} = \frac{p_{\text{FALSE ALARM}}}{p_{\text{FALSE ALARM}} + p_{\text{CORRECT REJECTION}}} \qquad \text{Formula 5.2}$$

Using HR and FAR based on each criterion which Subjects Q and W adopted under different experimental instructions we can plot their ROC curves in Figure 5.4. The departure of an ROC curve from a chance performance line is a measure of d'—as shown in the figure. The curves show that Subject W was more sensitive in signal detection than Subject Q when each operated under two different decision-making

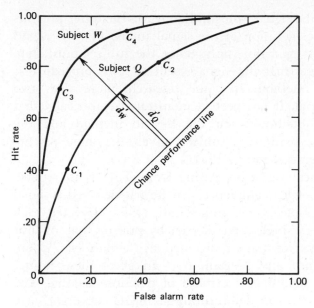

Fig. 5.4. ROC curves for Subjects Q and W, based on the hypothetical decision axes and criteria of Figure 5.3 and the illustrative performance data of Table 5.4.

criteria. Each ROC curve indicates the sensitivity which characterizes one subject. Points along the curve indicate his characteristic HR and FAR values as different criteria are adopted or elicited by experimental conditions.

Variations in Method

Like traditional psychophysics, TSD has given rise to a variety of different experimental procedures for generating ROC curves and determining a value of d' for an observer. In the example used to introduce basic concepts, the subject's choice of a "Yes" or "No" response on any trial was a critical part of his signal detection performance. The proportions of these two responses over a series of trials depended on his criterion or cutoff. Each trial comprised a single interval requiring his alert attention and his judgment or decision. A closely related method divides each trial into two intervals clearly differentiated for the subject. In this procedure the subject is made aware, through instructions, that one interval will contain the signal (plus noise) while the other presents noise alone. Of course the inclusion of the signal in the first or second interval of any trial is arranged randomly. Since the subject must state in which interval he judges that the signal occurred, this procedure is called the *forced choice* method. In some research, more than two intervals are used for a trial. It has been demonstrated empirically that corresponding data are obtained when the Yes-No method and the forced choice method are used with subjects given the same psychophysical task (e.g., Tanner and Swets, 1954).

Another methodological variation arising from TSD is to require a subject to give a rating of his confidence that he has detected a signal on a given trial. For example, Swets and Sewall (1963) directed each subject to respond on every single-interval trial by pressing one of four buttons. The four alternatives were designated as "certain yes," "uncertain yes," "uncertain no" and "certain no." In effect these ratings of confidence correspond to different criteria of decision making. The data therefore lend themselves to determining an ROC curve and a d' value for each observer.

Contributions to Psychological Research

Methods based on TSD have been used in numerous investigations of sensory and perceptual detection and discrimination tasks. Examples of such experiments are given abundantly in the general references cited earlier. In addition to their employment in empirical studies, the concepts of TSD have stimulated several analyses of earlier psychophysical approaches (e.g., Creelman, 1965; Hohle, 1965; Lee, 1969; Treisman and Watts, 1966). Finally, its dual consideration of a subject's perceptual system and his response system in decision making give TSD a great potential utility, according to Price (1966), in exploring the realm of personality.

Scaling Sensation and Perception

We saw how traditional psychophysical methods have been used to determine RLs and DLs for various dimensions of sensation and perception. In applying these measurement techniques, we vary the physical stimuli but the subjects respond in terms of the magnitude of their own sensory or perceptual experience. The RL may thus be considered an endpoint, and the DL an increment, on a psychological scale. A number of approaches have been taken to develop and refine such scales. We shall see that this work is sometimes based on the methods already examined and we shall discuss additional methods used in scaling sensation and perception.

DL or JND Scales

One of the techniques for scaling sensation is quite directly based on the basic constructs in psychophysical work, the RL and the JND or DL. By considering the JND or the DL as the unit of the sensory scale, we might start down at the RL and determine the magnitude of successive DLs. These could then be piled one on the other to create a sensory scale—an extremely laborious technique. Theoretically, it leads to a scale of sensation on which we can specify any point by stating how many JNDs it is above the threshold. This clearly indicates the adoption of the JND (or DL) as the unit of sensory measurement. Of course, our psychophysical work in constructing such a psychological scale would reveal the physical stimulus value which corresponded to each sensation value. Thus, physical values could be used to designate successive discriminable points on the psychological continuum.

The Weber-Fechner formulation

We have already seen how early psychophysical studies led Weber to assert that the just noticeable increment to any stimulus value is a constant proportion of that particular value. If we were to assume the Weber Formula, $\Delta R/R = K$, to be valid, we could create a ΔR scale (essentially a DL or JND scale) of sensory magnitudes without the time-consuming determination of successive DLs all the way up the scale. We would merely need to gather psychophysical data to determine ΔR values at a few points. From these we would calculate a value for K. Using this constant of proportionality, K, we could step off a sensory scale along the physical dimension beginning at the RL and carrying it as far as we wished. We know today, of course, that Weber's law is not valid over the entire range of any stimulus dimension. Therefore the hypothetical method we have discussed would not be considered appropriate.

Fechner, who did a great deal to codify some of the early psychophysical methods, accepted the Weber formulation, $\Delta R/R = K$. By integration over the series of Rs which makes up the sensory dimension, he transformed the equation to $S = k \log R$, where S is the sensory magnitude (actually the cumulative number of ΔRs above threshold), R is the physical stimulus value expressed as a multiple of the absolute threshold value, R_o, and k is a constant determined by the particular sensory dimension and modality. This Weber-Fechner law is, of course, no more valid than the Weber formula on which it is based. However, the Weber formula does seem to hold over a restricted range of stimulus values, those of moderate magnitude. For the middle range of intensities, then, the Weber-Fechner formula also has a measure of validity. The essential idea which it expresses is that linear increases in sensory magnitude will be aroused by logarithmic increases in the physical stimulus value. It suggests, for example, that a twofold increase in brightness will result from a hundredfold increase in light intensity, provided this physical change is measured in relation to the absolute threshold for vision.

The Fechnerian approach to scaling sensation via the JND has long been criticized on logical and mathematical grounds. A modern constructive criticism is set forth by Luce and Edwards (1958) who offer a mathematically complex functional-equation solution to the scaling problem to replace the solution in which Fechner employed the integration technique. The authors do not recommend the practical use of their equations, stating that a graphic method of placing JNDs one upon the other will yield a scale more simply.

The entire concept of the JND scale has been questioned by Stevens (1957, 1961). He objects to the indirectness of the Fechnerian approach in which an index of confusion, the DL or JND, is taken as the unit of a sensory scale. The logarithmic relationship between sensation and physical stimulus energy is questioned by Stevens who indicates that a modern reorientation of psychophysics reveals that for many stimulus dimensions a power function relates sensation level to stimulus intensity. In this formulation for scaling sensory experience a basic principle is that equal sensation ratios tend to be aroused by equal stimulus ratios. This is revealed empirically by the relatively direct ratio scaling methods which we shall consider next.

Ratio Scales

Techniques for *ratio scaling* of sensation share the essential feature of requiring subjects to make quantitative estimates of subjective events. Methods of *ratio estimation, ratio production*, and *magnitude estimation* are among those listed by Stevens (1957, p. 163). In ratio estimation two stimuli are presented to the subject and he must state the ratio of the sensory experiences which they arouse, for example, he might state that one of two luminances aroused a brightness sensation of ten times that which the other aroused—a 10:1 ratio estimate for the two sensations. Turning to ratio production, we find that *fractionation* is a common procedure. Given a tone of a particular loudness, for example, an observer should be able to indicate a tone half as loud as this standard by adjusting an attenuator which controls the energy level of a comparison tone. By such a process of bisection, which may vary widely as to procedural details, experimental subjects reveal a great deal about the scale of sensory magnitudes as they experience them. The technique of magnitude estimation approaches ratio scaling by having subjects assign numbers to different stimuli as they are presented, with the understanding that these numerical responses are proportional to the sensation levels aroused. A particular value may be initially assigned to one stimulus by the experimenter, but this is not always a part of the method.

Stevens (1957, p. 166) listed a number of sensory and perceptual dimensions which have been subjected to ratio scaling. Among them are loudness, brightness, visual distance, visual length, visual area, taste, and heaviness (of lifted weight). For these continua, and several others, the functional relationship between subjective sensory or perceptual magnitudes and the physical dimension being manipulated appears to approximate a power function. The general formula for such a relationship is presented by Stevens (1957, p. 162) as

$$\psi = kS^n$$

where ψ = the sensation magnitude,
  S = the physical stimulus intensity,
  k and n = parameters characteristic of the kind of experience being scaled.

When the equation is converted to logarithmic form, expressing $\log \psi$ as a function of $\log S$, the power function can be graphically represented by a straight line with n as its slope. A number of such linear plots on log-log coordinates are presented by Stevens and Galanter (1957) in order to compare the outcomes of several experiments. In another summary listing Stevens (1961b) gives the exponent values, n, as determined in some of these studies as well as explorations of still other psychological dimensions including electric shock, force of handgrip, smell, temperature, and tactile vibration.

A ratio scale of heaviness; fractionation method

An experiment by Harper and Stevens (1948) indicates how a fractionation technique yields a ratio scale of subjective magnitudes. The physical dimension that was varied in the study was the weight of stimulus objects, the aim being to construct a psychological scale for the sensory experience of heaviness when weights are lifted.

Each trial in this investigation consisted of presenting a standard weight, 100 g, and a series of comparison weights: 70, 75, 80, 85, 90 and 95 g. These comparison values were found in a preliminary study to cover a satisfactory range. The subject's task was to lift the standard and the different comparison weights (which were unmarked and all of identical size with the standard) until he could indicate which of the comparison weights he judged to be half as heavy as the standard. The scaling study thus employed a procedure somewhat analogous to that of the method of constant stimulus differences in order to obtain bisections on the subjective weight dimension. Here, of course, the comparison stimulus values bracketed the expected point of bisection rather than bracketing the physical equality value as in the search for the DL.

In the experiment we are describing, 12 subjects (designated *O*s for "observers") were given 3 trials each in selecting a bisection point from among the comparison stimuli. The median of the 36 values thus selected was taken as the bisection point for scaling purposes. Such a median bisection point was determined for each of eight standard weights: 20, 40, 70, 100, 300, 500, 1000, and 2000 g. The eight median bisection points that were obtained are plotted as a function of the standard weight values in Figure 5.5, with a straight line fitted by inspection. From this function we may determine, for example, that a weight of about 72 g would be judged half as heavy as the 100-g standard.

From the empirical data and the fitted function of Figure 5.5, Harper and Stevens derived a scale of subjective weight. They began by assigning a subjective value of 1.0 to the perceived weight that corresponds to the lifting of the 100-g weight. Since a 72-g weight is judged half as heavy as the 100-g weight, it is assigned a value of 0.5 unit on the subjective scale. From the graphic plot they determined that a 100-g weight would be judged half as heavy as a 140-g weight. Since 100 g

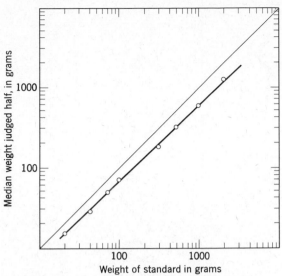

Fig. 5.5. The median weight judged half as heavy as the standard weight plotted as a function of the standard weight. Each plotted point represents the median of 36 judgments given by 12 observers, each giving 3 judgments. Values are scaled logarithmically on both coordinates. (After Harper and Stevens, 1948.)

has a sensory unit value of 1.0, then the subjective sensation aroused by 140 g was given a sensation value of 2.0. Starting with the arbitrary assumption of unit sensation value as being aroused by 100 g on the physical scale, the experimenters thus used the bisection data to assign sensation values to every other physical value.

   Proceeding as we have described, Harper and Stevens plotted sensation values for lifted weights as a function of physical values. Instead of presenting the curve which they obtained, we shall examine a more representative power function derived by Stevens and Galanter (1957, pp. 386–390) from the results of this and other studies. The name *veg*, from an old Norse verb for "lift," is given to the unit of experienced heaviness. In Figure 5.6 we see that the sensed magnitude of lifted weight is a power function of the physical weight. The equation for this idealized curve worked out by Stevens and Galanter is

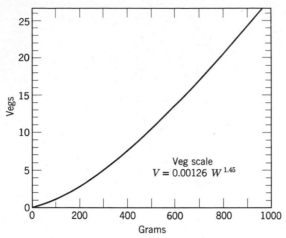

Fig. 5.6. Veg scale of subjective weight. (After Stevens and Galanter, 1957.)

$$V = 0.00126 \ W^{1.45}$$

where $\quad V =$ number of vegs,
$W =$ physical stimulus weight, in grams,
$0.00126 =$ the parameter k,
$1.45 =$ the parameter n.

This power function is an empirical example of the general equation which we examined earlier (p. 147).

A ratio scale of heaviness; magnitude estimation

In the fractionation method, as we have seen, the experimenter specifies the desired ratio of sensation, often 1:2, and the observer or subject then attempts to attain it or identify it as the physical stimulus dimension is manipulated. In the method of magnitude estimation *the numerical continuum is given to the subject to use.* The experimenter presents the stimulus intensities singly and in random order and the subject responds by assigning numbers to them in proportion to the sensation level they arouse. At the outset of a session the experimenter usually designates one numerical value to be assigned to one stimulus, taken as the standard. As the subject assigns numbers to the comparison stimuli he is, in effect, identifying them as arousing either multiples or fractions of the sensation level which the standard arouses. A ratio scale is thus approached quite directly through the magnitude estimations that are made.

Stevens and Galanter (1957, p. 387) describe how this method was applied to the ratio scaling of heaviness by three members of the Harvard Laboratory: Stevens, Nachmias, and Pertschonok. Keeping the standard weight always available for comparison, these experimenters required subjects to make magnitude estimates of the comparison weights. The weights used ranged from 19 to 193 g. In different parts of the study, different subjects were told that the 19-g weight was to be defined as having a value of 1, or that the 92-g weight was to be designated as 100, or that the 193-g stimulus was to be called 100. The method permits this flexibility in the one numerical value which the experimenter assigns in different phases of the same scaling effort. Using the one numerical referent given to him, the subject must assign numbers proportional to the experienced heaviness of the comparison weights. Upon examining the median values assigned to each comparison stimulus the experimenters found them to yield a power function of actual physical weight, in general agreement with the fractionation results of Harper and Stevens (1948).

The Harvard Laboratory studies employed certain procedural variations which illustrate the administrative flexibility of the method of magnitude estimation. In one part of the research the standard was presented only prior to every three comparison weights. In still other variations no standard value was designated at all. In the latter case the individual estimates were pooled only after a transformation to bring to 100 the value assigned to the 98-g stimulus. These procedural variations appear not to interfere with the attainment of a scale for subjective weight. Such details of method have been discussed by Stevens (1956) in connection with the psychophysical scaling of loudness. In this article several suggestions are made for the most effective employment of the method of magnitude estimation. Among the rules offered are the following, paraphrased from the original list:

1. Use a standard stimulus which impresses the observers as being moderate in sensation level.

2. Assign to the standard a number that is readily multiplied and divided, like 10.

3. Present additional stimuli for estimation that are both above and below the standard.

4. Use more than one standard, but only in separate scaling sessions.

5. Modify the random order of presentation to avoid very extreme values on early trials before subjects gain experience.

6. Keep the experimental sessions brief enough to avoid fatigue.

7. Let the subject present stimuli to himself, using self-pacing.

8. Use enough subjects or observers to obtain stable medians of the estimations, this statistic being less sensitive than the mean to the extreme values which some will give.

Ratio scaling of roughness and smoothness

As examples of methodological variations and of the investigative utility of psychophysical ratio scaling we may briefly consider two experiments dealing with the sensing of roughness and smoothness of textures like those of sandpaper or emery cloth. Using the grit number of emery cloth as a physical index, Stevens and Harris (1962) used magnitude estimation to determine exponents for a power function based on separate judgments for roughness and smoothness. (Grit number is inversely related to size of particles used in making emery cloth; thus a value of 24 refers to much coarser particles than does 320, these being the extreme values used in the study.) The two psychological dimensions were found in ratio scaling to be essentially reciprocal as their lexical designations imply. Subjects gave their numerical magnitude estimate after drawing the first and second fingers twice across the stimulus surface. The equation relating roughness to grit number was found to be $R = 5724G^{-1.5}$ with geometric means of roughness magnitude estimates ranging from about 1 to about 50. The experimenters compared two numerical scaling procedures. They concluded that better results are obtained when a subject is allowed to choose his own numerical modulus to assign to the first stimulus instead of having a number assigned by the experimenter. This recommendation represents a departure from the second of the rules listed earlier.

An experiment reported by Ekman, Hosman, and Lindstrom (1965) used different methods and stimuli in scaling the psychological continua of roughness and smoothness. Their procedure required ratio estimation, with samples of sandpaper, cardboard, and writing paper (which had been ordered physically by their coefficients of friction) being presented in pairs. For each pair, stroked with the two index fingers, subjects had to estimate the ratio of roughness (or smoothness) existing between the two stimuli as experienced. Examining the data for individual subjects, the investigators found that a power law represented a good approximation for the relationship of the psychological scale to the physical. Smoothness and roughness were found to be generally reciprocal in this study also. Requiring subjects to rate each surface for its pleasantness or preference, the experimenters found this psychological dimension to be directly proportional to scaled smoothness. The scaling sessions for roughness, smoothness, and preference were administered on different days.

Models for Magnitude Estimation Research

Reviewing numerous findings in experiments requiring magnitude estimation, Poulton (1968) offered a methodological and theoretical analysis of such psychophysical scaling efforts. He presented six graphic or pictorial models which represent the impact of different experimental variables on the resultant scales. Although we cannot include a full review of his contribution, we may profit from a summary listing of the independent variables which his analysis showed to be demanding of consideration if such psychophysical research is to progress. According to Poulton any experimenter must give due attention to the following independent variables. His treatise elucidates important reasons in each instance.

1. The range of stimuli.

2. Whether the range includes the threshold region.

3. The position of the standard (first stimulus) within the range.

4. The distance of the first variable (second stimulus) from the standard.

5. Whether the set of numbers used is infinite or finite.

6. The size of the modulus (the number given to the standard).

Poulton's graphic models show how the choice of these variables in designing an experiment can be expected to influence the psychophysical scale relationship to be expected as the outcome of the study. His theoretical interpretations point to the importance of such factors as numerical response bias and learning as influencing research findings.

Other theorists whom he cites have raised similar points about the psychological complexity of ratio scaling and other psychophysical procedures.

Cross-Modality Matching

In a notable departure from using numerical magnitude estimation, J. C. Stevens, Mack, and S. S. Stevens (1960) scaled several sensory dimensions by having subjects squeeze a hand dynamometer to match the stimuli as presented. Since handgrip had earlier been scaled by several different methods (J. C. Stevens and Mack, 1959), it was considered to be useful as a sensory-motor substitute for numerical responding. Several selected intensities were presented in the dimensions of electric shock, lifted weights, pressure on palm, vibration, light, noise, and tone of moderate pitch. The median dynamometer values were plotted against the physical stimulus values on logarithmic coordinates as shown in Figure 5.7.

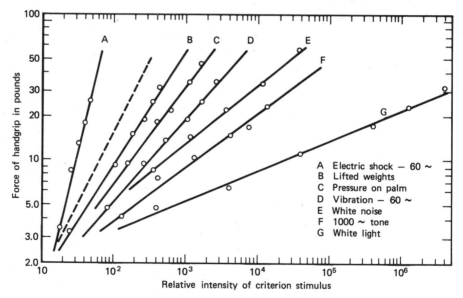

Fig. 5.7. Median handgrip force exerted in matching varied intensities of several kinds of stimulation. Since the stimulus intensities are plotted in a relative fashion along the abscissa, their horizontal positioning is arbitrary. The slopes of the straightline functions in this log-log plot are the exponents determined for the several power functions relating sensory intensity to handgrip force. These range from 2.13 (Function A) to 0.21 (Function G). (After J. C. Stevens, Mack, and S. S. Stevens, 1960.)

The investigators interpret the outcome of their cross-modality matching experiments in two different ways. In the first place, the intensities of squeezing the hand dynamometer are seen as a satisfactory means of having an observer report his magnitude estimates of stimuli presented to him in various sensory modalities. This may be considered to circumvent any problems which might stem from involving "number behavior" in a psychophysical scaling effort. On the other hand, the authors found that the relative results in estimating power law exponents on a comparative basis were in good agreement with earlier findings where numerical magnitude estimation had been used. It may be recalled that the exponent, n, of the power function is indicated by the value of the slope of a straight-line plotting of psychophysical data on log-log coordinates. Eliminating number behavior resulted in no change in the estimates of the exponents relative to the handgrip index and to each other. This finding helps to establish the validity of the simple procedure of numerical estimation in the psychophysical scaling of sensory and perceptual dimensions.

Category Scales

By using just one standard stimulus and its assigned numerical value in any particular phase of a magnitude estimation study, the experimenter gives the subject freedom to indicate ratios of sensation as he assigns values to the other stimuli. A true ratio scale can thus result. If, however, the experimenter were to fix numerical values for two different stimuli of the series, a ratio would be forced on the subjects and their further rating of sensory magnitudes could only indicate the intervals or categories into which they would put the sensory experiences aroused by the additional stimuli presented. Such *category scaling* has been attempted, with a variety of methods, for numerous sensory and perceptual dimensions.

Such interval scales have been shown by Stevens and Galanter (1957) to relate to ratio scales of the same continuum in a curvilinear fashion in many instances. As was the case for ratio scaling, category scaling may be attempted by a number of related approaches. These variations of technique bear such names as the methods of *single stimuli, absolute judgment,* or *equal intervals.* The method of *rating,* to be discussed at some length in Chapter 6, is another technique for category scaling. The essence of this kind of scaling is that the observer has to react to stimuli presented singly by assigning each to some category along the sensory continuum. Usually the subject is given some information about the upper and lower points of stimulation to be used, so that his task becomes that of partitioning the range into intervals to which he assigns the individual stimuli as each one is experienced.

Anchoring effects

An examination of Experiment I reported by Parducci, Perrett, and Marsh (1969) will serve both to illustrate some procedures in category scaling and to indicate some of the shifts in judgments which have been observed as effects of *anchoring* stimuli added to the regular series. The stimuli presented for size judgment were 9 dark squares projected on a white field for viewing from a distance of about 3 meters. The length of side was 5.4, 6.7, 8.3, 10.5, 13.3, 16.2, 18.7, 20.7, and 23.2 cm, respectively, for Stimuli I through 9. For different series of blocks of 5 trials, different sets of these stimuli were used as indicated in this tabulation:

Anchoring Condition	Trial Blocks		
	Pre-anchor Blocks 1–5	Anchor Blocks 6–9	Post-Anchor Blocks 10–14
High Anchor	Stimuli 3–7	Stimuli 5–9	Stimuli 3–7
Low Anchor	Stimuli 3–7	Stimuli 1–5	Stimuli 3–7
Control	Stimuli 3–7	Stimuli 3–7	Stimuli 3–7

The anchoring manipulations, as indicated, consisted of a shift in stimuli from Nos. 3 through 7 to Nos. 5 through 9 in the High Anchor condition and to Nos. 1 through 5 in the Low Anchor condition. These 20 anchoring trials were otherwise undifferentiated from the trials of the preceding and subsequent blocks.

In addition to the use of an altered stimulus set for inducing an anchoring effect on the judgments of stimulus size, 4 different instructions were used to structure the scaling task for different groups of subjects.

Instructional Condition	Summary of Instructions
Identification Task, *I*	Identify squares using the numerals 80, 90, 100, 110, 120 (and any others as needed) so as to indicate size of stimulus consistently as presentations continue.
Open Verbal-Numerical Scale, *O*	Judge each square using these scale labels: Very small—80; Small—90; Medium—100; Large—110; or Very Large—120. Add category labels as needed. For example, "Slightly larger than average—95" or "Very, very small—70." The scale was thus indicated to be open to interpolation or extrapolation.
Closed Verbal-Numerical Scale, *C*	(Same scale labels as Condition *O*, but without possibility of any addition.)
Fixed Verbal Scale, *V*	Judge each square using only the scale labels: Very Small, Small, Medium, Large, Very Large. To maximize anchoring effects, subjects were told to adapt these scale labels as desired if new stimulus sizes were encountered.

For all conditions, the subject groups were presented Stimuli 3–7 (without any judgment required) as background information before the instructions were given.

Two different analyses of the scaling data will be partially summarized here. First, a commonly observed anchoring effect of *contrast* was found when the changes in mean judgment from Block 5 (last pre-anchor block) to Block 10 (first post-anchor block) were examined and statistically tested. During the High Anchor condition, mean judgment of Stimuli 3–7 was found to have shifted downward; for the Low Anchor condition, experiencing the smaller stimuli led to an upward shift of assigned values. (In the case of the Fixed Verbal Scale, the experimenters transformed "Very Small"–"Very Large" to 80–120, respectively.) A second data analysis centered on the shifting of scale values assigned to Stimulus 5 as the blocks of trials continued. The trends are portrayed in Figure 5.8 for the High Anchor and Low Anchor conditions combined (after reversal of algebraic signs for the High Anchor groups). The plotted data are mean deviations from the numerical scale midpoint of 100.

As plotted functions clearly show, a contrast effect developed progressively over the anchoring trials. It persisted into Block 10, the early post-anchor trials. For three of the instructional conditions—*O*, *C*, and *V*—this contrast effect subsided as the anchoring stimuli were omitted from the post-anchor blocks of stimulus presentations. In the case of the Identification Task, Condition *I*, the post-anchor data actually showed a significant drop in Stimulus 5 values in the direction of the anchoring stimuli. Thus the contrast effect gave way to an *assimilation* effect. Such an effect has tended to appear only inconsistently in psychophysical scaling studies of anchoring. It occurred in this experiment under just one of four instructional conditions for the rendering of judgments.

Independent variables in category scaling

Numerous physical stimulus dimensions have been subjected to psychological category scaling. A diversity of independent variables have been manipulated by experimenters in this type of research. Space limitations

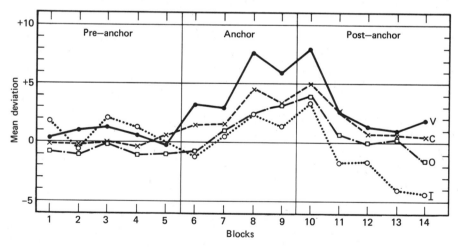

Fig. 5.8. Mean deviations from "100" for judgments of Stimulus 5 using identification judgments or the open, closed, or verbal scales. Data were pooled for the low-anchor and high-anchor (with algebraic sign reversed) conditions. (After Parducci, Perrett, and Marsh, 1969.)

allow us merely to list a few representative studies. In a series of experiments on the visual judgment of relative area Helson and Bevan (1964) varied such attributes of the stimuli as their absolute physical size and their orientation. Prior to their scaling of lifted weights, Tresselt (1965) had subjects engage in different anchoring tasks, including handing heavy books to the experimenter for reshelving. Presenting various configurations of lines and angles, Restle (1969) had subjects press 1 of 6 push buttons to signal categorical judgments relating to the Poggendorff illusion. Owen and Brown (1970) varied the complexity of irregular angular forms which they presented to subjects for either tactual or visual scaling. An examination of these and other category scaling efforts demonstrates both the great general utility of psychophysical methods for arriving at subjective scales of all sorts and the need for numerous procedural precautions if valid data are to be obtained.

Using Psychophysical Methods in Research

Their long history in psychological investigation has not lessened the vigor with which psychophysical methods have been applied to solving numerous research problems. In the earlier decades of their development and use they were heavily directed at exploring basic sensory functioning; more recently employment of them has proliferated into a variety of problems of perception. Renewed vitality of psychophysics followed the development of (1) direct scaling approaches like magnitude estimation and (2) the theory of signal detection (TSD). Among the older or the newer methods any investigator should find one suited to his particular purposes. Further, the flexibility in the methods allows for modifications if demanded in certain situations.

Wide Applicability

We have seen how psychophysical methods have been used in probing boundaries of sensation, in measuring discrimination abilities, and in scaling sensations and perceptions of many kinds. The TSD procedures have been used to delve into decision making as well as sensitivity in judgmental situations. A few examples of experiments should convince us of the continuing vigor of all these methods for laboratory studies of many psychological processes. Both ratio production and a category rating method were used by Chatterjea (1964) in studying the perception of time intervals. Creelman (1965) used both traditional psycho-physical methods and TSD procedures to examine the scaling and the discriminability of linear extents perceived visually. Methods based on TSD were also used by Halpern and Ulehla (1970) to investigate the visual discrimination of line tilt. In a study of importance for the scaling of heaviness, Ross and DiLollo (1970) varied the density as well as the weight of the physical stimuli. Magnitude estimation was employed by Moskowitz (1970) to scale the sweetness of various sugars. These few studies are a small fraction of the work that psychologists are conducting in psychophysics.

Special Suitability for Different Problems

It should always be kept in mind that a particular problem will probably be best studied by means of a particular psychophysical method. For example, if we are trying to determine olfactory DLs we might find the method of constant stimulus differences to be about the only one we could use. The method of adjustment could hardly be used because of the technical difficulties of gradually varying the strength of olfactory stimulus and because of rapid adaptation in the sense of smell. Our search to find the right method for a study should be conducted with deliberation. Our plan may involve details which preclude the use of the most conventional approach to the problem under investigation. A different psychophysical method may be better suited to our purpose. Of course, we should not expect that different methods will yield the same values for such constructs as the DL. Such computed values naturally depend upon the procedures through which they were obtained. On the other hand, TSD theory postulates a certain stability of the d' index of sensitivity in the face of procedural variations and different criteria or cutoffs used.

Flexibility in Use

We tend to speak of different psychophysical methods by conventional names and to describe the procedures in accord with certain stereotypes. Our complete appreciation of these techniques is demonstrated, however, in our willingness to modify them where the research demands it. For example, we may use only ascending series of trials in seeking the threshold during dark adaptation. Descending series would require supra-liminal stimuli which might destroy the adaptation process we were trying to plot.

There are few problems which can be investigated by only one psychophysical method. Some studies have actually applied different procedures to the same basic problem in a sort of comparative psychophysics. An example is an investigation of simultaneous brightness contrast by Diamond, Scheible, Schwartz, and Young (1955) in which several methods were used. Besides illustrating the comparing of different techniques, this study gives evidence of the suitability of the methods to modification for special purposes. Throughout the investigation, for example, the standard test field was presented to one eye while the comparison match field was presented to the other.

Precautions in Psychophysical Studies

As a complicated, indirect measurement of inner experience, research in psychophysics is very demanding of experimental rigor. All the guides to conducting psychological research which we considered in earlier chapters must be observed in psychophysical studies. In addition to respecting general procedural rules, we must often take special precautions in working with the stimuli and the responses they elicit if our measurements are to be valid.

General procedures

Preliminary studies can be very useful in a major psychophysical investigation. Such pilot experiments may be needed to establish an appropriate series of physical stimulus values for use in the later experiment. They may help to train both the experimenter and subjects for the complex performances required of them in some psychophysical procedures.

Detailed advance planning is required for good psychophysical research. The sequence of stimulus presentations should be prepared on the data record sheets if methods like limits or constant stimuli are to be used. Even for the method of adjustment we need to plan in advance the sequence of starting points to be used for the variable stimulus.

Precise quantitative control over stimuli is of paramount importance. Controlling the particular physical stimulus dimension that is being varied is a prime consideration, of course. Other physical dimensions of the stimulus cannot be ignored; they are usually held constant at values dictated by the general purposes of the investigation. Temporal dimensions of stimulation are important, too. There is evidence of many kinds that the duration of stimulus presentation and the interstimulus interval will affect psychophysical data. In addition to providing for adequate control over the stimuli being used, an experimenter must occlude unwanted stimulation while conducting a psychophysical study.

Many psychophysical investigations employ trained subjects since volunteer subjects, casually recruited, cannot perform the required task satisfactorily. A trained subject is familiar with the dimension of sensation being investigated. He can respond, for example, to changes in hue without being unduly influenced by differences in saturation. A trained subject will avoid making the "stimulus error." That is, he will not respond to what he knows to be the fact about the physical stimulus, but will respond on the basis of his sensation only. Besides his knowledge of how a subject ought to perform the assigned task, a person well-suited as a subject will bring the proper motivational level to psychophysical research. He will realize that his careful attention must be given each time he is called upon to make a response. He will also understand that a great number of data are required in most psychophysical work if the desired statistical values are to be computed reliably.

While a study in psychophysics is under way, the experimenter must be careful that unwanted processes like fatigue do not exert an effect on the data. In speaking of fatigue we refer actually to numerous possible processes that might reduce the validity of the results of the study. For example, boredom might set in during a long session, making the subject inattentive and careless in responding. By properly motivating our subjects, of course, we tend to prevent the development of boredom. We might find actual muscular fatigue, perhaps in visual accommodation, in some studies. To prevent fatigue from becoming an unwanted source of variance in a study, we might resort to the general rule of providing rest periods at reasonable intervals.

Another process that might distort psychophysical data is learning. One form of learning that might occur in a study of discrimination would be that of making judgments on the basis of cues other than the stimulus dimension being studied. If, in trying to vary saturation, the experimenter varied the intensity of visual stimuli, subjects might learn to respond to brightness cues while paying less attention to the dimension of saturation which was really the object of the investigation. A somewhat different form of learning might take place if a subject began to form impressions of the correctness of his responses. If such impressions were groundless, it is difficult to say what effect they might have had on the data. However, if the experimenter in some way was providing information that certain responses were right or wrong, the subject or observer might gradually improve his performance as he gained familiarity with the stimuli being employed. An experimenter must guard against giving any sign of approval or disapproval of responses made to stimuli.

Stimulus values

The choice of stimulus values to be used is important in any experiment, but in psychophysics it is a primary problem. What considerations would guide our choice of comparison stimuli to be used in determining the DL for lifted weights by the method of constant stimulus differences? We would conventionally choose three or four comparison stimuli on either side of the standard in order to yield a psychophysical function that would permit both a lower and an upper DL to be determined. For some of the more involved calculational procedures, the heavier and the lighter series of weights would have to be evenly spaced on the physical continuum. We would not want to use any comparison weights that were so different from the standard that they were judged heavier or lighter 100 percent of the time. Such data would not contribute much to our plotting of the psychophysical function. Our selection of stimulus values would usually be guided by previous findings or by some exploratory testing.

The potential influence on sensory and perceptual scaling of the values of the particular stimuli presented is widely recognized in psychophysics. One result of this context effect is that the middle portion of a range of stimulus values tends to take on a neutral value on a sensation scale as the stimuli are repeatedly presented. Helson (1964) formulated a concept of *adaptation level* (AL) to account for such phenomena. The experiment on anchoring effects by Parducci, Perrett, and Marsh, cited earlier, tends to illustrate the effect of an adaptation level although the investigators see their results as better explained by a range-frequency interpretation advanced by Parducci (1965). It appears that various theoretical approaches have merit and that influences on judgmental processes have yet to be fully elucidated.

After reviewing a number of investigations which revealed complex stimulus effects on observers' judgments, Harris (1948) reached the conclusion that even where a standard stimulus is presented on every trial, there may be influences from earlier stimulus presentations that affect the subjective experience. The subject may respond to a combination of the presented standard and temporally "remote" standards gradually developed in his experience on preceding trials. One suggestion that Harris offered after empirical study of the method of constant stimulus differences is that the fixed standard be replaced by a random series of standard values ranging very closely around the value that would normally be the standard. This proposal is further evidence of the fact that different aspects of psychophysical methods—in this case the choice of stimulus values—may be considered as problems requiring carefully considered and tested solutions rather than as procedural rules dictated by convention.

Control characteristics

Another precaution that must be taken in psychophysical research is to avoid having any bias introduced into the data by the characteristics of any control on the apparatus which must be operated by the subject. Suppose, for example, that in testing for the absolute threshold we required the subject to move a switch to the right if he detected a stimulus, to the left if not. If that switch were constructed so that it could be moved easily to the left but with considerable difficulty to the right, we might find that a subject resolved any doubt about detecting the stimulus by moving the switch left, indicating he had not detected anything. The percent of "No" responses might thus be artificially increased, with a resultant "raising" of the threshold we determined. Although our example might be somewhat exaggerated, it may serve to illustrate our need to consider the subject's task in every detail in planning a psychophysical study.

The method of adjustment typically calls for apparatus manipulation on the subject's part. In a study of loudness fractionation, Stevens and Poulton (1956) provided two different attenuation control knobs for the subjects to use. The amount of rotation of one control knob was related on a decibel scale to the intensity of the tone it controlled. Each 3° of rotation provided 1 dB of attenuation of the test tone. The other control knob was arranged to relate proportionally in its rotation to the sone scale of psychological loudness instead of to physical decibel scale. The results of the study indicated a definite influence of the differently connected control knobs on the estimation of half loudness, even though stimulus intensity was the primary determinant of the responses made.

Summary

A number of psychophysical methods have been devised to explore boundaries of sensation, to measure sensory and perceptual discrimination, and to scale the magnitudes of sensory experience aroused by stimuli of known physical values. Such techniques as the method of limits, the method of adjustment, and the method of constant stimuli are all useful for such research. Their procedures are flexible enough to permit their use for many experimental purposes. Besides a fairly complex statistical treatment of the data, the psychophysical methods demand many precautions as the data are being gathered. We saw, for example, how errors of anticipation or habituation might affect results if proper safeguards are not taken. In addition to learning experimental, statistical, and graphical procedures in psychophysics, we gave our attention to certain concepts like the RL, the DL, the JND, and the JUD. We noted, too, the futile attempt to summarize the data on differential sensitivities by means of Weber's law. The Weber-Fechner formulation, of historical importance in psychophysical scaling, was reviewed with some modern criticisms noted.

Having surveyed traditional psychophysical methods and noted some modern utilization in research, we turned next to signal detection methods. These newer procedures are based on a broadened theory of signal detectability (TSD). We saw how it includes decision processes as reflected in judgmental criteria in addition to sensory or perceptual sensitivities of subjects. Basic concepts of TSD were illustrated graphically and through hypothetical data treatments. These included the decision axis, hit rate and false alarm rate, and the receiver operating characteristic (ROC). Like the older psychophysical methods, TSD procedures were noted to be flexible in use.

Scaling sensation and perception was another major topic. Ratio scales may be constructed by using such methods as ratio estimation, ratio production, and magnitude estimation. Fractionation is a common form of the ratio production method. Numerous sensory and perceptual dimensions have been subjected to ratio scaling. An approximation to a power function, $\Psi = kS^n$, has generally been obtained as the relationship between subjective magnitudes and physical values. Studies which scaled the heaviness of lifted weights and the roughness of surfaces were summarized. General rules for ratio scaling were reviewed. Also noted were (1) models for magnitude estimation research and (2) the use of handgrip in cross-modality matching.

Category scales are established by using the methods of single stimuli, absolute judgment, equal intervals, or rating. An experiment on anchoring effects illustrated this special problem in category scaling. Several other studies of category scaling were briefly mentioned.

In our treatment of the traditional and modern psychophysical methods we reviewed evidence of their wide applicability. They can be used for basic studies and applied investigations in both sensation and perception. Their flexibility, however, does not mean that they can be employed carelessly. Many procedural precautions are required for valid work. The choice of subjects and of stimulus values are two primary problems. The task demanded of the subject, especially if he must operate any control device, is also a potential complication. In psychophysical work, as in all psychological research, we realize that the behavior under study is dependent on surrounding conditions in a complex way.

References

Chatterjea, R. G. Temporal duration: Ratio scale and category scale. *Journal of Experimental Psychology*, 1964, **67**, 412–416.

Cornsweet, T. N. The staircase-method in psychophysics. *American Journal of Psychology*, 1962, **75**, 485–491.

Creelman, C. D. Discriminability and scaling of linear extent. *Journal of Experimental Psychology*, 1965, **70**, 192–200.

Dallenbach, K. M. The staircase-method critically examined. *American Journal of Psychology*, 1966, **79**, 654–655.

Diamond, A. L., Scheible, H., Schwartz, E., & Young, R. A comparison of psychophysical methods in the investigation of foveal simultaneous brightness contrast. *Journal of Experimental Psychology*, 1955, **50**, 171–174.

Dinnerstein, D., Gerstein, I., & Michel, G. Interaction of simultaneous and successive stimulus groupings in determining apparent weight. *Journal of Experimental Psychology*, 1967, **73**, 298–302.

Egan, J. P., & Clarke, F. R. Psychophysics and signal detection. In J. B. Sidowski (Ed.), *Experimental methods and instrumentation in psychology*. New York: McGraw-Hill, 1966. Pp. 211–246.

Ekman, G., Hosman, J., & Lindstrom, B. Roughness, smoothness, and preference: A study of quantitative relations in individual subjects. *Journal of Experimental Psychology*, 1965, **70**, 18–26.

Green, D. M., & Swets, J. A. *Signal detection theory and psychophysics*. New York: Wiley, 1966.

Halpern, J., & Ulehla, Z. J. The effect of multiple responses and certainty estimates on the integration of visual information. *Perception & Psychophysics,* 1970, **7**, 129–132.

Harper, R. S., & Stevens, S. S. A psychological scale of weight and a formula for its derivation. *American Journal of Psychology,* 1948, **61**, 343–351.

Harris, J. D. Discrimination of pitch: Suggestions toward method and procedure. *American Journal of Psychology,* 1948, **61**, 309–322.

Helson, H. *Adaptation-level theory.* New York: Harper & Row, 1964.

Helson, H., & Bevan, W. An investigation of variables in judgments of relative area. *Journal of Experimental Psychology,* 1964, **67**, 335–341.

Hohle, R. H. Detection of a visual signal with low background noise: An experimental comparison of two theories. *Journal of Experimental Psychology,* 1965, **70**, 459–463.

Lee, W. Relationships between Thurstone category scaling and signal detection theory. *Psychological Bulletin,* 1969, **71**, 101–107.

Leibowitz, H. W., & Gwozdecki, J. The magnitude of the Poggendorff illusion as a function of age. *Child Development,* 1967, **38**, 573–580.

Luce, R. D., & Edwards, W. The derivation of subjective scales from just noticeable differences. *Psychological Review,* 1958, **65**, 222–237.

Moskowitz, H. R. Ratio scales of sugar sweetness. *Perception & Psychophysics,* 1970, **7**, 315–320.

Mote, F. A., Briggs, G. E., & Michels, K. M. The reliability of measurements of human dark adaptation. *Journal of Experimental Psychology,* 1954, **48**, 69–74.

Novak, S. Effects of free inspection and fixation on the magnitude of the Poggendorff illusion. *Perceptual and Motor Skills,* 1966, **23**, 663–670.

Owen, D. H., & Brown, D. R. Visual and tactual form complexity: A psychophysical approach to perceptual equivalence. *Perception & Psychophysics,* 1970, **7**, 225–228.

Parducci, A. Category judgment: A range-frequency model. *Psychological Review,* 1965, **72**, 407–418.

Parducci, A., Perrett, D. S., & Marsh, H. W. Assimilation and contrast as range-frequency effects of anchors. *Journal of Experimental Psychology,* 1969, **81**, 281–288.

Poulton, E. C. The new psychophysics: Six models for magnitude estimation. *Psychological Bulletin,* 1968, **69** 1–19.

Price, R. H. Signal-detection methods in personality and perception. *Psychological Bulletin,* 1966, **66**, 55–62.

Restle, F. Illusions of bent line. *Perception & Psychophysics*, 1969, 5, 273–274.

Ross, J., & DiLollo, V. Differences in heaviness in relation to density and weight. *Perception & Psychophysics*, 1970, 7, 161–162.

Stevens, J. C., & Mack, J. D. Scales of apparent force. *Journal of Experimental Psychology*, 1959, 58, 405–413.

Stevens, J. C., Mack, J. D., & Stevens, S. S. Growth of sensation on seven continua as measured by force of handgrip. *Journal of Experimental Psychology*, 1960, 59, 60–67.

Stevens, S. S. The direct estimation of sensory magnitudes—loudness. *American Journal of Psychology*, 1956, 69, 1–25.

Stevens, S. S. On the psychophysical law. *Psychological Review*, 1957, 64, 153–181.

Stevens, S. S. To honor Fechner and repeal his law. *Science*, 1961, 133, 80–86. (a)

Stevens, S. S. Toward a resolution of the Fechner-Thurstone legacy. *Psychometrika*, 1961, 26, 35–47. (b)

Stevens, S. S., & Galanter, E. H. Ratio scales and category scales for a dozen perceptual continua. *Journal of Experimental Psychology*, 1957, 54, 377–411.

Stevens, S. S., & Harris, J. R. The scaling of subjective roughness and smoothness. *Journal of Experimental Psychology*, 1962, 64, 489–494.

Stevens, S. S., & Poulton, E. C. The estimation of loudness by unpracticed observers. *Journal of Experimental Psychology*, 1956, 51, 71–78.

Swets, J. A. (Ed.) *Signal detection and recognition by human observers: Contemporary readings.* New York: Wiley, 1964.

Swets, J. A., & Sewall, S. T. Invariance of signal detectability over stages of practice and levels of motivation. *Journal of Experimental Psychology*, 1963, 66, 120–126.

Tanner, W. P., Jr., & Swets, J. A. A decision-making theory of visual detection. *Psychological Review*, 1954, 61, 401–409.

Treisman, M., & Watts, T. R. Relation between signal detectability theory and the traditional procedures for measuring sensory thresholds: Estimating *d'* from results given by the method of constant stimuli. *Psychological Bulletin*, 1966, 66, 438–454.

Tresselt, M. E. Similarity in stimulus material and stimulus task on the formation of a new scale of judgment. *Journal of Experimental Psychology*, 1965, 69, 241–245.

chapter 6
Psychological
Scaling

Experience can be quantified along many dimensions even when there is no specified physical stimulus attribute arousing it. In contrast to the psychophysical methods, which employ physical measurements as an indirect way of scaling experience, psychological scaling is accomplished in units that have no physical referent. The scales that are achieved reflect the quantitative aspects of judgmental responses like, "This picture is more attractive in composition than that one." It might be possible to scale the attractiveness of pictorial composition by means of certain physical measurements in complex combination, but we take a psychological approach when we ask subjects or observers to give us their comparative judgments of several pictures. By having them attend particularly to the artistic composition we obtain data which permit us to locate the stimulus pictures on an ordinal or interval scale* of this characteristic. Our capsule description has stressed the scaling of pictures as complex stimuli, with presumably representative observers selected to serve as subjects. In a theory dealing both broadly and thoroughly with such data Coombs (1964) has pointed out that the observers' responses may also be examined so as to reveal their judgmental characteristics or attitudes with respect to the set of stimuli which they evaluated. This duality of possible data interpretation points up

*Types of scale are discussed later in this chapter, p. 200.

the complexity and the far-ranging utility of psychological scaling in behavioral research and in applications.

As with psychophysical methods, psychological scaling techniques represent the summarizing of many data obtained by fairly conventional methods. We will not be seeking absolute or differential thresholds but will be establishing scales. Our study will require us to become familiar with common procedures for obtaining the judgmental data and for converting them statistically into scale values. In the *method of rating*, subjects are asked to give some sort of quantitative description to the stimuli that are considered singly. The responses given may be descriptive in a verbal way, or numerically, or even graphically. The *method of ranking* requires each observer to put all the stimulus items in order with respect to the attribute being scaled. In the *method of pair comparisons*, a subject must compare every stimulus with every other one. For each pair he must state which has the greater degree of the attribute being scaled. Most studies use many subjects, with statistical manipulations of the raw data being required to attain scale values for the stimuli —and sometimes for the subjects.

Even this brief introduction should suggest the complexity of psychological scaling. In a typical research effort an investigator generally finds it necessary to go through an extended series of demanding steps such as the following:

1. Identify population of potential stimulus items.
2. Select or construct a sample of stimulus items.
3. Define attribute to be scaled.
4. Postulate psychological processes and traits considered relevant.
5. Select and enlist sample of subjects.
6. Plan and administer selected scaling procedures, possibly including:
   (a) instructions to subjects
   (b) scale to be used
   (c) practice or training
   (d) presentation of items
   (e) recording of responses
7. Tabulate and treat data.
8. Compute scale values for the sample of items.
9. Determine scale values for subjects on relevant traits.
10. Interpret and report findings.

Detailed consideration of many of these facets of psychological scaling may be found in sources such as Guilford (1954), Torgerson (1958), Coombs (1964), or Garner and Creelman (1967) together with descriptions of various scaling methods and their rationales. Our treatment of topics here must necessarily be more circumscribed and less theoretical.

Research Applications

Before we turn to the methods of psychological scaling we shall survey the numerous uses they have. Not only are they techniques of value in laboratory research but they are among the foremost of psychological tools with respect to their general utility. They are used in clinical, industrial, and social psychology. Even beyond their employment by psychologists, they are used in government and business for many purposes. For example, personnel evaluation and opinion polling are two activities which have a psychological aspect. Unfortunately, the creation of questionnaires and other instruments related to scaling has sometimes been done in an inadequate fashion. Great care is required to obtain valid data. We shall here limit the applications we discuss, concentrating instead on the psychological scaling methods themselves as research instruments. As techniques for investigating judgmental behavior they serve well in the search for quantified relationships in psychology. We find them used in scaling stimuli, in quantifying complex behavior, and in the study of the judgmental processes themselves.

Scaling Stimuli

A primary use of the psychological scaling methods is to assign values to stimuli with reference to attributes or dimensions that are not scalable in physical units. Such intangibles as the beauty of a painting, the palatability of a cup of coffee, the friendliness of a smile, or the funniness of a cartoon can all be rated or ranked or otherwise quantified by these methods. In the psychological scaling of such stimuli we employ the human yardstick, the judgments of persons, since it is human appreciation toward which these qualities are directed. Having selected an appropriate group of subjects, observers, or judges, as they may be variously called, we accept their responses to the stimuli as the raw data from which our scale is constructed. Being aware of certain tendencies in judgmental behavior, we may instruct the observers and collect and treat their observations in such a way as to minimize distortion of the scale values by any extraneous process.

Esthetic stimuli

Considerable pioneer work on the psychological scaling methods was directed toward quantifying the degree of pleasure or approval aroused by different stimuli. What proportion of width to length makes for the most pleasing rectangle? The answer to this question would seem to be important to artists and architects. When it was sought experimentally by presenting rectangles of different proportions, no definitive result was obtained. As they were presented, without context or meaning, several different rectangles were judged most pleasing by different viewers. This result need not be disturbing since esthetic judgments made by different observers are based on divergent past experiences and should hardly be expected to coincide perfectly. In the older type of study described, lack of agreement was almost invited by assigning no potential application to the rectangles being judged. As an example of more carefully conducted scaling we may note a study by Ekman and Kuennapas (1962) who scaled the esthetic value of children's drawings using several different methods.

Personality traits

Although theories differ widely as to the direct measurability of key aspects of personality, they tend to agree that some observable or self-reportable traits may be important indicators of an individual's personality structure. This suggests the desirability of quantifying the degree to which certain traits are present in a person. The psychological scaling of aspects of personality can be useful in both clinical practice and research. As observers for the scaling of personality traits, one research design may demand trained judges such as clinical psychologists, whereas another investigation may require that the traits be rated by observers who spend considerable time in everyday situations with the person being rated. If self-report inventories are used, a modified form of rating is likely to be required in responding to the item. The complexities of psychological scaling are compounded when human beings are made the focus of study. Some of the intricacies of psychometric testing are listed and discussed by Fiske and Pearson (1970, 66–77).

Values

It is commonplace to state that different groups of persons have different standards of value. Psychological scaling is one way to describe value systems which exist for such diverse realms as ethics, social attitudes, sense of humor, fashions in clothes, and food preferences.. Different investigators have attempted scaling in all these domains, quantifying the judged severity of different crimes, preferences for different nationality groups, funniness of cartoons, appeal of necktie patterns, and choices among vegetables. In athletics we find scaling methods used in judging the diving at swimming meets and in voting the Most Valuable Player awards in baseball. The realm of politics was studied by Ekman and Kuennapas (1963) who scaled the conservatism of official statements issued by different political parties in Sweden.

Subjective states

Considerable use has been made of psychological scaling methods in quantifying affective arousal by various stimuli. Colors, odors, and tonal combinations have been scaled for their pleasantness or unpleasantness. Although we may refer to the stimuli as being pleasant or unpleasant, judges are actually scaling the quality and intensity of their own feelings as they attend to them.

A quantified description of a subject's current mood state is the aim of the adjective check list employed by Nowlis and Nowlis (1956). Given a list of about a hundred mood-descriptive adjectives like "drowsy" or "amused," the subject must rate each one on the degree to which it is applicable to him at that moment. This rating is quickly done by marking the check list opposite each adjective. Different code marks are used to indicate different points on a scale of applicability of the adjective to the rater's current mood.

Quantifying Behavior

Even though psychological scaling offers promise of quantifying subjective experiences like perceiving, valuing, and enjoying, it has its uses in the investigation of more overt behavior as well. Examples of such employment may be found in applied psychology as well as in research.

Merit rating

Supervisors in industry are sometimes asked to rate workers on their performance. Such ratings are particularly useful in evaluating for advancement those workers whose duties do not provide other performance indices such as number of items assembled. Ratings by supervisors sometimes provide the criterion measures for evaluating the validity of aptitude test scores. No matter what their purpose, merit ratings need to be based on competent instruction in the task of rating.

Behavior research

Scaling methods have potential application wherever behavior in an experimental situation is too complex to permit its quantification in some more direct way. For example, we might use ratings by judges to quantify the degree of aggression exhibited by subjects in a study to test the hypothesis that frustration leads to aggression.

Opinion-attitude assessment

Surveys or polls of opinions or attitudes may be considered to represent psychological scaling in at least three ways. We may have respondents rate themselves on the extent of their agreement with some statement, from "strongly disagree" to "strongly agree." In a more elaborate scaling effort we may assign a scale value to an individual indicating his position on some attitude continuum, like his attitude toward women in politics. His scale value will be based on his endorsing or rejecting numerous statements on this topic. Finally, psychological scaling is demonstrated in describing group opinion, as when we say that 73 percent of a sample of voters stated that they would vote for a woman as governor of their state. Whether attitude assessment is aimed at subjective states or at behavior may be debated. Here we have made the assumption that attitude expression is a form of verbal behavior that is quantified by psychological scaling methods.

Numerous technicalities in the devising and using of attitude scales have been discussed by Edwards (1957). Virtually every technique of psychological scaling finds its place in the measurement of people's attitudes. Ramsay and Case (1970) used a graphic rating scale, for example, to obtain subjects' attitudes toward a selected group of countries. A similar scaling method was employed in having the same judges rate these countries on their social and political characteristics such as authoritarianism, militarism, nationalism, and socialism. These subjects were a small group of undergraduates at McGill University in Montreal. The investigators were not interested in getting scale values that were representative of a broad population; their research was directed at the relationship of an overall rating of a stimulus item to the separate rating of some of its salient characteristics or properties.

Investigating Judgmental Processes

We have seen that psychological scaling methods may be used to quantify stimuli or behavior. In either of these applications we tend to take the ratings or rankings of the judges at face value. We realize, however, that the judgment that we require them to make is itself composed of complex psychological processes. Sometimes research which employs these scaling techniques is aimed at elucidating these judgmental processes, with no primary interest in the stimuli.

Idiosyncrasies in rating

Persons doing rating sometimes reveal particular persistent tendencies as they go about their task. Some judges, for example, tend to be unduly lenient in rating traits of others. Another idiosyncrasy that is sometimes observed is the tendency to avoid using either of the end points of the rating scale that is provided. A judge exhibiting this tendency will have a restricted variability in the ratings he assigns. Other persons have shown a tendency to use the extreme points of rating scales. Research on this tendency to polarization has been reviewed by O'Donovan (1965). The data that stem from these personal habits of rating may be dealt with in statistical treatment. Judges will be selected and trained to prevent any distortions in the scaling. The need for such caution in scaling efforts is highlighted by findings obtained by Light, Zax, and Gardiner (1965). Giving a rating task to students in the 4th, 8th, and 12th grades, they found that the use of the extremes on the scale was less frequent in the older children and in the brighter children at each grade level tested.

Influences on judgment

A general problem in the study of judging is to identify the numerous factors which may influence judgments. From past research on psychological scaling we may draw a few examples. Studies of many sorts have revealed that influences of a social nature can seriously affect judging behavior. If an individual knows the ratings that others are assigning, he may be swayed so that his ratings tend to correspond more closely to theirs than would otherwise be the case. The practice of having ratings given independently is a recognition of such a social influence, of course.

A judge may also be influenced by previous ratings that he himself has given to the same person or object being rated. In merit rating, for instance, if a supervisor rates an employee very high on "productivity," he may also give a high rating on "good will toward the company" even though evidence on which to base the latter rating is meager. It is as though the earlier rating provides a halo for the person being evaluated so that he is perceived thereafter as a superior being; the term *halo effect* has therefore been applied to this sort of influence of a readily made judgment on those less easy to determine. Although the terminology seems to imply positive bias, you can see that the same sort of interdependence of judgments might have an adverse effect in which a strongly negative response on the part of the rater would influence some of his other ratings in the negative direction.

Research on the processes of judgment is a source of aid in the improvement of psychological scaling techniques. As they are refined, these techniques will serve us better in many sorts of psychological investigations. Studies conducted by Harris (1969) are an example of the methodological probing into the behavior of subjects engaging in psychological scaling tasks. He required judges to use both a rating procedure and a pair comparison. In one study the stimuli being judged were personality-descriptive adjectives. In another they were phonograph recordings—judged by their covers. Through detailed examination of the data, Harris was able to show the appropriateness of certain models in describing judgmental processes.

The Method of Rating

The type of rating scale which a rater has to apply to the stimuli being judged may vary greatly. Verbal, numerical, or graphic scales have all been used. By locating stimuli at some point on such a continuum, the judges provide data which are used to establish a scale value for each of the stimuli. Sometimes called the method of successive categories or the method of graded dichotomies, the fundamental rating method is amenable to several variations in data analysis.

Criteria for Using Rating

There are a few considerations which favor the use of the rating method for psychological scaling as opposed to the method of ranking or of pair comparisons. When the use of these other two methods is precluded because the stimuli cannot be presented together for comparative judgments, some rating technique must be employed. Rating is to be preferred also for its economy of time when a large number of stimuli are to be judged. Comparing them pair by pair would be very time consuming.

The rating task, involving some kind of scale provided for the judges, is not overly simple; we must be confident of the judges' ability to use the scale properly before we turn to rating for psychological scaling. The method does have the important advantage of letting the judge indicate the distance separating different stimuli on the continuum. In the other methods, only comparative judgments are made although certain data treatments can yield interval scales.

Devising Rating Scales

A rating scale serves to aid judges in making a set of judgments and communicating them. Lacking such a device, it would be difficult to judge a series of items and to describe the judgments meaningfully. We shall examine some of the types of rating scales to see how they facilitate judgmental behavior and quantify it at the same time.

Numerical and verbal scales

Quantitative concepts are so much a part of our thinking that judgments may be expressed readily by the use of a numerical scale. Although most people find them easy to use, there are a few precautions to take in the establishment of such a scale. One rule is to provide a number of scale points or intervals appropriate to the needs of the rater. A three-point scale, for example, may not permit enough categories to which a judge may assign the items. On the other hand, a fifteen-point scale might imply finer differences than it would be possible to use in doing the rating. Since raters tend to avoid using the end points of a rating scale, it is useful to provide more points than would seem desirable for the ratings themselves to cover. Thus, a nine-point scale might yield a set of ratings that are largely confined to seven points.

Besides trying to fit the number of rating points or categories to the problem facing the raters, we need to think about an odd number of points vs. an even number for a rating scale. An odd number permits the center point to be used as a neutral index if that seems appropriate. Such a neutral point may be a zero, with positive and negative numbers arranged to represent degrees of judgment of desirable and undesirable traits or attributes. In the interest of simplicity, however, negative numbers are often avoided in setting up a scale. One of the series of positive numbers may then be verbally indicated as an indifference point if desired. Where such a neutral point is not considered appropriate, an even number of scale points may be provided to force judgments in one direction or the other.

Investigators sometimes give a verbal description of every point on a numerical rating scale. For example, consider the following scale for esthetic appeal:

9 Extremely appealing
8 Very appealing
7 Moderately appealing
6 Slightly appealing
5 Neither appealing nor unappealing
4 Slightly unappealing
3 Moderately unappealing
2 Very unappealing
1 Extremely unappealing

The scale points are identified by the graded series of adverbs—"slightly, moderately, very, and extremely"—which are assigned to the adjective "appealing" to form one part of the scale and to its opposite "unappealing" to form another part. At "5" on the scale the descriptive phrase indicates an indifference point. In a different numerical schema this point might have been considered "0," with the other values ranging up to "4" and down to "—4." For scaling in other value systems we might employ the same set of adverbs with pairs of adjectives like pleasant-unpleasant, or desirable-undesirable. Sometimes verbal labels are supplied only for certain numerical points such as the end points and perhaps the neutral point.

Numerical rating scales may be employed where the complexity of the material being judged would preclude simple verbal description. In a study of group behavior, for example, a judge might rate each observed group on the extent to which their morale level and their efficiency in communicating would lead him to predict success for them in cooperatively solving a difficult problem. In such an experiment in social psychology, the ratings might thus be applied to predicted behavior instead of observed behavior.

The rating scale that ranged from "extremely appealing" to "extremely unappealing" had every point verbally indicated so that these descriptions actually form a verbal scale. The numbers, convenient in recording judgments, might be discarded if we wished. It is common practice to use verbal statements like "agree" or "strongly disagree" when we scale a subject's degree of agreement with each of a series of attitude-indicating statements. In other types of psychological measurement a test may require a person to indicate by meaningful symbols, $+$, $-$, or ?, whether given statements are applicable or not to that which is being judged. Although not strictly verbal themselves, such symbols might be considered equivalent to terms like "applicable," "inapplicable," and "cannot say."

Graphic scales

In the graphic method of rating, judges are asked to indicate on a physical continuum—a straight line segment—the location which they feel represents the place of the item being rated on some psychological continuum or dimension. By placing a mark near one end of the line, for example, a rater may indicate his judgment that a painting has a great esthetic appeal. Various points along the line may be indicated by verbal statements as indicated below:

Very high	Moderate	Very low
esthetic appeal	esthetic appeal	esthetic appeal

Our sample graphic rating scale illustrates a number of principles that are felt to represent good practice. The line is a continuous one so that the rater may locate his mark at any point along it. This continuity imposes no restraints on the rater or on the numerical scoring that is done later. The verbal statements near the ends of the line are not so extreme as to cause raters to cluster their indicating marks near the center. It is considered better to have the "good" end of the scale at the left. A graphic rating scale may be a vertical line, too, permitting verbal statements to be readily placed alongside it at several points.

Graphic scales are interesting to use. They free the rater from some of the influences that might arise if he had to give numerical judgments repeatedly. They are readily scored with a scoring stencil or template which can, in some research uses, be adapted to the ratings that have been given. For example, if raters are found to have avoided the ends of the scale, the scoring divisions of the template can be adjusted so that a reasonable spread of numerical values results anyway. Another value of the graphic method is its extension into a series of parallel scales which yields a profile representation of the scaling of any item or person on several different dimensions.

Special scales

A number of variants of rating scale methods may lend themselves to application in research. One of these is the *standard scale* in which points along the continuum are designated by providing graded samples for the rater to use as he judges each item. For example, if we wanted ratings on the skill exhibited by different subjects in drawing a picture of a person, we might provide between six and twelve sample pictures of varying degrees of excellence. Judges could compare each subject's work with these standards in order to arrive at a rating.

A *sorting-tray* technique may be employed conveniently if verbal items are being judged. By printing the items on 3 x 5 cards we may require them to be sorted into a long tray containing perhaps 9 compartments. Having designated a numerical value and a verbal label for each compartment, we obtain ratings for the sorted items. With this technique it is feasible to allow subjects to relocate some items as the sorting proceeds. The scale can be evaluated continuously by the subject as he proceeds with his task. In this way, the ratings given to the earlier items do not distort the rating scale by exerting an anchoring effect, to be discussed later in this chapter.

A *check-list* procedure permits scale values to be developed in a cumulative process involving numerous judgments. Textbooks, for example, might be rated by checking the applicable items from a long list of descriptive words or phrases like "sturdy binding" and "useful index." The ultimate rating is based on the sum of all the value applied to the checked items for any particular book being judged. Different items may carry different weights, if desired, and negative weights may also be used.

A number of *forced-choice techniques* have been devised in an effort to reduce or eliminate subjective bias as raters give their judgments of stimuli or persons being rated. Two of the simpler formats involve presenting either a pair or a triad of items. Items might be statements descriptive of personality traits or behaviors, all favorable or all unfavorable. The rater would be required to choose the one which was most applicable to the person being rated. By using numerous such clusters of items, the technique tends to insure a more valid appraisal of an individual than might emerge if leniency in rating or a halo effect were permitted to operate freely. More elaborate forms use tetrads of items, sometimes mixed in connotation. Various aspects and implications of forced-choice psychological measurement have been discussed by Zavala (1965) and Hicks (1970).

Administrative Procedures

Having begun our use of a rating method by selecting an appropriate rating scale, we would continue by setting up proper conditions surrounding the collecting of the ratings. Primary problems confronting us would include the instructing or training of the judges and the presenting of the stimulus materials to them.

Instructions to raters

In experiments requiring that ratings be given by subjects or judges, the requirement that they be motivated to do their best is important, as in nearly all psychological research. In addition to arousing their interest, instructions to subjects should give them considerable information about how to perform their task. A prime requirement is that the dimension or attribute on which the ratings are to be given must be clearly defined. The validity of ratings might be ruined before they were even collected if judges misunderstand what they are to rate about the stimulus objects or persons presented to them. It is especially important to specify carefully the trait to be judged if it is a characteristic that is not too prominent in the total stimulus pattern. We must proceed carefully, however, in order not to define a stimulus dimension in such a way that we force some bias into the ratings given to the different stimuli. For example, it would be unwise to say, "You are to rate these paintings on their excellence in color harmony, as in a balanced presentation of deep purples, light tans, and fiery reds." The mention of particular hues might cause observers to give special attention to any painting that contained the three that were mentioned. The best instructions avoid any source of influence on the ratings (unless this is an experimental aim) while defining the attribute clearly enough to eliminate any misunderstanding on the part of the raters.

Besides making sure they know what they are rating, we must be sure that judges employ the rating scale properly. We saw that the proper devising of any type of rating scale can do much to insure its proper use.

We may wish to direct the judges to use the full extent of the scale, counteracting any tendency to avoid extreme values. Sometimes instructions are worded to suggest or even to dictate what proportion of the cases should be given each rating. This procedure might be used, for example, to assure a normal distribution for the assigned ratings. Such instructions should be given to judges only if the restraints are felt to impose no great difficulty on their performance of the rating task.

If there is any question about the adequacy of instructions for a rating task, they should be pretested on a group of persons similar to those who will be judges in the experiment. Such a preliminary tryout may reveal points of confusion which can be eliminated by clarifying the wording of the directions for judging. Some research may deal with perceptual judgments that are so difficult to make that some training of the observers must precede the actual collecting of the ratings. Such prior practice is often appropriate, but it should be remembered that the final scale values that are achieved are not the same as might have been obtained with untrained observers.

Presentation of stimulus items

Perceptual processes are so complex that many factors may affect the ratings which observers give to stimulus items. In the judging of paintings, for example, ratings related to color characteristics might be distorted if illumination were inadequate or too strong. Viewing distance also may seriously affect a judge's reaction to a picture. Which would be the sounder procedure, to keep viewing distance a constant or to let it vary at the desire of those who are rating a series of pictures? In a different judging task, what problems would you foresee in presenting musical selections to be rated?

One advantage of rating over some other methods of psychological scaling is that items to be judged can be presented successively rather than simultaneously. However, there are difficulties with an experimental design that presents stimuli singly, one after the other, for rating. As the judges rate the first few items they may employ a certain part of the rating scale. These early judgments may exert an *anchoring effect* for any similar stimuli judged later in the series. Such an anchoring effect may distort the assigned ratings from what they might have been if a different, and perhaps more representative, set of items had been experienced early in the task. To avoid introducing distortion, it is often good practice to give judges a preliminary acquaintance with the stimuli to be judged. Sometimes all the stimuli are presented in advance of actual judging; sometimes the judges are shown a sample of stimuli which is assumed to include representatives from all parts of the continuum that will be encountered in the actual rating. Either technique tends to offset the development of an anchoring effect.

Treatment of Rating Data

The data analysis which follows the collecting of ratings may range from a simple determination of central tendency to an elaborate series of calculations leading to the establishment of interval scale values. Our discussion will center on the simpler treatments of the data with a brief mention of more elaborate scaling techniques.

Distribution of the ratings

Although it is feasible to proceed immediately to the computation of measures of central tendency and variability when rating data have been collected, it is often well to make frequency distributions of the ratings assigned to each stimulus item first. Consider, for example, the contrasting sets of ratings on artistic merit given to hypothetical paintings *A* and *B* in the following frequency distributions:

	Rating							
	1	2	3	4	5	6	7	
Frequency distribution, Painting *A*:	0	2	4	12	19	3	1	$N = 41$
Frequency distribution, Painting *B*:	8	7	2	1	5	8	10	$N = 41$

We could compute the mean or median rating for each picture and the standard deviation of the ratings. These statistics would not reveal the entire difference, however, between the two sets of judgments. If we inspect the frequency distributions, we find that the distribution of the 41 ratings for Painting *B* is bimodal. Judges rated it either fairly high or else quite low. This aspect of the distribution adds to the information we would get from the computed statistics. In fact, it indicates any measure of central tendency to be somewhat misleading. The bimodality of ratings is the salient fact about Painting *B* requiring explanation. We might infer, for example, that there is some characteristic of this work of art which elicits strong approval from some viewers but evokes censure from others.

Central tendencies of the ratings

Often the use of ratings will not be oriented toward the determination of interval scale values, and a simple form of data analysis will be appropriate. As a measure of central tendency, the mean rating given to each stimulus item may be determined, to be statistically compared with the means for other items. In many studies there may be reasons for regarding the median as a more appropriate measure. If a number of judges particularly disliked a certain item, they might give extremely low ratings to it as "votes against" it. This would lower the mean rating unduly, but the median rating would not differ from the value it would have had if their dislike of the item had been expressed in moderation.

In other instances, extreme ratings may accurately reflect great approval or disapproval of an item. If a great number of ratings fall at one end point on the rating scale, we might infer that many of the judges would have rated even more extremely if this had been possible. In such a case a mean rating would not reflect the true central tendency of the judgments. A median would still do so, provided the median did not actually fall in this end category.

Variability of the ratings

The mean or median ratings given by a group of judges may be far less important in indicating their reactions to some stimulus items than a measure of variability of the ratings. If variability is extremely low, indicating very strong agreement among the judges in rating a stimulus item, this fact is likely to be noteworthy. If variability is great, the widespread disagreement indicated is a fact also requiring attention. In this case we would need to ask whether the lack of agreement stemmed from the nature of the stimulus item, from the composition of the group of judges, or from some sort of ambiguity in defining the rating task for them. By calculating the standard deviation, we may seek information about the experimental rating procedures as well as about the stimulus items.

Determining interval scale values

Computational procedures described by Guilford (1954, pp. 223–244) permit us to obtain interval scale values from rating data. The treatment of the rating data from a large number of judges represents a correction for the probable occurrence of inequalities in the intervals represented in the rating scale as it was employed. The assumption is made that ratings of each stimulus item would hypothetically be normally distributed. Wherever the distribution of ratings is empirically skewed, the application of this assumption of normal distribution represents a determination of either (1) the limits of the successive rating categories or (2) representative scale values. The latter approach to interval scale values is the one that Guilford recommends. Although many studies employing ratings may be carried out with simpler treatments of the data, it is well to be aware that there are procedures for more ambitious efforts at psychological scaling.

Precautions in Using the Method of Rating

In discussing administrative procedures we noted some rules concerning the instructing of raters and the presentation of stimulus items to them. Earlier, we discussed the care that must be taken in setting up rating scales. All these precautions represented our recognition of the complexity of the judgmental behavior situation. We may now consider a few additional precepts which deserve consideration if we are to use rating methods in research.

If each stimulus item is to be rated on a number of dimensions, it is desirable to consider one dimension at a time, rating all the stimuli on this factor. This is preferable to completing all ratings on a particular item at one time. The latter procedure tends to invite the operation of the halo effect which we discussed earlier.

By way of augmenting a good definition of the trait or dimension to be rated, it is desirable to select with care the verbal cues which identify points or regions on the rating scale. The wording employed in these cues should be clear, brief, and relevant to the dimension being rated. They should leave no doubt as to the degree of the trait which each of them implies. In brief, the labels attached to a rating scale should aid the rater rather than make his task difficult.

An Illustrative Experiment Using Ratings

A research report entitled "When is Aggression Funny?" offers an illustration of how ratings may be used as a tool in quantifying some rather complex sociopsychological processes. In their study of how humor is derived from a description of an aggressive act, Gutman and Priest (1969) used several different rating scales at different points in their investigation. Here we shall deal with just two aspects of their psychological scaling. After reading four experimentally prepared "squelch" jokes, subjects had to rate each one on its humor and on the justifiability of the aggression described in the brief anecdote. By preparing different versions of each joke the experimenters expected to vary the perceived humor and justifiability of aggression. This was done by manipulating the character or personality traits attributed in each story to the aggressor (A) and the victim (V) in the squelch. Among the interrelated expectations for the experimental findings was the hypothesis that a joke would be judged more humorous and its aggressive act more justified if A had been described as socially acceptable in his personal attributes while V had been portrayed in an unacceptable light. Different versions of each joke, presented to different college students, allowed the effects of such experimental manipulations to be examined in the ratings of the jokes that were obtained.

For the assessment of judged humor the experimenters asked the subjects to use a 9-point rating scale ranging from 0 (not at all humorous) to 8 (very humorous). For the scaling of justifiability of aggression the rating scale ranged from -3 (very unjustified) to $+3$ (very justified). The two different scales were chosen to relate to the conceptual dimensions being rated. "Justified" and "unjustified" each ranged over 3 scale points on either side of zero when aggression was to be rated. For humor, in contrast, a unidirectional scale ranging up from zero was used. As predicted by the experimenters, it was found that humor was rated as highest (4.31) when the aggressor (A) in the joke was portrayed as socially acceptable and when the victim (V) was unacceptable. Underlying this, according to the research report, was the corresponding finding that this experimental condition (version of joke) was the only one which led to a positive rating $(+1.11)$ for the justifiability of the aggressive squelch which was described.

The Method of Ranking

The *method of rank order*, sometimes called the *order of merit method,* is a simple technique for psychological scaling in which the items are merely placed in order with reference to the dimension being judged.

The data that are so obtained may be treated quite simply or may be subjected to elaborate transformations aimed at establishing a scale of some refinement.

Criteria for Using Ranking

Ranking is a useful technique in the judging of stimuli that may be moved around physically. If a collection of cartoons is spread out on top of a table, for example, it is convenient for a judge to arrange them in order of their excellence of humor. Ranking is not confined to situations where the stimuli are movable or even physically present. Subjects can assign ranks to famous authors, for example, or to makes of automobiles. The method is readily used when the number of stimuli is fairly small; it is not as convenient as rating when very many items must be judged.

An advantage in the use of ranking is that it forces every judge to use all parts of the scale that might hypothetically be considered as being applied. The highest ranks must be assigned to some of the stimulus items and the lowest must be given to others. Judges thus have no way of committing the error of central tendency that may occur in rating if they avoid using the extremes. Another advantage of ranking over rating is that it forces a decision among stimuli that may be hard to judge as different from each other. In rating, a judge might evade this difficulty by assigning the same rating to these items, often a legitimate thing to do in using rating scales. Ranking, however, demands decisions which, in effect, differentiate every item from every other one according to the judgments of the observer.

Administrative Procedures

With no rating scale requiring construction, an investigator finds himself with fewer preliminary problems if he decides to use the method of rank order. Its simplicity, however, does not mean that the method can be used carelessly with any prospect of getting valid results.

Instructions to judges

The initial instructions to judges in a ranking task may be considered even more important than in the rating method since cues that a rating scale provides are lacking in the method of rank order. This lack of cues requires special emphasis on the dimension with respect to which the ranking is to be done. This dimension must be especially carefully defined if it pertains to attributes of the stimulus items other than their major ones. Suppose, for example, we ask judges to rank popular singers on their enunciation of the lyrics in rendering their songs. As the ranking task is undertaken, our judges may slip unthinkingly into ranking these well-known singers according to their general appeal rather than on the specific dimension we indicated. The attribute to be scaled must be stated with emphasis at the beginning of the ranking task. These initial instructions may well be augmented by a printed reminder prominently displayed.

Another important point to cover in instructing judges is the indicating of which rank is considered most meritorious. Conventionally, of course, a rank of 1 symbolizes the best, with higher rank numbers designating inferior positions on the dimension being judged. It is especially important to stress this to judges who might be inclined to think of the numerical values as though ratings were being assigned to the stimulus items.

Presentation of stimulus items

For ranking purposes the stimuli all have to be available at once for comparison, whether physically present or symbolically represented. Thus, no problem as to sequence of presentation arises. If stimuli are physically arranged by each subject in order of merit, however, we must be sure that the arrangement is not permitted to influence the ranking done by the next subject. The items need to be randomly mixed between presentations to judges.

Treatment of Data

Where a hundred or more judges have engaged in ranking the stimulus items, we might wish to use elaborate computational procedures for scaling which are described by Guilford (1954, pp. 183-188). For many research purposes simpler treatments of rank data will suffice and we shall discuss them here.

Distribution of the ranks

For each stimulus item we might make a frequency distribution showing how many times it was ranked in each position. The series of such frequency distributions covering all the stimuli could be combined into one matrix for convenient summary of the ranking. A sample of such a matrix is found in Guilford's Table 8.2 (1954, p. 180). Examination of the distribution of the ranks assigned to each stimulus will reveal any stimuli which were ranked with good agreement or with great disagreement among the judges.

Central tendencies in the ranks

Since the assignment of ranks represents only ordinal scaling, it is not proper to compute mean ranks for the stimuli as if the ranks were interval scale values. The median rank assigned each item thus becomes a preferred descriptive statistic. The whole rank number where the median falls may be taken as an index of central tendency. Refining such a median by interpolation may not be sound in view of uncertainty about the scale widths of the different ranks.

Variability of the ranks

Inspection of the frequency distribution matrix of ranks assigned to stimulus items will indicate the degree of agreement among judges. If a descriptive statistic is desired, the semi-interquartile range is appropriate to use. Without being permitted to calculate a mean rank we should not take the standard deviation as a measure of variability.

Transformation to C scale values

One way to refine ranking is to apply the assumption that the trait or attribute that was judged was one that was normally distributed in the sample of items presented for judging. Under such an assumption the endmost ranks are considered to represent a fairly wide separation of interval scale values. The middlemost ranks are assumed to represent scale values that were closer to each other than those represented by the ranks at either end of the set of ranks. By applying mathematical relationships represented in the normal distribution it is possible to transform ranks into centiles. After describing such a transformation, Guilford (1954, p. 182) suggests another convenient transformation, to his C scale values. This C scale is based on the normalizing transformation of the ranks with the additional convenience that a mean C value of 5.0 and a standard deviation of 2.0 are utilized. The transformation of ranks to normalized C values is readily accomplished by use of Table 6.1, adopted from Guilford (1954).

Since the normalized C values are considered to be interval scale values, we can find mean C values for each stimulus item as a way of refining our psychological scaling. This transformation to C values does not demand the large number of judges that are required in some of the more elaborate scaling procedures. A point to keep in mind, however,

Table 6.1 Ranks Corresponding to C Scale Values for Different Numbers of Items Ranked (After Guilford, 1954)

Number Ranked	C Scale Values								
	1	2	3	4	5	6	7	8	9
10	...	10	9	7–8	5–6	3–4	2	1	...
11	...	11	9–10	8	5–7	4	2–3	1	...
12	...	12	10–11	8–9	6–7	4–5	2–3	1	...
13	13	...	11–12	9–10	6–8	4–5	2–3	...	1
14	14	...	12–13	9–11	7–8	4–6	2–3	...	1
15	15	14	13	10–12	7–9	4–6	3	2	1
16	16	15	13–14	11–12	7–10	5–6	3–4	2	1
17	17	16	14–15	11–13	8–10	5–7	3–4	2	1
18	18	17	15–16	12–14	8–11	5–7	3–4	2	1
19	19	18	16–17	12–15	9–11	5–8	3–4	2	1
20	20	19	16–18	13–15	9–12	6–8	3–5	2	1
21	21	20	17–19	14–16	9–13	6–8	3–5	2	1
22	22	21	18–20	14–17	10–13	6–9	3–5	2	1
23	23	22	19–21	15–18	10–14	6–9	3–5	2	1
24	24	22–23	20–21	15–19	11–14	6–10	4–5	2–3	1

is that we *assume* the normal distribution of the attribute over the sample of items being judged. Such an assumption may be valid for samples of handwriting from 20 second-graders, selected at random. It is probably not a valid assumption to make about the humorous appeal of 20 cartoons from *The New Yorker*.

Precautions in Using the Method of Ranking

In discussing the rank ordering of stimuli in psychological research we noted the care which must be taken in instructing the judges, in presenting the stimuli, and in treating the data. A general rule which may be added is to use ranking only when the number of stimulus items is reasonably small. To demand that very many items be placed in rank order is to invite frustration on the part of the judges with subsequent unreliability of rank data. Where many stimuli must be judged it is better to provide a good rating scale. When assigned ranks are examined it must be remembered that the highest rank does not necessarily reflect strong approval by the subject. Nor do very low ranks mean that disapproval may be safely inferred. In rank ordering we *force* the subject to employ the highest rank, the lowest, and all others. Again, a good rating scale is preferred if we need to determine the level of evaluation assigned to items by our subjects.

The Method of Pair Comparisons

In using scaling methods like ranking or rating we ask a judge to assign a numerical value, directly or by implication, each time he considers a stimulus item. In the method of pair comparisons judgments are in themselves less quantitative than in these other methods. Stimuli are paired and compared with each other instead of with any numerical rating scale or set of ranks. Judges merely say which member of each pair is preferred or possesses more of the quality being scaled. This comparative judgment of the various pairings of stimuli gives the method its name. From the expressed preferences we obtain scale values by a series of computational steps.

Criteria for Using Pair Comparisons

This method may be used when it is desired to obtain an interval scaling of some psychological dimension. If we merely desired a rough ordinal scale, we would employ ranking or rating with a minimum of elaboration on the raw data. We further restrict our choice of pair comparisons to a scaling task where the stimulus items to be judged are not too numerous. As the number of stimuli to be compared rises, the number of pairings increases much more rapidly. Thus, it takes 10 trials to present 5 stimuli in all possible pairs whereas 45 trials would be needed for 10 stimuli. If there are 15 stimuli, it takes 105 trials to present all possible pairs. It taxes the motivation of observers to be asked to make even this many comparative judgments. It would be practically impossible, in most studies, to require such pair judging when stimuli are more than 15 in number. It should be noted, though, that the method does not actually require all possible pairs to be judged. A reduced number of pairings may yield good results if there is some knowledge of approximate rank order, perhaps gained in preliminary research.

Administrative Procedures

Many of the general rules for obtaining opinions from judges or observers apply to the method of pair comparisons as well as to the other methods we have discussed. A clear definition of the dimension or trait on which judgments are to be based is the essential initial step in all psychological scaling. Judges must be motivated too. To these general requirements we add the special techniques that typify the pair comparison method.

Presentation of stimulus items

It is in the pairing of the stimuli as they are presented for judgment that this method is unique. For ranking, we make them all available for the judges to place them in order of merit. For rating we present them singly, but usually only after a wide sample has been given to the raters to acquaint them with the range covered. In contrast, the method of pair comparisons minimizes the impact of the entire group of stimuli on the judges. The stimulus items are to be considered just two at a time. Ideally, a choice is made between these two without reference to any of the other stimuli, whether previously experienced or anticipated. This comparative judgment within a pair can be encouraged by isolating the pairs from each other as they are presented, perhaps by spacing the presentations in time. Some applications of this method, it is true, present lists of paired words or names to be judged so that all the stimuli are before the observers at once. Such a technique seems to invite a tacit rank ordering of the stimuli as a guide to the judging of the various pairs. While this might enhance the consistency of the preferences within pairs, it is not required by the rationale for the method of pair comparisons. As long as the stimuli are to be judged in pairs it seems appropriate to present them that way, rather than instructing the judges to give their attention to just a pair at a time when all pairs are in front of them during the judging.

Another procedural rule is to present each stimulus as often on the right as on the left, to keep a space error from distorting the data. If stimuli are paired successively in time instead of contiguously in space, then of course a similar counterbalancing of first and second presentations would be used; in this case to control for possible time error.

Instructions to judges

If we strive to keep judgments confined to within-pair evaluations by the way we present the stimuli, we would do well to augment this procedure by instructions. Judges must be told to take each pair as a new problem. Preference must be expressed at the time of presentation with no specific effort made to recall previous stimuli.

Judges must make a choice from every pair in this method of pair comparisons. There is no provision in the basic computational techniques for any failure to select one stimulus of each paired presentation as the superior one on the quality being scaled. Even if a judge feels it impossible to make a choice in any instance, he must be instructed to express one anyway. Some suggestions have been made (e.g., Glenn and David, 1960; Greenberg, 1965) that would modify this requirement and allow "equal" preferences or judgments. Different data treatments are suggested.

Assumptions—The Law of Comparative Judgment

Since each judgment in the method of pair comparisons is not a quantitative value, we do not arrive at psychological scale values for the stimuli by any simple statistical process. Instead, we use the relative frequencies with which each stimulus is preferred in its comparisons with every other stimulus. The proportions of times that each is chosen provide data from which interval scale values may be derived. We shall briefly examine the rationale that underlies the treatment of the data.

Thurstone (1927) formulated a *law of comparative judgment* which describes how preference data arise from judgmental processes that are assumed to operate when two stimuli are compared. A fundamental assumption is that the judgmental responses made to any stimulus vary in a normally distributed fashion around a central response value which characterizes the judgments of that particular stimulus. The variations in judging a stimulus are assumed to arise from a large number of internal and external factors whose random fluctuations contribute small increments or decrements to the judgment being made. On most occasions the increments and decrements will nearly cancel each other so that the given judgment will not deviate far from the "true" judgmental response. Less frequently, most of the factors will contribute increments so that the judgment that is made will be somewhat higher than usual. Equally rarely, it is assumed, will there be a piling up of decremental factors so that an unusually low judgment results. By assuming the contributory factors to be uncorrelated in their positive or negative effects from moment to moment, we find it possible to assume further that the distribution of resulting judgments is normally distributed around some central value. Such a distribution is termed a *discriminal dispersion* in discussions of comparative judgment.

Thurstone's law of comparative judgment consists of a series of assumptions that relate hypothetical response value separations and their discriminal dispersions to the proportion of judgment favoring either of two stimuli which are repeatedly compared. The assumptions differ in particular cases subsumed under the general law. We may assume that individual differences may be taken as one factor contributing to discriminal dispersions. Thus we often treat judgmental data gathered from many observers in the same manner as we would treat data based on repeated judgments made by a single observer.

The method of pair comparisons uses the law of comparative judgment as its basis for psychological scaling. As different stimulus items are considered in pairs, the proportion of times that one is preferred over another is an indicant of the scale separation of the items. For example, if stimulus G is preferred over stimulus R on 520 comparisons out of 1000, this indicates the scale values of these two items to be quite close. In contrast, if stimulus W is preferred over stimulus J in 831 out of 1000 judgments, then W is indicated to be much higher on the scale than J. The different proportions obtained from the comparison of all possible pairs of stimuli can be converted to estimates of the different scale separations of the judgmental responses to the stimuli. By pooling these estimates we arrive at scale values. Guilford (1954, pp. 154-177) provides discussion of the law of comparative judgment and computational guidance for the investigator who wishes to use pair comparisons to accomplish interval scaling for some psychological dimension.

Precautions in Using the Method of Pair Comparisons

The method of pair comparisons should be avoided if the stimuli are so numerous as to make the judgmental task very long and tedious. It may be noted in this regard that a reduction can be made in the number of pairings employed if the scaling effort is planned to provide for such a modification in procedure (Guilford, 1954, pp. 168-169; Coombs, 1964, pp. 32-58).

To insure that judgments are made within each pair of stimuli as presented, it is good practice to keep the other stimuli out of the subject's field of attention. One advantage of this method over ranking is that it demands the consideration of only two stimuli at a time. This advantage might be lost, however, if judges have access to other stimuli while a particular pair is supposedly under comparison.

For the most exacting applications of the pair comparison method we would have to determine which assumptions under the law of comparative judgment could properly be applied.

A commonly observed precaution in treating pair comparison data is to omit from consideration any preference proportion value more extreme than .977 and .023. Such extreme proportions are likely to introduce unreliability into the estimates of scale separation. Where such values are disregarded, we may take scale separation estimates from each of the more moderate preference proportions. These scale distances may then be averaged to obtain the final scale.

Multidimensional Similarity Scaling

Up to this point we have been concerned with the psychological scaling of stimulus items with reference to only one defined attribute or dimension. In everyday life people engage quite readily in the multidimensional scaling of complex stimulus configurations. We are not at all puzzled if someone says, "Chris looks a lot like Pat." This judgment of similarity takes place quite naturally. Presumably it reflects a comparison of Chris and Pat on a number of aspects of their appearance—complexion, eye color, hair color, shape of face, and possibly numerous other facial features. Since many important stimulus items are a collection of different attributes, psychologists have been interested in devising methods for scaling similarity and then transforming and analyzing the data to obtain insights into the perceptual and judgmental processes underlying these reactions. Also of interest of course are the psychological distances separating different stimuli—the converse of similarity. Among the materials so scaled have been colors, odors, visual forms, and words.

Aims

Multidimensional scaling is aimed at the construction of models of similarity for particular stimulus domains. These quantitative models are representations of the psychological distances separating judged items or objects. They are also analytic, indicating the component dimensions or factors which appear to contribute to the similarity or separation of items which have been rated (or otherwise assessed by subjects) for their general resemblance to each other. Thus multidimensional scaling seeks to determine the psychological structure underlying certain complex judgments. In addition to this analytic approach there is sometimes a synthetic technique used in probing perceptual processes. In such a method stimuli such as visual forms are generated by combining various attributes such as geometrically defined and measured elements—angles, arcs, and lines, for example. Then the investigator requires the general scaling of similarity among the pairs of these forms. Finally, he analyzes the psychological distances which are derived from the data. In doing this he seeks to learn how the original physical dimensions and their ranges of values were perceived and processed by the subjects in their global comparisons of the synthetic stimuli.

Models

Distinctiveness or differentiation among a set of stimulus objects is considered to be a kind of psychological distance in perception or cognition. It is quite natural then to formulate a model in which physical distance between points is used to represent such scaled separations. This is a logical extension of using points along a line to represent differences among items which have been subjected to interval scaling. The easy acceptance of graphic rating scales in which a psychological continuum is represented by a line is another indicant of the natural character of linear representation of psychological quantity. Separations of points along such a line represent psychological distances or scaled differentiations.

In multidimensional scaling, the quantitative models are often comprised of sets of axes or coordinates in two-, three-, or n-dimensional space. Points located in this space represent items or objects which have been scaled. The distances between pairs of points are inversely representative of the scaled similarity among the corresponding pairs of items. Further, the coordinates defining the space in such a geometric model represent the psychological dimensions reflected in the judgmental processes of the subjects. The Euclidean spatial representation of similarity is only one of several models which have emerged from multidimensional scaling. Torgerson (1965) has suggested that the Euclidean model relates best to the similarity scaling of stimuli such as color, a multidimensional attribute which includes the dimensions of hue, intensity, and saturation as discussed in Chapter 7. For other stimuli, such as geometric forms, he reports on research which suggests that an additive spatial representation of psychological distances seems more appropriate. Still another spatial representation of multidimensional scaling has been set forth by Ekman (1963) who uses vectors to represent psychological qualities of different items being compared, say two colors. The judged similarities of the two stimuli are represented as the projections of each vector on the other. This hypothetical representation is an early stage of Ekman's theoretical development. After the judgmental data have been obtained, they are transformed and subjected to factor analysis. The final representations of stimuli are points in space defined by the factors as coordinates.

Data Collection and Treatment

The transformations of data involved in multidimensional scaling are quite complex, usually requiring computer processing to accomplish the iterative procedures expeditiously. Many substantial contributions to this kind of research have been mathematical in character. Despite the complexity of data transformation, the basic scaling of similarity by experimental subjects is often a relatively simple task. A few examples will illustrate this. In some experiments, pairs of multidimensional stimuli are presented to subjects who are asked to use a rating scale to indicate the similarity they perceive between each two items. In other work, triads of items may be considered together. Here the task is to say whether *B* or *C* is more similar to *A*. In Ekman's procedure the stimuli are presented in pairs, say items *J* and *K*. A subject is required first to consider *J* as a standard and to report what proportion of this unit is perceived in *K*. Then he takes *K* as the standard unit and indicates what proportion of it he experiences in examining *J*. These proportions, based on all stimulus pairs, comprise the raw data for the analytic scaling. In still other methods a subject may be asked to estimate the ratios of psychological distances between pairs of stimuli presented two pairs at a time.

An Illustrative Multidimensional Analysis

One of the experiments summarized by Torgerson (1965, pp. 385-386) may serve to illustrate some aspects of multidimensional scaling. The asymmetric stimulus forms, shown in Figure 6.1, were created by manipulating two physical dimensions. These were the sizes of the two circles used as a basis for the forms and the distance separating their centers in the construction of the stimulus shapes. The circle sizes are expressed as a ratio of the left circle's radius to that of the right circle in establishing the ordinate of Figure 6.1. The abscissa is a scale of the distance between the centers of the circles. Once two values were selected for these physical variables, each form could be completed by connecting the circles with short arcs as the figure with its 15 stimuli suggests. Although they are

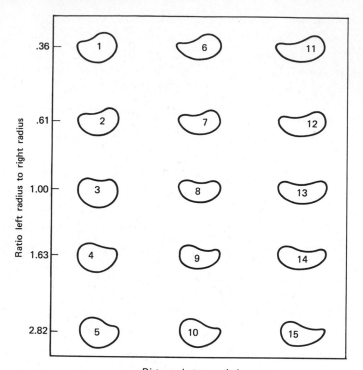

Fig. 6.1. Asymmetric stimulus forms used in multidimensional scaling of similarity. (After Torgerson, 1965.)

shown as outline forms with numerical designations for convenient reference, the actual stimuli were solid figures presented without numerical designation. As each pair was shown to a subject he was asked to rate the similarity of the two stimuli to each other. Sixteen subjects each gave the 105 similarity ratings required by all of the pairings.

Two subjects were found to have rated similarities in such a way as to locate the stimuli in two-dimensional space in about the same way as they are arranged in Figure 6.1. It was almost as if these subjects had made a cognitive analysis of these shapes into dimensions such as those used in constructing them. The similarity judgments given by the remaining 14 subjects seemed upon multidimensional factor analysis to reflect three perceptual dimensions in comparing the forms. One dimension was related to the width of the shapes and thus corresponded to the distance between the circles used in forming them. The ratios of the circles seemed to yield two different subjective factors—the degree of asymmetry of the figures and the sign or direction of the asymmetry where it was present. In Figure 6.2 these factors II and III have been used as coordinates. The plotted points in the two-dimensional space are the locations of the 15 stimulus forms. The interpoint distances represent the psychological distances among the stimuli that emerged through factor analysis of the similarity ratings. It can be seen that the points occupy a U-shaped portion of the two-dimensional plot. This would extend along a third axis—for factor I, width of form—in three-dimensional Euclidean space. This complete multidimensional scaling thus would yield a surface resembling the letter U turned on its side and extended in thickness. Other experiments summarized by Torgerson gave further evidence of the utility of the experimental approach and the data treatment used.

Psychological Scaling Methods Evaluated

Having completed our survey of various procedures for psychological scaling, we conclude our discussion with a general evaluation. Our attention will range across the major methods of rating, ranking, pair comparisons, and multidimensional scaling.

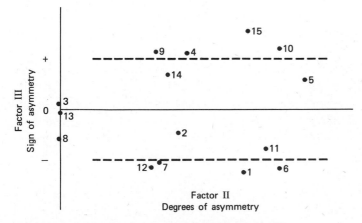

Fig. 6.2. Location of the 15 stimulus forms in two-dimensional space representing two of three subjective factors; Factor II corresponds to the degree of asymmetry and Factor III corresponds to the sign of the asymmetry. (After Torgerson, 1965.)

Scales of Measurement

According to measurement theory our quantification of behavior may yield scales of different types—*ordinal, interval,* or *ratio* scales. Although it may represent an oversimplification we may say that a ratio scale is exemplified in psychological research only when we measure behavior in terms that a physical scientist might commonly employ. The number of responses made, their duration, their rate, their amplitude or their force would be examples of this. In contrast, psychological scaling—the quantification of values and judgments—is considered to yield only ordinal or interval scales. Unlike ratio scales, these lack any meaningful zero point; they therefore cannot support any expressions of ratios among the data obtained. Ordinal scales indicate only how the items judged are sequenced along the quantitative dimension under study. More refined interval scales permit the comparison of distances that separate various pairs of items.

Choice of Method

In choosing a method for unidimensional scaling we may be guided by the stimulus dimension to be studied and by the persons available as judges. We would also consider the purpose of our research, whether it aimed toward establishing an interval scale or required only ordinal scale values. The number of stimuli to be judged and their availability for simultaneous or successive presentation also bear upon our choice of procedure.

Rating scale techniques are preferred when there is so large a number of stimuli to be judged that other methods would be prohibitively time consuming. By proper selection or construction of a rating scale, we may do much to assure that the judgmental data we collect will actually serve the purposes of our investigation. Ratings may be obtained even when stimuli are not all available at once, a condition usually required by the other methods.

Ranking has the advantage of forcing judges to exhibit a maximum number of discriminations among the stimuli. It can be accomplished quickly for a small number of stimuli, particularly if these can be moved around physically. It requires the consideration of all the stimuli for comparative purposes. The pair comparison method is a good one if accurate and dependable scaling is desired for a small number of stimuli. It becomes too time consuming if the number of items is much beyond a dozen, unless a technique reducing the number of pairings is adopted. A general guideline for choosing among methods is to consider the matter thoroughly, weighing disadvantages and advantages of each one.

Scales Achieved

The methods of rating, ranking, and pair comparison can all yield ordinal scale values. Ordinal scaling is represented directly in the rank order method. In rating, too, an ordering occurs although several stimuli may be given the same value. The complete treatment of pair comparison data yields an interval scale with ordinal sequence as one of its properties, even though complete ordinal consistency may be lacking in the judgments of individual judges. Interval scales can also be achieved by appropriate treatment of the data obtained by rating and ranking. Such scaling should be attempted only when a large number of judgments has been made. In dealing with ranks we may employ the normalizing process to get interval scale values or we may first obtain from the rankings a pair comparison set of proportions of preference. This set then becomes the basis for determining interval scale values as in the pair comparison method. If the intricate data treatments of multidimensional scaling are used, a model of stimulus perception may emerge. This spatial representation of psychological values will itself be more complex than a simple linear scale of course. It will suggest the complexity of perceptual or cognitive processes which generated the original observations.

General Precautions in Psychological Scaling

Perhaps the best guide to using psychological scaling in research is the general formulation that behavior is a function of the person with his past experience, and the environmental situation in all its aspects. Judgmental behavior will depend on our choice of judges, the instructions, and the training we give them. It will depend on the particular set of stimuli we give them to rate or to compare. Finally, the scale values we obtain will depend on all the operations involved in the scaling. These operations include our definition of the dimension to be scaled and the treatment we give to the data that are collected.

Counteracting the stimulus error

The *stimulus error* is said to occur whenever a judge's knowledge of the stimulus is permitted to alter the judgment he would make solely on the basis of perception of the stimulus dimension being scaled. For example, if a series of weights to be judged was constructed by varying the size of stimulus objects, the size cue would be a source of information that might strongly influence the judgments of the weights as they were lifted. Any extraneous source of information about the stimuli is a potential contributor of stimulus error. To counteract this error, then, we must prevent judges from knowing anything about the stimuli except what is gained through perceptions of the dimension to be scaled.

Avoiding anchoring effects

Anchoring effects must be remembered as we plan stimulus presentation for almost any psychological scaling. Where these arise from sampling a restricted range of stimuli early in the judging, they may be precluded by presenting all stimuli first, before judging actually begins. We must also avoid setting up anchoring effects by revealing our own evaluations of stimuli during the course of the investigation. Scale distortions may also be precluded by appropriate treatment of data. Jones (1967) has shown, for example, how scaling stability may be attained even when the ranges of stimuli being judged are quite different.

Guarding against distorting processes

Some of the behavior processes which can occur in many situations are potential sources of error in psychological scaling. Learning, for example, might give a spurious consistency to the data if we asked a judge to rate or rank the same set of stimuli over and over again. Fatigue might introduce a careless attitude in a prolonged pair comparison session. Another possible mechanism for the introduction of error would be the suggestions regarding stimulus values that might come from the experimenter if he were to talk informally to judges about the stimulus items.

Summary

Methods like rating, ranking, or pair comparison can be used in scaling experience aroused by stimulus dimensions which may lack a physical referent. By applying the conventional procedures and calculations we may arrive at ordinal or interval scale values for esthetic qualities, personality traits, mood states, or other evaluative judgments. Psychological scaling is accomplished properly only through careful attention to a lengthy series of steps which are listed in introducing this investigative methodology. The conventional methods have numerous

applied uses as well as utility in research. In laboratory studies they may
be employed to measure stimulus attributes, to evaluate certain traits
and states of persons, to describe some aspects of behavior, or to
investigate judgmental processes.

Verbal, numerical, or graphic scales may be used in the method of
rating. These devices must be carefully constructed and administered.
The method is particularly appropriate when many stimulus items are to
be evaluated. Special techniques like the standard scale, the sorting tray,
and the checklist illustrate the variety of formats in which rating may
be utilized. Instructions to raters must indicate clearly the dimension to be
scaled and the proper use of the rating scale. Sometimes forced-choice
techniques are used to reduce rater bias. The presentation of stimulus
items must be planned to avoid any distorting influences such as the halo
effect or the anchoring effect. Simple treatment of rating data will
yield ordinal scale values, whereas interval scaling may be accomplished
by more elaborate computations. An illustrative experiment showed
how rating was used in studying the psychology of aggression and humor.

Ranking may be employed conveniently for stimulus items that are
not too numerous. It requires each judge to discriminate among all the
items. Like other methods, it requires care in instructing the judges and
presenting the stimuli. Ranking data can be simply treated to yield an
ordinal scale. Transformation to C scale values provides an interval scale
if the assumption of normal distribution is reasonable.

The method of pair comparisons is somewhat time consuming, but it
yields interval scale values that may be regarded as quite accurate,
assuming adequacy of procedure. Practical only for small numbers of
stimuli, this scaling technique is based on various assumptions of the
law of comparative judgment. Careful administration of procedures is
demanded. Basic pair comparison data are proportions of times that each
stimulus in various pairs is chosen or preferred. From these proportions,
scale separations of each stimulus from the other stimuli can be estimated.

Multidimensional scaling of stimulus similarity is accomplished by
treating judgmental responses according to theoretical quantitative
models. In this way an empirical model is obtained. It shows how complex
stimuli are differentiated from one another in the perception or cognition
of the judges. We did not attempt any deep probing of the intricate data
transformations demanded in these methods. We did examine the visual
stimuli and the graphic outcome of one multidimensional scaling effort.

A general evaluation of the major psychological scaling methods was attempted in concluding this chapter. The judges to be used and the stimuli to be scaled are among the first factors to consider in choosing a psychological scaling method. Special considerations include the fact that ratings may be given even when stimuli cannot be brought together for comparative purposes. Ranking of a small number of stimuli is usually accomplished with facility, especially if the stimuli can be moved around physically. Pair comparison is generally reserved for more elaborate efforts at psychological scale construction. All the methods can be made to yield interval scales as well as ordinal scales. Psychological scaling certainly requires complex behavior and therefore demands as careful attention to detail as does any other laboratory research. Special precautions include safeguards against stimulus error, anchoring effects, and distorting processes.

References

Coombs, C. H. *A theory of data.* New York: Wiley, 1964.

Edwards, A. L. *Techniques of attitude scale construction.* New York: Appleton-Century-Crofts, 1957.

Ekman, G. A direct method for multidimensional ratio scaling. *Psychometrika,* 1963, **28**, 33–41.

Ekman, G., & Kuennapas, T. Scales of aethetic value. *Perceptual and Motor Skills,* 1962, **14**, 19–26.

Ekman, G., & Kuennapas, T. Scales of conservatism. *Perceptual and Motor Skills,* 1963, **16**, 329–334.

Fiske, D. W., & Pearson, P. H. Theory and techniques of personality measurement. *Annual Review of Psychology,* 1970, **21**, 49–86.

Garner, W. R., & Creelman, C. D. Problems and methods of psychological scaling. In H. Helson & W. Bevan (Eds.), *Contemporary approaches to psychology.* Princeton, N.J.: Van Nostrand, 1967. Pp. 1–33.

Glenn, W. A., & David, H. A. Ties in paired-comparison experiments using a modified Thurstone-Mosteller model. *Biometrics,* 1960, **16**, 86–109.

Greenberg, M. G. A modification of Thurstone's law of comparative judgment to accommodate a judgment category of "equal" or "no difference." *Psychological Bulletin,* 1965, **64**, 108–112.

Guilford, J. P. *Psychometric methods.* (2nd ed.) New York: McGraw-Hill, 1954.

Gutman, J., & Priest, R. F. When is aggression funny? *Journal of Personality and Social Psychology*, 1969, **12**, 60–65.

Harris, R. J. Deterministic nature of probabilistic choices among identifiable stimuli. *Journal of Experimental Psychology*, 1969, **79**, 552–560.

Hicks, L. E. Some properties of ipsative, normative, and forced-choice normative measures. *Psychological Bulletin*, 1970, **74**, 167–184.

Jones, L. V. Invariance of zero-point scaling over changes in stimulus context. *Psychological Bulletin*, 1967, **67**, 153–164.

Light, C. S., Zax, M., & Gardiner, D. H. Relationship of age, sex, and intelligence level to extreme response style. *Journal of Personality and Social Psychology*, 1965, **2**, 907–909.

Nowlis, V., & Nowlis, H. H. The description and analysis of mood. *Annals of New York Academy of Science*, 1956, **65**, 345–355.

O'Donovan, D. Rating extremity: Pathology or meaningfulness? *Psychological Review*, 1965, **72**, 358–372.

Ramsay, J. O., & Case, B. Attitude measurement and the linear model. *Psychological Bulletin*, 1970, **74**, 185–192.

Thurstone, L. L. A law of comparative judgment. *Psychological Review*, 1927, **18**, 289–293.

Torgerson, W. S. *Theory and methods of scaling*. New York: Wiley, 1958.

Torgerson, W. S. Multidimensional scaling of similarity. *Psychometrika*, 1965, **30**, 379–393.

Zavala, A. Development of the forced-choice rating scale technique. *Psychological Bulletin*, 1965, **63**, 117–124.

part 2
Selected Areas
of Investigation

chapter 7
Visual
Processes

We experience visual phenomena in rich variety. Although there are generally few light sources in any environment, the absorption, reflection, diffusion, and transmission of the light, with respect to numerous objects and surfaces, create a complex visual field for the viewer. When the light enters the eye, all of these physical processes continue within the receptor itself, together with the optical refraction which results in the focusing of the retinal image. The photochemical and neural activity of the retina itself plays a major role in visual experience. Seeing has motor aspects, too, involving the muscular control of pupillary diameter and the positioning of the eyes. The anatomy and physiology of the neural optic tract also contribute to visual sensation. All of this complexity of visual sensation is compounded when we turn to the topic of perception. Perceptual processes depend on sensory mechanisms but they also involve learned habits and motives as well. In this chapter we consider both sensory and perceptual aspects of vision.

Background Facts

One mark of the expert is the great number of facts and concepts at his command as he thinks about a problem or reads reports of research. Even though it is not our aim to become specialists in visual investigation, we do aspire to some understanding of research that has been conducted. We shall need at least a few facts as we review some studies in the psychology of seeing.

Physical Stimulus Attributes

There are two specifications that must be given to designate the light that stimulates visual sensation. They are the amount of luminous energy and its distribution among the wavelengths of electromagnetic radiation that fall within the visible spectrum. In many experiments on vision we must also specify the size, location, and duration of the visual stimulus.

Aspects of light energy

There are a number of terms now conventionally used to describe light energy in various aspects. We refer to the energy level of the light generated at a source as the *luminance* of that source. If the energy is emitted from a point source, we speak of the *luminous intensity* of the point source. As the light energy radiates out in all directions we refer to it as the *luminous flux*. When it falls upon a surface we speak of the *illuminance* of the surface by the light energy. Most surfaces will absorb part of the light and reflect part of it, the latter part of the energy being called the *luminous reflectance*. If light falls on a surface that has some degree of transparency, the energy which passes through is termed the *luminous transmittance*. Notice that we have not referred to the "brightness" of a light source or the "brightness" of an illuminated surface. After years of ambiguity in the use of this term, scientists dealing with light and vision have agreed to reserve it for the psychological experience aroused through the activation of the visual receptors by light. Our sensing of brightness depends on *retinal illuminance* and on the receptive status of the retina.

Photometric measurement

Light energy is measurable at many points in its pathway from its source to the retina, with different units of photometric measurement conventionally used for its different aspects. These conventional units are identified in Table 7.1 together with quantitative definitions. Good research on vision requires specification of stimulus values which have been measured in a standard fashion using calibrated instruments.

Spectral distribution of light energy

We noted earlier that a complete description of light requires specification of the distribution of its energy over the wavelengths of radiation

Table 7.1 Units of Measurement for Different Aspects of Light Energy

Aspect of Light Energy	Unit of Measurement	Quantitative Definition of Unit
Luminous flux, F	Lumen	4.12×10^{15} quanta per sec per unit solid angle*
Luminous intensity of point source, I	International Candle	Generating 1 lumen of flux
Luminous intensity of extended source, B	†Lambert	Generating 1 lumen of flux per sq meter
Surface illuminance, E	(a) Foot-candle	1 lumen per sq ft at 1 ft from source
	(b) Lux	1 lumen per sq meter at 1 meter from source
Reflectance or transmittance, B	†Lambert	1 lumen per sq meter
Retinal illuminance, E	Troland	$B \times A$, where A is pupillary area in sq mm

*Quanta (singular: quantum) are fundamental units of physical light energy. A unit solid angle (steradian) is equivalent to a cone of light large enough to illuminate a square meter at one meter from its point source.

†The millilambert (mL), equal to 0.001 lambert, is the unit more commonly used.

which comprise the visible spectrum. A stimulus from many kinds of light source, or reflectance from a white or gray surface, is a broad band of energy with many wavelengths intermixed in roughly equal proportions. However, light passing through a colored filter or reflected from a pigmented surface will have its energy somewhat concentrated, a preponderance of it in some one or two portions of the wavelength spectrum. We shall consider spectral distribution more fully later as we relate it to the sensations of hue and color saturation to which it gives rise.

The Receptor

The morphology or structure of the eye is probably somewhat familiar to you. Light entering the eye passes through four transparent media before reaching the retina. Both the cornea and the crystalline lens, by virtue of their shape, contribute to the refraction of the light and the formation of an image on the retina. This image is usually resolved or focused by the reflex action of the ciliary body or muscle whose contraction and relaxation change the thickness and curvature of the lens for viewing near and distant points, the lens becoming thicker and more curved for near vision. This focusing adjustment for any distance is called *accommodation*.

The pupillary response

Another aspect of ocular structure and function that must often be considered in conducting visual research is the pupil and its reflex response to light. As you know, the pupil constricts in bright light and dilates in dim illumination, its size ranging from about 2 mm diameter when fully constricted to about 8 mm diameter when completely dilated. Keep in mind that the amount of light entering the eye is proportional to pupillary area and not diameter. The extremes in pupil size thus represent a ratio of 16 to 1, the square of the diameter ratio, in the amount of retinal illuminance. The change in the amount of light reaching the retina due to pupillary action sometimes poses a problem in experimentation that may be met by having subjects look through a small aperture called an artificial pupil whose constant diameter simplifies the computing of retinal illuminance.

The fovea

It is useful to consider the location in the retina of the foveal pit or *fovea*. The fovea lies in the optical axis of the eye; it is aligned, that is, with the center of the cornea and the lens. The image that falls on the fovea thus corresponds to whatever point in space the eye is *fixating*, looking at directly. This fact makes the fovea a convenient reference point for mapping points on the retina that are subject to stimulation. These retinal stimulation points are controlled in some experiments by providing a *fixation point* for the subject to look at. While this fixation is maintained by the subject, the experimenter may present stimuli at some predetermined angular displacement in the visual field, thus assuring the stimulation of a point in the retina of similar angular displacement from the fovea.

Location of the blindspot

The *blindspot,* sometimes called the *optic disk,* is a small area about 3 mm from the fovea on the nasal side of each retina. Here there are no retinal rods or cones since nerve fibers leave the eye at this point to become the optic nerve. Any point in the visual field that throws an image on the nasal retina of one eye forms an image on the temporal side of the other retina. It is impossible, therefore, for any point to throw its image on both blindspots simultaneously. When we engage in monocular viewing, of course, there is a tiny portion of the visual field that corresponds to the blindspot and might be expected to appear as an empty space in our visual pattern. There seems to be a perceptual filling-in, though, so that it is usually necessary to seek out the effect of this gap in the retinal mosaic in order to be aware of it.

Retinal structure

Although we do not intend to study the retina in great detail, either as to its complex cellular structure or its photochemical and neural functioning, we do need to review a few basic facts to complete our foundation for the understanding of some of the visual mechanisms. The light-sensitive elements of the retina are the rods and the cones, each named for its cellular shape. These cells are located toward the back of the retina, their tips pointing toward the choroid coat. The light that reaches them travels first through a layer of nerve fibers and connecting cells. Through synaptic connections the activation by light of rods and cones excites activity in several types of neural elements—amacrine cells, horizontal cells, bipolar cells and ganglion cells. Both convergent and divergent neural pathways create a retinal organization which is represented functionally in such visual phenomena as lateral effects between nearby points of stimulation.

Rods and cones differ markedly in their distribution over the retina. Centered on the fovea is a 3° area composed exclusively of cones, the fovea itself comprising midmost 1.5° of this area. Outside this central portion of the retina the density of cones is greatly reduced. As we move out from the fovea, the cones become less numerous and rods are found more and more frequently, reaching a peak density about 20° out from the center and then gradually becoming less frequent near the periphery. These anatomical facts are also reflected in common visual experience. Since the cones mediate color vision (technically called *chromatic vision,* the experiencing of hues), it is best in the foveal and near-foveal areas. Acuity or sharpness of vision is also best at the fovea where the densely packed cones each have a representation in neural impulses. In contrast rods are more likely to have multiple interconnections in neural response generation. This, in addition to their greater photochemical sensitivity, makes the detection of extremely low levels of light energy most detectable about 20° from the fovea where rod concentration is greatest.

Some Visual Mechanisms

As additional background for reviewing research reports of visual studies and conducting experiments of our own, we need to discuss some of the facts about the visual process that might play a role in almost any investigation. These facts were themselves determined by research, of course, and the phenomena we cite are the topic for current study as visual scientists seek even greater refinement of knowledge.

Spectral sensitivity curves

A fact of great importance in vision is that the eye is not equally sensitive to all wavelengths of light. This phenomenon has been explored by applying psychophysical methods, our topic in Chapter 5, to the determination of thresholds or limits of vision for different wavelengths. The *spectral sensitivity curves* are shown in Figure 7.1. As plotted, these functions may be better termed threshold curves since they indicate the minimal radiant flux at any wavelength that is needed to arouse *rod vision* or *cone vision*. For rods, the lowest threshold occurs at about 510 mμ, whereas for cones the threshold is lowest at 555 mμ. If these curves were inverted to become direct representations of sensitivity, then the values would represent peak sensitivity. Both rod and cone reactivities are much lower for wavelengths at a distance from their peak sensitivities, with much greater amounts of radiant flux needed to reach threshold and excite a sensation.

The threshold data for cone vision forming the *photopic visibility curve* of Figure 7.1 were obtained by applying a test stimulus to the rod-free area at the fovea. This had to be done, of course, to avoid arousing sensation in the more sensitive rods, thus making it virtually impossible to determine at what intensity value the cones would become functional. The data for rod thresholds forming the *scotopic visibility curve* were taken at some distance from the fovea. The presence of cones at that locus was no problem since the testing values were well below cone threshold as the curves indicate. What would a subject's sensation be if we presented him with a spot of light of 500 mμ wavelength directed 10°

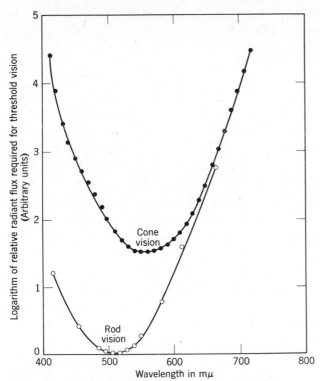

Fig. 7.1. The absolute threshold curves for rod vision and for cone vision as a function of wavelength of the test stimulus. The photopic visibility curve (cone vision) differs from the scotopic visibility curve (rod vision) in general level of radiant energy required to arouse sensation, in point of lowest threshold or peak sensitivity, and in extent of responsiveness to longer wavelengths. (After Chapanis, 1949.)

from the fovea, and gradually increased it from well below threshold value? Since both rods and cones are present in that area of the retina, we see from Figure 7.1 that the rods would be activated first, this wavelength actually being very near their peak sensitivity. The figure also shows that the intensity of the test light would have to be increased by about two log units, a hundredfold increase in luminance, before the activation of the cones began. Inspection of the curves reveals that the rods are much more sensitive than the cones for all wavelengths below

600 mμ. At about 650 mμ, however, there is not much difference in their sensitivities, and in the region of 700 mμ and beyond, the rods are generally considered unresponsive.

Adaptation

The eye is capable of functioning in a wide range of light intensities, from the absolute rod threshold where it is responsive to an intensity of less than a millionth of a millilambert to the upper limit of tolerance for very bright light at about 16,000 mL. The increase from threshold to upper limit, then, is more than a ten billionfold change in intensity. The eye has to adapt to the illuminance impinging on it in order to function over so great a range. The constriction or dilation of the pupil can change retinal illuminance by a factor of sixteen. The remainder of the adaptive process takes place in the retina, the rods, cones, and associated neural cells.

The retinal adaptive processes, either light adaptation or dark adaptation, require some time to bring the eye to an optimal functioning point. The temporal course of adaptation, particularly to darkness, has been studied extensively. Adaptation to light appears to take place in just a minute or so after the eye encounters a higher intensity value. Dark adaptation, which is actually a decline in threshold or an increase in sensitivity as the eye remains in darkness, requires about 20 min to approach completion and often shows a slow change even beyond that interval.

Figure 7.2 shows a family of dark adaptation curves. The experimental parameter that differentiated the curves was the intensity of the preadapting light to which the eye was exposed for 2 min just prior to beginning the period in the dark. Absolute threshold determinations were made after different intervals in the dark in order to obtain these curves. We see that the preadapting intensity had a great effect on the level of the absolute threshold during the whole period of dark adaptation. The curve numbered 3 shows that after the most intense prior stimulation, the threshold was at a high point. The first segment of this curve indicates that the cones increased in sensitivity from the very first moment of darkness, leveling off at the absolute cone threshold after about 10 min in the dark. After about 12 min of dark adaptation the rods recovered enough from their previous impairment of responsiveness by the preadapting light to continue the lowering of the threshold for a long period of time. The middle curve of the figure shows cone adaptation first and then rod adaptation beginning after about 5 or 6 min in the

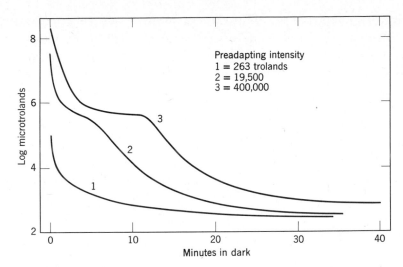

Fig. 7.2. Dark adaptation curves showing declining absolute visual threshold as a function of time in the dark, with intensity of the 2 min of preadapting light as the parameter differentiating the three curves. (After Hecht, Haig, and Chase, 1937.)

dark. This threshold curve numbered 2 indicates greater sensitivity or lower threshold throughout the plotted course of dark adaptation when compared with the curve numbered 3. The lesser preadapting intensity permitted speedier recovery of sensitivity. The lowest curve in the figure indicates a sensitivity of the rods from the very beginning of the dark period. There is no cone segment to the curve because the preadapting luminance was weak enough to permit the rods to remain partly functional from the very beginning of the dark period. This curve also shows speediest attainment of full sensitivity by these receptor elements after the weakest preadapting luminance.

The need for stating how the plotted values were obtained is highlighted by the fact that the shape of dark adaptation curves can be materially affected by changes in the locus and size of the retinal area tested, and the intensity and duration of the preadapting light. If the test light were limited to a 3° area located at the fovea, we would obtain only the first portion of the dark adaptation curve since there are no rods in that locus to carry the threshold lower than the cone threshold. As to size of the test stimulus, it is found that both portions of the dark adaptation curve drop more sharply and to lower values if the test stimulus is increased in size from about 3° to about 20° or more of subtended visual angle. If the preadapting light field is very weak, then the cone adaptation, represented in the first segment of the curves numbered 2 and 3 in Figure 7.2, does not appear. The rod adaptation curve, now assuming we are stimulating a retinal area where rods as well as cones are present, drops more steeply than it does after strong preadapting intensities, as the curve numbered 1 in the same figure shows. This sharper drop in the dark adaptation curve also occurs if briefer exposure to the preadapting field has taken place. Numerous procedural complexities of experimentation on dark adaptation have been described by Boynton (1966, 274-277).

Visual masking

Numerous investigations of visual masking were reviewed by Kahneman (1968). Selected parts of his paper can guide our brief consideration of this important phenomenon. In visual masking experiments the effect of a *test stimulus* (TS) is reduced by the presentation of a *masking stimulus* (MS) which is temporally overlapping or proximal to TS. An important variable affecting masking (the reduction of TS effectiveness) is *stimulus-onset asynchrony* (SOA) or interval between the onsets of the two visual stimuli. By defining SOA as the time of TS onset minus the time of MS onset, we see that SOA is negative if MS follows TS, a situation termed *backward masking*. If MS onset precedes TS, the condition is called forward masking, with SOA a positive value. SOA would be zero, of course, if the two stimuli had simultaneous onsets. *Masking* is the term used when the two stimuli are presented to spatially overlapping areas of the retina. Typically TS is smaller than MS in area and briefer, under 100 milliseconds (msec) in duration. When the two retinal areas stimulated are close to one another but not overlapping the terms *metacontrast* and *paracontrast* are used; these correspond, respectively, to backward and forward masking. Other variants of masking are found when the TS is a form or pattern to be identified, while MS is either homogeneous illumination or a regular or random stimulus pattern.

Returning to the temporal variable, SOA, we can comprehend the masking phenomenon better if we examine a schematic masking function which Kahneman presented as a generalized hypothetical outcome of research. It is assumed that the experimenter was determining the luminance threshold for a brief (e.g., 50 msec) TS when SOA was varied. The

MS is a more intense flash of light covering a larger retinal area and lasting 500 msec. The masking function shown in Figure 7.3 represents a typical finding. In the figure the logarithm of the luminous energy needed to reach the TS threshold of detection is plotted as a function of SOA. TS intensities below the curve were generally not detectable in the psychophysical testing that determined the function.

The major effect of masking is a striking elevation in the threshold for detecting the TS when it immediately precedes, overlaps in time, or immediately follows the MS. The curve shows forward masking as elevating the threshold by about two log units (a hundredfold increase in TS intensity needed for its detection) just after MS onset. From its peak the threshold curve drops, showing some recovery of visual sensitivity. At MS offset it rises slightly then drops gradually toward full recovery from the masking effect. Notice that the curve shows backward masking also, where SOA is a negative interval just prior to MS onset. Backward masking is not the paradoxical retroactive effect of MS on TS detection that it might seem; since the visual response to a stimulus outlasts the presentation of the light, backward masking is an interaction between responses

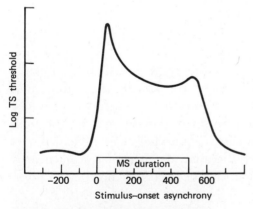

Fig. 7.3. A schematic masking function showing the elevation of the threshold for test stimulus (TS) detection as it depends on the stimulus-onset asynchrony (SOA) of the masking stimulus (MS) onset and the TS onset. (After Kahneman, 1968.)

that overlap in time even when the physical stimuli do not. These temporal aspects of interactions within the responding system make masking experiments a powerful tool for probing certain perceptual processes.

Visual Research Techniques

A primary technical problem in experimentation on vision is the exercise of strict control over stimulation. At this point, we shall cite some of the general ways of controlling various important dimensions of visual stimuli, including retinal illuminance, size of stimulus, retinal locus of stimulation, duration of stimulation, and retinal state induced by other illumination. Boynton (1966) has described and illustrated numerous laboratory procedures very thoroughly.

Controlling luminance

If we are engaged in psychophysical research aimed at the determination of brightness thresholds, then control over the luminance of the test stimulus is obviously of paramount importance. Even in attacking other problems, with luminances well above threshold, it is important to specify and control light intensity. Techniques for the control of luminosity naturally vary in their suitability. Some of the ones we mention are cited for their ease of employment even though they contain flaws which preclude their use in serious work demanding great rigor in the specification and control of the light stimulus.

One way to control the luminous intensity of an incandescent source is to vary the applied voltage with a resultant variation in light intensity; a drawback of this method is that it alters the spectral distribution of the light produced. Another convenient method for varying the illuminance of a test surface or the luminance transmittance of a translucent test stimulus is to utilize the physical inverse square law by moving the light source toward and away from the surface being viewed. A difficulty here is that the law may not strictly apply because of reflectance from nearby surfaces and also that the lamp which may be used will not be the point source that is theoretically required.

Another class of techniques for controlling light intensity calls for interposing something in the light path between the source and the eye, usually between the source and a transilluminated surface of high diffusing quality like flashed opal glass. One method is to interpose a sectored disk rotating at high speed in the light beam. Openings in the disk allow the light to pass through intermittently. At a high rate of intermittence, the effect is one of a steady light of lessened intensity. Another way of reducing the intensity of a light beam is to insert into it one or more neutral density filters. The percent of light transmitted by these is specified so that their use in combination can often achieve a desired value. They are termed neutral to indicate that their transmission characteristics do not alter the spectral composition of the light passing through.

Retinal state

The luminance of a source or test stimulus is often not as important as the retinal illuminance. Since pupillary dilation serves to let more light in when intensity is low, retinal illuminance in such a circumstance is controlled by providing an artificial pupil, a viewing aperture with a small fixed diameter. In addition to retinal illuminance, the adaptive state of the rods and cones need to be considered. This is often controlled by letting the eye become completely dark adapted before testing or else specifying the intensity and duration of a preadapting field which is viewed prior to the presentation of the test stimulus. The importance of retinal state for reactivity was illustrated by the dark adaptation curves of Figure 7.2 and the masking function of Figure 7.3.

Specifying stimulus size

The size of a test stimulus employed in visual research is usually specified in terms of the visual angle it subtends. It is often useful to state the viewing distance and whether it was measured from the corneal surface or elsewhere. An important reason for specifying size of stimulus is that brightness varies with the size of small stimuli. That is, larger stimuli appear brighter even for the same retinal illuminance. The effect is considered due to a spatial summation deriving from the neural interconnections in the retina.

Specifying retinal location

Specifying the retinal location of a point of stimulation is necessary in view of what we know of the distribution of rods and cones over the retinal surface. The specification is usually made in terms of visual angle from the center of the fovea, often measured along the horizontal nasal or temporal meridians or perhaps up or down on a vertical meridian passing through the fovea. The fovea is a convenient reference because the image of any point fixated falls upon it. Thus, the visual angle on the retina from fovea to image point is the same in size as the angle formed in space by the fixation point, the eye, and the test stimulus. The angular direction is reversed, of course, by the inverting of the image optically. Thus, points in the upper half of the visual field impinge on the lower part of the retina and vice versa. Points in the temporal portion of the field fall on the nasal half of the retina and vice versa. It is obviously important to use terms like "nasal" and "temporal" with careful reference to either visual field or to the retina.

A very special problem in retinal stimulation is that the eye is always in motion. Small involuntary movements (usually just a few angular minutes of arc) and tremors (under one-half minute of arc, at a rate up to 150 cycles per second) keep the retinal image constantly moving with respect to the mosaic of rods and cones. Actually, it is found, this eye movement (of which we are not aware) is necessary for good vision. But a complete technical study of how the eye responds to patterns of light sometimes requires that the motion of the retinal image be reduced or eliminated. Visual scientists have devised some ingenious techniques for stabilizing the retinal image. These techniques and the phenomenal effects they produce were reviewed by Heckenmueller (1965). Here we mention one method and a representative finding. A mirror attached to a contact lens is in the optical path used in delivering a test stimulus to the eye. As the eye moves, the motion of the mirror in this system of optical geometry is such as to compensate for it and thus keep the retinal image relatively stable. A striking effect of image stabilization is that test lines, for example, actually disappear from view in a few seconds—often reappearing and fading again intermittently. This special phenomenon of the stabilized retinal image suggests that the involuntary eye movements are actually quite beneficial in normal vision through their maintenance of continuing experience. It is felt that this is accomplished when different rods and cones are excited by the unstable retinal image, thus preventing the complete fatiguing of particular receptor elements.

Duration of stimulation

When visual capacities are explored by means of very brief test flashes of light, the duration of such stimulation is an important determiner of indices of visual performance such as the absolute threshold. The threshold will not be found as low in luminance value if the test flash is extremely brief. The effective brightness of a test flash at threshold levels is a product of its luminance and its duration, these two factors being reciprocally contributory to the sensory effect as indicated in the formulation that a constant threshold effect, K, is achieved by the product of retinal illuminance, I, and duration of flash, t. $K = I \times t$, known as Bloch's law or the Bunsen-Roscoe law, is considered to hold for small test areas, less than 1°, and for flashes briefer than 50 msec at threshold intensity.

Visual Acuity

The ability to detect fine spatial detail in the visual field is termed *visual acuity*. Various acuity targets like letters of the alphabet or broken circles are presented in different sizes and at different distances, the subject's task being to detect a small critical detail like the break in the circle. The visual acuity rating is the reciprocal of the visual angle in minutes of arc subtended by this just detectable detail. If the break in the circle, for example, subtended 2 min of arc, the acuity rating would be 0.5, the reciprocal of 2.0. An acuity rating of 1.0, corresponding to the detection of a detail subtending 1 min of arc, is considered to be "normal," but a number of factors need to be specified before this becomes particularly meaningful. Among the determinants of measured acuity are retinal position stimulated, illuminance of the target viewed, and contrast of the light and dark areas of the target. In clinical testing of vision, of course, well-illuminated targets of high contrast are generally presented to the foveal area. Here the tester is using optimal values of the variables so as to assess the eye's powers of accommodation and refraction in a standardized way.

Acuity Targets

Among the types of acuity targets that have been employed are fine wires viewed against an illuminated background, gratings through which light is directed at the eye, and pairs of parallel bars or rectangles. Samples of the latter type of acuity target are shown in Figure 7.4 together with the Landolt ring, as the broken circle is usually called. The bars are shown in two different contrasts, white on black as well as black on white, since it has been found that this is a determinant of the detectability of the separation between them which is the detail actually used in measuring acuity. For the Landolt ring it is conventional to have the break or separation equal to one-fifth the outside diameter of the ring. Most geometrical types of acuity targets may be considered superior to the alphabet letters used, for example, on the Snellen eye chart. The letters are perceptible or distinguishable on the basis of several different

Fig. 7.4. Geometrical targets for measuring visual acuity. The critical details to be detected are the space between the parallel rectangles and the break in the Landolt ring. By detecting the detail a subject can state the orientation of the bars, horizontal or vertical, or of the ring. His acuity rating is computed as described in the text.

cues rather than a single detail. Suggestions have been advanced to use letters selected for their equivalent recognizability.

Fundamentals of Color Vision

Although we have neglected it to this point we need to turn our attention to the sensing of hue and the manipulation of the spectral composition of light in research on vision. We previously identified energy level and the distribution of wavelengths as important specifications of light. We may now pair these with the quantitative and qualitative aspects of visual sensation to which they contribute. Table 7.2 indicates the corres-

Table 7.2 Relationships between Characteristics of Light and Basic Attributes of Visual Sensation

Characteristics of Light	Basic Attributes of Visual Sensation
1. Luminous energy level	1. Brightness
(a) Luminance	
(b) Illuminance	
(c) Luminous reflectance	
(d) Luminous transmittance	
2. Dominant wavelength	2. Hue
3. Purity of spectral composition	3. Saturation

pondence of visual sensory attributes to the characteristics of the light which are usually associated with their arousal. We have mentioned brightness before as the quantitative sensing of the light energy level or luminance value. We saw of course that the sensation aroused is greatly dependent upon the state of adaptation of the eye as well as on the impinging energy value. The table indicates that hue and saturation depend on the spectral composition of the light.

Chromatic and Achromatic Colors

Hue and *saturation* which are attributes of *chromatic visual sensation* need to be discussed in their relation to the spectral composition of light. It is now customary to think of all vision as color vision, the term "color" having been broadened to take in whites and grays. A distinction is still maintained by applying the term chromatic vision to the sensing of hues like green and yellow and using an opposed term, *achromatic vision,* to apply to the sensing of gray and white. Notice that the word hue is the generic term now applied to what are commonly called colors. Saturation is the qualitative intensity of a hue, the redness of a red or the greenness of a green. A so-called deep red is a highly saturated red; a pink is a desaturated red.

Brightness is an aspect of both chromatic and achromatic sensation. We can have greens and reds of different brightnesses, essentially independent of their saturation. We can also have grays of greater or lesser brightness, commonly called lighter or darker grays. Being achromatic or hueless, whites and grays do not differ qualitatively but only in their brightness value. As a sensation, brightness depends on the level of retinal illuminance among other things.

Sensations Mediated by Rods and Cones

In very dim illumination, below the threshold for activating the cones, only white, gray, and black images are experienced. The mediators of this scotopic vision, the rods, do not give rise to any sensations of hue even though they are differentially sensitive to wavelength as their spectral sensitivity curve in Figure 7.1 showed. Only cone vision is chromatic, giving rise to sensations of hue; rod vision is achromatic, yielding hueless visual experience. We can now give a more complete answer to our question (p. 214) regarding a person's sensations if a light of 500 mμ wavelength impinging 10° from the fovea were gradually increased in intensity from below threshold. After its luminosity was equal to the rod threshold it would be seen as a white light, becoming gradually brighter as luminosity increased but evidencing no hue at first. Only after the cone threshold was reached would the subject begin to experience the green hue associated in cone functioning, or photopic vision, with that wavelength of light. The difference in luminosity values between the rod threshold and the cone threshold is known as the *photochromatic interval*. The area between the scotopic and photopic sensitivity curves in Figure 7.1 is thus a representation of the changing values of the photochromatic interval as we proceed along the spectrum. You can see that the interval is greatest for the shorter wavelengths.

Hue and saturation correspond to the spectral composition of the light that reaches the eye. Because of the selective transmittance of a filter or the selective reflectance of a surface, the energy reaching the eye may be unevenly distributed among the various wavelengths with a particular band of values predominant. It is usually the predominant wavelength in the mixture that determines the hue that is experienced. A concentration of energy at the longest visible wavelengths arouses the sensation of red, whereas a concentration at about 450 mμ gives rise to blue. The colors of the spectrum thus correspond to particular bands of wavelengths. The hues of the familiar listing, red, orange, yellow, green, blue, and violet, are arranged in order from the longest to the shortest wavelengths. An experiment reported by Sternheim and Boynton (1966) combined color naming and psychological scaling of chromatic sensations. For the longer wavelengths used in the study, it was found that the label "orange" was somewhat dispensable for adequate sensory description and scaling.

Mixture and Specification of Colors

A number of psychophysical relationships have emerged from many decades of research on color vision. Some of the fundamental laws provide the researcher with metrics and techniques for additional investigation. An acquaintance with some of these will serve as a partial basis for understanding the continuing discoveries of color science.

Additive Color Mixture Principles

The addition of any two hues will result in a hue that is intermediate in its spectral position and of lesser saturation than the hues employed in the mixture. The additive mixture of blue and green, for example, results in a blue-green or aqua, where as a mixture of red and green gives yellow. We are speaking here of the *additive* mixing of light of different predominant wavelengths and not of the mixing of paints or pigments which is called *subtractive* mixture. The mixture of complementaries such as blue and yellow will result in white or gray. The hues complement each other so perfectly that they yield an achromatic sensation. If two hues are mixed that are almost complementary, the mixture will be greatly desaturated but will not actually be achromatic.

Tristimulus mixture

Besides the principles of two-color additive mixture which we have been discussing, there is an important principle of tristimulus mixture. It is that white may be achieved by the additive mixture, in proper proportions of luminance, of any three wavelengths provided that one is from the violet-blue region of the spectrum, one from the green region, and one from the red region. Attaining white by the tristimulus method may be conceptualized in terms of the mixture of complementary hues. For example, if we are given a particular wavelength in the red region, we mix the blue and the green to obtain the blue-green hue that is the complementary of the given red. The tristimulus mixture thus appears to reduce to a mixing of just two hues. However, the principle of tristimulus mixture does not impose the rigid specification upon the particular wavelengths employed that we mentioned as a requirement in the principle of complementaries.

An additional feature of tristimulus mixture, besides its ability to yield white, is that *any hue whatsoever* may be attained by mixing in required proportion just three wavelengths, each one chosen from one of the three broad regions of the spectrum. These regions of the spectrum thus provide us with physical primaries, one that is violet or blue, one that is green, and one that is a red with a yellowish tinge to it. It is important to note that none of these primaries is defined with reference to a specific wavelength. Various sets of primaries might be selected that would demonstrate the principle of tristimulus mixture.

Color science finds in the trivariant principle more than just an interesting phenomenon. With every possible hue and saturation specifiable in terms of the proportionate mixture of three primaries, you can see how conveniently a color may be described by stating the proportions of the three primaries in a mixture that matches the particular color. A particular blue-green, for example, might be specified by the equation, $BG = .06R + .31G + .63B$, where R, G, and B represent specified primaries and their coefficients indicate the proportion of each one required in the mixture to match the blue-green. Such primaries were specified by the International Commission on Illumination (ICI*) in order to permit a conventional method for giving color specifications. With reference to these ICI primaries it is possible to write an equation for any color: $X = xR + yG + zB$. The equation we used to specify the blue-green in our example was of this precise form, with particular coefficients specified for the proportions of the primaries in the mixture. Since the coefficients in the three terms of the equation always sum to unity, the specification of any color is actually complete when the first two terms are given. Our sample blue-green is adequately identified by the equation $BG = .06R + .31G$. The coefficient indicating the proportion of the blue primary in the mixture, .63, is determined by the relationship, $x + y + z = 1$, and therefore need not be stated.

The ICI Chromaticity Diagram

Since any hue, together with an indication of its purity, may be described by two coefficients, x and y, of the ICI red and green primaries mixed with the ICI blue to match the given hue, a single point on a two-dimensional plot can give a graphic representation of the color. Such a graph, called the ICI *chromaticity diagram*, is shown as Figure 7.5. Along the abscissa is scaled the coefficient, x, indicating the proportion of the red component in any matching mixture. The scale for the green coefficient, y, forms the ordinate of the graph. The solid curved line in the figure represents the locus of points representing the colors of the spectrum. The violet end of the visible spectrum is at the lower left of the diagram where the wavelength 400 mμ is shown. The spectral greens occupy the top portion of the curve, whereas the red end of the spectrum is represented at the right of the chromaticity diagram as indicated by the notation, 700 mμ, at the long wavelength end of the visible spectrum. The straight line connecting this point to the other end point of the spectral curve at 400 mμ is the locus of points representing the non-spectral reds and purples. This straight line and the spectral curve above it may be considered to form a sort of distorted color circle since all of the hues are arranged in order around the perimeter. The roughly triangular area bounded by these lines includes all the points which rep-

*The abbreviation CIE, after the French equivalent, is commonly used.

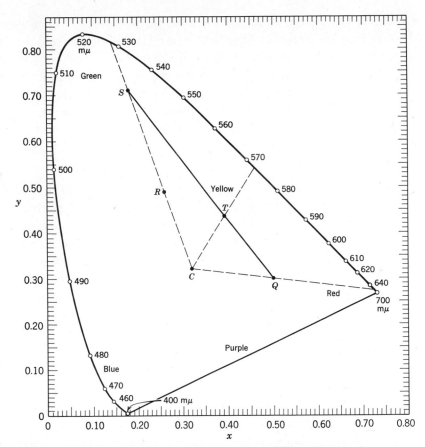

Fig. 7.5. The ICI chromaticity diagram, used in specifying illuminants and colors and in predicting the results of additive color mixtures. (After Judd, 1951.)

resent the characteristics—the hue and the purity—of any color that can be achieved with spectral stimuli. The ICI chromaticity diagram thus represents a convenient way of representing the chromatic aspects of any color likely to be used as a stimulus in an experiment.

The ICI standard observer

The chromaticity diagram of Figure 7.5 has its empirical basis in the ICI *standard observer*. This construct, the standard observer, represents international agreement on particular data on color matching obtained with representative subjects and specified primaries. The chromaticity diagram assumes these primaries as the ones being mixed and indicates the proportions of the primaries needed by the standard observer (actually a particular set of experimental subjects) to match the different spectral hues and the purples. Once the primaries had been agreed upon and the locus of these basic hues had been plotted, the diagram became the reference for further indexing of hues by other research workers. The earlier psychophysical work had been used to forge a very useful tool for subsequent investigations.

White illuminants

We stated that white may be achieved by a tristimulus mixture of proper proportions, so we should expect that some point on the chromaticity diagram would represent the three coefficients of the ICI primaries needed in a formula for white. The point marked C near the center of the diagram is the index point for ICI *Illuminant C* which is a standard white resembling daylight. You see that its graphic coordinates indicate that it contains about equal proportions of each of the ICI primaries. Other whites are located near this point. The chromaticity diagram thus includes achromatic color points as well as points which describe chromatic hues.

Spectral purity

With spectral saturations of the hues represented along the curved boundary line in the diagram of Figure 7.5, and white represented at the point marked C, we may infer that points out near the curve represent hues of purer spectral composition than points nearer to C. Points nearer to C are indicated to have a more uniform distribution of energy over the spectral range. These, then, have a lesser spectral purity and would tend to be seen as less saturated.

Complementaries

Although our usual sensation of white is aroused by light containing about equal proportions of all the wavelengths in the spectrum, the principle of complementaries must be understood to mean that a similar experience is stimulated by a mixture of just two complementary wavelengths in proper proportions. Such pairs of wavelengths include 671 and 493 mμ, which would appear red and blue-green, respectively, when viewed separately. Blue and yellow, represented by wavelengths of 477 and 579 mμ, respectively, are also complementaries. Wavelengths up to 492 mμ have their complementaries beyond 568 mμ in the visible spectrum. In the chromaticity diagram complementary hues lie at the opposite ends of straight lines drawn through the white region. Wavelengths between 492 and 568 mμ do not have any complementary wavelength. These hues, the greens, have as their complementaries various purple hues which are attained only by mixing two spectral hues, a red and a blue. In passing we may note that a hue that has a fundamental red appearance, one of the so-called psychological primaries, is actually a nonspectral hue attained by adding a little violet to a spectral red. The spectral red alone is too yellowish to be judged a real red. The other psychological primaries, blue, green, and yellow, correspond to wavelengths of about 480, 510, and 580 mμ, respectively.

Details of color specification

If we take some color and match it with a color-matching device which permits us to specify how much of each ICI primary we put into the matching mixture, then we can plot the locus of the matched color on the diagram. The plotting of such a point permits the determination of further facts about the color in question. To illustrate these, we have placed the points marked Q, R, and S in Figure 7.5. These points represent three different colors for which the ICI primary proportions have been determined. We see that color Q was matched by proportions .50, .30, and .20 of the ICI red, green, and blue, respectively. For color R the corresponding coefficients were .26, .49, and .25, whereas for color S they were .18, .71, and .11. The straight dotted line drawn from Illuminant C through the point representing any color intersects the boundary curve at a point that represents the dominant wavelength of the color being described. To indicate the purity of the color in question we determine how far its index point is from white and then express this distance as a percent of the total distance from white to the dominant wavelength of the color. For example, we note that the dotted line that passes from C through Q intersects the boundary at 670 mμ, indicating the dominant wavelength in color Q to be a spectral red. Q is located over four-tenths of the way out from C along this dotted line and it is calculated to have a spectral purity of about 45 percent. Looking at points R and S we see that they fall on the same straight line drawn from C to the perimeter and therefore they have the same dominant wavelength, 528 mμ, corresponding to a green. R and S differ in their purity, however, with R having a value of 33 percent and S 75 percent. Thus, S would appear to be a more saturated green than R would seem to be.

Predicting additive mixtures

Another illustration of the usefulness of a standard chromaticity diagram is also given in Figure 7.5. It can be employed to predict the result of the additive mixing of any two colors. The prediction is based on an extremely simple graphic procedure. Suppose we want to predict the outcome of mixing Q and S in certain proportions. We simply connect those two points in the diagram with a straight line segment. All colors resulting from a mixture of these two will fall somewhere on this line, depending on the proportions of Q and S that went into the mixture. If we want to predict the outcome of mixing just two parts of Q with one part of S, we would locate the mixture point nearer to the preponderant constituent, Q. In fact, it would be located one-third of the distance from Q to S, as indicated at T in the diagram. The rule for predicting the result of a two-color mix in any proportion, then, is to locate a point on the connecting line whose distance from each of the constituent points is inversely proportional to their proportions in the mixture. This rule locates the mixture point nearer to the greater contributing color in the diagram. Once the mixture has been located, we may use the diagram to determine its dominant wavelength and its purity by drawing a line, as shown in Figure 7.5, from the locus of the illuminant, C, through the mixture point, T. In our example, this leads to the prediction of a dominant wavelength of 572 mμ, indicating a yellow resultant when Q and S are mixed in the indicated proportions. The proportionate distance of T from C along this radial line gives us a prediction of the purity of the yellow, about 52 percent in our example.

Color Mixture Techniques

We have indicated that the principles of color mixture that we have discussed are those which apply to the additive mixing of different wavelengths. To experiment with additive mixture, then, we need to obtain samples of light composed of different dominant wavelengths and to mix these samples as they stimulate the eye. A direct approach to our problem is to obtain two light sources, like slide projectors, and two filters of different colors, like a red and a green Wratten filter. By aiming the two projectors at the same white screen and putting one filter in the beam of each, we are effectively mixing the two different wavelength bands which these filters transmit. As we view the screen, our eye is stimulated by the mixed light. The resultant hue that we experience may be anywhere between a red and a green in the spectral series, depending upon the relative amounts of light reaching the screen through each filter. This can be controlled for each projector beam separately, using any of the techniques we suggested for the control of luminance. In the demonstrations we are discussing, another feasible method of controlling the screen illuminance from each projector, and hence the relative proportions of the colors being mixed, is to put an adjustable camera aperture in each beam of light as it emerges from the projector. The stop settings of such a camera diaphragm provide a means of specifying the relative proportion of the constituent colors used.

With three projectors and red, blue, and green filters it is possible to demonstrate tristimulus mixture by projecting three overlapping circles of light on the screen, one coming through each filter. If some sort of luminance control is included in each of the three optical systems, it should be possible to show that white can be achieved by mixing three primaries in proper proportions. When white is perceived in the center of the cloverleaf of overlapping circles, it will be found that the mixture of each possible pair of colors has been adjusted to yield the complementary of the third color. In the outer portion of the pattern, where the circles of color overlap in pairs, we find that the mixture of each pair yields an intermediate hue that is the complementary of the third color. There will be a blue-green complementary of the red, a purple complementary of the green, and a yellow complementary of the blue. Gregory (1969, p. 219) has described a simpler way of demonstrating tristimulus mixture. A box with a translucent front surface (flashed opal glass or similar material) has 3 lamps mounted inside its back wall. Each lamp is arranged to shine through a different filter (red, green, blue), each aligned with a hole in a baffle plate. The 3 holes are arranged so that overlapping circles of light are cast onto the translucent screen. Some method of luminance control can be used to vary each component contribution to the mixture.

The color wheel

Another way of verifying the principles of color mixture is to place different colored papers on a disk or *color wheel*. The overlapping sectors of different colors can be adjusted so that their angular proportions represent the proportional contribution that each color will make to the mixture. The mixture is achieved by spinning the disk at a high rate of speed with a motor. The spectral distributions of wavelengths reflected from each colored paper do not actually mix as the light travels from the disk to the eye. Light striking any portion of the retina on which the image of the disk falls is actually coming alternately from the two colored sectors of the disk, assuming just a two-color mixture. The retinal excitation resulting from light from one colored paper does not cease instantaneously when that sector of the disk gives way to the other colored sector. Instead, it persists and combines with the excitation aroused by the second color. As the disk whirls, the result of this process is a fusion of the two colors that is functionally equivalent to mixing the light reflected from the surface of each and sending the mixture steadily into the eye. The spinning disk of the color mixer will thus appear to have a surface of uniform color, the resultant of the mixture. By adjusting the angular proportions of the two colored sectors on the disk we can explore the range of intermediate hues attainable.

Color Vision Phenomena

Despite the fact that the realm of color is a highly subjective one, a number of laboratory approaches have revealed some solid facts about it. We have already cited the principles of color mixture and indicated the progress that has been made in standardizing color specifications. These mixture principles, and a number of other color phenomena, provide topics for student investigation that give us an excellent means for getting better acquainted with visual research.

Contrast

A visual phenomenon in which a portion of the visual field is changed in appearance as a result of stimulation in another part of the field is known as *contrast*. Laboratory studies have revealed a number of principles which are operative as this phenomenon is experienced. We shall mention a few of these which you may wish to verify for yourself.

A procedure which may be regarded as an operational definition of achromatic contrast is to place small samples of a medium gray paper upon backgrounds of white, light gray, dark gray, and black. The contrast effect will be experienced in the different surface brightnesses that the sample gray assumes when viewed against these different backgrounds. Against the white background the test patch of gray will appear darkest and it will also appear darker when seen against the light gray. Against the dark gray background the medium gray patch will appear lighter than "usual" and on the black it will appear lightest of all. The contrast principle seems to be that the background brightness induces an opposite or contrasting brightness in the test patch. For this reason, contrast effects are said to occur through *induction*, a term which is applied also to a somewhat different phenomenon associated with the blindspot.

Chromatic contrast may be studied by a procedure similar to the one just described for achromatic contrast. We may take samples of the same neutral gray and place them on red, blue, green, or yellow backgrounds of fairly high saturation. The achromatic gray test patch will now be seen as having a chromatic tinge to it which will be a hue that is complementary to the background. Viewed against red, the gray will be seen to have a blue-green tinge. Against blue it will appear slightly yellowish and against yellow it will seem to be a blue of very low purity, that is, having an appearance of extremely low saturation. When colored papers are used to demonstrate contrast, the effect may be enhanced by placing a thin tissue paper over the test patch and background. Another way is to hold the stimulus papers so near to the eye that the edges of the test patch cannot be clearly perceived. Both these techniques weaken the objective perception of the test patch; such objective viewing seems to reduce contrast. An additional principle of contrast is that it is best when the test area is small and the surrounding background is large. It has also been found that chromatic contrast is greater when the background is of high purity.

Peripheral Hue Sensitivity

Peripheral portions of the retina vary with respect to their sensitivity to different wavelengths of the spectrum. We find that chromatic sensation is absent in the peripheral portions of the visual field furthest from the foveal point, presumably due to the reduced density of cones in the outer retina. Exploration of the portion of the retina where chromatic sensitivity is present reveals that certain hues are sensed more peripherally than others. Blue and yellow, for example, are sensed farther from the fixation point than are red and green. These different areas of differential hue sensitivity are sometimes called the *color zones* of the retina.

The extent of the different hue-sensitive zones along any meridian of the retina is determined by exploring the corresponding meridian of the visual field with a stimulus patch of particular dominant wavelength.

This is conveniently done by using a *retinal perimeter,* a device with a semicircular arc along which the test patch may be moved. At the center of the arc is a fixation point which the subject fixates steadily during the perimetry. He reports the hue of the test patch as soon as he senses it while the experimenter moves it slowly in along the arc toward the fixation point. With the arc calibrated in degrees from the fixation point, a direct indication of the outer limit of sensitivity for that hue is obtained, expressed in degrees from the fovea. It is commonly found that some hues are rather regularly misidentified as the test patch is moved inward, the correct hue being named only after the patch is moved farther in toward the fixation point.

The actual locus of correct hue identification along any meridian of the retina depends on a number of factors in the test situation. Besides the hue itself, other determinants of the identification point include the purity of the test patch, its luminance, and its degree of contrast with the background. If the test stimulus is only momentarily presented, its exposure time will also determine how peripherally the hue will be correctly sensed. Below a certain value, the area of the test patch also is a determinant of peripheral hue sensitivity measurements.

An experiment by Boynton, Shafer, and Neun (1964) explored chromatic vision in peripheral locations 20° and 40° from the fovea as compared with foveal hue sensitivity. Presenting subjects with a flash of light (of various wavelengths, 1000 trolands in intensity, 3° in subtended angle, 300 msec in duration) the investigators required color-naming responses and saturation estimates from the dark-adapted subjects. It was found that color names were generally retained at the 20° test location though saturation was much less than in the fovea. At 40° from the fovea saturation was even less and the hues named were generally either blue or yellow (and a few red) for the different spectral wavelengths presented. These findings are in accordance with other mappings of retinal color zones.

Afterimages

With the stress that we place on vision as a psychophysical process one might suppose that we are interested in the functioning of the visual system only while it is undergoing physical stimulation. We can easily show, however, that visual experience outlasts the stimulation that initiates it. To various sensations that occur after the termination of the physical stimulus we give the name *afterimages*. A study of afterimages, both achromatic and chromatic, may yield additional information about the visual sense.

Positive afterimages

Essential for the production of most afterimages is some pattern of the relative illuminances in the visual field that provides the stimulus for the aftersensation. If this aftersensation has the same pattern of relative brightnesses as was being experienced when the eye was still stimulated, we refer to a *positive afterimage*. The term is analogous to our reference to a snapshot as a positive print, one that maintains the light-dark relations of the original scene. You have probably experienced a positive afterimage after viewing an intense source of light, perhaps the sun. As you averted your eyes because of the discomfort, you are likely to have seen a persistent bright spot which remained in your visual experience for a few seconds even if you closed your eyes. This was a positive afterimage. They are seen most often after a brief exposure to a very strong light.

Negative achromatic afterimages

At much lower luminance levels than are needed for positive afterimages it is possible to generate a *negative afterimage,* one which has its light-dark relationships reversed from their appearance in the original scene, as in a photographic negative. The particular requirement for producing a good negative afterimage is to fixate a particular point in the visual field or on a test pattern for about 30 to 60 sec and then to turn the eyes toward a uniform field against which the afterimage may be seen. To demonstrate the phenomenon to yourself, if you are not already familiar with it, you might stare at the center point of a black triangle located on a white background. After the greater part of a minute has elapsed while you hold this fixation, you need merely to shift your gaze to something like a gray piece of cardboard. Seemingly superimposed on this surface you will see a light gray triangle surrounded by a darker gray field. This negative image may persist for a few seconds, fade from sensory experience, and then reappear again. Such waxing and waning are typical of the afterimage experience. The vividness of a negative afterimage depends on such factors as the luminance contrast in the original stimulus pattern, the duration of the original fixation, and the luminance of the background upon which the afterimage is "projected."

Chromatic afterimages

If a stimulus target has a dominant wavelength so that it appears as having a particular hue, it will be found that its afterimage viewed against an achromatic surface has a complementary hue. A red target arouses a blue-green afterimage and a blue target a yellow afterimage. A fairly simple explanation may be offered for this hue reversal. If a blue target is viewed, a certain amount of adaptation to this hue takes place in the cones that are responding to it. They gradually become less responsive to it. As the blue target is fixated, in fact, it is likely to appear to lose saturation due to adaptation. When a white or gray background is then viewed, its reflected light finds the target portion of the retina to be somewhat less responsive to the wavelengths in the blue region of the spectrum. Since responsiveness is still normal in the green, yellow, and red regions of the spectrum, the retinal activity approximates that which would be aroused by such a distribution of incoming light energy. The yellow afterimage that is sensed is the normal accompaniment of such a pattern of retinal activity. We see, then, that an afterimage is the joint product of the ongoing physical stimulation at the time of its perception and the state of the retina created by the prior stimulation.

Visual Perception and Its Study

Perceptual processes such as attention, discrimination, and interpretation are considered to intervene between the sensing of external stimulation and the generating of responses to it. Our perceptions are so dependent on our sensations that perceptual processes may be considered as natural extensions of sensory events. On the other hand, our perceptions are so powerful in determining our responses in any situation that a perception may be characterized as a readiness to respond in a particular way.

Relation to sensation

Perceptions often seem to be either a synthesis or an analysis of sensations, sometimes incorporating sensory cues from several modalities. We perceive a blazing hearth when we simultaneously see the flames in the fireplace, hear the twigs crackling, and smell the smoke from the green wood. Even "seeing" the flames is a perception resulting from the synthesis of the hues, and the spatial and temporal patterns of the incandescence. Perception of an analytic sort occurs when we search through a sea of visual sensations until we locate something, perhaps a familiar face, to which we can respond.

What are the sensory elements out of which percepts are constructed in our experience? Reasoning from the facts of optical image formation and the retinal mosaic of rods and cones, early workers argued that a multitude of points of color, varied as to brightness, hue, and saturation, were the building stones from which our visual perception of the environment was constructed. These pioneer elementarists, knowing that visual stimulation was a pinpoint process at the retina, introspected mightily to see these points of color in their percepts.

Professor James Gibson (1966) has offered a different conception of sensation and perception. For him the sensory organ is the detector portion of a perceptual system. In his ecological optics it is not patches of luminance but actively variable edges and outlines which provide information for the guidance of behavior.

Relation to response

It may be appropriate, for some purposes, to define a perception as a tendency to respond. If we place a slide in a projector and very gradually bring it into focus, a subject who has been instructed to report what he sees may say, "I see *something* now . . . it's a *circle* . . . it's a *bicycle wheel.*" We may infer that he experienced three successive perceptions. We might go further and say that a perception is a tendency to make a particular response. A tendency to respond is still part of private experience which may be inhibited or which may be changed before an overt response occurs. Therefore, in accepting a response-tendency definition of perception, we do not commit ourselves to accepting any response as a direct indication of the perception aroused by the stimulus situation.

Relation to learning

The view that perceptual processes are strongly influenced by experience or learning is widely held, being supported by much experimental evidence. An extended treatment of perceptual learning has been offered by Professor Eleanor Gibson (1969). Unfortunately, by the time a person is old enough to participate as a subject in research, the experience that contributes to basic perceptual processes is long since past. The effects of experience which immediately precedes perception are easier to investigate. Such experience may establish a perceptual *set*, a readiness to make responses of a particular type.

Past learning may also fortify a particular perception by providing an associative filling-in for any cues that may be missing. In our earlier example, for instance, it is not necessary to draw every spoke to obtain a perception of a bicycle wheel. In the case of an ambiguous stimulus, past experience may even be the principal source of any perception that occurs. This fact underlies the use of projective tests in psychology, of course.

Phenomenological Studies

The study of psychological phenomena by directly experiencing them is the *phenomenological* method. Reflecting upon their visual experiences, phenomenologists were able to formulate principles that appeared to operate in their perceptions. Men of the gestalt school, particularly, worked out rules that governed the perceiving of stimulus configurations, or *Gestalts*. Other investigators worked with stimulus materials like geometrical figures, creating perceptual illusions like apparent curvature in a physically straight line. Besides using oneself as subject, it is possible to extend the phenomenological study of perception by getting reports from others on how they perceive stimulus material. Typical use of phenomenal reports is found in studies of the *Ganzfeld* (entire visual field) as summarized by Avant (1965).

Functional Relationships

In contrast to those experiments which seek to describe certain perceptual phenomena are studies which *seek functional relationships* between the determinants of the perceptions and the responses to which the perceptions give rise. The gestalt principles that are often demonstrated by means of illustrative examples are amenable, along with many other perceptual processes, to this quantitative approach. Besides the commonly used manipulations of physical stimulus dimensions, we may mention a few special techniques that are useful for the study of a variety of perceptual problems.

Stimulus impoverishment

One way to study the interrelated effects of environmental and other factors on perception is to reduce the external stimulation in some important respect. We can reduce the duration of presenting a stimulus word to subjects, for example, to determine the limiting length of presentation which still permits the word to be perceived correctly by the majority of persons. We would thus be determining a sort of absolute threshold for word recognition. In addition to exploring limits of perception, various impoverishment techniques may be used to reduce the stimulus contribution to perceptual processes in order to permit other factors like the past learning or the motivation of the subjects to reveal their impact upon the perception.

There are a number of ways of impoverishing visual stimulation. Devices of various kinds which limit stimulus exposure to very brief durations are called *tachistoscopes*. In the *fall* tachistoscope the stimulus is momentarily revealed by having a cutout window pass in front of it as an opaque screen falls. In the *Dodge* tachistoscope a subject looks at a semitransparent mirror, with the stimulus shown briefly by a quick change in illumination on the two sides of the mirror. Tachistoscopic stimulation can be given to a large group of subjects at one time by using a projector whose beam is briefly permitted to pass through a sector disk or a camera shutter. Besides using tachistoscopic exposure, we may impoverish stimuli by reducing the brightness contrast in projected stimuli by cutting down the projection lamp intensity or by increasing the room illumination. Blurring the focus of a projected image will also reduce its perceptibility.

Training or establishing a set

Besides looking for the effect on perception of whatever a person's past experience may have been, a more direct study of the relationship of learning to perception may be undertaken by administering training to experimental subjects and noting how it affects their perceptual processes. Somewhat akin to giving perceptual training, in that it manipulates the subject's experience, is the use of instructions or some other means to establish a set—an expectancy or a readiness to perceive or respond in a certain way. Exactly how a mental set influences a perception is a topic for debate among psychologists. Discussions have been presented by Haber (1966) and by Steinfeld (1967).

Psychophysical methods

How round is a circle? Most views we get of circular objects are from an angle so that the retinal image in mose cases is actually elliptical, yet we perceive the object as round. Our objective knowledge of the probable situation is a potent determiner of our perceptions in such cases. Without the benefit of such actual knowledge, how much elliptical distortion could a circle be given while still being perceived as perfectly round? We are asking here about the differential threshold for circularity. This might be determined by applying the method of constant stimuli, described in Chapter 5, with a number of almost circular ellipses used as comparison stimuli. Ellipses and circles might be presented at various angles of regard, the subjects being asked to state whether the stimulus object was circular.

Form Perception

Discrimination and recognition of two-dimensional forms or shapes have been common tasks in visual perception research. In early experiments geometric forms such as triangle, ellipse, rectangle, circle, hexagon, crescent, cross, and star were commonly used as stimulus figures. Such items have two disadvantages for such investigations. First, they are familiar to subjects and this familiarity may contribute to their discriminability. Second, there exist only a limited number of such forms—not a large enough population of stimuli to permit extensive systematic work on form perception.

Prepared Stimulus Materials

Various combinations of definitional constraints and random-numbers techniques have been used to generate several types of irregular forms and patterns. Their great number and their unfamiliarity gives experimenters a useful pool of stimulus materials. Further, such materials have been analyzed and investigated so as to provide more information about their psychological aspects. Some of this developmental work needs to be briefly reviewed as we consider research on form perception.

Attneave and Arnoult (1956) explicitly described several methods by which stimulus shapes could be generated in an essentially random manner. Figure 7.6A shows 2 sample forms prepared through using 2 of their methods. This work stimulated further research, much of this effort analyzed by Michels and Zusne (1965). Using one of the techniques of Attneave and Arnoult to generate 180 random shapes, Vanderplas and Garvin (1959) went on to scale these for their association value. They had 50 subjects report what each shape reminded them of, if anything. With shapes ranging in complexity of perimeter from 4 points to 24 points, they found that the simpler shapes more frequently elicited numerous associations from subjects. Two of the shapes are shown in Figure 7.6B. The simpler four-point form evoked associative responses: triangle, kite, sail, pyramid. The 24-point shape in Panel B elicited different responses: church, nun, branch, city.

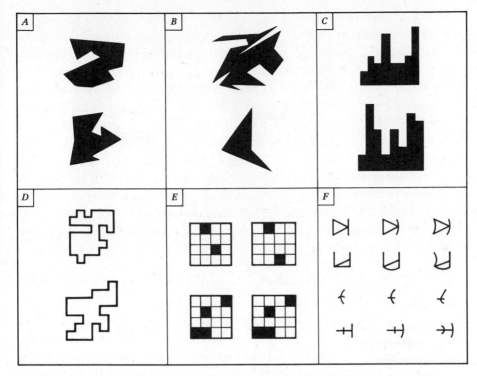

Fig. 7.6. Representative examples of some of the different stimulus materials used in studies of form perception. Forms in *A* are constructed in accordance with one of the methods described by Attneave and Arnoult (1956). Forms in *B* represent 2 levels of complexity as operationally defined by Vanderplas and Garvin (1959). in *C* are histographic forms of a type used by Fitts et al. (1956). Forms in *D* are two which were employed by Hake and Eriksen (1956). In *E* are representatives of matrices used in research on pattern recognition by Sekuler and Abrams (1968). The letter-like forms in *F* were among those used for both visual and tactual form discrimination by Pick (1965).

Brown and Owen (1967) conducted a metrical descriptive analysis of a sample of 1000 forms generated by one of the Attneave and Arnoult methods, slightly modified. After creating irregular polygons of 4, 8, 12, 16, and 20 sides (200 of each) they measured these to obtain descriptive data on a number of dimensions. Upon factor analysis, these data revealed such factors as compactness, jaggedness, and skewness. Such detailed study of stimulus materials will hopefully contribute to research on form discrimination.

Other materials for use in experiments on form or pattern perception are represented in Figure 7.6, most of them created through randomized methods. In Figure 7.6C are shown two variations of forms resembling histograms such as those devised by Fitts, Weinstein, Rappaport, Anderson, and Leonard (1956). Forms of the type created by Hake and Eriksen (1956) are shown in Figure 7.6D. An investigation by Sekuler and Abrams (1968) used patterns like those in Figure 7.6E. When paired patterns were presented, as in the figure, it was found that subjects could more quickly identify identical patterns than similar patterns, defined as having just one cell in common among those filled or blackened as shown. Experiments on form discrimination in school children were conducted by Pick (1965) who used forms such as those in Figure 7.6F, representing a type devised by Gibson for studies related to the form recognition required in learning to read.

Form Recognition in Visual Noise

A common laboratory procedure for investigating form perception is to employ a tachistoscope (p. 241), a device which permits very brief controlled exposure times in stimulus presentation. Munsinger and Gummerman (1967) used tachistoscopic presentation of stimulus forms in an experiment to determine how form perception is affected by visual noise or interference in the viewed field. Their stimuli were 3 sets of random shapes of the type described by Attneave and Arnoult (see examples in Figure 7.6A), with 4 different shapes in each set. The 3 sets differed in the number of turns forming the perimeter of the form, either 5, 10, or 20 turns characterizing the 3 levels of stimulus complexity or variability. The visual noise was introduced into the viewing situation by superimposing over the form to be recognized a grid or matrix composed of black horizontal and vertical lines. Several versions of the grid were drawn on glass to achieve 4 noise conditions: high or low density of noise achieved by narrower (1/16 in.) or wider (1/8 in.) spacing of the lines, and systematic (equal) or random (uneven) spacing of the lines. The black-on-white forms occupied 1/4 sq in. in the tachistoscopic field, being viewed from a distance of 18 in. as a subject looked into the tachistoscope.

As a trial began the subject saw a small x used as a fixation point on an illuminated field. When he pressed a button, the fixation field went dark instantly to be replaced by a test shape with one of the noise grids placed directly in front of it. As the test form flashed on briefly the subject tried to perceive its shape and call out its number from a card which showed the 4 forms of the set, printed in enlarged versions. The stimulus exposure times used in the experiment are not reported but presumably they were established so as to allow recognition on a fair percentage of trials without making the task so easy as to have 100% recognition of the test forms. The experimenters devised a derived score for performance. Their index of recognition was the percent correct divided by the exposure time in milliseconds, multiplied by a constant of 100. This index averaged from around 50 to around 400 for the various experimental treatments. Another variable in Study I, reviewed here, was the age level of subjects. Eight college students, 8 fifth-grade children, and 8 second-grade children were tested for their form perception abilities under the 4 visual noise conditions.

All variables in Study I showed statistically reliable main effects. The data were combined in several ways to show the significant interactions among the variables as portrayed in Figures 7.7, 7.8, and 7.9. Each

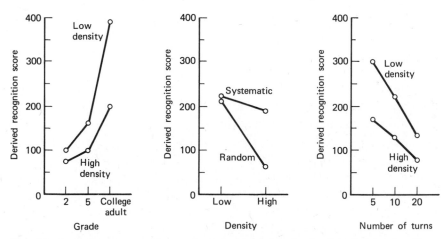

Fig. 7.7. (*Left*) Form recognition under 2 levels of visual noise density as a function of age level of subjects. (After Munsinger and Gummerman, 1967.)

Fig. 7.8. (*Middle*) Form recognition as a function of visual noise density of the systematic or the random type. (After Munsinger and Gummerman, 1967.)

Fig. 7.9. (*Right*) Form recognition as a function of stimulus complexity (no. of turns in perimeter of the forms) with high or low density of interfering visual noise as a parameter. (After Munsinger and Gummerman, 1967.)

graph shows the form recognition index plotted as a function of some variable with a different variable serving as the parameter which differentiates the two curves. The data presented were all based on the last 10 trials of the 20 trials given under each experimental condition.

Figure 7.7 shows that form recognition under visual noise is a performance which increases markedly with age of subject. College students did better at the task than fifth-graders who did better, in turn, than the second-grade children. The curves suggest an interaction between age of subjects and density of visual noise in determining form recognition. This interaction, statistically significant, resulted in age of subject being particularly important for task performance when the low density grids were used to introduce visual noise. With high density noise (systematic and random combined in the plotted points) the older subjects still exceeded the scores of the younger but not as strikingly.

Another interaction may be seen in Figure 7.8, this time between the two characteristics of the visual noise, its density and its systematic or random nature. Pooling data for all subject groups, it is seen that when density of the grid lines was low (1/8 in. spacing) performance was better, but that it made very little difference whether this spacing was systematic or random (lines averaging the 1/8 in. spacing). When the grid density was high, however, with twice the number of lines used to create visual noise, form recognition was greatly reduced when the line patterning was random. Statistical analysis of the data under systematic grid spacing showed no significant difference when high grid density was compared to low. The investigators felt that subjects were able to filter out the systematic visual noise, even at the higher level, so as to permit form recognition.

Significant information about the perception of visual forms under visual noise conditions may be found in Figure 7.9. As expected, the more complex forms constructed with 10 or 20 turns, were harder to recognize. Again there was a significant interaction, this figural variable showing a greater effect under the lower density of visual noise. When noise density was high, recognition scores were reduced more for the stimulus forms of lesser complexity. This study by Munsinger and Gummerman is notable for its uncovering of these several interactions as well as for the finding of the main effects of age and visual noise on tachistoscopic form recognition.

Some Metrics of Spatial Perception

As we explore our surroundings we rely on our vision very heavily to inform us about objects and surfaces nearby and at a distance. Our knowledge about numerous familiar things we see gives size cues useful in unconsciously estimating their distance from us. Conversely, cues concerning distance may help us in judging the size of unfamiliar objects— a tree at the far edge of a field, a stranger coming down the street. Our numerous judgments of spatial extents are usually relative, known facts influencing new estimates. One part of our visual field affects our perception of another. This relativism in visual perception is illustrated in two different experiments to be summarized as examples. In each investigation subjects had to make judgments of a quantitative sort, but the test stimuli being judged and the variables influencing the visual estimation were all quite different. Considered together, our selected studies prove the vigor of modern research interest in the metrics of visual perception of space, one of the oldest topics in experimental psychology.

Linear Extent Judgments and Surrounding Magnitudes

We have indicated that metric judgments tend to be comparative or relative. Another way to express this general idea is that the estimate made of any visual magnitude will be influenced by a subject's adaptation to the values of nearby magnitudes in his visual field. Restle and Merryman (1969) tested this notion by asking subjects to judge the length of a test line segment, the ends of which were flanked by squares or boxes of different sizes at different distances in the different display patterns. A general representation of the visual display may be seen in Figure 7.10 which

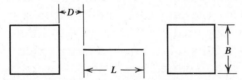

Fig. 7.10. Typical stimulus display showing the test line of length *L*, boxes of size *B*, and distance *D* separating the test line from each box. (After Restle and Merryman, 1969.)

indicates the three independent variables of the experiment: *L*, the length of line to be judged; *B*, the size of the square box outline which appeared near either end of the horizontal line; and *D*, the distance separating the ends of the line from the nearest point on the boxes. Forty-five of these stimulus fields were carefully constructed for projection on a screen 130 cm square. The screen was viewed by subjects at a distance which averaged 2.5 m. The projected values for the 3 variables, used in each possible combination, were as follows:

$$L = 13, \quad 16, \quad 19 \quad cm$$
$$B = 6.4, \quad 13, \quad 19 \quad cm$$
$$D = 0, \quad 1.6, \quad 3.2, \quad 6.4, \quad 13 \quad cm$$

To indicate their judgments of the test stimulus (the horizontal line) in each presented pattern, a subject was asked to press one of six response buttons located in a horizontal row in front of him. In preliminary training with this response scale, a subject was taught that the buttons, from left to right meant, "very short, medium short, slightly short, slightly long, medium long and very long." Although used in acquainting the subject with his judgmental task, the verbal labels were not stressed. Subjects reported using the response buttons as general indicators of magnitude without specific reference to the verbal designations for the scale points. For compilation of response data, the experimenters assigned the numbers 1 through 6 to the buttons, left to right. The 45 test patterns were presented in random sequences with a 5-sec dark interval between the projected stimuli. Six different sequences of all 45 patterns comprised a testing session, and 9 undergraduate subjects served in at least 10 sessions each, a small group of them typically responding in individual test cubicles at the same time while viewing the projected stimulus patterns. The random-access slide projector was operated, all timing accomplished, and responses collected and stored by a fully automatic computer system. Nothing could go wrong. Nothing could. Nothing.

Before examining the influence of the visual surround on the judgments of the line, Restle and Merryman first determined how the judgments were influenced by the three values of the variable *L* itself. This result is pictured in Figure 7.11 which shows that the mean response judgment, R, was linearly related to the objective length of the test line. The straight line function was fitted by the investigators to the three means to estimate certain theoretical parameters of the function. In Figure 7.12 the data are regrouped to show how mean judgments of length were affected by the other two variables in the stimulus configuration, B being used to scale the abscissa and D being the parameter which differentiates the five plotted curves.

In their original formulation of the experimental problem, the investigators considered the size of box, B, to be the principal variable having an effect on the judgments of line length. The variable of the distance, D, between the boxes and the line was considered to be a modifier or modulator of the effect of B on the response, R. If this had been the case, then only the slopes of the curves in Figure 7.12 might have varied. Instead D showed itself as a second variable with a main effect of its own. As a perceptible distance or extent in the visual field, it also contributes to the adaptation state of the subject or to the relativity of his judgments. Restle and Merryman indicate that individual differences in judgmental tendency were found among their subjects. One subject evidently was not influenced by B and D in his judgments of the line (perhaps using the projection screen as a reference constant) while another showed influences approaching twice the group average. Adopt-

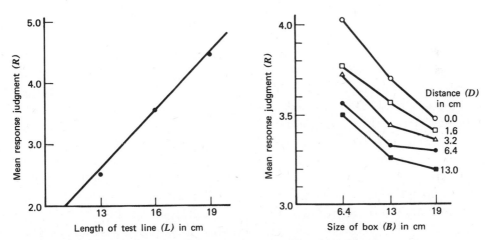

Fig. 7.11. (*Left*) Mean response judgment, R, as a function of length of test line, L. (After Restle and Merryman, 1969.)

Fig. 7.12. (*Right*) Mean response judgment, R, as a function of size of box, B, with separation distance, D, as a parameter. (After Restle and Merryman, 1969.)

Some Metrics of Spatial Perception   **249**

ing a particular perceptual set or problem-solving approach may affect a subject's responses in spatial judgments, but such a tendency can itself be detected if data are carefully collected and analyzed.

Instruction Effects on Size-Matching

Much of the research on size perception indicates, either more or less directly, a close relationship between the perceiving of size and the perceiving of distance. Stressing this relationship, Schlosberg (1950) reviewed the geometry of the viewing situation to show that the retinal image size is always proportional to the quotient of object size divided by viewing distance: $a = A/D$. Thus, if a man's height, A, is 6 ft, the retinal image, a, formed when we look at him will be halved when his distance from us, D, is doubled. This relationship between retinal image size and distance is useful in perceiving the size of unfamiliar objects. If we were to go for a walk in the country and encounter a board fence some distance away, we might perceive the height of the fence as a particular value on the basis of the experienced retinal image and the perceived distance from us to the fence. Our perception of the height of the fence might be arrived at by a swift process of *unconscious inference,* Schlosberg's paper suggests, borrowing the term from early discussion of perception by Helmholtz. This conceptualization of the perceptual process, Schlosberg indicated, is not to be considered an exposition of the mechanism that is operative.

The perception of size involves mechanisms which lead to a constancy effect. As we drive along the highway, a billboard always appears to be billboard-sized no matter what changes occur in the retinal angle that it subtends. This *size constancy* phenomenon may be demonstrated and quantified in experimental studies. If constancy is a fact of size perception, then perceived size should be invariant with viewing distance. This postulation may be tested by having subjects judge the size of test objects viewed at different distances. When such studies have been undertaken, it is found that the particular instructions given to subjects for the performance of their task are a powerful influence on the data obtained. We shall briefly review one experiment which made different instructions a major independent variable.

From a series of experiments on size perception reported by Leibowitz and Harvey (1969) we may consider their Experiment I, limiting our summary to a part of their investigation. They displayed a test object

—a board 6 ft high painted bright red—on separate trials at different distances of 340, 680, 1020, 1360, and 1680 ft, the site being the campus mall viewed from the library steps. A subject did not see the board being put in place for a trial. When it was on view, he was required to compare it with an adjustable rod placed 51 ft away on his left. The subject's task was to indicate his comparisons of the rod with the test board as the experimenter adjusted the rod through a series of comparison values.

For the part of this experiment we are considering 3 groups of 10 undergraduates served as subjects. Each group was given a different set of instructions, termed *objective, apparent,* or *retinal* to indicate the emphasis in each description of the task to be performed. After stressing the importance of following the specific directions exactly, here is what subjects in the different groups were told:

Objective Instructions: Suppose I were to place the rod on the left (comparison object) beside the board (test object); how big would the rod have to be so that it would be exactly the same size as the board? I am going to set the rod at various heights and I want you to judge which would be taller if they were placed side by side, the rod or the board.

Apparent Instructions: I am going to set the rod on the left (comparison object) at various heights and I want you to judge which appears taller, the rod or the board. Please disregard any knowledge you may have about the real height of the object, and base your judgment on the way it appears.

Retinal Instructions: As you know, the farther away an object is from you, the smaller is its image . . . Now imagine that the field of view is a scene in a picture or a photograph. Every image in the picture is fixed in size. If you were to cut out the fixed image of the board and paste it on the image of the variable rod, how big would the variable rod have to be so that the two images would be exactly the same size? I am going to set the rod at various heights and I want you to judge which photographic image would be larger, the rod or the board.

The results of this part of the experiment may be quite simply described. Under the Objective condition the size-matching data averaged very close to the physical height of the board, actually exceeding it by around 10 percent. Further, the size-matching data did not vary significantly over the 5 different viewing distances. This shows that size constancy was operative in the subjects' judgments despite the changes in retinal image size. They were able to comply quite well with the Objective Instructions. Next considering the group given the Retinal Instructions, it was found that their data indicated magnitudes far below objective size but still far above an equating of retinal image size. Their average values were lower at greater viewing distances, in correspondence with instructions, and tended to approach a retinal image matching more closely. The group given the Apparent Instructions showed average response values which were in between those of the Objective and the Retinal groups, somewhat closer to the latter. With the greater viewing distances their values also became lower. These instructions (Apparent) were said by the investigators to be somewhat ambiguous. The findings seem to indicate that subjects perform the task in a way which conforms somewhat to the retinal guide to size-matching.

Tachistoscopic Recognition of Words

Perceptual processes have been studied with variables in the realm of time as well as of space. When a tachistoscope (p. 241) is used to present a stimulus in a very brief exposure, this may constitute a real challenge to a subject's powers of perceptual recognition. When the stimuli are words presented tachistoscopically the demand on perception may blend with a demand on associative or cognitive processes as well. This is illustrated in two different studies we are to consider.

Word Frequency and Verbal Ability

Numerous studies have found that recognition thresholds are found at lower exposure durations for words of relatively high frequency of usage and presumed greater familiarity to subjects. Spielberger and Denny (1963) reported a tachistoscopic recognition experiment which varied word frequency while testing two groups of subjects who scored either high or low in verbal ability on a college entrance examination. Their study represents a utilization of the psychometric approach in conjunction with laboratory experimentation, as advocated by Cronbach (1957).

The two groups of subjects, High Verbal Ability ($N=16$) and Low Verbal Ability ($N=16$) were run individually to determine their tachistoscopic recognition thresholds for 12 selected words. There were 4 words at each level of frequency of occurrence in English as listed in compilations by Thorndike and Lorge (1944). The words were:

High Frequency	Moderate Frequency	Low Frequency
NECESSARY	RECOMMEND	BARRISTER
AFTERNOON	ASSISTANT	NOCTURNAL
CONDITION	CURIOSITY	AFFLUENCE
IMPORTANT	SENSATION	HIBERNATE

After visual acuity testing subjects were given practice with the testing of tachistoscopic recognition using 6 practice words of high frequency of occurrence. For testing with each word, 5 presentations were made at each exposure time, beginning at 0.01 sec and increasing exposure by 0.01 sec after each 5 presentations at the prior level. Recognition threshold was defined as the total number of exposures required to reach 2 correct identifications, not necessarily consecutive. Special letter-reporting criteria were also established to cover cases where an occasional subject was unfamiliar with a word in the list. The words of different frequency levels were intermixed irregularly in the sequence of testing, the same order being used for all subjects.

Results of the experiment are portrayed in Figure 7.13 which shows separate curves plotted for the two groups, High Verbal Ability and Low Verbal Ability. The mean number of tachistoscopic exposures identifying the defined recognition threshold is seen to vary inversely with word frequency level for both groups. This effect of the word frequency variable is in agreement with much past research. The plotted curves suggest an interaction of this variable with verbal ability. Statistical analysis showed this to be significant. The High Verbal Ability subjects had significantly lower thresholds for the low frequency words than did those in the Low Verbal Ability group. In discussing this threshold difference as related to verbal ability, Spielberger and Denny saw two possible interpretations. Subjects of high verbal ability may possess verbal habits and greater familarity with rare words which facilitate their word recognition performances. Or, those of higher verbal ability may also possess greater skills of perceptual organization. Regardless of interpretation, the experiment demonstrates the utility of working with

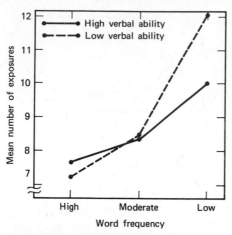

Fig. 7.13. Mean number of tachistoscopic exposures required for recognition of words of high, moderate, or low frequency by subjects of high or low verbal ability. (After Spielberger and Denny, 1963.)

psychometrically tested groups of subjects in conducting laboratory investigations.

Contextual Information

In considering the task of recognizing or identifying tachistoscopically presented words Tulving and Gold (1963) noted that a subject's task may be conceptualized as selecting a response word on the basis of information gained during the experiment. In some experiments aimed at determining perceptual thresholds all of the information may come from the tachistoscopic exposures. However, in certain experiments there may be a second general source of information about the response words to be selected. For example, a study of tachistoscopic recognition thresholds as a function of familiarity might require earlier familiarization presentations of words before tachistoscopic testing. The familiarization experience might serve as a source of information about appropriate response words. Such pretest information may be said to establish a set or expectancy in subjects.

For a situation in which there are two types of information source, the tachistoscopic and the contextual, Tulving and Gold assumed that the two sources were complementary in helping the subject arrive at his response. Thus the more information provided by the context, the less would need to be obtained from tachistoscopic exposures and hence the lower would be the measured threshold for recognition of the word presented. In postulating a lowering of the threshold, it is assumed that the contextual information is congruous with the test word. The experimenters also postulated an opposing relationship in the information sources; if context is incongruous, its information will oppose the tachistoscopic information and elevate the recognition threshold.

The stimulus material for their Experiment I consisted of 10 selected 3-syllable nouns which were used as the final word in 9-word sentences to create the needed verbal context. These contexts and associated test words are presented in Table 7.3. The investigators used the full 8-word context as one contextual condition. They reduced context length by omitting the first 4, 6, or 7 words to create other conditions. With the first 7 words of Sentence 1 omitted, for example, the context was reduced to "outstanding." Omitting the first 4 words of Sentence 2 reduced the context to

Table 7.3 Contexts and Corresponding Test Words
(After Tulving and Gold, 1963)

Sentence	Context	Test Word
1	The actress received praise for being an outstanding	performer
2	Three people were killed in a terrible highway	collision
3	The escaped soldier was captured and court-martialed for	desertion
4	Far too many people today confuse communism with	socialism
5	She likes red fruit jams of strawberry and	raspberry
6	The skiers were buried alive by the sudden	avalanche
7	Many colorful flowers and stately elms lined the	boulevard
8	Medieval knights in battle were noted for their	gallantry
9	More money buys fewer products during times of	inflation
10	The loud piercing screams occurred with regularly increasing	frequency

"in a terrible highway." When all context was omitted the condition of zero context length was created. In addition to the values of 0, 1, 2, 4, and 8 for context length, the investigators made pre-exposure context either congruous with the test word or incongruous with it. The congruous combinations were based on the sentences of Table 7.3. Incongruity was obtained simply by following any context with a tachistoscopic exposure of a different test word than the one paired with it in the prepared sentences.

The combination of 5 context lengths with either the congruity or incongruity relationship to test words yielded 10 experimental conditions. Subjects were 10 female college students who were each tested under every condition for tachistoscopic recognition of each of the 10 test words, 100 threshold determinations per subject. These tests were preceded by visual duration threshold determinations for 4 practice words to familiarize subjects with the tachistoscope and the testing procedure. Thresholds were determined by using the psychophysical method of limits. For the ascending series of exposures, 10 milliseconds (msec) was used first, and then exposure durations were increased in 10-msec steps until recognition was achieved. Two exposures were made at each duration step. If the second exposure was the one on which word recognition occurred, 5 msec was added to the exposure in recording the visual duration threshold. Of course the critical experimental treatment for each threshold determination was the presentation of one of the 10 context conditions in the pre-exposure field of the tachistoscope just before each exposure of the test word. Irregular sequences of conditions were employed for the series of 100 threshold determinations.

The group mean values for the visual duration thresholds are plotted in Figure 7.14 for the relevant and irrelevant context conditions over their 5 different lengths of pre-exposure context. The mean threshold is seen to be just above 70 msec for the zero context conditions when the test words had no word or phrase preceding them. Under conditions of relevant or congruous context, recognition thresholds are seen to be lower, increasingly so as context length increases. In contrast, adding incongruous context is seen to elevate the threshold, with greater irrelevant context raising it more. Statistical analyses reported by Tulving and Gold bear out these interpretations of the plotted means.

The investigators went on to perform additional experiments as reported in their article. They obtained measures of the information con-

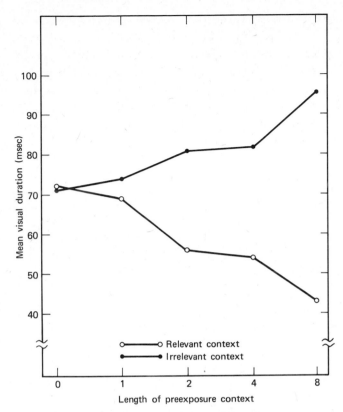

Fig. 7.14. Group mean visual duration thresholds for test words as a function of length of relevant or irrelevant preexposure context. (After Tulving and Gold, 1963.)

veyed in the 50 contexts used in Experiment I and also indices of congruity of these contexts with the designated test words. They then tested 2 groups of subjects, getting threshold determinations for each of the 10 words under congruous conditions of either 4- or 8-words contexts. Correlational analysis of the data showed that the contribution to lowered thresholds stemmed principally from the congruity of the context with its test word rather than from the information level. The 2 mean thresholds found in Experiment III were 69.2 and 63.9 msec for the 4- and 8-word contexts, respectively. These are not as low as those plotted for Experiment I in Figure 7.14. It seems probable that repeated threshold determinations on each test word in Experiment I gave subjects still another contextual source of information about the response words to be selected during tachistoscopic testing. This interpretation seems consistent with the investigators' view that response selection is influenced by different sources of information in an experiment. An alternative explanation might be that subjects in Experiment I achieved lower thresholds by virtue of their greater amount of practice in the tachistoscopic task. The use of practice words probably reduced greatly any such practice effect, however.

Visual Search

A perceptual process which is very prominent in the major sensory modalities of vision and audition is attending selectively in a complex stimulus situation and picking out the stimuli of interest for further perceptual processing. In a review of several types of research on selective attention, Egeth (1967) identified visual search as a systematically studied task for which laboratory studies have yielded some impressive principles of performance and postulations concerning underlying processes. He cites the experimentation of Neisser and his associates in a program of research which Neisser (1964) himself has also summarized and interpreted. This particular type of visual search experiment requires a subject to scan a vertical list of printed items from top to bottom to find a target item or element. The target might be a specified word placed somewhere in a list of 50 words, or it might be an alphanumeric character (numeral or letter) in one of the 50 items each consisting of random strings of 5 or 6 characters. The measure of performance is the time required to search the items and find the target. It has been found that this response time relates linearly to the distance down the column to the location of the target, permitting search rate to be estimated. Egeth listed several facts characterizing the performance of subjects well-practiced at this task. Subjects report that they do not "see" the irrelevant items, and they seem to have no memory of them. Search rate is slowed when the field of items has high similarity to the target being sought, e.g., Q as a target in a field with numerous other round letters. Subjects can visually search for several different targets at the same rate they search for one.

Letter Search in Words and Nonwords

Consideration of Experiment III in a series reported by Kru</er (1970) will acquaint us with procedures differing somewhat from those just

summarized and will indicate another finding in selective attention. The 6-letter items comprising the 2-line display to be searched provided the experimental variation in this part of the research. The 2 items to be searched in looking for a designated target letter were either common words, rare words, pseudowords or corresponding nonwords randomly constructed from the letters of the first three classes of item. Pseudowords were constructed by random selection of 2 trigrams (3-letter sequences) from a set of 10,000 words. The experiment was conducted to see if these different types of stimulus array would be searched at different rates to find the target which was a single letter of the display, specified as the target letter just before the display was presented for the search task.

The 6 types of words, pseudowords, or nonwords plus the 12 potential locations for the target letter comprised 82 experimental conditions. Two more conditions were trials on which a target letter was designated but was not present in the 2-item display. Such catch displays required a different response button to be pushed from the one which signalled a successful finding of the target letter. A computer controlled the sequence of the 84 conditions, selected the items for the display, designated the target letter, and timed the presentation of first the target letter (1.4 sec) and then the display to be searched for it. There was a 1-sec intertrial interval. Five replications of the 84-condition set gave 420 trials for the single session used. Eighteen Harvard students served as paid subjects in this experiment. Each was given a few practice trials before data collection began.

Search times for the 6 different types of stimulus items were averaged across all target locations (using geometric means for the 5 replications of each condition within a session and arithmetic means thereafter). These summary data are plotted in Figure 7.15. Display context or field to be searched was clearly a determinant of time taken to locate a target letter visually. Words were searched most readily, with common words yielding shorter search times than rare words. Pseudowords of trigram construction were searched less readily than words but faster than the nonwords which, as the figure shows, took considerably longer to search. Statistical analyses confirmed these interpretations of the plotted data. The results of this and related experiments are interpreted by Krueger as indicating an active analytic processing of information in visual search which broadly attends to items like real words rather than being limited to a letter-by-letter inspection of items displayed.

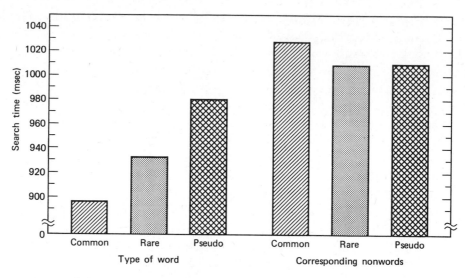

Fig. 7.15. Mean search time for the different types of words and nonwords averaged across all target locations. (After Krueger, 1970.)

Summary

The richness of visual experience depends on numerous sensory and perceptual processes. Our background for the understanding and conducting of research on this complex topic begins with the study of light, and the terms and units of measurement used in specifying visual stimuli. Luminance, in various aspects, and spectral composition are two major dimensions of light. The structure and functioning of the eye constitute a second factual area which must be mastered as part of a foundation for the study of research in vision. A knowledge of the retina is particularly useful in understanding visual phenomena.

Certain visual facts, arising from research, must be kept in mind when pursuing further investigations. The facts about photopic and scotopic vision, represented in the spectral sensitivity curves, must be kept in mind when working near threshold values of luminance. Adaptation and masking are two areas for investigation from which we drew brief illustrations of basic studies.

Numerous experimental studies of vision provide evidence of the need for careful research techniques. Control of the physical stimulus and consideration of the adaptive state of the retina are especially important. The luminance of the stimulus may be controlled in a number of ways. The size of stimuli and the retinal location at which they impinge need to be specified if research is to extend our knowledge. Another physical dimension, duration of stimulation, must also be considered in many experiments. Problems of visual acuity, of considerable interest in vision testing, must be explored more fully. A prime consideration in such work is the nature of the acuity target used.

Our understanding of color vision begins with our knowledge of how chromatic and achromatic sensations depend on the distribution of spectral wavelengths in the stimulating light. Two fundamental aspects of chromatic sensation are hue and saturation. The activity of the retinal cones mediates chromatic sensation, whereas rod functioning yields only achromatic experience.

We reviewed some of the empirical facts about color mixture and complementaries. Principles of tristimulus mixture were also described. For precise specification of color, we utilize the ICI chromaticity diagram with its rectangular coordinates. Stating the coordinate values of any point in the diagram is a way of indicating a tristimulus mixture of the ICI primaries that we would need to match the color we are describing. The chromaticity diagram permits the graphic determination of the results of additive color mixture, with the dominant wavelength and the spectral purity of the mixture being determinable. The diagram, based on psychophysical research which defines the "standard observer," may also be used to locate various white illuminants.

The color wheel, or other mixing apparatus, can be used to explore the rules of additive color mixture. Other visual phenomena with which we may experiment include contrast, peripheral hue sensitivity, and afterimages.

Perceptual processes like attention, discrimination, and interpretation intervene between sensation and response. Although they are closely related to sensory processes, perceptions show marked dependence on past learning. As determinants of behavior percepts may sometimes be considered as tendencies to respond.

Perception may be studied phenomenologically or with more conventional experimental methods used in seeking functional relationships. Among the techniques that have been used are the psychophysical methods for scaling perceptions, stimulus impoverishment for determining limiting factors, and special training for exploring the dependence of perception on past experience.

The perception of form constitutes a vast problem area for the study of perceptual processes. Quantitative specification of various prepared stimulus materials has contributed to advances in research. The tachistoscopic recognition of forms under visual noise conditions was an illustrative multivariate experiment.

Some metrics of spatial perception were examined in different studies we reviewed. One experiment quantified the judging of linear extent as affected by the stimulus configuration. Another examined linear size judgments as modified by experimental instructions. Tachistoscopic perception of words in two experiments and the study of visual search behavior were the final topics in our consideration of visual processes as investigated in the psychology laboratory.

References

Attneave, F., & Arnoult, M. D. The quantitative study of shape and pattern perception. *Psychological Bulletin*, 1956, **53**, 452–471.

Avant, L. L. Vision in the Ganzfeld. *Psychological Bulletin*, 1965, **64**, 246–258.

Boynton, R. M. Vision. In J. B. Sidowski (Ed.), *Experimental methods and instrumentation in psychology*. New York: McGraw-Hill, 1966. Pp. 273–330.

Boynton, R. M., Shafer, W., & Neun, M. E. Hue-wavelength relation measured by color-naming method for three retinal locations. *Science*, 1964, **146**, 666–668.

Brown, D. R., & Owen, D. H. The metrics of visual form: Methodological dyspepsia. *Psychological Bulletin*, 1967, **68**, 243–259.

Chapanis, A. How we see: A summary of basic principles. In National Research Council, Committee on Undersea Warfare, Panel on Psychology and Physiology. *Human factors in undersea warfare*. Washington: National Research Council, 1949. Pp. 3–60.

Cronbach, L. J. The two disciplines of scientific psychology. *American Psychologist*, 1957, **12**, 671–684.

Egeth, H. Selective attention. *Psychological Bulletin*, 1967, **67**, 41–57.

Fitts, P. M., Weinstein, M., Rappaport, M., Anderson, N., & Leonard, J. A. Stimulus correlates of visual pattern recognition: A probability approach. *Journal of Experimental Psychology*, 1956, **51**, 1–11.

Gibson, E. J. *Principles of perceptual learning and development*. New York: Appleton-Century-Crofts, 1969.

Gibson, J. J. *The senses considered as perceptual systems*. Boston: Houghton Mifflin, 1966.

Gregory, R. L. Apparatus for investigating visual perception. *American Psychologist*, 1969, **24**, 219–225.

Haber, R. N. Nature of the effect of set on perception. *Psychological Review*, 1966, **73**, 335–351.

Hake, H. W., & Eriksen, C. W. Role of response variables in recognition and identification of complex visual forms. *Journal of Experimental Psychology*, 1956, **52**, 235–243.

Hecht, S., Haig, C., & Chase, A. M. The influence of light adaptation on subsequent dark adaptation of the eye. *Journal of General Physiology*, 1937, **20**, 831–850.

Heckenmueller, E. G. Stabilization of the retinal image: A review of method, effects, and theory. *Psychological Bulletin*, 1965, **63**, 157–169.

Judd, D. B. Basic correlates of the visual stimulus. In S. S. Stevens (Ed.), *Handbook of experimental psychology*. New York: Wiley, 1961. Pp. 811–867.

Kahneman, D. Method, findings, and theory in studies of visual masking. *Psychological Bulletin*, 1968, **70**, 404–425.

Krueger, L. E. Search time in a redundant visual display. *Journal of Experimental Psychology*, 1970, **83**, 391–399.

Leibowitz, H. W., & Harvey, L. O., Jr. Effect of instructions, environment, and type of test object on matched size. *Journal of Experimental Psychology*, 1969, **81**, 36–43.

Michels, K. M., & Zusne, L. Metrics of visual form. *Psychological Bulletin*, 1965, **63**, 74–86.

Munsinger, H., & Gummerman, K. Identification of form in patterns of visual noise. *Journal of Experimental Psychology*, 1967, **75**, 81–87.

Neisser, U. Visual search. *Scientific American*, 1964, **210**, 94–102.

Pick, A. D. Improvement of visual and tactual form discrimination. *Journal of Experimental Psychology*, 1965, **69**, 331–339.

Restle, F., & Merryman, C. Distance and an illusion of length of line. *Journal of Experimental Psychology*, 1969, **81**, 297–302.

Schlosberg, H. A note on depth perception, size constancy, and related topics. *Psychological Review*, 1950, **57**, 314–317.

Sekuler, R. W., & Abrams, M. Visual sameness: A choice time analysis of pattern recognition processes. *Journal of Experimental Psychology*, 1969, **77**, 232–238.

Spielberger, C. D., & Denny, J. P. Visual recognition thresholds as a function of verbal ability and word frequency. *Journal of Experimental Psychology*, 1963, **65**, 597–602.

Steinfeld, G. J. Concepts of set and availability and their relation to the reorganization of ambiguous pictorial stimuli. *Psychological Review*, 1967, **74**, 505–522.

Sternheim, C. E., & Boynton, R. M. Uniqueness of perceived hues investigated with a continuous judgmental technique. *Journal of Experimental Psychology*, 1966, **72**, 770–776.

Thorndike, E. L., & Lorge, I. *The teacher's word book of 30,000 words.* New York: Teachers College, Columbia University, 1944.

Tulving, E., & Gold, C. Stimulus information and contextual information as determinants of tachistoscopic recognition of words. *Journal of Experimental Psychology*, 1963, **66**, 319–327.

Vanderplas, J. M., & Garvin, E. A. The association value of random shapes. *Journal of Experimental Psychology*, 1959, **57**, 147–154.

chapter 8
Auditory
Processes

Language communication and the enjoyment of music are two outstanding characteristics of our day-to-day life. Our understanding of speech and the pleasure we derive from listening to music both depend, of course, on our sense of hearing. This auditory sense stands with vision in posing a multitude of problems for the experimental psychologist. Since the experience of hearing normally begins with the impingement of physical energy on the auditory receptors, we shall begin our discussion of audition by considering the physical stimuli. We shall then review the receptor anatomy, going on to describe basic hearing phenomena. Finally, we shall study some experimental investigations of auditory perceptual processes like localization of sound sources, masking, recognition of timbre, and perception of speech.

Background Facts

As a link with our surroundings, hearing originates with physical energy changes in the environment. To understand auditory research we must know something of how experimenters generate, transmit, and measure the sound energies they use as controlled stimuli in their laboratory studies of hearing. We need to know the major facts about the response of the ear to such physical stimulation, including phenomena that need to be considered in planning almost any investigation into auditory processes.

Physical Stimuli

Sounds originate in the mechanical vibration of objects like violin strings, vocal cords, or diaphragms in telephone receivers or loudspeakers. These vibrations set up disturbances in the adjacent air that are propagated through this medium as waves of alternate compression and rarefaction. These waves of pressure, or sound waves, are transmitted in the mechanical action of the air molecules until they beat repetitively upon the eardrum to initiate the receptor activities that result in hearing.

The vibrating sound source

Musical instruments and tuning forks produce sound that has a *tonal* quality. Other sources of sound, like a hissing radiator or a stereo record clattering to the floor, yield noise that is *atonal* in quality. Tonal quality is generated by regularly repeated vibrations of a sound source, whereas noise comes from irregular and heterogeneous mechanical action. Simple harmonic motion of a vibrating body such as a tuning fork yields pure tones. Musical notes result from mechanical disturbance patterns of greater complexity than this when different parts of the vibrating instrument make their differing contributions to the pressure exerted on nearby air molecules. Speech contains both tonal and atonal qualities.

Besides the distinctiveness of their vibratory patterns, two musical instruments, like the violin and the clarinet, may both produce a great variety of vibrations that differ in two other major respects—their frequency and their force. These physical dimensions of the vibration depend on how the instrument is constructed and how it is played. All the physical characteristics of the sound source, its vibratory pattern, its frequency, and its force per unit area, are represented in the sound waves that travel through the transmitting medium.

Transmission through a medium

Sound waves can travel through any medium that has some degree of elasticity, like air, water, metal, or bone. Our discussion concentrates on the propagation of sound waves in air. A vibrating object alternately compresses and rarefies the air that is immediately adjacent to it. As the air molecules are struck and pushed together, they strike other molecules that are adjacent to them, and so on. The region of compression in the air thus moves out from the sound source in a traveling wave even though the air molecules themselves merely vibrate back and forth over a very short distance in replication of the vibrations of the sound source. One direction of motion of a vibrating object compresses nearby air and the other direction rarefies it, causing a slight partial vacuum. This partial vacuum draws air molecules from somewhat farther away to fill it, and this leads to rarefaction farther on, and so on. A complete sound wave traveling out from a source consists, then, of regions of relative compression and regions of relative rarefaction of the air. As the source continues to vibrate many times per second it generates wave upon wave traveling out through the propagating medium.

Figure 8.1 presents a schematic representation of several sound sources with the waves they send out through the air. The molecules of air are represented by the dots, close together to represent a region of compression and far apart to represent rarefaction. In Figure 8.1*A*, the point *w* designates a location where compression is maximal and point *x* designates an identical location in the adjacent pattern. The distance from *w* to *x* thus encompasses one complete sound wave, or cycle. A complete sound wave is also designated by the distance from *y* to *z* in Figure 8.1*B*, the terminal points in this instance having been chosen at corresponding regions of rarefaction. Having indicated the terminal points of two sound waves, it might seem natural to go on to specify their wavelengths. Sound travels about four times as fast through water as through air, with wavelengths that are correspondingly four times as great for the same frequency of vibration. Rate of propagation and wavelength also vary for air transmission with temperature and barometric pressure. Due to these variations, it is not customary to refer to the wavelength of sound waves but only to their frequency, the number that pass a given point in a second. This corresponds, of course, to the frequency of vibration of the source.

Assume the tuning fork in Figure 8.1*A* is vibrating at 512 cycles per second, or 512 Hz. The term *Herz* is used for *cycles per second* of sound vibration frequency. It is abbreviated as Hz and pronounced with a *t* sound as in *hurts*. A symbol used in older sources to indicate cycles per second is ∿. Another earlier abbreviation for the term is *cps*. Our diagram indicates that the tuning fork in Figure 8.1*B* is generating sound

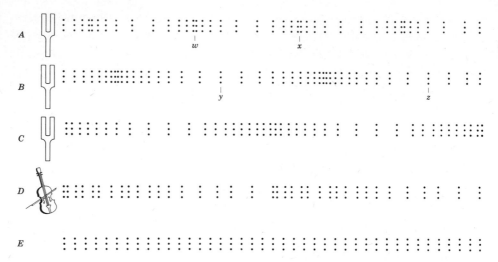

Fig. 8.1. Schematic representation of several vibrating objects and the sound waves that they produce in the air.

waves at only half the rate that they are initiated by the tuning fork A. Thus the frequency for B is 256 Hz, corresponding to the frequency of middle C on the piano. The tuning fork in Figure 8.1C also has a vibration rate of 256 Hz, but since it was struck about a millisecond later than tuning fork B, its waves are out of correspondence with those from B by a quarter of a cycle. We say that the waves from B and C are *out of phase*. Our schematic representation of the air molecules in the sound waves indicates another difference in the waves from tuning forks B and C. In the waves from C the molecules, represented by dots in the figures, are less densely concentrated in the regions of compression and are more numerous in the regions of rarefaction. We might infer that tuning fork C is not vibrating as vigorously as B, possibly because it was struck less sharply to set it in motion. Its rate of vibration is the same, due to its identical dimensions, but the force it exerts on nearby air depends on the force applied in setting it vibrating.

The violin string represented in Figure 8.1D is represented as also generating sound waves of 256 Hz, but the distribution of regions of compression and rarefaction within each wave is more complex. Although a pure tone of a tuning fork has waves with just one region of compression and one of rarefaction, a wave from the violin string contains several alternations of pressure higher and lower than normal for the undisturbed air represented in Figure 8.1*E*. Such complexity results from the vibration of the string as a whole and by separate parts. Special patterns of vibration are characteristic of different musical instruments and of the human voice in producing particular sounds.

Representation of sound waves

Figure 8.1 employs dots to represent air molecules in an arrangement which they assume at any instant when sound waves are radiating out from a vibrating object. Although this schema has the merit of close analogy with the actual momentary positioning of molecules when sound waves are being transmitted, it does not permit us to perceive readily the dimensional details of the waves. Another method of representation is shown in Figure 8.2 which represents in the conventional way all the waves which we saw in Figure 8.1. The height of any of the four curves represents, in arbitrary units, the momentary pressure at any point in the waves. The light horizontal line in each part of the figure represents the normal air pressure. Points on the curves that are above this line therefore represent various degrees of compression whereas portions of the curves below the line represent rarefaction in different amounts. All the features of the different waves that could be determined by inspection of Figure 8.1 can be seen even more readily in Figure 8.2. We can see that tuning fork *A* is producing sound waves at twice the rate that *B* and *C* are vibrating. We can see that *B* and *C* are out of phase, and also that the regions of pressure and rarefaction produced by *C* are not as far from normal air pressure as those produced by tuning fork *B*. It can be seen very clearly, too, that the violin string is producing a wave of some complexity every 1/256 sec.

With the conventional way of representing sound waves that is shown in Figure 8.2 we speak of the maximum deviation of the curve from the baseline as the *amplitude* of the wave. For each tone represented in the figure this maximum amplitude has been indicated by the vertical dimension line marked *A*. With *A* representing the maximum height of the curve, the lower case *a* may be used to designate an amplitude at any other point on the curve. Considering each waveform as a time analysis of the auditory stimulus, we have suggested that any amplitude may be considered to represent the pressure of the air at a given place and time.

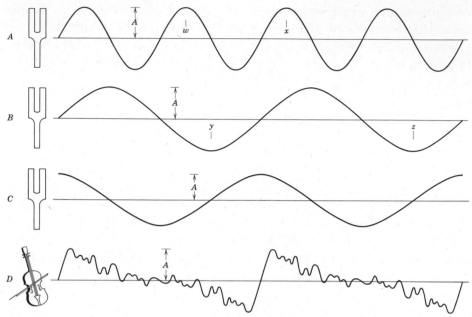

Fig. 8.2. Conventional portrayal of the sound waves of Figure 8.1.

The Receptor

Since hearing is a psychological experience that depends on the functioning of the auditory sense organs as well as on physical stimuli, we must turn our attention to some of the details of structure of the ear. The different parts of the ear serve to gather in the sound waves and to transmit their patterns inward to the auditory nerve endings which must be activated if we are to hear.

The outer ear and tympanic membrane

The part of the ear that is external to the head is the *pinna*, which serves to help in localizing sound sources. Sound waves entering the outer ear pass through the conducting and amplifying canal termed the *auditory meatus* until they impose their temporal patterns of pressure upon the eardrum or *tympanic membrane*.

The middle ear

Behind the tympanic membrane lies an air-filled chamber of about 2 cc volume, called the *middle ear*. Suspended by ligaments in the middle ear are the auditory *ossicles*, the body's three smallest bones called the *malleus, incus,* and *stapes,* or hammer, anvil, and stirrup, respectively. Their principal purpose is to amplify the pressures that impinge upon the eardrum in transmitting them to the fluid-filled inner ear. A part of the malleus rests on the inner side of the tympanic membrane so that the vibratory displacement of the membrane causes the malleus to "hammer" on the incus, with which it interlocks. The motion is imparted from the incus to the stapes, the footplate of which presses on the *oval window* which leads into the inner ear.

The inner ear

Labyrinthine fluid-filled cavities in the skull comprise the inner ear. Two portions, the *vestibule* and the *semi-circular canals,* function in our sensing of head position and motion, whereas a third part, the *cochlea,* contains the sensitive receptors for hearing. Coiled in its bony cavity that is shaped like a spiral snail shell is the *cochlear duct,* which would measure about 35 mm in length if straight. The cochlea or the cochlear duct is divided into three channels by the *basilar membrane* and the *vestibular membrane* which extend the length of the spiral. The foot of one channel is the oval window where the stapes imparts pressure to the cochlear fluid, called *perilymph.*

The basilar membrane and associated structures are the parts of the inner ear which function to transform the imparted mechanical energies into the neural energies of the *auditory nerve.* The basilar membrane is about 0.04 mm wide at the stapes, broadening to about 0.5 mm as it spirals inward. Several thousand *hair cells* rest on the basilar membrane. Collectively comprising the *organ of Corti,* these cells are connected to the fibers of the auditory nerve. It is their stimulation that is the final mechanical step in the functioning of the inner ear.

Research Techniques

The multidimensional nature of physical stimuli for hearing and the anatomical and functional complexities of the ear place numerous technical demands on quantitative auditory experimentation. Hirsh (1966) has dealt with some of the major problems of measurement and methodology which are posed. His block diagrams of apparatus suggest the role played in auditory research by electronic equipment. It demands accurate calibration and appropriate linking of components for good laboratory work. We can deal only briefly here with selected topics in the instrumentation of investigations in audition.

Stimulus presentation

Experimenters sometimes use tape-recorded musical selections or samples of speech in studies of auditory perception. For more basic sensory investigations they employ simpler stimuli such as pure tones or brief clicks. These controlled inputs make it possible to observe and infer more about the mechanisms of hearing than complex stimulation would. Tones of moderately complex waveforms may be specially generated for particular purposes. Another type of stimulus used frequently is *white noise*. Named for its analogy of white light, this is a random mixture of many frequencies. It is heard as a hissing or roaring sound.

Special electronic devices generate the sounds needed for research. For example, the *beat frequency oscillator* produces the sinusoidal waves that are heard as pure tones. They are controllable as to amplitude and frequency. While the oscillator has some amplification and attenuation, it is common to use additional amplifiers and attenuators to achieve desired intensity levels. Transmission of clicks, tones, noise, music, or speech is accomplished directly through the air from a loudspeaker or through earphones which are generally cushioned to occlude unwanted sounds. Prevention of extraneous stimulation also demands sound-conditioned laboratory rooms or anechoic (sound-absorbent) chambers.

Testing the hearing of subjects—in research as well as in clinical examination—can be done with a standard *audiometer*. Such an instrument presents attenuated tones at sampled frequency values so that a plot of threshold values termed an *audiogram* may be obtained. A modified method of limits with slowly changing test frequencies is used in the audiometer devised by Békésy (1947) whose creative research on cochlear functioning and psychoacoustics won the Nobel prize in medicine.

Measuring sound intensity

The pressure developed in a sound wave leads to an index of the sound intensity. Of course the average pressure in a complete sound wave will simply equal the air pressure of the undisturbed air. Instead of a mean value, we use the standard deviation around this average of the instantaneous pressures in the wave. In a hypothetical calculation we take each pressure value in the wave, square it, add all the squared values, divide by the number of values, and finally extract the square root of this sum of squares. We have been following the statistical formula for calculating the standard deviation. In engineering this statistic is called the *root mean square*, abbreviated *rms*. It is rms pressure, then, which is used in specifying sound pressure level, SPL. The physical unit of pressure measurement applied to SPL is the dyne per square centimeter. (This is roughly equivalent to the microbar of atmospheric pressure.) SPL values are typically not expressed directly in dynes/cm² but are converted to a logarithmic expression of a ratio between the designated SPL and a reference level. The reference level conventionally used is 0.0002 dyne/cm² which approximates the SPL of the absolute threshold of hearing for a 1000-Hz tone. The formula for this relative expression of sound intensity is:

$$dB_x = 20 \log_{10} \frac{SPL_x}{SPL_{ref}} \qquad\qquad \text{Formula 8.1}$$

where dB_x is the intensity expressed in decibels, SPL_x is the rms pressure of the sound being measured and SPL_{ref} is the reference sound pressure. This reference level should always be specified where decibel values are cited. If not given in a report, it may be assumed to be the conventional 0.0002 dyne/cm².

With reference to this conventional reference pressure some representative sounds are found to have the dB values indicated below:

Sound	Decibel Value
Pneumatic drill	125 dB
City traffic	90 dB
Conversation	60 dB
Quiet whisper	20 dB

The measurement of such environmental sound levels as well as those in some laboratory situations is often accomplished through the use of a *sound-level meter* scaled directly in decibels. Other laboratory work may require microphonic pick-up of sound intensity in the ear canal itself. A different approach to intensity measurement works with the voltages found at different points in the circuitry of sound generating and amplifying equipment. These are converted to decibel values through established conversion tables or graphs.

Specifying frequency and waveform

An investigator also relies heavily on calibrated instruments in determining and controlling the frequencies and waveforms of tones used as stimuli. A direct-reading *frequency meter* may be used; a *cathode ray oscilloscope* can aid in determining tonal frequency as well as providing a visual display of the waveform. For the frequency characteristics of voices, a *sound spectrograph* can be used in analytic work. The cited chapter by Hirsch deals with such laboratory instrumentation as well as with auditory research in general.

Dimensions of Hearing

As a sensory experience hearing has certain dimensions which correspond to different aspects of physical stimuli. Some attributes of hearing correspond quite closely to particular aspects of sound waves, whereas others seem more dependent upon interactions of different physical characteristics of the stimulus.

Correlates of intensity, frequency, and waveform

These physical dimensions of sound tend to give rise to particular attributes of auditory experience, although we shall see that the simple relating of one psychological dimension to one physical characteristic is not possible. We begin, however, by reviewing the relationship of each aspect of hearing to its principal physical determinant.

Loudness is a psychological attribute of every kind of experienced sound, whether pure tone, musical note, speech, or noise. Its principal determinant is the physical intensity or sound pressure level of the stimulus. It is mediated by the amount of physical displacement of the moving portions of the ear. The greater this physical movement, the more fibers of the auditory nerve that are activated. The vigor of the action initiated by sound waves is also represented in the rate at which the nerve fibers initiate neural impulses.

Pitch is the sensory aspect of tonal sounds which is determined principally by the frequency of the sound waves. Low pitched tones result from low frequency stimulation and high pitch is experienced when vibration frequency is high. The mediation of low pitch is generally believed to occur through the firing of volleys of nerve impulses in synchrony with the frequency of physical stimulation. For high pitch the mechanism is thought to be the occurrence of maximum stimulation at particular points along the length of the basilar membrane, each region corresponding to particular degrees of pitch.

A qualitative dimension of auditory sensation is *timbre*, that characteristic by which we distinguish the voice from a violin, and perhaps one violin from another, even though each one is sounding a note of the same intensity and frequency. Timbre, sometimes termed *quality*, is dependent on the waveform of the sound waves.

Interaction of intensity and frequency

Although we were quite correct in identifying intensity as the principal determinant of loudness, and frequency as the chief determinant of pitch, careful scaling of these two attributes of sensory experience shows that they are dependent on an interaction of the two physical dimensions of sound. When an 8000-Hz pure tone is raised about 40 dB in intensity, for example, it will be heard as becoming considerably higher in pitch. The change in this sensory attribute is so great as to require a decrease of about 14 percent in frequency if the tone is to seem of the same pitch when it is so intensified. Pure tones that are low in pitch seem to become lower when they are intensified. Tones between 2000 and 3000 Hz do not change much in pitch when they become louder.

Loudness, principally dependent on sound intensity, changes quite markedly with changes in frequency. Tones between 1000 and 5000 Hz may be considered as sounding loudest for a given physical intensity level. An intensity level that makes a 100-Hz tone barely audible, for example, will be about 40 dB above threshold for a 2000–Hz tone.

Other auditory attributes

Auditory phenomenology has a long history of naming tonal attributes in addition to loudness and pitch. Two such aspects of hearing which survived the test of psychophysical investigation are *volume* and *density*. Volume, as a technical term in audition, should not be confused with intensity or loudness to which we refer when we speak of the "volume control" on a radio. As a dimension of auditory experience, volume is defined as the bigness or space-filling quality of a tone. Density is the experienced degree of concentration of a tone. Both of these dimensions of auditory experience were found by Stevens (1934) to depend strongly on interaction between intensity and frequency of the test tones. In comparison with a standard tone, if a test tone of the same intensity was increased in frequency, its volume was lessened while its density was increased. Intensity and frequency contribute more equally to these qualities of hearing than they do to loudness (primarily dependent on intensity) and to pitch (primarily dependent on frequency). In experimental scaling of narrow bands of noise, Stevens, Guirao, and Slawson (1965) found that loudness is proportional to the product of volume and density.

Limits of Hearing

Not all disturbances of the air which would seem to qualify as sound waves actually arouse tonal experience. Both major dimensions of vibration, intensity and frequency, have absolute thresholds in hearing. As in other senses, too, there are differential thresholds. In audition there are limits to our discriminatory abilities for both loudness and pitch.

Absolute thresholds

One absolute threshold or *limen* is reached when intensity level or sound pressure level becomes too weak to activate the receptor sufficiently to arouse any sensation. An important fact about the intensive threshold is that it varies with the frequency of the test stimulus. From about 1500 to about 4000 Hz the threshold is at or near a minimum physical intensity which may be conveniently considered to be a sound pressure level of 0.0002 dyne/cm². The dependence of the threshold on frequency is illustrated by the fact that with a test tone of 10,000 Hz, the absolute threshold is found to be around 15 dB higher than the reference level of 0.0002 dyne/cm². For a tone of 100 Hz, the threshold is almost 40 dB higher than this reference value. A plot of the absolute intensive threshold as a function of frequency, then, yields a U-shaped curve that is higher at the low-frequency end than at the high-frequency end, with minimal values reached around 2500 Hz.

Measurement of intensive thresholds may show slight effects of practice and motivation level of subjects. For example, Swets and Sewall (1963) used a brief 1000-Hz tone heard against a white noise background of approximately 50 dB re 0.0002 dyne/cm². Detection of the signal was found to improve slightly from Day I to Day II when 500 trials per day were experienced at a relatively low level of motivation. Later in the experiment, increasing the level of motivation in two steps was found to improve signal detection by small amounts. Returning to practice effect, it may be noted that Zwislocki, Maire, Feldman, and Rubin (1958) found a 100-Hz tone to show greater practice effects in threshold determination than did a tone of 1000-Hz.

Frequency of vibration also affects hearing limits. When frequency drops below about 20 Hz, tonality disappears from auditory experience giving way to a variety of repetitive auditory sensations instead of a single sound. When frequency exceeds 16,000 or 18,000 Hz a tone is also no longer heard, the ear being effectively unresponsive to such high rates of vibration.

An upper auditory threshold is considered to exist at the point where sound intensity becomes so great that audition gives way to a variety of tactile sensations in the ear, usually somewhat unpleasant. This limit, not varying as much as the absolute limen with vibration frequency, is reached at from 120 to 150 dB above the reference pressure level of 0.0002 dyne/cm^2.

Differential thresholds

We have seen that there are absolute limits of audibility that depend on both the intensity and the frequency of the test tone. There are also limits on the ability of the ear to discriminate between tones that differ only slightly in intensity or frequency. Psychophysical studies have shown that discrimination of *loudness*, like absolute sensitivity to tones, is best from frequencies between 1000 and 3000 Hz. Tones in this frequency range are distinguishable if they differ by 1or 2 dB, provided their absolute intensity is 20 dB or more above threshold. If they are only about 5 dB above the absolute limen, a difference of about 3 dB is needed to discriminate loudnesses in this frequency range. For tones of higher or lower frequency, intensity differences have to be somewhat greater to be detectable. Differential thresholds, like absolute thresholds for intensity, thus depend on the frequency of the test tone.

The differential threshold or limen for the discrimination of *pitch* also varies with intensity and with the frequency of the standard tone used in testing. Pitch discrimination is best for tones below 1000 Hz. For these lower tones a difference of about 5 Hz is usually detectable when intensity is fairly low and at higher intensities the just noticeable difference drops to about 3 Hz. For tones above 2000 Hz, the just noticeable difference tends to be a roughly constant proportion of the standard frequency used in the test. At about 10 dB above threshold, a frequency difference of about a half of 1 percent is required for discrimination. With intensity raised to 40 dB above threshold, a frequency difference of about a fourth of 1 percent is detectable when the frequencies being compared are above 2000 Hz. Campbell and Small (1963) found that frequency discrimination improves somewhat with practice.

Auditory Phenomena

Hearing includes many experiences besides the sensing of tones with simple attributes like loudness, pitch, and timbre. A few of these auditory effects may be briefly considered before we review research on special topics in audition.

Temporary threshold shift (TTS)

As it undergoes stimulation the ear loses sensitivity which it gradually regains when the stimulation has ceased. Such decreases in hearing acuity are referred to as *temporary threshold shift* (TTS) since an elevation in threshold for test tones is found when the phenomenon is measured in the laboratory. The accumulated data subdivide the threshold elevation and the recovery of sensitivity into short-term TTS, intermediate TTS, and long-term TTS. Short-term effects after low intensity levels of stimulation last only around a fraction of a second. Such elevations of threshold, probed with brief test tones or clicks, are greater after stronger or longer lasting stimulation. When moderate stimulation intensities are used, for example, 40 to 70 dB SPL, the resultant TTS is intermediate in duration—lasting somewhere between a second and one or two minutes. One finding is that tonal stimulation produces the greatest TTS for tones of the same frequency. Long-term TTS, lasting up to a day or more, is produced by intense stimulation. Pure tones tend to cause a greater TTS for their frequencies than do noise bands at the same pitch.

Combination tones

When two pure tones of different frequencies are sounded together, certain auditory phenomena arise on the basis of the response characteristics of the ear. The nonlinearity of response, failure to follow the stimulus pattern with complete accuracy, gives rise to *combination tones*. The frequency of various combination tones derives from the addition and subtraction of the frequencies of the two stimulus tones.

Let us suppose that two intense pure tones are sounded, one of 800 Hz and one of 100 Hz. We find that in listening to this combination we may be able to hear a *summation tone*, so-called because its frequency, 900 Hz, is the sum of the frequencies of the two tones. A second-order summation tone would have a frequency of 1000 Hz, stemming from a summation of the 800-Hz frequency and twice the frequency of the 100-Hz tone. There are also summation tones like 1700 Hz and 1800 Hz, involving twice the frequency of the 800-Hz tone plus some multiple of the 100-Hz tone. Although some of the summation tones are detectable by a listener, the existence of others can be demonstrated only by special experimental techniques.

Analogous to the creating of summation tones by summing various combinations of the stimulus frequencies is the creation of *difference tones* whose frequencies may be calculated by subtraction. For example, the 800-Hz and the 100-Hz stimulus tones would give a difference tone of 700 Hz. To compute the frequencies of other difference tones we might double the frequency of either component before substracting. This would lead to 1500 and 600 Hz as second-order difference tones. Again, some difference tones may be heard and others may be detected by special means.

Beats

The simultaneous sounding of two intense pure tones that are not far apart in frequency results in *beats*. Beats are heard as alternate waxing and waning of loudness. For example, if a 256-Hz tone and a 258-Hz tone are presented together, they will arouse an auditory sensation that will be alternately louder and softer twice each second. The periodicity of this loudness cycle is calculated by subtracting one of the component frequencies from the other. Tones of 1004 Hz and 1000 Hz would thus yield 4 beats per second if sounded together. With small frequency differences giving rise to beats and large ones creating difference tones, some intermediate values of frequency difference yield a rough intermittent quality of sound.

Localization and Lateralization

The direction from which sounds reach our ears can be identified with some accuracy under ordinary listening conditions. Auditory cues guide our attention to the sound source. When an external source is perceived, locating it is termed *localization*. If earphones are worn and a sound seems to originate inside the head, locating its apparent left or right point of origin is known as *lateralization*. Both processes have been extensively studied by laboratory investigators.

Monotic, Diotic, and Dichotic Stimulation

In everyday life the same sounds impinge on both ears so that localization of sources is based on binaural reception. Laboratory study of auditory localization and lateralization sometimes requires special manipulation of sound presentation. If a sound is delivered to just one ear, we speak of *monotic* stimulation. Presenting the same stimulus to both ears is *diotic* stimulation. The stimulation is termed *dichotic* when stimuli that differ in one or more respects are applied separately to the two ears. Such special arrangements for stimulation are sometimes used for studying other auditory phenomena such as masking, as we shall see.

Physical Bases for Sound Localization

With normal diotic stimulation from a sound source that is located on one side or the other of the median plane of the head, the cues to localization are differences in the sound that reaches each ear. If a sound source is to the left of the listener, the sound reaching the left ear is slightly more intense than that reaching the right ear. This difference in intensity is due to the partial blocking of sound waves by the head. The intensity difference serves as a cue chiefly for high frequency tones since these are more effectively blocked by the head. Another difference with diotic stimulation is temporal; tones reach the left ear first in our example. If a tone is continuous there is generally a phase difference in its reception by the left and right ears. The results of research indicate that these temporal cues are important for tones below about 2000 Hz. In the case of complex sounds there are higher frequency overtones so that intensive and temporal differences in diotic stimulation both serve as cues for localization. Complex tones, and clicks or brief pulses as well, have been found to be more accurately localizable in space than pure tones. With diotic differences serving as the cues to localization we might expect—and it can be demonstrated—that monotic stimulation leads to markedly inferior localization.

Discrimination of Points in Auditory Space

Although left-right localization can be quite readily achieved on the basis of diotic differences in the intensive or temporal dimensions of the sound that is heard, such cues are not available for discriminating the elevation of sound sources. Discrimination of different locations is particularly poor when the sound source is in the median plane of the head, equidistant from both ears. If the sound is a familiar one it may be localized as coming from in front of us or from in back on the basis of its intensity, the pinnas acting to reduce slightly the loudness of sounds originating in back of our heads. In laboratory studies, with somewhat unfamiliar sounds presented, we sometimes find confusion of the front-back direction when the source is in the median plane. In everyday life we would rarely make such localization errors because of the extra cues that our surroundings give us. When we are seated at our desk studying, the familiar voice of a friend is more likely to be perceived as coming from the doorway behind us than from the wall in front of us.

Localization with Dichotic Stimulation

Presentation of sounds through earphones generally leads to a perception of the stimulation as arising within the head. In dichotic stimulation, a source may be lateralized as on one side of the midline depending on the different cues to the two ears. An experiment was conducted by Jeffress and Taylor (1961) to see if subjects could "localize" a sound source as originating from somewhere out in front of them if time differences in the binaural stimulation were provided to simulate differential arrival times at the two ears. Zero time difference in the dichotic cues was simulative of a sound arising from directly in front of the subject in this study. Origin points at 15, 30, 45, 60, and 75° to the left and right of the median plane were simulated by introducing temporal differences in cueing of 135, 261, 378, 486, and 576 msec, respectively.

For his testing and training, a subject experienced in psychoacoustic research sat facing a horizontal semicircle of small lamps about 6 ft in front of him. Using a rotary switch, he could illuminate any lamp to indicate his perceived localization of the "sound source" on any trial. The experimenter could also flash any lamp to confirm or correct any response in certain series of trials. With his head gently but firmly clamped to prevent movement, the subject heard a series of 2-sec bursts of wide-band noise (100 to 3000 Hz at 60 dB spectral level) as the stimulation to be localized.

Four subjects familiar with psychoacoustic investigations each gave 4 series of 110 localization responses, 10 for each of the 11 "sources" located (simulated) from 75° left to 75° right at 15° angular intervals. Sound sources were simulated in random order. For the first two series, no informative feedback or knowledge of results was given. After Series I, however, the experimenter had the subject listen to 10 training presentations simulating each sound source as the appropriate lamp was flashed. For Series III and IV, confirmatory or corrective feedback was given after each response.

The results of the experiment may be summarized very simply. Subjects given the appropriate dichotic cues tended to "localize" the external "sound source" very easily and naturally. Combining all locations, the mean constant error for the 4 series of trials was $+1.0$, $+2.5$, $+3.0$, and $+1.9$, respectively. Here the $+$ sign indicates a clockwise error tendency. As evident in the 4 successive values no steady improvement with practice was observed although there may be a hint of benefit from feedback in the reduction of error from Series III to IV. According to Jeffress and Taylor the sounds were perceived as generally arising in the head, only occasionally as originating from a lamp position as an external source. The study shows, then, that dichotic cues simulating different source locations can be matched with subjects' "simulated" localizations.

Head Movements in Localization

In most studies of auditory localization the head of the subject is immobilized so that binaural reception of the cues will not be complicated by distance and directional changes. In natural situations, however, for example locating a jet flying overhead, a person may turn his head to use binaural differences to best advantage. The head movements which subjects use in trying to localize sound sources were investigated in a laboratory situation by Thurlow, Mangels, and Runge (1967). They made motion pictures of college students trying to identify the loudspeaker source of 5-sec bursts of 48 dB noise, either high in pitch (at bandpass 7500–8000 Hz) or low (500–100 Hz). The speakers were placed to the left or right, or in front, of the subject as he was seated in an anechoic chamber. They were above and below ear level as well. At the end of each "sh" sound, the subject had to point to its source as he judged it, though these localizations were not actually recorded. The experimenters' interest was in the head movements used in attempting the localization task.

For analysis of the motion picture records, movements of over $3°$ were categorized in three types: rotate, pivot, or tip, as illustrated here. Since some subjects were evidently unable to use head movement in localizing the 5-sec stimuli, the response analysis was limited to 23 subjects. The data, shown in Table 8.1, indicate the percent of these using different movement patterns in attempting the localizations. Rotating and also tipping the head was the commonest pattern used. Rotation

Pivot

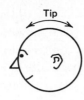

Tip

Rotate

alone was quite common as well. Many subjects were seen to rotate the head from side to side by 10° or more in an effort to identify the sound source. This type of head motion is effective of course in varying the binaural differential in the diotic stimulation reaching the ears. It should thus be beneficial to accurate localization.

Table 8.1 Percent of Subjects Showing Each Pattern of Head Movement in Localization Effort (After Thurlow, Mangels, and Runge, 1967)

	Placement of Loudspeakers	
Movement Pattern	High	Low
Rotate—tip—pivot	36	39
Rotate—tip	63	70
Rotate—pivot	19	22
Tip—pivot	6	4
Rotate	41	49
Tip	15	13
Pivot	5	3

Masking

Interference with the hearing of a sound due to another sound which stimulates the same ear is called *masking*. We commonly contend with auditory masking when we have difficulty hearing in a noisy environment. If we are trying to make ourselves heard in such a situation, we raise the intensity of our voice so that our speech sounds will exceed the masking threshold of our hearers. This common experience parallels the laboratory measurement of masking. An investigator determines the amount by which he must intensify a test sound in order to make it audible to a subject who is also experiencing a masking tone or noise. Among the common findings in studies of masking we may cite one related to the intensity of the mask tone and one based on its frequency. As we might expect, a more intense mask (or masking) tone or noise will cause a greater elevation in the threshold of the masked stimulus. A mask tone of a particular frequency is most effective in masking tones of similar frequencies. However, test tones of nearly identical frequency will not show a peak elevation of threshold since the test tone and the mask tone will produce beats which enhance the detectability of the test stimulus.

Temporal Course of Masking

The masking of a brief click stimulus by noise lasting a fraction of a second was investigated by Osman and Raab (1963). Their research was particularly aimed at investigating the masking effect on the detection of a click which preceded the onset or followed the offset of the mask noise. Their test click of 0.1 msec duration was introduced at intervals from 50 msec before the onset of the noise to 10 msec after its cessation. This permitted the plotting of the temporal course of threshold elevation. A parameter of the study was the intensity of the masking noise, 60, 75, 85, or 95 dB SPL. The noise was band-limited to 100–7000 Hz and was gated in its presentation to create a burst with sharp onset and offset.

Using themselves as experimental subjects, the investigators carried out right-ear testing using a forced-choice version of the psychophysical method of limits. Two noise bursts were presented on each trial and the subject had to say whether the first or the second had been accompanied by the click. The click was raised in intensity until chance level scores gave way to an indication of the intensity threshold for hearing the click despite the noise interference. The elevated threshold values were plotted as a function of Δt, the interval from the onset of the mask noise to the presentation of the click.* Of course Δt was a negative value when the click preceded the noise onset. The results of the testing of one subject using a masking noise of 100 msec duration are shown in the family of curves of Figure 8.3.

There are four segments in the temporal course of these masking

---

*This interval, Δt, corresponds to the stimulus-onset asynchrony, SOA, in visual masking research (p. 218).

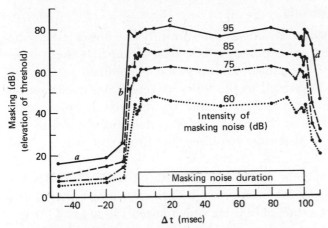

Fig. 8.3. The amount of masking (elevation of threshold) for the detection of a click as test stimulus as dependent upon its temporal relationship to a 100-msec masking noise. These masking functions for an individual subject are discussed in the text. (After Osman and Raab, 1963.)

data which are of interest, lettered *a*, *b*, *c*, and *d* in the figure. The portion of the curve marked *a* indicates that there is a slight, slowly rising elevation in threshold during the period from about 50 to about 10 msec before the onset of the masking noise. In the final 10 msec before the noise, segment *b* of the curves shows a great rise in threshold for the click to about the same level which prevails during the noise, shown in segment *c* of the curves. Segments *a* and *b* represent backward masking. This does not refer to a backward action of the masking noise in time, but indicates that a slightly preceding click is masked when the two stimuli interact during the processing of the stimulation by the auditory system. Segment *d* shows that the threshold shift persists after the cessation of the masking noise. It rapidly approaches normal sensitivity again, the curves suggesting negative acceleration in recovery. These curves for the temporal course of auditory masking also portray the very general fact mentioned earlier, that more intense masking stimulation produces greater threshold shift for the masked stimulus. The 95-dB noise raised the threshold for the click much more than did the 60-dB noise, the other noise levels falling into intermediate places in their masking effects.

Other-Ear Effect on Masking

Ordinarily a masking stimulus and a test stimulus are presented to the same ear in masking research. In fact, it has been found that there is almost no masking effect when the masking sound is confined to one ear and the test stimulus is presented to the other. A remaining combination of stimulation is to test for masking in the regular way by presenting masking and test stimulus to one ear while also delivering noise to the other ear. This was the situation explored by Blodgett, Jeffress, and Whitworth (1962).

While presenting one ear with a steady masking noise of 41 dB per cycle re 0.0002 microbar (approximately 58 dB effective level), they tested its threshold for hearing a tone of 500 Hz which lasted 150 msec. This test tone was varied at 2 dB intervals to find a 50 percent threshold. The experimental treatments consisted of using noise in the opposite ear at several levels ranging from 22 to 62 dB re 0.0002 microbar, with an "off" condition used also in which this other-ear stimulation was not employed. The outcome of this study is shown in Figure 8.4.

Plotted in Figure 8.4 are mean masked threshold values for the test tone rather than elevations in the threshold as in Figure 8.3. Each data point is based on 200 judgments made by each of 3 subjects experienced in psychoacoustical work. As the graph shows, it was found that the thresh-

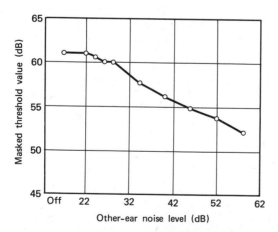

Fig. 8.4. Stimulus threshold for a 500-Hz tone of 150 msec duration as a function of effective noise level presented to the other ear. (After Blodgett, Jeffress, and Whitworth, 1962.)

old for a masked tone actually is lowered when a noise of some intensity is introduced into the other ear. Further, the more intense this other-ear stimulation, the greater its reduction of the masking effect at the tested ear.

Recognition of Timbre

Different musical instruments are characterized by their own tonal quality or timbre even when played at the same frequency and intensity. Identification of a musical instrument by its tone is not a simple process. Besides the differences in waveform they produce, different instruments may vary in formants, transients, and vibrato—depending on their construction and the style of play. Some musical instruments may be harder to recognize than others, particularly under the reduced-cue conditions which are often a part of psychological research. Two studies reported in the same year used similar yet contrasting methods of investigation. Results were generally in agreement despite the different methods of obtaining and reporting the data.

Multivariate Experimentation

A complex experimental design used by Saldanha and Corso (1964) included such variables as musical instruments played, tonal frequencies, style of play, and repeated testing. Experienced musicians recorded test tones of 9 sec duration, playing either with or without a vibrato. The tonal frequencies were 261.1, 349.2, and 440 Hz corresponding, respectively, to the musical notes C_4, F_4, and A_4. The instruments recorded were the bassoon, cello, clarinet, flute, French horn, oboe, saxophone, trombone, trumpet, and violin. Twenty college student musicians served as subjects in trying to identify the instrument used for each test tone.

Each experimental variable was found to have a significant effect when percent of correct recognition was examined. For example, correct judgments increased from 36.5 percent for the first testing session to 41.9 percent for the second. The instruments were found to differ widely in their recognizability under the restricted stimulus presentation. Combining across conditions the percent of correct identifications of the different instruments were as follows: clarinet, 84; oboe, 75; flute, 61; French horn, 46; saxophone, 35; trumpet, 29; trombone, 23; violin, 19; cello, 9; bassoon, 9.

Stimulus Alterations

In an analytic effort to determine which cues were more important in recognizing instruments, Berger (1964) used several alterations of the tape-recorded sample note. This basic stimulus was a concert F_4 on the treble staff with a frequency of about 349 Hz. A number of experienced instrumentalists from the Southern Illinois University Band made recordings of this note at an intensity level of 80 dB re 0.0002 dyne/cm^2 with a duration of 5 sec. The experimenter used these stimuli in an unaltered fashion as Condition 1 of his experiment. The stimuli for Condition 2 were created by deleting the first and last half seconds of the recorded tones, eliminating the attack and decay which characterize the sounding of a musical note. Condition 3 was obtained by playing the tape-recorded notes backwards. Condition 4 was created by using a 480-Hz low-pass filter to eliminate the partial overtones, leaving only the fundamental frequency of the tone. Instruments used in this study were the alto saxophone, baritone, B-flat clarinet, cornet, flute, French horn, oboe, tenor saxophone, trombone, and trumpet.

The percent of exact identifications made by 30 band students was 59 percent for Condition 1 with the stimulus notes unchanged. For Conditions 2, 3, and 4, the reduced cues lowered the identification levels to 35, 42, and 18 percent, respectively. The drastic reduction in recognizability under Condition 4 is understandable when we realize that the filtering of the tones cut out their characteristic waveforms and converted them nearly to pure tones without any timbre to be recognized. The score attained was hardly above a chance level. The exact identification results we have considered may be supplemented by other data given by Berger. When responses were tabulated within instrument groups such as brasses and woodwinds, the percent of "group" recognitions was much higher in all conditions, approaching 90 percent for Condition 1 and exceeding 60 percent even for Condition 4.

Perception of Speech

Besides serving us esthetically as we listen to music, our sense of hearing functions as the receiver in speech communication. Although most of our use of speech involves the speaker and the hearer in a face-to-face situation, important segments of our use of spoken words involve devices like public address systems, telephones, television, and radio—as used in general broadcasting and in special communication networks.

Speech Perception Under Distortion and Noise

As sound, speech is characterized by great complexity. Physical analysis of even elementary units like phonemes reveals a succession of changes in sound pressure patterns. The sound changes that rapidly succeed each other as we speak involve different amplitudes, frequencies, timbres, and durations. This complexity does not make speech perception more difficult but makes it easier instead. The fundamental dimensions of pure tones, amplitude and frequency, do not play major roles in making speech intelligible. They can greatly be interfered with while speech perception remains high.

Three ways of interfering with speech are amplitude peak-clipping, interruption, and masking with noise. The hearing of speech has been found quite resistant to masking by noise. The noise level must be raised quite high to reduce transmission scores. In other words, the signal-to-noise ratio, abbreviated S/N, may fall quite low before intelligibility is greatly reduced. Speech is also resistant to the effects of periodic or aperiodic interruption. As much as 50 percent of a message can be "chopped out" without reducing the transmission of the message by more than 10 percent, provided the intermittency of sound and silence is at a high rate like ten times per second. Many audio communication devices distort speech by clipping its amplitude peaks, since the power is not available for faithful following of the sound waves through these peaks. Later in the system amplification may boost power again but, of course, the sound wave will have had its form changed in the peak-clipping part of the system. Research has shown that peak clipping can be quite severe with out materially reducing speech intelligibility.

The Articulation Test

An *articulation* test assesses the effectiveness of a speech communication system by measuring the intelligibility of the spoken messages that are transmitted. The people who do the talking and listening, as well as the electrical and mechanical devices, are considered as factors in experimental work. The articulation score is the percent of the spoken material that is correctly reported by the listener. A great number of variables can affect scores attained in such a situation.

The person who speaks may be considered to be a source of variables in an articulation test, and the material he is required to deliver is a contributing factor of several dimensions also. The equipment used in the speech transmission can influence the sound patterns of the message in numerous ways. The listeners, too, may vary in their speech perception abilities. Speakers and listeners selected for articulation tests might simply be persons who were free from defects of speech and hearing. Poor qualities of voice, aside from outright defects, might be sufficient reason for not using some speakers. Auditory tests might be employed to screen listeners. The selection and training of personnel for their tasks are obviously part of such research requiring careful consideration.

The material comprising the "messages" in speech communication research can importantly affect test results. If the listener hears parts of words he may reconstruct the message that was transmitted. If we merely use the digits from one to nine, we find that most of them can be distinguished on the basis of the vowel sound alone. Thus, hearers might frequently miss the consonant sounds but still make high scores. Nonsense syllables are sometimes the material of choice because each *phoneme,* each vowel or consonant sound, must be heard if the item is to be correctly recorded.

The importance of the kind of spoken material used in articulation tests is illustrated in the data from an experiment by Miller, Heise, and Lichten (1951). A microphone-amplifier-earphones system was used to deliver the test messages from speaker to listener at an intensity of about 90 dB re 0.0002 dyne/cm². Also introduced into the earphones was a variable level of noise. By using the intensity of the message signals as a reference, the various values of the S/N were expressed in decibels, ranging from -18 with noise at the maximum value employed to $+18$ with noise at the minimal level used in the study. With type of material as a parameter, functional relationships between the percent of items correctly recorded and the S/N were determined. These curves, for digits, words in sentences, and nonsense syllables, are shown in Figure 8.5. In looking at the figure, remember that it is the S/N that is plotted on the abscissa. With the message signal intensity held constant, the noise level decreases as we proceed from left to right along this scale. As expected, the percent of items recorded goes up as this decrease in noise occurs. We see that the three plotted functions in Figure 8.5 differ markedly, indicating that the intelligibility of speech in the presence of masking

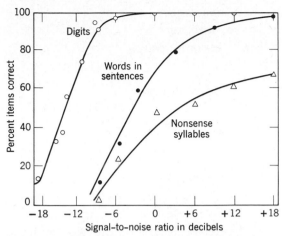

Fig. 8.5. Percent of items correctly identified in articulation tests as a function of signal-to-noise ratio with type of test material as the parameter differentiating the curves. (After Miller, Heise, and Lichten, 1951.)

noise varies with the different types of material used in the articulation test.

Word Frequency and Intelligibility

In an experiment that was unusual for its using two modern languages as sources of stimulus words, Rosenzweig and Postman (1957) determined how the auditory perception of words was affected by their frequency of occurrence in the language. Grouped by frequency level, the English and French words listed here were used in testing 87 American students and 60 French students, respectively.

Low-Frequency   English words: flange, prism, dram, larch, thrall, tithe, cull, hoot
French words: guidon, hernie, notice, pliant

Low-Moderate   English words: cud, jab, foe, pelt, pew, gem, hash
French words: visage, bouton, cabine, niveau

Moderate	English words: cheat, ridge, rouse, lump, apt, barn, curve, bean, ray
	French words: besoin, malade, dedans, argent
Moderate-High	English words: age, price, chair, reach, walk, next, find, put
	French words: enfant, jamais, petite, moment

To measure the intelligibility of the words, they were tape recorded in several random sequences. Each word was introduced by the carrier phrase, "You will write. . . ." Both this phrase and the test words were masked by white noise. While the intensity level of the test material was held constant, the noise level was decreased on successive trials to obtain an increasing likelihood of word recognition as trials continued. The final trial presented a recording of the test words in the carrier phrase without any interfering noise. The intelligibility score was taken as the mean number of trials to achieve recognition. Therefore the better the intelligibility of any group of words, the lower the mean score. Since 7 trials were given, under decreasing masking noise, a score of 8 was assigned arbitrarily if a word was never recognized by a subject.

The intelligibility of the words of both languages was found to increase (fewer trials to recognition) as a function of their frequency of occurrence. Mean intelligibility scores are presented in Table 8.2 for the four frequency levels for each language. The statistically significant relationship between word frequency and auditory intelligibility over noise

Table 8.2 Mean Intelligibility Scores for the Four Frequency-of-Usage Levels (After Rosenzweig and Postman, 1957)

Test Stimuli	Frequency-of-Usage Levels			
	Low	Low-Moderate	Moderate	Moderate-High
English words	6.87	6.10	4.14	4.08
French words	6.72	6.16	5.22	5.48

yielded correlations of about .70 which is in general agreement with similar studies. This finding must be given due consideration when words are selected for inclusion in articulation tests.

Speeded Speech

Tape-recorded speech can be accelerated or compressed in time so as to shorten communication time. A question naturally arises as to whether such speeded speech remains intelligible and comprehensible. This is a significant challenge to investigators since accelerated speech has at least three major potential utilities—communication with the blind at a rate which compares with visual reading, information transmission in general educational efforts, study of problems of auditory speech perception. Foulke and Sticht (1969) reviewed and discussed the methods and findings which have emerged from laboratory experimentation. Their treatment offers several points for our briefer consideration of accelerated speech.

Three basic methods of achieving time-compressed speech yield quite different stimulus material. The simplest technique is merely to have a speaker accelerate his speech or oral reading in making a recording. Only a moderate increase in speed can be attained without substantial changes in speech characteristics such as phoneme sounds, inflection, and even intensity. A second way of compressing message time is using a higher rate in playback of speech which was recorded at a lower rate. Here the difficulty is that the frequencies of all the vocal tones are elevated in proportion to the speed-up. Vocal pitch is raised by one octave, for example, when playback speed is twice the recording speed. Since the method has a practical simplicity in view of the availability of multiple-speed tape recorders, it has been used in a number of experiments. A third method of accelerating tape-recorded speech is to "cut out" many brief portions, abutting the remaining segments to form a continuous message. The deleting of sections of the original recording may be done by cutting and splicing the experimental tape and then duplicating it, or by using special apparatus for transformation to time-compressed speech of this sort. The deletions may be random or selective on the basis of sampling rules which may be computerized. The deletions in any case are typically very frequent and very brief; for example 10 deletions per second, each of 50 msec duration, might be used to achieve a doubling of the speed of message transmission. When Garvey (1953) accelerated speed by this sampling method, intelligibility was maintained at above 90 percent for rates up to 2.5 times that of the original speech. In contrast, merely increasing playback speed to 2 times the recording speed led to a drop in intelligibility to around 65 percent. A number of experiments which used articulation tests and other methods of assessing intelligibility were reviewed by Foulke and Sticht.

Also to be considered is the effect of compressed speech on comprehension, typically measured by administering an objective test covering the content of a passage presented to listeners. With a normal oral reading rate found to be around 175 *wpm* (words per minute), Foulke and Sticht report on some of their own research testing the comprehension of accelerated speech using the deleted-segment method of compression. Only slight reduction in comprehension is found in speeding the message up to 275 wpm. However, comprehension deteriorates as transmission rates higher than this are tested. These investigators found a 6 percent loss in comprehension in comparing 325 wpm with 225 wpm and 14 percent more loss when the rate went up to 425 wpm.

Variables which affect comprehension of accelerated speech include the material presented and the characteristics of the listeners themselves. Among the individual factors for which positive findings have emerged, two or three cited by Foulke and Sticht may be mentioned. Comprehension of compressed material increased with the age and grade level of school children in two different studies. Two other experiments found a positive correlation between individuals' comprehension scores and their reading rates. Faster readers are better able to comprehend faster compressed speech. Finally, comprehension has been found to improve during initial experience with the unfamiliar task of listening to speeded speech. However, more extended efforts to achieve comprehension improvement have not been notably successful. It appears that more research is needed on the perceptual and cognitive aspects of speech perception and comprehension if successful training methods are to be devised.

Summary

Numerous facts about human hearing have emerged from psychophysical investigations. Basic foundations for our knowledge of audition exist also in the physics of sound and the anatomy of the ear. The external stimuli for hearing are sound waves. Their pressure levels, frequencies, and waveforms give rise to key aspects of auditory experience: loudness, pitch, and timbre. A partial understanding of how this occurs is to be found in a study of the ear, particularly the tympanic membrane, the ossicles of the middle ear, and the basilar membrane with associated cochlear structures. Auditory functioning is studied by means of a variety of stimuli: pure tones, clicks, complex tones, and noise.

The amplitude or intensity of a sound is measured by comparing its pressure level with that of some reference pressure level, often 0.0002 dyne/cm^2. Since such pressure ratios may become very great, a logarithmic scale of bels or decibels is employed.

Although loudness is primarily dependent upon intensity or sound pressure level, it depends to a lesser degree on frequency. Pitch, dependent primarily on frequency, is also affected by the sound intensity. Timbre is a third quality of many tones. Psychophysical studies have shown the existence of two other attributes of auditory sensation, volume and density.

There are absolute limits to hearing, found at both high and low extremes of intensity and at high and low frequencies of sound vibration. Sensation disappears when intensity is too low or frequency becomes very high. When intensity gets very great, hearing gives way to painful sensations in the ear. When frequency gets too low, tonality disappears. Besides these absolute thresholds, hearing has its differential thresholds, quite thoroughly investigated for loudness and pitch. Difference limens for these two attributes vary with both frequency and intensity.

A number of auditory phenomena must be taken into account in planning experiments on hearing. Among those which have been studied quantitatively are temporary threshold shift, combination tones, and beats. Sometimes these processes pose problems for designing simple investigations. On the other hand, they may be used as tools for exploring the domain of hearing.

Problems in audition which have been examined with varied experimental techniques are sound localization and lateralization. The auditory cues that normally permit our localizing of a sound source are binaural. In research, however, diotic stimulation has been augmented by monotic and and dichotic stimulation to aid in delineating the localization process. In dichotic stimulation the binaural differences in intensity and phase are sometimes simulated to elicit a localization response. An illustrative experiment demonstrated this approach in auditory research.

In another study the role of head movements in localizing sound sources was studied.

The masking of one sound by another has been repeatedly studied by investigators of audition. The elevation of the detection threshold for the test stimulus, as brought about by the masking noise, was traced over time in one experiment we reviewed. In another, a laboratory study revealed that a masking effect in one ear is actually lessened when a noise is introduced into the other ear.

Illustrative experiments on auditory perception of musical tones and of human speech concluded this chapter. Two of the studies that were briefly compared and contrasted were carried out with experienced musicians providing recordings of tones to be judged later by subjects. Recognition of the various instruments was found to depend on a variety of factors. For studies of speech perception the articulation test is widely used. It permits quantified investigation of how distortion, noise, and speeded transmission of speech affect its reception by a hearer. One of our illustrative experiments showed that speech intelligibility has a cognitive aspect; both French and American students showed that their word recognitions varied with the frequencies of usage of the articulation test words.

References

Békésy, G. v. A new audiometer. *Acta Oto-Laryngologica Stockholm*, 1947, 35, 411–422.

Berger, K. W. Some factors in the recognition of timbre. *Journal of the Acoustical Society of America*, 1964, 36, 1888–1891.

Blodgett, H. C., Jeffress, L. A., & Whitworth, R. H. Effect of noise at one ear on the masked threshold for tone at the other. *Journal of the Acoustical Society of America*, 1962, 34, 979–986.

Campbell, R. A., & Small, A. M., Jr. Effect of practice and feedback on frequency discrimination. *Journal of the Acoustical Society of America*, 1963, 35, 1511–1514.

Foulke, E., & Sticht, T. G. Review of research on the intelligibility and comprehension of accelerated speech. *Psychological Bulletin*, 1969, 72, 50–62.

Garvey, W. D. The intelligibility of speeded speech. *Journal of Experimental Psychology*, 1953, 45, 102–108.

Hirsh, I. Audition. In J. B. Sidowski (Ed.), *Experimental methods and instrumentation in psychology*. New York: McGraw-Hill, 1966. Pp. 247–271.

Jeffress, L. A., & Taylor, R. W. Lateralization vs. localization. *Journal of the Acoustical Society of America*, 1961, 33, 482–483.

Miller, G. A., Heise, G. A., & Lichten, W. The intelligibility of speech as a function of the context of test materials. *Journal of Experimental Psychology*, 1951, 41, 329–335.

Osman, E., & Raab, D. H. Temporal masking of clicks by noise bursts. *Journal of the Acoustical Society of America*, 1963, 35, 1939–1941.

Rosenzweig, M. R., & Postman, L. Intelligibility as a function of frequency of usage. *Journal of Experimental Psychology*, 1957, 54, 412–422.

Saldanha, E. L., & Corso, J. F. Timbre cues and the identification of musical instruments. *Journal of the Acoustical Society of America*, 1964, 36, 2021–2026.

Stevens, S. S. The volume and intensity of tones. *American Journal of Psychology*, 1934, 46, 397–408.

Stevens, S. S., Guirao, M., & Slawson, A. W. Loudness, a product of volume times density. *Journal of Experimental Psychology*, 1965, 69, 503–510.

Swets, J. A., & Sewall, S. T. Invariance of signal detectability over stages of practice and levels of motivation. *Journal of Experimental Psychology*, 1963, 66, 120–126.

Thurlow, W. R., Mangels, J. W., & Runge, P. S. Head movements during sound localization. *Journal of the Acoustical Society of America*, 1967, 42, 489–493.

Zwislocki, J., Maire, F., Feldman, A. S., & Rubin, H. On the effect of practice and motivation on the threshold of audibility. *Journal of the Acoustical Society of America*, 1958, 30, 254–262.

chapter 9
Verbal
Behavior

Learning our native language, listening, speaking, reading, and writing are verbal activities that especially mark us as humans. Experimental psychologists were historically rather limited, perhaps self-limiting, in their approaches to this domain. Recent decades have seen a moderate broadening of investigative aims and methods, partly as a result of interactions with scholars of other disciplines such as communication and linguistics. At the same time traditional problems are being studied with ingenious refinements of old methods and with newly invented techniques.

Deferring consideration of memory and problem solving to later chapters, we shall be concerned here with fairly elemental verbal behavior. *Association is a central concept.* It is explored in word association studies; it enters into the scaling of certain verbal attributes such as meaningfulness; and it tends to be used descriptively or analytically in treating the processes of verbal learning. These topics will occupy our attention as experimentalists concerned with the methods and materials for research in verbal behavior. An illustrative sampling of reported results should demonstrate continuing opportunities to design and conduct further experiments.

Word Association

Word association is investigated by presenting a subject with a word (or other stimulus) after directing that he respond as quickly as possible with the first word or words which come to his mind. Studies of word association are conducted by experimental psychologists for two principal reasons. First, these investigations explore the orderly associative processes and structures which evidently underlie a significant part of verbal behavior. Such experimentation has been systematically reviewed in a book by Cramer (1968). Second, research in word association yields normative information about groups of subjects and scaled values descriptive of the verbal items studied. These data guide the selection of verbal materials for other experiments in areas such as verbal learning, memory, and problem solving. Using materials scaled for their associative and semantic characteristics has proved to be effective in permitting more penetrating analyses of performance by human subjects in verbal tasks.

Materials

Associative verbal responses may be elicited by almost any sort of stimuli, for example, abstract shapes presented visually (Vanderplas & Garvin, 1959). Generally, however, stimuli used in word association studies are words or quasi-verbal combinations of letters such as bigrams, trigrams, nonsense syllables, and paralogs. As the designations imply, bigrams and trigrams are configurations of two and three letters. Nonsense syllables are often of trigram format—either CVCs such as BIF, GAJ, and ZOP or CCCs such as DWF, HBL, and XHQ. Paralogs are usually longer items such as NEGLAN or GOJEY.

Nonlexical items such as nonsense syllables have long been favored by experimenters in verbal learning research because such material—lacking real meaning—is less likely than words to introduce unwanted associational influences. Nonsense syllables and paralogs are not devoid of all associative character, however, especially as they resemble or suggest real words. Consequently, investigators into verbal processes now prefer to employ items which have been scaled along certain dimensions—sometimes using word association techniques.

Our mention of nonlexical items as stimuli should not obscure the fact that real words have been presented to subjects in most word association studies. And, of course, real words are given as the responses to be tabulated. A classical list of 100 fairly common words has often been used as stimulus material in word association research. This Kent-Rosanoff list, named for its original users, is presented in Table 9.1

Table 9.1 The 100 Stimulus Words of the Kent-Rosanoff List (After Rosanoff, 1927)

TABLE	SWEET	HIGH	MEMORY	BUTTER
DARK	WHISTLE	WORKING	SHEEP	DOCTOR
MUSIC	WOMAN	SOUR	BATH	LOUD
SICKNESS	COLD	EARTH	COTTAGE	THIEF
MAN	SLOW	TROUBLE	SWIFT	LION
DEEP	WISH	SOLDIER	BLUE	JOY
SOFT	RIVER	CABBAGE	HUNGRY	BED
EATING	WHITE	HARD	PRIEST	HEAVY
MOUNTAIN	BEAUTIFUL	EAGLE	OCEAN	TOBACCO
HOUSE	WINDOW	STOMACH	HEAD	BABY
BLACK	ROUGH	STEM	STOVE	MOON
MUTTON	CITIZEN	LAMP	LONG	SCISSORS
COMFORT	FOOT	DREAM	RELIGION	QUIET
HAND	SPIDER	YELLOW	WHISKEY	GREEN
SHORT	NEEDLE	BREAD	CHILD	SALT
FRUIT	RED	JUSTICE	BITTER	STREET
BUTTERFLY	SLEEP	BOY	HAMMER	KING
SMOOTH	ANGER	LIGHT	THIRSTY	CHEESE
COMMAND	CARPET	HEALTH	CITY	BLOSSOM
CHAIR	GIRL	BIBLE	SQUARE	AFRAID

(Rosanoff, 1927). In a later part of this chapter there are references to a number of normative studies of word association responses. Some of these employed the Kent Rosanoff list, in whole or in part, as the stimulus items. Other investigations have begun with new lists of words as stimuli.

A special kind of stimulus item for eliciting associative responses is the designation of a class or category of items. For example, subjects might be asked to respond with words belonging to the class of things designated by "a type of music" or "a college or university" or "a city." Obviously, some category designations require proper nouns as responses while others do not. Responses obtained from college student subjects when numerous category labels were presented to them have been tabulated. Such normative data are valuable to investigators of verbal processes as well as being research findings in their own right. Again, these studies are indicated later—with illustrative data drawn from their results.

Methods

Relatively standardized methods have evolved for the investigation of word association; variations can be devised to extend their utility as needed. The task requirements and the procedures used to run subjects offer considerable latitude to any experimenter. Of course the designing and conducting of any study will be guided by its purpose, whether testing some hypothesis about associative processes or establishing normative data for a subject population or a sample of stimulus materials.

Table 9.2 illustrates the fourfold classification of procedures which

Table 9.2 Four Subject-Running Procedures Obtained by Requiring Free or Controlled Responses in Discrete or Continued Word Association Tasks

	Free: Unrestricted as to Type of Verbal R	Controlled: Restricted as to Class or Category of R
Discrete: Single Verbal R Required	1. S is instructed to give the first verbal R which the stimulus brings to his mind.	3. S is told to give his single R within a defined class or category.
Continued: Multiple Verbal Rs Required	2. S is asked to continue giving his verbal associations to the stimulus through a specified number or until given a timed termination signal.	4. S is required to give continuing Rs within a designated category as indicated by the stimulus.

may govern response elicitation. Under the free-discrete procedure (arbitrarily designated No. 1 in the table) a subject is instructed to give the first word that comes to mind when each stimulus item is presented. Speed of reaction is stressed. Procedure 2 calls for free-continued association. Responses to the stimulus are given as they come to mind in a sequence which is terminated when a predetermined number or a time limit has been reached. This condition explores a hierarchy of associations elicited from subjects as each stimulus is presented. In Procedure 3 the subject is instructed to limit his single response to a defined class. Under this controlled-discrete classification of responses, for example, subjects might be required to give the opposites of adjectives presented as stimuli, that is, stimulus: *hot*, response: *cold*. Since the responses would presumably be predictable, the investigator might be interested in the speed of response, the reaction time, as compared with reactions in the free-discrete procedure. Procedure 4 probes semantic inner space by requiring controlled-continued responses to be given, often to a category-designation stimulus as mentioned earlier.

Having matched one of the four procedures of Table 9.2 to his experimental purpose, an investigator has some additional decisions to make in planning his investigation. Depending again on his aims, he may need to run subjects individually or in groups. With individually tested subjects the word association responses may be oral or written and reaction times may be obtained if required by the research goals. With subjects run in groups responses are typically written. Reaction times are not easily obtained, but the rate of production of continued responses over time can be measured with satisfactory precision.

Indices of Associative Strength

The stimulus-response behavior that is studied in word association is generally supposed to reveal the strength of association existing between the stimulus word and the response word that is given. Some of the frequency measures that are taken are indices that represent general associative tendencies in the group being studied, whereas other measures refer more specifically to the verbal habits of the individual being tested.

Frequency of common response words

It is usually found that one or more particular words will commonly be given as responses to a stimulus item by several members of any group of subjects in an association test. The simple index of this communality in response tendencies is the proportion of subjects giving each popular response. Besides the occurrence of common responses, it is typical to observe a great variety of words elicited from just one or two subjects each.

Frequencies within response categories

The diversity of individual response words that may be given to a particular stimulus word has led investigators to devise categories for the description of responses. A fourfold classification presented in Woodworth and Schlosberg (1954, p. 52) illustrates such an attempt. It is given here with slight changes in class labels and different examples:

Class 1. Definition

This class would include synonyms, supraordinates, and probably subordinates.
Examples:
To the stimulus AFRAID, a synonym response might be SCARED.
To TABLE, a supraordinate response might be FURNITURE.
To FISH, a subordinate response might be FIN.

Class 2. Completion or predication

Many associations in this class might be of the adjective-noun or the noun-verb sort, expressive of a descriptive or a functional association.
Examples:　WHITE—SNOW
　　　　　　TABLE—EAT
　　　　　　AFRAID—DARK

Class 3. Coordinates and opposites

Similar or contrasting responses are classed together because they have been found to go together in the responses made by particular subjects to a large number of stimulus words. If many coordinates are given by a subject, many opposites are usually given also; if one of these types of response is scarce, the other is likely to be infrequent as well.
Examples:　TABLE—CHAIR
　　　　　　WHITE—BLACK
　　　　　　AFRAID—BRAVE

Class 4. Unique responses

These are less often governed by semantic relations between stimulus and response. Many types of unique response may occur. The associations may stem from the personal experience of the person responding. The responses may be evaluative in relation to the stimulus. Another variety is the so-called *clang* association, with the response tending to echo part of the stimulus sound.
Examples:　TABLE—MABEL (clang)
　　　　　　WHITE—ALMOST (personal)
　　　　　　AFRAID—BAD (evaluative)

The preceding system of classification, like others which have been suggested, is not without its difficulty of application in some instances. However, categorization is useful in describing some word association phenomena.

Reaction time

The response latency between stimulus and response has been considered an index of associative strength just as RT has been taken as a measure of reaction potential in other research. This temporal measurement of the interval from presenting the stimulus word to giving the response word in discrete association can be obtained through the use of voice-activated electrical switches, termed *voice keys*. These are operated as experimenter and subject say the stimulus and response word, respectively. Voice-key reaction times may be affected by extraneous verbalization on the part of a subject, as when he says "uh . . ." before giving the response word itself. This difficulty may be overcome by having the experimenter do all timing with a stop watch. This method, too, has possibilities for error but is satisfactory for some purposes.

Rate of response production

In the method of continued association, the number of items produced in each successive interval is one measure of performance. If oral responses are tape-recorded, such counting of responses may be done when the tape is played back, dividing the verbal production into segments of any desired duration. If subjects are required to write their continued associations, they may be asked at regular intervals to draw a line under the word just written in order to designate the passage of time. With time intervals indicated throughout the verbal production we can plot the response rate for various parts of the task. Total response production in a designated time interval may be considered a special index reflecting the psychological character of the stimulus item. We shall see later in discussing meaningfulness that its index may be defined as the number of associations which an item elicits in a unit of time.

Clustering

If free-continued association is a subject's task, we are likely to observe *clusters* of words in sequence at various points in the performance. Such clusters have to be identified on the basis of independent information about associative values or semantic scaling of the words. Once these facts have been determined, the description of verbal behavior in free association is enhanced by cluster analysis.

Clustering may also occur within a controlled sequence of associations. Within the category assigned for the task there may be subcategories. These may give rise to special clusters in the sequence of word production. Thus, if asked to name scientists, a subject might tend to cluster the names he produced by scientific specialty or by nationality of scientist. When items can be identified as associated with a particular category or subcategory, quantitative indices of clustering many be calculated as explained in Chapter 11, pp. 407–409.

Associative Hierarchies

When a continued word association method is used, the tabulation of a group's responses to a single stimulus word tends to reveal a hierarchy of response probabilities. There is a variation in probability values (p) for the occurrence of different responses and also for the giving of these responses in different ordinal positions in the sequence of associations. Two continued word association studies may be mentioned to indicate this finding. The experimenters employed somewhat different structuring of the task for subjects even though both studies required responses to be written in stimulus booklets.

In their continued task, Bilodeau & Howell (1965) had their subjects write three different responses to each stimulus word which was repeated three times across the booklet page. Andreas (1966) did not limit the number of responses; he allowed subjects one minute to write their continued responses to a stimulus word which was arrayed on a booklet page in two double-spaced columns of 10 repetitions each. Despite procedural differences, the two investigations show moderate agreement in the probabilities of occurrence of various response words to the five stimuli which were common to both studies. The data are presented in Table 9.3. Careful study of the p values will show that the results of the Andreas study were in greater agreement with the Bilodeau and Howell data when tabulation was limited to the first three responses, as one might expect. The informational value of letting subjects go on in a full minute of responding is illustrated in the finding, for example, that "dance" is given to the stimulus MUSIC by 40 percent of subjects even though only 15 percent give it as one of their first three responses. Andreas also determined the median ordinal position of responses, as shown in the final

Table 9.3 Probabilities of Occurrence (p) and Median Ordinal Position (o) of Common Responses to Five Selected Stimulus Words Under Continued Word Association (After Andreas, 1966)

Stimulus	Response	B & H 1 - 3	Andreas 1 - 3	1 - n	Median Ordinal Position
COLOR	red	.53	.47	.63	2.42
	blue	.51	.28	.60	3.80
	black	.20	.21	.41	3.50
	green	.20	.22	.51	4.13
MUSIC	song(s)	.23	.15	.21	1.50
	note(s)	.18	.16	.28	2.40
	sound(s)	.15	.09	.21	3.83
	dance	.07	.15	.40	4.38
RIVER	water	.56	.41	.62	2.20
	stream	.24	.24	.31	1.46
	lake	.17	.13	.18	2.50
	boat	.16	.16	.60	4.45
WATER	wet	.44	.15	.28	2.00
	drink	.41	.40	.65	2.30
	swim	.18	.12	.50	7.17
	river	.04	.22	.44	3.50
WOMAN	man	.47	.35	.44	1.39
	girl	.36	.25	.32	2.00
	wife	.25	.16	.28	3.20
	sex	.21	.32	.53	2.70

column of Table 9.3. Since this index does not correlate significantly with the probabilities of occurrence, it may be regarded as a separate indicant of the hierarchical structure of word association tendencies.

Another fact about word association networks that is illustrated in the table is the nonsymmetrical relation of certain stimulus and response words. The data from both studies show that "water" is a strong associate given in response to RIVER but that "river" is less strongly elicited by WATER. This differential directionality of the *river-water* pair was also found by Duncan (1966) in a task structured as guessing at word associates. It is reflected as well in published norms for discrete word association.

The continued method would seem to be the preferred approach to exploring hierarchies of word association responses. There is danger in using data drawn exclusively from the discrete method to create ordinal relationships artificially. Shapiro (1966) has presented findings that illustrate this. Using the discrete method, this experimenter found, for example, that PAY elicited "money" from 53 percent of the adolescent subjects and MONEY, now a stimulus word, elicited "dollar(s)" from 16 percent. Should this be taken to mean that a "chain of association" links PAY with "dollar(s)"? Evidently not, since no subject gave "dollar(s)"? in response to PAY in the study. This is not to say that such an association does not exist. Rather, our suggestion is that explorations of hierarchies or chains be conducted more directly with the continued method wherever possible.

Stability of Associative Responses

Are the data on word associations reliable? Can they be expected to show consistency when subjects are retested with the same stimulus words being repeated? Putting the question in still another form, are word associations sufficiently stable phenomena for psychological investigation? A number of illustrative studies may be cited to suggest a cautious affirmative answer to these questions.

Using the 100 Kent-Rosanoff stimulus words (Table 9.1) plus 58 others, Brotsky & Linton (1967) used the free-discrete procedure to test college students who were required to write their responses to the stimuli printed in a booklet. Ten weeks later, the same 158 stimulus words were presented again in a different random sequence. The probability of occurrence of an identical response was found to be .32. Identical associates tended to be those of high response frequency or dominance, particularly when given to stimulus words of low frequency of usage.

A much longer interval intervened between testing and retesting in a study conducted by Gekoski & Riegel (1967). They used both free-discrete and controlled-discrete methods in testing University of Michigan students on two occasions a year apart. In the controlled conditions, subjects had to give responses that related in various grammatical and logical ways to the stimuli. Intra-individual stability was indicated in a nearly 30 percent repetition rate for free association. This rate was slightly higher for logical associations and somewhat lower for grammatical relations in the controlled tasks. Group tabulations showed considerably higher tendencies for particular responses to be repeated to the stimuli. As in much of psychological research, group data may be needed to demonstrate principles which may be lost in the lesser reliability of individual performance. The work task imposed on subjects in this study might be questioned. In the test booklet they had to respond to each of the 33 stimulus words 17 times—once in free association and the rest of the times under one control requirement or another. Such repeated encountering of a stimulus and so many changes in response demand may have had unwanted effects on the associative behavior under study.

Determining the stability of response hierarchies in a free-continued word association task was the aim of a study carried out by Andreas & Mills (1967). They used nonsense paralogs as well as words as stimuli. The interval between a subject's first and second encounters with the same stimulus item was just a few minutes. The retest situation was accomplished within a single experimental session by simply inserting extra booklet pages for 3 stimuli of the 17 used, thus creating a 20-page booklet. To prevent confusion which might otherwise arise and to try to neutralize any tendency to strive for repetition (or its avoidance), subjects were told: "Some of the items may be repeated in your booklet. If you do happen to find a stimulus item repeated, pretend that it is a new stimulus. Don't try to remember what you put down the first time and don't try to purposely omit previous responses."

The percent of individual subjects repeating each response was calculated. This indicant was generally quite substantial although it varied greatly for different responses as shown in the right-hand column of Table 9.4. Also calculated for each response at each encounter were the group response probabilities (p) and median ordinal position (o) in the sequences of responses to each of the items: MELON, MAYIR, NUSIR. A comparison of the columns of data for these two encounters with the three stimuli shows that performance of continued association tends to be fairly stable. The correlation between response probabilities (p) tended to be fairly high for each repeated stimulus. For ordinal position (o) the correlations based on repeated responding to each stimulus were moderately positive.

Table 9.4 Probability of Occurrence (*p*), Median Ordinal Position (*o*), and Percent Repetition of the Commonest Responses to Three Stimuli (After Andreas and Mills, 1967)

Stimulus	Response	First Encounter		Second Encounter		Per Cent Repetition
		p	*o*	*p*	*o*	
MELON	watermelon	.77	1.21	.80	1.50	74
	canteloupe	.46	2.38	.60	4.13	81
	honeydew	.40	3.10	.38	3.33	78
	fruit	.34	3.50	.29	4.83	50
	green	.34	7.50	.26	6.75	42
	seed	.34	6.50	.38	5.25	67
	rind	.26	5.00	.11	6.55	45
	eat	.23	4.00	.20	7.00	50
	sweet	.23	4.50	.20	4.75	62
	juice	.20	6.25	.23	5.83	62
	red	.20	7.00	.11	6.00	43
	ripe	.20	5.75	.20	7.25	71
	round	.20	7.00	.09	2.25	14
MAYIR	mayor	.77	1.34	.77	1.06	85
	May	.38	3.25	.14	4.75	31
	may	.31	2.67	.26	3.33	55
	year	.26	3.00	.14	2.33	40
	ear	.23	3.50	.17	2.17	86
NUSIR	sir	.57	3.30	.57	2.79	60
	new	.51	4.70	.31	3.00	28
	music	.46	1.30	.31	2.00	44
	noose	.31	4.00	.23	4.00	64
	nurse	.31	1.75	.26	1.14	91
	news	.23	3.00	.26	4.25	38
	nuisance	.23	1.90	.17	2.50	25

Other Illustrative Studies

Examining two different experiments will demonstrate the diversity of approaches to probing associative processes. One study examines the producing of clusters of responses in continued word association. The other investigates how different verbal contexts given to subjects affects their responding in both discrete and continued testing.

Associative clusters

When subjects produce continued word association responses over an extended period, the cumulative production of the group may be plotted against time as a rising negatively accelerated curve (Bousfield & Sedgewick, 1944). In considering the performance of any individual subject, however, Pollio (1964) reasoned that groups of response words should share a high interitem associative strength as well as a certain congruence or overlap in meaning. Such a group of words, which he terms an associative cluster, should be emitted more rapidly than less cohesively organized responses. Pollio designed an experiment to test this hypothesis which relates production rate to clusters of responses: production rate is higher when clusters occur in continued word association, while lower response rates occur as less interconnected, less semantically similar responses are given by the individual subject.

A three-session experiment was conducted. In the first session subjects were run individually to permit the recording and timing of their vocal responses during four minutes of continued word association to each of four projected verbal stimuli: TROUBLE, THIEF, JUSTICE, and HOUSE. By recording each vocal response on a constant-speed pen recorder tape as well as on audio tape, Pollio was able to analyze the response latencies or interword intervals for each subject. He identified parts of each record which were characterized by fast, medium, and slow production. These groups of words were then studied by two different methods when subjects returned in four weeks.

In Sessions 2 and 3, with appropriate sequential counterbalancing, each subject gave word associations to his three groups of response words from Session 1 and rated them on semantic differential scales.* These two techniques yielded an assessment of the associative cohesiveness and the semantic similarities among the words produced by each subject at his fast, medium, and slow rates of continued word association. The quantitative derivation of these indicants, necessarily quite complex, provided the data to test the hypothesis under investigation.

It was found, as predicted, that associative cohesiveness was much higher for responses elicited by each stimulus at a faster rate of response. Semantic distance (inverse of semantic similarity) was lower for the faster

*Semantic differential scaling is described later in this chapter, pp. 320–322.

sequences of responding. Both tests of the hypothesis yielded positive results. This study is in agreement with others in revealing a functional orderliness in verbal behavior.

Contextual priming

Word association testing represents a fairly simple probing of verbal behavior tendencies. A number of stimulus items are presented and a number of verbal responses are given. A natural question for the experimental psychologist is "Just what does determine the particular response given by a subject, considering that any one of a number of words might be expected on the basis of semantic relationships and actual tabulations of responses in past studies?" One way to investigate the determinants of response tendencies is to try to manipulate them experimentally. Can experimental procedures be devised which will influence, if not determine, the response words given?

One manipulation designed to affect responses in word association has been termed priming. This is accomplished by assigning some task to subjects which exposes them to selected material, possibly requiring that they study or recite certain words. Such a learning task may prime the evocability of these words. Then when the word association test is administered, these words may appear as responses more frequently than in a control condition where they have not been primed. Procedures may be of many sorts with extensive possibilities for manipulating temporal and frequency variables. The effects of priming are often tested through the use of stimulus words which are homophones (BARE and BEAR; PAIR and PEAR) presented orally or homographs (BANK meaning either *edge of stream* or *financial institution;* PLANT meaning *botanical specimen* or *manufacturing facility*) which may be presented in printed stimulus form as well as orally. Since these "ambiguous" stimulus items each have contrasting potential response pools, the priming of one of these *before* word association testing can influence actual responding with demonstrable effect. The preliminary material or task used for priming might involve stimulus items, particular response words, or associative combinations of stimuli and responses.

Segal (1967) reported a series of experiments in which fourteen homographs were selected as potential response items in one of their meanings. These potential responses were primed for some experimental subjects by embedding them in a verbal analogies test in various forms. Other experimental groups were given rote learning tasks for priming purposes while an unprimed control group provided response norms for comparison purposes. Table 9.5 shows the stimulus items, the critical potential response words which were primed, and some sample problems from the analogies test used for priming some of the subjects.

Table 9.5 Materials Used in Experiments on the Use of Different Verbal Contexts to Prime Word Association Responses. (After Segal, 1967)

Stimulus Items	Critical Potential Responses
GREEN	plant
SICKNESS	well
JUSTICE	scale
CITY	state
KING	ruler
HARD	rock
BUTTERFLY	net
LIGHT	bulb
MOUNTAIN	top
STOMACH	organ
RIVER	bank
FRUIT	bowl
DEEP	down
MUSIC	sound

Sample Problems from Analogies Tests Used in Preliminary Priming of Some Subjects

1. PLANT is to GREEN as BANK is to (a) Stream, (b) Wet, (c) Sandy, (d) Lake.
2. SICKNESS is to WELL as TOP is to (a) Below, (b) Bottom, (c) Valley, (d) Peak.
3. TENNIS is to NET as BOWL is to (a) Alley, (b) Strike, (c) Ball, (d) Tenpin.

The problems in the analogies tests were carefully structured by Segal to incorporate three forms of priming: identical, congruent, and incongruent. These may be examined in the sample problems of Table 9.5. In Problems 1 and 2, the first part of the analogies represent the identical form of priming since they contain both the stimulus item and the critical potential response (GREEN–plant and SICKNESS–well). In Problem 3 the first part of the analogy represents the congruent form of priming. The critical potential response "net" is paired with the word "tennis" so that the ambiguous word "net" is given the implied definition of "a group of holes tied together with string" rather than an alternate meaning such as "remainder" as in "net cost." Also illustrative of congruent priming are the second parts of Problems 1 and 2 involving critical potential responses "bank" and "top" in contexts which are congruent with the intended response meaning in the word association test to follow. The second part of Problem 3 is an example of incongruent priming. Here the potential response word "bowl" is presented to subjects but as a verb in a context of the sport of bowling rather than as a noun meaning a container.

Several forms of the analogies tests were devised by Segal so that different critical potential responses were given the three different forms of priming—identical, congruent, or incongruent. The word association data collected in the second part of his experiments were then examined in correspondence to the form of analogy-test priming which had been given to particular response items for particular subgroups of subjects. The responses of other experimental subjects were examined for the priming that may have occurred in their attempts to memorize either the 14 critical potential responses or the 49 words of a seven-problem analogies test including some of the word association stimulus items and all of the 14 critical potential responses. A norm group took the word association test without any priming.

The results of Experiment I, which employed a discrete word association test, are given in Table 9.6. After studying the basic data, if we direct our attention to the right-hand column of differences between the mean number of critical and control responses we can examine the net effects of priming as these occurred in the experimental groups. (Control responses had been selected for their equal frequency of occurrence with critical responses in the data of the unprimed normative control group.) The data indicate that incongruent priming had a minimal effect. Congruent priming was about as effective as the learning tasks. Identical priming, which involved critical responses and their stimuli paired in the analogy problems, was most potent in its effect on the word association task.

In his Experiment II, Segal found similar effects of the several types of priming when the test task was continued word association. An additional finding was that the priming effects persisted over the 14 minutes of responding (one-minute per stimulus item) when the identical form of priming had been applied. His graphs indicate that priming of the congruent and incongruent forms was functioning for about five minutes.

Table 9.6 Priming Effect in Experiment I (After Segal, 1967)

Cond.	N	Mean Number Critical Responses	Mean Number Control Responses	Critical Responses Minus Control Responses
Norms	70	.77	.76	.01
Learning (Controls)				
14 word	50	1.46	.92	.54
49 word	38	1.16	.63	.53
Experimental	240			
Identical	(80)	3.45	.64	2.81
Congruent	(80)	1.15	.64	.51
Incongruent	(80)	.80	.64	.16

The learning groups showed a strong priming effect which tended to be limited to the first minute of responding. In these two experiments (and a third one described in the journal article) Segal has amply demonstrated the effects of priming on word association performance and has revealed some of its characteristics. This area of investigation should be challenging to the inventiveness of additional investigators in devising probes for verbal behavior mechanisms.

Tabulated Associations

A number of experimenters have used selected stimulus items to elicit word association responses from large groups of subjects, typically college students. The tabulation of these associates and their relative frequencies or percents of occurrence is useful in other investigations of verbal behavior where items of known associative relations are desirable. Lists of common or popular responses to selected stimuli may be found in the studies listed in Table 9.7.

A word or two about the special characteristics of some of these tabulations may help to suggest their utility in further research. Two studies used designations of *categories* as stimuli, requiring the continued associations to be instances of the category. Such category norms have been tabulated by Battig and Montague (1969); and by Cohen,

Table 9.7 Reports of Word Association Studies
Presenting Extensive Response Tabulations

Investigators	Stimulus Items	Method of Association	N Per Item
Battig & Montague (1969)	56 category labels	Continued (30 sec)	442
Bilodeau & Howell (1965)	138 words	Continued (3 Rs)	108
Bousfield et al. (1961)	400 words	Discrete	150
Cohen, Bousfield, & Whitmarsh (1957)	43 category labels	Continued (4 Rs)	400
Cramer (1970)	100 homographs	Discrete	109
Keppel & Strand (1970)	234 words	Discrete	182
Marshall & Cofer (1970)	328 words	Discrete	100
Paivio, Yuille, & Madigan (1968)	925 nouns	Continued (30 sec)	25
Palermo & Jenkins (1964)	200 words	Discrete	1000
Postman (1970)	96 words	Discrete & Continued (50 sec)	1000, 96
Taylor & Kimble (1967)	320 words & paralogs	Discrete	100
Underwood & Richardson (1956)	213 nouns	Controlled-discrete	153

Bousfield, and Whitmarsh (1957). In building upon the earlier work, Battig and Montague extended the number of categories from 43 to 56 and allowed 30 seconds for responding instead of limiting subjects to four responses as Cohen et al. had done.

The study conducted by Bilodeau and Howell (1965) resulted in a tabulation with several distinctive features and considerable potential for additional investigation. As basic stimulus items the experimenters selected 45 words from the Kent-Rosanoff list (Table 9.1, p. 301) on which some previous work had been done. Fifteen of the stimuli had elicited no predominantly strong associates in earlier discrete association tests; 15 had elicited two fairly strong associates; and 15 had evoked one very dominant primary associate. This selection of stimuli set the stage for different patterns of responses when continued association was studied. Besides the original stimulus words, their three most common associative responses were themselves used as stimuli with a new subject group, airmen in technical training. By using erstwhile responses as stimuli, the investigators could examine the characteristics of networks of association. Written responses were obtained from about 108 subjects per stimulus word in either discrete or continued association. Due to overlapping with the earlier studied responses this investigation used 138 different words as stimuli, 45 from the Kent-Rosanoff list and 93 of their strongest associates.

Bousfield et al. (1961) present a full tabulation of written free-discrete responses they obtained from college students. Their 400 stimulus words included about 60 of the Kent-Rosanoff list and 177 words from published semantic differential profiles stemming from an associative scaling of meaning discussed later.

Palermo and Jenkins (1964) obtained discrete responses to 200 words from 1000 subjects. Their published norms include tabulations of response frequencies based on subjects of elementary and high school ages as well as college students.

A volume edited by Postman and Keppel (1970) has brought together the word association norms collected in a number of studies conducted earlier. Several of these chapters are indicated in Table 9.7. The special stimulus words used by Cramer (1970) were 100 selected homographs, words with two or more distinct meanings in English. Examples are *bat, beam, carp,* and *club.* Tabulated data showed that a particular meaning was strongly predominant in some associative reactions, while in some cases both meanings appeared to be about balanced in their response elicitation. In another study Keppel and Strand (1970) sought to explore associative networks or chains. To do this they used 234 stimulus words which had been found to be primary (strongest) or strong responses tabulated by Palermo and Jenkins. Since 64 stimulus words were actually common to both studies (having been responses in the earlier norms), the chapter includes comparisons and discussion of the two investigations. Another study in the collection of norms was also based upon earlier response tabulations. Marshall and Cofer (1970) used as their stimuli 328 of the words given to 21 of the category labels of the

Cohen et al. investigation. Most categories were explored with over a dozen of the earlier responses now used as stimuli. The associations tabulated thus represent an approach to mapping out certain concepts. From this collection of reports, the final one to be noted here was a study by Postman (1970). He employed college students as subjects with different groups being administered either a written discrete association test or a continued response requirement which allowed 50 sec for production of written responses. Four sets of stimulus words were sampled from four different Thorndike-Lorge frequency-of-usage levels. These items were randomly sequenced into lists of 96 items for presentation in test booklets. Besides using both Procedures 1 and 2 (Table 9.2) this investigation was designed to compare the word association performance of men and women and of students of high and low language aptitude. The tabulated data afford numerous insights into linguistic associative mechanisms.

A tabulation of response productivity in 30 sec of continued word association is contained in a report by Paivio, Yuille, and Madigan (1968) who used 925 nouns as stimulus items. Although not listing the responses given to each word, their table contains the Thorndike-Lodge frequency of each stimulus and mean ratings obtained for each of these nouns on concreteness (C) and imagery (I). These indicants are useful supplements to meaningfulness (m) which is defined as the mean number of responses given during the continued production period.

Several associative indices were obtained by Taylor and Kimble (1967) for selected stimulus words and paralogs of CVCVC format. Running subjects individually, they used Procedure 1 (free-discrete responding) with stimulus items presented in printed form and responses given orally. Their procedure allowed them to obtain response latencies as indicants of association value. More comparable to the data of other studies listed in Table 9.7 was their tabulation of the word most frequently given in responding to each stimulus item and the percent of subjects giving it (F). The investigators discussed the utility of the various indices as their stimulus items might be considered for use in research on verbal behavior.

Underwood and Richardson (1956) carried out their study so that verbal materials of known relationships might be available for experiments on concept formation. Using the method we have designated Procedure 3 (controlled-discrete association), they required that the response to each stimulus noun be a descriptive adjective; a sense impression. Their response tabulation includes about 50 or 60 sense impression categories elicited by 213 of their original stimulus words. For example, responses in the categories Shiny, Metallic, and Light were elicited by the stimulus noun ALUMINUM. In their article these experimenters indicate the utility of the categorical information in grouping items for concept formation tasks which are discussed in Chapter 13, pp. 489–492. In Table 13.4, p. 490, may be found the distribution of responses to a sample of the stimulus nouns.

In closing our review of tabulations of word association responses, two final points may be made. First, as indicated by Jenkins and Palermo (1965), adult word association norms have changed over the decades since normative responses were first tabulated. Extending an earlier analysis by Jenkins and Russell (1960) they confirm these trends in responses to the stimulus words of the Kent-Rosanoff list since the early decades of this century:

1. The frequency level of popular responses has tended to increase.

2. The responses of highest frequency tend to remain the same although the three most frequent responses to each stimulus exhibit some shifting in relative frequency.

3. Superordinate responses ("color" to RED; "animal" to LION) have tended to decrease in frequency.

The slow drift in the most common responses demonstrates the need for new normative data to be collected at reasonable intervals. On the other hand, it may be noted that responses of highest frequency seem to be reliably stable. This suggests confident reliance on word association norms as other experiments in verbal behavior are designed.

A second point to be made concerning tabulated data is that we must note carefully the methods used in each investigation. Any index of associative strength needs to be scrutinized for its reliability and its significance. An article by Marshall and Cofer (1963) offers guidance in its critique of the various methods by which associative indices are obtained.

Attributes and Dimensions of Verbal Materials

Besides counting and describing the responses which they elicit in word association tests, there are a number of other ways in which theorists and investigators have examined and measured verbal items. The scaling procedures they have devised, their findings on the interrelated nature of verbal attributes, and the scaled pools of materials they have provided will be our topics in this section. As we move into the final part of the chapter we shall find that these scaled characteristics of verbal materials are salient variables in determining the course of verbal learning, just as word associations are. In later chapters we shall find that these dimensions of verbal items also operate very strongly in the processes of verbal memory, transfer, and problem solving.

Meaning: The Semantic Differential

Osgood (1952) has discussed meaning and its measurement at considerable length, offering the *semantic differential* technique for the quantified description of meaning. This method combines associative and psychological scaling techniques. A series of seven-point rating scales are identified by pairs of adjectival opposites like ANGULAR-ROUNDED, WEAK-STRONG, and ROUGH-SMOOTH. The seven steps of the scale for such a semantic dimension as WEAK-STRONG, for example, would range as follows:

WEAK ____: ____: ____: ____: ____: ____: ____: STRONG
     (1)   (2)   (3)   (4)   (5)   (6)   (7)

where (1) is "very closely related to WEAK."
     (2) is "quite closely related to WEAK."
     (3) is "only slightly related to WEAK."
     (4) is "equally related to WEAK and STRONG."
        or "completely irrelevant."
     (5) is "slightly related to STRONG."
     (6) is "quite closely related to STRONG."
     (7) is "very closely related to STRONG."

In its employment, this scale would not show the numerical values that we have placed in parentheses. It would simply be a graphic scale with 7 intervals provided for checking. A number of such scales, perhaps 10, would appear under each other. The word or concept to be differentiated semantically would be printed on top of the page. Figure 9.1 shows such a page with the rating check marks of an experimental subject or judge filled in to show his reactions to the word POLITE. Looking at the third scale, we see that this judge has rated POLITE as very closely related to SMOOTH. This illustrates the associative aspect of the semantic differential technique. The profile that we would obtain by connecting the check marks in Figure 9.1 would tend to describe the meaning of POLITE as it is perceived by this subject. Similar sorts of profiles may be based on median group ratings.

The semantic differential technique yields a picture of the connotative meaning of a word with respect to whatever associative dimensions are represented in the adjectival scales which an investigator chooses to employ. Osgood has pointed out that both SIMON LEGREE and WAR might yield similar profiles on some scales even though their denotative meanings are poles apart. If it suited our research purposes we might obtain different connotative profiles for two such concepts by utilizing other descriptive scales. It is important to understand that the semantic

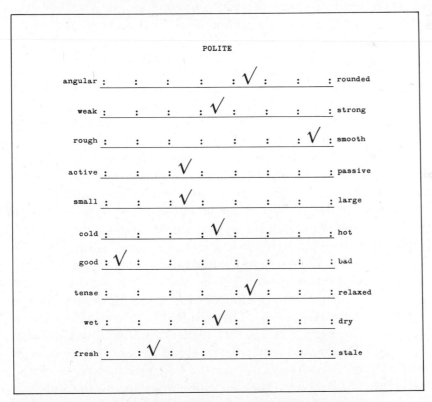

Fig. 9.1. Sample page in administering a semantic differential scaling of "POLITE" with check marks of a hypothetical judge indicated. (After Osgood, 1952.)

differential technique does not prescribe a particular set of scales which must be used. Osgood, Suci, and Tannenbaum (1957) do offer their basis for using seven-point bipolar scales with opposite adjectives as end labels.

A large number of psychological studies have employed the semantic differential technique. Following Osgood's lead, the scale data have often been treated with the complex quantitative operations of factor analysis. This has permitted the postulation of certain meaning factors which may be used to indicate the location of a scaled concept in hypothetical semantic space. Factors that have emerged prominently include the semantic dimensions of *evaluation, potency,* and *activity.* Employment of the semantic differential technique has ranged very widely in psychological studies. Its use in dozens of different investigative applications is illustrated in a collection of research reports brought together under the editorship of Snider and Osgood (1969). Their book also includes the early description of the semantic differential, its rationale, and some critical examinations of the technique.

Meaningfulness

An attribute of verbal items termed *meaningfulness* has been devised by Noble (1952) and shown to be useful in scaling both real words and paralogs (pronounceable wordlike configurations of letters) by applying the identical technique. This quantitative index is obtained through the use of the free-continued procedure of word association that we designated Procedure 2. Meaningfulness, m, is defined as the mean number of acceptable written responses given to an item in one minute. The original investigation determined m for 96 two-syllable nouns and paralogs using 119 enlisted airmen in calculating the final group mean values. A subgroup split of the data yield a coefficient of reliability for m of .975.

Noble and Parker (1960) determined m values for the same 96 items with 100 college students contributing the data which were tabulated. Verbal productivity of the college students was greater than that of the airmen tested in the earlier study. This resulted in elevations of the m values obtained. The average m was 2.11 higher, a statistically significant difference when overall productivity of the two groups was compared. Despite the differences, the m values for the 96 items showed a correlation of .965 when the data from the two different groups were compared. This indicates a general stability of relative m values even when verbal fluency may affect the data obtained from particular subject groups.

The author has used the general method devised by Noble in determining *m* for a different set of 75 two-syllable CVCVC items: words of different frequencies of usage, altered-word paralogs, and randomly generated paralogs, plus six items from Noble's list which conformed to the specified length and spelling format. The *m* values obtained when 120 college students were given the written continued association task are given in Table 9.8.

Table 9.8 Values of Meaningfulness (*m*) Based on One-Minute Response Production to Each Listed Stimulus Item in Categories 1 through 6

Category 1. High Frequency Words

cabin	11.19	final	9.71	naked	8.86
canal	10.30	honey	10.40	robin	10.76
decay	9.76	motor	11.23	sugar	10.96

Category 2. Moderate Frequency Words

boxer	11.17	genus	8.29	nasal	9.40
cider	10.08	haven	8.98	pivot	8.85
defer	7.48	lever	9.02	viper	8.56

Category 3. Low Frequency Words

befog	7.55	ducal	6.93	ravel	8.04
borax	9.38	facet	7.75	rebut	6.77
diner	9.21	mucus	8.13	vixen	6.92

Category 4. Altered-Word Paralogs

bosum	7.34	labar	7.77	repen	6.93
cixar	6.33	menor	6.76	royel	9.42
dobut	6.44	metaz	6.12	siven	6.86
favow	6.62	metel	9.24	sugax	6.83
fumor	7.46	muney	8.20	tawen	7.01
gaked	6.77	perih	6.42	totor	7.72
hukan	6.04	pusil	6.29	wagot	6.64
juyer	6.79	relew	6.21	xamel	7.07

Category 5. Randomly Generated Paralogs

bakov	7.16	gupac	5.80	varuc	6.02
bimor	5.90	guroy	5.98	wayot	6.85
cifur	6.76	kuwil	6.65	wikor	6.54
davoh	5.82	mudov	6.09	wiluf	6.58
gikel	6.23	peluy	5.60	wusah	6.33
gowip	6.66	subav	6.32	yiwan	6.72

Category 6. Items from Noble's List

carom	7.05	gojey	5.39	kupod	6.94
gamin	7.35	jewel	10.72	money	11.78

The random selection of the words from specified Thorndike-Lorge frequency levels and the randomized method of constructing the paralogs should make these items useful in designing studies of verbal learning. Additional words or paralogs with similar m values may be selected or constructed as needed. The definitions of the categories that are designated in Table 9.8 are as follows:

Category 1. High Frequency Words

Selected at random from CVCVC words of Thorndike-Lorge frequency of 26 times or more per million words.

Category 2. Moderate Frequency Words

Selected at random from CVCVC words of Thorndike-Lorge frequency of 3 to 7 times per million words.

Category 3. Low Frequency Words

Selected at random from CVCVC words of Thorndike-Lorge frequency of 2 times or fewer per million words.

Category 4. Altered-Word Paralogs

Created by randomly changing one vowel or consonant of a CVCVC word selected at random from words of frequency of 9 times or more per million words.

Category 5. Randomly Generated Paralogs

Created by random selection of the needed consonants (excluding j, q, x, z) and vowels.

Category 6. Items from Noble's List

Items of CVCVC format from high, medium, and low m values of Noble's list.

Familiarity and Frequency

The familiarity to subjects of particular verbal items would seem to be of importance as we select material for research purposes. A method of rating has been one way to scale words for familiarity. Haagen (1949) had 40 undergraduates use a 5-point scale in rating 400 adjectives for their familiarity. Familiarity has also been approached indirectly through estimates of frequency of past encounters with each item to be scaled. Noble (1953) had subjects rate their frequency of past contact with the 96 items of his m-scaling. The points on the scale describing number of times an item had been experienced were: Never, Rarely, Sometimes, Often, and Very Often. The obtained scale values (f) correlated very highly with the m values for the item.

In a later study Noble (1954) demonstrated the validity of the assumption that frequency of experiencing an item generates familiarity with it. Choosing items rated very low on the earlier f scale, he projected them on the screen different numbers of times for subjects to read. Later subjects rated the items for familiarity. Appropriately transformed f values were found to depend upon the number of times an item had been experienced in the first part of the experiment.

Without necessarily invoking the concept of familiarity, it is possible to obtain frequency data on verbal items merely by counting their number of occurrences in printed sources. A classical source of frequency of word usage is the compilation by Thorndike and Lorge (1944) of the frequency of occurrence of several thousand words. Bigrams and trigrams (two- and three-letter combinations) have been subjected to several counts from different sources. A compilation of these may be found in Underwood and Schulz (1960). Another count that relates to familiarity is the brief tabulation by Lindley (1960) of the frequencies of some trigrams occurring as the first three letters of words in the Thorndike-Lorge list.

Association Value and Associability

The nonsense syllable was invented to reduce the variance which would be introduced into rote memory experiments by words of varied familiarity and meaning. However, it was found that nonsense syllables themselves differed in connotative meaning as revealed by the extent to which they suggested associated words. Accordingly, associative techniques were used to classify numerous syllables with respect to the number of associations they elicited. Classified lists based on the studies of several different experimenters—Glaze, Hull, Krueger, and Witmer—have been presented by Hilgard (1951, pp. 540-546). These lists have provided a ready source of material for research in verbal processes. We should rely on such association values cautiously, however. For example, the percent figures cited as association values for the Glaze lists are based on how many subjects out of 15 offered associations to each syllable. The response, or failure to respond, of just one person thus represents a 7 percent change in association value. The unreliability of the values has led most investigators to utilize widely spaced values in designing experiments. A second reason for caution in relying on associative descriptions of this sort is that certain syllables may rise or fall in apparent meaning as the verbal environment changes over the years.

More recent scalings of trigrams for association value (or meaningfulness) have required question-answering or rating by subjects. Archer (1960) scaled 2480 CVCs (using Y as both vowel and consonant) by projecting each one for four seconds while subjects considered four questions pertaining to the stimulus:

Is it a word?

Does it sound like a word?

Does it remind me of a word?

Can I use it in a sentence?

The percent of subjects answering "Yes" to any one or more of these questions was taken as the index of meaningfulness for each CVC.

Noble (1961) scaled 2100 CVCs (all permutations possible without consonant duplication in any trigram and using Y as a consonant only) by having subjects indicate the number of things or ideas suggested by each one when given a five-point scale:

1. None.

2. Below average.

3. Average.

4. Above average.

5. Very many.

Association value, a, was calculated for each CVC as the percent of subjects responding to it with any of the response categories 2 through 5, above. Rated association, a', was computed by using 1–5 as values for the rating categories. Both of these indices relate to scaled meaningfulness, m', in a nonlinear fashion.

Over a broad range of values there is a fairly high correlation of values assigned to CVCs by the different operations employed by Archer ($N=216$ subjects) and by Noble ($N=200$ subjects). This can be seen by inspection of the values related to the low, medium, and high CVCs as grouped in a sample compiled by Runquist (1966) and presented here in Table 9.9.

Table 9.9 Trigrams Scaled for Association Value and Meaningfulness (After Runquist, 1966)

Low Items	Association Value (Noble, 1961)	Meaningfulness (Archer, 1960)	Medium Items	Association Value (Noble, 1961)	Meaningfulness (Archer, 1960)	High Items	Association Value (Noble, 1961)	Meaningfulness (Archer, 1960)
cij	25%	8%	beh	53%	44%	bim	98%	100%
foj	24	11	boh	60	53	cat	100	100
gaq	22	11	beq	50	42	don	100	100
jih	23	13	ciy	57	40	for	100	100
huj	24	7	luq	49	42	gem	100	100
kuq	17	11	jat	56	41	hut	98	100
qah	22	14	fip	58	42	joy	98	100
qaz	21	10	foh	47	43	lag	98	100
qef	22	8	deh	52	44	mat	100	100
qiy	20	8	moy	60	45	pin	100	100
que	24	19	toh	58	46	wig	100	100
wij	22	13	siq	56	47	pub	97	100
wuq	22	8	jir	58	41	gil	98	95
xab	17	8	nef	54	49	jog	92	95
xak	22	17	raj	60	44	lam	99	95
xaw	15	8	yom	48	51	nat	100	96
xin	16	10	yuh	43	45	dol	98	94
xiq	17	5	zin	50	47	cal	100	96
xep	22	13	wiy	52	42	wag	98	99
xev	16	6	neq	56	42	bor	97	92
xoc	16	9	vem	59	46	lob	94	92
yix	22	9	gez	58	42	dik	92	90
zeh	24	14	pif	59	57	sel	98	90
zih	16	6	soq	48	49	bur	98	91
zuf	22	8	weh	56	41	rin	93	92

Beyond the association value of individual CVCs, experimenters in verbal learning may have reason to be interested in the *associability of pairs* of such items. Montague and Kiess (1969) undertook to scale pairs of CVCs for their associability (*AS*), choosing the items to be paired from all levels of association value or meaningfulness as scaled by Archer (1960). Creating hundreds of such pairs (for example, GEX-sij, VEM-lig, BIP-von, FAS-woz, BEG-fad, SEW-fig), they projected these one pair at a time for a 15-sec. inspection and response period. Subjects were asked to write in a booklet any associative device or idea which they might use to associate the items comprising each pair. The index (*AS*) of associability was the percent of subjects identifying some natural language mediator (*NLM*) by which the CVCs of each pair might be mentally connected. The *AS* values were found to range from 11 to 98 (percent) with female students showing *AS* values which averaged 5 (percent) higher than males.

It was expected that scaled *AS* values would prove to be important determiners of memorization when paired associate verbal learning experiments were conducted. Within several studies, however, the experimenters observed only minimal effects. In a final experiment reported in their monograph, Montague and Kiess did obtain a significant effect of *AS* level on pair memorization. This study involved relatively long exposure time for the pairs, possibly providing an adequate opportunity for subjects to formulate and fix in mind the natural language mediators (NLM) that might assist the associating of the items for the test to be given 24 hr later.

Real words, paired both randomly and systematically, were studied for their associability (*Asb*) by Kammann (1968). Also concerned with the prediction and explanation of the phenomena of paired associate learning and recall, he included words for which there were available data obtained through word association, the semantic differential, the scaling of meaningfulness, and word frequency counts. Groups of subjects were asked to rate, on a 10-point scale, the likelihood that the two words of each listed pair would occur together in the same sentence or line of poetry, or that one word would call the other to mind, or how easy it would be to relate the two words. Scaled associability (*Asb*) was found to relate in various ways to other indices which deal with words and word pairs. It was found—in verbal learning studies that are reported in the monograph—to correlate more highly than the others with the learnability of the word pairs. Kammann also shows its utility in analyzing intrusion errors.

Pronounceability

Since audiolingual processes may be operative as subjects engage in learning or memory tasks, the degree to which verbal materials are pronounceable may be an influence on their learnability. Recognizing this Underwood and Schulz (1960) gave subjects a 9-point rating scale to use in assessing the pronounceability of a large number of trigrams including words as well as nonlexical CVCs and CCCs.

Concreteness, Imagery, and Meaningfulness

As a final reference to dimensions on which experimenters have tabulated scale values for verbal items, we may consider an investigation by Paivio, Yuille, and Madigan (1968). Taking 925 nouns as their pool of words, the experimenters determined the meaningfulness, m, of each item. Their scaling of this dimension differed from the original method of Noble in allowing 30 sec instead of 60 sec for subjects to write their responses to each item in a 50-page booklet. For the other two dimensions, *concreteness* and *imagery,* this study employed 7-point rating scales with end points given appropriate labels: Highly Abstract, Highly Concrete; Low Imagery, High Imagery. Extensive instructions and examples were used to be certain the subjects understood their rating task in each case. Besides the group means and standard deviations for these three scalings the authors also list the Thorndike-Lorge frequency count for each of the alphabetically listed nouns.

Another investigation of the relationships among scalable attributes of words was reported by Spreen and Schulz (1966). They also used a 30-sec response period for m quantification and 7-point rating scales for concreteness, c, and specificity, s. These three indices were tabulated for 329 common nouns of the "A" frequency level in the Thorndike-Lorge count. The words were 1 to 3 syllables in length. It was found that m correlated positively in moderate degree with c and s, and somewhat negatively with word length.

Verbal Learning: Acquisition of Associations

The concept of an association between verbal items serves to relate the processes of verbal learning to areas of investigation such as word association and meaning. In word association we investigate certain functional connections between words. When we present a stimulus item, most subjects can readily respond with a related or associated word. Their associations are presumably based on past experience or learning outside the research situation. In experiments on verbal learning, in contrast, we study the acquisition or strengthening of associations under controlled conditions. In paired-associate learning, for example, we prepare a list of stimulus-response pairs and then have our subjects learn to give each response to the appropriate stimulus item.

Material

One of the principal determinants of associative learning is the nature of the material being presented for study. Whether they are meaningful words or nonlexical items, the stimuli and responses of the assigned task very significantly affect the ease or difficulty of associating them. This is due in considerable measure to the fact that the elements presented to subjects must undergo certain processing of various sorts before they can be associated appropriately. If stimuli are very similar they require *discrimination* prior to associating responses with them. If responses are relatively low in familiarity and meaningfulness, they may require *integration* and perhaps *encoding* before they are readily stored in memory and available for retrieval. Much of the recent research into verbal learning has investigated these cognitive processes that are thought to precede or accompany the forming of stimulus-response associations.

Subjects

Any verbal material presented to a subject for learning will have a degree of familiarity and possibly some meaning for him. The perceptual, cognitive, mnemonic processes which he brings to bear on this new associative task will reflect his own learning history, his past experience with words. In placing great emphasis on the nature of the material to be learned, we are actually emphasizing the learner as entering actively into the assigned task, bringing to it his earlier acquired repertory of associations, habits, cognitive processes, and problem solving skills. In studying and scaling verbal materials along several related dimensions we have actually been probing the verbal behavior histories of individuals who resemble our learners. What we learn about the words and wordlike items through the normative cataloging and counting of responses given by a sample of persons will help us to predict behavior of verbal learning subjects—their acquisition or strengthening of associations in a new situation.

The relatively recent resurgence of interest in scaling verbal items to be employed in research on learning is one sort of blending of two quantitative traditions in psychology—psychometric testing and laboratory experimentation—as called for by Cronbach (1957). Studies of verbal learning which we shall examine later have proved the efficacy of this approach in analyzing subjects' accomplishments. This should encourage two natural extensions of this endeavor. First, careful scaling of larger pools of diverse items on a variety of dimensions with representative samples of subjects being used in data collection. Second, the verbal testing of subjects as a first stage of verbal learning studies. This closer juxtaposition of the psychometric and the experimental approaches might or might not involve identical verbal units in the testing and learning stages. In any case it should be preferable to interpret the results of a learning experiment on the basis of known facts about the subjects' verbal repertories and processes than on the basis of inference drawn from the testing of other—somewhat similar—individuals. Such interpretation, of course, would consider the stimulus-response activities of verbal testing as part of each subject's recent history as he undertook the learning task.

Task formats

Verbal items to be learned may be organized and presented to a subject in several possible ways, with differing modes of stimulus presentation and a variety of requirements for overt responses to be made. Two long-used formats for items are the serial list and the paired associates task. In serial learning a subject must learn to respond with each item at the time that the prior item in the ordered list is presented to him. In paired associate learning a subject learns to give each response at the time that its designated stimulus item is presented. In either instance the subject learns to anticipate the presentation of the response item so the technique is the method of anticipation. Regular timing, as with an exposure device such as a memory drum, paces the task. As an alternative to the anticipation method, an experimenter can successively expose the items (in either serial or paired associate format) and then allow a recall period for subjects to write their responses. Such a recall requirement might also follow whole-list study instead of item or pair presentation. Still another task arrangement is to require a subject to discriminate or choose among two or more responses presented with a stimulus on repeated trials. On earliest trials, of course, the subject can only guess. As he is informed of the correct choice each time, however, his learning will soon have him responding above the chance level and ultimately attaining errorless performance in most cases.

In point of fact, there are a variety of fairly standardized methods for the laboratory investigation of verbal learning. Many technical facets of such research are reviewed by Runquist (1966). While standardization of materials and some aspects of methods have their utility, we must be aggressive in developing new approaches to exploring problem areas and testing new hypotheses. This is one strong plea of Tulving and Madigan (1970, p. 442) who lament the tendency to take standard methods of experimentation as phenomena to be studied as problems in their own right.

Treatment of data

The general problem in treating results in verbal learning studies is to portray the progress of subjects in mastering the material, that is, forming the required associations. We shall consider two techniques for describing this memorization process. Our illustrative data may be assumed to have come from the paired-associate learning of a ten-pair list, with six subjects performing by the anticipation method.

A common measure of a group's progress is the mean number of correct responses as a function of trials. Our hypothetical group of subjects would be making more and more correct anticipations as trials continued. Such a series of means is presented along the bottom of Table 9.10 to represent the central tendencies of the columns of data. In calculating these means, it was assumed that once a subject had reached the criterion of ten correct anticipations he would continue to perform at that level if trials were continued. The data of this table are represented graphically in Figure 9.2, a curve of verbal learning.

The data of Table 9.10 are characterized by considerable variability in the number of trials required by different subjects to reach the criterion of ten correct anticipations. As a result, it is the performance data for the slower learners which contribute strongly to the shape of the final portion of the curve in Figure 9.2. The curve reaches the mean of ten correct anticipations at the twelfth trial because that is how long the

Table 9.10 Number of Words Correctly Anticipated on Successive Trials

						Trials						
S No.	1	2	3	4	5	6	7	8	9	10	11	12
1	0	2	2	4	6	5	6	8	9	10		
2	0	1	2	3	3	4	7	8	8	10		
3	0	1	2	5	6	9	9	10				
4	0	0	1	2	4	5	4	5	7	8	8	10
5	0	2	4	7	8	9	10					
6	0	1	3	6	7	8	8	10				
Mean No. of Words:	0	1.2	2.3	4.5	5.7	6.7	7.4	8.5	9.0	9.7	9.7	10.0

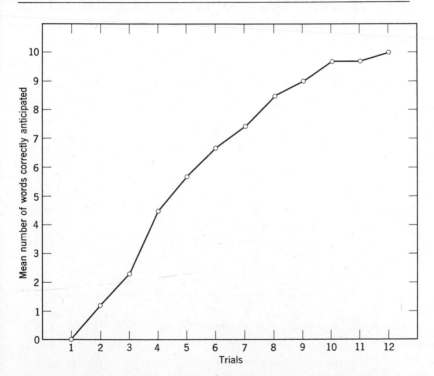

Fig. 9.2. Illustrative verbal learning curve showing the mean number of responses correctly anticipated as a function of trials. The hypothetical data represent the learning of a ten-pair list by six subjects, as presented in Table 9.10.

Verbal Learning: Acquisition of Associations   **333**

slowest subject, No. 4, took to learn the list. The curve might have been either shortened or lengthened by a trial or two had this subject performed somewhat differently.

As we examine the performance of our learning task we might ask a different question about the progress that subjects have evidenced. Instead of asking, "How many responses did S No. 2 get correct on Trial 2 or Trial 4?" we might ask, "How many trials did S No. 2 require to get two responses correct, three responses correct, four responses?" We can examine Table 9.10 for the answers. We find that S No. 2 required three trials to reach two correct anticipations, four trials to anticipate three responses correctly, and six trials to get four correct. By asking how many trials each subject took to reach successive criteria, from one response correct up to ten responses, we can transform the data of Table 9.10 into a new set of descriptive data. This technique for treating the data stems from an analysis of learning curves by Melton (1936). We see such transformed data in Table 9.11.

Table 9.11 Trials Required to Reach Successive Criteria—Number of Words Correct

	Successive Criteria—Words Correct									
S No.	1	2	3	4	5	6	7	8	9	10
1	2	2	4	4	5	5	8	8	9	10
2	2	3	4	6	7	7	7	8	10	10
3	2	3	4	4	4	5	6	6	6	8
4	3	4	5	5	6	9	9	10	12	12
5	2	2	3	3	4	4	4	5	6	7
6	2	3	3	4	4	4	5	6	8	8
Mean No. of Trials:	2.2	2.8	3.8	4.3	5.0	5.7	6.5	7.2	8.5	9.2

If we look at the successive scores reported in Table 9.10 for S No. 1 we can see how they were transformed in filling in Table 9.11. S No. 1 had two correct anticipations in his second trial. For the criterion of two correct in Table 9.11 (the column headed "2") we have shown an entry of two for this subject, indicating it took him this number of trials to reach this performance level. Actually, he also reached and surpassed the criterion of one correct on that same trial, so we have shown the same entry of 2 in the column headed "1." This subject did not reach the criterion of three correct until the fourth trial when he actually anticipated four responses correctly. We have therefore made the entry of 4 to indicate the trial on which these two criteria were reached or surpassed. By the next trial, the fifth, he had reached the criteria of five and six correct so a 5 is entered in the table for those two columns. S No. 1 did not reach seven correct until the eighth trial when he also reached the level of eight correct. This fact is indicated by the entry of 8 in the two columns for the seventh and eighth criteria. The criterion of nine correct was reached on the ninth trial and ten correct was achieved on the tenth trial, so these trial numbers become the final entries for S No. 1. Looking back at his performance record in Table 9.10, we see that his slipping back on Trial 6 to only five responses correct is not reflected in the transformed data.

The transformed data indicate the earliest trial number when a particular criterion of responses correct was reached or surpassed. By following this rule you should be able to see how every entry in Table 9.11 was obtained from some entry in Table 9.10. The numbers in the two tables are not the same, of course, since one set of data refers to responses recited and the other to trials experienced. The data naturally do not correspond by columns in the tables since twelve columns were required in Table 9.10 to accomodate data for S No. 4, whereas Table 9.11 has just ten columns to represent the successive criteria at which we chose to examine the progress of the learners. The correspondence of these two tables simply stems from the application of our transformation rule.

At the bottom of Table 9.11 we have presented the mean number of trials required by the subjects to attain the successive criteria of mastery of the list. Every subject has contributed to each of these means. These values also permit the plotting of a performance curve, shown in Figure 9.3. As is conventional in functions representing behavioral data, the ordinate represents the units of performance, the successive criteria of mastery of the material being memorized. The abscissa resembles conventional learning curves in representing the succession of trials experienced by the subjects. The function simply departs from conventional graphs in that we have plotted a group mean to the right of each value on the ordinate instead of plotting a group mean above each value on the abscissa.

We noted that the curve of Figure 9.2 reached a mean of ten re-

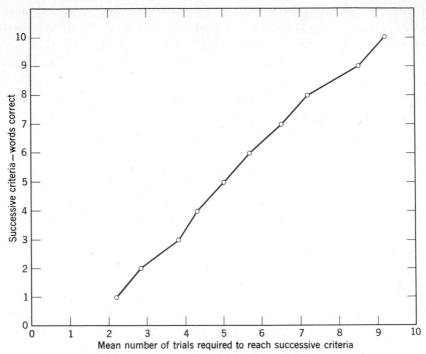

Fig. 9.3. Illustrative verbal learning curve plotting the mean number of trials required to reach successive criteria of mastery of a ten-pair list. The hypothetical data which yield this function are presented in Table 9.11.

sponses correct at the twelfth trial, this fact being dependent on the performance data of S No. 4. Since this mean represents an errorless performance which was not indicated in any earlier portion of the group curve, we might be tempted to conclude that twelve trials were required, on the average, to master the ten-pair list. But we know this conclusion would not be valid, because most of the subjects achieved a perfect trial earlier. Once they had made ten correct anticipations we subsequently credited them with that level of attainment in computing the group means. Even though additional trials would have led to a greater degree of mastery, to overlearning, we used a score of ten in our calculations. This is another way of pointing up the later part of this function as chiefly dependent on the slower learners.

The means of Table 9.11 plotted in Figure 9.3 are more representative measures of central tendency. Consider, for example, the mean number of trials required to attain ten correct anticipations. To the mean, each subject has contributed an empirical datum. In its calculation we did not use any value which really reflected a different stage of the memorization process, as was partly the case when we computed the means of Table 9.10 and Figure 9.2. From these considerations it would seem that the functional relationship of Figure 9.3 is a better reflection of the group's performance.

Either of the curves we have been discussing has a weakness in reflecting the learning process. Certain empirical facts, evident in the data of individual subjects, tend to be suppressed when group means are taken. This is true whether we consider the mean number of responses correct or the transformed data, mean trials required to reach successive criteria. The empirical facts obscured are the occurrences of either plateaus or sudden increases in the performance data of some subjects. If we regard these parts of the records as mere chance deviations from a smooth learning curve which characterizes the learning of the hypothetical ideal individual, then our averaging is merely an aid to recapturing a valid representation of memorizing. If, however, these aspects of individual data represent subprocesses which are parts of the learning process, then they deserve our attention.

Paired Associate Learning

Early systematic explorations of verbal learning and memory are exemplified in the work of Ebbinghaus which has been insightfully reviewed by Postman (1968).* The pioneer experimentalist used serial learning as the format of memorization tasks that he prepared for himself as his own subject. The serial list method has continued to be a commonly chosen procedure and also a source of questions about the processes and variables which function as items are associated (for example, Ebenholtz, 1966; Heslip and Epstein, 1969; Slamecka, 1964; Voss, 1968). For some purposes, however, the serial method has limitations. If we are interested in the separate effects of verbal items as stimuli and as responses, the serial list has the disadvantage that each item serves as both a stimulus and a response. For studying processes such as stimulus differentiation or response availability, the paired associate method is preferred. In the remainder of this chapter, then, we shall focus our atten-

*See pp. 389–390 of Chapter 11, Memory.

tion on research in paired associate learning, sometimes abbreviated in research reports as PA learning or PAL.

In addition to the separate roles given to items as either stimuli or responses, the paired associate format permits the study of response acquisition or association in separate pairs or in specially constructed subsets of items in the list. Such use of mixed lists for testing certain hypotheses within the performances of a single group of subjects is another advantage of the paired procedure. Serial lists cannot be so fractionated without inviting rather serious complications such as interaction with order effects. It must be emphasized that in noting the experimental assignment of different types of items to stimulus and response roles, a common practice, we are not claiming that these items do not interact or that there are no processes which reflect effects of both types of item. In fact, it is this very complexity of processes which makes it desirable to be able to create lists with deliberate choice of items to be stimuli and those required as responses. Similarly, the forming of mixed lists for certain analytic purposes does not mean that the different list pairs are thought to be completely free of any effects on one another. The technique simply gives us another way of examining the phenomena which can otherwise be studied in homogeneous lists of pairs constructed in the same way within any list.

Stimulus variation

Some ingenious paired associate experiments have been designed to take advantage of the latitude which the method allows in the manipulation of stimulus and response side of the pairs to be associated. A few of these may be mentioned illustratively. Dukes and Bevan (1967), for example, made a rather distinctive choice of stimulus and response items to suit the special purposes of their investigation. They wanted to determine how variations in the stimuli from trial to trial would compare with the usual identical repetitions. The responses to be learned were "names of people"—actually items prepared by the experimenters. The stimuli were colored photographs of these 20 hypothetical individuals—actually pictures of fashion models from mail order catalogs. In the learning task these individuals' pictures were projected from slides made up into different sets. A person given the name "Frank Oliver" would be differently dressed when his picture appeared in each set.

The major experimental conditions of the study are summarized in

Table 9.12. Subjects were trained by viewing either *one set* of 20 photographs or by seeing each person in *four different sets* with varied clothing and pose each time. Each picture-name exposure lasted five seconds. The 4, 8, or 16 trials given each group of subjects involved either repeated exposure of Set A or successive exposures of Sets *A*, *B*, *C*, and *D*. Testing required written responses—the names of the 20 persons—when either Set *A* or a new Set *E* was viewed for 15 sec per photograph.

Table 9.12 Design of Experiment with Learning of Names of Persons as Responses to their Repeated or Varied Photographs

Training Trials	Recall Test	
(4, 8, or 16)	Same Set (*A*)	New Set (*E*)
Single set of 20 photographs (Set *A*)	Single set—Same, = Condition I	Single set—New, = Condition II
Four sets of 20 photographs each (Sets *A, B, C, D*)	Four sets—Same, = Condition III	Four sets—New, = Condition IV

Recall scores obtained from 12 independent groups of subjects are shown in Figure 9.4. Response scoring gave one point for each name, first or last, of each person of the twenty studied so that the maximum possible score on the test was forty. As the plotted points show, recall was superior for Condition I after any amount of training, being nearly perfect when 8 or 16 trials had been given on the same set of photographs as were used in testing. When subjects had seen only one set of photos and then were tested on a completely new set, Condition II, performance on the recall test was poorest, significantly lower than the groups under Conditions III and IV after 8 or 16 trials as the figure suggests.

Most paired associate studies do not involve stimuli as colorful as photographs of fashion models. Typically stimulus items are verbal, or at least symbolic in form, as are the usual response items of the pairs. Many manipulations of verbal stimuli have been made in order to examine their role in the accomplishment of the learning task. One approach has been the use of compound stimuli (for example, Horowitz et

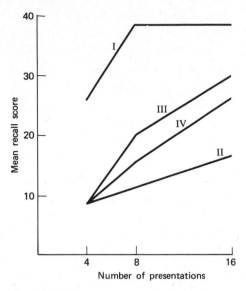

Fig. 9.4. Mean recall score obtained after different numbers of presentations under Conditions I–IV as described in Table 9.12. (After Dukes and Bevan, 1967.)

al., 1964; Musgrave and Cohen, 1964; Saltz, 1963) in order to investigate how the stimulus elements are involved when the associations within the pairs are developed. Many other inventive approaches in paired associate learning have involved special treatments of the stimulus terms (for example, Bernbach, 1967; Brown and Battig, 1965; Postman and Greenbloom, 1967).

Response analysis

On the response side of the paired associate task, two different reports may be cited as examples of analytic approaches. Using two-syllable nouns as stimuli, Postman (1964) departed markedly from standard procedure by having subjects provide their own responses to be learned. Subjects were told to decide on some word to give as the response to any particular stimulus whenever it appeared in the memory drum window. They might change some responses during practice but they would have to continue the trials until a consistent S-R pattern appeared for the entire list. Subjects tended to choose responses for their own learning which corresponded with normative word association data for the stimulus words used. Learning was faster for pairs developed from the stimuli of medium Thorndike-Lorge frequency of use than for stimuli of higher or lower frequency.

In a paper which analyzes the problem of assessing response learning as one stage of paired associate learning, Ekstrand (1966) pointed out the difficulty of using the trial on which a response is first given as an index of when it has become available or integrated. The trouble is that a subject may withhold a response until he has a certain level of confidence in its correctness. In view of the subjectivity and hence unreliability of this approach, the article suggests alternatives. These involve using free learning or free recall requirements in the experimental design. If carefully obtained and interpreted, free learning or recall data may be taken as estimates of response learning while conventional paired associate measures assess the completion of the associative task.

Temporal variables

As a standardized laboratory technique, the paired associate procedure offers the experimenter rigorous control over temporal aspects of the learning task. The commonest temporal variation which can strongly affect performance is the rate of presentation of the stimulus-response pairs. A commonly used pacing of the anticipation method is a 2:2 rate; the stimulus alone is presented for the 2-sec anticipatory interval and then both stimulus and response are presented together for a 2-sec study interval. No matter whether this standard rate or another is adopted, it must be realized that the rate of S-R presentations may be a determinant of the experimental outcome.

Two reports may be cited where the temporal dimension was found to interact with other task dimensions as an influence on performance. Underwood and Ekstrand (1967) conducted a series of experiments in which they used three different intertrial intervals: 0 sec representing massed practice and 15 sec and 45 sec representing two degrees of distributed practice. Among the stronger effects noted was the superior performance obtained over the course of 40 acquisition trials under distributed practice when trigrams of high intralist similarity were the responses to common 3-letter words used as stimuli. Despite this particular finding (Underwood and Ekstrand, 1967, p. 16) the experimenters note that with paired associate learning the effect of distributed practice is usually not large (p. 21).

A very different manipulation was introduced by Nodine (1969). His temporal arrangement of presentations of stimulus-response trigram pairs represents a combining of the conventional anticipation format and the conventional recall format, as indicated in Figure 9.5. The temporal variable of the experiment was the interstimulus interval $I(S,R)$ between the offset of the stimulus and the onset of the response presentation during the study phase. Values of 0, 1, 2, 4, and 6 sec were used for this independent variable. Different groups of subjects were run at each interval under one of three different conditions: instructed to repeat numbers as heard from a loudspeaker during $I(S,R)$; instructed to repeat the stimulus item just seen as paced at a 1-sec rate by a blinking light; uninstructed as to any activity during $I(S,R)$. Durations of the separate presentations of stimulus and response items during the study phase were 0.5 sec each. In the test phase 2.5 sec was allowed for each response, the spelling of the trigram. Every third test trial was followed by a free recall trial with 40 sec allowed for the writing of the PA units as far as possible.

When the trials-to-criterion data were analyzed, Nodine found that the 1-sec value for $I(S,R)$ had led to the slowest learning. The zero and 6-sec intervals led to the quickest attainment of criterion generally, with 2-sec and 4-sec performance being generally intermediate. Other main effects were that number naming and low-M value of stimuli each led to poorer learning.

Other Illustrative Studies

Learning scaled items

An experiment by L'Abate (1959) illustrates two points that were stressed earlier: (1) that the paired associate format permits the separate manip-

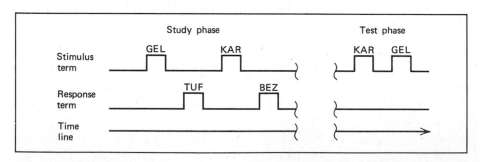

Fig. 9.5. Schematic representation of the temporal course of presentations of stimulus and response trigrams in a modified recall format as described in the text. (After Nodine, 1969.)

ulation of stimulus and response dimensions, and (2) that scalable characteristics of the verbal materials are among the most potent determinants of verbal learning as studied in the laboratory. The experimenter constructed four 9-pair lists from nonsense syllables which had been identified by Glaze as either very high or low in association value, *a*. This allowed four different conditions to be created by placing high or low items in either stimulus or response positions of the pairs: Condition *H-H* with both stimulus and response high in association value; Condition *H-L* with high stimuli, low responses; Condition *L-H*, the reverse; and Condition *L-L* with both elements drawn from the items of low *a* value. Presenting these lists to different groups of subjects, L'Abate determined the course of learning under the different conditions as shown in Figure 9.6. The course of learning was speediest in Condition *H-H* and by far the slowest in Condition *L-L*. Condition *H-L* required more

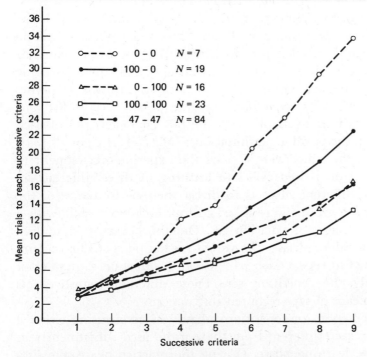

Fig. 9.6. Course of paired associate learning of nonsense syllables with stimulus and response terms with either very high or low association values. (After L'Abate, 1959.)

trials to reach the criterion than did Condition *L-H*. This indicates that dropping the response *a* values from high to low is more detrimental than reducing the *a* values of the stimuli.

Numerous other studies have shown that scaled characteristics of the materials can significantly affect verbal learning, in either serial or paired associate tasks. Two examples may be cited in which experimenters have usefully presented the scaled items. Lindley (1960) gives 4 groups of CVCs which are segregated according to their association values, pronounceability, and familiarity as based on their occurrence as the first part of common words. Saltz (1967) presents 5 lists of 20 nouns segregated by Thorndike-Lorge frequency count which he then scaled for *m* value.

Learning strategies

The role of mental imagery as a strategy in associative learning has been treated in depth by Paivio (1969). Having worked earlier on the rating of nouns as to *concreteness* versus *abstraction*, Yuille and Paivio (1968) examined the impact of this dimension on paired associate learning. Keeping the selected nouns comparable on Thorndike-Lorge frequency and on *m* value, they prepared needed lists with stimuli being either concrete and high in imagery or abstract and low in imagery and responses being from the opposite category. Other lists had both stimuli and responses drawn from the same category, either concrete or abstract. Thus four types of 16-pair lists were available with the S-R characteristics of each type being of one of the possible permutations; *C-C, C-A, A-C,* or *A-A.*

In addition to the scaled verbal pairs the experimenters sought to determine the effect on paired associate learning of three different instructions given to different subjects to direct their performance of the task. One-third of the groups were asked to link each noun pair with a mental image—the imagery mediation set. One-third were told to link the nouns with a word or phrase—the verbal mediation set. The remaining third were asked to repeat each pair of words out loud a number of times during study—the repetition set. These different cognitive sets were induced by means of tape-recorded instructions.

A practice mediation (or repetition) phase was given using either a *C-C* or an *A-A* list, each different from those to be used subsequently in the paired associate learning phase. During the practice phase, the subjects given either mediating set had to press a button when they found a mediator for each pair of nouns as it was presented. They then briefly described this mental image or verbal mediator, reflecting their instructions. Subjects from repetition groups simply repeated each pair while it was on the screen.

The learning phase which followed mediation practice consisted of four study-test trials. For study or learning, each noun pair was projected for 4 sec. For recall testing each stimulus noun was projected for 7 sec during which the subject attempted to give the correct response word orally. With 4 types of word pairs, 3 instructional sets, and either of 2 contrasting practice lists, there were 24 combinations of experimental variables. Ten different college student subjects were run individually under each combination.

In the mediation phase subjects given the *verbal* set found mediators about as readily for the *A-A* noun pairs as for the *C-C* pairs. However, the *imagery* set led to longer response times in getting mediators for the abstract noun pairs as contrasted with the concrete.

In the paired associate task the learning of the *A-A* pairs was less effective than with the *C-C*, *C-A*, or *A-C* pairs when mean number correct was combined over all trials. The subjects given the mediating sets for imagery or verbal linking did about the same, better than the repetition groups on Trials 1 and 2. The learning sets showed a significant interaction with concreteness of stimulus item when Trial 1 data were examined, as shown in Figure 9.7. A postexperimental inquiry showed that

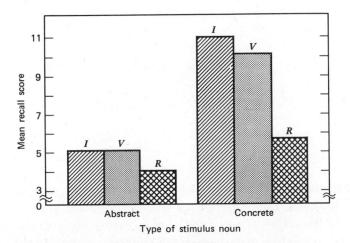

Fig. 9.7. Mean recall score on Trial 1 under instructional set for imagery mediation (*I*), verbal mediation (*V*), or repetition (*R*) for pairs with either abstract or concrete stimulus nouns. (After Yuille and Paivio, 1968.)

subjects given different instructional sets had generally adopted the learning strategy intended by the experimenters. In discussing the results the investigators stress the poorer learning of the *A-A* noun pairs despite their equivalence with other lists in *m* and in frequency. They note that abstractness versus concreteness is a dimension to be given due attention when nouns are used in verbal learning studies.

An experiment carried out by Martin, Boersma, and Cox (1965) stands in contrast to that of Yuille and Paivio with respect to the method of studying associative strategies. It shares their subsequent finding, however, of the superiority of mediational strategies over mere repetition. Giving the learning of 8 paralog pairs as the initial task, these researchers obtained each subject's reports later as to the pair-by-pair strategy he had employed. Classifying the various techniques as to complexity, the experimenters found a positive relationship between this index and number of correct responses attained during learning.

Acoustic characteristics and learning

There is evidence that acoustic aspects of verbal material may affect verbal learning even though hearing and speech are not always directly or overtly involved. In concluding this chapter we shall briefly allude to two studies which involve certain linguistic concepts. Jenkins, Foss, and Greenberg (1968) used the following stimulus-response pairings of syllables as the learning task for their experimental subjects:

Stimuli	Responses
pa	ba
ta	da
ka	ga
fa	va
sa	za
cha	ja

According to the distinctive features system of classifying speech sounds as employed by some linguists, these pairs have initial consonant sounds which differ in only one basic way. The stimuli begin with voiceless consonants and the paired responses are the voiced counterparts of these initial sounds. Thus there is an articulatory or phonological basis for the pairings. Paired items are more similar as phonemic items than are non-pairs. The experiment was designed to determine if this would aid learning when compared to a control condition where the same syllables were paired randomly. Three of the four experimental groups, to learn the pairs as presented above, were given special instructions. The *System* group was told to look for systematic relations between stimulus and response terms. The *Sound* group was told to pay attention to the sound of the syllables. The *Mouth* group was instructed to look for a system and to pay attention to their mouths as they pronounced the syllables. The other experimental group was referred to as *Standard,* being given regular paired associate instructions with no hint as to how to learn the pairs. Subjects of a *Control* group each had to learn one of five different random pairings of the stimuli and responses.

The general outcome of the experiment is indicated by the mean number of trials taken by each group to attain the criterion of two successive errorless trials:

Group	Mean Trials to Criterion
Control	19.75
Standard	18.00
Mouth	10.25
Sound	16.80
System	15.35

It is evident (and statistically supported) that the learning of the *Control* group was slower than that of the four experimental groups. The plotted learning curves of the original report show the *Standard, System,* and *Sound* groups as learning at about the same rate. The *Mouth* group was shown statistically to be faster in learning than these three. A postexperimental questionnaire revealed that the approach taken by subjects to the memorization task had been influenced by the special instructions about as intended. Both the linguistic system of S-R pairings and the linguistic strategies suggested to the learners had proved effective when compared with the control condition.

In the study just reviewed phonological similarity was facilitative when used as the basis for pairing the syllables to be associated with each other. We turn now to an experiment by Runquist (1970) in which the acoustic similarity was introduced among six words used as stimulus items. Responses were the pressing of six push buttons, each arbitrarily paired with a stimulus word to create a paired associate task. Stimulus items projected on the wall for three different groups of subjects were as follows:

Similar	Different	Control Group
mad	man	man
map	may	mop
mat	mar	mid
hem	hem	hem
hen	her	hug
hep	hew	hod

In the spelling of the items the stimuli for the two experimental groups show the same degree of intralist similarity of items. However, in the *Similar* group, the vowel sounds of "a" or "e" are more similar than they are in the *Different* group where the consonants change the phonemic nature of either vowel from item to item.

Intralist similarity, highest for the *Similar* group, was expected to produce interference that would hamper learning. As predicted, this group averaged about 20 percent fewer correct responses over the course of 20 learning trials and made about 50 percent more overt errors in pressing the response buttons. The other two groups did not differ significantly on these two measures of performance. The interference that probably reduced the effectiveness of the *Similar* group was attributed by Runquist to acoustic or articulatory representation of the stimulus syllables as they were encountered by the learners. Once again linguistic considerations appear to be relevant to the interpretation of verbal behavior even when speech and hearing are not overtly involved in the task.

Summary

Association has been a central concept in much of the psychological research on verbal behavior. Word association investigators have presented stimuli and required verbal responses which were either discrete or continued, and free or controlled. Stimulus items have included abstract shapes and quasi-verbal letter combinations, but usually they have been individual words or category labels. Indices of associative strength include frequency of occurrence, reaction time, response rate, clustering, and ordinal position. Repeated testing has revealed response hierarchies to be fairly stable.

Studies of word association have provided normative data on stimulus-response tendencies. References to several studies were tabulated. The data these provide may help other investigators to select verbal materials for many kinds of experimentation into verbal processes. Illustrative studies we reviewed were probing the mechanisms of priming and clustering.

Attributes and dimensions of verbal materials have been explored in numerous ways. The data obtained offer promise of refining further verbal behavior research. Different investigators have quantified association norms, meaning, meaningfulness, familiarity and frequency, associability, pronounceability, and imagery.

The acquisition and strengthening of associations among verbal items has been studied in various verbal learning tasks. Data obtained in a typical experiment may be summarized as mean number of items correct or as mean trials to successive criteria. We saw that either method of treating the data can give us a learning curve. Paired associate learning experiments provided us with varied examples of research methods and findings. Among the problems investigated were the effect of multiple vs. single photographs of persons as stimuli, stimulus and response attributes, temporal dimensions, association values, imagery, mediational strategies, and acoustical or phonological properties of items to be paired.

References

Andreas, B. G. Indicants of response strength hierarchies in continued word association. *Psychonomic Science*, 1966, **6**, 447–448.

Andreas, B. G., & Mills, M. Stability of response strength hierarchies in continued word association. *Psychonomic Science*, 1967, **7**, 129–130.

Archer, E. J. Re-evaluation of the meaningfulness of all possible CVC trigrams. *Psychological Monographs*, 1960, **74**, (10, Whole No. 497).

Battig, W. F., & Montague, W. E. Category norms for verbal items in 56 categories: A replication and extension of the Connecticut category norms. *Journal of Experimental Psychology Monograph*, 1969, **80**, No. 3, Part 2.

Bernbach, H. A. Stimulus learning and recognition in paired-associate learning. *Journal of Experimental Psychology*, 1967, **75**, 513–519.

Bilodeau, E. A., & Howell, D. C. *Free association norms by discrete and continued methods.* Washington, D.C.: Office of Naval Research, 1965.

Bousfield, W. A., Cohen, B. H., Whitmarsh, G. A., & Kincaid, W. D. The Connecticut free associational norms. Technical Report No. 35, Contract Nonr 631(00), University of Connecticut, 1961

Bousfield, W. A., & Sedgewick, C. H. W. An analysis of sequences of restricted associative responses. *Journal of General Psychology*, 1944, **30**, 149–165.

Brotsky, S. J., & Linton, M. L. The test-retest reliability of free association norms. *Psychonomic Science*, 1967, **8**, 425–426.

Brown, S. C., & Battig, W. F. Effects of successive addition of stimulus elements on paired-associate learning. *Journal of Experimental Psychology*, 1965, **70**, 87–93.

Cohen, B. H., Bousfield, W. A., & Whitmarsh, G. A. Cultural norms for verbal items in 43 categories. Technical Report No. 22, Contract Nonr 631(00), University of Connecticut, 1957.

Cramer, P. *Word association*. New York: Academic Press, 1968.

Cramer, P. A study of homographs. In L. Postman & G. Keppel (Eds.), *Norms of word association*. New York: Academic Press, 1970, Pp. 361–382.

Cronbach, L. J. The two disciplines of scientific psychology. *American Psychologist*, 1957, **12**, 671–684.

Dukes, W. F., & Bevan, W. Stimulus variation and repetition in the acquisition of naming responses. *Journal of Experimental Psychology*, 1967, **74**, 178–181.

Duncan, C. P. Problem solving within a verbal response hierarchy. *Psychonomic Science*, 1966, **4**, 147–148.

Ebenholtz, S. M. Serial position effect of ordered stimulus dimensions in paired-associate learning. *Journal of Experimental Psychology*, 1966, **71**,132–137.

Ekstrand, B. R. A note on measuring response learning during paired-associate learning. *Journal of Verbal Learning and Verbal Behavior*, 1966, **5**, 344–347.

Gekoski, W. L., & Riegel, K. F. A study of the one-year stability of the Michigan free and restricted association norms. *Psychonomic Science*, 1967, **8**, 427–428.

Haagen, C. H. Synonymity, vividness, familiarity, and association value ratings of 400 pairs of common adjectives. *Journal of Psychology*, 1949, **27**, 453–463.

Heslip, J. R., & Epstein, W. Effectiveness of serial position and preceding-item cues in serial learning. *Journal of Experimental Psychology*, 1969, **80**, 64–68.

Hilgard, E. R. Methods and procedures in the study of learning. In S. S. Stevens (Ed.), *Handbook of experimental psychology*. New York: Wiley, 1951. Pp. 517–567.

Horowitz, L. M., Lippman, L. G., Norman, S. A., & McConkie, G. W. Compound stimuli in paired-associate learning. *Journal of Experimental Psychology*, 1964, **67**, 132–141.

Jenkins, J. J., Foss, D. J., & Greenberg, J. H. Phonological distinctive features as cues in learning. *Journal of Experimental Psychology*, 1968, **77**, 200–205.

Jenkins, J. J., & Palermo, D. S. Further data on changes in word-association norms. *Journal of Personality and Social Psychology*, 1965, **1**, 303–309.

Jenkins, J. J., & Russell, W. A. Systematic changes in word association norms: 1910–1952. *Journal of Abnormal and Social Psychology*, 1960, **60**, 293–304.

Kammann, R. Associability: A study of the properties of associative ratings and the role of association in word-word learning. *Journal of Experimental Psychology Monograph*, 1968, **78**, No. 4, Part 2.

Keppel, G., & Strand, B. Z. Free-association responses to the primary responses and other responses selected from the Palermo-Jenkins norms. In L. Postman & G. Keppel (Eds.), *Norms of word association*. New York: Academic Press, 1970, Pp. 177–239.

L'Abate, L. Manifest anxiety and the learning of syllables with different associative values. *American Journal of Psychology*, 1959, **72**, 107–110.

Lindley, R. H. Association value and familiarity in serial verbal learning. *Journal of Experimental Psychology*, 1960, **59**, 366–370.

Marshall, G. R., & Cofer, C. N. Associative indices as measures of word relatedness: A summary and comparison of ten methods. *Journal of Verbal Learning and Verbal Behavior*, 1963, **1**, 408–421.

Marshall, G. R., & Cofer, C. N. Single-word free-association norms for 328 responses from the Connecticut cultural norms for verbal items in categories. In L. Postman & G. Keppel (Eds.), *Norms of word association*. New York: Academic Press, 1970, Pp. 321–360.

Martin, C. J., Boersma, F. J., & Cox, D. L. A classification of associative strategies in paired-associate learning. *Psychonomic Science*, 1965, **3**, 455–456.

Melton, A. W. The end-spurt in memorization curves as an artifact of the averaging of individual curves. *Psychological Monographs*, 1936, **47**, No. 2 (Whole No. 212).

Montague, W. E., & Kiess, H. O. The associability of CVC pairs. *Journal of Experimental Psychology Monograph*, 1968, **78**, No. 2, Part 2.

Musgrave, B. S., & Cohen, J. C. Effects of two-word stimuli on recall and learning in a paired-associate task. *Journal of Experimental Psychology*, 1964, **68**, 161–166.

Noble, C. E. An analysis of meaning. *Psychological Review*, 1952, **59**, 421–430.

Noble, C. E. The meaning-familiarity relationship. *Psychological Review*, 1953, **60**, 89–98.

Noble, C. E. The familiarity-frequency relationship. *Journal of Experimental Psychology*, 1954, **47**, 13–16.

Noble, C. E. Measurements of association value (*a*), rated associations (*a'*), and scaled meaningfulness (*m'*) for the 2100 CVC combinations of the English alphabet. *Psychological Reports*, 1961, **8**, 487–521.

Noble, C. E., & Parker, G. V. C. The Montana scale of meaningfulness (*m*). *Psychological Reports*, 1960, **7**, 325–331.

Nodine, C. F. Temporal variables in paired-associate learning: The law of contiguity revisited. *Psychological Review*, 1969, **76**, 351–362.

Osgood, C. E. The nature and measurement of meaning. *Psychological Bulletin*, 1952, **49**, 197–237.

Osgood, C. E., Suci, G. J., & Tannenbaum, P. H. *The measurement of meaning*. Urbana, Ill.: University of Illinois Press, 1957.

Paivio, A. Mental imagery in associative learning and memory. *Psychological Review*, 1969, **76**, 241–263.

Paivio, A., Yuille, J. C., & Madigan, S. A. Concreteness, imagery, and meaningfulness values for 925 nouns. *Journal of Experimental Psychology Monograph Supplement*, 1968, **76**, No. 1, Part 2.

Palermo, D. S., & Jenkins, J. J. *Word association norms*. Minneapolis: University of Minnesota Press, 1964.

Pollio, H. R. Composition of associative clusters. *Journal of Experimental Psychology*, 1964, **67**, 199–208.

Postman, L. Acquisition and retention of consistent associative responses. *Journal of Experimental Psychology*, 1964, **67**, 183–190.

Postman, L. Hermann Ebbinghaus. *American Psychologist*, 1968, **23**, 149–157.

Postman, L. The California norms: Association as a function of word frequency. In L. Postman & G. Keppel (Eds.), *Norms of word association*. New York: Academic Press, 1970, Pp. 241–320.

Postman, L., & Greenbloom, R. Conditions of cue selection in the acquisition of paired-associate lists. *Journal of Experimental Psychology*, 1967, **73**, 91–100.

Postman, L., & Keppel, G. (Eds.) *Norms of word association*. New York: Academic Press, 1970.

Rosanoff, A. J. (Ed.), *Free association test (Kent-Rosanoff)*. New York: Wiley, 1927.

Runquist, W. N. Verbal behavior. In J. B. Sidowski (Ed.), *Experimental methods and instrumentation in psychology*. New York: McGraw-Hill, 1966. Pp. 487–540.

Runquist, W. N. Acoustic similarity among stimuli as a source of interference in paired-associate learning. *Journal of Experimental Psychology*, 1970, **83**, 319–322.

Russell, W. A., & Jenkins, J. J. The complete Minnesota norms for responses to 100 words from the Kent-Rosanoff word association tests. Technical Report 11, Contract N8 onr 66216, University of Minnesota, 1954.

Saltz, E. Compound stimuli in verbal learning: Cognitive and sensory differentiation versus stimulus selection. *Journal of Experimental Psychology*, 1963, **66**, 1–5.

Saltz, E. Thorndike-Lorge frequency and *m* of stimuli as separate factors in paired-associates learning. *Journal of Experimental Psychology*, 1967, **73**, 473–478.

Segal, S. J. Priming of association test responses by differential verbal contexts. *Journal of Experimental Psychology*, 1967, **74**, 370–377.

Shapiro, S. S. Word association norms: Stability of response and chains of association. *Psychonomic Science*, 1966, 4, 233–234.

Slamecka, N. J. An inquiry into the doctrine of remote associations. *Psychological Review*, 1964, **71**, 61–76.

Snider, J. G., & Osgood, C. E. (Eds.) *Semantic differential technique: A sourcebook*. Chicago: Aldine, 1969.

Spreen, O., & Schulz, R. W. Parameters of abstraction, meaningfulness, and pronunciability for 329 nouns. *Journal of Verbal Learning and Verbal Behavior*, 1966, **5**, 459–468.

Taylor, J. D., & Kimble, G. A. The association value of 320 selected words and paralogs. *Journal of Verbal Learning and Verbal Behavior*, 1967, **6**, 744–752.

Thorndike, E. L., & Lorge, I. *The teacher's word book of 30,000 words*. New York: Teachers College, Columbia University, 1944.

Tulving, E., & Madigan, S. A. Memory and verbal learning. *Annual Review of Psychology*, 1970, **21**, 437–484.

Underwood, B. J., & Ekstrand, B. R. Effect of distributed practice on paired-associate learning. *Journal of Experimental Psychology Monograph Supplement,* 1967, 73, No. 4, Part 2 (Whole No. 634).

Underwood, B. J., & Richardson, J. Some verbal materials for the study of concept formation. *Psychological Bulletin*, 1956, **53**, 84–95.

Underwood, B. J., & Schulz, R. W. *Meaningfulness and verbal learning.* Chicago: Lippincott, 1960.

Vanderplas, J. M., & Garvin, E. A. The association value of random shapes. *Journal of Experimental Psychology*, 1959, **57**, 147–154.

Voss, J. F. Serial acquisition as a function of number of successively occurring list items. *Journal of Experimental Psychology*, 1968, **78**, 456–462.

Woodworth, R. S., & Schlosberg, H. *Experimental psychology.* (Rev. ed.) New York: Holt, 1954.

Yuille, J. C., & Paivio, A. Imagery and verbal mediation instructions in paired-associate learning. *Journal of Experimental Psychology*, 1968, **78**, 436–441.

Note: Data of Table 9.9 on page 327 were taken from the chapter by W. N. Runquist in *Experimental methods and instrumentation in psychology* edited by J. B. Sidowski. Copyright 1966 by McGraw-Hill, Inc. Used with permission of McGraw-Hill Book Co.

chapter 10
Perceptual-Motor Performance

Perceptual-motor performance is a term we use to describe coordinated activity usually involving the use of arms, hands, and fingers in performing a variety of tasks. Although the phrase is often shortened to "motor performance" in emphasis of the motion involved, the designation "perceptual-motor" gives proper recognition to the perceptual guidance of the movements that we make. Visual perception guides much of our motor activity, but always in conjunction with another important sense—kinesthesis. Our actions are so dependent on this sense of motion that some investigations of motor performance are interpreted as studies of kinesthetic perception.

A few examples will remind us that perceptual-motor performance deserves considerable study in a science of behavior. When we sign our name, drive a car, or tap to the rhythm of our favorite melody, we are engaging in perceptual-motor behavior. The quarterback flipping a short pass, the marksman steadying the rifle, the surgeon wielding the scalpel—these, too, are performing motor tasks guided by their perceptions. Of course we do not necessarily go to the football field, the rifle range, or the operating room for scientific studies of motor behavior, although psychologists have conducted studies in the first two of these situations. Conventionally, we use standard tasks to be performed by experimental subjects in the laboratory. The study of their achievement under different conditions is the way we attempt to clarify the principles of perceptual-motor performance.

Taxonomy of Performances

The domain of perceptual-motor performance under laboratory investigation ranges almost as widely as our examples of motor activities in real life. We need to subdivide our topic in order to review it systematically. In considering the problem of task classification Fitts (1964) drew attention to the elements which comprise the required actions, to task continuity (contrasted with discrete responses or periodicity in reacting), to spatial-temporal coherence (redundancy or repetition), and to stimulus-response complexity. The taxonomy of performances which we shall consider here represents a similar approach by way of task analysis. As a descriptive method it contrasts with the empirical-theoretical approach to categorizing human abilities represented in the work of Fleishman (1954, 1969). In dealing with various performance descriptions we shall sometimes review particular tasks used in psychology laboratories and we shall occasionally consider some of the determinants of scores made on them.

Static Motor Performance

One kind of motor behavior is actually aimed at minimizing motion. We have already mentioned the rifle marksman who maintains an essentially motionless posture as he prepares to fire a round. We may think, too, of the diver poised on the high board, immobile just before he springs into the air. Despite their lack of motion, these performances are characterized by a high degree of muscular coordination. Such static motor performance, then, is a proper topic for laboratory study.

We may wish to investigate the static motor performance involved in posture. The measurement of such behavior often involves the making of a graphic record of body sway. By fitting a subject with a headband and linking this by threads and pulleys to recording styluses, we can make a continuous record of his postural sway on a kymograph drum or tape. Later this record may be analyzed to determine such things as the amplitudes and the periodicity or frequency of his motion.

Most of us have noticed that our hand shakes slightly when we extend it and attempt to hold it motionless. A simple apparatus devised for testing hand steadiness provides a convenient task for investigating the effect of any independent variables that an experimenter might select. The apparatus consists of a stylus and a metal plate in which there are nine holes of graded diameters. In the standard procedure for measuring steadiness, the subject is required to begin with the largest hole, inserting the stylus to the required depth and then withdrawing it without touching the metal plate. He then proceeds to the next smaller hole, and so on, until he touches the plate while attempting to insert or withdraw the stylus. His steadiness score is determined by how far down through the series of holes he proceeds successfully before touching the metal plate.

Discrete Motor Responses

Discrete responses like pushing a button or releasing a telegraph key are among the simplest motor performances investigated by psychologists. The time lag between a stimulus and the response to it is often the focus of study. This response latency is referred to as *reaction time* (RT) in many laboratory experiments. Both simple reaction time (one response associated with one stimulus) and choice reaction time (multiple responses correlated with multiple stimuli) have been subjected to decades of research.

Simple reaction time

In a typical experiment on simple RT the subject is required to release a telegraph key as soon as he detects the onset of a light or tone, whichever is being used in the study. Simultaneously with stimulus onset a clock or chronoscope is started, to be terminated on release of the key. With the chronoscope calibrated in hundredths of a second, or perhaps in milliseconds, an accurate determination of RT is possible on each trial.

Since it is generally desired that a subject be attentive and ready for the critical stimulus each time, a warning signal usually precedes the stimulus. The interval separating the warning signal from the stimulus is an important determiner of RT so it should be carefully controlled. Numerous experiments have probed the effect of this variable—termed the *foreperiod* or *preparatory interval*. For example, Botwinick (1969) found shorter RTs to auditory stimuli after a preparatory interval of 0.5 sec compared with 6.0 sec when tonal intensity levels were approximately 8 or 81 dB above the reference level of 0.0002 dynes/cm^2 as set individually through audiometric testing of subjects. For weaker tones averaging around 6 dB, however, it was the longer foreperiod which resulted in shorter RTs. In correspondence with earlier work, Botwinick found that RT is shorter at increased stimulus intensity levels, averaging 715, 518, and 194 milliseconds for the tonal intensities of approximately 6, 8, and 81 dB, respectively.

A series of reports by Simon (1967, 1968, 1969) indicates some other aspects of RT to auditory stimulation. In one group of experiments Simon (1967) found that binaural stimulation led to faster key pressing than did a monaurally presented tone. When uncertain as to which ear would be stimulated, subjects responded more quickly when the tone was delivered to the right ear. When instructions eliminated the uncertainty, however, RT to left-ear stimulation was as short as to right-ear stimulus presentation. In a different task—moving a handle either to the left or right on command—Simon (1968) found that RT was shorter when the command "Right" was presented to the right ear (as compared to left-ear presentation of the command "Right"). However, when the command was "Left" the left-ear presentation led to shorter RT. In still another experiment, Simon (1969) found that RT in initiating a right or left movement was shorter when the handle had to be moved toward the side stimulated by an auditory tone presented monaurally.

Choice reaction time

In the series of studies conducted by Simon, the task of key pressing measured simple RT. When two responses were possible, moving the handle left or right at either command, the situation became one of *choice reaction time.* Another form of choice reaction time is found when instructions are given subjects to respond to one of two stimuli but not to the other. Whether involving one or two responses, the task calls first for stimulus discrimination, then for response selection. With this greater task complexity, choice RT exceeds simple RT by up to a fifth of a second. Choice RT is greater when stimuli to be discriminated are more similar or when the number of stimuli and responses is greater.

Positioning Reactions

When a task calls for some degree of accuracy in arm, hand, or finger movements, we may speak of *positioning reactions.* Such responses are often required in operating the controls on equipment as in adjusting a knob (rotary positioning), setting a lever (linear positioning) or reaching out and touching a button at some spatial location. Some positioning reactions involve the use of objects or tools as in indicating something with a pointer or picking up or placing a small item with pliers or tweezers.

The typical demands for speed and accuracy provide a way of measuring performance in positioning reactions and also a dilemma for the investigator. He may build a particular accuracy demand into his laboratory task and then measure reaction time and movement time as the response is performed. This is quite common in research. However, speed and accuracy are competing demands to some extent. If subjects tend to ignore an accuracy requirement (assuming they may be free to do so) their response times may be reduced. On the other hand, if they pay undue attention to accuracy—perhaps making their positioning movements more precise than required—they may sacrifice speed. In the face of these possibilities, an investigator devises the task, designs the experiment, phrases the instructions to subjects, and collects the data in ways which yield interpretable results. Numerous studies have compiled a great number of findings on positioning responses. As one might expect, performances are found to be influenced by a diversity of variables such as physical dimensions of tasks, age and sex of subjects, informational feedback or knowledge of results given to them, and environmental conditions under which performance is tested. A review by Keele (1968) summarizes and discusses many findings concerning skilled movement control. We shall here consider a study which exemplifies a systematic quantitative approach to the investigation of positioning reactions.

Movement amplitude and target width

A study reported by Fitts and Peterson (1964) demonstrated how physical task dimensions affected reaction time (RT) and movement time (MT) as a subject reached out to tap a metal target plate with a stylus. An overhead schematic view of a subject seated at the test apparatus is shown in Figure 10.1. Careful study of this diagram will indicate several common aspects of the experiments, which were carried out using 6 male subjects, ages 18 to 25, who were paid for their participation. Wearing headsets, subjects heard a continuous loud white noise. A momentary interruption of this noise was the ready signal. Then, exactly 2 sec later, either the left or right stimulus light flashed on. To this point the procedure resembles a test of choice RT. Following his instructions, the subject moved the stylus he had been holding on a start button and struck the target plate on the same side as the stimulus light. Immediately the knowledge of results (KR) lights showed whether he had hit the target or had undershot or overshot it. The two physical variables in the experiments were the movement amplitude required (3, 6, or 12 in.) and the

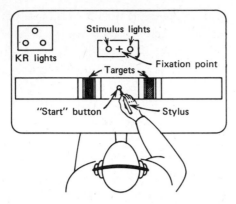

Fig. 10.1. Overhead schematic view of subject seated at apparatus designed to measure perceptual-motor choice reaction time and movement time for positioning reactions. (After Fitts and Peterson, 1964.)

target width (1.0, 0.5, 0.25, 0.125 in.). These two task dimensions were used jointly in determining an index of difficulty* (*ID*) which ranged from 2.58 bits (a unit borrowed by Fitts from information theory) for a 3-in. movement to a 1-in. target up to 7.58 bits for a 12-in. movement to a target 0.125 in. wide.

The reaction time (RT) and movement time (MT) were found in Experiment II to be linear functions of *ID,* as shown in Figure 10.2. The slope of the straight line fitted to the MT data was found to be 74, indicating that this measure depends heavily on *ID*. In contrast the RT function has a lesser slope, 5.4, indicating that choice RT is less affected by these task dimensions.

Repetitive Responses

In contrast to the single response in RT experiments and positioning reactions, perceptual-motor performance can be investigated by means of tasks in which an action is repeatedly performed. In these tasks the subject works as quickly as possible, his score usually being the number of units accomplished in a fixed amount of time. Each trial or session is

*$ID = \log_2 2A/W$, where *ID* = index of difficulty, in bits, *A* = amplitude of movement, in inches, and *W* = width of target, in inches.

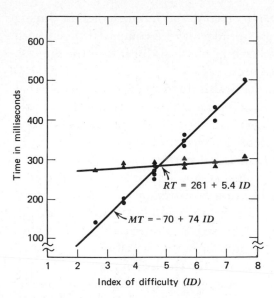

Fig. 10.2. Choice reaction time (*RT*) and movement time (*MT*) as functions of the index of task difficulty (*ID*). RT data are indicated by triangular symbols and MT data by circular symbols. (After Fitts and Peterson, 1964.)

short enough so that scores are not unduly affected by fatigue. A number of these procedures have been borrowed by experimental psychologists from the batteries of psychomotor aptitude tests devised for the selection of military or industrial personnel. In some research these may be administered in about the same way as originally employed. In other investigations the test materials, apparatus, or procedures must be modified to seek the effects of particular independent variables.

Tapping

One of the simplest of repetitive performances employed in the study of motor behavior is tapping. A simple motion of limited amplitude, involving wrist, hand, and fingers, is repeated as fast as possible. Despite its simplicity this kind of activity can be approached by means of several different techniques which differ in their task dimensions. One method for the study of tapping is to have the subject repeatedly tap a telegraph key that is connected to a counter to record the number of taps during a fixed interval so that the rate of tapping may be computed. Even with this simple arrangement there are several physical dimensions of the task which might affect performance scores.

To eliminate some of the mechanical influences on performance that are introduced by the telegraph key, tapping is frequently studied by providing a metal stylus that the subject uses to tap on a metal plate. Each contact of stylus and plate completes an electrical circuit and advances the counter one unit. A weakness in this technique, as with the key, is that the subject may vibrate the stylus in contact with the plate so that the counter score evidences rate of voluntary tremor instead of tapping rate. This difficulty is avoided in a different version of the task by providing two metal plates which have to be struck alternately by the stylus. Such a two-plate tapping board not only prevents the vibratory response, but introduces two physical task dimensions which may be varied to determine their effect upon the rate of response. These dimensions are the separation of the plates, which determines the travel of the hand and arm in performing, and the size of the plates, which influences the accuracy with which the response must be terminated at each end of the oscillatory motion. These two variables were studied by Fitts (1954) who used the apparatus represented in Figure 10.1 to test two-plate tapping speed.

Minnesota Rate of Manipulation Test

This standard aptitude test provides a repetitive motor task in which the repeated action is a manipulatory one, considerably more complex than tapping (Ziegler, 1933). In addition to requiring quite different manual involvement from tapping, the task also requires much more visual guidance. The test apparatus consists of 60 cylindrical blocks and a 60-hole board. Two different speed tasks may be administered. In the first, the subject is timed as he places the blocks in the holes. For the second task, all the blocks are initially in the holes and the subject must pick up one at a time with one hand, transfer them to the other hand, and replace them inverted in the same hole. The scores earned, of course, depend on the time taken to place or turn the cylinders. One could modify some of the dimensions or procedures of this test to study effects on performance in laboratory experiments, but even with apparatus dimensions retained in standard form, the test can be a useful research tool for studying the influence of variables like age and sex and of environmental conditions such as lighting and temperature.

Pegboard tasks

Another type of performance test that can be used in laboratory studies of perceptual-motor performance is one which calls for eye-hand coordination and fingertip manipulation of small objects. This kind of task is represented by a variety of pegboard tests in which subjects have to pick up small pegs or metal pins and place them as rapidly as possible in the holes arranged in rows on the pegboard. The motion pattern required is thus a repetitive one, although it is obviously more complex than tapping because of the manipulative requirement. Among the physical dimensions of such tasks that we would expect to influence the scores attained would be size of pins and size and spacing of holes in the pegboard. Two methods have been used in scoring performance on these tasks. In the work limit method, subjects must perform a stated amount of work—that is, fill a set number of holes, usually one hundred. The score for this method is the time, often expressed in seconds, that was taken to accomplish this amount of work. In the time limit method, the subject is allowed a fixed amount of time—perhaps 4 min. Here the score is the number of holes filled within the time limit. Note that in the work limit method, the score made is a time score; in the time limit method, the score is the amount of work done.

Selective Serial Actions

In everyday life—in playing a musical instrument, in athletic competition, in clerical and industrial work—perceptual-motor performance is less often strictly repetitive than it is serial in nature. That is, different actions succeed one another sequentially. One response leads to another, usually with perceptual feedback or guidance quite evident. Psychological research has been carried out on such serial motor performances as typing or piano-playing as well as industrial tasks like machine operation or light assembly work. For basic studies a number of laboratory tasks have been devised. In listing and describing some of the psychomotor test devices Noble (1969) stressed another characteristic of such tasks. They tend to provide multiple-choice situations in which learning may develop S-R associations between particular stimuli and responses. Feedback or knowledge of results guides the selection of appropriate responses to different stimulus conditions as selective learning proceeds. Think about the S-R learning possibilities as we review a few serial action tasks.

Card sorting

In the usual card-sorting task subjects are given a pack of numbered cards, thoroughly shuffled, to be sorted into a sorting tray divided into bins, each bin identified by a number which appears repeatedly in the set of cards. The tray might contain from 16 to 30 bins, and the pack of cards might contain from about 60 to 120 cards with each number included from four to eight times. The bin numbers are generally arranged randomly in the tray so that some searching is required on early trials to locate the bin into which a card must be tossed. As you can see, this card-sorting task is one that is likely to exhibit a strong practice effect as subjects become familiar with the bin locations. The performance measure for this task is the time taken to sort the entire pack of numbered cards. Very important is the requirement that the cards be shuffled thoroughly between trials, since they are taken in sorted groups from the bins. (It is much sounder research if improvement in scores from trial to trial can be interpreted as a practice effect in the subject's sorting rather than as a fatigue effect in the experimenter's shuffling!) To avoid another source of distortion of apparent practice effect it is well to cover the sorting tray immediately on the completion of a trial so that the subject may not study the bin locations during the intertrial interval.

Inverted-alphabet printing

Another serial motor task quite suitable for laboratory studies is inverted-alphabet printing. In this paper and pencil task, subjects begin at the right side of a page and work toward the left, printing letters of the alphabet upside down and in sequence so that if the page were rotated 180° the letters would appear as normal. Trials are set at some convenient length; 30-sec trials have been used, for example. On each successive trial the subject is required to begin with the next letter after the one with which he ended the previous trial. When Z is reached, the subject continues from A again. The score for each trial is the number of letters printed in the correct inverted fashion.

Maze tasks

Although most psychological experiments on learning maze pathways have used albino rats, we shall focus here on maze performance in which a human subject is required to trace a small maze manually. Most maze-learning procedures prohibit visual guidance. A person is forced to rely on tactual and kinesthetic cues as he moves his finger or a stylus through the pathways. Other maze techniques may permit the use of vision. A subject may look through a viewing tube, for example, which allows him to see only a small portion of the maze at a time as he attempts to master the entire pattern through repeated trials. Or a printed maze to be traced with a pencil may be of such complexity as to allow complete visual inspection. Still another full-vision procedure employs a letter maze in which letters of the alphabet are scattered in a seemingly random pattern on a printed page. Subjects have to use a pencil to connect the letters in some specified sequence.

Multiple light-and-key tasks

More illustrative of the S-R associative demands in selective serial actions are the laboratory tasks in which lights are typically used as discrete stimuli and array of keys or buttons must be pushed selectively in responding. In effect such apparatus demands many choice RTs in succession as performance proceeds serially. A special problem—the trade-off between speed and accuracy in such tasks—was studied by Howell and Kreidler (1963). Giving subjects a 10-light, 10-key task with complete correspondence or compatability in the stimulus-response arrays, these investigators varied task instructions. In briefly reviewing their experiment we shall consider the instructions given to just 3 groups of subjects.

Group I

"You are to respond as fast as possible . . . speed is the important thing and accuracy is definitely a secondary consideration."

Group II

"You are to respond so as to make as few errors as possible . . . speed is definitely a secondary consideration."

Group III

"You are to respond as fast and as accurately as you can . . . speed and accuracy are of equal importance in performing your task."

Subjects were given 4 blocks of 5 trials at the selective response task with each trial presenting the 10 stimulus lights in a randomized sequence. Performing under their different instructions, Groups I–III showed these accuracy (percent correct) and average speed (Rs per sec) scores for the final block of trials.

Group	Accuracy (%)	Speed
I (Speed)	87.3	1.84
II (Accuracy)	97.8	1.72
III (Both)	95.9	1.76

Accuracy scores differed significantly among the groups and were reflective of the special instructions given. Speed scores seemed also to be ordered as expected but were not significantly different when tested statistically.

Continuous Adjustive Performance

A kind of perceptual-motor performance which typically calls for continuous responding instead of discrete repetitive or serial actions is called tracking. This kind of task requires a subject to move a control in such a way as to minimize the positional discrepancy between two elements of a display that he is watching. Tracking is performed by astronauts, for example, when they engage in the visually guided docking maneuver which brings two spacecraft together. Not limited to the esoteric realm of space exploration, tracking is involved as a pilot lands a plane on a runway or as we drive a car down a winding road. Steering the car is a specific instance of the continuous adjustive performance called tracking.

In laboratory research and in numerous man-machine systems, two kinds of tracking are often contrasted and compared—*pursuit tracking* and *compensatory tracking*. In effecting a rendezvous with another spacecraft an astronaut might use first the one and then the other. He would use pursuit tracking in controlling his own craft to follow the target craft as both moved through space. Then as the craft became generally aligned he would make small corrections with his controls to compensate for any detectable misalignment as he completed the docking and link-up.

In pursuit tracking an operator of controls sees two moving elements, the target and the target follower (variously termed a cursor, pointer, ring, or stylus in different devices). He uses his controls to guide the follower in pursuit of the moving target, attempting to achieve and maintain their alignment. In compensatory tracking the moving element in the display actually represents the misalignment between the target and follower. Its motion combines the target motion and the compensatory control movements as well. The operator's task is to try continually to keep this element as near to a null reference point in the display as he possibly can. He tries, in other words, to compensate for any drift of the moving element away from the reference mark which represents zero error.

In laboratory studies as well as in other man-machine situations a wide variety of visual displays and of controls (cranks, knobs, and levers or sticks) are used in performing tracking tasks. Research on both pursuit and compensatory tracking, as well as other forms, has been reviewed and discussed by Poulton (1969). Here we shall go on only to mention a common laboratory task which represents a special kind of pursuit tracking— one in which the control handle and the target follower are directly linked instead of through some electronic or mechanical mechanism.

Rotary pursuit performance

In this tracking task the target is a small metal disk set in the surface of a turntable which rotates at a constant speed, usually sixty revolutions per minute. The subject tries to keep the tip of a metal stylus in contact with the target as it travels its circular pathway. The pursuit rotor, as the apparatus is usually called, thus requires following tracking. The linkage between stylus handle and tip which are the control and target follower, respectively, is a direct one in the rotary pursuit task. In most other tracking tasks this linkage between control and target follower is indirectly accomplished by mechanical or electrical means. The measure of performance for the rotary pursuit task, as for many other tracking tasks, is time on target, usually measured in milliminutes, seconds, or hundredths of a second. The clock accumulating the subject's score is operated by current passing through the stylus and the metal target so that it runs only when the subject is on target.

As a relatively standardized laboratory task, the pursuit rotor serves investigators as a tool for studying the effects on perceptual-motor performance of environmental variables and subject characteristics. For example,

Teichner and Wehrkamp (1954) studied the influence of ambient (environmental) temperature on rotary pursuit performance. Subjects were tested at a room temperature of 55, 70, 85, or 100° Fahrenheit on 5 successive days. Analysis of time-on-target scores indicated that performance is best at about 70° with significant detrimental effects observed at the higher or lower temperatures. An example of the role of subject characteristics is found in a study performed by Ammons, Alprin, and Ammons (1955). Testing boys and girls from Grades 3 through 12, they found that boys made superior rotary pursuit scores at all grade levels. The boys' superiority was greater for the older subjects. Both sexes showed performances which were higher with chronological age, except that girls' scores declined in the eleventh and twelfth grades.

Learning and Fatigue

Almost any perceptual-motor performance exhibits measurable changes as it is practiced repetitively. Such changes may reveal increments in level of skill or they may indicate decrements in quality of the performance. The incremental process we might call *learning* and the decremental process we might term *fatigue*. Either process is an inference which we draw from the performance curves as practice continues under prescribed conditions. In many cases just one type of process is considered to be the major determinant of performance change, and the empirical curve is called either a learning curve or a fatigue curve. In other instances the rate of improvement is considered to reflect a decremental process going on concurrently with an incremental one. The problem in such a case is to infer properly how much of a contribution each of the opposing forces, learning and fatigue, is contributing to the data. We shall see that the inference needs to be based on measurements obtained under several experimental conditions if it is to be more than a mere guess.

Drawing inferences from empirical data is a tricky business. We must be careful not to infer learning or fatigue too quickly from different performance curves obtained under different conditions. We may be looking at performance differences due to processes, for example, motivation, which do not reflect learning or fatigue at all. A complete test for fatigue may require that performance be studied again after a rest interval has been given so that fatigue may dissipate. A full investigation of learning may involve a test for retention or transfer of training to be sure that relatively permanent learning and not some transient effect led to the difference observed in original performance under given conditions. Changing the difference between the experimental conditions is a fundamental way to determine if an observed effect was merely in performance or is indeed indicative of differential learning. After briefly describing two performance phenomena that may mimic learning, we shall go on to consider some experiments which reveal learning or fatigue, or both.

Two other processes that may affect performance are *warm-up* and *end spurt*. Warm-up is the improvement that occurs early in a performance session as the subject settles down to the task at hand. As we conceptualize it, warm-up is not the same as learning although the initial effects of the two processes may be practically indistinguishable in a task about which the subject has something to learn. In a task that may be considered very well learned, like tapping, we would consider any improvement in rate over the first minute or two as attributable to warm-up. The muscular warm-up familiar to us from athletics would be a likely part of the warm-up effect observed in motor performance, but the phenomenon is thought to consist of other factors as well. We find that the warm-up effect is observable in mental activity like doing arithmetic problems. End spurt refers to the improved performance that is noted sometimes when a subject knows he is nearing the end of an experimental session or a performance interval. Anticipating the termination of the session, or at least the occurrence of a rest period, he makes an especially strong effort at the task for a period of time. End spurt is most likely to affect the data, of course, when performance has slumped or has proceeded along a plateau due to fatigue or boredom. If it is considered undesirable, end spurt can be eliminated in some experimental designs by the simple expedient of not letting the subject know what the length of the session will be. If there are repeated trials of the same length, though, a subject is likely to learn to anticipate the end of a trial. End spurt may not really be an undesirable phenomenon in an experiment. It represents a lift in a motivational state that may have dropped a bit as the session wore on. Because it gives information about what a person *can* do under certain conditions, it may even be desirable in some studies to induce an end spurt by telling subjects, as they begin the final portion of performance, to do their best since the trial or session is drawing to a close.

Knowledge of Results

Our summaries of studies have suggested how many different independent variables affect the scores made on perceptual-motor tasks. Many of these also are contributory to the incremental growth of skill as practice continues. Feedback or knowledge of results (KR) has been declared the most potent determinant of performance and learning. This postulation is presented and strongly supported by Professor Ina Bilodeau (1969) in a chapter entitled "Information Feedback." Noting that KR has long been considered to play a dual role of motivator of subjects and informative guide for their subsequent responses, Bilodeau stresses the latter contributor to improvement of performance, that is, to learning. She defines KR—or information feedback, IF—as a stimulus event under control of the experimenter. KR is given with the frequency, quantative characteristics, and temporal locus in task sequence which suits the experimenter's investigative purpose. Its impact on subsequent performance is great, as Bilodeau's research review shows. Our space limitation will allow us to review just one illustrative study.

A lever positioning response with discrete trials given to subjects provided a test situation very conducive to systematic study of KR. Twenty-four trials were given to 4 groups of men in the experiment conducted by Bilodeau, Bilodeau, and Schumsky (1959). A subject's task on each trial was to attempt the positioning of a lever which required a 20-lb pull to move. The only guidance which might help improve performance was quantitative KR such as "9 units high" or "12 units low" which was given to different groups after certain trials. The Control Group received this KR after each positioning response. Group Zero was given no KR in the first 20 trials which concern us here. Group 2 received KR only for the first 2 trials, after which it was no longer given them. Similarly, Group 6 got KR for the first 6 trials only. There were 40 men in each group, performing a lever positioning response each 20 sec. Absolute positioning errors—positive or negative discrepancy from the 33° displacement considered to be correct—were averaged for each group trial by trial. Performance curves are presented in Figure 10.3.

The Control Group is shown to have reduced absolute error to near 2° when they received KR each trial. In contrast, Group Zero—given no KR at all—drifted in the neighborhood of 10° to 12° of absolute error for all 20 trials. Errors on Trials 1 and 2 for Group 2 and Trials 1 through 6 for Group 6 were combined with the Control Group data for graphing

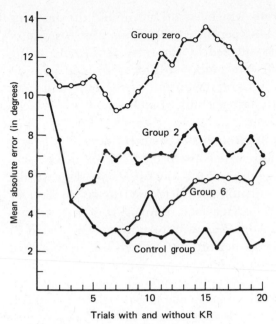

Fig. 10.3. Mean absolute error in lever positioning as a function of trials with and without knowledge of results (KR) for different groups. (After Bilodeau, Bilodeau, and Schumsky, 1959.)

purposes, yielding the most reliable record possible of how early KR benefited performance. When KR was terminated, both groups drifted back toward greater errors. It should be noted, though, that they appeared to continue to respond more accurately than Group Zero. The findings demonstrated the potency of KR in three ways, the experimenters noted. First, no improvement was shown without KR. Giving KR each trial led to progressive improvement of a substantial amount. Finally, as soon as KR was terminated, performance deteriorated on subsequent trials though showing some residual benefit of earlier KR.

Fatigue Decrement in Manual Cranking

A study of repetitive crank-turning conducted by Bilodeau (1952) will illustrate the direct approach to fatigue decrement in motor performance with continued practice. In his research report the author pointed out that the task was selected as one which would minimize the learning factor, or incremental process. This permitted the direct investigation of the motor performance as it was affected by the force requirements imposed on the subjects. Two different crank loadings were used, one demanding about three times the horsepower output of the other. In both cases the output increased with faster crank rotation and, conversely, lessened as cranking became slower.

A partial review of the findings of this experiment reveals different decremental affects for two groups which performed continuously for 5 min, each turning the crank against one of the two loads. During the first minute of work the crank-turning rate decreased more rapidly for the group performing with the heavier load. During this first minute this group decreased from about 80 to about 55 revolutions completed in a 20-sec period, whereas the group performing against the lighter load dropped from about 80 to about 65 revolutions per 20 sec in the same period. In the subsequent 4 min of work, both groups declined at about the same rate, somewhat more gradually than in the early decline of output. The group turning against the heavy load tended to level off at about 50 revolutions per 20 sec, whereas the group given the easier task showed a nearly asymptotic performance at about 60 revolutions per 20 sec. When a 40-sec rest interval was given at the end of 5 min of continuous work, both groups showed a partial recovery of their earlier output rate. In about 1 min of the resumed continuous performance, work output had again dropped to the asymptotic values cited.

Massed and Distributed Trials

It was noted earlier that a perceptual-motor task performance curve might reflect both learning and fatigue. If scores improve with trials learning is evident, but fatigue may be hidden in such a curve. It takes comparisons across conditions to reveal decremental as well as incremental processes in rising performance scores.

Rate of improvement over trials in many tasks depends on the extent to which rest is permitted, allowing for the dissipation of fatigue. Archer (1954) used inverted-alphabet printing as a task for which different groups of subjects were given different degrees of spacing of trials. All groups were given 20 trials of 30-sec duration. In one group a 30-sec rest interval was given after each trial, providing the greatest degree of distributed practice in this study. Another group received an intermediate degree of spacing of trials with 15-sec rest after each trial. A third group was given massed practice in which the "trials" were strung together with no rest interval at all, thus demanding 10 min of continuous performance from these subjects.

That these three degrees of distribution of practice led to different patterns of performance is clearly shown in the empirical curves of Figure 10.4. These curves represent just a portion of the findings pre-

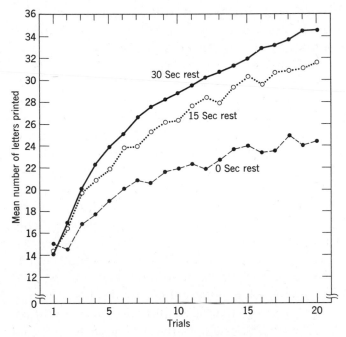

Fig. 10.4. Performance curves for inverted-alphabet printing under three different degrees of distribution of practice. (After Archer, 1954.)

sented by Archer since we are centering our attention on how spacing of practice affects the performance of perceptual-motor tasks as trials continue. The introduction of different rest intervals, 15 sec and 30 sec, is clearly facilitating with respect to scores subjects can make in inverted-alphabet printing. Further, the amount of facilitation is related to the amount of rest given, although this relationship is not necessarily a linear one.

Response Probability as Learning Index

Performance measures commonly used in motor tasks include amplitude of movements, number of responses per unit time, or time required to complete an activity. In several theories of learning another index of habit strength or response tendency is prominent. This is the probability, p, that a given response will occur on a particular trial or stimulus occasion. Probability may be defined empirically as relative frequency: $p = n_0/n_t$ where n_0 is the number of observed instances of the response being assessed, and n_t is the total number of opportunities for the response to have occurred. If learning of the particular response is occurring, p should be increasing. In a study of selective serial actions Andreas and Miller (1965) sought to determine how p was dependent on N, defined as the number of previous responses of the critical type. The investigation differed from most of the experiments we have reviewed in that only one group of subjects was run, all under a single condition. Their performance patterns were examined to determine the nature of their group learning function, $p = f(N)$.

Forty-four right-handed college students served as subjects. Their repeated performance on a letter maze gave rise to the learning data being sought. To create the maze, the experimenters arranged 110 upper-case letters in rows on the 10 identical pages of a test booklet. Some letters appeared just once in the maze, some 3, 4, or 6 times, and some several more times. The maze is presented in Figure 10.5. In the figure choice point letters (T, Q, I, K, W, X, M, L) that occur just once are underlined, and numerical subscripts are shown on alternative responses represented by 3, 4, or 6 maze locations for the same alphabet letter (H, U, C, B, N, J, P, A). The underlinings and subscripts did *not* appear when the maze was used in the study; they are shown only to aid in description of the task and the investigation of maze learning. Examination of the maze shows that six alternatives of H, U, N, and J are arranged in a circle around unique choice points T, Q, W, and X, respectively. Also, multiple alternatives (3 or 4) of C, B, P, and A are aligned horizontally or diagonally with choice points I, K, M, and L, respectively.

Subjects were told that trials would be timed as they used one page

Fig. 10.5. Arrangement of letters on each page of letter maze test booklet, as discussed in the text. Underlining and numerical subscripts in this figure were not included in the maze as given to subjects. (After Andreas and Miller, 1965.)

per trial to attempt tracing out the sentence THE QUICK BROWN FOX JUMPS OVER OUR LAZY DOG. Starting with the circled T at mid-page, they were told, the task is first to find an H and to draw a connecting line from T to H, then to an E, then to a Q, and so on. In other words, the maze was to be traced by a continuous line passing through each letter of the sentence in order, or as far as an individual could go in the 50-sec time limit for each trial page. Since pages were identical, it was expected that subjects would progress further and further through the maze as trials continued.

The mean number of letters connected on successive trials bore out this expectation. This molar measure of task learning rose from 5.2 letters reached on Trial 1 to 21.2 letters connected on Trial 10. The investigators were interested in a more molecular measure of learning as well, one of potential theoretical significance. For every choice point in the maze, they determined the empirical probability, p, defined as the relative frequency ratio of the number of times a particular response was a recurrence of the response made there on the immediately preceding trial (n_0) divided by the number of opportunities for such recurrence (n_t). This ratio was calculated separately for each number of previous occurrences (N) of that response—not necessarily consecutive. In other words, $p=f(N)$ was determined for each choice point in the maze as subjects became more and more consistent in their serial selection of a pathway as trials continued. The learning functions which emerged from the first four choice points are shown in Figure 10.6 as four determinations of $p=f(N)$.

Both the molecular index, p, and the molar measure of number of letters reached were in agreement in revealing that learning was taking place as trials progressed. The increasing number of letters connected was probably reflective of decreased response latencies or movement times. Andreas and Miller point out in their report that relative frequencies of

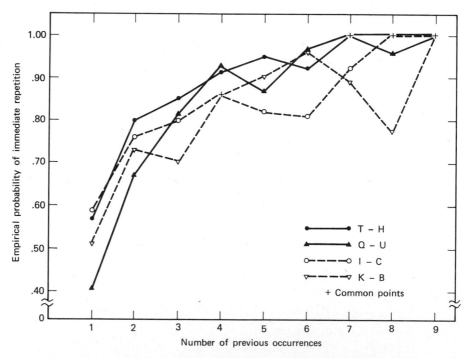

Fig. 10.6. Empirical probability (relative frequency) of immediate repetition of a particular response as a function of number of previous occurrences of that response. (After Andreas and Miller, 1965.)

a response (for example, a right turn at a maze choice point) have typically been cumulated for each ordinal trial number, disregarding the actual number of prior occurrences of the particular response. They feel that the definition of N as number of prior occurrences or reinforcements of the particular response yields a more appropriate independent variable for examining learning curves.

Other Illustrative Research

From a wide variety of investigations into perceptual-motor performance we may examine a few more examples. One study explored the effects on choice RTs of the preparatory sets or expectancies which subjects form as they experience repeated trials with certain regularities in the foreperiods used. Another experiment used television technology to permit the probing of complex positioning responses under varied conditions of visual feedback. The final example of research was a study of how stimulus-response compatibility affects performance levels in selective serial activity.

Preparatory Set in Choice Reaction

In a reaction time (RT) experiment a subject is faced with uncertainty. In simple RT he is uncertain, in some degree, as to when the stimulus will be presented on a particular trial. The presentation of a warning signal reduces this *time uncertainty* to some extent. It tends to build, over trials, an expectancy or preparatory set that the critical stimulus will follow the warning signal at an interval which may be somewhat predictable. This depends on experimental regularity or variation in the preparatory interval or foreperiod. The development of an effective preparatory set to respond at a certain point in time is revealed in shorter RTs than are attained without such a set.

In studies of choice RT a subject faces *event uncertainty* as well as time uncertainty. He cannot be certain as to which stimulus event will occur in addition to not knowing the exact time of the presentation. Again, it is possible that a preparatory set or expectancy may develop as a subject gains experience with the conditions under which he is being tested. A mental set which tends to reduce event uncertainty will lead to a concentration of attention on the expected stimulus. If appropriate, this preparatory set for the event to come should reduce choice RT.

The purpose of an experiment reported by Moss (1969) was to extend past findings on the development of preparatory set under testing conditions which permitted subjects to overcome time uncertainty and event uncertainty to some extent. The choice RT task required subjects to press one of two response keys as quickly as possible whenever one of two event lamps flashed on. Mounted in the vertical panel just above the two white event lamps was an amber lamp which served as the warning signal. It flashed on for a half second to initiate the foreperiod or preparatory interval which lasted either 1, 3, or 5 sec until one of the event lamps came on to elicit the pressing of the key aligned with it on the table top. Eight blocks of 30 trials each were given to 32 male undergraduates at 10-sec trial intervals. Within each block of trials, a given experimental condition was in effect; 3 of the conditions are treated in this summary. In the complete study, every subject experienced each condition during 2 separate series of trial blocks.

The design of the experimental conditions afforded Moss the desired study of preparatory set. During a block of 30 trials, each of the two stimulus events was equally probable on any trial, 15 of each occurring in a random sequence. The foreperiod was treated differently for the two stimulus event lamps, however, depending on experimental condition. One stimulus event had a fixed foreperiod preceding it (1, 3, or 5 sec), while the other event occurred after any of these intervals used equally often. Under experimental Conditions 1, 3, and 5 the foreperiod for the Fixed Event was 1, 3, or 5 sec, respectively. During a block of 30 trials, then, with just one of the experimental conditions in effect, a subject had a chance to develop an expectancy or preparatory set for *this* event at the particular fixed time following the warning lamp. Also a subject might learn when to expect the *other* event as more probable, reducing event uncertainty *to some extent*.

The experimental conditions, then, had the potential of reducing both time uncertainty (through regular foreperiods) and event uncertainty (through keeping one event at a fixed foreperiod). An alert subject could build preparatory set in a block of trials because each block carried its own pattern of conditional probabilities of event occurrence at different times after the warning lamp. These time-dependent probabilities are shown in Part I of Table 10.1 for each of the three experimental conditions we are considering.

The RT data for the final block of 30 trials under any condition were treated most fully in the report by Moss since these trials had the benefit of earlier practice and greater acquaintance with the various experimental conditions. Accordingly, we shall examine the median RTs to each event after each foreperiod. These medians are arranged in Part II of Table 10.1 in a way which parallels the presentation of the time-dependent event probabilities in Part I. The data in the table may be scrutinized to see if they tend to support 4 predictions the experimenter had made.

Prediction 1
RT to the fixed event should generally be shorter than RT to the variable event since the fixed event has less time uncertainty in a block of trials.

Table 10.1 Selected Experimental Conditions and Median Reaction Times as a Function of Event and Time Uncertainty (After Moss, 1969)

Part I. Probabilities Associated with Each Experimental Condition and Event Conditionalized on the Foreperiod Intervals

Condition	Event	Foreperiod Interval (in sec)		
		1	3	5
1	Variable	.167	.500	1.000
	Fixed	.500	.000	.000
3	Variable	.167	.250	1.000
	Fixed	.000	.500	.000
5	Variable	.167	.250	.500
	Fixed	.000	.000	.500

Part II. Median RT to Each Event in Second Block of Trials Under Each Condition as a Function of Foreperiod Interval (Median RT in milliseconds)

Condition	Event	Foreperiod Interval (in sec)		
		1	3	5
1	Variable	299.1	259.0	240.0
	Fixed	263.6	—	—
3	Variable	330.1	302.3	265.8
	Fixed	—	295.1	—
5	Variable	327.8	311.0	299.4
	Fixed	—	—	277.6

Prediction 2
Longer foreperiods for the fixed event should lead to generally greater
RT values in responding to it.
Prediction 3
RTs for the variable event should be shorter for the longer foreperiods
since the probability of that event tends to increase markedly as time
passes following the warning signal.
Prediction 4
Longer RTs to the variable event should occur when the foreperiod
matches the foreperiod for the fixed event under a particular experimental
condition.

The data of the table appear to confirm Prediction 1, and statistical
analysis reported by Moss corroborates this impression. RTs to the fixed
event were significantly lower than those to the variable event. Prediction 2 was not borne out. Although RT for the fixed event was higher
at the 3-sec foreperiod compared to the 1-sec value, when the foreperiod
was 5 sec the RT was shorter than at 3 sec. Prediction 3 is seen to be
confirmed on examining the rows of tabled RT values for the variable
event. As the foreperiod value goes up, RT goes down in every experimental condition. It is not easy to assess Prediction 4 on the basis of
these median RTs. However, a consideration of all the experimental
data led the experimenter to conclude that a special state of expectancy
for the two alternative events was developed at the interval when either
one might be expected under a particular experimental condition.

A very general postulate concerning preparatory set is that this
anticipatory readiness to respond increases as the probability of an expected event rises. Heightened readiness leads to lower RT values. This
means that lower median RT values in Part II of Table 10.1 should be
associated with higher probability values in Part I. When Moss computed
a rank order correlation (rho) to assess this inverse relationship, a negative value of 0.805 was found. This strong inverse relationship tends to
confirm the postulation that preparatory set, reflected in RT, is dependent
upon event probability over time.

Differential Visual Feedback

The technology of television was employed by Gould (1965) to study how
the visual feedback available to subjects guides their manipulative positioning reactions. The task assigned to female college students was to

use a pair of long-nose pliers to move 6 plastic-and-steel pins from one set of holes to another. Three pins had to be placed in 5⁄8-in. holes and 3 went into 3⁄8-in. holes, demanding greater precision of movement. The all-important control over visual feedback was achieved by having subjects view their actions by means of closed-circuit television instead of directly. Under a Control Condition, the television screen showed subjects a normal picture of their hand, pliers, pins, and target holes outlined in white. For the seven experimental conditions feedback was varied by including only certain selected components of the task performance in the visual feedback. This was done by adjusting the television system so that only white objects were visible. Then by providing either a black or white glove, black or white pliers, and black or white pins, the experimenter could control the elements which subjects could see on the television monitor, giving them reduced visual feedback in a variety of experimental combinations. Some visual cues were always available from the white outlining of the target holes.

In his task analysis, Gould designated the hand as the *reactive* component (R), the pliers as the *instrumental* component (I), and the pins as the *operational* component (O). Thus, Condition RI was one in which visual feedback of the reactive and instrumental components was provided by having subjects wear a white glove and use white pliers (while the pins were black and therefore invisible on the television screen). In Condition IO the pliers and pins were white and therefore visible while the hand was black-gloved and not seen. Some experimental conditions gave visual feedback of a single component alone (R, I, or O). One condition, similar to the normally viewed Control Condition, provided vision for all the components—Condition RIO. The seven experimental conditions and the control are summarized on the next page.

Subjects were given 32 trials per day, 4 under each condition, for 10 days. Each trial required that a pin be moved into each of the 6 target holes under normal viewing or reduced feedback conditions. The measure of performance was the time required to move the pins into each set of target holes, of smaller and larger diameters. The results showed that scores attained were significantly affected by days of practice, target hole size, and by the visual feedback condition. Performance curves are presented in Figure 10.7 with times for both target sizes averaged. Combined with the Control Condition are Conditions IO and RIO under which performance was very similar.

Operational feedback—seeing the pins—was most beneficial. Condi-

Condition	Components in Visual Feedback	Elements Visible on TV Screen*
Control	All	All
RIO	Reactive-instrumental-operational	Hand, pliers, pins
RI	Reactive-instrumental	Hand, pliers
RO	Reactive-operational	Hand, pins
IO	Instrumental-operational	Pliers, pins
R	Reactive	Hand
I	Instrumental	Pliers
O	Operational	Pins

*In addition to the target holes.

tions *O*, *RO*, *IO*, and *RIO* did not differ significantly from the Control Condition in overall performance. Next best were the scores attained under Conditions *I* and *RI*. Performance was worst under Condition *R*. The different feedback conditions showed significant interactions with days of practice and with target hole size. The more difficult feedback conditions showed greater gains over days of practice, as is evident in the slopes of the learning curves of Figure 10.7 At the same time, the more difficult feedback conditions were found to be more affected by target hole size than were the operational feedback conditions in which the pins as well as the holes were visible to subjects. The experiment showed —in main effects and interactions—the roles of visual component feedback in guiding positioning reactions. Further, at the end of the study, Gould tested subjects' ability to perform the task without component feedback and found them much poorer in performance with only visual information from the target holes to guide them.

Stimulus-Response Compatibility

Efficiency in performing selective serial actions depends on the stimulus-response (S-R) compatibility that characterizes the arrangement of perceptual-motor tasks. This hypothesis was investigated by Fitts and Biederman (1965) using a group of information-processing tasks which required choice reactions from subjects. The 4 stimuli presented on separate trials were Circle, Square, 2 Circles, and 2 Squares. Responses were key presses performed using 2 or 4 fingers, either on 1 hand or both hands in the 8 tasks assigned to the different groups of 10 subjects each. The fingers

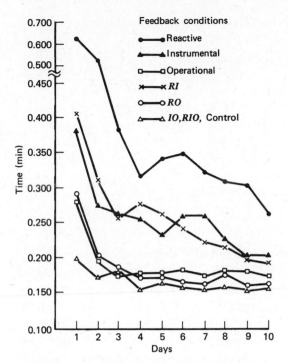

Fig. 10.7. Performance curves obtained under 8 visual feedback conditions. (After Gould, 1965.)

and hands required for the several tasks represented variations in stimulus-response compatibility. The investigators postulated that these task differences would lead to different values in the measurement of choice RTs. In Table 10.2 are shown the requirements for using the different fingers of 1 or both hands in pressing the 2 or 4 keys in response to the 2 or 4 stimuli in the tasks assigned to the several groups. The odd-numbered tasks required only the right hand to be placed on the response keys. In the even-numbered tasks both hands were used.

An example of S-R compatibility may be seen in the response requirements for Task 8, assigned to Group 8. A Circle as stimulus calls for a key press by the left forefinger. A Square requires response by the right forefinger. Two Circles call for left-hand response, the middle finger. Two Squares demand response by the right middle finger. Compatibility exists in that the left hand is always used for circular stimuli, right hand for the square stimuli. Also, a forefinger is used whenever a

Table 10.2 Hands and Fingers Used in the Tasks Assigned to Different Groups
(After Fitts and Biederman, 1965)

Task Number

Stimuli	1	2	3	4	5	6	7	8
●	*1–R	1–L	1–R	1–L	1–R	1–L	1–R	1–L
■	2–R	1–R	2–R	1–R	2–R	1–R	2–R	1–R
● ●			1–R	1–L	2–R	1–R	3–R	2–L
■ ■			2–R	1–R	1–R	1–L	4–R	2–R

*1 indicates first or forefinger; 2 is second or middle finger, etc. R represents
right hand; L is left hand.

single geometric figure is presented, a middle finger when the stimulus
is a double form. This consistency or S-R compatibility was expected to
lead to better performance among tasks of the same general difficulty
level. In Task 6 for Group 6, compatibility of responses with stimulus
characteristics is notably less than in Task 8. In Task 6 only the forefinger of each hand is required in responding. However, the left forefinger must press its key when the stimulus is either 1 Circle or 2 Squares,
while the right forefinger responds to 1 Square or 2 Circles. Despite fewer
different responses, this task lacks compatibility.

Subjects were given 7 blocks of 16 RT trials on Day 1 and 8 blocks
of trials on Day 2, with a simple RT task being administered initially on
Day 1 for practice and warm-up purposes. Throughout the 15 blocks
of trials each group of subjects was kept at its own assigned task. The
median RT for each subject was determined for each block of trials.
Then these medians were used in computing the group mean RTs which
are plotted in Figure 10.8.

The performance curves indicate that learning occurred for every
task over the two days of practice. The 8 groups are readily seen to have
been divided into two clusters. Tasks 1–4 led to the lower RT values,
while RTs were notably longer for Tasks 5–8. It was in these more difficult tasks that the investigators expected to find a benefit from stimulus-
response compatibility. The RT data, analyzed statistically, confirmed
this expectation. As may be seen in the performance curves, Task 8
yielded the lowest RTs in the cluster of more difficult tasks. Its compatibility was evidently facilitative of quick responding. Such performance
differences were not detectable in the cluster of easier tasks.

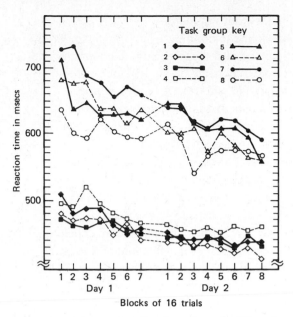

Fig. 10.8. Group mean RT values over the 15 trial blocks administered for each task. (After Fitts and Biederman, 1965.)

Summary

An important segment of human behavior, perceptual-motor performance, is studied in the psychology laboratory by requiring subjects to perform one of a variety of tasks. Static motor performance is studied by measuring body sway or hand steadiness. Latency of response is investigated in experiments on simple or choice RT. Other simple performances that have been required in research are linear and rotary positioning reactions and repetitive tapping. Serial motor activity is represented in psychomotor tests and laboratory tasks such as performing with pegboards, card-sorting, inverted-alphabet printing, mazes, and manipulation of switches or keys. Continuous adjustive reactions are studied in compensatory and pursuit tracking tasks, including rotary pursuit performance.

    As a task is performed repeatedly over a series of trials, a trend toward higher or lower scores is often evident. From such performance data we may draw inferences about processes like learning or fatigue. The problem of arriving at correct inferences is complicated by the fact that incremental and decremental effects are often intermixed, with numerous variables contributing to their development.

Knowledge of results has been found to contribute importantly to the development of many perceptual-motor skills. It serves both to inform the subject of the effect of his actions and to motivate him to continue trying to improve. This factor was manipulated in one illustrative experiment in which the task was positioning a lever. Decrements in performance have been observed when subjects were assigned a motor task like repetitive cranking. Other studies that we reviewed gave evidence of both incremental and decremental processes. The massing or distribution of practice trials provided one approach to the description of these processes. A task studied in this way was inverted-alphabet printing. In another research example we examined, the investigators used a letter maze to determine how the probability of a particular response at a choice point depended on the number of previous occurrences of that response.

Other studies provided us with additional insights as to how perceptual-motor behavior is investigated by research psychologists. One experiment sought to determine how choice RT would be affected by subjects' expectancies for the two different stimuli. Another experiment manipulated visual feedback by using television technology in setting up a manipulative positioning task. Finally we saw how selective serial activity was found to depend on stimulus-response compatibility.

References

Ammons, R. B., Alprin, S. I., & Ammons, C. H. Rotary pursuit performance as related to sex and age of pre-adult subjects. *Journal of Experimental Psychology*, 1955, **49**, 127–133.

Andreas, B. G., & Miller, L. Probability of response repetition in serial motor performance as a function of number of previous occurrences. *Perceptual and Motor Skills*, 1965, **20**, 609–613.

Archer, E. J. Postrest performance in motor learning as a function of prerest degree of distribution of practice. *Journal of Experimental Psychology*, 1954, **47**, 47–51.

Bilodeau, E. A. Decrements and recovery from decrements in a simple work task with variation in force requirements at different stages of practice. *Journal of Experimental Psychology*, 1952, **44**, 108–113.

Bilodeau, E. A., Bilodeau, I. McD., & Schumsky, D. A. Some effects of introducing and withdrawing knowledge of results early and late in practice. *Journal of Experimental Psychology*, 1959, **58**, 142–144.

Bilodeau, I. McD. Information feedback. In E. A. Bilodeau (Ed.), *Principles of skill acquisition*. New York: Academic Press, 1969. Pp. 255–285.

Botwinick, J. Joint effects of stimulus intensity and preparatory interval on simple auditory reaction time. *Journal of Experimental Psychology*, 1969, **80**, 348–352.

Fitts, P. M. The information capacity of the human motor system in controlling the amplitude of movement. *Journal of Experimental Psychology*, 1954, **47**, 381–391.

Fitts, P. M. Perceptual-motor skill learning. In A. W. Melton (Ed.), *Categories of learning*. New York: Academic Press, 1964. Pp. 243–285.

Fitts, P. M., & Biederman, I. S-R compatibility and information reduction. *Journal of Experimental Psychology*, 1965, **69**, 408–412.

Fitts, P. M., & Peterson, J. R. Information capacity of discrete motor responses. *Journal of Experimental Psychology*, 1964, **67**, 103–112.

Fleishman, E. A. Dimensional analysis of psychomotor abilities. *Journal of Experimental Psychology*, 1954, **48**, 437–454.

Fleishman, E. A. Human abilities. *Annual Review of Psychology*, 1969, **20**, 349–380.

Gould, J. D. Differential visual feedback of component motions. *Journal of Experimental Psychology*, 1965, **69**, 263–268.

Howell, W. C., & Kreidler, D. L. Information processing under contradictory instructional sets. *Journal of Experimental Psychology*, 1963, **65**, 39–46.

Keele, S. W. Movement control in skilled motor performance. *Psychological Bulletin*, 1968, **70**, 387–403.

Moss, S. M. Changes in preparatory set as a function of event and time uncertainty. *Journal of Experimental Psychology*, 1969, **80**, 150–155.

Noble, C. E. Outline of human selective learning. In E. A. Bilodeau (Ed.), *Principles of skill acquisition*. New York: Academic Press, 1969. Pp. 319–353.

Poulton, E. C. Tracking. In E. A. Bilodeau (Ed.), *Principles of skill acquisition*. New York: Academic Press, 1969. Pp. 287–318.

Simon, J. R. Ear preference in a simple reaction-time task. *Journal of Experimental Psychology*, 1967, **75**, 49–55.

Simon, J. R. Effect of ear stimulated on reaction time and movement time. *Journal of Experimental Psychology*, 1968, **78**, 344–346.

Simon, J. R. Reactions toward the source of stimulation. *Journal of Experimental Psychology*, 1969, **81**, 174–176.

References   **387**

Teichner, W. H., & Wehrkamp, R. F. Visual-motor performance as a function of short-duration ambient temperature. *Journal of Experimental Psychology,* 1954, 47, 447–450.

Ziegler, W. A. *Minnesota Rate of Manipulation Test.* Minneapolis: Educational Test Bureau, Inc., 1933.

chapter 11
Memory

In a commemorative address on Hermann Ebbinghaus, who was a pioneer investigator of memory, Postman (1968) reviewed the liberal approaches of the German scholar to research and theory before commenting on his specific contributions in laboratory experimentation. Postman then recounted briefly the trends that developed in the study of verbal learning and memory during the decades since the early work and particularly in more recent years. A brief review of these points should prepare us for our description of theory and research in the domain of human memory.

For Ebbinghaus, Postman feels, research on memory exemplified a scientific approach to problems in psychology. Together with other early laboratory investigators, he contributed to the intellectual climate of experimental psychology as it took directions which are still evident today. First, Ebbinghaus was more willing than some to depart from the old philosophical approaches to mind; he was eager to use empirical methods in the systematic elucidation of mental processes. He departed also from the doctrinal constraints of the earlier laboratory psychologists who insisted that physical stimulus manipulations be made the avenue to the study of psychological events. In his search for laws of memory he defied this prohibition of direct study of higher mental processes. Ebbinghaus was eclectic in accepting contributions of different methodologists and theorists. He did not slavishly follow any single tradition. Instead he borrowed and blended methods and theoretical constructs. For example, he saw in psychophysical research a possibility of quantifying retention and forgetting in a way which might parallel the scaling of sensation. Finally, Ebbinghaus found relevance in his work as he sought to assist educators in the realm of mental measurement. In a number of recent emphases in research on memory to be examined in this chapter, we shall find echoes of the creative and liberal approach to psychological investigation that is exemplified in the writings and work of this innovator.

In contrast to his general influences on the shaping of experimental psychology, the specific contributions of Ebbinghaus have almost all been seriously questioned as the psychological study of learning and memory has matured. That is as it should be, of course, and is quite consonant with the views of Ebbinghaus as an experimentalist. Innovations that he introduced or stressed in his work include the nonsense syllable, serial learning, criterion measures, the saving method, and curves of forgetting, as Postman has listed and discussed them. Although every one of these approaches to memory study has been significantly modified since the early work, they nearly all find some reflection in the more refined methods of today's investigators.

In recent years there has been a new wave of innovations in thinking about memory and in probing its nature. Within the limitations of textbook treatment this chapter exemplifies a number of the trends. Postman concluded his tribute to Ebbinghaus by noting some of them which are prominent in work on verbal learning and retention. First, he points to the inventive proliferation of methods of experimentation, a departure from the too-narrow constraints of standardized approaches of earlier decades. Second, there is greater concern with describing mechanisms and processes of memory, and less with simple quantification of stimulus-response relationships over time. In the third place, experiments in verbal behavior have begun to take their place alongside animal studies for their bearing on learning theory. It might even be argued that memory has emerged as a stage for the presentation of new psychological hypotheses and theories somewhat apart from the topic of learning, though not unrelated to it. Next there has been—almost forced upon psychologists—a recognition of linguistic habits and processes of subjects as pertinent to their verbal behaviors in laboratory experiments. Finally, memory research and theory have begun to be related to the psychology of problem solving.

The conceptual complexities with which we must wrestle in considering research on memory should have begun to emerge by now. This area of investigation promises continuing change in concepts and methods. In view of this it may be best to approach the topic with two open-ended questions:

What processes make up the phenomenon of memory?

How do investigators probe these processes to test their hypotheses?

A number of students of memory have offered answers to the first question by formulating descriptive theories. We shall examine these in the next section of the chapter. Then, in later sections we shall examine some examples of experiments on long-term memory, free recall, and short-term memory—partially answering our second question.

Theories of Memory

Any reflection on the remembrance of things past naturally brings to mind the dimension of time as prominent in our concept of memory. In early studies of retention and forgetting the intervals over which the phenomena were studied were measured in minutes, hours, days, weeks, or even months. Today, such investigations must be termed experiments on long-term memory. Emerging very prominently in recent years has been the study of short-term memory, retention over periods of less than a minute, often of only a few seconds. Some investigators have sought similarities in the laws and processes of short-term memory (STM) and long-term memory (LTM). In contrast, some experimenters and theorists have adduced evidence that there are fundamental differences between STM and LTM so that each requires special treatment in a theory of memory. This does not mean, of course, that such a theory will not include important functional linkages between STM and LTM. Indeed, the theories that have emerged have actually stressed such a relationship. These theories have as their substance the postulation of processes rather than quantitative relationships among variables. Quantification in research is not abandoned. Rather, data are collected to confirm or disconfirm the operation of the mechanisms postulated. This quantitative exploration of processes has been a major approach to comparing, contrasting, and relating STM to LTM.

To expedite our consideration of memory theories, we shall examine one set forth by Shiffrin and Atkinson (1969) and relate some other theoretical viewpoints to it. Although their article emphasizes long-term memory, the model they present includes a short-term store and assigns to STM processes a strong contribution to the establishing and utilizing of LTM. Since we cannot review the theoretical treatise in its entirety, we must concentrate on the relationships among events and postulated processes as memory research is conducted. These relationships are suggested in Figure 11.1 which is a flowchart nearly identical to one presented by Shiffrin and Atkinson.* Events in an experimental test of memory may be examined in temporal sequence by following the arrows across the chart from left to right and then back across the top to the left again—from stimulus through intervening processes or hidden events back to an overt response. It may be seen that processes of STM and LTM are heavily involved, with STM playing an intermediary role for information flow to and from LTM. The control processes listed below the flowchart are believed to be complexly operative in different parts of the memory system at different times. We shall encounter some of these processes as we summarize (and simplify) some of the aspects of memory functioning which the theorists postulate. They indicate at many points that particular experiments have yielded data to support their hypotheses. We shall not cite this evidence since our interest in the model is confined to using its description to organize our thinking about research into memory that will occupy our attention later.

Figure 11.1 indicates that auditory or visual stimulus input (such as the presentation of a word to be remembered) goes first into the sensory register in which it is rapidly processed for transmission to the short-term memory. Information in STM is postulated to decay in a period of 30 sec or less if the individual does not attend to it and process it by some mechanism such as rehearsal. Information may be retained in the rehearsal buffer, or otherwise maintained for as long as a person continues active in processing it. At the same time, rehearsal or other treatment given to items in STM automatically transfers information to LTM which the theorists assume to be permanent memory storage (except for brain damage of various sorts).

*In Figure 11.1 the terms short-term memory (STM) and long-term memory
(LTM) have been used where Shriffrin and Atkinson used
short-term store (STS) and long-term store (LTS).

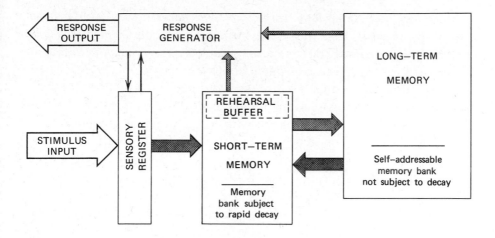

CONTROL PROCESSES

- Stimulus analyzer programs
- Alter biases of sensory channels
- Activate rehearsal mechanism
- Modify information flow from SR to STS
- Code and transfer information from STS to LTS
- Initiate or modify search of LTS
- Heuristic operations on stored information
- Set decision criteria
- Initiate response generator

Fig. 11.1. Flowchart indicating some of the elements and processes of information transfer in active memory as discussed in the text. (After Shiffrin and Atkinson, 1969.)

Information goes into LTM as a self-addressed code or memory trace. That is, the nature of the item to be stored determines in what location (by computer analogy) it is to be stored. By analogy with library shelving, the topic and perhaps the form of the item determines where it is to be kept until needed. Information is stored according to its characteristics and is searched out and retrieved on a similar basis. This stress on the salient characteristics of material in memory to be recalled or recognized later gives the theory of Shiffrin and Atkinson a point of contact with the multicomponent theory advanced by Bower (1967) for the memory trace and with the attributes listed by Underwood (1969) as the functional units of memory. Also relevant is the emphasis given by Paivio (1969) to the role of imagery in mnemonic storage.

Since any code, image, or trace is placed permanently in LTM according to Shiffrin and Atkinson, the form and timing of its transfer into storage and the retrieval processes used to search it out and formulate an overt response are the real determinants of whether or not retention will actually be demonstrated in any given test of memory. These authors give an ingenious hypothetical account of these processes—especially search—which they find to be congruent with many findings and phenomena of research on memory. For example, in paired associate learning and retention, suppose that a subject has been given the S-R pair GAX-3. During the brief trial of its presentation, the subject may generate in his STM the "incomplete" code G**-3, for storage in LTM. This memory trace will suffice to yield the response "3" when GAX is next encountered as a stimulus. However, suppose that our subject is later presented with GEK-7 and manages only to store G**-7. Now if he later is tested with GAX, his search may turn up both G**-3 and G**-7. Barring any storage or utilization of other attributes he will have to guess at "3" or "7" in formulating his response. This example is one of the simpler ones given by the theorists in expounding on the memory processes they postulate.

Our incomplete review of the article by Shiffrin and Atkinson should suggest an active interplay between theory and research in memory. Mention of the influence of theory on experimentation suggests that we might have alluded to other theoretical articles, for example, Waugh and Norman (1965), Peterson (1966), Kintsch (1967), Norman (1968). Descriptive theory construction and the quantitative demonstration of its postulated processes has burgeoned in the past decade. Unfortunately, space limitations will prevent our full consideration of theoretical implications as we review methods and research findings in the remainder of this chapter. It would be necessary in some cases to review several related experiments reported in one article as an investigator pursued an elusive clarification of theoretical mechanisms of memory. Since that is impossible, we must set a more moderate goal here. Students interested in pursuing studies of memory will naturally need to consult the journal literature in depth.

Methods of Investigation

Since our later section on free recall includes information on the characteristic materials and quantitative methods used in its study, we shall here concentrate on the materials, methods, and measurement procedures which are prominent in experiments on LTM and STM. Even though similar processes are sometimes studied, there is a tendency to contrast LTM and STM as modes of memory and to use contrasting procedures in their study. We shall make these methodological contrasts by describing in turn the typical experimentation in each case, with some mention of alternative techniques.

Long-Term Memory Methods

A study of LTM for verbal material might, in its simplest form, involve requiring subjects to learn a list of nonsense syllables or words and then testing different groups for their retention after different amounts of time had elapsed since learning. Two decisions required of the experimenter would be the level of learning to be accomplished by subjects during the acquisition phase and the form of retention testing to be used to collect the memory data—conventionally *recall, recognition,* or *relearning.* Equating the level of learning across groups is often accomplished by having learning proceed to some specified criterion of performance, two successive trials with all items correct, for example. This is satisfactory for most purposes, though the actual amount of learning may be underestimated and may vary for different individuals who approach the criterion at different rates. Similar problems of precise quantification may occur as well in using some measure of retention. The brief descriptions given here should also suggest the undesirability of comparing retention results across studies which used different indices or measures to arrive at percent retained.

Recall

When a subject has previously learned a serial list of verbal items, we may require him to demonstrate his retention of the material by recalling as much of it as possible. We may score his responses, given orally or written, with respect to serial order or we may ignore this and merely count the correct items. We may or may not include a penalty for erroneous intrusions in the list he gives. In contrast to such free recall, the anticipation method (using serially presented cards or a memory drum) requires the subject to give the next item in the list as each one is presented. There are, then, a variety of possibilities for administering and scoring a recall test, but the essential aspect of this method is that the subject is given a specific opportunity to recall whatever he can of the previously learned material.

Recognition

In a recognition test a subject is given a different type of opportunity to demonstrate what he has retained. The items that he has previously learned are all presented to him again, but they are interspersed among numerous other items of a similar nature. In a recognition test, then, the subject must recognize previously seen material, discriminating it from material which has not been studied. This is a somewhat easier task than free recall. The recognition score depends in part, of course, on the degree of similarity between the items that are correct and those that are provided as distractors or foils. In setting up such a study it would seem advisable to draw the items to be learned randomly from a larger pool of items, with those not chosen for the learning task being retained as foil items in the recognition test. The difficulty level of such a test would probably then depend on the degree of similarity or heterogeneity of the items in the original pool.

Relearning

The relearning method of measuring retention is one in which each subject relearns the material he has learned earlier. The percent of time or trials saved in this relearning effort, when compared with original learning, is the measure of retention. If original learning to a specified criterion took 15 trials, for example, and relearning after 1 day takes only 5 trials, we find that the 10-trial difference represents a saving of 67 percent, the index of retention after this interval. If a different group of subjects took 15 trials to learn the list and 9 trials to relearn it after 1 week, the 6-trial difference would indicate a 40 percent saving as the measure of retention at this point on the retention curve. A special advantage of using the relearning method for measuring retention is that the first of the relearning trials may provide a recall index of the amount remembered. Obtaining both a recall and a saving score at the same interval after original learning represents a potential bonus of information about the retention process.

Sources of interference

As we shall see in reviewing LTM theory and research, much of the forgetting that is observed to take place for a test list of items is attributed to either prior learning activity or to learning activity which intervenes between critical list study and subsequent recall. Another important part of LTM research design, therefore, is to provide appropriate materials and learning opportunities for tasks either preceding or following the critical list learning. The selection of such items and their administration as an interfering task must be guided by theoretical considerations. Therefore, simple procedural guidelines cannot be prescribed. In our examination of LTM research we shall find some multiple-list studies which were designed to test interference theory.

Short-Term Memory Methods

Methods—and methodological variations—for the investigation of STM have been devised in some profusion. Besides the briefer interval of retention, they typically contrast in a number of respects with LTM. Again our review of studies in a later section will exemplify at least some of the techniques. Here we suggest some of the salient procedural differences from LTM study which many STM experiments embody.

First, STM may focus on the retention of a single critical item which has been briefly presented either in isolation or as part of a list. If part of a list, an item typically has to be identified by some "probe" such as the serially preceding item to indicate what response is required. In our simple example, it appears we would be testing the serial association between the presented probe and the required item as well as the response integration of the required item. When single items are sought, the individual's index of retention cannot be the percent retained as with LTM lists, of course. It is usually the percent or proportion of responses which are correct, tabulated for a group of subjects.

Second, a special characteristic of many STM experiments is the use of a distractor task. Since retention intervals are quite short, say 15 sec, a subject would almost certainly recall a single item if allowed to rehearse it. To prevent rehearsal, a distractor task is usually provided and explained to subjects as a regular part of the experimental procedure. For example, a subject might be required to read numbers, to name colors, to add 3 or subtract 4 consecutively when given a starting number by the experimenter. Used as a distinct alternative to the distractor task arrangement has been requesting a subject to attend to (and rehearse) only the latest one in serially presented items. This should preclude rehearsal of blocks or sequences of items. Of course, postexperimental inquiry would be used to try to rule out any subjects who did not comply.

Finally, STM may be studied using a continuous presentation technique with a recognition response required from subjects to distinguish those items, say 3-digit numbers, which he recognizes from earlier presentation. In such a running-list technique, then, a subject responds "Old" or "Yes" each time he recognizes an item seen or heard earlier in the list. He replies with "New" or "No" to items he feels have not been experienced earlier. The technique permits numerous experimental manipulations of variables. Frequency data fall into a fourfold table based on two classes of stimulus item and two types of response:

	Response	
Stimulus	"New"	"Old"
New:		
Old:		

Long-Term Retention

Research on long-term retention may examine memory over intervals as short as a few minutes or as long as several hours, days, weeks, or even months. Over the longer periods the individuals being studied pursue their normal activities before returning to the psychology laboratory for testing. For the shorter durations subjects remain in the experimental situation, often being asked to perform interpolated tasks during the retention interval. A primary research question in long-term studies is how much forgetting (memory loss) occurs over the retention interval. Or, by testing subjects (usually different individuals) after different intervals we might determine the course of decline in retention. The data obtained should permit the plotting of a curve of forgetting.

Interference Theory

The decline in amount retained over minutes, hours, or days does not mean that the memory loss is to be considered as dependent merely on the passage of time. Some decades ago forgetting was thought to be due in large measure to time-dependent internal physiological processes which weakened memory traces. More recently the events or experiences—especially learning—of the retention interval have been implicated as determinants of memory loss. Broadly speaking this interaction of ongoing activities with the retention of earlier learned material is dealt with by interference theory. This active-process theory displaced the more passive decay-of-memory-strength-over-time hypothesis as a result of numerous experiments, now largely of historical interest. The investigative approaches which gave general support to interference theory have been refined in recent years with consequent refinement of the theory and with new understanding of memory processes. We shall need to examine the methodological paradigms and also to review some research in which these designs are used to increase our knowledge of memory and forgetting.

Retroactive inhibition

A classical three-stage paradigm for retention studies may be represented as follows:

Experimental Group: OL—IL—Test
Control Group: OL———Test

where OL represents original learning and IL stands for an interpolated learning task required of the experimental group but not the control group. Comparison of the memory tests for retention of the original learning permits us to determine how much interference was generated by the interpolated learning. In experiments of this type the IL task is usually designed especially to generate interference and thus to depress the test performance of the experimental group as compared to the control group. The test of retention might be a recall, recognition, or relearning method or some combination or variation of these. The interfering effect of IL on the tested retention of OL responses is termed *retroactive inhibition*.

Retroactive inhibition (RI) was considered by psychologists for a number of years to be the prime example of interference between two learning experiences. RI is the interference of a later learned task with the retention of an earlier one, as we have seen. In cases where no IL task was required in the laboratory, decrement over time was believed to be due to interference with the retention of OL which stemmed from everyday activities of subjects between the initial learning or acquisition of material and its subsequent testing.

Proactive inhibition

In an insightful and incisive examination of both old and new data from verbal memory studies, Underwood (1957) discovered that retention depended heavily upon the number of *previous* lists which subjects had memorized. After a retention interval of 24 hours the recall was around 75 percent for subjects who had not engaged in prior laboratory learning. However, the performance declined markedly when other data were studied which had come from subjects who had learned several lists (ranging from 1 to 21) earlier. Evidently prior learning is a powerful impediment for the recall of later learned verbal material of a similar sort.

Interference theory now embraces two interfering paradigms which reduce retention of learned material—retroactive inhibition (RI) and proactive inhibition (PI). As Underwood noted, our task of explaining a given instance of forgetting in our research subjects is now made easier when we consider the contribution of PI from their past learning histories. Their earlier-learned verbal habits would seem to be a much more substantial source of interference than any learning which might occur in a relatively short retention interval. Experimental evidence has now been accumulated which shows that a number of phenomena of verbal forgetting can indeed be explained by considering past language habits. We shall later consider some studies of this sort.

A test of interference theory

When an originally learned list of paired associates is found to have undergone a loss in its retention the question arises, "What happened to those verbal responses during the interval when interpolated learning of other responses was taking place?" One hypothesis prominent in interference theory indicates that first-list responses are extinguished in some manner perhaps analogous to the extinction of a conditioned response. Barnes and Underwood (1959) performed a carefully designed experiment to test this hypothesis. (Another part of their investigation dealing with proactive facilitation and mediation will not be treated here.) In accordance with the retroactive inhibition concept of interference theory they used an OL-IL-Test design. The original learning task was memorizing an eight-pair list with nonsense syllables of moderate association value as stimuli and two-syllable adjectives as responses. Care was taken to minimize similarity among items. Letting "*A*" stand for the stimuli and *"B"* for the responses, the investigators designate this OL task as the *A-B* list. It was learned by four experimental groups and a control group to a criterion of one perfect trial using the anticipation method. Each experimental group was then required to begin the interpolated learning task, memorizing a new list which should interfere with retention of the *A-B* items. This List 2 IL task was designated *A-C* to show that the identical stimuli of List 1 were retained but that completely different and unrelated adjectives were now used as responses to the old nonsense syllables. This 2-list *A-B, A-C* paradigm is designed to produce interference from List 2 with the retention of List 1.

The experimental question, it may be recalled, was whether the responses of List 1 actually get extinguished as the learning of List 2 proceeds. To test this, Barnes and Underwood interrupted the learning of List 2 at four different points, one in each experimental group. These different groups were stopped after 1, 5, 10, or 20 anticipation-method trials in their List 2 learning. They were then given a written test by presenting them a list of the 8 stimulus syllables and asking them to recall all of the adjectives which they could from either list. They were instructed to put down their responses as these occurred to them, whether from List 1 or List 2. The control group simply took a recall test for its retention of the *A-B* pairs after the longest experimental retention interval, 13 minutes. It yielded a mean score of 7.75 responses correct, nearly perfect recall, The results of the recall test of retention for the four experimental groups are shown in Figure 11.2. The data clearly showed that as interpolated learning of List 2 responses led to their strengthening, the List 1 responses were being weakened in memory. This finding is consonant with the hypothesis that an extinction-like process weakens originally learned responses as new responses are learned to the same stimuli in the OL-IL-Test paradigm. The interference theory of memory loss receives support and elucidation from this experimental outcome.

Response set interference

Research into interlist interference phenomena has continued to proliferate. Another illustrative experiment may serve to show how new findings have led to modification of the basic theory with new processes being postulated. If the *B*-response weakening in the *A-B, A-C* test paradigm is analogous to extinction of a conditioned response, then

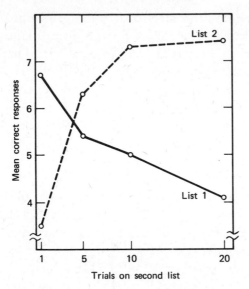

Fig. 11.2. Mean number of responses correctly recalled from List 1 and List 2 as the learning of List 2 proceeded. (After Barnes and Underwood, 1959.)

recovery of the response over time might be expected. This would parallel the so-called spontaneous recovery of an extinguished conditioned response.

Postman, Stark, and Henschel (1969) performed a series of experiments to explore different aspects of the interference-recovery phenomena. Our brief review will focus on Experiment III of their report. They used an *A-B, A-C, A-D* paradigm for two experimental groups, testing each group for recovery of the weakened earlier list responses after a different interval following List 3 learning: either 2 min or 18 min. As the paradigm designation suggests, stimuli were kept the same from list to list but responses became different with each new list. Two other experimental groups learned three lists with less direct response competition presumably generated because different stimulus items were used for each successive list. This paradigm is designated *A-B, C-D, E-F.* Two control groups learned List 1 alone and were then tested for recall after the appropriate total intervals, 14 or 30 min. The 8-pair lists learned in this study were comprised of single-letter stimuli and 2-syllable adjectives as responses. The method of anticipation, with a 2:2-sec rate, was used for the memorization. Retention of the sets of responses was tested by a method of modified free recall. Subjects were handed a list of the alphabet letters used as stimuli (8 or 24, as appropriate) and were asked to recall orally all the responses which they could.

Besides the stimulus-related response competition of the *A-B, A-C, A-D* paradigm, a second phenomenon was under test in the *A-B, C-D, E-F* paradigm. Here, without repeated stimuli from list to list, subjects learning the later lists do not have direct response competition but they may have a problem in suppressing responses from earlier lists as the later ones are learned. It is postulated that they establish a selective response set for each list which suppresses the response set for the earlier list or lists. This strong suppressive mechanism may also be considered a part of interference theory. Further, the weakening of such a suppressive set over an extended retention interval may result in a general recovery phenomenon in recall test results.

Postman, Stark, and Henschel had some reason, then, to expect more recovery and therefore higher recall scores in the experimental groups after the longer retention interval. The suppression of response set and its weakening over the longer retention interval should occur in both paradigms. However, the *A-B, A-C, A-D* group should show *an added effect* if direct extinction and spontaneous recovery of earlier learned responses to particular stimuli is operative. Both groups should show early loss and later recovery in their List 1 recall when compared with the control group. The recall data for the two paradigms are shown side by side in Figure 11.3. The control group means (for the retention of the *A-B* list alone) show very little memory loss and this tends to be the case also for the retention of List 3 within each experimental group. For Lists 1 and 2, however, the groups show reduced retention at the shorter test interval presumably followed by recovery to a higher performance level as evidenced in the groups tested at the 18-min interval following the completion of the second IL task. Since both paradigms show similar magnitudes of effect, the experimenters indicate that the outcome is consistent with the postulation that the recovery phenomenon is due solely or principally to the dissipation of response set interference. Reduced recall at the earlier test point, then, is presumably due to a general suppressive effect of the response sets adopted as the successive lists had to be memorized.

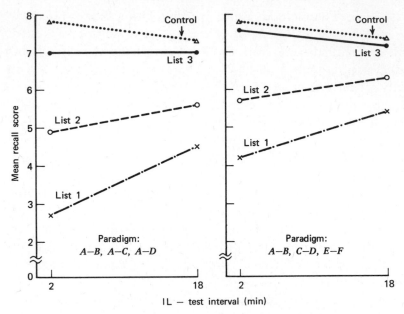

Fig. 11.3. Mean recall scores at different test intervals for Lists 1, 2, and 3 of the experimental paradigms compared with control group scores on List 1 which they learned exclusively. (After Postman, Stark, and Henschel, 1969.)

Mixed Motor and Verbal Responses

Long-term memory over several very different retention intervals has been studied relatively rarely in recent years. In an experiment reported by Bilodeau and Levy (1964), however, we find retention intervals ranging from 3 minutes to 6 weeks. Further, their research is a distinctive combination of simplicity and complexity in the investigation of both motor and verbal (or symbolic) memory. Of necessity we must examine here only a small portion of their findings. (The design and procedures by which these data were generated will be described as if they constituted the entire study; in actuality the investigators used several more experimental manipulations and data analyses.)

The simple motor activity required of subjects was a lever-positioning response. The nature of this task may be better understood by reference to Figure 11.4 which shows the apparatus used. During training a subject first moved the lever—without viewing it—through arcs of 20°

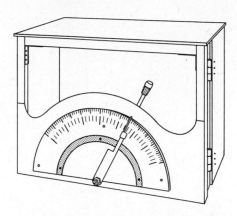

Fig. 11.4. Schematic view of the experimenter's side of the lever-positioning apparatus. The lever in the box was not seen by a subject as he moved it. (After Bilodeau, Jones, and Levy, 1964.)

and 60° which were delimited by mechanical stop pins. Then he was given a single training trial in which he attempted to move the lever through one of these arcs, whichever he guessed was "correct." In the part of the experiment which we are considering here, the subject was then told, "You chose the correct target." This concluded the training procedure, the experimenter having noted the magnitude of the subject's setting, designated R_1.

At the end of the retention interval—3 min, 20 min, 2 days, or 6 weeks, depending on group assignment—a subject was called upon to repeat his response as accurately as possible. This recall response was designated R_2. This tested for the retention of a once-practiced positioning response. Subjects were also called upon to recall the knowledge of results (KR) given them by the experimenter. This was sometimes quantitative in form (although arbitrary in value for experimental purposes) but we are dealing here only with subjects who were arbitrarily told that they were "correct" after R_1. About 99 percent of these subjects remembered being given this KR information.

In attempting the R_2 lever-positioning response as a duplication of their R_1 effort, subjects proved to be fairly accurate also, at least through the 2-day retention interval. As the plotted values of Figure 11.5 show, it

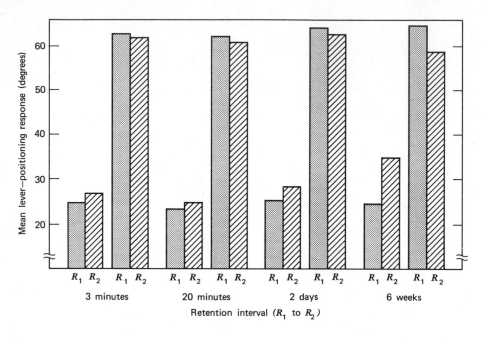

Fig. 11.5. Lever-positioning responses R_1 and R_2 for 8 groups tested for R_2 after different retention intervals. (Data from Bilodeau and Levy, 1964.)

was only the two groups tested after 6 weeks who showed a notable amount of error. The 20-degree group showed an increased tendency to overshoot in their blind positioning of the lever. The 60-degree group tended to undershoot their R_1 responses (actually becoming more "accurate" in moving the lever through the 60-degree arc demonstrated in training prior to R_1). These data on mean magnitude of R_2 tend to reflect an often-reported stability of motor performance memory over extended periods. Earlier work typically gave subjects extended practice on complex tasks. This experiment typifies a new approach in memory research in which the task is simplified to allow a more penetrating analysis of how the different events experienced by subjects affect their retention.

Free Recall

The method of free recall has been used prominently in recent years. Its aim is more to probe certain processes of memory than to determine the amount retained over time. Although there are many variations used in research, several features seem to characterize free recall experiments.

1. A specially contrived list of words is presented to subjects, usually in a random or quasi-random sequence.

2. A single presentation of the list followed immediately by a single written free recall is common, although repeated study-recall trials are also used.

3. Free recall of the words—in any order—is asked of subjects and recall sequence by each subject is examined.

4. Intrusions of words from extra-list sources are sometimes observed and tabulated to reveal encoding or retrieval processes.

These general features of free recall research, as well as variations on the theme, will be illustrated in the experiments to be reviewed.

Clustering of Responses

Since its observation by Bousfield and Sedgewick (1944), the sequential *clustering* of responses in free recall has become the phenomenon most used by experimenters and theorists as they attempt to infer processes of organization in memory. Shuell (1969) has reviewed much of the research and has presented and criticized the several indices devised to measure clustering.

Clustering may be illustrated by reference to an early experiment. Bousfield (1953) created a list of 60 words by selecting 15 from each of 4 categories: animals, vegetables, men's first names, and professions or occupations. His items included, for example, giraffe, reindeer, camel; radish, spinach, lettuce; Amos, Gerald, Howard; and milkman, printer, dentist. The 60 words were randomly mixed to create a sequence of presentation for reading the list to subjects at the rate of 1 word every 3 sec. When the single reading of the list was completed, subjects wrote down in a column as many of the words as they could recall. It was found that the written responses contained many instances where sequences or clusters of words from the same category were produced from memory. This categorical clustering in free recall has been observed in numerous other studies using a variety of item categories and procedures. The observation leads theorists to infer an organizing process as a prominent mechanism of memory. We shall later review some studies which pursue this line of inquiry. We need first to examine two of the formulas devised to provide indices of the degree of clustering found in any subject's response sequence.

A clustering index must be calculated for each individual subject since some subjects will naturally show a greater degree of clustering than others. For our example of the calculation of two indices of clustering we shall begin with the response records of three hypothetical subjects from an experiment in which the words of a 20-item, 4-category (A,B,C,D) list were presented once in random order. The written response sequences of Subjects 12, 15, and 17 are given in Table 11.1, Part

Table 11.1 Calculation of Two Indices of Clustering for Each of Three Hypothetical Subjects in Free Recall of a 20-Item Four-Category List

Part I. Individual Response Sequences Showing Each Response Category (A, B, C, D), Number Recalled (N), and Number of Repetitions (r) within Same Category as Preceding Response (Note: * identifies each repetition)

S No. 12: C C^* C^* A B B^* A A^* A^* B D D^* A D C B ($N=16$, $r=6$)
S No. 15: B B^* B^* C C^* C^* C^* A A^* A^* A^* A^* D D^* D^* ($N=15$, $r=11$)
S No. 17: D A B B^* D C A D B A A^* B D C ($N=14$, $r=2$)

Part II. Calculation of Ratio of Repetition (RR) for Each Subject

$$RR = \frac{r}{N-1}$$ Formula 11.1

where RR = the ratio of repetition
      r = the number of repetitions made by S
      N = the number of items recalled by S

S No. 12: $RR = \dfrac{6}{15} = .40$

S No. 15: $RR = \dfrac{11}{14} = .79$

S No. 17: $RR = \dfrac{2}{13} = .15$

Part III. Calculation of $r - E$, Observed Repetitions in Excess of Expected Chance Level

$$E = \frac{\Sigma m^2}{N} - 1$$ Formula 11.2

where E = expected chance number of repetitions
Σ = the summation sign
m^2 = the square of the number of items recalled in each category by S
N = the number of items recalled by S

Category	S No. 12		S No. 15		S No. 17	
	m	m^2	m	m^2	m	m^2
A	5	25	5	25	4	16
B	4	16	3	9	4	16
C	4	16	4	16	2	4
D	3	9	3	9	4	16
Σm^2 =		66		59		52
E =		3.1		2.9		2.7
$r - E$ =		2.9		8.1		-0.7

I. Also indicated are two basic data needed in computing either index of clustering: the number of items recalled (N), and the number of repetitions (r). Part II of the table shows the calculation of the *ratio of repetition* (RR) which is often used as an indicant of the amount of clustering exhibited by any subject. Part III presents another index of clustering, the amount by which any subject's repetition within categories exceeds a chance-expected level, given his production of items from each category. Both of these indices have the merit of taking the individual's recall performance level into account as his clustering is assessed. Shuell (1969) discusses these and other measures of clustering and gives their correlations with each other and with number of items recalled as determined by him in earlier research.

Before examining some experiments on *categorical clustering*, we should briefly note two other paradigms for research on organization in memory as revealed in other forms of clustering. An investigator may devise a list of words based on normative tables from word association studies. The four responses of highest frequency to each of four different stimulus words would yield, for example, a sixteen-word list with four associational subsets or networks selected so as to be unrelated directly to each other. This component creation of the list parallels Bousfield's category approach, described earlier. By presenting the sixteen-word list in random sequence the experimenter can observe the extent to which the associative networks are grouped in sequential clusters at the time of free recall. This paradigm for memory study is termed *associative cluster-*

ing. In the third paradigm, the original study list is composed of words selected to be evidently unrelated. In this type of research, *subjective organization* is sought in the response listings of individual subjects given repeated trials with varied stimulus sequences. Subjects have been observed to develop their own repeated sequences in trial-to-trial responding. This is considered evidence of an idiosyncratic organizing tendency, possibly related to habit formation or associative linking of successive items during responding. Table 11.2 summarizes three experimental

Table 11.2 Three Experimental Paradigms for the Study of Clustering as an Indicant of Organization in Free Recall (After Shuell, 1969)

Experimental Paradigm	Composition of List	Typical Mode of Presentation	Response Tendency
Categorical clustering	Words from two or more conceptual categories	Random sequence; one or more trials	Clustering by category
Associative clustering	Words from two or more associational networks	Random sequence; one or more trials	Clustering by associational links
Subjective organization	Unrelated words	Random sequence; multitrial presentation and response	Developing and using own sequences in responding

paradigms for the study of organization in free recall, as outlined by Shuell (1969, 353-354).

Dominance level in conceptual categories

An experiment by Bousfield and Puff (1964) serves to demonstrate the investigation of clustering in free recall. It also illustrates a slightly different approach to stimulus list formation. These experimenters based their critical sublists on the scaling of words by Underwood and Richardson (1956) for their dominance level with respect to certain sensory adjectives associated with them, in this case, the adjective *smelly*. Words with high dominance level for association with smelly were *ammonia, manure, garbage, skunk, gardenia, sewer, garlic,* and *cheese.* Words of lower dominance level associated with smelly were *sardine, hospital, hog, vinegar, daffodil, coffee, diaper,* and *cinnamon.* It may be noted that the concept of smelly here includes items of both pleasant and unpleasant odors.

Bousfield and Puff ran two groups of subjects who listened three times to a 24-word list and performed written free recall after each presentation. List *A* included the 8 words of high dominance level in the concept smelly plus 16 buffer words moderately related to 2 other concepts, *round* and *soft.* List *B* contained the 8 words of low dominance level for smelly plus the same 16 buffer words. (The buffer words, intermixed with the critical words to form different random sequences of presentations, did not figure in the response analyses.) It was hypothesized that response clustering would be observed in the critical words of Lists *A* and *B,* with the high dominance level words of List *A* showing the phenomenon more prominently.

For the data analysis a formula was devised to compute the expected-by-chance number of successive appearances of critical items in the response lists, adjusted for the number of such critical words recalled (Formula 11.2, p. 408). This chance-expected value was calculated separately for each subject, based on his response productivity of critical items. His actual number of critical-item repetitions in sequence was also computed. This was done, of course, separately for the two groups of subjects who had been given the high dominance level or the low dominance level in the critical words. For each group the observed mean repetition level was compared with the chance-expected mean. In Group *A,* the difference was statistically significant, indicating that the words of high dominance level on the concept *smelly* had clustered in response more frequently than a chance formula would predict. For the words of low dominance level, the amount of clustering was calculated to be not statistically significant.

This study by Bousfield and Puff, it may be noted, tends to blend the categorical clustering and the associative clustering paradigms. The critical words were instances of a concept or category—smelly—but they were scaled by Underwood and Richardson using a controlled or restricted word association technique.

Associative frequency and block presentation

Words used in another study of free recall by Cofer, Bruce, and Reicher (1966) can also be viewed as probing both categorical clustering and associative clustering. Using the Connecticut word association norms (Cohen, Bousfield, and Whitmarsh, 1957) the experimenters selected 10 high-frequency (HF) and 10 low-frequency (LF) associates given in response to each of four category names used as stimuli in compiling the association data. These four category designations were: occupations, weapons, four-legged animals, and articles of clothing. Two 40-word lists were formed, the HF List from the high-frequency associates in each category and the LF List from the low-frequency responses. In Experiment I (selected from a series of three for review here), the experimenters also varied the sequence of word presentation. They used either a random order or a *block presentation* in which all 10 associates from any given category were presented in succession, followed by 10 from a different category, and so on. Both the random and the block presentation were used with both the HF List and the LF List, requiring 4 subject groups to accommodate the 4 combinations of material and method of presentation. The words were projected individually with an exposure time of 4.4 sec each. They were viewed by subjects who were told in advance to expect a free recall test.

There was a further division of groups in the design of the experiment for the recall testing. For each combination of list and sequence of presentation, two different recall test plans were followed. One set of 4 groups was given a 5-min written recall test and then a second test after a 5-min interval filled with a word-rating task. Another 4 groups were given a delayed recall test only, the word-rating task filling a 10.5 min interval to match the interval prior to the second testing of the other 4 groups.

Cofer, Bruce, and Reicher were interested in measuring three different aspects of performance in free recall: mean number of words recalled, frequency of intrusions (written responses not appearing in the presented list), and mean ratio of repetition (*RR*—an index of clustering described earlier in Formula 11.1, p. 408). Some of these descriptive statistics are presented in the three-part Table 11.3.

When the mean number of words recalled was examined, the HF List was found uniformly to yield significantly better retention scores. Block presentation led to better recall than did random presentation.

Table 11.3 Indicants of Recall, Categorical Intrusion, and Clustering in the Different Presentation and Test Conditions of Experiment I (After Cofer, Bruce, and Reicher, 1966)

Part I. Mean Number of Words Recalled

Condition	HF List	LF List
Random presentation		
Immediate test	25.9	20.5
Second test	25.7	20.3
Delayed test	22.2	16.4
Block presentation		
Immediate test	26.3	21.2
Second test	27.3	20.4
Delayed test	25.3	21.7

Part II. Number of Categorical Intrusions

Condition	HF List Categories	LF List Categories
Random presentation		
Immediate test	2	14
Second test	4	20
Delayed test	12	25
Block Presentation		
Immediate test	1	5
Second test	4	11
Delayed test	9	26

Part III. Mean Ratio of Repetition (RR)

Condition	HF List	LF List
Random presentation		
Immediate test	.60	.53
Second test	.65	.56
Delayed test	.57	.53
Block presentation		
Immediate test	.80	.69
Second test	.81	.73
Delayed test	.72	.68

Most of the intrusion errors made in recall could be identified with one of the four categories of the lists. Only these categorical instrusions are tallied in Table 11.3. The more frequent categorical intrusions into LF List recall were generally high-frequency associates of the category designations.

The third part of the results tabulation is of interest as we consider where clustering was prominent under the different experimental conditions. As the mean RR scores indicate, greater clustering occurred in the recall of the HF List. Perhaps high frequency associates are more strongly associated with each other as well as with their category designation. Greater clustering also occurred after block presentation. Subjects benefit from the categorical organization of the material as opposed to the random sequencing of item presentation. In this study, though not in all experiments of this sort, superior recall is associated with greater clustering. In the groups given a second recall test, clustering was significantly greater than in the immediate test. There was evidently a persistent—even increasing—tendency to organize the retained items by category. The delayed test groups showed the lesser amount of clustering which characterized the immediate tests of the other groups.

Including category names in lists

A study by Segal (1969) resembled the one just reviewed in its use of either high- or low-frequency associates to category names as the words comprising its two basic lists. As before, high-frequency associates were found to cluster more readily and to yield higher mean recall scores. In our brief review of the Segal experiment we shall concentrate on two aspects of the study which contrast with the research of Cofer, Bruce, and Reicher. One of these differences was Segal's giving subjects a series of 6 study-test trials and the other was his inclusion in two 55-item lists of the 11 category names under which the other 44 words (either high- or low-frequency associates) could be grouped. Other lists (of 44 words) omitted these names or substituted one more associate per category to give 55-item lists for comparison.

The two frequency levels and the three compositions of the lists required that six groups of subjects be run. The word lists were pre-recorded on audio tape with a 3-sec separation of items and a different randomization of word order for each of the 6 trials. A trial consisted of the list presentation followed by a 4-min period for a written free recall.

Some salient results may be noted in addition to the greater clustering and better recall of high-frequency associates mentioned earlier. The inclusion of the category names led to greater clustering as measured by the mean ratio of repetition (RR). However, recall of category members was enhanced by the presence of the category labels only for the group studying the low-frequency list. Recall of the high-frequency associates, Segal suggests, seemed to be inhibited by the inclusion of the category designations. Returning again to clustering, it was found that the RR index increased over trials, indicating a kind of learning-to-organize in recall. Further, where category names were included for study, they tended to appear more frequently at the beginning of their clusters as trials went on—another sign of their functional utility, especially where low-frequency associates had to be retrieved from memory.

Subjective Organizing

Even when semantic or associative categories are not used in presenting verbal materials to be memorized, it is found that subjects engage in organizing processes which affect their later recall. This concept of organization has been discussed in depth by Mandler (1967). Two methodological approaches to such organizing of information are represented in illustrative studies to be mentioned here. Neither investigation employed a direct measure of organizing in recall. Instead, each sought to infer its operation in an initial task on the basis of its transfer to a second task. Both studies yielded reliable results which supported such an inference. In the first, subjective organization was first beneficial and then detrimental as the second stage of a learning task was undertaken. In the second study, success in recall was related to the number of categories into which subjects sorted items which they were later requested to recall.

Organizing in part-learning

Two tasks of learning and recall were administered to subjects in the third and fourth experiments reported by Tulving (1966). Both experiments were very similar, differing only in the number of words to be learned and the number of trials given to subjects. The general patterns of results were quite similar too, so the two studies may be briefly summarized together. The second task for both experimental and control subjects was to study and recall over repeated trials a list of familiar words. For the experimental group, the prior task was to study and recall a first list comprised of just half the words to be encountered in the second list. Control subjects were administered an irrelevant list of this length to be studied as their first learning task. Experimental subjects were not forewarned, of course, that the words they first studied would comprise half of the items of the second list.

On the basis of earlier research, Tulving postulated that all the learners would tend to engage in subjective organization of items as they studied and recalled the words of their first task. As he puts it, they would organize the material into subjective units designated as S units. His investigation was to determine how these hypothetical S units would affect second-list learning and recall when experimental subjects (who might need to reorganize their S units) were compared with the control subjects whose first-list S units would presumably be irrelevant to second-list study. The outcome, in short, was that experimental subjects first showed a benefit of the earlier learning when they worked on the second list but later demonstrated a detrimental effect when compared to control subjects. Presumably S units formed from the first list imposed a pattern on their recall which caused difficulty as they attempted mastery of the total second list. The earlier benefit was a natural increase in their scores derived from the earlier memorization of a number of the words. These findings lend emphasis to the process of subjective organizing in memory since they show that it can be a source of difficulty in special circumstances as well as a source of aid in recall.

Categorizing and subsequent recall

A two-stage experiment was also used by Mandler and Pearlstone (1966) in exploring how the activity of organizing may affect the recall of words. The first stage of the experiment required subjects to sort stimulus materials into categories, either self-selected or specified for different groups. The items of interest to us were sets of words of either high or low frequency of usage. These were the items which had to be recalled in the second stage of the study, following the conceptual categorizing. The investigation sought, in part, to see how recall scores might be related to the earlier performance of sorting these words into categories.

In both kinds of sorting—free and subjective or constrained and imposed—the number of organizing categories was found to relate to the recall of the high-frequency words. The correlations between initial number of sorting categories and later number of words recalled ranged from +.79 to +.96 as different computations were performed. Recall of these common words seemed to depend upon the number of categories into which they had to be consistently sorted on the repeated categorization trials, even when the number of sorting trials was held constant. For the rare words, of low frequency of usage, no significant correlation was obtained. These unfamiliar words had commonly been sorted on an alphabetical basis, not affording enough response integration for good recall. For the high-frequency words, their familiarity had presumably allowed a more meaningful sorting so that this categorizing could contribute to memory for the items through the organizing mediation afforded by the conceptual coding into classes.

Short-Term Memory

Intensified research work, often with creative new experimental designs and procedures, accompanied the development of two-stage theories of memory. In the theoretical emphasis on the contributory role played by short-term memory (STM) in getting information into long-term memory (LTM), there was a demand to learn more about those critical first few seconds after item presentation. There was, too, the question of how congruent short-term retention might be with LTM in the mechanisms operating. So processes like interference had to be explored. In brief, short-term retention studies invigorated research on memory in recent years. They should appeal to students of experimental psychology due to the lack of demand for elaborate instrumentation and for the invitation they offer to contribute original investigations or replications of key studies.

Intake Processes

With briefly presented material to be remembered for only a brief time, the nature of the material, the conditions of its presentation, and the subject's processing of the information given to him all become important areas to examine. From numerous reported studies we shall first consider a few which stress intake processes.

Grouping and encoding

One information processing mechanism that individuals appear to use in placing material in memory is to group items into convenient units or chunks for storage and retention or to encode items in ways that aid retention while preserving item sequence accurately. A commonplace example of this is the encoding of telephone numbers by some mnemonically motivated individuals into meaningful words using the phone dial as the code key. Thus, 779 2465 can be encoded as PSYCHOL. Unfortunately the dial does not give us alphabetic equivalents for "zero" and "one" so the code key has limits.

Grouping of items subjectively has a parallel in grouping items as they are presented. We often attempt this when we give a phone number to another person. Our grouped presentation of the digits facilitates his grouping for immediate memory purposes or for rehearsal and long-term retention. An experiment reported by Bower and Springston (1970) used an optimal and a shifted three-letter grouping of alphabet letters presented to subjects for short-term memory. Two kinds of material were used in the optimal grouping, either easily pronounced CVC trigrams (but not meaningful words) or abbreviations and acronyms such as TWA, IBM, or FBI. Four items of either type were used in sequence to create a string of 12 letters which could be tape recorded with appropriate pauses (approximately 1 sec) and intonations for the four groupings of letters.

In order to create a shifted grouping of 3-letter items, each string of 12 letters was simply altered by moving the last letter up to the initial position. When pauses and intonation now broke the string into 3-letter groups these became unpronounceable CCVs or meaningless clusters of letters. The four types of 12-letter strings comprised the four experimental treatments of the study (Experiment I):

Pronounceable—Optimal Grouping
    DAT   BEC   JAX   PEL
Meaningful—Optimal Grouping
    FBI   PHD   TWA   IBM
Pronounceable Items—Shifted Grouping
    LDA   TBE   CJA   XPE
Meaningful Items—Shifted Grouping
    MFB   IPH   DTW   AIB

Each subject listened for 10 sec to a string of 12 letters—with pauses as indicated above—and immediately wrote his recall of the letters on a 12-space line of a response sheet, being allowed a 15-sec silent period for this responding. Different types of strings followed one another until 80 strings had been presented, 1 of each type in each block of 4 strings.

The outcome of this Experiment I in the study by Bower and Springston was clearly supportive of the hypothesis that optimal grouping of the material presented would facilitate STM. The mean number of letters correctly recalled from the different types of 12-letter strings were:

Type of String	Mean Number Recalled
Pronounceable—Optimal Grouping	9.2
Meaningful—Optimal Grouping	9.7
Pronounceable Items—Shifted	7.6
Meaningful Items—Shifted	7.4

Statistical analysis confirmed the evident facilitation of memory for both kinds of items by the optimal grouping in presentation. It also showed a significant interaction, with the meaningful abbreviations showing the greater effect of the different groupings when compared with the nonsense trigrams.

The auditory modality

Considerable evidence from different types of research has accumulated to support the theoretical position that the auditory modality is strongly operative in STM. Two kinds of findings are represented in the studies we shall examine. First, intrusion errors in short-term recall tend to indicate acoustic confusion of items. Second, several comparisons have been made of memory for items presented to the ear or to the eye. Intake through audition generally is found to yield better short-term retention, especially when a relatively high rate of presentation of items is used. Even when visual presentation yields better performance, the auditory modality is interpreted as contributing to the encoding process.

Expanding on earlier studies by Conrad, an investigation by Wickelgren (1965) sought clues in intrusion errors as to the nature of encoding in STM. Subjects listened to 8-item lists composed of alphabet letters and numerical digits, four of each, randomly selected and sequenced. The auditory presentation was prerecorded at a rate of one item every 0.75 sec. Subjects in one condition had to copy the lists during presentation and then to cover what they had written and to write the items as recalled from memory. By using this copy + recall method the experimenter insured that any error appearing in recall was not merely the result of an error in perception. Any misperceptions were detected as copying errors and ruled out of recall analysis.

Thirty-six MIT students were given 50 different 8-item lists under the copy + recall condition. The letter-for-letter intrusion errors which occurred in their recall responses are tallied in Table 11.4. The intrusions

Table 11.4 Frequency of Same-Sound and Different-Sound Intrusions of Letters for Letters in Recall After Correct Copying (After Wickelgren, 1965)

Sound	Letter Containing Sound	Same-Sound Intrusions	Different-Sound Intrusions	p
a = /ey/	A H J K	9	7	.001
e = /iy/	B C D E G P T V Z	52	29	.001
e = /e/	F L M N S X	14	16	.001
i = /ay/	I Y	2	7	.05
u = /yuw/	Q U W	4	8	.001
Vowel total		81	67	.001
/b/	B W	0	10	
/d/	D W	1	10	
/k/	K Q X	0	13	
/l/	L W	1	10	
/s/	C S X	6	15	.01
/j/	G J	8	8	.001
Consonant total		16	66	.001
Total		97	133	.001

Notes: p = probability of obtaining this frequency of same-sound intrusions by chance. // indicates the phonemic representation of the sound.

were segregated into same-sound and different-sound categories, as the column headings indicate. The p values in the right-hand column indicate those totals of same-sound intrusions which are significantly greater than expected on a chance basis. These data clearly confirm and extend Conrad's earlier finding that acoustic confusions produce errors in immediate recall. The evidence supports the hypothesis that short-term memory encoding is auditory (or speech-motor) in nature.

Turning now to a direct test of the auditory intake channel (as compared to the visual modality) for short-term memory, we may briefly consider an experiment (Experiment I) reported by Murdock (1968). He used both recall and recognition testing to determine if immediate memory for serial order of items was better after one type of sensory intake than the other. Subjects were presented with 10-word lists either projected at a rate of ½ sec exposure per word or played from a tape recorder at a comparable rate. The words were common two-syllable words. For recall testing, about ½ sec after the tenth item was presented a single word from the list (excepting the tenth) was repeated as a probe for recall of serial order. A subject was required to recall if possible the subsequent word in the list. For recognition testing, there were two kinds of probes—target pairs of words (actually successive in the list) or lures (nonsuccessive pairs of words from ordinal list positions 1-3, 2-4, 3-5, 4-6, 5-7 or 7-6, 8-7, 9-8). In the recognition test, of course, a subject tried to respond "Yes" to any pair presented in the sequence of the list (for example, 1-2, 6-7, 4-5) and "No" to any of the false lures.

Twenty-four subjects were tested individually with 72 lists, separated by intervals of 15 sec. Blocks of 18 lists were counterbalanced for sensory modality with the *AVVA* or *VAAV* orders each being given to 12 subjects. The results of the experiment favored the auditory intake as yielding better STM. In the recall test, hearing the words led to better performance than seeing them for every probe position in the serial lists. Performance for both sensory modalities was much better for the later list positions, possibly indicating that an intralist retroactive inhibition may have hampered recall of earlier sequences of items. In the recognition test, performance curves for both audition and vision fluctuate around the 50 percent chance level for the earlier part of the list. For the later part of the serial list, especially for stimulus positions 8 and 9, performance data show much better retention with clear superiority for the auditory intake channel. The general advantage for audition in short-term memory for serial order was statistically significant in both recall and recognition test results.

Another experiment on STM also compared the auditory and visual modalities for processing the stimulus information but the experimenters devised procedures very different from those we just examined. Laughery and Fell (1969) used the same subjects in two different phases of their study. In Phase One subjects were presented with stimulus sequences of 8 letters of the alphabet in random order. *Within any sequence*, some of the letters were presented over a loudspeaker for auditory intake and some appeared on a television screen for visual perception. For different groups of subjects the rate of presentation was set at values ranging from 0.5 to 3.0 sec per letter. Subjects responded at the end of each sequence by writing down the letters which they recalled as heard or seen. Fifteen sequences were given to each subject at his assigned presentation rate. The first 5 were considered as practice trials, while data from the last 10 were analyzed. Analysis of variance showed that sensory modality and rate of presentation significantly affected the percent of items recalled. As Figure 11.6 indicates, the auditory modality yielded a greater percent of letters recalled at every presentation rate. At the slower rates the visually-presented items were recalled almost as well as the auditory items. This evident interaction between modality and rate of presentation was statistically significant as were the main effects of sensory channel and rate.

In Phase Two of their investigation Laughery and Fell used a different way of mixing the auditory and visual inputs and of examining their impact on STM. Using the same groups at the same rates of presentation they had experienced before, the experimenters now presented sequences of 5 consonants. The *same* letters were presented on the screen and through the speaker but *in a different sequence*, with no consonant at the same ordinal position in the auditory and visual lists. By telling the subject to write down the letter *in any order* after the two-channel presentation ended, the investigators hoped to determine which channel

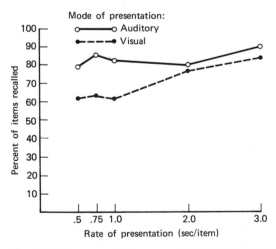

Fig. 11.6. Percent of items recalled in Phase One by groups given auditory and visual presentations at particular rates. (After Laughery and Fell, 1969.)

was preferred for intake into STM. Some response sequences followed the auditory order, some the visual, and some were classified as mixed. The results, plotted in Figure 11.7 revealed a strong preference for the auditory modality at all presentation rates except the 3-sec rate where no clear preference is evident. In a postexperimental inquiry subjects were found generally to express preference for hearing the items rather than viewing them. This choice of the auditory modality was preponderant after the three fastest rates of presentation, but not following the two slowest rates where preferences tended to be more evenly divided.

It was further found that recall performances in Phase One of the investigation tended to correspond with subjects' expressed preferences. However, 8 subjects expressing a preference for the visual modality were found to have recalled more items that they had heard; the reverse relationship of better performance on items seen despite an expressed preference for hearing the items was found for only 2 subjects. The two types of mixed-modality presentations and the expressions of subject

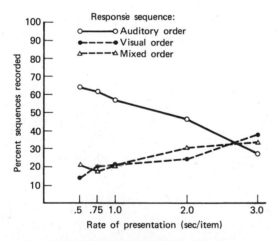

Fig. 11.7. Percent of sequences recorded in auditory, visual, or mixed orders by subjects given simultaneous but differently sequenced sets of consonants in the auditory and visual modes of presentation. Rates of presentation in this Phase Two were the same as the groups had earlier experienced. (After Laughery and Fell, 1969.)

preference in this study indicate, as did Murdock's data, a superior contribution to STM of auditory intake where the information processing must be rapid.

For our final consideration of intake modality we may briefly consider an experiment by Sherman and Turvey (1969). Subjects were presented lists of 9 digits for immediate serial recall with separate groups receiving either auditory or visual presentations. Stimulus durations were 0.3 sec and interstimulus intervals were 0.6, 1.2, or 2.0 sec for different groups. The score for each of the 6 lists presented to any subject was the number of digits recalled aloud in correct serial order, counted from the beginning of the 9-digit series.

The investigators found that the two groups tested at the 0.6-sec interstimulus interval did not differ significantly in serial recall scores, with just over 3 items recited correctly from the initial part of the list. At the slower rates, the two visual presentation groups did somewhat better, approaching 4 correct. The two auditory groups dropped slightly below 3 correct at the slower rates. At these rates statistical analysis indicated that the visual group scores were significantly higher.

The experimenters offer an interpretation for this finding. Subjects receiving the digit series visually are able to rehearse early items in the acoustic code typical of short-term memory while still viewing later items. Early-item rehearsal and later-item intake are considered to involve different modalities. For individuals hearing the digits presented, however, a conflict or interference is postulated between auditory intake and auditory involvement with early-item rehearsal. It is felt that these subjects delimit this rehearsal to avoid confusion with items still being received. This is the explanation given for their lower scores in serial recall of the initial part of the 9-digit series.

Processes During Retention

Even though the interval of short-term retention is only a few seconds, there are numerous research results which delineate certain processes occurring in it. Some processes are detrimental to retention; some are facilitative. We shall examine a selection of three studies which represent markedly different experimental approaches to describing and quantifying events and mechanisms related to STM.

Interpolated inputs and outputs

In many experiments on memorizing, the study, retention, and testing of any particular item is interwoven with similar events pertaining to other items in the list. With this complexity of sequential activities it is difficult to determine just what is taking place as STM is examined. Experimenters and theorists have turned to analytic procedures—often centered on the learning of a single item—to clarify the effect on memory of various kinds of behavioral events which are part of typical experimental procedures. Tulving and Arbuckle (1966) carried out the research which gives us our example. We shall examine only Test 1 of their complex design. It involved 9 different conditions of paired associate list construction with 144 subjects tested twice with each condition or type of list. The interest of the experimenters and the analysis of data was limited exclusively to the short-term retention of a single paired associate item. This item, a word-number pair like the others, was always the fifth pair in the list so that any proactive effect from studying the earlier pairs would be comparable across conditions. It was the interval just following this pair presentation and just prior to its testing that was the focus of the study. During this period—the retention interval for the critical unit —subjects experienced different numbers of input-output events in the 9 experimental combinations indicated here.

Condition	Number of Inputs	Number of Outputs
1	0	0
2	0	1
3	0	2
4	1	0
5	1	1
6	1	2
7	2	0
8	2	1
9	2	2

Some definitions, followed by examples, may be helpful. An input was simply a word-number pair presented at the regular exposure duration for study as were the other items in the list. It was an input to memory storage. An output (required from the subject) was called for by presenting a stimulus word alone; this was from a pair presented earlier and required an output of effort to recall the associated number, as per instructions. The nine conditions which we have described in the abstract are illustrated in the presentation sequences of Table 11.5.

Table 11.5 Illustrative Sequences of Study-Test Events Comprising the Nine Conditions of Test 1 (After Tulving and Arbuckle, 1966)

Condition 1		Condition 2		Condition 3	
unknown	9	faultless	2	conscious	4
divine	1	crafty	7	perfect	9
silly	5	fatal	6	silent	7
severe	4	evil	5	clumsy	3
*tired	8	*dismal	3	*quiet	2
**tired		crafty		silent	
		**dismal		perfect	
				**quiet	

Condition 4		Condition 5		Condition 6	
cheerful	6	upright	8	awkward	7
willing	7	hostile	6	verbal	3
steady	2	deadly	2	silent	6
happy	8	active	1	steady	2
*witty	4	*gentle	4	*fluid	5
vacant	3	hostile		silent	
**witty		unseen	9	dirty	4
		**gentle		steady	
				**fluid	

Condition 7		Condition 8		Condition 9	
polite	3	beastly	1	pressing	5
healthy	4	open	7	empty	2
ready	1	fiery	2	perfect	1
formal	6	sturdy	6	gloomy	4
*hearty	7	*random	9	*lively	6
exact	2	able	4	comic	9
playful	9	manly	3	pressing	
**hearty		fiery		gloomy	
		**random		timid	3
				**lively	

In each condition exemplified in the table the first four pairs are buffer items and a source of output test events as needed. The fifth pair is the critical unit for data analysis. It is starred with an asterisk in the table. The stimulus word of this critical pair occurs again as Test 1 of short-term retention. The critical test presentation is double starred in our sample sequences. Between the study exposure of the critical unit, in fifth ordinal position, and its stimulus test presentation a short time later the input-output events are interpolated to determine their effect during this retention interval. Sample events are shown in the illustrative sequences of Table 11.5. Following Test 1 for recall of the critical number response, the subject received a few other study and test items which are not relevant to our review of the study, and not illustrated in the table.

For the paired associate learning procedure the subjects, tested individually, were asked to read aloud each word and number which appeared on a 3 x 5 index card displayed in the aperture of a screen separating the experimenter from the subject. The card sequence was presented at a 2-sec exposure per card with no interval between cards. When an output card appeared showing a stimulus word only, the subject had to give the number which had been paired with it on an earlier input exposure. If he could not recall the number confidently, he was required to guess one of the digits from 1 to 9. Despite the presentation and testing of several pairs, the investigators were interested only in STM for the critical unit of each series.

The proportions of critical unit responses correctly recalled are shown in Figure 11.8 for each of the 9 input-output conditions. In Condition 1 with no intervening events and no time interval between study of the critical unit and its testing only 1 error occurred in 288 tests so its proportion of recall is shown as 1.00 on the graph. Conditions 2 and 4, with one output or one input respectively, yielded p values of .83 and .80. Condition 3, after two intervening outputs, gave correct recall in about half the cases (.48) as did Condition 5 after one input and one output (.49). Condition 7, with two intervening input events, gave a significantly smaller proportion of recalls (.36) than did Condition 3 where both interpolated events were outputs. Conditions 6, 8, and 9 yielded recalls in about thirty percent of the tests. In discussing these findings of Test 1 the authors of the report stress the comparison of Conditions 3 and 7 which indicate two new inputs to be more interfering during retention than two output demands.

Transpositions in three-word items

When complex items are retained in short-term memory, the juxtaposition or transposition of their component parts is one form which imperfect recall may take. Though transpositions had been found in earlier studies to occur rarely, Murdock and vom Saal (1967) investigated them for their dependence on retention interval and their relation to errors in memory for trigrams composed of monosyllabic words. These three-word items were derived from the associative norms tabulated by Cohen,

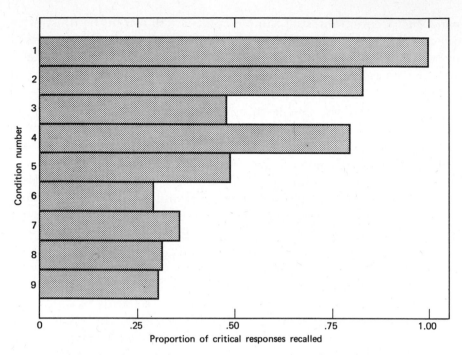

Fig. 11.8. Proportion of critical responses recalled for each of the 9 input-output interpolation conditions described in the text and illustrated in Table 11.5. (Data from Tulving and Arbuckle, 1966.)

Bousfield, and Whitmarsh (1957) for numerous conceptual categories. Here are trigram samples as given in the experimental report:

Same-Category Word Trigrams

GRAY	BROWN	RED
SKULL	THIGH	WAIST
OWL	DUCK	LARK
SPEAR	AXE	CLUB
SLOOP	TUG	RAFT

Different-Category Word Trigrams

EEL	SCREW	LOUNGE
ALE	BOMB	STEAL
YACHT	BEAM	FLOOD
WINE	COAT	PIG
BIRCH	CORN	PINK

Each of the 48 subjects in the experiment was tested with both types of word trigram at three different retention intervals—3, 9, and 18 sec. Eight trigrams of each type were presented at each interval for a 48-trial retention experiment. Counterbalancing and randomization were used to assure unbiased results. Each word trigram was presented visually for a 1.3-sec study exposure. The retention interval then began, with subjects required to perform a previously practiced distractor task of adding 3 to numbers presented by the experimenter in rapid succession. A gong signalled the end of this interval. The subject then recalled the three-word item in sequence, guessing as necessary to complete a trigram.

Superior retention was observed for the same-category trigrams with 67, 46, and 43 percent correctly ordered items recalled at the intervals of 3, 9, and 18 sec. In contrast, the corresponding data were 44, 28, and 21 percent correct recalls of different-category word groups.

Transpositions of the correct (ABC) sequence of words occurred rarely as expected, but their frequencies show some interesting patterns in the data. Transpositions of same-category items occurred three times as often as transpositions in the different-category word trigrams. Further, adjacent transpositions (ACB or BAC) heavily outnumbered remote transpositions (BCA, CAB, or CBA).

As a further examination of STM, the experimenters studied the relationship of transposition to word errors (any noncorrect response—for example, ABX, XXC, or XBA). Sometimes errors occurred without transposition, of course, as in our first two examples just given. However, there was a tendency for errors and transpositions to occur together as in our third example, XBA. That is, item information and order information seem to be somewhat interdependent in memory processes. Transpositions may be disruptive of recall of one or more of the trigram elements, as the report's authors suggest, or possibly the memory loss of an element interferes with retention of the sequence or locus of elements correctly retained. In any case, it is clear that misrecall of various kinds has potential for the continuing analysis of memory processes.

Natural language mediators

In studies of learning and memory it has often been found that the subjects report using previously acquired language to help them apprehend and retain new material, particularly if it lacks meaningfulness. This use of natural language mediators (NLMs) was investigated intensively in a study conducted by Kiess (1968). We shall review his Experiment I to see how the use of NLMs facilitates short-term memory. We shall also learn how this facilitation relates to the association value of the CVC trigrams as scaled by Archer (1960).

Each subject was given 25 memory trials or tests by Kiess with different blocks of 5 trials incorporating the 5 retention intervals of Experiment I—0, 5, 10, 15, and 30 sec. Each different group of 50 subjects was tested for retention of individual CVCs drawn from either a high, medium, or low association value. A distractor task of reading visually presented random digits during the retention intervals was used. The single CVC to be retained on each trial was presented for 3 sec of study and NLM selection by the subject. (The trigram was projected on the screen for 2 sec and 1 sec was taken for a slide change.) If the retention interval was 0 sec, the next slide showed an asterisk—the signal for recall of the CVC during the 5 sec allotted. For the other intervals a random digit group was projected so the subject could read the digits. Then the asterisk slide called for recall of the CVC. A very important procedural aspect of this experiment was requiring the subject to indicate during the 3-sec study period any NLM he might consider useful in remembering the CVC of the current trial. The response latency for giving any NLM was measured from the start of the CVC presentation. Further, after the recall of the CVC, or its attempted recall, the subject was given 10 sec to recall also the NLM he had earlier stated. Using these ways of observing the NLMs was directed at clarifying their role in facilitating short-term retention.

It was found that the CVCs of high association value elicited NLMs 87 percent of the time, while 61 and 32 percent were used with the trigrams of medium and low association value, respectively. The subjects reported NLMs at shorter latencies for the higher association trigrams with the mean latency values, in sequence, being 1.77, 1.91, and 2.09 sec. Having found that some CVCs elicited NLMs and some did not, Kiess examined the recall data for these two classes of trigrams at each level of association value and at each retention interval. The results of this partitioning of the recall scores are portrayed in Figure 11.9. Inspection of the retention curves reveals several salient facts. Percent correct recall of the CVCs declined over time in a manner suggestive of some of the forgetting curves of long-term memory studies. Items of higher association value were retained better, probably due to superior learning or encoding in the brief study time. Next—the main effect sought in this experiment—CVCs which elicited NLMs were better retained than those presumably learned in rote fashion without evident mediation.

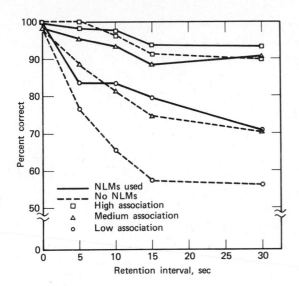

Fig. 11.9. Percent of CVCs correctly recalled as dependent upon retention interval, association value, and elicitation of NLMs vs. rote memorization. (After Kiess, 1968.)

Besides the convincing data plotted in Figure 11.9 for CVC retention (and the supporting statistical analysis), additional evidence for the facilitation stemming from NLMs is reported by Kiess. First, 98.8 percent of all the NLMs reported at the study time were retained and recalled when the retention interval and CVC recall test had been completed. This is evidence of the continuing availability of the NLMs and suggests that they may be functional as an aid to CVC retention (as the CVC recall data also imply). Out of only 28 instances of forgotten NLMs, furthermore, the corresponding CVC had not been able to be recited in 27 of the cases—a performance level even below that attributed to rote memorization. Kiess also found significant NLM facilitation of CVC retention in his Experiment II, not reviewed here. The contribution of past language experience to verbal STM appears to be strong, even though more must be discovered about precisely how it operates.

Cueing for Retrieval

The processes of STM range over time from the anticipatory set or expectancy which may be established prior to the presentation of material to be memorized, through the encoding and storage, to retrieval from memory by recall or recognition. Post-retrieval processes such as judgments of confidence to be placed on one's accuracy or adequacy of memory performance extend the time span even further. To conclude this chapter we shall examine two studies in which the cueing for retrieval was treated as the experimental variation.

Delayed cues

An experiment performed as an undergraduate independent study project demonstrated how retrieval from STM was facilitated by giving subjects cues or prompts part way through the interval devoted to attempted recall. The report by Russ and Loess (1969) describes the investigation as building upon earlier research which Professor Loess had directed. In this sequel, subjects were given 12 sec to recall the 3 words of a triad, for example, BEAR-CANADA-SPINACH, which had been presented to them 10 sec earlier. This retention interval was filled with a digit-naming distractor task. At the time of retrieval, three groups of subjects were given differentiating treatments. Forty subjects received no cue (NC) to aid memory, just the word "Recall" projected as their command to report the word triad. Another 40 subjects received an immediate cue (IC) in the form of three category names, for example, ANIMAL-COUNTRY-VEGETABLE, corresponding to the triad of category members they had seen 10 sec earlier. The other 40 subjects saw the "Recall" slide at the end of the retention interval and began to report the words they remembered—either correctly or possibly with error. After 6 sec had elapsed, if any category had not been represented by some reported word, a subject from this delayed cue (DC) group was told the category name corresponding to any unrecalled part or parts of the triad. Then a few more seconds were available for the aided retrieval before the recall period ended, as for all groups, after 12 sec. (In this review we are not considering the use of high and low frequency words from the categories, another variable in the design of the research.)

The recall data given by Russ and Loess have been condensed for presentation in Table 11.6. It shows the proportion of words correctly recalled during each half of the 12-sec recall period—before and after the special cueing of the DC group. In the first half of the recall period, the three groups did not differ significantly, statistical analysis showed. However, in the second half of the period, the delayed cue (DC) group recalled more words than did the other two groups. The authors point out that the DC group did not appear to wait for its special cueing. It

Table 11.6 Proportion of Words Correctly Recalled During Each
Half of a 12-Sec Recall Interval (After Russ and Loess, 1969)

	Recall Group		
Recall Interval	No Cue	Immediate Cue	Delayed Cue
First half	.69	.63	.69
Second half	.04	.06	.13
Total	.73	.69	.82

recalled as much as the other groups in the first 6 sec, then added more
correct responses after the category prompts were presented. This result
suggests that recall alone may not retrieve all the available material from
memory. Appropriate cueing seems to make more of it accessible.

Differential retrieval

In research examining STM as affected by special retrieval instructions,
Epstein (1969) conducted a series of experiments. Experiment I from
his report will be reviewed for its examination of competing demands for
retrieval of one list of items and continued retention of another list in
one experimental condition. Subjects were required to listen to a list of
8 tape-recorded two-syllable words and a list of 8 two-digit numbers.
Half of the subjects heard the word list first, then the numbers. The other
half listened to the numbers first, then the word list. The rate of presentation was 1.5 sec per item with a 6-sec pause between lists. At the end of
the second list, a subject heard one of four possible instructions for recall:

"Words only."
"Numbers only."
"Words, then numbers."
"Numbers, then words."

These differential retrieval instructions, in addition to the alternative
list presentation sequences, comprised the major experimental manipulations. Subjects had no way of knowing what recall demand would be
placed on them as they listened to the lists. Presumably they attended
carefully to all the items knowing that they might be expected to give
free recall (any sequence within a list permissible) of either the words,
the numbers, or both.

The retention results are presented in Table 11.7 which gives the mean number of items correctly recalled under the different retrieval requirements and following one or the other sequence of list presentation. As the data suggest, statistical analysis showed that the words were uniformly recalled better than the numbers. Both list sequence and output requirement at recall showed significant effects on performance in certain combinations of input-output conditions. Under Conditions O and F (requiring a particular list only or first, respectively) recall was better for the list which had been presented second. However, for recall second, Condition S yielded equivalent scores regardless of the earlier sequence of presentation. For the list presented first, the tabled means under different recall requirements did not differ significantly. The patterning of results for the second list studied, parallel for both words and numbers, suggests that its recall (as compared with Condition O) suffers when the other list must still be maintained in memory for recall second, and shows even greater decrement when it must be retained while the earlier-studied list is recalled first. This experiment, like others in its series and in the research literature on memory, shows that retention to the point of actual recall is partly dependent upon events and demands of retrieval.

Table 11.7 Mean Number of Words (*W*) and Numbers (*N*) Recalled for the Two List Input Sequences and Three Output Requirements (After Epstein, 1969)

List Input Sequence	Output Requirement		
	Only— Condition *O*	First— Condition *F*	Second— Condition *S*
	Word Recall		
WN	4.05	4.18	4.00
NW	5.64	5.00	3.93
	Number Recall		
NW	2.97	2.32	2.43
WN	3.62	2.84	2.45

Summary

With its roots in the early history of experimental psychology, research on memory exemplifies the renewed invigoration of modern theory construction and penetrating experimentation. Both theory and research focus on elucidating the processes of intake of information, storage, and retrieval. In the approaches that are taken we find subdivision into studies of long-term memory (LTM), free recall, and short-term memory (STM). LTM and STM are related functionally in some theories. At the same time, they are found experimentally to embody somewhat different psychological laws.

Methods of measurement of LTM include the conventional retention indices based on testing through recall, recognition, or relearning. Special designs to examine interference are commonly used also. The newer methods devised to study STM include the probe technique for determining if a particular single item has been retained, the use of distractor tasks, and the continuous presentation technique.

Plotting the course of forgetting (or retention) over time is a common aim of traditional LTM studies. Multitask designs to test certain interference hypotheses were cited as well. Both proactive inhibition and retroactive inhibition are now seen as important kinds of interfering with retention. Some investigations on the processes and mechanisms of interference were reviewed. Another illustrative experiment looked at LTM for a motor response of lever positioning.

Free recall experiments have been oriented toward revealing subjects' organizing tendencies such as clustering responses sequentially on a semantic basis. Quantitative indicants of such tendencies have been developed—such as the ratio of repetition (*RR*). The associative basis for clustering leads to a useful joining of research on word association with research on memory. Among the particular experiments reviewed was one which showed that including category names in memory lists led to special effects in clustering and in recall. The use of two-stage experiments was seen as helping to reveal the occurrence of subjective organizing in memorization.

STM research on intake processes was first examined. Grouping of items during encoding was shown to be both natural and facilitative for retention. Several intake experiments gave emphasis to the role of auditory processes in STM. In some of these studies, the auditory modality was pitted against the visual in certain experimental manipulations. During retention itself, however brief in STM, it has been possible to investigate the ongoing processes. Illustrative experiments did this by varying the input-output events which occurred, by examining transpositions in three-word items, and by examining the role of natural language mediators (NLMs). Cueing for retrieval from STM was a final kind of investigation we reviewed. One example of research considered the timing of retrieval cues as a key variable. The other study manipulated retrieval cues for different segments of the material which had been presented earlier.

References

Archer, E. J. Re-evaluation of the meaningfulness of all possible CVC trigrams. *Psychological Monographs*, 1960, **74** (10, Whole No. 497).

Barnes, J. M., & Underwood, B. J. "Fate" of first-list associations in transfer theory. *Journal of Experimental Psychology*, 1959, **58**, 97–105.

Bilodeau, E. A., Jones, M. B., & Levy, C. M. Long-term memory as a function of retention time and repeated recalling. *Journal of Experimental Psychology*, 1964, **67**, 303–309.

Bilodeau, E. A., & Levy, C.M. Long-term memory as a function of retention time and other conditions of training and recall. *Psychological Review*, 1964, **71**, 27–41.

Bousfield, W. A. The occurrence of clustering in the recall of randomly arranged associates. *Journal of General Psychology*, 1953, **49**, 229–240.

Bousfield, W. A., & Puff, C. R. Clustering as a function of response dominance. *Journal of Experimental Psychology*, 1964, **67**, 76–79.

Bousfield, W. A., & Sedgewick, C. H. W. An analysis of sequences of restricted associative responses. *Journal of General Psychology*, 1944, **30**, 149–165.

Bower, G. H. A multicomponent theory of the memory trace. In K. W. Spence & J. T. Spence (Eds.), *The psychology of learning and motivation*. Vol. 1: New York: Academic Press, 1967. Pp. 229–325.

Bower, G. H., & Springston, F. Pauses as recoding points in letter series. *Journal of Experimental Psychology*, 1970, **83**, 421–430.

Cofer, C. N., Bruce, D. R., & Reicher, G. M. Clustering in free recall as a function of certain methodological variations. *Journal of Experimental Psychology*, 1966, **71**, 858–866.

Cohen, B. H., Bousfield, G. A., & Whitmarsh, G. A. Cultural norms for verbal items in 43 categories. Technical Report No. 22, Contract Nonr 631(00), University of Connecticut, 1957.

Epstein, W. Poststimulus output specification and differential retrieval from short-term memory. *Journal of Experimental Psychology*, 1969, **82**, 168–174.

Kiess, H. O. Effects of natural language mediators on short-term memory. *Journal of Experimental Psychology*, 1968, **77**, 7–13.

Kintsch, W. Memory and decision aspects of recognition learning. *Psychological Review*, 1967, **74**, 496–504.

Laughery, K. R., & Fell, J. C. Subject preferences and the nature of information stored in the short-term memory. *Journal of Experimental Psychology*, 1969, **82**, 193–197.

Mandler, G. Organization and memory. In K. W. Spence & J. T. Spence (Eds.), *The psychology of learning and motivation.* Vol. 1. New York: Academic Press, 1967. Pp. 327–372.

Mandler, G., & Pearlstone, Z. Free and constrained concept learning and subsequent recall. *Journal of Verbal Learning and Verbal Behavior*, 1966, **5**, 126–131.

Murdock, B. B., Jr. Modality effects in short-term memory: Storage or retrieval? *Journal of Experimental Psychology*, 1968, **77**, 79–86.

Murdock, B. B., Jr., & vom Saal, W. Transpositions in short-term memory. *Journal of Experimental Psychology*, 1967, **74**, 137–143.

Norman, D. A. Toward a theory of memory and attention. *Psychological Review*, 1968, **75**, 522–536.

Paivio, A. Mental imagery in associative learning and memory. *Psychological Review*, 1969, **76**, 241–263.

Peterson, L. R. Short-term verbal memory and learning. *Psychological Review*, 1966, **73**, 193–207.

Postman, L. Hermann Ebbinghaus. *American Psychologist*, 1968, **23**, 149–157.

Postman, L., Stark, K., & Henschel, D. Conditions of recovery after unlearning. *Journal of Experimental Psychology Monograph*, 1969, **82**, No. 1, Part 2.

Russ, D., & Loess, H. Taxonomic cues as aids to recall in short-term memory. *Journal of Experimental Psychology*, 1969, **80**, 394–396.

Segal, E. M. Hierarchical structure in free recall. *Journal of Experimental Psychology*, 1969, **80**, 59–63.

Sherman, M. F., & Turvey, M. T. Modality differences in short-term serial memory as a function of presentation rate. *Journal of Experimental Psychology*, 1969, **80**, 335–338.

Shiffrin, R. M., & Atkinson, R. C. Storage and retrieval processes in long-term memory. *Psychological Review*, 1969, **76**, 179–193.

Shuell, T. J. Clustering and organization in free recall. *Psychological Bulletin*, 1969, **72**, 353–374.

Tulving, E. Subjective organization and effects of repetition in multi-trial free-recall learning. *Journal of Verbal Learning and Verbal Behavior*, 1966, **5**, 193–197.

Tulving, E., & Arbuckle, T. Y. Input and output interference in short-term associative memory. *Journal of Experimental Psychology*, 1966, **72**, 145–150.

Underwood, B. J. Interference and forgetting. *Psychological Review*, 1957, **64**, 49–60.

Underwood, B. J. Attributes of memory. *Psychological Review*, 1969, **76**, 559–573.

Underwood, B. J., & Richardson, J. Some verbal materials for the study of concept formation. *Journal of Experimental Psychology*, 1956, **51**, 229–238.

Waugh, N. C., & Norman, D. A. Primary memory. *Psychological Review*, 1965, **72**, 89–104.

Wickelgren, W. A. Acoustic similarity and intrusion errors in short-term memory. *Journal of Experimental Psychology*, 1965, **70**, 102–108.

chapter 12
Transfer

A transfer of training effect is the action that learning one task has upon the subsequent learning or performance of another task. A transfer effect will usually be either *positive,* that is, beneficial or facilitating, with respect to the second task, or *negative*, that is, detrimental or interfering. For example, the steering practice one gets in riding a tricycle might facilitate learning to ride a bicycle, a positive transfer effect. However, a negative transfer effect might be experienced in trying to stop a bicycle equipped with hand brakes when one has been trained earlier on a bicycle with a pedal-operated brake. In transfer research we also encounter *zero* transfer effects, where the first task has no measurable effect on the second. *Transfer* is the term applied to the process underlying *transfer effects*, and often "transfer" is used to refer to the effect instead of the process.

Kinds of Behavior Investigated

The definition of a transfer effect places no limitation on the kinds of activity in which the transfer process may be studied. Any sort of behavior may be a potential source of transfer or may reveal transfer effects from prior activity. The operation of transfer in everyday life, particularly as we go through the early developmental and educational years, may be considered as common as the learning process. In psychological research we necessarily select certain laboratory tasks as tools for studying transfer of training. Our consideration of different studies will show that these include a variety of verbal and perceptual-motor tasks. Transfer processes are often too complex to permit casual observational analysis. We need the controls that the psychological laboratory offers if we are to discover how the mechanisms of transfer work.

Hypotheses Concerning Transfer Mechanisms

We should not expect to find transfer between any two tasks that were merely selected at random. The mechanisms of transfer are usually sought in tasks that are related to each other in some particular way. We shall briefly survey some of the relationships to which transfer effects have been credited. The experimental approach to the precise identification of such factors operating in transfer involves systematic varying of the content and the practice conditions for the two tasks.

Identical elements

When we examine many instances of positive transfer we find that there are elements in the second task which were found also in the first. The acquisition of these elements as the first task is learned permits their use when the second task is undertaken. The identical elements which subserve transfer may be specific habits, methods of work, or principles which are applied in the second activity.

Similarity and generalization

Performance on a second task may be benefited by an earlier activity even when there are no mutual identical elements. Facilitation may occur when similar stimuli and responses are involved. Sometimes positive transfer effects may stem from a combination of identity and similarity of elements in the two tasks concerned. Explanation of transfer effects involving similarity of stimuli or responses is usually based on a process termed *generalization*. This is observed to occur in experiments on learning or conditioning when a response associated with one stimulus is found also to be elicited by similar stimuli. This is called *stimulus* generalization. Quantitative studies show that the response tendency aroused by a generalized (similar) stimulus is greater when this test stimulus is more similar to the original stimulus. This functional relationship is termed a *gradient of generalization*. *Response* generalization is a tendency for similar responses to be strengthened when a particular response is learned. A gradient of generalization based on response similarity may be noted here as well as in stimulus generalization.

Generalized response tendencies, based on either stimulus or response generalization or both, are considered to develop in practice on any task. If a second task then involves similar elements, these generalized tendencies operate to facilitate its learning and performance. Similarity of tasks thus resembles identical elements as a frequent basis for transfer except that generalized tendencies instead of identical tendencies are involved.

Stimulus-response relationships

In our foregoing discussion of transfer based on identical elements or on generalization, positive transfer was assumed to result from similar or identical stimulus-response associations in the two tasks. Patterns of stimulus-response relationships between two tasks that tend to yield positive transfer include the following:

I. Identical stimuli elicit identical responses.
II. Similar stimuli elicit identical responses.
III. Identical stimuli elicit similar responses.
IV. Similar stimuli elicit similar responses.

When stimulus-response associations are markedly different in the two tasks, identical or similar elements can lead to negative transfer effects. An especially potent source of interference occurs with reversal of these associations which demands that opposite responses be made when the second task is undertaken. With reversed associations encountered, identical elements may contribute strongly to negative transfer instead of positive. We may list two conditions contributing to negative transfer:

V. Identical stimuli elicit different or opposite responses.
VI. Similar stimuli elicit different or opposite responses.

Our consideration here of how the relationships or similarities between tasks may influence transfer has been both brief and very general. More explicit discussion of how task relationships contribute to transfer effects may be found in Ellis (1965) and Mandler (1954).

Design of Transfer Experiments

As is the case with numerous areas of scientific study, transfer research has developed designs for experiments which provide a framework for planning specific studies. Murdock (1957) has presented an evaluative review of numerous designs used in transfer experiments. We shall consider a few variations of the designs which have been principally employed. In outlining the plan of any transfer study, it will usually be convenient to use Task *A* as a label for the task *from which* transfer effects are considered to arise, and Task *B* as the designation of the task *to which* transfer is accomplished. The fundamental investigation of transfer from Task *A* to Task *B* involves the comparison of Task *B* performance in a group (experimental) who had previously been trained on Task *A* with the performance on Task *B* in a group (control) without the prior practice on Task *A*.

Randomly Assigned Groups

Quite commonly subjects are assigned at random to an experimental and a control group in a study of the transfer from Task *A* to Task *B* in a basic design:

Experimental: Task *A* then Task *B*
Control: Activity *X* then Task *B*

In this paradigm we have used Activity *X* to represent anything that control group subjects might have been doing before engaging in, or learning, Task *B*. Such activity might be assigned by the experimenter, who selects a task for control subjects which is assumed to have no transfer effect to Task *B*. An alternative possibility is that nothing specific is required of control subjects before undertaking Task *B*.

The design represented in the foregoing paradigm should yield information about the empirical transfer effect from Task *A* to Task *B* when the second task performance of the two groups is compared. Both the direction and amount of transfer are represented in the Task *B* scores of the groups. The effect as measured may represent transfer of several sorts, general and specific, and it may be confounded with warm-up effect as well. In order to determine the transfer effects that are based specifically on relationships of Task *A* to Task *B*, a molecular analysis requiring more groups may be required. We shall see later how more extensive designs permit such analysis to help identify warm-up effects and general positive transfer effects like learning how to learn.

Only the transfer from Task *A* to Task *B* is represented in the schema we have examined. It may often be desired to determine transfer from Task *B* to Task *A* as well. We depart from the rule that Task *A* is the source and Task *B* is the recipient of transfer, and map out the following:

Group I: Task *A* then Task *B*
Group II: Task *B* then Task *A*

Still using only two randomly assigned groups of subjects we can now examine transfer effects bidirectionally, from Task *B* to Task *A* as well as from Task *A* to Task *B*. In the fundamental comparison to examine empirical transfer effects from Task *A* to Task *B*, we would use the performance of Group II on Task *B* to provide us with the control data. To find transfer from Task *B* to Task *A* we use Group I as a control, comparing its Task *A* performance with that of the transfer group, II, on Task *A*. In this bidirectional assessment of transfer effects, then, each randomly constituted group contributes control data from its first performance and experimental data from its second task. If differences are found between the two directions of transfer, these may permit us to draw some cautious inferences about the mechanisms of transfer. Whether differences are found or not, this design provides the same information we might get from the first design we listed, plus the dividend of a second assessment of transfer. This is accomplished at minimal extra cost by merely having subjects who begin with Task *B* go on to take practice on Task *A*. Any desired Activity *X* may be inserted in the plan of the study prior to first task practice for both groups.

Matched Groups

A more precise experiment may result if we employ matched experimental and control groups instead of setting up two groups by random assignment. Especially useful if the number of available subjects is small, matching is often based on data from some pretest. A common design is represented in the following schema:

Experimental: Pretest *B'*—Task *A* then Task *B*
Control: Pretest *B'*—Activity *X* then Task *B*

Of course, the two groups are not actually established until the pretest scores are available for use in matching.

The matching factor

We have used the designation B' for the pretesting in the matched group design since this matching factor may often resemble Task B quite closely. Not infrequently, the pretest may actually consist of a few trials on Task B. If this task is not itself employed in pretesting, the matching factor should at least correlate with Task B performance or else it is of no value for matching the two groups. The whole purpose in matching is to equate the groups so that differences in their performance on Task B may be attributed to their prior activity, either Task A or Activity X. Although we have referred to pretesting as a part of the experimental procedure, it is also possible that the matching factor may not be a performance score which the experimenter obtains but may be something like IQs or aptitude scores that are available for the subjects who are to be used. The B' symbol is still appropriate for the paradigm since some correlation with Task B scores must exist if the use of the matching factor is to be justified.

Molecular Analysis of Transfer

We have considered a number of designs for transfer of training experiments. In the elementary form in which we reviewed them, most of them featured a single comparison; a single difference between groups was sought which might be attributed to differential prior treatment. Extensions of the basic design often involve several variations of Task A or Task B in the same study, with numerous groups of subjects being run.

One reason why a single molar comparison of data tells us little about transfer is that there may be many factors that contribute to an empirical transfer effect between Task A and Task B. Transfer based on specific perceptual-motor habits may be confounded with transfer stemming from general work methods and with warm-up effects. The molecular analysis to separate these different sources of influence involves running several groups of subjects under different conditions. For example, to separate warm-up effect from positive transfer based on identical elements or on stimulus generalization, we might vary the interval between Task A and Task B in several different groups so that the warm-up effect from Task A would have a chance to dissipate over the longer intervals. The residual benefits appearing in Task B, with warm-up assumed to have dissipated, might be attributed to learned elements which were more persistent over time.

Where several different kinds of habit are presumed to underlie a transfer effect, several different variations of Task *A* may be used to delineate the contribution of several factors. Another approach to this problem is to vary the amount of training given to different groups on Task *A*. This would prove useful when different Task *A* habits were acquired at different rates or reached asymptotic strengths after different amounts of practice. A different way of studying transfer in detail is to employ several different measures to Task *B* performance. These may provide different information about the transfer process.

Measurement of Transfer Effects

The quantitative description of transfer involves multiple comparisons which must be made properly. A further goal of the data analysis is sometimes to describe the transfer effects in relative terms so that different experiments may be compared without reference to specific units of performance measurement.

Two General Principles

Before we examine several ways of measuring and describing transfer effects we should note two general rules which apply to the treatment of transfer data. First, each different performance measure taken on Task *B* may yield information on the transfer process and therefore each measure may warrant separate analysis. For example, in a paired associate learning study we may obtain the number of responses correct on each trial and the number of intrusion errors as well. Data analysis may be performed on each of these indices of Task *B* performance, comparing the experimental and control conditions. It is entirely possible that two such measures may not agree perfectly in the picture of transfer effects which they present. There may also, of course, be close agreement. Where there are divergent indications of the transfer that has occurred, these may help to delineate the process itself by suggesting some of its mechanisms.

A second principle about transfer measurement is that the experimental and control groups should often be compared at more than one point on their Task *B* performance curves. As practice continues on Task *B*, an initial transfer effect may change or disappear. *Since almost all performance curves ultimately approach an asymptote, it is particularly likely that transfer effects will finally approach zero magnitude as experimental and control subjects carry on their practice of Task B.* This means that our description of any transfer effect will often involve stating its initial magnitude and direction and telling how long it persisted into the repeated trials of Task *B*. Information about the persistence of a transfer effect is an important reason for providing several trials of Task *B* practice.

Combining the two rules for the description of transfer effects we may say that a separate index for the sign and magnitude of a transfer effect may be separately computed for each performance measure at each stage of practice on Task *B*.

Comparison with Control Data

There are a number of different ways of assessing the amount of transfer from Task *A* to Task *B* (and from *B* to *A* if a balanced design is used). Data from an experiment by Bilodeau (1965) will be used to illustrate two ways of looking at transfer effects. Her experiments will be partially summarized here to provide the needed example; her study was itself somewhat more complex in design.

Bilodeau studied transfer effects in the acquisition of a perceptual-motor skill, turning two crank controls to follow a designated pathway. She examined transfer from one target size or precision demand to another. Here we shall consider just two of these treatments. Treatment *P* (precise) required the pathway to be followed quite precisely, with a deviation tolerance of only about a quarter of a turn of either crank. Treatment *F* (free) allowed a much greater latitude in following the pathway, almost 10 times as great as Treatment *P*. The score for each 1-min trial was the number of pathway circuits completed per trial. For original training, under one treatment or the other, subjects were given 30 trials. Then half of them were switched to the opposite treatment as a transfer task while half continued with the same condition to provide further control data. Fifteen more trials were given in either the transfer or the continuation condition.

The results of the experiment are shown graphically in Figure 12.1 which indicates the mean number of pathway circuits completed per trial during the original training and the transfer or continuation testing. We may examine transfer by inspection of the figure and then go on to use certain formulas for quantifying the transfer effects.

Initial control performance

One conventional way to assess any transfer effect is to compare the transfer performance with the performance of the task under the same

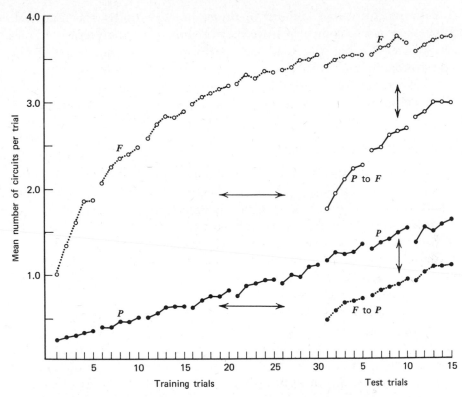

Fig. 12.1. Mean number of circuits completed during training trials and transfer under the free (*F*) and precise (*P*) treatments. (After Bilodeau, 1965.)

treatment during original learning. Using the graph to make this comparison (see the double-headed horizontal arrows), we find that the performances under both transfer conditions (*P* to *F*, *F* to *P*) appear superior to the scores made on the original training trials under Treatments *F* and *P*. Inspection of the plotted data, then, indicates moderate positive transfer from Treatment *P* to *F* and also from *F* to *P*. Under either treatment, in other words, a beneficial transfer effect is observed when performances are compared with those of subjects performing without prior experience in the task.

Extended control performance

Another way of examining the performance curves of Figure 12.1 is directed at answering the question, "How does the transfer effect compare with an equivalent amount of direct practice under the final task condition?" For this comparison we may be guided by the vertical arrows in the figure. We see that final task performances by the two transfer groups are below the levels attained by the continuation groups. Neither transfer effect, though positive by conventional assessment, is equivalent to the level attained by investing the same amount of prior practice in the final task.

Conversion to Percent Estimates

We have seen that transfer group scores on Task B may be compared with initial control group scores on the same task or with extended control performance. One difficulty with any direct attempts at assessing the amount of transfer is that their numerical expression will reflect the units of measurement employed in scoring performance. In trying to compare the results of one transfer study with another, raw score expression may render meaningful comparison impossible if the studies involved different performance measures. Gagné, Foster, and Crowley (1948) pointed out the desirability of expressing amount of transfer as a percent, thus facilitating comparisons between different studies. The decision to express transfer as a percent still permits considerable leeway, represented in the question, "Percent of what?" After reviewing numerous studies of transfer of training, these authors present several alternative formulas for expressing amount of transfer as a percent. The various limitations which they point out for each formula indicate that we need to consider, at the design stage of any transfer experiment, what way of expressing amount of transfer seems desirable. Then we can be sure to utilize the necessary groups, conditions, and measures. After discussing some of these formulas, Murdock (1957) has offered another way of computing percent transfer. We shall examine some of these different computational guides without attempting to review the extensive discussion found in these two articles. We need to recall that a measurement of the amount of transfer may be taken for each performance measure obtained at each stage of practice. The percent formulas we examine here are similarly applicable at more than one point in many experiments.

Percent difference from control group

One way to express the amount of transfer is as a percent of the accomplishment of the control group which performed the task without prior special training. We take the mean scores on Task B made by the experimental group, E, and the control group, C, and express the difference between these two means as a percent of the mean score made by the control group, C, at a similar point in Task B practice. The computational formula is as follows, assuming a score that increases with practice:

$$\text{Percent transfer} = \frac{E - C}{C} \times 100 \qquad\qquad \text{Formula 12.1}$$

This arrangement of the formula is for scores like number of words correct or time on target—measures that increase as proficiency is gained. For behavior measures like errors or time to complete a task—scores that decrease as skill increases—the numerator is reversed: $C - E$.

To illustrate the use of Formula 12.1 we shall examine the data obtained by Bilodeau to determine the percent transfer effect at the beginning and end of the transfer test performance (Trials 1 and 15), using the corresponding trials of training to provide the needed control values. The mean number of circuits completed by subjects on these trials was as follows:

Treatment	Trial 1 of Training (C)	Trial 1 of Transfer (E)	Trial 15 of Training (C)	Trial 15 of Transfer (E)
P	0.26	0.46	0.70	1.08
F	1.13	1.74	2.88	3.00

Applying the formula to the Trial 1 data for Treatment P, we get

$$\text{Percent transfer} = \frac{0.46 - 0.26}{0.26} \times 100 = 77$$

For treatment F the Trial 1 transfer is calculated to be 54 percent. On Trial 15, at the end of the transfer test, the transfer for Treatment P is also 54 percent. In contrast, it is calculated to be only 4 percent for Treatment F. In this case direct practice for 15 trials has brought control subjects to about the same level of proficiency as that attained by the experimental subjects after 30 training trials (Treatment P) followed by 15 transfer trials. In other words the initial positive transfer effect has not been sustained because the control score has overtaken the transfer score, not an unusual finding in transfer studies.

Percent of direct practice increment

Performance of many tasks will benefit maximally from prior *direct* practice on the task as compared with any positive transfer from an equal amount of practice on *another* task. We may take the increment in scores made through direct practice as a working estimate of 100 percent transfer. An increment in mean score attributable to practice on a different task may then be compared with it to determine a percent transfer value. The formula for this method of calculating amount of transfer is as follows:

$$\text{Percent transfer} = \frac{E - C_i}{C_e - C_i} \times 100 \qquad \text{Formula 12.2}$$

where E is the experimental group score on a particular transfer trial; C_i is the mean score at the initial level of control group practice; and C_e is the mean score of a control group given extended practice equivalent in amount to the total practice in the transfer group up to the comparison trial.

Formula 12.2 is most appropriately applied to the final transfer trial in the Bilodeau study, using the first control score on original training as C_i for each treatment and the last continuation score as C_e. The relevant data are as follows:

	Initial Control Score (C_i)	Final Continuation Trial (C_e)	Final Transfer Trial (E)
P	0.26	1.62	1.08
F	1.13	3.73	3.00

For Treatment P the computation is:

$$\text{Percent transfer} = \frac{1.08 - 0.26}{1.62 - 0.26} \times 100 = 60$$

A parallel calculation for Treatment F yields a value of 72 percent. These percentages indicate how effective the two-task transfer sequences have been in comparison with the performance gains due to direct practice.

Similarity Between Tasks

As we noted earlier, the relationships between Task A and Task B are strong influences upon the transfer from A to B. In conformity to our earlier statements (I–VI, p. 441) we can represent several of these task relationships in stimulus-response (S-R) terms for Tasks A and B.

Paradigm	Task A	Task B		Transfer
I.	S–R	$S_{iden.}$	$R_{iden.}$	+
II.	S–R	$S_{sim.}$	$R_{iden.}$	+
III.	S–R	$S_{iden.}$	$R_{sim.}$	+
IV.	S–R	$S_{sim.}$	$R_{sim.}$	+
V.	S–R	$S_{iden.}$	$R_{diff.}$	−
VI.	S–R	$S_{sim.}$	$R_{diff.}$	−
VII.	S–R	$S_{diff.}$	R_{any}	0

Paradigm No. VII has been added to the earlier list, indicating that a zero transfer effect is to be expected for any response comparison between tasks provided the stimuli are distinctly different between them.

The Transfer Surface

Osgood (1949) used several principles of specific transfer like these, and the data from a number of experiments, in creating a graphic representation of how transfer effect depends upon both stimulus similarity and response similarity between tasks. ("Similarity" is here considered a dimension ranging from identity through lessening degrees of resemblance to no resemblance and perhaps on to an antagonistic or opposite relationship.) The tricoordinate figure—the transfer surface—is shown in Figure 12.2 with axis labels and Roman numerals located so as to exemplify the several S-R relationships which we have identified as leading to positive transfer (I–IV), negative transfer (V–VI), or zero transfer effect (VII). Constructed on the basis of earlier research, Osgood's transfer surface has served a theoretical function in predicting the transfer outcomes of experiments designed with identifiable degrees of stimulus and response similarities between Tasks A and B. Precise quantitative predictions cannot be generated of course, since the coordinates are scaled only ordinally and since the sign and amount of transfer may be affected by other influences besides task similarity. Studies conducted since Osgood's formulation have shown results that correspond generally to the predictions of relative transfer which the surface suggests (for example, Dallett, 1962). Complete correspondence of new data to theoretical expectation has not always been found, of course. Nevertheless, our familiarity with Osgood's work should be helpful as we examine examples of more recent attempts to explore such surfaces empirically.

Separate surfaces

A report by Martin (1965) exemplifies the attempt to extend transfer

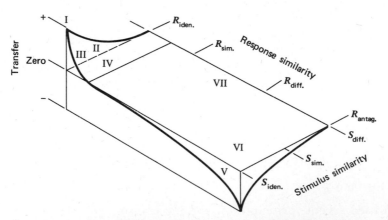

Fig. 12.2. The transfer (and retroaction) surface of Osgood; the addition of the Roman numerals indicates how the 7 transfer paradigms listed in the text relate to the coordinates along which stimulus similarity of tasks and response similarity are considered to be ordinally scaled. (After Osgood, 1949.)

theory in verbal paired associate learning to achieve greater correspondence with accumulating empirical findings. While still recognizing stimulus and response similarity as contributory to specific transfer effects, Martin begins his theoretical development by identifying two other relevant variables of considerable potency—degree of Task *A* learning and response meaningfulness. As his argument unfolds he takes note of several research results which seem not easily accommodated by the Osgood transfer surface.

Although we cannot here review the complex considerations of the theorist's creative work, we shall mention the outcome of his deliberations. He indicates that paired-associate learning has been seen as involving a response-learning phase and an associative S-R bonding. Further, besides forward S-R connecting, it is found that backward (R-S) connections are also formed and strengthened as learning proceeds. These facts must also be incorporated in transfer theory. The final result of Martin's thinking is his postulation of three different transfer surfaces which predict, for different task relationships, the components of a transfer effect in terms of response availability, forward (S-R) association, and backward (R-S) association strength. These surfaces are modified by the degree of Task *A* learning and by response meaningfulness. When all of these elements—both theoretical and empirical—are taken into account, then an estimate or prediction of a net or summary transfer effect can be made.

Empirical exploration

Besides leading to theoretical extensions, Osgood's transfer surface has led to a number of experimental explorations of transfer effects. From a series of experiments reported by Shea (1969) we may consider as an example his Experiments I and II. Conducting his investigation under the Undergraduate Research Participant Program of the National Science Foundation, Shea used the learning of a paired associate list as Task *A* and taking an S-R multiple choice test as Task *B*. The stimuli and responses in both tasks were adjectives which had been scaled by Haagen (1949) for their similarity in meaning to each other. For 18 adjectives, Shea chose 18 others with high similarity and 18 with slight similarity. Identity of a stimulus or response adjective was also used in order to probe the end point of the similarity dimensions of the Osgood transfer surface. As an example of the ordering of the adjectives along either the stimulus or response similarity dimension, consider this example.

		High	*Slight*
Adjective	*Identical*	*Similarity*	*Similarity*
LITTLE	LITTLE	PETITE	SLIGHT

For the paired associate learning of Task *A*, 9 pairs of adjectives comprised the list. With 3-sec exposures used for testing on a pair and for its study, trials were continued in Experiment I until a subject performed perfectly on 3 successive trials. When he reached this criterion, he was then told he would be given a difficult multiple-choice test based on the pairs just learned. For example, if one of the pairs learned in Task *A* had been ANGRY-LITTLE, the Task *B* test item might take one of these forms, among others.

ANGRY	CENTRAL	(Identical S,
	LITTLE	identical R)
	HEAVY	
ANGRY	HEAVY	(Identical S,
	CENTRAL	high similarity of R)
	PETITE	
ENRAGED	LITTLE	(High similarity of S,
	HEAVY	identical R)
	CENTRAL	

With either stimulus or response similarity taking on any of 3 values, a total of 9 types of test items were included in Task *B* with each subject responding to one item of each type in the 9-item test. Several combinations of adjectives were used so that different subjects received different types of item corresponding to each adjective pair of Task *A*.

Seventy-two undergraduates participated in Experiment I and another 72 served in Experiment II. In the latter experiment, the Task *B* test was of the same multiple-choice format. However, Task *A* procedure was different in that the learners were all given just 10 study trials and 2 test trials in memorizing the 9 adjective pairs. Further, they were required to read aloud the stimulus and response words on every trial. In Experiment I it required an average of 10.3 trials to reach the criterion of mastery. In Experiment II an average of 7.7 responses were given on the second test trial, completing Task *A* performance.

The results on Task *B* comprise the test of a part of the Osgood transfer surface, the portion near the "identity" origin for both the stimulus and response dimensions of similarity. For each of the 9 different task relationships investigated, the critical datum was the percent of correct responses given on the corresponding test items of Task *B*. These data are presented in Table 12.1 Statistical tests—analyses of variance—

Table 12.1 Percent Correct Responses on the Task *B* Multiple Choice Test for Different Stimulus and Response Similarity Relationships Between Tasks (After Shea, 1969)

Relationship of Task *B* S-R Units to Task *A*	Percent Correct Responses	
	Experiment I	Experiment II
Both S and R identical	97.2	95.8
S identical, R high similarity	79.2	73.6
S identical, R slight similarity	69.4	73.6
S high similarity, R identical	59.7	56.9
S slight similarity, R identical	45.8	44.4
S high similarity, R high similarity	45.8	47.2
S high similarity, R slight similarity	54.2	40.3
S slight similarity, R high similarity	37.5	31.9
S slight similarity, R slight similarity	25.0	43.1

showed that the effects of varying stimulus and response similarity were significant in each of the experiments.

In conformity with the presentation of results by Shea, the pooled data from the two experiments are represented in the tricoordinate graph of Figure 12.3. The orientation of this figure differs from that of Figure 12.2 in that the origin of the three dimensions is here at the far side of the diagram. Keeping this in mind, we can see that Shea's findings correspond to the Osgood transfer surface. Positive transfer effects decrease in a negatively accelerated fashion as the testing conditions range out from the identity origin along the dimensions of stimulus and response similarity. Besides its correspondence with earlier transfer data and the transfer surface representing and predicting them, perhaps the most interesting aspect of this study is its use of a simple 9-item test instead of a learning performance as Task *B*.

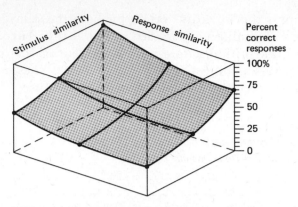

Fig. 12.3. Percent correct responses on Task *B* in Experiment I and Experiment II as a function of stimulus similarity and response similarity to Task *A*. (After Shea, 1969.)

Transfer Determinants in Verbal Learning

Two experimental reports offer good examples of how certain determinants of transfer have been explored in other verbal studies. These investigations required subjects to learn successively two paired associate lists. For different groups the lists were related in paradigms designed to test for transfer. For both lists one experimenter used adjectives as stimuli paired with CVC trigrams as responses; the other used CVC trigrams as stimuli and adjectives as responses. Both studies are reported here only partially.

Response Meaningfulness

Two levels of meaningfulness (*m*) of nonsense items were used for the response items in a transfer study of paired associate learning carried out by Jung (1963). The response items for the List 2 learning illustrate the two *m* levels.

High *m*:	JAK,	ENT,	XYW,	IMP,	UVR,	HOS
Low *m*:	SBL,	MQK,	OCJ,	HFW,	RDG,	TXP

Stimuli for the 6-pair Lists 1 and 2 were two-syllable adjectives. For both levels of *m* in the responses, 2 experimental and 1 control paradigm were used to create a 6-condition design for the experiment. A summary of the task relationships for the 3 paradigms is given here. The *C-D* paradigm provides the control condition; with both the stimuli and responses of List 2 different from those encountered on List 1, there is no basis for specific transfer effects between the two tasks. For the *C-B* paradigm no transfer is expected on the basis of associative *S-R* learning. However, on the basis of response learning, Jung predicted that this paradigm would lead to positive transfer for the groups learning low *m* responses, identical in both lists. The acquaintance gained with these responses in List 1 should enhance their availability as List 2 was learned. For the *A-C* paradigm with identical stimuli encountered in List 2 but with different responses to be associated (No. V, p. 441), a negative transfer effect was predicted, its magnitude about the same for both *m* levels.

Paradigm Designation	List 1 S-R Pairs	List 2 S-R Pairs
C-B	*C-B*	*A-B* (S different, R identical)
A-C	*A-C*	*A-B* (S identical, R different)
C-D	*C-D*	*A-B* (S different, R different)

Six subject groups of 20 students each were used in the experiment, each group being assigned to one paradigm and one of the two *m* levels of responses. List 1 was learned by the anticipation method to a criterion of one perfect trial. Items were presented at a 2:2 sec rate with a 4-sec intertrial interval. Five different list orders were used to preclude serial learning of the responses. About a minute after completing the first task, participants in the study were asked to learn the second list using the same procedures for 10 trials under all conditions. Subject groups and the first-task lists were found to be satisfactorily equivalent in the List 1 learning at either *m* level. With high *m* responses, an average of about 10 trials was needed to reach the criterion, while about 24 trials were needed to learn low *m* responses.

The transfer results of the experiment are presented in Figure 12.4 which shows the performance of all 6 groups on Trials 1 and 2 in learning List 2. (Similar results were found in the data for all 10 trials.) With the control group's performance on the *C-D* paradigm considered as a

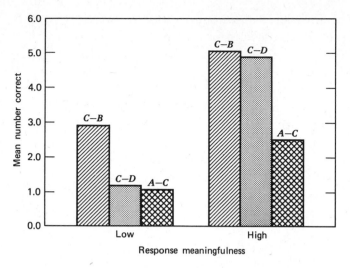

Fig. 12.4. Mean number of correct anticipations on Trials 1 and 2 as a function of response meaningfulness and transfer paradigm. The *C-D* paradigm provided the control data or baseline values. (After Jung, 1963.)

baseline value for comparisons, it was found that the *C-B* paradigm yielded a significant positive transfer effect for subjects learning low *m* responses. This confirmed Jung's prediction. As expected, the *A-C* paradigm led to a significant negative transfer effect. However, contrary to expectation, this appeared only for the group learning the high *m* responses.

As is often the case, the data of the study were partly in agreement with prediction, partly not. The positive transfer found for low *m* responses in the *C-B* paradigm tends to support the postulated operation of a response availability effect, also found in other research. The *A-C*, *A-B* interference effect was not found for low *m* responses although it appeared strongly at the high *m* level. It may be that the baseline performance of the control group run at the low *m* level was so poor due to task difficulty or to subject morale (after a quarter hour of rote memorization) that there was little possibility for significantly lower scores to be made by the *A-C* experimental group. (In concluding this brief review of the transfer study, it should be noted that the error analysis conducted by Jung has been omitted from this summary.)

Semantic Relations

An experiment designed and conducted by Slamecka (1967) explored the role of semantic relations among words as a determinant of transfer effects. In summarizing this study with a view toward brevity and clarity of exposition, we shall concentrate only on the use of the homogeneous (unmixed) lists which were constructed to test the semantic contribution to positive transfer in paired associate learning. Both List 1 and List 2 were formed by pairing CVC trigrams as stimuli with adjectives as responses. For the usual transfer control group (designated Paradigm *C-D*), List 1 consisted of completely different pairs from List 2. In the 3 experimental groups which concern us, however, the List 1 pairs bore 3 different special relations to List 2 pairs. All stimulus CVCs were identical for all these lists. The responses paired with them in List 1 were semantic counterparts of the corresponding responses of List 2. For Paradigm *A-B*, the response adjectives of Lists 1 and 2 were identical (as were their stimuli) so that "transfer" here simply meant continued learning or testing. For Paradigm *A-Syn* the List 1 adjectives were synonyms of their counterparts in List 2. For Paradigm *A-Ant* the List 1 responses were antonyms of their corresponding List 2 responses. It is these two special paradigms, then, that comprised a test of the semantic relations between list items as contributors to transfer. Examination of the sample response adjectives listed under their paradigm designations in Table 12.2 will illustrate these relations.

Separate groups of 10 subjects were run under each paradigm. Alternate training (S-R) and testing (S-) trials were administered using

Table 12.2 A Sample of the Response Words Used in Different Lists, According to Paradigm (After Slamecka, 1967)

List 1, by Paradigm				List 2
A-B	*A-Syn*	*A-Ant*	*C-D*	All *A-B*
precise	exact	vague	secret	precise
fatal	deadly	harmless	spotless	fatal
drowsy	sleepy	awake	gallant	drowsy
comic	funny	serious	scornful	comic
famous	noted	obscure	absurd	famous

decks of 20 3 x 5 cards. For study trials each CVC-adjective pair was shown to the subject at a rate of 2 sec per pair. Then in a test trial the experimenter presented each CVC for up to 8 sec for the verbalization of the response if possible. The List 1 training proceeded until the subject achieved 2 consecutive errorless test trials. Then he was told that a second list was to be learned. A similar alternation of training and testing trials was used for a transfer list, the one called for by the subject's assignment to a particular paradigm. This List 2 learning was carried to a criterion of 1 errorless trial. All groups learned List 1 in about 7 trials.

The List 2 results of the experiment clearly showed positive transfer attributable to the semantic relations of Paradigms *A-Syn* and *A-Ant*, where responses in the transfer list were either synonyms or antonyms of the originally learned responses to the same stimuli. Three different performance means for each group are given in Table 12.3. The group

Table 12.3 Mean Scores in Learning List 2 (After Slamecka, 1967)

Mean Score	Paradigm			
	A-B	*A-Syn*	*A-Ant*	*C-D*
Trials to criterion	1.0	3.4	3.9	5.6
Correct Rs per trial	20.0	17.6	16.6	13.2
Correct on first trial	20.0	14.6	12.3	3.5

in Paradigm *A-B*, given an identical paired associate list for its second task, performed with no error on the first study trial; its scores may be considered 100 percent positive transfer. According to convention, the means for the control group, Paradigm *C-D*, represent baseline performance or zero specific transfer effect. In comparison, the two semantic test groups for the effects of synonyms and antonyms showed a moderate degree of overall positive transfer. A beneficial effect was strongly evident in the first trial scores which these groups made on List 2. For all of the tabled indices, these semantic relations groups were statistically superior to the control group. They did not differ significantly from each other.

In discussing his findings, Slamecka considered two different mechanisms to account for the positive transfer based on semantic relations. In one possibility, subjects might have perceived the semantic relations between the List 1 and List 2 responses to the same stimuli and deliberately used these relations in mediating their responses as List 2 learning proceeded. The other possibility is that when a meaningful response is learned, some response tendency accrues automatically to other words which are semantically related. Other psychologists have suggested this possibility. As Slamecka considers all of his data, some from groups and conditions not reviewed here, he suggests that his study supports the latter view.

Negative Transfer Effects

Consider a learning task in which two groups of subjects are required to learn a list of words in serial order. If one group had just experienced these words in a free recall memory task, and the second had performed such a task using entirely different words, which group would do better at the serial learning? Would it be the first, with its recent encounter with these words, or the second? This question was explored empirically by Wood (1969). From his report we shall summarize Experiment II in which he also varied the amount of practice or training on List 1, a variable to be considered in designing any study of transfer.

Ninety-six students were assigned at random to 3 experimental conditions and 3 control conditions. All groups engaged in the same transfer task at the end of the experiment—learning List 2, nine familiar 2-syllable nouns, in serial order. The 3 experimental groups had first worked in a free recall (unordered) task at memorizing 18 such words, including the 9 they were later to learn serially; the different experimental groups were given 1, 3, or 6 trials at the first task on List 1 before switching to List 2 learning. The three control groups were treated in similar fashion, except that their 18 nouns for the first task were a different set—containing none of the words to be found in List 2.

For the serial learning of the 9-word List 2, all subjects were given a study trial followed by 10 anticipation trials with the words presented at a 2-sec rate. The progress of the 6 groups in memorizing these words in sequence is depicted in the learning curves of Figure 12.5. The experimental and control curves are paired according to the amount of training received on the earlier free recall task. It may be seen that after 1 trial at

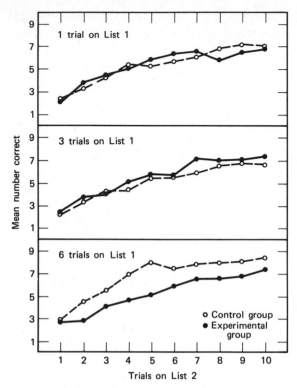

Fig. 12.5. Mean number of words correct as a function of the 10 trials given on List 2 after different numbers of trials on List 1. (After Wood, 1969.)

free recall, the two groups exhibited similar learning curves for List 2. After 6 trials, as the curves in the lowest part of the figure show, the experimental group lagged behind its control group in the serial learning task. Here we have a clear instance of negative transfer of training for the group which had been given 6 prior exposures of the 9 words, included among the 18 of the free recall task. In the center part of the figure are plotted the data of the 3-trial groups whose performances, like the 1-trial groups, did not differ significantly. It is evident that the effect of the two different first task conditions interacted with level of practice. Statistical analysis confirmed this significant interaction and showed only the 6 trials on the free recall words to have affected List 2 serial learning.

How can the negative transfer shown by the 6-trial experimental group be explained? One hypothesis is that the experimental group engaged in subjective sequential organization of the 18 words as they orally recalled them after each of the 6 randomly ordered presentations of List 1. Such subjective organization has been observed to develop in free recall memorization. By incorporating the 9 critical words in various sequential linkages during the first task, the experimental subjects may have found it more difficult to learn them in the List 2 serial order imposed by the experimenter. To test this hypothesis, Wood split his 3-trial as well as his 6-trial groups into high and low organizers on the basis of an index of intertrial repetitions of sequences in their free recall performances. His question was whether those in the experimental groups who showed a greater tendency to organize in the first task actually were the ones to do more poorly on the transfer task. The basic data of this analysis are presented in Table 12.4.

Table 12.4 Mean Correct Responses on the Last Three Trials of List 1 and Trials 1–10 of List 2 for High and Low Organizers Who Received Three or Six Trials on List 1 (After Wood, 1969)

Number of Trials on List 1	Type of Organizer	Free Recall of List 1		Serial Learning of List 2	
		Control	Experimental	Control	Experimental
Three	Low	25.38	30.62	45.25	59.88
	High	27.88	30.00	57.25	50.75
Six	Low	33.25	35.75	60.38	54.75
	High	39.75	37.88	75.50	50.87

Examination of the right-hand column of means gave the investigator a direct answer to his question. In their List 2 learning, those experimental subjects who had been higher in their first task subjective organization showed lower serial memorizing in the transfer task. This evidence becomes more impressive when the control groups' data for List 2 learning are studied. When the words encountered in the transfer task were completely different the data show that better serial learning was accomplished by those control subjects who had been high organizers on the free recall task. Since their subjective organization had not involved the

9 words of List 2, they were not hampered by it in transfer. The free recall scores in the table show that the high organizers in the different groups generally did better in the initial memory task. This lends emphasis to the fact that the high organizers of the experimental group were inadvertently acquiring their negative transfer tendency even while performing satisfactorily on the initial task.

Verbal Chaining and Mediation

Subjects who participate in rote memorization studies come to the experiments with long histories of verbal behavior. It has been proposed by a number of theorists that the forming of new verbal associations is facilitated by a mediational role played by associations established earlier in the learner's history. Again we see that the state of the learner is considered important, this time as a result of experience antedating the memorizing session by many years. Interest in mediation processes has led to numerous experiments in verbal learning and transfer. Jenkins (1963) has surveyed the concept of mediated associations, reviewing the early research and presenting the numerous multistage paradigms used in various investigations. We shall here briefly summarize a significant early study and two more recent experiments. All of them examine verbal associative chaining as a mediational mechanism.

Implicit Verbal Chaining

In paired associate learning, mediate associations may form an implicit verbal chain which connects the two members of a pair in such a way as to aid the memorizing. Russell and Storms (1955) identified such verbal chains as OCEAN-WATER-DRINK by an examination of word association data which indicated WATER as the most common response to OCEAN and DRINK as the commonest response to WATER. Following the mediation hypothesis, they postulated that if OCEAN were linked with a nonsense syllable like ZIL in a paired associates task, it should subsequently prove easier to connect that same nonsense syllable to the word DRINK than to some other word like DOCTOR. Restating this in general symbols, we label the word association chain B-C-D, the nonsense syllable A, and the neutral or control word X. The hypothesis is, then, that A-B learning will facilitate subsequent A-D learning when the latter is compared with the A-X type of paired associate.

These experimenters presented an *A-B* set of ten paired associates to a group of women students. After this task had been mastered, each subject was given a test list employing the same ten nonsense syllables as stimuli. The response words were chosen so that five items were *A-D* pairs and five were *A-X* pairs. These two groups of pairing were counterbalanced through the use of two subgroups of subjects. Examples of the verbal materials used by Russell and Storms are the following:

Original Paired Associates		Implicit Mediator	Alternatives for Test List Response	
A	*B*	*C*	*D*	*X*
CEF	STEM	FLOWER	SMELL	JOY
YOV	SOLDIER	ARMY	NAVY	CHEESE
JID	THIEF	STEAL	TAKE	SLEEP
ZIL	OCEAN	WATER	DRINK	DOCTOR

In a comparison of *A-D* memorizing with *A-X* memorizing, each subject served as her own control. It was found that the *A-D* pairs were memorized somewhat more readily than the *A-X* pairs, thus offering support to the hypothesis that implicit verbal chaining can play a mediational role in the forming of new associations. A different group of students constituted a control group who learned the *A-D* and *A-X* pairs without the prior *A-B* learning. Their performance served to show that *A-D* pairs were not inherently easier to master than *A-X* pairs.

Explicit Nonchained Mediation

In discussing their experimental results Russell and Storms pointed out that their demonstration of mediational influences is not actually an explanation of how the effect was achieved. Since they had determined the *D* responses through the associative *B-C-D* chains, they naturally inferred that such chains must be involved in mediating the better learning of the *A-D* pairs. When postexperimental inquiry indicated that subjects often could not verbalize the mediating *C* word, it appeared justified to label the inferred chaining as implicit or unconscious.

Martin and Dean (1964) carried out two experiments patterned after the Russell and Storms study to see if the mediation used by learners could be detected in postexperimental inquiry and to determine if the mediation made explicit in subjects' reports could be classified as involving a C-term chaining in A-D pair learning. In addition to the procedures used by the earlier investigators, now termed the RS (Russell-Storms) condition, they used a "Pronounce" condition for the second list learning. In this Pronounce condition, subjects had to say aloud the B response of the first list and then try to anticipate the D or X response newly paired with the nonsense syllable stimulus. Only the two conditions mentioned were common to Experiments I and II by Martin and Dean, so these alone will be treated in summarizing the two experiments together.

We must first consider the learning of the A-D versus the A-X pairs in the transfer list. It may be recalled that Russell and Storms had found A-D pairs to be learned more easily, attributing this to mediation in the form of implicit B-C-D chaining. Under their replication condition (RS) Martin and Dean found A-D pairs learned no more readily than A-X pairs. Under their Pronounce condition, however, A-D pairs were more readily learned in both experiments. They also sought to determine what mediation processes the subjects could make explicit at the end of each experiment. Their tabulations of replies are listed in Table 12.5 by mediation category for A-D and A-X pairs and for each condition common to the two experiments.

In these postexperimental reports by subjects a number of interesting aspects of mediation are indicated. First of all, A-D pairs evoked more total mediation reports than A-X pairs. Second, A-D pairs elicited more mediations involving B terms, while A-X pairs evoked more non-B mediators. Third, in Experiment II, the Pronounce condition led to a significantly greater amount of reported mediation for A-D pair learning than did the RS condition. Pronouncing the B and the D responses evidently enhanced mediation.

In examining the relation of reported mediation to the learning of the final paired associate task, Martin and Dean found that the A-D and the A-X pairs that were reported as nonmediated were learned more slowly. Mediation facilitated learning, they found, and it occurred more frequently for A-D pairs as contrasted with A-X. However, they consider this to be explicit mediation, reportable by subjects, and not the implicit verbal chaining that had earlier been postulated.

Table 12.5 Mean Number of Pairs in Each Mediation Category
(After Martin and Dean, 1964)

| Pairs | Condition | Mediated | | | Non-mediated |
		B	Non-B	Total	
Part I. Experiment I					
AD	RS	3.3	1.4	4.7	0.3
	Pronounce	4.6	0.1	4.7	0.3
AX	RS	1.3	2.2	3.5	1.5
	Pronounce	2.1	0.4	2.4	2.5
Part II. Experiment II					
AD	RS	1.9	1.6	3.5	1.5
	Pronounce	4.5	0.1	4.6	0.5
AX	RS	0.6	2.1	2.7	2.3
	Pronounce	2.3	0.2	2.5	2.5

Unwanted Transfer Effects

We have reviewed a number of experiments in which transfer effects were deliberately sought since transfer was the topic of study. In closing this chapter it may be well to note that unwanted transfer effects are sometimes present in experiments of certain two-stage designs and procedures. Every experimenter who plans studies in which subjects perform sequentially at different tasks must be alert to the possibility that transfer will influence the data obtained.

Counterbalanced Treatments

As we saw in Chapter 2, some experiments are designed so that two different treatments are administered to the same subjects. Since there may be learning or transfer effects, half the subjects get the two conditions in one order and half in the other order. The assumption made here, of course, is that any transfer from Treatment A to B will be matched by transfer from B to A. In other words, it is assumed that any transfer effect will be symmetrical. Poulton and Freeman (1966) have pointed out that this assumption of symmetry in balanced designs may not always be valid. They cite a number of studies where asymmetrical transfer or one-way transfer was found between similar tasks. Their analyses indicate that results of many experiments may be contaminated by such unwanted transfer. The findings of those who have examined such effects serve as a warning to those who use presumably balanced designs without due attention to unwanted distortion of data by transfer.

Familiarization in Verbal Studies

A procedure used in numerous experiments on verbal learning has been to familiarize subjects with the material by presenting the words or quasi-verbal items to them prior to the required memorization task. Although the investigators try to rule out the formation of interitem associations during familiarization with materials, some such learning is likely to occur. Pointing this out, Jung (1967) went on to examine the parallels between the familiarization procedures and the paradigms used in verbal transfer research. He concluded that unwanted transfer effects may be especially difficult to control or eliminate in studies of verbal familiarization. Here again we see that a knowledge of transfer principles and a sensitivity to the operation of transfer is indispensable to the designer of psychological research.

Summary

Transfer is the effect, either beneficial or detrimental, that learning one activity has upon the performance of another task. Laboratory experimentation permits the necessary controls and measurements to delineate transfer mechanisms in all kinds of tasks. The elements that are identical or similar from task to task are hypothesized to be important in transfer of training. Such elements foster the carryover from task to task of the same, or generalized, response tendencies which are the basis for the observed transfer effects.

A number of experimental designs have been generated in research on transfer. A simple design involves subjects randomly assigned to either an experimental group, experiencing both Task *A* and Task *B*, or a control group, doing Task *B* alone. If the latter group subsequently is given Task *A*, the design permits study of two-way transfer, Task *B* to Task *A* as well as Task *A* to Task *B*. A different design involves equated groups of subjects, pretested and matched on some performance related to Task *B*, the second task in the simple transfer paradigm. If this plan is used, considerable attention must be given to the pretest or matching factor and the amount of experience afforded the subjects as they are pretested.

A complete investigation of transfer mechanisms is likely to necessitate the running of more than two groups of subjects. Multiple groups permit the systematic manipulation of several different variables in the same study. Different variations of Task *A*, different performance measures on Task *B*, different amounts of training, and different intertask intervals may all be possible sources of information about the processes underlying transfer.

Two principles of transfer measurement should be kept in mind as research is planned. First, different indices of performance may yield different pictures of transfer. This principle suggests that multiple measures may enhance the description of transfer between two tasks, and that discrepancies in what the different indices portray need not be a cause for alarm. The second principle is that measured transfer effects can be expected to change as different stages in the practice of the second task are reached.

Besides comparison with control values, experimental measures may sometimes be compared with extended performance curves. Often the observed differences in any sort of comparison will be converted to percent estimates of transfer. Transforming empirical findings to the percent values may permit general comparisons of transfer effects between experiments in which different raw measures may have been employed. We noted different formulas for converting group statistics to percent estimates. A choice among these should be made in the planning stages of a research effort so that the required measurements may be taken properly.

The transfer surface and some related models were examined. They blend empirical findings with theoretical analyses of transfer. Two-list tasks for quantifying transfer in verbal learning was the methodological approach in several exemplary studies. One of these revealed negative transfer from List 1 to List 2.

A special kind of transfer is observed when a chain of earlier learned associations is found to be operative, implicitly or explicitly, in some laboratory tasks of verbal learning. Selected studies illustrated the research methods and the findings. The chapter concluded with a warning that unwanted transfer effects may distort the data obtained when an experimenter relies on counterbalancing or preliminary stimulus familiarization in some experimental designs.

References

Bilodeau, I. McD. Transfer of training across target sizes. *Journal of Experimental Psychology*, 1965, **70**, 135–140.

Dallett, K. M. The transfer surface re-examined. *Journal of Verbal Learning and Verbal Behavior*, 1962, **1**, 91–94.

Ellis, H. C. *The transfer of learning*. New York: Macmillan, 1965.

Gagné, R. M., Foster, H., & Crowley, M. E. The measurement of transfer of training. *Psychological Bulletin*, 1948, **45**, 97–130.

Haagen, C. H. Synonymity, vividness, familiarity, and association value ratings of 400 pairs of common adjectives. *Journal of Psychology*, 1949, **27**, 453–463.

Jenkins, J. J. Mediated associations: Paradigms and situations. In C. N. Cofer & B. S. Musgrave (Eds.), *Verbal behavior and learning*. New York: McGraw-Hill, 1963. Pp. 210–245.

Jung, J. Effects of response meaningfulness (m) on transfer of training under two different paradigms. *Journal of Experimental Psychology*, 1963, **65**, 372–384.

Jung, J. Transfer analysis of familiarization effects. *Psychological Review*, 1967, **74**, 523–529.

Mandler, G. Response factors in human learning. *Psychological Review*, 1954, **61**, 235–244.

Martin, E. Transfer of verbal paired associates. *Psychological Review*, 1965, **72**, 327–343.

Martin, R. B., & Dean, S. J. Implicit and explicit mediation in paired-associate learning. *Journal of Experimental Psychology*, 1964, **68**, 21–27.

Murdock, B. B., Jr. Transfer designs and formulas. *Psychological Bulletin*, 1957, **54**, 313–326.

Osgood, C. E. The similarity paradox in human learning: A resolution. *Psychological Review*, 1949, **56**, 132–143.

Poulton, E. C., & Freeman, P. R. Unwanted asymmetrical transfer effects with balanced experimental designs. *Psychological Bulletin*, 1966, **66**, 1–8.

Russell, W. A., & Storms, L. H. Implicit verbal chaining in paired-associate learning. *Journal of Experimental Psychology*, 1955, **49**, 287–293.

Shea, M. Formulation of a generalization surface for the simultaneous variation of stimulus and response similarity. *Journal of Experimental Psychology*, 1969, **80**, 353–358.

Slamecka, N. J. Transfer with mixed and unmixed lists as a function of semantic relations. *Journal of Experimental Psychology*, 1967, **73**, 405–410.

Wood, G. Whole-part transfer from free recall to serial learning. *Journal of Experimental Psychology*, 1969, **79**, 540–544.

chapter 13
Problem Solving

Like many other activities, problem solving is not a unitary behavior but a combination of psychological processes. A typical problem situation might demand that motivational, perceptual, associative, retentive, and transfer processes be used to arrive at a solution. Instead of attempting any psychological definition of problem solving, then, we need to consider briefly the essential aspects of a problem situation. These aspects tend to recur in the variety of problems or tasks employed in studying this area of behavior.

1. A specified goal or goals.

2. A variety of stimuli or cues.

3. A number of possible responses.

4. Varied associative strengths linking different stimuli and responses.

5. Sources of information indicating particular stimulus-response combinations to be correct or incorrect.

In research these elements are found in the instructions given to subjects and in the task materials as they are perceived and manipulated. Once the problem is posed, responses to the stimuli tend to occur sequentially with gains and losses in associative strength resulting from the information feedback obtained. This responding may be covert, involving cognitive processes that can only be inferred by the experimenter on the basis of procedures used and data collected. For some tasks, however, the problem-solving performance may be quite overt—with the trial-and-error variety of behavior quite prominent. The discovery or gradual acquiring of goal-attaining responses terminates the behavioral sequence. In a review of research and theory Davis (1966) stressed the possibility of using the overt-covert behavior dichotomy to categorize problem-solving experiments which have employed a variety of problem tasks.

Materials and Methods Used in Research

In order to study how people solve problems psychologists have used a diversity of materials and methods. Essentially, we give a problem task to subjects and then observe and measure the behavior that follows. You may get a subject's-eye view of such investigations if you attempt to solve the problems posed for you here as illustrative examples.

Examples of Problem Tasks

Since we are using these sample tasks only for illustration, we are not considering them in a complete form. Some of the examples will, in fact, only suggest the nature of the problem as it might occur at some stage in an experiment. Several of the tasks are multidimensional, permitting the manipulation of more than one variable in research. Later we shall see how some of the problem tasks we pose here have actually been used by experimenters.

Task I. Concept Identification

From the examples given below, determine the characteristics of the letter clusters which define a Beta, a Gamma, and a Delta. *Note*: Only the letters J, Q, V, X, and Z were used in setting up the patterns. It is a combination of the *presence or absence of one or two* of these letters which defines each concept. Letter sequence or multiple use of any letter in a cluster does *not* enter into the concept definition.

Concepts defined by the presence or absence of letters in such clusters were employed in an experiment by Neisser and Weene (1962). Their subjects were shown each example of a concept separately, a technique that differs very much from the way in which the problem was put to you. We shall review their study later in this chapter.

Examples of Beta			Examples of Not-Beta		
ZVXJ	VVJX	ZXJX	QVXX	JQVZ	VVXQ
JXZZ	JJZV	VXVZ	ZJJQ	VXQQ	XZQX

Examples of Gamma			Examples of Not-Gamma		
ZVXJ	QVJX	XZJQ	QJZV	VQXX	ZXVQ
JZZX	JQXQ	XJJX	VZZX	VJZJ	ZQQJ

Examples of Delta			Examples of Not-Delta		
QQZJ	VXXJ	ZJQX	XJXQ	JJQX	QXXJ
JQVX	VJXQ	QXXZ	JXJJ	QQJX	QXJX

Task II. Anagrams

Rearrange each group of five letters to form a meaningful word:

AEPHS   OSHRE   GNHTI   ECNAO

Did you notice that two different words could be formed from each letter group? Look at the words below; try to rearrange the letters of each one to form a *different* five-letter word:

GROWN   BLEAT   TREAD   TRAIL

Both nonsense and word anagrams were used in a study by Mayzner and Tresselt (1966). Their experiment required many controls in the selection of words to be used and in the sequencing of the anagram letters as one variable in the research.

Task III. Word formation

Add the missing letters to these items to form meaningful words:

S__R__   P__ __G   M__L__G__
D__A__   CL__ __   __EM__ __IS__

The problems that are posed for you here represent possible stages in a task used by Battig (1957). Working on just one word at a time, a subject had to guess various letters while the experimenter showed him the location of each guessed letter if it did appear in the word. As given to you, each word problem is possibly open to more than one solution. Your task differs, too, in your not receiving any letter-by-letter information as you proceed to fill in the gaps.

Task IV. Twenty Questions

Read the sequence of questions and answers below and decide what question would be best to ask next in playing this familiar game.

Q: Is it human?
A: Yes.
Q: Is it living?
A: Yes.
Q: Is it a man?
A: Yes.
Q: Is he in politics?
A: No.
Q: Is he in show business?
A: Yes.

This task has been used in several psychological experiments. For example, it was employed by Faust (1958) to investigate the improvement an individual shows as he repeatedly solves the problems posed in Twenty Questions. In your opinion, does the above series of questions represent a high or a low level of skill?

Task V. Water jar problems

For each problem below, decide how you would measure out the exact amount of water required, using the jars whose capacities are indicated:

Problem Number	Jar *a*	Jar *b*	Jar *c*	Amount Desired
1	6 pt	13 pt	2 pt	3 pt
2	10 pt	2 pt	9 pt	5 pt
3	4 pt	7 pt	2 pt	1 pt

Materials such as this have helped to reveal the habits formed as people solve many problems of a similar nature. Gardner and Runquist (1958) investigated how a particular way of solving such problems could be learned and then abandoned as the problem patterns changed.

Task VI. Three-term series problems

Read each problem below and see how quickly you can arrive at the answer to the question.

If Chris is better than Brian, and Brian is better than Adam, then who is best?

Brian   Chris   Adam

If Mary is shorter than Sue, and Mary is taller than Ellen, then who is tallest?

Ellen   Sue   Mary

If Heinz isn't as bad as Gino, and Bob isn't as good as Gino, then who is worst?

Gino   Heinz   Bob

Problems like these, which call for simple deductive reasoning, were used in experiments conducted by Huttenlocher (1968) and Clark (1969). One finding is that linguistic format is a determinant of solution time.

Task VII. Reaching a decision

On the basis of the numbered cards which are presented here, decide whether the mean value of the entire set of 12 cards is above or below 87. Assume the cards were thoroughly shuffled before the eight were turned.

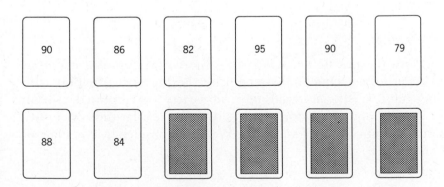

How confident are you in the correctness of your judgment? In a study by Little and Lintz (1965) subjects had to express their confidence by checking a graphic rating scale after each number was seen.

Desirable Task Attributes

It might seem that almost any challenging task could be used in the study of problem solving. The investigator would only have to require that subjects "think aloud" as they attempt to solve each problem. Although this use of introspection might suggest some of the mechanisms of thought which were operating, it is likely that such subjective reports would be very incomplete and unreliable. Our discovery and description of the processes of problem solving must depend on our ingenuity in devising tasks and stimulus materials and in obtaining reliable and valid performance measures. From the data obtained we may infer the covert behaviors of the subjects under different experimental conditions. The relationships we seek are not necessarily fundamental behavior laws. They may be quantified relationships among variables which reflect basic principles of perception, learning, memory, or transfer, for example. Problem solving is an area where such processes may interact in very intricate ways. That is why it poses a challenge in devising experimental procedures which will permit underlying phenomena to be uncovered.

Ray (1955) has called for systematic manipulation of independent variables and measurement of different facets of problem solution. In reviewing some of the commonly used laboratory tasks, he called for greater attention to the use of scaled task attributes and quantification of observed behaviors as a way to improve research. The experimentation of recent years has exemplified these desirable trends to a considerable degree, as shown by some of the studies presented in Ray's book (1967) and in this chapter.

Stimulus Materials

Together with the instructions given to subjects, the stimulus materials given to them—often sequentially—comprise the problem situation with which they must wrestle. Materials of great variety are employed. And in stimulus items of almost any sort there is usually great latitude for multidimensional manipulation of variables. We shall consider briefly some of the commonly used types.

Verbal or numerical items

Symbolic materials have great utility. Besides the ease with which they may be prepared and presented, they have the advantage of being the materials in which many problems of everyday life are cast. By presenting words or numbers in a controlled fashion and setting the guidelines for their utilization by the subject, an experimenter can explore many different thought processes.

Verbal materials, both words and nonsense items, have been scaled along many dimensions as indicated in Chapter 9. They provide researchers with an enormous pool of stimuli. Scaling efforts have ranged from associative descriptions of meaningfulness to the molecular determination of frequency of occurrence of each bigram making up the spelling of a word. Investigators of problem solving may profit from this quantification of stimulus characteristics just as students of verbal learning have done. Indeed such research refinement is already evident in studies of anagram solving.

Numbers and numerical aspects of problems also promise the discovery of problem-solving principles. Although mathematical problems have been generally avoided due to unequal formal training or past experience of subjects, numerical values have been effectively used in probing behavior in probabilistic situations like those faced in games of chance. Numerals, as ultra-familiar symbols, may be used to form chains or arrays as alternatives to alphabet letters for some problem presentations. Certain numerical puzzles may have utility where special mathematical training can be ruled out as an unwanted influence on their solving.

Geometric or pictorial items

Discrete types of stimuli are afforded by geometric forms or symbols—circle, rectangle, triangle, cross, or star. Their diversity is extended by the use of different coloring or shading. A further extension to multidimensionality is found in the cards of the Wisconsin Card Sorting Test in which *color, form,* and *numerosity* of symbols are all independently variable. One to four copies of a triangle, star, cross, or circle may be printed on a card in red, green, yellow, or blue. Each card thus has three dimensions with four possible values on each.

As another kind of multivariate stimulus item Hovland (1953) suggested a series of line drawings of plants or flowers. These may vary as to the number of petals or forms of leaf, for example. Their identification on the basis of such features closely resembles the classification task performed by the botanist. Such stimulus materials have been used in research on concept attainment.

Common Research Methods

Over the years psychologists have themselves been creative problem solvers as they invented different research procedures with which to investigate this area of behavior. Standardized methods have not emerged but certain general approaches have found increasing use. A wide-ranging methodological survey and critique was prepared by Bourne and Battig (1966). Here we may consider a few of the more prominent approaches.

Concept identification

A frequent topic has been concept attainment, also designated concept identification or concept learning. The experimenter sequentially presents numerous examples or instances of several concepts until the subject has learned which label applies to each. Knowledge of results (KR) is given as feedback to assist in the learning. This type of study offers many opportunities for quantitative manipulations of stimulus attributes and of temporal aspects of the test situation. Sometimes trials are arranged so as to establish a certain mental set in experimental subjects in the first part of a study; its effect on later performance is then assessed through comparing experimental data with that of control subjects. Our first reviews of experiments will deal with concept attainment.

Reasoning tasks

Logical syllogisms and verbal puzzles may be used to test subjects' reasoning powers. Instead of mental evaluation, though, the experimenter is interested in illuminating various influences on reasoning processes. Although reasoning is considered to be logical in nature, studies have shown that psychological factors, such as verbal habits, are important determinants of the course taken in solving problems.

Games and puzzles

Our survey of methods must include games and puzzles, long used in the psychological laboratory. Their employment has tended to decline as more quantifiable tasks have been sought. The outstanding survivor of their declining use has been the anagram or scrambled word puzzle. This form of verbal problem has remained popular, particularly as verbal scaling techniques have helped to refine quantification.

Probability situations

Experimenters have studied how people behave in the face of uncertainty as exemplified in gambling situations. Both the probability and reward associated with a correct response or a winning bet can be quantified. So, too, can the probability and amount of loss. Measures of behavior range widely. The number of subjects who bet in a certain way, accepting a risk for a possible gain, is a common datum. For the individual subject, the measures may vary from the response latency or the amount risked to the confidence expressed in the decision or judgment. Over many trials, with their consequences, an experimenter may plot the course of learning, change in the behavior exhibited.

Tasks resembling real problems

Since problem solving is demanded quite frequently in real life, psychologists have sometimes posed simulations of practical problems for their laboratory studies. In one line of investigation a desired accomplishment is described to the subject and various objects or tools are made available for use in the task. The goal is not to be reached by making direct use of these implements, however. A common requirement is that new relationships among the objects or a new utilization of a tool must be perceived before solution of the problem occurs. Making novel use of an item is sometimes hampered when a subject has to use it in a customary way first. For example, if a hammer is used to drive a nail from which a string is hung, the use of the hammer as a weight on the lower end of the string will be less likely to occur than in a situation where the hammer did not have to be employed first in its normal function. According to Duncker (1945, p. 85) the first use of the hammer would result in "functional fixedness," a strengthening of the tendency to perceive it for conventional employment. This recent strengthening of the perception of normal utilization would render a novel use less likely to occur later on. Glucksberg and Weisberg (1966) found that labeling of the functionally fixed object was contributory to problem solution in a different task of this type.

Another simulation of real life occurs when a subject is given a piece of apparatus or equipment to operate or to troubleshoot. Special arrangements of conditions pose problems of different sorts. Task dimensions are systematically varied for different groups of subjects and the effects on their problem solving are noted. These special apparatus problems give the experimenter great control over independent variables and permit his ready measurement of responses. In such manipulable problems we may have a powerful tool for the determination of general laws of behavior in problem situations.

Concept Identification

Research exploring how individuals identify concepts when presented with varied positive and negative examples has been prominent in the study of problem solving. Progress has been made in theory development as well as in empirical findings. One analysis by Haygood and Bourne (1965) indicates that conceptual behavior should be considered as dependent on both attribute learning and rule learning. Experiments we shall later review exemplify the varied investigative approaches to concept attainment. We shall not be able to consider, however, the prominent topic of concept shift in discrimination learning; the research literature, methodological questions, and theoretical development are very extensive (for example, Wolff, 1967; Slamecka, 1968; Kendler and Kendler, 1969).

Levels of Complexity

The ease or difficulty with which a concept can be attained depends on the complexity of its definition. This hypothesis was tested by Neisser and Weene (1962). As stimulus items they used clusters of letters such as those presented on p. 475 as an example of a concept identification task. Subjects were fully informed in advance about the several kinds of concept definitions—or criterial attributes—which might constitute their goal on any given task. They were told that the presence or absence of just one or two letters per cluster would be relevant to concept identification.

An example of a sequence of stimulus presentations and possible responses may be helpful before we consider details of the study. We see a series of possible trial presentations with the covert hypotheses and responses of one hypothetical subject. Also indicated is the knowledge of results (KR) given by the experimenter after a response has been made. This serves to confirm tentatively or to disconfirm any hypothesis.

In our example, the subject first guessed the presence of both X and Z might define the concept so he responded "Plus" and received KR which could be considered confirmatory. Trial 2 gave him a chance to

Trial	Stimulus	Hypothesis	Response	KR
1	JXQZ	(X&Z?)	"Plus"	Plus
2	QQZJ	(X&Z)	"Minus"	Plus
3	VVQZ	(Q&Z?)	"Plus"	Minus
4	XJJQ	(J&Q?)	"Plus"	Plus
5	XZQZ	(J&Q)	"Minus"	Plus

test his hypothesis decisively since X was missing from the letter cluster. His response of "Minus' was followed by KR of Plus, thereby disconfirming his X & Z hypothesis. On Trial 3 he switched to another hypothesis which he thought could be correct, Q & Z. However, the KR of Minus disconfirmed this immediately. On Trial 4 he tried a new hypothesis, J & Q. He might have been guessing or he might have remembered that J and Q were both present on earlier positive instances, Trials 1 and 2, but not in the negative stimulus of Trial 3. His hypothesis seems valid so he retains it for Trial 5, responding "Minus" because J is missing. Now he finds that this third hypothesis is also invalid when KR turns out to be Plus. Every hypothesis tested in the example was of a *conjunctive* type, the subject postulating that two letters must both be present to define the concept being sought. In turn, his hypotheses X & Z, Q & Z, and J & Q were each found untenable. Actually the correct definition for this particular concept identification task was one involving the presence of one letter (Q) *and* the absence of another (V). This definition, symbolized as Q & —V, represents a two-feature concept of the Exclusion type, according to the classification of concept types given by Neisser and Weene. Ten different one-feature or two-feature types of concepts, organized according to complexity level, comprised the experimental task manipulation of their study. These 10 types of concepts are listed in Table 13.1 together with positive and negative instances of each.

Stimulus clusters of consonants were printed on cards for presentation, one per trial, to small groups of subjects. Each subject used a toggle switch to signal his own response, "Plus" or "Minus", to the experimenter for recording. After all had responded, the experimenter informed the group of the correct answer, and then presented the next stimulus card. Subjects were allowed up to 15 sec or so for a response. Successive stimuli were independently sequenced, with positive and negative instances equally probable. Trials on any one of the 10 concept types continued up to 100 stimuli or until each subject had attained the criterion for concept

Table 13.1 Types of Concepts Defined by Presence or Absence of One or Two Features* (After Neisser and Weene, 1962)

Type of Concept	Positive Instances			Negative Instances		
Level I						
Presence (Q)	QJJV	XJZQ	ZQQX	JYYZ	XJXV	VJXJ
Absence (–Q)	ZXVJ	JZXJ	XXZZ	QVXJ	XZQX	QQJV
Level II						
Conjunction (Q & J)	JXVQ	VXQJ	ZJZQ	JVXZ	XVQV	XXVZ
Disjunction (Q or J)	QXZV	ZXXJ	JVQQ	ZVVX	XXZV	VXZX
Exclusion (Q & –J)	XZQV	XVQQ	ZXXQ	XXVV	JVZV	QJXX
Disjunctive absence (–Q or –J)	XVJZ	XVZX	QVXZ	ZQJJ	XQVJ	JVXQ
Conjunctive absence (–Q & –J)	XZVV	ZVXZ	VXZX	JZVV	XQQZ	QVZJ
Implication (–Q or J)	XVJZ	QVJV	JVJX	XQVZ	QXQV	ZVXQ
Level III						
Either/or (Q & –J) or (–Q & J)	QVZV	XVVJ	XJVV	JXQV	JVZQ	QXJJ
Both/neither (Q & J) or (–Q & –J)	QZJV	XZVX	XJQV	JVZV	VZQX	XJJZ

*Features varied in the table are Q and J. In the actual experiment these features in any particular problem were one or two of the 5 letters used in creating the 4-letter concepts: J, Q, V, X, Z.

identification—25 consecutive responses with only a single error. Three practice problems preceded 2 cycles through the 10 concept types in varied orders for different subject groups. In all, 20 college students served as subjects.

The results of the experiment are presented in Table 13.2 in the form of median trials to concept attainment for each type of problem on each cycle of testing. The data confirmed the hypothesis that the ease or difficulty of attaining these concept types depended on the level of complexity of their definitions. The median scores were clearly different for the 3 levels defined by the investigators. The data also reveal a practice effect, Cycle 2 scores being substantially lower than Cycle 1 in most cases. In further support of their hypothesis concerning complexity levels, Neisser and Weene made 56 interlevel comparisons and found that in all but one a greater proportion of subjects had done better on the lower

Table 13.2 Median Number of Trials Prior to Criterion
Sequence for Each Cycle on the Ten Types of
Concepts (After Neisser and Weene, 1962)

Type of Concept	Cycle 1	Cycle 2
Level I		
Presence (Q)	11.0	4.0
Absence (–Q)	7.0	1.5
Level II		
Conjunction (Q & J)	13.0	18.0
Disjunction (Q or J)	21.0	24.0
Exclusion (Q & –J)	28.0	17.0
Disjunctive		
absence (–Q or –J)	50.0	23.0
Conjunctive		
absence (–Q or –J)	29.0	8.0
Implication (–Q or J)	*	19.5
Level III		
Either/or (Q & –J)		
or (–Q & J)	68.0	41.5
Both/neither (Q & J)		
or (–Q & –J)	*	53.5

*Median not determinable since fewer than half the subjects
attained the concept on this cycle of trials.

level of concept complexity. Of these 55 differences, 39 were statistically significant.

The investigators entertained the possibility that more complexly defined concepts would *logically* require examination of more instances before concept attainment. However, they found that a computer program could identify *any* of the concepts in an average of 8 to 10 trials. They conclude, therefore, that the experimental results with the college students point to psychological processes and not to logically necessary operations.

Sequencing of Relevant and Irrelevant Cues

As stimuli are successively presented in a concept learning task a subject tends to gain information from the various instances given to him and from his responses and the knowledge of results (KR) which follows them.

The amount of repetition of the same cues from trial to trial, as compared with alternation of possible cue values, would be expected to have some effect on concept attainment. The constant (repetitive) or alternating presentation of stimulus attributes might affect performance differently depending on whether these attributes were relevant or irrelevant cues.

Anderson and Guthrie (1966) carried out an experiment in which 4 experimental training conditions (and a control) were designed to explore how concept identification would be accomplished under such manipulations of cues. The introduction of their report indicates two expectations for the outcome of the research. First, with alternating presentations of relevant cues, concept attainment would be better when fewer stimulus values were changed from trial to trial. Second, with a constant series of relevant cues, a facilitation of performance should accompany the greater number of stimulus dimensions changing values during training.

Multidimensional stimuli were drawn on 3 x 5 in. file cards for presentation in the small window cut in the screen which separated subject and experimenter. Stimuli were characterized by 5 dimensions, each of which could take on 1 of 3 values as indicated in Table 13.3. For example, a stimulus card might contain 3 blue rectangles with striped shading and a horizontal black bar. Of the 5 dimensions just one was relevant for the concept learning of any particular subject and 4 were irrelevant. With respect to the relevant dimension, 1 cue value was arbitrarily designated as requiring the concept identification "Alpha" while

Table 13.3 Relevant or Irrelevant Stimulus Dimensions and
Three Possible Cue Values of Each
(After Anderson and Guthrie, 1966)

Stimulus Dimension	Three Stimulus Values
Color	Red, Blue, or Green
Number	One, Two, or Three Figures
Form	Rectangle, Diamond, or Oval
Shading	Outline, Solid, or Striped
*Bar	Vertical, Horizontal, or Absent

*Bar was black, $1\frac{1}{2}$ in. long, centered on the 3 x 5 stimulus card.

either of the other 2 values required the response "Bravo." For example, in the color dimension—if it were the relevant one—red stimulus forms might represent Alpha, while either blue or green would correctly be identified as Bravo.

Five groups of subjects, run as individuals, were given 6 training trials followed immediately by test trials until 10 consecutive correct responses (or 80 trials) were completed. It was in the sequencing of stimulus presentations for the 6 training trials that the groups of subjects were given their differential treatments.

Group | Treatment During Training

A1   Relevant Dimension: The Alpha cue and one of the Bravo cues were alternated.

Irrelevant Dimensions: All dimensions were held constant using some particular cue value of each.

A3   Relevant Dimension: Same as Group A1.

Irrelevant Dimensions: Two dimensions changed value each trial and each dimension changed at least twice.

C1   Relevant Dimension: The Alpha cue value was constantly present on each trial.

Irrelevant Dimension: One dimension changed value each trial and each dimension changed at least once.

C3   Relevant Dimension: Same as Group C1.

Irrelevant Dimensions: Three dimensions changed value each trial and each dimension changed at least twice.

Control   Given 6 randomly selected stimulus cards.

The test trials which followed the training trials without any break consisted of randomly sequenced presentations from a deck of all the stimulus cards. All trials were run at a 15-sec interval. A single reading of the instructions covered both the training and test series.

In a moment, I will show you a series of cards. They will appear one at a time in the little window in front of you. Your task will be to classify the cards into one of two categories. You should try to learn the basis of the correct classification as quickly as possible. Each time you see a card in the window, you are to say either Alpha or Bravo. I will tell you whether you are correct. Alpha will be the correct word for some of the cards and Bravo will be the correct word for some of the cards. Your task is to learn which word goes with which kind of card.

Anderson and Guthrie present their results in the form of mean number of errors made by the different groups during training and test trials. Their tabled values are represented graphically in Figure 13.1. The major finding for both series of trials was an interaction effect which confirmed their expectations. Where relevant cues were alternated during training, concept learning was superior when fewer stimulus changes

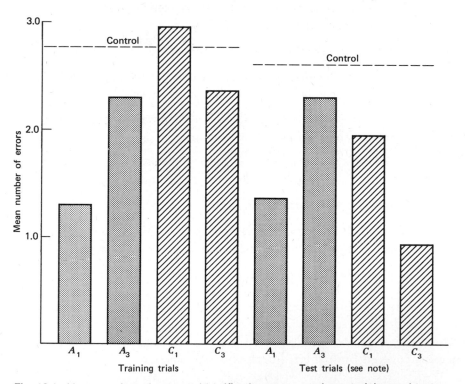

Fig. 13.1. Mean number of concept identification errors made on training and test Guthrie, 1966.) *Note.* For test trials, the plotted values are means of square roots of trials by four experimental groups and the control group. (Data from Anderson and errors, a transformation of the original data.

Problem Solving   **488**

were made (Group A1 showing fewer errors). Where relevant cues remained the same, in a constant series, concept attainment was facilitated when more irrelevant cues were varied (Group C3 showing fewer errors).

Associative Rank of Stimuli

As subjects undertake a concept identification task, their problem is to learn to make a certain response to each of the different stimuli presented. Studies of transfer suggest that the ease with which a stimulus and a response become associated is dependent on the previously developed tendency of the stimulus to evoke this response. In preparation for research on concept learning, Underwood and Richardson (1956) scaled the associative strength linking a large number of concrete nouns to adjectives which were descriptive of the sensory impressions that might be aroused by the objects to which the nouns referred. It was found, for example, that the stimulus noun *baseball* elicited the adjectives *round, white, hard,* and *small* in an association test. Since *round* was the response given to the word *baseball* by a great majority of subjects, this adjective is considered to have high *response dominance* to this stimulus.

Since these scaled verbal materials have been demonstrated to be useful in research on concept learning, we may examine the scaling procedure more closely. The experimental subjects, 153 college students, were first given instructions and preliminary training. These were aimed at insuring that the responses given were descriptive of *sense impressions.* A set of 328 nouns was then presented, being pronounced by the experimenter and flashed on a screen, each word being succeeded by the next one after 6-sec exposure. Subjects wrote down the first sensory impression which they associated with each noun.

In categorizing the responses for tabulation, synonymous adjectives like *big* and *large* were combined. The final list of stimulus words tabulated by the authors contains 213 nouns, with 115 having been eliminated because they had been perceived ambiguously or had yielded too few common responses for categorization. For the 213 nouns, the percent of subjects giving each adjective as a response is presented in the original article. Any response which was not given by at least 5 percent of subjects was thrown into a miscellaneous category, along with responses which were not sense impressions. The distribution of responses to a sample of the nouns is presented in Table 13.4. In the original tabulation, a datum on frequency of usage of each noun in written English was also given.

Mednick and Halpern (1962) conducted a study of concept attainment using as stimuli some of the nouns which Underwood and Richardson had scaled for response dominance. Included in the lists of nouns to be presented were some which had as either their first-rank or second-rank associations the responses *round* or *white*. Table 13.4 includes three of the nouns used. *Bread* may be seen to have the response *white* as its first-rank response, as does *goat*. *Dime* has *round* as its first-rank response. Although not used in this experiment, *apple* is an example of a noun having *round* as its second-rank response. It was hypothesized by Mednick and Halpern that when sensory associate adjectives like *round* and *white* were used as concepts to be learned as responses to nouns, learning would proceed faster where the noun-adjective associations had been found to be of first rank when compared to those of second rank. To test

Table 13.4 Selected Sample of Stimulus Nouns Scaled for Response Dominance on the Basis of Percent of Subjects Offering Different Sensory-Impression Responses in Word Association (After Underwood and Richardson, 1956)

Stimulus Word	Response Categories and Percent Occurrence	Miscellaneous Responses
Aluminum	Shiny 59%; metallic 14%; light 12%	14%
Apple	Red 67; round 19; sweet 5	9
Atom	Small 87	13
Auditorium	Big 84	16
Barrel	Round 72; woody 15; big 6	7
Baseball	Round 70; white 11; hard 10; small 5	4
Bread	White 35; soft 31	28
Cave	Dark 66; deep 6; damp 14; hollow 5	9
City	Big 72; noisy 5	23
Dime	Round 30; metallic 23; small 15; shiny 13; thin 9	9
Ether	Smelly 70	30
Goat	White 29; smelly 20; hairy-furry 18; dirty 5	29
Ivory	White 65; hard 14; smooth 12	9
Lips	Red 59; soft 24	18
Needle	Sharp 53; pointed 15; small 9; metallic 5; thin 9	10
Pin	Sharp 55; small 22; pointed 10; metallic 5	9
Rice	White 54; small 24; hard 6	15
Stone	Hard 63; small 7; round 6; heavy 6	19
Zoo	Big 32; smelly 30; noisy 7	31

this prediction, they compiled the two lists of stimulus nouns presented in Table 13.5. List I contained 4 nouns with *round* as their Rank 1 re-

Table 13.5 Concept Lists with Associative Rank, Response Dominance, and Mean Dominance Level Indicated (After Mednick and Halpern, 1962)

Associative Rank in Hierarchy	List I Nouns	Response Dominance (%)	Concept and Mean Dominance (%)	List II Nouns	Response Dominance (%)	Concept and Mean Dominance (%)
1	Pot	29		Hospital	32	
	Eye	32	Round	Enamel	28	White
	Dime	30	27	Goat	29	31
	Grape	18		Bread	35	
2	Frost	34		Badge	21	
	Gardenia	28	White	Pill	28	Round
	Lard	27	31	Waist	24	24
	Bone	34		Capsule	22	

sponse in the associative hierarchy and 4 nouns with *white* as their Rank 2 associations. List II had *white* as the Rank 1 response to 4 stimulus nouns and *round* as the Rank 2 *response* to 4 others. For experimental purposes both lists were expanded to 12 items by adding 4 nouns related to the concept *long:* EEL, BEAK, ALLEY, CUCUMBER.

Three different random orders were used in presenting the 12 stimulus nouns of either list to a subject, with a memory drum used to achieve a 4-sec rate of exposure per noun. Each subject had been told that 4 of the nouns could be described by the same adjective, 4 by another adjective, and the remaining 4 by still another. Responding aloud, a subject tried to give an appropriate adjective as each noun was presented. He was told immediately by the experimenter if he was correct or wrong as he responded to each item. Either 12-noun list, then, required the attainment of 3 concepts, *round, white,* and *long,* as responses.

Upon analyzing the data for the critical 2 sets of nouns from each list, Mednick and Halpern found that the adjectival concepts having associative Rank 1 were attained more readily than the same concepts having a Rank 2 association with 4 stimulus nouns in the other list. Rank 1 concepts were learned in 5.90 trials on the average with 12.17 errors being made. The learning of the Rank 2 concepts took an average of 8.09 trials during which 18.14 errors were made. These results confirmed the investigators' predictions for the experimental outcome.

Additional Studies of Problem Solving

In the area of concept identification, which we have just examined, investigators have demonstrated trends toward the employment of standard methods and materials. Other regions of the vast realm of problem solving have been explored by a great diversity of techniques. In the remainder of this chapter we shall consider this research effort by examining a number of illustrative experiments.

Associative Influences on Syllogistic Reasoning

Deductive reasoning has long been known to be influenced by psychological factors rather than being a purely logical process. Pezzoli and Frase (1968) carried out an experiment designed to explore how associative relations among words encountered in different configurations might affect judgments of validity of logical syllogisms. For example, an invalid syllogism—Some Y are X; Some Y are Z; therefore Some X are Z—might be erroneously judged to be valid if certain associated words were substituted for X, Y, and Z in the two premises and the conclusion. As test items, the experimenters used syllogisms of the 10 different formats of Table 13.6 (in which every syllogism is invalid). Words of either high or low associative connection were used in place of X, Y, and Z in forming 20 syllogisms. Ten more had nonsense CCC trigrams in place of X, Y, and Z. To these 30 invalid syllogisms, 12 valid ones were added to create a 42-item test. The 2 premises and the conclusion of each syllogism were projected for 6 sec each. Fifty-four subjects recorded their judgment of the validity of each conclusion on a prepared response sheet. Manipulations of certain time intervals and verbal embellishments of the syllogisms were parts of the study which are not to be included in this summary.

It was noted by the experimenters that syllogisms of the second figure (see footnote of table) contained a sequencing of elements which suggested the equivalence of two stimuli, X and Z, each paired with the same response, Y. They considered this figure therefore to be S-equiva-

Table 13.6 Syllogisms of Second and Third Figures Each Used in Five Different Syllogistic Modes* (After Pezzoli and Frase, 1968)

Mode of Syllogism	Syllogisms of Second Figure	Syllogisms of Third Figure

EAI	No X are Y.
	All Z are Y.
	   Some X are Z.
		No Y are X.
		All Y are Z.
		   Some X are Z.

EEI	No X are Y.
	No Z are Y.
	   Some X are Z.
		No Y are X.
		No Y are Z.
		   Some X are Z.

AOI	All X are Y.
	Some Z are not Y.
	   Some X are Z.
		All Y are X.
		Some Y are not Z.
		   Some X are Z.

III	Some X are Y.
	Some Z are Y.
	   Some X are Z.
		Some Y are X.
		Some Y are Z.
		   Some X are Z.

IEI	Some X are Y.
	No Z are Y.
	   Some X are Z.
		Some Y are X.
		No Y are Z.
		   Some X are Z.

*The terms "figure" and "mode" refer in formal logic to the properties of syllogisms. *Figure* refers to the sequencing of elements in the premises and conclusion. *Mode* refers to the use of the logical words, such as *all, some, no, not.*

lent. In contrast, the arrangement of elements in the third figure suggested that X and Z were equivalent responses to Y as a stimulus. This figure was therefore designated as R-equivalent. It was felt that the S-equivalent figure should facilitate reasoning especially with high associations of X and Y, and Z and Y. The R-equivalent figure was viewed as inviting interference which would increase as association strength increased, thus being detrimental to syllogistic reasoning and causing more errors in judgment.

The results of the experiment are pictured in Fig. 13.2 which shows how the number of reasoning errors was related to associative strength between the words placed in the syllogisms of either the S-equivalent or R-equivalent types. The data points at the far right are of primary interest. When highly associated words were inserted, the R-equivalent syllogisms showed an upsurge of errors. In the S-equivalent syllogisms, the

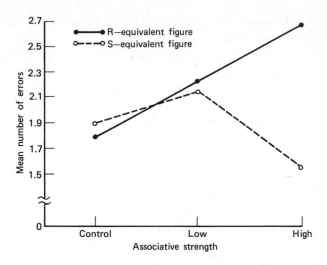

Fig. 13.2. Mean number of judgmental errors as a function of associative strengths of words used in syllogisms of two types. (After Pezzoli and Frase, 1968.)

words of high relationship reduced the mean number of errors. Pezzoli and Frase concluded that associative relations exert an influence on deductive reasoning. Verbal learning research and word association studies thus appear to be significant sources of principles and processes for the student of problem solving or thinking.

Solving Anagrams

The anagram task, challenging subjects to rearrange a group of letters to form a word, represents a convenient format for studying problem solving with solution time providing an index of performance. Johnson (1966) has reviewed much of the research, emphasizing recent progress in refined identification of the determinants of anagram solving. Analytic work has tended to relate this task to various parts of the realm of words and verbal behavior. As we noted in Chapter 1, this special form of problem solving may be considered one example of how systematic research has yielded behavior laws. Variables ranging from frequency of word usage to frequencies and positions of bigrams in words have been found relevant. On the subjective side, an induced mental set in subjects for certain types of solution has been shown to be quite powerful.

An experiment carried out by Ekstrand and Dominowski (1968) provides us with an example of this type of research. It was directed at an old question: "If an anagram to be rearranged to form a word is itself in the form of another word, does this facilitate or hinder solution?" These investigators designed an experiment with a number of variables carefully controlled so that they might get an unequivocal answer to this question. A quick understanding of the investigation may be gained by examining Table 13.7 which lists the 11 words used as anagrams (*W*), the nonsense

Table 13.7 Word Anagrams (*W*), Nonsense Anagrams (*N*), and Solutions (After Ekstrand and Dominowski, 1968)

W Anagrams	*N* Anagrams	Solutions
Froth	Frtho	Forth
Cheat	Athce	Teach
Thorn	Hontr	North
Shrub	Bhsur	Brush
Canoe	Eanoc	Ocean
Beard	Berad	Bread
Diver	Deriv	Drive
Bleat	Bleta	Table
Shelf	Heslf	Flesh
Sauce	Ceusa	Cause
Sleet	Etesl	Steel

anagrams (*N*) formed from the same letters, and the solution word for each *W* or *N* anagram. The *W* and *N* lists were devised to provide equivalence of the problem items on such formal indices as number of moves to rearrange letters for solution and total frequency of bigram occurrences for the anagrams.

Although the 2 anagram lists (*W* and *N*) might suggest just 2 experimental treatments and groups, the experiment was somewhat more complex in design. For the *N* anagrams, different instructions were given to different groups of subjects. One condition required that 1 solution word be sought; the other asked that subjects look for 2 solution words —for example, TEACH and also CHEAT, from ATHCE. *N1* and *N2* were the designations given to these conditions, while *W* indicated the condition where words were the original anagrams to be rearranged. On these 3 conditions, 2 different preliminary treatments were imposed. Half of the subjects under *N1, N2,* and *W* were primed by having read to them a list of the solution words just before they began work on their anagrams; the remaining half, of course, were not primed in this manner.

Subjects from the 6 groups were tested individually. Each anagram from the appropriate list was presented on a 3 x 5 card, typed in lower case letters. A stopwatch was used by the experimenter to time the solutions, which were given orally. A time limit of 120 sec was imposed, this value being recorded if an anagram was not solved. Thirteen different orders of problem presentation were used for the 13 subjects in each group. Table 13.8 gives the results for the 6 conditions in mean solution time for those solutions which were achieved.

Table 13.8 Mean Time Score (Sec) on Critical Problems That Were Solved (After Ekstrand and Dominowski, 1968)

	*N*2	*N*1	*W*
Primed	12.46	7.85	14.15
Not primed	20.92	13.00	22.54

Inspection of the data quickly shows that priming did speed anagram solving for each kind of instruction and stimulus item. On the question of words as anagrams, the data require some interpretation. The most appropriate comparison for Condition *W* is with *N1*. Statistical analysis indicated that *W* stimuli required significantly greater solution times than *N1*. The word configuration seems to hinder rearrangement. The reason for not considering *N2* as a comparison is that the mean solution times are inflated by those cases where the critical solution was found as the second one. Further analysis of their data convinced Ekstrand and Dominowski that the evident hampering of solutions under Condition *W* was a genuine difference from the anagram solving of Condition *N1*.

Gambling Choice

A special kind of problem solving occurs when no response is correct for sure and reaching a satisfactory solution is by no means certain. This is the situation faced in gambling where risk and possible reward must be considered in decision making. Behaviors governed by probable outcomes have been studied in a number of psychological investigations, often devised as simulated games of chance. In most studies the risky opportunities offered to subjects have been artificial, unrelated to real gain or loss. In the research we shall review, however, such hypothetical gaming was compared to betting behavior with actual monetary gain or loss as possible outcomes.

To play or not to play, that was the question faced by a subject in the duplex gamble used in the experiment by Slovic (1969). An example of a duplex gamble is presented in Figure 13.3. The two discs are considered to have spinning pointers on them. Each pointer must be spun to complete a play—the left one to determine possible winnings, the right one to ascertain possible loss. On any play, an individual might win and not lose, both win and lose, lose but not win, or neither win nor lose. The dollar labels and the fractional sector sizes of the discs indicate the values of payoff and risk for this particular duplex gamble. These were the four variables of the experiment:

P_W = the probability of a win.
$\$_W$ = the amount to be won.
P_L = the probability of a loss.
$\$_L$ = the amount to be lost.

It was the aim of the study to see how these risk dimensions would affect the subjects' choices among pairs of duplex gambles. Such choices—which gamble to play—were studied under two different conditions. Group H played under *hypothetical* conditions, the subjects knowing that no monetary risk was actually involved. Group RP engaged in *real play* on a portion of the gambles they chose; they actually might lose if their plays were poor risks or if luck ran against them, or they might be lucky and win some amount of money.

A total of 18 pairs of duplex gambles were constructed. One of these is shown in Figure 13.4. Within each pair a subject had to indicate his preference for playing the upper or the lower duplex gamble as portrayed with its four values of P_W, $\$_W$, P_L and $\$_L$. The pairs had been devised so that each tended to pit one variable against another. For example, in Pair 1 as shown in Figure 13.4 the upper duplex gamble features $\$_W$ as an attraction while the lower pair offers P_W as particularly attractive. In choosing between them a subject tends to indicate whether $\$_W$ or P_W is

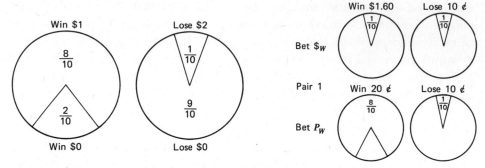

Fig. 13.3. (*Left*) Example of a duplex gamble. Both discs would have pointers on them for real play. Both would be spun. The dollar labels indicate the possible amounts to be won or lost and the fractional sector sizes indicate the likelihood of each of the possible outcomes. (After Slovic, 1969.)

Fig. 13.4. (*Right*) One of the pairs of duplex gambles used in the experiment (upper or lower pair to be selected by subject). (After Slovic, 1969.)

stressed in his gambling choice. In the entire 18 pairs each such direct test of two variables was included 3 times. A subject whose choice of duplex gamble favored one variable over another at least twice was identified as considering the more selected variable as more important.

Group H subjects ($N=184$), whose gambling was only hypothetical, were run in a group. They merely indicated their choice between paired duplex gambles by checking a printed version of the task. Group RP subjects ($N=29$) were run individually, being informed that some of their choices would actually be played. They were given $1.50 to start the game when real play began.

The data tabulation took the form of percent (or proportion) of subjects evidently favoring one variable as more important than another as their choices were made. Table 13.9 shows the results for the two groups. Three underlined values in the table indicate where one group showed a significantly stronger preference than the other. In Group H the variable of $\$_w$ appears to have been dominant. Group RP showed no such dominant choice. The risk of real play made subjects give relatively more attention to variables other than the amount to be won. It is evident that gambling behavior differs substantially in real play when contrasted with merely hypothetical situations. As Slovic had expected, subjects boldly play to maximize *hypothetical* winnings but strive more to protect against

Table 13.9 Percent of Subjects Who Preferred the Row
Dimension over the Column Dimension (After Slovic, 1969)

Part I. Group H—Hypothetical Play

Dimension Preferred over:	$\$_W$	P_W	$\$_L$	P_L
$\$_W$		65	77	70
P_W	35		$\overline{56}$	67
$\$_L$	23	44		51
P_L	30	33	49	

Part II. Group RP—Real Play

Dimension Preferred over:	$\$_W$	P_W	$\$_L$	P_L
$\$_W$		41	52	55
P_W	59		34	55
$\$_L$	48	66		48
P_L	45	$\overline{45}$	52	

loss when real money is at stake. His findings pose a problem for further studies of risk-taking behavior. Simulated situations seem not to yield results that are generalizable to real life conditions.

Response Chaining

Problem solving often involves trial-and-error behavior before a solution is achieved. Psychologists have devised some laboratory tasks which make such behavior observable and measurable. Such tasks permit the experimental manipulation of certain independent variables which influence the learning and problem solving. In introducing the research from which we shall examine one experiment, Davis (1967) pointed out that the task variables may parallel the hypothetical variables of certain learning theories. A laboratory task constructed to pose artificial problems of a specific sort may thus have a general utility in exploring the processes of problem solving behavior.

Davis constructed an apparatus in which the pressing of lever switches would turn different lights in a 3 x 4 display matrix either on or off. This laboratory task offered great versatility in posing problems for subjects and in arranging the conditions governing the required learning and problem solving. We shall review Experiment II of his report in which the major variable was the number of switches required to illuminate the two red lights in the 12-light matrix. A second condition was the presence or absence of an extra distractor switch which operated a red light but was not relevant to the problem solution. The dependent variable which concerns us was the mean number of switch presses which subjects made in solving the five problems assigned under each experimental condition.

Forty-eight students at the University of Wisconsin served as subjects. They were assigned to one of eight experimental conditions. The five problems given to each group of 6 required 2, 3, 4, or 5 switches to solve; there either was or was not a distractor switch for different conditions. A total of 10 switches was available under each condition, the extra ones affecting some of the white lights but not relating to problem solution. In the analogy which Davis made with behavior theory, the relevant switches were symbolic of the number of responses which must be chained together to solve a particular problem. The distractor switch represents a response which may receive reinforcement but is actually not needed in the solution.

The results of Experiment II are portrayed in Figure 13.5. It is very

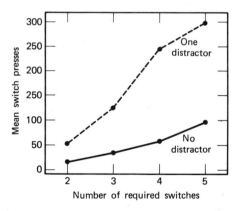

Fig. 13.5. Mean number of switch presses used in problem solution as a function of the number of required switches in the problem-solving chain. The number of distractor switches (0 or 1) was the parameter which led to the two different functions shown. (After Davis, 1967.)

Problem Solving   **500**

evident that having more switches in the problem-solving chain of responses resulted in a much-lengthened series of switch presses to arrive at a problem solution. The presence of a distractor switch greatly increased the amount of switch pressing, especially as the number of required switches increased. This interaction between the variables was statistically significant as were the main affects.

Summary

Problem solving is not a single psychological process but a complex kind of behavior which is, in part, situationally defined. The elements of the situation usually include a specified goal, various stimuli or cues, several response possibilities, and some means of guiding progress toward the goal. Problem tasks of great variety, incorporating these basic aspects, have been used in laboratory experiments. These were introduced by means of samples ranging from Concept Identification to Reaching a Decision. Our research aims include the description of all the processes which interact as our subjects work at solving problems. These aims are best served through interrelated experiments that provide tasks having manipulable dimensions and permitting one or more meaningful measures of behavior. Numerical, verbal, and pictorial materials, as well as apparatus tasks, can meet these criteria for laboratory studies. Commonly used research methods fall into classes that include concept identification, games and puzzles, probability situations, and tasks requiring reasoning or practical accomplishment.

The heart of concept identification research is the manipulation of cues that are a part of complex stimulus patterns. One way to vary task difficulty is through using concepts which differ in the logical simplicity or complexity of their definitions. Another task characteristic is the sequence in which the different relevant and irrelevant cues are included in the concept instances displayed to subjects. Response tendencies, tested in prior research, may be woven into the fabric of a study by proper choice of stimulus items. These may be varied with respect to their dominance in eliciting specific verbal associations. All of these experimental approaches were illustrated in different studies we examined.

Besides reviewing research on concept identification we examined studies of many sorts that clearly showed the great number of ways in which problem solving may be investigated. In some cases the selected experiments employed methods and variables that had already been partially tested. Our attention was given to the following examples of investigations: associative aspects of syllogistic reasoning, solution of word versus nonsense anagram arrangements, gambling choices in hypothetical and real play, and response chaining as influenced by task complexity.

References

Anderson, R. C., & Guthrie, J. T. Effects of some sequential manipulations of relevant and irrelevant stimulus dimensions on concept learning. *Journal of Experimental Psychology*, 1966, **72**, 501–504.

Battig, W. F. Some factors affecting performance on a word-formation problem. *Journal of Experimental Psychology*, 1957, **54**, 96–104.

Bourne, L. E., Jr., & Battig, W. F. Complex processes. In J. B. Sidowski (Ed.), *Experimental methods and instrumentation in psychology*. New York: McGraw-Hill, 1966. Pp. 541–576.

Clark, H. H. Linguistic processes in deductive reasoning. *Psychological Review*, 1969, **76**, 387–404.

Davis, G. A. Current status of research and theory in human problem solving. *Psychological Bulletin*, 1966, **66**, 36–54.

Davis, G. A. Detrimental effects of distraction, additional response alternatives, and longer response chains in solving switch-light problems. *Journal of Experimental Psychology*, 1967, **73**, 45–55.

Duncker, K. On problem-solving. *Psychological Monographs*, 1945, **58**, No. 5 (Whole No. 270).

Ekstrand, B. R., & Dominowski, R. L. Solving words as anagrams: II. A clarification. *Journal of Experimental Psychology*, 1968, **77**, 552–558.

Faust, W. L. Factors in individual improvement in solving Twenty-Questions problems. *Journal of Experimental Psychology*, 1958, **55**, 39–44.

Gardner, R. A., & Runquist, W. N. Acquisition and extinction of problem-solving set. *Journal of Experimental Psychology*, 1958, **55**, 274–277.

Glucksberg, S., & Weisberg, R. W. Verbal behavior and problem solving: Some effects of labeling in a functional fixedness problem. *Journal of Experimental Psychology*, 1966, **71**, 659–664.

Haygood, R. C., & Bourne, L. E., Jr. Attribute- and rule-learning aspects of conceptual behavior. *Psychological Review*, 1965, **72**, 175–195.

Hovland, C. I. A set of flower designs for experiments in concept-formation. *American Journal of Psychology*, 1953, **66**, 140–142.

Huttenlocher, J. Constructing spatial images: A strategy in reasoning. *Psychological Review*, 1968, **75**, 550–560.

Johnson, D. M. Solution of anagrams. *Psychological Bulletin*, 1966, **66**, 371–384.

Kendler, H. H., & Kendler, T. S. Reversal-shift behavior: Some basic issues. *Psychological Bulletin*, 1969, **72**, 229–232.

Little, K. B., & Lintz, L. M. Information and certainty. *Journal of Experimental Psychology*, 1965, **70**, 428–432.

Mayzner, M. S., & Tresselt, M. E. Anagram solution times: A function of multiple-solution anagrams. *Journal of Experimental Psychology*, 1966, **71**, 66–73.

Mednick, S. A., & Halpern, S. Ease of concept attainment as a function of associative rank. *Journal of Experimental Psychology*, 1962, **64**, 628–630.

Neisser, U., & Weene, P. Hierarchies in concept attainment. *Journal of Experimental Psychology*, 1962, **64**, 640–645.

Pezzoli, J. A., & Frase, L. T. Mediated facilitation of syllogistic reasoning. *Journal of Experimental Psychology*, 1968, **78**, 228–232.

Ray, W. S. Complex tasks for use in human problem-solving research. *Psychological Bulletin*, 1955, **52**, 134–149.

Ray, W. S. *The experimental psychology of original thinking*. New York: Macmillan, 1967.

Slamecka, N. J. A methodological analysis of shift paradigms in human discrimination learning. *Psychological Bulletin*, 1968, **69**, 423–438.

Slovic, P. Differential effects of real versus hypothetical payoffs on choices among gambles. *Journal of Experimental Psychology*, 1969, **80**, 434–437.

Underwood, B. J., & Richardson, J. Some verbal materials for the study of concept formation. *Psychological Bulletin*, 1956, **53**, 84–95.

Wolff, J. L. Concept-shift and discrimination-reversal learning in humans. *Psychological Bulletin*, 1967, **68**, 369–408.

chapter 14
Motivation

Motives are the energizers of behavior. Their conceptualization in psychological theory has for decades been quite fragmented. Echoing the theorists, lecturers in psychology classes have filled chalkboards with lists of numerous motivational states. There are the basic biological drives such as hunger, thirst, and sex. There are learned motives such as acquisitiveness, competition, and social affiliation. In the emotional realm there are positive feelings ranging from mild pleasure to euphoria and ecstasy and negative states of anger, anxiety, disgust, fear, and frustration—all with great potential for giving thrust and direction to behavior.

Research on motivation has often dealt with one particular state or another—biological drive or learned motive, positive affective tone or negative emotion. Although they are usually investigated one at a time, these variables are typically not studied in isolation but in their natural impact on processes such as conditioning, learning, memory, perception, and social interaction. For example, dozens of experiments that investigated the impact of motivation on memory have been reviewed by Weiner (1966). The contributions of level of motivation to psychological processes have been inferred from data collected under a variety of experimental conditions. Much of the research has been directed at examining physiological indicants of drives and affective states, and much of it has used animal subjects so that deprivations, harsh stimulation, and long-term treatments could be used. There has been a substantial amount of investigation with human subjects as well, and it is these studies that will occupy our attention in this chapter. The great scope of experimentation on motivation is exemplified in the research reports collected and presented by Haber (1966).

Beyond the experiments on particular motives there has emerged a more general concern with certain functional roles in which these states interact with psychological processes such as learning. Prominent in this refinement of theory and research are the topics of activation or arousal, incentive, and reinforcement. These have been extensively treated in reviews by Berlyne (1967) and Appley (1970). We may briefly consider these concepts here; experiments in which they are investigated will concern us later.

Reinforcement

Berlyne claims that any serious student of learning must deal with *reinforcement* no matter what his theoretical predilection. Although it is difficult to define and it takes on many guises, he sees it as a necessary condition if learning is to occur. Reinforcement relates to motive states in a variety of ways. A reinforcement may be a satisfier of a basic drive, for example, food obtained by a hungry organism. Or it may relate to acquired motives such as are reflected in the act of paying attention or exploring out of curiosity, rewarded by gaining new information. Besides reward or positive goal attainment psychologists use "reinforcement" to cover the negative situation of punishment, which tends to strengthen avoidance rather than approach responses. The relationship of reinforcement to motivation and emotion in a behavior sequence might be something like: *Motive State—Response—Reinforcement*—possible change in *Emotion* (or *Affect*), either positive or negative—possible change in *Motive State,* either intensifying or reducing it in some degree.

Incentive

An *incentive* might be briefly defined as an indication (with resultant expectation) of a reinforcement that may be obtained. As discussed by Appley, the concept is closely parallel to motivation since its effect on behavior is said to be energizing. It relates also to reinforcement in that it is viewed as an anticipation of reinforcing events, based on experience. We might consider that incentive-motivation is a motive state acquired by the organism through interaction with the environment. As a concept it has been enmeshed in theoretical debates which may have obscured its general utility.

Arousal

A state of *activation* or *arousal* has much to recommend it for a place in behavior theory. It tends to parallel the older notion of drive level. It can encompass emotions as well as motive states, possibly blending the two. Reinforcement may be defined as either an increase or a decrease in arousal level. Finally, various physiological indices, and even subjects' reports, may be sought as indicants which are related to the behavioral manifestations of arousal level in learning and performance. All this is not to suggest that the concept is without debate. Berlyne makes it clear that controversy continues to stem from both research findings and theorizing dealing with arousal or activation. In his own view, experimentation shows arousal level to be affected by three classes of variable:

1. *Psychophysical* (stimulus intensity and other characteristics of stimulation);

2. *Ecological* (internal visceral and hormonal changes);

3. *Collative* (relational properties of stimulus configurations as in complexity and incongruity).

Arousal Level

As a theoretical concept arousal level has the potential for bringing together a wide variety of empirically observed effects. The experiments we shall review exemplify each of the three classes of independent variable which Berlyne listed—psychophysical, ecological, and collative. One study dealt with hunger drive, its level of arousal being inferred from the time since the last meal. This would be an ecological variable with its basis in internal bodily states. Also representing ecological variables are arousal states of anxiety and general activation as compared in a different study. These variables were not experimentally manipulated but were assessed by administering self-report inventories to subjects; then the effect of reported arousal level on task performance was examined. An example of a psychophysical variable for elevating arousal level is the use of noise directed at subjects as they engage in a task. Still a different way of manipulating arousal is the use of a long period of sensory deprivation, subjects being kept in an isolation chamber. Finally an example of a collative variable is the use of stimulus complexity or variation to elevate affective arousal or pleasant feelings. All of these techniques were used in the different investigations we shall review.

Hunger in Learning and Recalling Food Words

Manipulation of the hunger drive has been far more common in animal research than in studies of human subjects. The college student has "volunteered" for some experiments, however. Saugstad (1966, 1967) has examined a number of investigations which sought the effects of food deprivation on perception-cognition. Here we shall consider an experiment in which Epstein and Levitt (1962) determined how the learning and retention of food-designating words were affected by two amounts of food deprivation.

Sixty fraternity brothers at the University of Massachusetts served as paid participants in the study. At the time of paired associate learning 30 were hungry (just before the evening meal) and 30 were not hungry (just after the meal). At recall a day later each of these groups was subdivided so that the 30 tested for recall when hungry came equally from the hungry and not-hungry groups of the learning sessions. Similarly, the two levels of hunger at learning contributed 15 men each to the not-hungry recall test. The paired associate word list contained 4 food-word pairs, 4 nonfood pairs, and 4 mixed pairs with a food word as either the stimulus or the response. The 12 pairs were: Fruit-Apple, Cheese-Cracker, Waffle-Steak, Cake-Ham, Carpet-Rug, Lamp-Light, Room-Sofa, Bed-Window, Egg-Stair, Stew-Ceiling, House-Butter, Screen-Potato. High associative strength, deliberately included within certain pairs, contributed to ease of learning as expected, but this finding will not concern us further.

The results for the original learning were that the hungry group learned significantly faster than the nonhungry group. Also, both groups learned the food words more readily than the nonfood words. Here the hungry group did not differ from the control group. When the mixed-item pairs were examined in another data analysis, Epstein and Levitt found a significant interaction. As may be seen in Figure 14.1 the hungry students (4–5 hours without food) did better on pairs with a food stimulus. The nonhungry students did better when the food word was the response. The authors of the report caution that this interaction might have depended on the use of particular words in the list.

At recall testing the day after learning, another interaction was found as shown in Figure 14.2. It was found that level of hunger at recall

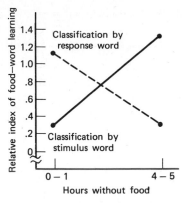 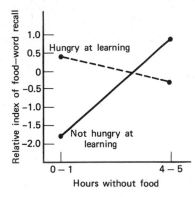

Fig. 14.1. (*Left*) Relative index of food-word learning for stimulus or response items as a function of hours without food. (After Epstein and Levitt, 1962.)
Fig. 14.2. (*Right*) Relative index of food-word recall as a function of hours without food at recall testing as determined for subjects who were hungry or not hungry at time of original learning. (After Epstein and Levitt, 1962.)

made no significant difference in selective recall of food words for those subjects who had been hungry at learning. For those who had not been hungry for the original learning, however, food-word recall was significantly better for the group who were hungry at the recall test than for those tested just after their meal. Although statistically significant, the two different interactions found in this experiment are not easy to interpret. Certain cautions are offered by the investigators. In view of the relatively mild drive state, the high association word pairs, the short list, and the small number of subjects who were tested in groups, it would appear that further research is desirable.

Activation and Anxiety

Motivational effects of individuals' anxiety states have been tested in a variety of conditioning and learning situations. Theoretical considerations and empirical findings have been treated by Spence and Spence (1966). With particular reference to verbal learning methodologies and processes, Goulet (1968) has called for more precise studies of how the level of anxiety plays a motivational role in learning. Since we cannot here review the extensive literature, which involves several measures of anxiety and numerous learning tasks, we may examine just one experiment which gaged arousal level in two different ways in a verbal learning session.

Experiment I from a study conducted by Thayer and Cox (1968) demonstrates two different forms of arousal measurement—the Manifest Anxiety (*MA*) scale and the Activation-Deactivation Adjective Check List (*AD-ACL*). Using these two instruments to divide subjects into high and low groups on each scale, the experimenters analyzed verbal learning scores to test certain theoretical predictions. We may briefly consider the two different testing procedures and then see how the learning study was carried out.

The *MA* scale explores the manifest anxiety level which characterizes any individual by having him respond to statements which comprise the functional part of a self-report inventory. By taking the inventory a person reveals whether he is moderate, low, or high in anxiety with respect to group scores. Since anxiety level is considered to correlate with drive or arousal, experimenters have been interested especially in the performances on learning tasks of High Anxious (*HA*) and Low Anxious (*LA*) subjects.

The *AD-ACL* consists of a set of self-descriptive adjectives each accompanied by a 4-point scale. For each adjective, an individual checks its applicability to his present feeling state by checking 1 of the 4 statements:

_____ Definitely do not feel

_____ Cannot decide

_____ Feel slightly

_____ Definitely feel

Seven of the adjectives such as *energetic* or *lively* form a General Activation scale which was used to segregate high and low activation groups in this study.

Thayer and Cox gave a paired associate learning task to a group of 74 male college students. The list to be learned contained dominant response items and very few competing responses. Learning theory and past findings suggested that such a list should be learned more readily by subjects of higher arousal level (or drive level) as measured in past work using the *MA* scale. Just before the 4 learning trials, subjects responded to the Activation-Deactivation Adjective Check List. After the learning task had been presented, with responses recorded in prepared booklets, the investigators administered the Manifest Anxiety scale.

In accordance with past research, subjects were divided to segregate the learning data into *HA* and *LA* groups and also independently into groups highest and lowest on General Activation. Their performance on the 3 learning trials that were scored was then examined; (an earlier trial was a study trial). The percent of responses which were correct for these subgroups were as follows:

	Trial		
	1	2	3
High Anxiety	61.3	77.8	87.5
Low Anxiety	69.7	87.3	94.3
High General Activation	72.4	89.2	94.3
Low General Activation	61.4	81.0	89.7

Contrary to past findings with this list construction, the *HA* group actually did more poorly than the *LA* group, although differences between them were not statistically significant. For the General Activation subgroups a different picture emerged. The High General-Activation group performed better on every trial, the difference in learning scores being significant. Although the prediction consonant with past findings on Manifest Anxiety was not borne out, the check list scores indicating the subgroup activation or arousal levels proved to be a determinant of learning performance in accordance with theory.

Timing of Arousal

As contrasted with examining data from selected subjects whose self-reports indicate different levels of arousal, the experiment we shall review next was one in which arousal was manipulated by external stimulation. Pursuing earlier indications that white noise (a mixture of numerous vibration frequencies) had arousal properties, Berlyne, Borsa, Hamacher, and Koenig (1966) sought to determine its effect on paired associate verbal learning and recall. More particularly, they investigated the effects of the timing of the noise presentation and its resultant elevation of arousal. The timing of the loud noise (75 dB) with respect to the stimulus-response presentations and/or the 6-sec interval between a pair and the next stimulus is indicated in Figure 14.3, which defines the 4 experimental conditions.

Sixty-four female undergraduates, serving as subjects, had to learn 40 adjective-male name pairs by the anticipation method. For each block of 10 pairs, subjects received a different one of the white noise conditions as accompaniment to the word presentations. The conditions and the different sublists of words were varied in sequence over several subgroups of subjects. Recall test trials without noise were conducted either immediately after three training trials on the 40-pair list or 24 hr later. The test scores emerging from the different experimental conditions were studied to see if white noise arousal in some particular temporal correspondence with training events had affected immediate or delayed recall, i.e., original learning or 24-hr retention.

Mean numbers of correctly recalled response terms are shown in Table 14.1 for each condition separately and for certain combinations of conditions (covering 20 pairs instead of 10). In studying the anticipation

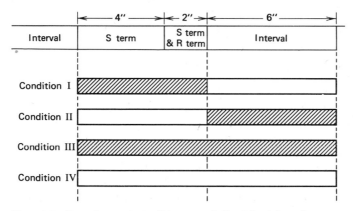

Fig. 14.3. Experimental conditions as defined by interval during which noise (cross-hatching) was present during paired-associate training. Under Condition I noise accompanied S-R presentation. Under Condition II it occurred during the interval between pairs. Under Condition III it lasted for both these brief periods. Under Condition IV it was not employed. (After Berlyne et al., 1966.)

Table 14.1 Mean Number of Correct Responses in Immediate and Delayed Recall Tests for Different Single and Combined Experimental Conditions (After Berlyne et al., 1966)

Experimental Condition	Immediate Recall	Delayed Recall
I	6.3	4.1
II	6.1	3.6
III	5.9	4.0
IV	6.2	3.6
I and III	12.2	8.1*
II and IV	12.3	7.2*
I and IV	12.5	7.7
II and III	12.0	7.6

*Significantly different from each other, $p < .025$.

scores made during training, the experimenters had found no differential effects due to the white noise conditions. As the first column of means in the table shows, this was also the case for the immediate test of recall. At the 24-hr test, however, there was significantly greater recall for the sublists learned under Conditions I and III when compared with Conditions II and IV. Reference to Figure 14.3 shows that I and III were the conditions in which the white noise was being presented during the exposure of the stimulus and the response for study. During Conditions II and IV the S-R exposures had been unaccompanied by the noise. The data show that the presence or absence of white noise *after* the response made no significant difference.

Returning to the difference that was found in 24-hr recall, the investigators interpret it as a beneficial effect of arousal upon retention since the data for original training and immediate testing had shown no differences among conditions. The lack of immediate effect cannot be taken as a generalization, though, since the report indicates that past research has sometimes revealed a beneficial effect and sometimes a detrimental effect in immediate recall after training under arousal. The authors suggest that the degree of arousal and its timing are probably interactive with other variables in their impact on immediate recall.

Sensory Deprivation

A distinctive and somewhat drastic method of manipulating motivation was used in an experiment by Suedfeld, Glucksberg, and Vernon (1967). These investigators used sensory deprivation (SD) of subjects as a drive-arousing operation. Male college students in 4 SD groups experienced 24 hr of isolation, lying on a bed in a darkened sound-deadened chamber before engaging in the assigned problem-solving task. Four other groups were assigned to NSD conditions which involved no sensory deprivation. Another motivational manipulation used for half the conditions was the offering of a financial incentive for speedy solution of the problem. The combinations of sensory deprivation (or lack of it) with monetary incentive (or none) provided the experimental conditions which were considered to represent three drive or arousal levels.

Low Drive Level
    No sensory deprivation and no monetary
    incentive
Moderate Drive Level
    No sensory deprivation; monetary incentive
    given, or
    Sensory deprivation; no monetary incentive
High Drive Level
    Both sensory deprivation and monetary incentive

The monetary incentive for the paid volunteer subjects was an extra $5.00 given to the best 25 percent in the problem solving, with $20.00 awarded for the speediest performance of all. The motivational manipulations were combined with 2 task variations so that 8 conditions comprised the experiment.

The problem assigned to be solved at the end of sensory deprivation (or without SD, depending on the experimental condition) was to use some objects in order to affix a candle to the wall. This task was performed by all subjects in the dark chamber used for SD. This was done to preserve the SD state of those subjects who had been in 24-hr isolation. The objects placed on a table for use in solving the problem were a candle, a book of safety matches, and a box of thumbtacks. Actually, this listing represents the task condition of High Response Competition (HRC) since the pasteboard box tends to be perceived as merely the container for the tacks. This perception competes with perceiving the pasteboard box as very useful in getting the candle mounted on the wall. In the condition of Low Response Competition (LRC) the tacks were strewn on the table and the box was empty. It could be readily considered as available to use in solving the candle problem.

Nine or ten men served in each of the 8 experimental conditions combining drive level and task variation, HRC or LRC. As expected HRC made the problem difficult to solve in the 15 min allowed. In the subgroups of HRC the percent of subjects completing the task ranged from 40 to 80. In contrast the results showed 78 to 100 percent of LRC subjects arriving at the solution. Median solution times were determined for the 2 task variations in combination with the 3 drive levels. These are plotted in Figure 14.4 which shows a V-shaped function relating performance to drive level for each task variation. This finding is consonant with the Yerkes-Dodson law which states that for any task there will be an optimal range of motivation level which yields superior performance when compared to levels much lower or higher. In the findings of Suedfeld, Glucksberg, and Vernon we see that the moderate level of drive

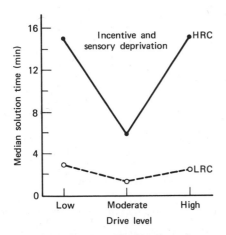

Fig. 14.4. Median solution time (in minutes) as a function of drive level with Conditions HRC or LRC as a parameter yielding different V-shaped relationships. (After Suedfeld, Glucksberg, and Vernon, 1967.)

or arousal—achieved in two different ways, either sensory deprivation or monetary incentive—led to faster problem solving than did the high or low levels.

Stimulus Variation and Arousal of Affect

A general hypothesis concerning affective arousal level is that people tend to prefer, or find most pleasant, a moderate amount of stimulus variation in their environment. Either too little or too great variation in stimulation tend to be less pleasant or even unpleasant. In a test of this postulation Vitz (1966) used tape-recorded sequences of tones which ranged from a minimal level to a very great amount of variation in frequency, loudness, and duration of the pure tones comprising the sequences. Each tone sequence was comprised of randomly ordered pure tones (with the required variation in characteristics) separated by a silent interval of 0.05 sec. The variations in the different tonal dimensions are indicated in Table 14.2 for each tone sequence. Actually the experimenter used three different random series for each different tone sequence designation, providing for testing with 18 different orders.

Table 14.2 Number and Range of Variations in Frequency, Duration, and Loudness in the Six Tone Sequences (After Vitz, 1966)

Tone Sequence Designation	Frequencies (Hz)	Durations (sec)	Loudnesses
1	2 (398, 447)	1 (0.5)	1 (medium)
2	4 (355–501)	2 (0.4, 0.5)	2 (medium-low, medium)
3	6 (316–562)	4 (0.2–0.6)	3 (low, medium-low, medium)
4	8 (282–631)	6 (0.1–1.2)	3 (low, medium-low, medium)
5	12 (224–794)	6 (0.1–1.2)	4 (low-high)
6	17 (100–2512) plus a silent interval	8 (0.05–1.5)	4 (low-high)

From the experimental report we shall consider the data from Study I and the crucial Study II. The first study was used to obtain subjective verification of the objectively created levels of stimulus variation represented in the 6 tone sequences. Thirty-six college students rated the tone sequences on "variation or unexpected change" using a 5-point scale: None (0), A Little (1), Moderate (2), Very Much (3) and Very, Very Much (4). The resultant group mean ratings were found ordered as expected on the basis of objective variation. Sequences 1 through 6 received mean ratings, respectively, of 0.63, 1.36, 2.13, 2.45, 2.90, and 3.47. These mean ratings were used as the index of stimulus variation when the findings of the second study were plotted.

Study II tested the initial hypothesis regarding the affective pleasantness of moderate stimulus variation. A different group of 36 men and women students were asked to rate the pleasantness or unpleasantness of the 6 tone sequences (each presented in 3 different random orders). A 9-point scale was used ranging from Very, Very Unpleasant (-4) through Neutral (0) to Very, Very Pleasant ($+4$). The mean ratings were then plotted against the judged stimulus variation of the 6 tone sequences as determined in Study I. The curvilinear function is presented in Figure 14.5.

As the curve clearly shows, the experimental hypothesis was con-

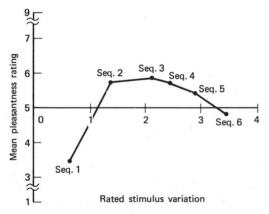

Fig. 14.5. Mean pleasantness rating (Study II) of tone sequences as a function of their rated stimulus variation (Study I). (After Vitz, 1966.)

firmed. Ratings indicating greater pleasantness were given to stimulus variations at the moderate levels. Sequence 1, with minimal variation, was actually judged to be unpleasant to a significant degree. Departures from the trend of the group curve were found, to be sure. Two subjects actually gave their highest rating to Tone Sequence 1; five liked Sequence 6 the most. But the majority of judges preferred the sequences of moderate variation. In Study III, to be summarized here only in its outcome, Vitz found that subjects with musical training and interests rated the sequences more highly on the average than did students with little or no training and no more than a moderate interest in music. Further, the musically trained subjects showed a relatively greater preference for those sequences of higher stimulus variation or complexity.

Incentive

Since incentive is considered to be the anticipation of reinforcement, the most direct way to vary it in human subjects is to indicate in advance that a particular amount or kind of reinforcement is to be contingent on their performance of a task. This may immediately suggest a simple research design with one or more experimental groups being given incentives at the time of task instructions and a control group given no special incentive. A somewhat more complex plan makes each subject serve as his own control. Different incentives are indicated to an individual as each particular trial or test is administered. Then his performances on certain trials may be studied to see which incentives were more effective in elevating task accomplishment.

Both positive and negative incentives have been studied in research using human subjects. Common forms taken by these are the promising of monetary gain for positive incentive and the threat of monetary loss or of mild electric shock as negative incentives. Of course if monetary rewards or electric shocks are actually given during performance trials, the study is actually examining the effects of both incentive and reinforcement as these are usually defined. Manipulating both of these tends to direct the investigation more generally at motivational level. Returning to incentive research, besides seeing how incentive affects performance it is of some interest to see how its removal or termination affects achievement as a task continues in a subsequent period. Incentive effects have been examined in a variety of psychological processes. Our exemplary experiments deal with short-term memory and with vigilance in a visual monitoring task.

Incentives in Short-Term Memory

Two different experiments sought the effects of both positive and negative incentives on short-term memory (STM). We may examine these studies for their similarities in using procedures for introducing incentive levels into STM trials and for their different aims and findings.

Retention interval

Two different retention intervals—4.67 and 15 sec—were investigated by Weiner and Walker (1966). Their 20 subjects had to remember a consonant trigram while engaging in the interpolated activity of reading random single digits from a screen. Of the 80 stimulus CCCs projected for 0.75 sec each in the successive separate memory tests, 10 in each block of 40 trials were projected with each possible background color—red, yellow, green, or white. These colors served as codes to cue the subject as to what reinforcement would be associated with the correct or erroneous recall of the trigram at the end of the retention interval for the trial. The colors accompanying the CCCs thus served as either positive, negative, or control condition incentives. Prior to his memory testing which intermixed trials with each retention interval and each incentive, each subject was well rehearsed in the color-incentive code under which he would be examined, for example:

Color	Incentive
Red	1¢ to be awarded for correct R
Yellow	5¢ to be awarded for correct R
Green	Electric shock on arm if wrong R
White	Neither money nor shock to be given

The percent correct responses at each STM interval is indicated in Figure 14.6 with incentive conditions as the parameter for each separate plotted curve. At the shorter retention interval, trigrams recalled ranged around 80 to 90 percent and there was no significant effect due to incentive variation. At the 15-sec interval, however, retention was less good and two of the incentives yielded significantly better recall than the control. The promise of 1¢ reward yielded performance no better than the control condition, but both 5¢ reward and the threat of shock elevated per-

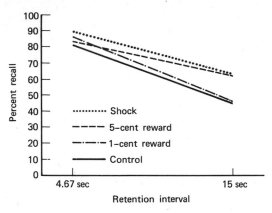

Fig. 14.6. Percent correct recall of CCCs as a function of retention interval under different incentive conditions. (After Weiner and Walker, 1966.)

cent recalled for those trials on which they were used.

Since no differences were found for the shorter retention interval, Weiner and Walker suggest that the different incentives acted during the storage stage of STM as revealed in the 15-sec test data. This led them to the next question, "Did the incentive-motivation conditions produce differential recall by means of their effects on rehearsal?" They indicate that in the paced performance of the interpolated digit-reading task there was no evidence that subjects used different rehearsal strategies under different incentive conditions.

Timing of incentive cues

An experiment related to the preceding one was conducted by Wickens and Simpson (1968). They sought to measure the interpolated activity on the distractor task under different incentive conditions so that they might interpret the recall data on the basis of differential rehearsal if this could be inferred. In addition, they presented the color cue for the incentive at different times in the STM procedure. The incentive was color-coded on the stimulus trigram (CCC) slide, or on the distractor task slide, or on the recall signal slide. In this way it was hoped to determine whether incentives have their differential effect on memory trace formation (TF), trace storage (TS), or trace utilization (TU) at recall, respectively.

In many procedural respects this study by Wickens and Simpson resembled the one by Weiner and Walker which we just reviewed. As an economy in description we may list only the ways in which this experiment differed from the earlier. Wickens and Simpson tested for 15-sec retention of 20 CCC trigrams under three different incentive conditions, color-coded as follows:

Color	Incentive
Red	Electric shock on fingertips if wrong R
Green	5¢ to be awarded for correct R
White	Experimenter's verbal acknowledgment of correct R

The slide administering the interpolated activity showed a 3-digit number from which the subject was to subtract 3 successively until a "?" slide appeared 15-sec later to signal a recall attempt.

The three curves of Figure 14.7 show the percent correct responses for each incentive condition with the timing of the color cue as a parameter distinguishing the functions. Statistical analysis showed that recall was superior under the later incentive cues, Conditions TS and TU. The interaction among the major variables was marginal. However, separate analyses for the 3 timing conditions indicated that only in the TF condition was recall significantly affected by the type of incentive used. Inspection of Figure 14.7 suggests that performance was noticeably reduced when only verbal acknowledgement was promised for a correct response.

In Figure 14.8 are plotted the data on interpolated task performance. Wickens and Simpson recorded the number of backward counting responses given under each experimental condition. In these data they sought to account for differential effects of incentive on recall. As inspection of the curves suggests, it was found that for Conditions TF and TS, the early signal of monetary reward or shock to be anticipated had the effect of reducing the amount of distracting activity in which subjects engaged as compared with their performance under the verbal incentive. Further, backward counting was lower for the shock incentive than for the monetary reward. The experimenters took these data as evidence that early incentive information leads subjects to shirk the distracting task, presumably in favor of rehearsing the stimulus trigram. Some additional evidence for this was the occurrence of some recitation of letters in place of numbers in the successive subtractions. Under Condition TU, with the incentive cue given only as recall is required, the backward counting has

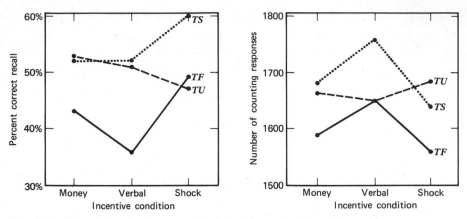

Fig. 14.7. (*Left*) Percent correct recall of CCCs as a function of incentive condition as signalled at time of trace formation (*TF*), trace storage (*TS*), or trace utilization (*TU*). (After Wickens and Simpson, 1968.)

Fig. 14.8. (*Right*) Number of interpolated counting responses as a function of incentive condition as signalled at time of trace formation (*TF*), trace storage (*TS*), or trace utilization (*TU*). (After Wickens and Simpson, 1968.)

ended and cannot be differentially affected by the incentive promised. The data showed no effect as the TU curve of Figure 14.8 indicates.

Monetary Incentives and Vigilance

Vigilance is studied by placing subjects in a monitoring task in which infrequent signals—visual or auditory—have to be detected. Over extended time periods like an hour or two a vigilance decrement is typically observed, the data showing a decreasing percent of signals detected in successive blocks of time. In the vigilance experiment we are considering here, Bergum and Lehr (1964) studied the effect of giving and later withdrawing a monetary incentive for signal detections in a visual monitoring task.

A subject was seated facing a panel on which 20 lights were mounted in a circular array. During the monitoring task the lights were individually illuminated in sequence at a rate which completed the circle 12 times a minute. In this vigilance test a signal to be detected consisted of the failure of any lamp to light up in its turn. Only 12 such signals occurred in an hour, at somewhat irregular intervals. The subject had to push a response button whenever he detected a signal.

Two groups of subjects were run with the following testing schedule: brief instructions; 20-min pretest; 10-min rest and instructions; one-hour monitoring session; 20-min rest period; 90-min monitoring session. The Control Group, 20 U.S. Army trainees, received no special motivational treatment. The experimental subjects, 20 trainees assigned to the Incentive Group, were told just prior to the first monitoring session that they would receive 20¢ for each signal they detected during the session and that they would be penalized 20¢ for each signal they failed to detect. At the beginning of the second session this group was told that this reward and penalty system would no longer be in effect. The experimenters thus sought to determine the effect of a special incentive on monitoring performance in Session 1 and the effect of withdrawing it in Session 2.

Scores for this vigilance testing were the percents of signals detected by each group in each one-third of Session 1 and Session 2. These data are as follows:

Group	Section 1			Section 2		
	a	b	c	a	b	c
Incentive	98	74	66	84	61	59
Control	84	75	68	85	75	85

Bergum and Lehr were interested in the effect on performance of the monetary incentive during Session 1 and its withdrawal for Session 2. As the tabulated data show, the Incentive Group was superior to the Control Group in just the first third of Session 1, a 20-min period. An incentive effect was present but it was evidently quite transient, both groups performing at about the same level during the last 40 min of Session 1. In Session 2 both groups began well but the scores of the Incentive Group, no longer performing with reward or penalty in prospect, fell significantly below the Control Group during the last two-thirds of the testing, 60 min of the 90-min session. Actually the control subjects performed remarkably well in Session 2, not exhibiting a steady decrement in vigilance. The investigators concluded that monetary incentives have only a relatively brief facilitating effect on vigilance test performance. They note further that an incentive condition may actually be detrimental when withdrawn. They feel that theories of activation are too generally stated to account for these results.

Reinforcement

In studies of motivation and learning using animal subjects, reinforcements very often take the form of a quantity of food or water obtained by the hungry or thirsty animal as a consequence of a correct response. With human subjects, as our summaries of experiments will indicate, a reinforcement may often be given in a verbal form or as a token. Statements of "right" or "wrong" are symbolic equivalents of reward and punishment in some learning situations. Token rewards, such as poker chips, may also be considered symbolic or they may be exchangeable for desired items. In this case they are considered to be secondary reinforcers. Some experiments investigate vicarious reinforcement, the rewards observed or heard to be given to another individual. Even self-reward has been studied as a form of reinforcement. Our illustrative examples have been selected to represent this diversity of approaches to reinforcement as studied in the human subject.

Verbal Reinforcers—"Right" and "Wrong"

One of the simplest forms which reinforcement may take when a subject gives a response is for the experimenter to say "Right" (R) if it is correct or "Wrong" (W) if it is incorrect. It must be noted, of course, that such feedback is informative as well as motivational. Besides the RW alternatives for reinforcement there are two related patterns, RN and NW— where N stands for the experimenter's saying nothing at all. In the study we shall examine Buchwald (1959) used all three patterns in the two-choice "coding task" of Experiment I. Subjects were shown 3 x 5 in. cards one at a time. On each card were two nonsense syllables, one above the other, and a 3-digit number. It was the task of the subject to select one of the syllables and respond by saying it aloud. The experimenter would then give informative verbal reinforcement in one of the patterns (RW, RN, NW) *depending under which condition the particular syllable pair had been placed* in the experimental design. Three syllable pairs were used and each was paired with three different numbers on different cards. The numbers were really irrelevant, the two syllables of any pair having been split arbitrarily into a "correct" one and an "incorrect" one. A pack of 216 cards had been prepared to give each subject 72 trials with each syllable pair and its associated reinforcement pattern. Counterbalancing procedures were used for which syllable of a pair was correct for different subjects and which was printed in the upper position on different cards.

When a reinforcement pattern such as RN or NW is used by itself, as in previous research, the meaning of the N event (where the experimenter says nothing at all after a response) can easily be inferred by a subject. In the present study no comment was given, however, for a wrong choice in certain pairs (RN) and for a correct choice in certain others (NW). This made for more difficult learning, since these two patterns of reinforcement gave opposite meanings to the experimenter's silence in different instances.

Buchwald analyzed the incorrect responses given during the 72 trials for each feedback pattern and its associated syllable pair. He tabulated descriptive statistics on the total number of errors made under each reinforcement combination and on the trial number when the last error occurred. These results are presented in Table 14.3.

Table 14.3 Descriptive Statistics on Errors Made Under Each Reinforcement Combination (After Buchwald, 1959)

Part I. Total Number of Errors				
Reinforcement Combination	Mean	Median	Standard Deviation	Range
RN	17.2	8.0	21.0	0–71
NW	10.4	7.0	10.5	1–52
RW	6.2	3.0	6.1	0–22
Part II. Trial Number of Last Error				
Reinforcement Combination	Mean	Median	Standard Deviation	Range
RN	29.3	14.5	28.3	0–72
NW	32.2	31.5	21.0	2–72
RW	15.8	7.5	16.0	0–57

The statistical analysis of Part I of the table showed that the RW combination of reinforcement events led to fewest errors as the tabled values clearly suggest. The RN and NW conditions were not differentiated from each other by two different statistical tests plus a subject-by-subject examination of errors. Analysis of Part II of the tabled data showed that the last error under RW occurred earliest by a reliable amount. Also, the last error under RN occurred reliably earlier than under NW. Buchwald notes that these data depart markedly from results of experiments where a subject received only one reinforcement combination, depending on group assignment. His evaluation of the various experiments leads him to postulate that the N event (silence of experimenter) in this mixed-event design actually takes on reinforcing properties as the study proceeds.

Token Reinforcers

A token reward is considered to be a secondary reinforcer; it generally can be exchanged later for some primary reinforcer such as a candy bar. In a study by Kanfer and Matarazzo (1959) blue poker chips were used as token reinforcers in paired associate verbal learning tasks. Three groups of student nurses were asked to learn two successive lists. List 1 was composed of 6 adjective pairs and List 2 was made up of 6 pairs of nonsense syllables. The learning of each list was carried out by the anticipation method until a subject had earned 20 poker chips by giving 20 correct anticipation responses. A token was sent down a metal chute into an open box beside the subject every time she gave a correct response. The 3 treatment groups differed in the reinforcing value of these tokens. In the Control Group the poker chips were collected by the experimenter at the end of the learning task; there was thus no real secondary value of the tokens for this group. For Group SR, secondary reinforcement value was indicated for the tokens since two of the chips could be exchanged for one kind of small prize as arbitrarily predetermined by the experimenter: a candy bar, or a sample packet of cigarettes, or a sample flask of hand lotion. Group GR was told that the tokens might be exchanged for *any* of the prizes, at the rate of two tokens each; for this generalized reinforcement group, the poker chips had a broader utility. For Groups SR and GR the small prizes for which they were eligible (1 kind for SR; 3 kinds for GR) were on display as they undertook the learning of the lists.

The mean numbers of trials taken to achieve 20 correct responses are shown in Table 14.4 for each group in learning each list. Statistical analysis showed that there was no significant difference among the groups

Table 14.4 Mean Number of Trials Taken in Achieving 20
Correct Responses (After Kanfer and Matarazzo, 1959)

Group	List 1	List 2
Control	47.1	70.9
Group SR	45.1	58.4
Group GR	46.9	52.7

in learning List 1. Evidently the promised redemption of the tokens had no differential incentive value for Groups SR and GR as compared with the Control Group even when the prizes to be won were on display. At least the performance of this rote learning task revealed no difference. For List 2, however, these two secondary reinforcement groups—after cashing in their chips from List 1 learning—showed speedier progress in learning the nonsense syllables than the Control Group exhibited. This was a clearcut result confirming the power of token reinforcement value. Group GR's slight superiority over Group SR was not statistically significant. The expected superiority of generalized reinforcement value was thus not found. (Maybe the girls in Group SR were figuring on trading prizes among themselves later on; the wiles of the women may have offset the wills of the experimenters.)

Direct and Vicarious Reinforcement

One effect which reinforcement can have upon behavior is to increase the probability, or relative frequency, of occurrence of responses of the reinforced class or category. This effect has been investigated in experiments where subjects engaged in the operant behavior of saying words. As a particular class of words is reinforced by the experimenter's saying "Good" it is often found that the frequency of that class of words increases as the performance period continues. In Experiment I reported by Phillips (1968) this direct reinforcement (DR) was compared with two other experimental treatments. One of these was vicarious reinforcement (VR) in which the subject was permitted to listen to the tape-recorded performance of the word production task by another person. The reinforcement "Good" was given to the taped model subject each time he gave a word from the category being reinforced. A third condition was no reinforcement (NR) either direct or vicarious. Each subject did listen to the taped performance of the model subject, but no reinforcement was given. This control condition was required to see how much performance change might occur through imitation of the changing performance of the model subject. The opportunity to imitate was quite inviting since the pacing of the trials was synchronized with the performance being overheard. A tendency to imitate should show an increase of responses in the critical class since the model subject increased in relative frequency of giving such words over the 54-trial blocks of the experiment. These relative frequencies of the critical response were 0.20, 0.40, 0.60, 0.70, and 0.80 in successive blocks of trials. The tape-recorded "subject" and the real subject alternated in saying their response words for a total of 270 trials at 10-sec intervals. Ten earlier trials with the subject saying words were used to examine the base rate of saying words from the critical response class. This category was *human* words—those which might pertain to a human being.

To recapitulate the experimental procedures and the 3 treatments, all subjects performed the task under instructions to say a word each time a small signal light flashed on. All subjects heard words produced by "another person performing the same task." This other person, tape-recorded, showed a marked increase in production of words of the critical response class. Forty-five subjects received no special reinforcement (NR) as they said their words. In another group of 45 a subject heard "Good" over the intercom from the experimenter whenever he produced a critical response, thus getting direct reinforcement (DR). The third group of 45 overheard the experimenter saying "Good" each time a critical response was given by the tape-recorded subject, this condition constituting vicarious reinforcement (VR). Other conditions in the experiment involved varied instructions, but these will not be considered here.

The performances of the three reinforcement groups in giving critical responses (CRs) are shown in Figure 14.9. All groups showed a notable rise in CRs over the 45 min of responding. Statistical analysis showed that the CR production by the direct reinforcement group (DR) was reliably greater and increased at a faster rate than shown under the other conditions. Vicarious reinforcement (VR) led to no better production of CRs than did the imitation presumed to have occurred in the no reinforcement (NR) condition.

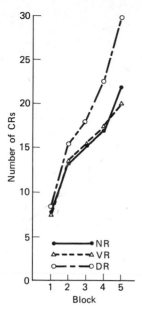

Fig. 14.9. Number of critical responses during each 54-trial block under different conditions of reinforcement as described in the text. (After Phillips, 1968.)

Self-Reward

While most studies of reinforcement naturally have the administering of rewards or punishments arranged by the investigator in accordance with experimental conditions, it is possible to place reinforcement under a subject's own control and still examine its effect on his behavior. This allowing of self-reward (SR) was a prime feature of an experiment by Montgomery and Parton (1970) in which 76 school children were the subjects. After we review the experimental instructions and procedures we shall see how response analysis can indicate if self-reward has a detectable reinforcement effect on responding.

Each child was asked to be seated in front of a panel similar to the schematic representation of Figure 14.10. On every trial the square translucent screen was illuminated from behind in one of 5 hues—blue, orange, red, turquoise, or yellow. The subject then selected and pushed 1 of the 3 response buttons, which turned off the stimulus hue. There ac-

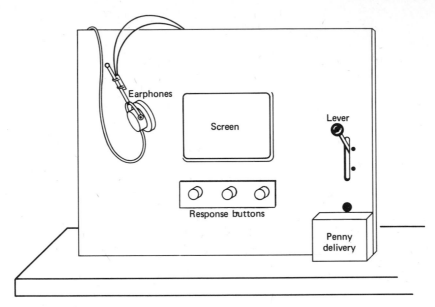

Fig. 14.10. Schematic representation of panel at which the child was seated in the investigation of the reinforcing effect of self-reward.

tually was no correct or incorrect response to be learned. However, the instructions had informed the subject that "each color goes with one button" and that "these earphones will help you learn the game." The earphones were used to deliver a continuous prerecorded white noise (mixed frequencies) at a moderate intensity. It was assumed that this ambiguous signal might make the entire procedure plausible to the children of the third through sixth grades who were subjects.

After making his pushbutton response a subject was to depress the lever at the right if he thought he had pressed the button that was correct. He was also instructed not to operate the lever unless "very sure you pressed the right button for that color." Self-reward (SR) was thus under each subject's own control in accordance with these instructions. Pressing the lever served as its own reward for half the subjects; for the other half, a lever press delivered a penny into the clear plastic box below the lever. The latter subjects were told in advance that pennies would accumulate in the box but that they would not be able to keep the pennies. It was expected that the SR involving the pennies would show a greater reinforcement effect than lever pressing alone. Eighty-five trials were administered with each stimulus hue presented once in each five trials, the hues appearing in random order within the block of trials.

The events in repeat-of-color sequences were examined and segregated into one of 4 categories according to whether or not SR had followed the first response and whether that same response was made the next time that the same hue appeared as the stimulus. Here are examples of the categories.

Category	Sequence of Events for a Repetition of Hue
1	Hue B, R_3, SR . . . . Hue B, R_3
2	Hue B, R_3, no SR . . . . Hue B, R_1 or R_2
3	Hue B, R_3, SR . . . . Hue B, R_1 or R_2
4	Hue B, R_3, no SR . . . . Hue B, R_3

Although our example refers to Hue B and R_3 particularly, it must be understood that these arbitrarily selected symbols refer to any hue and to any particular response since all were involved in the analyses. The experimenters tallied all occurrences of Category 1 and Category 4 over Trials 6 through 85, divided into 4 20-trial blocks.

Before we examine the resulting performance curves, we need to consider why Categories 1 and 4 are of significance according to reinforcement doctrine. Notice that in Category 1 a particular response followed by self-reward (SR) was repeated the next time the same stimulus hue appeared. Reinforcement theory states that a response to a stimulus will have a heightened probability of being elicited by that stimulus again if a reinforcement followed its earlier occurrence. Category 1 conforms to this sequence of events. Since relative frequency is an empirical index of probability of occurrence, reinforcement theory indicates that event-sequences of Category 1 should become more frequent as self-reward continues to operate.

In contrast we need to examine the sequence of events of Category 4. Here no SR follows the earlier response, yet that same response is repeated the next time the stimulus appears. Reinforcement theory postulates a decreasing probability of occurrence of nonreinforced responses. Consequently we should expect a decreasing frequency of Category 4 sequences as self-reward operates over trials.

Montgomery and Parton were thus interested in two probabilities (or relative frequencies). These were (a) the frequency of a matching (same) response (*M*) following *SR* as a proportion of all *SR* occurrences, and (b) the frequency of a matching response following no *SR* as a proportion of all non-*SR* occurrences. Their designations for these two probabilities and the computational formulas in terms of our category labels are as follows:

(a) is designated *Pr (M/SR)* and is

computed as $\dfrac{\text{Frequency of Category 1}}{\text{Frequencies of Categories } 1+3}$

(b) is designated *Pr(M/no SR)* and is

computed as $\dfrac{\text{Frequency of Category 4}}{\text{Frequencies of Categories } 2+4}$

In parallel with our discussion of reinforcement theory, the investigators reasoned that $Pr(M/SR)$ should increase over blocks of trials if self-reward (*SR*) is actually reinforcing, while $Pr(M/\text{no } SR)$ should decrease. The results they obtained are represented in Figure 14.11 which shows confirmation of their expectations in both reward levels.

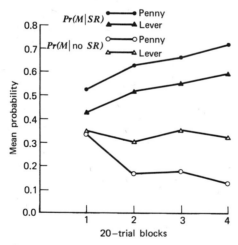

Fig. 14.11. Trends in mean probabilities of matching responses following self-reward or no self-reward when reward involved either a penny or only a lever response. (After Montgomery and Parton, 1970.)

The plotted curves show that $Pr(M/SR)$ increased over blocks of trials while $Pr(M/\text{no } SR)$ decreased. Further, the more extreme curves (highest and lowest in the figure) were obtained under the extra reinforcement condition in which a penny was released for each lever press. In addition the penny condition showed a higher overall percent of SR trials than the no-penny condition, 86 to 74 percent. The plotted curves with the extra impact of the penny condition suggest very strongly that self-reward (SR) is to be considered a valid instance of reinforcement.

Summary

Both biological and learned motives have been studied as they interact with numerous other psychological processes. Key concepts which have emerged from research and theory are arousal or activation, incentive, and reinforcement. Several approaches to experimentation on arousal level were illustrated. One study sought to determine the affect of hunger on the learning and recall of food words. Verbal learning was also the task in other experiments. One assessed anxiety and activation in the subjects. Another manipulated arousal with a loud noise used at different points in the memorization trials. Two other investigations manipulated arousal in quite different ways—one through the sensory deprivation of isolating subjects, and the other through stimulus variation in synthetic musical sequences.

Both positive and negative incentives, promises and threats, have been studied for their effects on various performances. We surveyed two similar studies of short-term memory. Findings of the second one reviewed suggest that early incentive cues act to reduce subjects' activity in an interpolated distractor task, thus elevating memory scores indirectly. A final experiment tested the effect of monetary incentive on performance of a vigilance task. Promise of a money reward led to better performance for a time, but when it was withdrawn, performance became comparatively poorer.

With human subjects reinforcement is often of a secondary sort—verbal approval, token rewards, or even self-reward for a response thought to be correct. When "right" and "wrong" are paired with no verbal reinforcement in different combinations, one study indicated that the silence of the experimenter came to serve as a positive reinforcement. In another experiment tokens as reinforcers in verbal learning were found to attain a degree of effectiveness, but were less influential than anticipated. In a different illustrative study—of verbal operant conditioning —direct reinforcement of responses was found more powerful than vicarious reinforcement or imitation. Self-reward by children in a "learning" task was the final experiment we considered. It was found to affect response rates in the way that external reinforcement does.

References

Appley, M. H. Derived motives. *Annual review of psychology*, 1970, **21**, 485–518.

Bergum, B. O., & Lehr, D. J. Monetary incentives and vigilance. *Journal of Experimental Psychology*, 1964, **67**, 197–198.

Berlyne, D. E. Arousal and reinforcement. In D. Levine (Ed.), *Nebraska Symposium on motivation: 1967*. Lincoln: University of Nebraska Press, 1967. Pp. 1–110.

Berlyne, D. E., Borsa, D. M., Hamacher, J. H., & Koenig, I. D. V. Paired-associate learning and the timing of arousal. *Journal of Experimental Psychology*, 1966, **72**, 1–6.

Buchwald, A. M. Experimental alterations in the effectiveness of verbal reinforcement combinations. *Journal of Experimental Psychology*, 1959, **57**, 351–361.

Epstein, S., & Levitt, H. The influence of hunger on the learning and recall of food related words. *Journal of Abnormal and Social Psychology*, 1962, **64**, 130–135.

Goulet, L. R. Anxiety (drive) and verbal learning: Implications for research and some methodological considerations. *Psychological Bulletin*, 1968, **69**, 235–247.

Haber, R. N. (Ed.) *Current research in motivation*. New York: Holt, Rinehart and Winston, 1966.

Kanfer, F. H., & Matarazzo, J. D. Secondary and generalized reinforcement in human learning. *Journal of Experimental Psychology*, 1959, **58**, 400–404.

Montgomery, G. T., & Parton, D. A. Reinforcing effect of self-reward. *Journal of Experimental Psychology*, 1970, **84**, 273–276.

Phillips, R. E. Comparison of direct and vicarious reinforcement and an investigation of methodological variables. *Journal of Experimental Psychology*, 1968, **78**, 666–669.

Saugstad, P. Effect of food deprivation on perception-cognition. *Psychological Bulletin*, 1966, **65**, 80–90.

Saugstad, P. Comments on the article by David L. Wolitsky: "Effect of food deprivation on perception-cognition: A comment." *Psychological Bulletin,* 1967, **68**, 345–346.

Spence, J. T., & Spence, K. W. The motivational components of manifest anxiety: Drive and drive stimuli. In C. D. Spielberger (Ed.), *Anxiety and behavior.* New York: Academic Press, 1966. Pp. 291–326.

Suedfeld, P., Glucksberg, S., & Vernon, J. Sensory deprivation as a drive operation: Effects upon problem solving. *Journal of Experimental Psychology,* 1967, **75**, 166–169.

Thayer, R. E., & Cox, S. J. Activation, manifest anxiety, and verbal learning. *Journal of Experimental Psychology,* 1968, **78**, 524–526.

Vitz, P. C. Affect as a function of stimulus variation. *Journal of Experimental Psychology,* 1966, **71**, 74–79.

Weiner, B. Effects of motivation on the availability and retrieval of memory traces. *Psychological Bulletin,* 1966, **65**, 24–37.

Weiner, B., & Walker, E. L. Motivational factors in short-term retention. *Journal of Experimental Psychology,* 1966, **71**, 190–193.

Wickens, D. D., & Simpson, C. K. Trace cue position, motivation, and short-term memory. *Journal of Experimental Psychology,* 1968, **76**, 282–285.

chapter 15
Social Processes

Imagine a hundred people listening to a partisan speech advocating organized political action. Now try to picture a somewhat different situation in which a half dozen college students argue some controversy currently capturing their attention. Either one of these group activities might seem too complex to permit objective behavioral investigation. It is just such social processes, however—the persuasion of an audience by a speaker, and free discussion of a problem in a face-to-face group—that are among the targets of investigations which social psychologists are conducting. Admittedly, a total description of what is occurring in either of these situations would be so detailed as to defy analysis, especially to the extent that the past experience of each participant would have to be considered. The student of social interaction, however, can follow the lead of those who investigate other aspects of behavior, abstracting certain features to be measured and to be examined for interrelationships, instead of trying to deal in global fashion with a welter of phenomena.

The actions of individuals in a group constitute a realm of behavior of great proportions. A major part of any person's activity is carried on in a social context. Furthermore, our dealings with other people often involve such major processes as perception, motivation, learning, remembering, and problem solving. To some extent, then, we are studying all these topics in complex relationship when we investigate how people act and react in group situations. The interactions of personalities in group situations compound the complexity further. Numerous questions and problems have challenged investigators and theorists alike. Nearly three hundred reports were cited, for example, in a review by Lott and Lott (1965) of studies relating interpersonal attraction to group cohesiveness.

Much of the research directed at social processes is aimed at bridging the territory between the two disciplines of sociology and psychology. We seek to determine the psychological mechanisms that underlie social phenomena which the sociologist may have observed in various groups in the community. Research efforts are often interdisciplinary. The specialists who pool their talents may come not only from psychology and sociology, but also from fields like economics and political science and from scenes of group action like government and industry. Our general aim of a unified science of behavior is thus more prominent here than in some special areas in psychology. This is not to suggest that such unity is close at hand. Even within psychology there is a diversity of approaches to studying social processes. In the area of small group theory, for example, DeLamater, McClintock, and Becker (1965) found great heterogeneity in conceptual orientations and their supporting experimentation.

In this chapter we must limit our consideration of research on social processes to two major areas of investigation—persuasive communication and group dynamics. Within these areas we are forced to be very selective, examining only a very few illustrative experiments. Before turning to these special topics and particular methods of study by which they are probed, we may note some very general approaches to the study of behavior in group situations. These and other methodological matters have been reviewed and referenced by Hare (1962) in an appendix outlining small group research methods.

Field Observation

One way to study behavior in group situations is to investigate the composition and activities of groups already in existence. Numerous aspects of this approach were discussed by Whyte (1951) who used it in an intensive study of a street corner gang. Such studies generally involve a long-term investigation rather than a brief perusal of the group's activity. This general method of field observation may employ one or more special techniques for gathering information, in addition to direct observation at gatherings of the group being studied. Besides recording the interactions of group members, we may employ opinion polls, attitude scaling, and depth interviews to obtain a picture of the psychological forces at work. The technicalities of these approaches, beyond the scope of our discussion, must be understood and carefully considered if these methods are to enhance a research effort.

Sociometry

Sociometry, a method of analyzing the interpersonal structure of an existent group, requires that individuals choose or reject other group members as potential associates. As a basis for choosing, rejecting, or ignoring other persons, the individual is asked to consider a hypothetical situation where he might be associated with those he indicates as his choices. This situation is often either a task requiring cooperative work or a period of leisure time which may be shared with others.

A tabulation of each individual's choices and rejections provides the raw data in sociometry. Together with the pattern of cases where neither choice nor rejection was made between two persons, these data can be used to construct a *sociogram*, which is a graphic representation of group structure based on the data of sociometric choice. Each individual is represented at one point, or circular symbol, in the sociogram, with solid lines indicating choices and dotted lines rejection. This schematic representation is further refined by having distances between the person-points represent the different degrees of choice and rejection between pairs of individuals. Two people who mutually chose each other would be represented close together, whereas a pair who mutually rejected each other would be widely separated. Intermediate relationships, like mutual ignoring and nonmutual choice and rejection, would be shown as intermediate distances in the diagram of the group. Such a graphic schema readily reveals the existence of subgroups or cliques, of highly popular group members, and of persons isolated in the structure of the group.

Persuasive Communication

A key role is played in social behavior processes by communication of many sorts: an executive issues directives to his subordinates, a small boy pesters his uncle with questions, a popular singer hits his hearers with a new beat. Still another sort of social interaction is the communication of a message from a speaker to an audience. In many cases the person speaking is attempting to persuade the audience to change their opinions on some set of issues, whether he be delivering a keynote political speech, a sermon, or a football pep talk, to say nothing of a sales pitch.

One analysis of research on persuasive communication points to three major aspects of the process as places where experimental manipulations of variables have been undertaken. These are the *communicator,* the *communication,* and the *audience.* A typical study involves choosing a particular group to serve as the audience. Various social and psychological characteristics of this group are noted. A specially selected communication—a speech, a tape-recorded panel discussion, or perhaps a motion picture—is presented to them. The communicator is either present as an element in the situation or he, or they, may be identified for the audience. Since we are dealing with persuasive communication, another procedural detail is the assessment of opinions of audience members after the communication has been delivered. This pattern of opinions is compared with that of the same group prior to receiving the message or with that of a different control group of similar composition.

Some Methodological Considerations

There is a compounding of the psychological dynamics when social processes are made the object of laboratory investigation, itself a social process. Alerting ourselves to special problems of experimentation may be useful before we turn to illustrative studies.

The communicator

If two or more communicators are brought separately into direct contact with the audience, any variable that is assumed to be introduced by the way in which each one delivers his speech may be confounded with numerous variables of his personality as the audience reacts to it. If the same person plays different communicator roles, his portrayal of one speaker may be more valid than his impersonation of another type of communicator. Again, a straightforward interpretation of results may be hindered.

Often the complexities introduced by using a speech delivered in person are avoided by using a tape-recorded presentation or a printed copy. In this way, an identical communication can be attributed to two or more sources. It thus becomes the task of the experimenter to persuade the audience, for each presentation, that the communication is coming from the source he names. If his attributing of the message to some source should be doubted for any reason, then the outcome of the experiment might be questionable in proportion to the existence of this doubt in one or more of the audience groups.

The communication

It would seem that devising a communication to be used in research might pose less of a problem than creating a communicator's role. However, this part of an investigation can offer difficulties of its own. Primarily, these may stem from the fact that a communication is a multidimensional pattern of stimulation. Among the facets of the message that may represent important variables are its logical and verbal structure, its factual content, its motivational and emotional appeals, and its sequential organization as a series of persuasive arguments. For the investigator this wealth of variables again poses problems of interpreting results. It is unlikely that any one class of factor can be manipulated without some shift in the value of other factors.

Even prior to planning how we will vary a communication to suit our experimental purpose we must make a decision on the general topic of the message. Usually we will want the message to be one which has a fair amount of interest for the audience. Persuasion to the point of opinion change will hardly stem from exposure to a communication which fails even to arouse interest. Picking a very interesting topic has its pitfalls too, however. Such a topic may have been widely discussed among the audience to be employed. This may mean that many individuals have firmly held opinions on the issues involved. There may be general knowledge of the group's views, with attendant pressure to conform. If the topic is timely, it introduces the risk that day-to-day news stories may affect opinion strongly. Research on persuasive communication is obviously not very easy to plan and execute.

The audience

Having seen that a communication may be quite complex, we must now note that an audience is complex in the extreme. Each individual brings numerous perceptual, motivational, and associative predispositions to the experimental situation. We thus would face many unknowns if we tried to persuade even one person to alter his opinion on some matter. When we take great individual differences into account, we would face a formidable task if we tried to account in detail for the ongoing processes of the experiment. As in other research efforts in psychology, we take the easier course of treating group statistics, letting individual differences cancel out to some extent.

Most groups which constitute audiences for research in persuasive communication have a measure of homogeneity. Classroom groups, for example, would have a much narrower range on many psychological dimensions than would a random sample of persons from the general population. This similarity among individuals might even extend to the opinions which entered into the experiment. A degree of such convergence of viewpoints might be appropriate for some studies, whereas other experiments would benefit more from employing a group whose views diverged markedly, covering a broad spectrum of opinion.

Besides selecting a communication that is appropriate to the audience, the experimenter must create plausibility for his request that it be given their attention. Why should they listen to this tape recording, and why should they fill out an opinion questionnaire on the topic? An investigator may have to invent some reason for conducting the experiment other than to see how the message causes opinion change. To admit his true purpose would invite resistance on the part of many people and defeat his aims. The gaging of opinions must similarly be conducted in a way calculated not to alter response tendencies in an undesired way. Later, when the data have been collected, the experimenter may explain the study fully without danger of introducing distortion into his findings.

Measuring attitudes and opinions

An attitude or opinion may be defined as an evaluative response which a subject makes, or indirectly indicates his readiness to make. Being evaluative, opinions are measured through psychological scaling techniques such as we considered in Chapter 6. Examples of items designed to assess an opinion are the following two:

Intercollegiate football should be abolished.
_____ Agree strongly
_____ Agree
_____ Neither agree nor disagree
_____ Disagree
_____ Disagree strongly

Intercollegiate football . . .
_____ 1. should be given greater emphasis in college life.
_____ 2. should be maintained at the present level of emphasis in college life.

_____ 3. should be given less emphasis in college life.

_____ 4. should be abolished.

Either of these techniques for scaling opinion provides a means of measuring opinion change in a group. Some other scaling method, such as a graphic rating scale, might be selected instead if the experimental topic seemed to require it. In research on persuasive communication we may measure the average amount of shift along the opinion scale, or we may note the percent of subjects who shift their opinion in either direction.

Attitude measurement cannot be regarded as simple to achieve. All stages of preparing and administering the testing instrument must be guided by the best technical advice available. Standard attitude scales and their uses have been discussed by Shaw and Wright (1967). Valid expressions of opinion must be encouraged by stressing the research orientation of the investigator. Anonymity may usually be promised to participants to elicit frank opinions. Communication topics may be chosen which do not arouse strong tendencies to shrink from revealing true opinions.

Communicator Characteristics

How persuasive a communication may prove to be depends heavily on how the communicator is perceived by those whose opinions are to be changed. Experimental tests of this hypothesis have generally relied on using instructions or other techniques to create different characteristics for the presumed communicators. These methodological manipulations are assumed to affect the credibility or persuasive powers of the individuals who deliver identical messages to different groups. In addition to examining opinion change, investigators typically require subjects to react also to the communicator so as to check on their assumptions as to how he has been evaluated. Some illustrative studies will show the diversity of research on communicator variables.

Credibility and communication discrepancy

Besides creating two levels of credibility by attributing vastly different prestige levels to their communicators, one research group also varied the discrepancy of the position advocated in the message from the subjects' original judgments. More specifically, the communication was directed at securing a greater or lesser change in the subjects' ranking of a stanza of poetry. Aronson, Turner, and Carlsmith (1963) first required each subject to rank nine different alliterative stanzas of poetry on how the poet used form to express his meaning. The subject was then required to study a two-page essay entitled "The Use of Alliteration in Poetry." After a general treatment of the topic, the communication used as an example the stanza which the subject had ranked eighth in her earlier task. (The experimenters were obviously ready with several different versions of the persuasive message.) A further experimental variation in the communication was the discrepancy between the rank the subject had given the illustrative stanza (Rank 8) and the rank assigned to it in the essay on alliteration, as indicated here:

Assigned Rank	Discrepancy
5	3
3	5
1	7

For half the subjects, the author of the essay was indicated to be a highly credible expert, the prestigious poet T. S. Eliot. As a mildly credible source the essay was attributed to an English major at Mississippi State Teachers College, a Miss Agnes Stearns. In each case the subjects were told that the experimenter was interested in seeing if the essay would assist them in evaluating poetry. After reading it, each subject was again asked to rank the nine poetry selections. Any elevation in rank of the critical stanza would indicate a persuasive effect of the communication. Further, each subject was requested to indicate degree of agreement on a 7-point scale with 14 evaluative statements concerning the essay and its author. Once these data were collected, the experimenter revealed the purpose of the study and discussed the need for deception in conducting the research. Subjects for this "experiment in esthetics" were 112 female college students who were paid to participate, reporting in small groups for the tasks we have reviewed.

The amount of opinion change or elevation of ranking of the crucial stanza is shown in Figure 15.1 for the 2 levels of communicator credibility and the 3 values of discrepancy from original ranking. Besides the solid lines connecting the data points, the figure contains two dotted lines representing the hypothetical amount of opinion change to be expected if either a perfectly credible communicator or a perfectly incredible one were to advocate a given elevation in rank (or discrepancy from a subject's earlier ranking). The amounts of obtained opinion change clearly

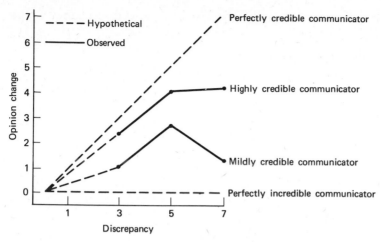

Fig. 15.1. Opinion change as a function of discrepancy. Hypothetical limits and observed data for highly credible and mildly credible communicators. (After Aronson, Turner, and Carlsmith, 1963.)

show that the highly credible communicator, alleged to be T. S. Eliot, was more effective in elevating opinions of the critical stanza. Statistical analyses showed the differences to be significant at each discrepancy value. The credibility or prestige of the communicator was thus found to be a determinant of persuasiveness, as in other experimental studies.

The influence of discrepancy of the communicator's advocated ranking from the subject's original ranking shows a more complex result. With Discrepancy 5, compared with Discrepancy 3, there is a greater opinion change elicited by both communicators. When the discrepancy value was set at 7, however, the highly credible communicator evoked only a nonsignificant difference in opinion change when compared with Discrepancy 5. In the case of the mildly credible source, Discrepancy 7 induced a significantly lesser change than Discrepancy 5. Actually the amounts of opinion change were not statistically different for Discrepancies 3 and 7 for this communicator. The investigators suggest that when a communicator of lesser prestige advocates too large a change in opinion, the audience tends to reject or derogate the communicator rather than be influenced by his message. On analyzing subjects' scaling of their agreements and disagreements with the evaluative statements concerning communicator and message they found that the mildly credible source was indeed derogated more than was the highly credible communicator. However, the amount of derogation did not rise with the discrepancy value as expected.

Communicator-audience similarity

Both intuitively compelling and experimentally verified is the hypothesis that a communicator will be more persuasive if the audience members perceive him as similar to themselves in certain respects—perhaps in background, interests, or values. The study we shall next consider tested this hypothesis in a rather indirect way. Mills and Jellison (1968) created not only fictional communicators but fictional original audiences as well, either matched or unmatched with the indicated speakers in presumed patterns of interest. The speaker was described as either an acoustical engineer or an accomplished pianist. His audience was described as composed of either engineering students or music students at the *alma mater* of the communicator. Each speaker was indicated as presenting his speech to each of the two audiences, thus forming 4 different experimental conditions which were administered to different subjects from this study, women psychology students. The intent of the investigation was to determine how these subjects would themselves be influenced by reading the speech when it was indicated as having been earlier delivered by an experienced alumnus of either similar or dissimilar interests from his indicated college audience. The speech advocated that a college curriculum should assure a broad, general education for every student.

The experimenter told each group of subjects that his investigation concerned the forming of impressions about a person. They would read a speech, he said, and then rate the personality traits of the person who had delivered it. The introductory part of the material which was then distributed identified the speaker as engineer or musician and his original audience as either engineering or music students. Each communicator-audience combination was described for about a quarter of the 202 subjects. After reading the copy of the speech the subjects were asked to rate its author on a number of traits: biased, competent, earnest, frank, friendly, impartial, likeable, obliging, selfish, sincere, sympathetic, and unconventional. A 20-point rating scale from 0 (extremely inappropriate) to 20 (extremely appropriate) was used to indicate how aptly each adjective seemed to fit the author of the talk. When this rating task was finished the experimenter announced another purpose of the study—to see how the ratings given to a speaker might relate to memory for what he had said. Subjects then took a multiple-choice memory test for the content of the communication. Included in this were items which tested their perception of the profession of the speaker and the college major of his original audience. These two items had to be correct to retain a subject in the later analysis of opinion data. Around 7 percent of subjects were dropped for missing one of these items, making them inappropriate to use in testing the hypothesis about communicator-audience similarity.

On the final page of the memory test were some items which were explained as testing the relation of reactions to the speech to memory for its content. These 10 items contained 6 favorable to general education and 4 unfavorable. Subjects had to indicate their degree of agreement with each statement on a 7-point scale ranging from "Strongly Disagree" to "Strongly Agree." Positive values up to $+3$ were assigned to positions favoring general education and negative values to -3 were given to opposing views. Over the 10 items a cumulative index could have ranged from -30 to $+30$ as a measure of agreement with the communicator's views. Mean scores attained by the 4 groups given the different introductions to the printed speech provided the test of the hypothesis that perceived similarity of speaker and audience would render the communication more persuasive when it was read by the experimental subjects.

The mean opinion scores for the 4 subject groups were as follows:

Group Reading Speech—	Mean Agreement Score
By musician to music students	10.1
By engineer to engineering students	8.2
By musician to engineering students	6.0
By engineer to music students	7.4

On the average, the "musician" and the "engineer" did not differ in their persuasive powers as measured by subjects' agreement with the speech they read. However, there was a statistically significant interaction between the presumed speaker and the supposed original audience. When these were paired—engineer with engineering students and musician with music students—the speech was found to be more persuasive in the view of the experimental subjects. A mismatch of speaker and audience led to less persuasiveness of the identical message. Indirectly, then, the investigation suggests further confirmation of the hypothesis that similarities of communicators and their audiences add persuasibility to communications.

Sex of the communicator

A study using communications in Arabic, Cantonese, English, Hindi, and Portuguese was conducted by two collaborators in a 'round-the-world investigation of whether a male or female communicator is more credible or persuasive. Whittaker and Meade (1967) prepared a thousand-word communication with the title "Evaluation of the United Nations Since Its Founding." It offered a favorable opinion of the UN's activities without claiming the organization to be perfect in its work. Using professional radio commentators—one male and one female in each country—tape recordings were made which simulated radio broadcasts of the translated essay. One tape or the other was played, in the appropriate language, to different groups of college students in Brazil, Hong Kong, India, Jordan, and Rhodesia. The purposes of the study were to assess reactions to the speakers of either sex, judged as communicators, and to determine how effective each sex was in eliciting opinion change.

There was some variation in the questionnaires used in the different countries. In general, however, there was a 30-item instrument used both before and after the communication to gage opinions of the United Nations and a second questionnaire to get reactions to the communicator's completeness, fairness, and logic in covering the topic. The pretest with the opinion questionnaire was administered by a professor of the students about a week before the major part of the experiment. Listening to the tape recording was also presented as a classroom exercise with reactions to the speaker collected immediately afterward. Then the 30-items of the opinion assessment were administered again, the explanation being offered that not everyone had followed directions the week before. The complete study involved using written forms of the communication in some countries but our review treats only the oral presentation by a male or a female communicator.

The results of the investigation may be briefly described since differing assessment procedures reduce the direct comparability of the data obtained. The evaluations of the communicators favored the male speaker in Brazil, Hong Kong, and India. In Jordan and Rhodesia smaller differences were not statistically significant. On the matter of opinion change as induced by the male or female broadcaster, only the Brazilian students were more persuaded by one than the other. For them, statistical analysis showed the male speaker to have been slightly more persuasive. A similar result had been obtained in an earlier experiment in the United States.

Aspects of the Message

A communication intended to bring about opinion change has numerous aspects which might be varied in an attempt to make it more persuasive. Advertisers and politicians use the art and science of opinion molding as they prepare messages for their audiences. Although the stakes are not as high, experimentalists have also shown great ingenuity in constructing persuasive communications to test their hypotheses about the relevant variables. Two illustrative studies show us how language and logic have been manipulated on the one hand, while fear arousal has been varied on the other.

Language variables

In creating four different versions of their brief persuasive essays, Kanouse and Abelson (1967) varied the semantic nature of certain verbs (positive or negative) and the kind of evidence (abstract or concrete) which was incorporated. Also varied was which type of verb and which form of evidence were paired together as the first and second premises of the syllogistic argument of the messages. The four versions (A, B, C, D) of the constructed arguments are suggested in the following table:

Form of Evidence Used with Positive Verb*	Order of Verb Utilization	
	Positive First and Negative Second	Negative First and Positive Second
Concrete	Version A	Version B
Abstract	Version C	Version D

*Opposite form of evidence was used with the negative verb.

Here is an example of Version A of one of the brief essays:

Figures released by U.S. Wildlife officials show that Nebraskan hunting regulations are producing a large increase in the number of Nebraskan crested hawks. This indicates that the regulations are producing a large increase in the number of legally protected birds.

A recent issue of the Farm Journal reports that Nebraskan farmers fear a large increase in the number of government-preserved wildlife, because of the danger of destruction of crops and livestock. From this it is apparent that Nebraskan farmers fear a large increase in the number of legally protected birds.

Therefore, the laws against hunting legally protected birds are too strict.

Note that in the two premise paragraphs the verb order is positive verb (producing) used first and negative verb (fear) used second. The evidence accompanying the positive verb is concrete (Nebraskan crested hawks) while evidence given with the negative verb is abstract (government-preserved wildlife). This combination of verb order with accompanying form of evidence defines what we are here designating as Version *A*. These combinations were varied to produce the 4 versions possible for each of 4 essay topics: hunting, toys, Central America, and Alaska. Persuasive essays were built around these topics since they were judged to involve unfamiliar issues yet be perceived as meaningful to college students.

Forty-eight Yale University students were randomly subdivided into 4 experimental groups. The booklet handed to members of each group used a different version of the persuasive argument—*A, B, C,* or *D*—for each of the 4 essay topics included. After reading each essay in his booklet a subject had to indicate on a 31-point scale how much in agreement he was with the conclusion reached on the basis of the evidence presented. On a similar scale he then had to rate the communication he had just read on its convincingness. Based on earlier research that they had conducted, the experimenters predicted that greater agreement would result when concrete evidence was used with positive verbs (Versions *A* and *B*) while lesser agreement would be elicited when the abstract evidence accompanied the positive verbs (Versions *C* and *D*). Similarly, Versions *A* and *B* were expected to be rated as more convincing than Versions *C* and *D*. The means obtained on the scaling of agreement and convincingness are presented in Parts I and II of Table 15.1 for each version of the messages and for each essay topic.

Both the means of subjects' agreements with the argument of the essays and their ratings of convincingness are supportive of the hypothesis. Versions *A* and *B* fared better than Versions *C* and *D*. Statistical analyses bore out what inspection of the data suggests. The interaction of type of verb and kind of supporting evidence was a significant determinant of

Table 15.1 Mean Response Ratings Given to Each Version of the Communications on Each Topic (After Kanouse & Abelson, 1967)

Part I. Mean Agreement with Conclusions by Topic and Version of Communication

Communication Version	Topic			
	Toys	Hunting	Central America	Alaska
A	18.92	9.25	12.83	13.75
B	12.50	10.25	16.75	17.25
C	12.67	6.58	8.33	9.75
D	15.25	8.42	9.17	13.00

Part II. Mean Rating of Convincingness of the Evidence by Topic and Version

Communication Version	Topic			
	Toys	Hunting	Central America	Alaska
A	17.00	7.75	12.50	11.58
B	13.42	8.42	18.33	15.00
C	10.00	6.42	9.00	7.75
D	9.67	6.83	9.33	9.42

both the degree of agreement elicited and the rated convincingness of the essays. Specifically, Versions A and B which paired concrete evidence with positive verb form and abstract evidence with negatively toned verbs, were more persuasive than Versions C and D with the opposite pairings. Kanouse and Abelson noted that this agrees with their earlier findings and encourages a further exploration of how language forms contribute to the persuasiveness of communications.

Fear arousal

A dimension of many attempts at persuasion is the amount of emotional arousal of the audience which is generated by the communication. A number of studies have sought to create different levels of fear arousal in subjects in order to determine if greater arousal leads to greater persuasion. This has been found to be the case in several experiments. In reviewing the research literature, however, Leventhal and Singer (1966) pointed out that one study had found that high fear arousal seemed to make subjects resistant to the message. They set up an experiment on the same topic—recommending good dental hygiene practices—to examine further the hypothesis that greater fear arousal would lead to greater acceptance recommended practices. They also investigated the timing or sequencing of the recommendations with respect to the fear arousal but this complicated aspect of their research need not concern us in this limited review.

Psychological research moved off the college campus when Leventhal and Singer went to a state fair to conduct their research. Subjects were fair-goers who wandered into the Hall of Health and agreed to serve in the evaluation of a program on dental hygiene. Our summary will concentrate on 4 groups exposed to a high-fear version of the audiovisual communication and 4 groups given the low-fear treatment, a total of 284 persons ranging widely in age and vocation. Assembled in small groups the subjects listened through earphones to a tape recording and viewed slides appropriate to the experimental treatment assigned to them. For high arousal of fear, the communication emphasized the fearsome consequences of dental neglect as it dealt with tooth decay, gum disease, and spread of infection. Vivid, fear-arousing vocabulary in the taped talk was augmented by color slides depicting cavities, gum inflammation, bleeding extractions, and the lancing of an abscess. The low-fear version of the communication discussed the teeth and dental disorders but did not mention the consequences of dental neglect. The accompanying slides included only drawings, diagrams, and dental X-rays. Incorporated in either version of the audiovisual presentation were a set of illustrated recommendations on several steps to be taken for good dental health. It was the indicated acceptance of these that would give the experimenters a measure of how persuasive either version of the communication had been.

Our review of this research will deal with two aspects of subjects' reactions to their version of the dental hygiene message—their scaled reports on their emotional arousal and their ratings of their intentions to follow the recommendations given. Although this latter assessment is the indicant which tests the hypothesis that high arousal of fear makes the message more persuasive, it is important first to discover if the two versions of the presentation did indeed arouse negative emotion to different degrees. The arousal elicited was measured by asking subjects to use a 7-point rating scale to indicate how applicable to their state of mind as they viewed the program were 6 descriptive adjectives—angry, tense, unhappy, disgusted, anxious, and fearful. On the scale used, the definition of points was 1 = "Not at All," 4 = "Not Sure," and 7 = "Very." The sum of the ratings given served as an index of emotional arousal. For the

4 high-fear groups the results graphed in the research report indicate an average score of about 18 while the low-fear groups averaged about 12. The difference in scaled arousal level was statistically significant.

Finding that the two versions of the communication had aroused negative emotion in differing degrees, Leventhal and Singer could then see if the ratings of intent to follow the recommended dental practices were different. A 7-point scale allowed subjects to describe their intentions in response to 5 questions such as "Do you intend to brush with an up and down stroke?" When the summed ratings were separately averaged for the two levels of arousal, the high-fear groups showed rated intentions which averaged about 3 points higher than the data for the low-fear groups. This difference was also statistically significant. In contrast with occasional divergent findings in the past, this experiment is added to those which demonstrate that a higher level of emotional arousal makes a communication more persuasive.

Forewarning the Audience

In the several studies of persuasive communication we have reviewed, the subjects were never informed in advance that an attempt was to be made to influence their attitudes or opinions. Usually the task described to them posed some other interpretation of their participation. In theorizing about persuasion the hypothesis has been advanced that forewarning an audience that they are to receive a communication directed at changing their opinions will reduce the chance of any change being effected or will lessen its measured amount. Research has given some confirmation to this hypothesis. We shall briefly summarize two investigations into this matter. Both of them extend the previous findings by going on to inquire into the timing of the warning given to different audience groups.

Forewarning versus after-warning

Accepting the fact that forewarning can nullify the persuasive impact of a communication, Kiesler and Kiesler (1964) questioned whether it is the content of the warning or its timing which is effective in this way. They designed a means of delaying the warning to one group of experimental subjects while forewarning another group. A third experimental group received no warning but was exposed to the same written communication. A control group was subjected to the same attitude assessments as the experimental groups but read only a neutral communication.

The data were collected from junior college students in two separate sessions a week apart. A survey research questionnaire administered at the first session by one experimenter included an item on the attitude of each respondent toward foreign aid extended to other countries by the United States. An identical item was incorporated into a different questionnaire on news events which was given to subjects at the second session following their reading of the communication which strongly advocated liberal foreign aid. This essay was prepared in three versions which differed only by a footnote so as to achieve the three desired experimental treatments. To accomplish forewarning the footnote was placed at the bottom of page 1, with an asterisk at the beginning of the article to call immediate attention to it. The footnote read, "This article was taken from the recent book, *Techniques of Persuasion,* by R. J. Friedley. It was designed to make you change your opinion." The same footnote appeared at the end of the 2-page communication for the after-warned experimental group. The no-warning group read the article without any footnote, while the control group read a neutral article on education.

The attitude-measuring item in the pretest and posttest was a statement advocating liberal foreign aid. It was accompanied by a graphic scale with one end marked "Strongly Disagree" and the other marked "Strongly Agree." An arrow placed somewhere along the line by each subject was his method of expressing his degree of agreement with the statement. For scoring purposes the experimenters later divided each line into 16 segments and determined the number of units of attitude change revealed through comparing the posttest with pretest response of each subject. With almost 50 subjects in each group, the mean opinion change scores were examined.

Kiesler and Kiesler had hypothesized that an after-warning of the subjects would not prevent their revealing an attitude shift attributable to the communication they read. For the forewarned group they predicted a resistance to the persuasive message which would preclude any expressed change of opinion. The data presented below confirmed these expectations.

Group	Mean Opinion Change
Forewarned	−0.13
After-warning	2.11
No warning	2.29
Control	0.85

The results show that the forewarned subjects were indeed resistant to the message. They actually showed a slight decrease in agreement with the test statement while the control group showed a slight increase, presumably by chance or perhaps reflective of influences during the interval between questionnaires. The afterwarned group showed a substantial shift of opinion, almost as great as the group receiving no warning about the communication. Statistical analysis confirmed the overall trend evident in the group means. The results of the study show the importance of the time when subjects are alerted to the persuasive intent of the communication.

Timing of forewarning

The amount of time by which a forewarning precedes a persuasive communication may affect the amount of opinion change it accomplishes. This was one hypothesis tested in an experiment conducted by Freedman and Sears (1965). They reasoned that an earlier forewarning of persuasive intent would allow audience members more time to prepare their defenses against persuasion. Their study involved an oral presentation on highway safety delivered to high school students by a man introduced as an expert on cars and driving. For two different groups of subjects the forewarning of the speaker's intent to sway them was included in written instructions presented 10 minutes in advance of the talk, or 2 minutes in advance. No advance warning was given to a third group of subjects who learned of the intent of the talk only at the time the guest speaker was introduced. The warning took this form:

The title of the talk is "Why Teen-Agers Should Not Drive." Dr. Allen will tell you why he thinks that teen-agers should not be allowed to drive.

Questions on teen-age driving were embedded in 12-item questionnaires administered several weeks before and immediately after students heard the 12-minute talk. Responses were given on the graphic scales accompanying the items. On the pretest the mean score was 3.75 for all students out of a possible 14. This indicated their favoring almost no restrictions on teen-age driving and showed considerable opportunity for opinion change. The actual changes evoked by the talk were not very great but they tended to confirm the hypothesis being tested. The group with no advance forewarning showed a change of 1.54 points on the scale. With a 2-min warning, a second group showed only 0.94 points change.

With 10 min of advance warning on the topic and intent of the speech, students of the third group showed a change of only 0.55 points. Although statistical analysis of these three means fell short of conventional levels for confidence, the trend in the values was clearly suggestive that the hypothesis concerning the development of defense against persuasion is one that deserves further study.

Group Dynamics

As we turn to group dynamics, the topic of communication as an important social process is by no means left behind. Rather, the one-way communication of speaker to audience is replaced by multiple channels of communication. In most research, group members are brought into face-to-face contact and each person can converse with everyone else. In some studies communication is given special attention by limiting the channels by which group members may deal with each other. In either form of experiment, the frequency, direction, and content of "messages" sent and received are of considerable interest to the investigator.

In an extensive treatment of research on small group functioning Hare (1962) indicated some major classes of variables to be personal and social characteristics in the composition of the group, assigned task, size of group, communication network, and leadership. We shall be able to illustrate only a small part of the ongoing investigation of these topics. Work on leadership has also been reviewed by Hollander and Julian (1969).

Methods of Study

Our methodological discussion of group dynamics research will necessarily be limited. We must omit any discussion of how group dynamics research is carried out in established groups in business and industry, in schools, and in the military. Within the domain of laboratory study of small groups assembled for experimentation, we shall further exclude from consideration those studies which center on the personal characteristics of the group members—age, sex, intelligence, abilities, and traits of personality. Factors that will occupy our attention will range from assigned task to communication net imposed on the group.

Assigned task

The tasks assigned to experimental groups have tended to fall into two main classes—topics to be discussed and problems to be solved. In some instances a discussion may have a problem-solving aspect, as when a group is required to arrive at a consensus on how some problem should be solved. In these cases there is usually no right or wrong answer, so that these discussions still differ from attempts to solve problems where an objectively correct solution exists. In some discussion groups, performance data are sought in the opinion changes registered by individuals. Other studies may involve little interest in the outcome of the discussion but may concentrate attention on the social processes taking place as the group members interact.

Many experiments on problem solving by groups have used the number of groups achieving the solution or the time taken to solve the problem as indices of effectiveness, while varying such factors as size of group or channels of intragroup communication. Such molar measures of performance have often revealed little of the processes taking place as the group solved the problem. Furthermore, when a principle as to the most efficient group size or structure was sought, discussion of experimental results has often included the unhappy conclusion that it depends on the type of task or problem involved. It is precisely in this lament that we can detect a powerful resource for the investigator of social processes in recent and future studies. If the outcome of a problem-solving effort and the group interactions leading to that outcome differ as a function of the type of problem assigned, then the experimenter should be able to use problem tasks of such variety as to create a wealth of interactions of various sorts among the members of the group. Putting the matter somewhat more empirically, an investigator may hope to find numerous aspects of behavior varying as a function of the independent variables which he manipulates in devising problem tasks and presenting them to his subjects. As this approach is employed, more attention can be paid to measuring different facets of the individuals' behaviors as well as to the final outcome of the group effort.

Inspiration for the foregoing stress on the assigned problem as a pool of experimental variables has been largely derived from an article by Roby and Lanzetta (1958). These authors suggest the analysis of complex tasks into input variables of two kinds, those initiated by the experimenter and those that arise as group members receive communications from each other. They would also deal with output variables of two kinds, the communicative acts and the actions directed toward solving the problem. This detailed task analysis should lead to the identification of critical demands made on the group by different problem tasks. A program of research may incorporate tasks that feature different sets of critical demands so that different patterns of behavior are elicited from the group members. Some tasks, for example, might place special demands on group members for perceiving and remembering the stimulus information which might be gradually offered to them as the task progressed. Other tasks might stress a cooperative effort in logic to obtain a problem solution.

Tasks assigned to groups composed of just two or three persons have often been certain kinds of games which offer an experimenter a considerable latitude in control of variables and measures of performance. At the same time the competitive games are usually quite motivating to experimental subjects. An interpretive survey of the use of games in small-group research has been presented by Vinacke (1969) who deals with both research and theory in a thorough treatment of the topic. A different method of investigating interpersonal behavior in a dyadic (two-person) situation is to provide for game-playing through a communications link. This affords the experimenter control over numerous events and variables as two subjects engage in competition or cooperation. Such a laboratory approach to interpersonal dynamics is represented by the Interaction Screen described and illustrated by Sawyer and Friedell (1965). Sitting at separate consoles, the subjects communicate and interact in restricted ways under surveillance of the investigator. The apparatus allows great choice in designing assigned tasks and variables.

Returning to tasks which may be given to several subjects cooperating in a group performance, Morrissette, Pearson, and Switzer (1965) described a mathematically defined problem. It may be assigned to a group operating within various sorts of restricted communication networks, as commonly used in past research. It has the merit of allowing several quantitative variations so that their effects on group problem solving may be studied. In their article the authors report two validation experiments which demonstrate the utility of this research tool.

Communication net

A general method for studying the interactions of group members as they solve a problem has been to establish different communication nets which restrict the sending and receiving of messages. Certain group members are permitted to send messages directly to others. Contrastingly, direct communication between certain persons in the communication net is prohibited. They may exchange information only indirectly, transmitting messages through intermediaries in the net. Two-way communication over each of the channels which comprise the net is generally permitted, although one-way lines connecting certain persons may also be introduced as a variant in this method. Written messages are usually required so as to restrict communication to designated channels. This slows down the interaction processes and permits the experimenter to examine them in complete sequential detail. Sometimes electronic intercommunication involving microphones and earphones or loudspeakers is used. The experimental technique of restricting the interaction of group members contrasts markedly with the free face-to-face discussion that is permitted in many experiments on group dynamics.

The employment of different communication networks in experiments on group dynamics has been discussed extensively by Shaw (1964). Figure 15.2 shows a number of the networks which have been used for networks of intercommunication among three and four persons. Shaw also illustrates five-person networks of these and other types. An inspection of the three-person networks in Figure 15.2 shows the restrictions imposed on communication by all but the Comcon network. The Wheel has a single hub location representing a person through whom the others must go in communicating with each other. The Alpha, Beta, and Pinwheel networks differ from Comcon in having certain channels restricted to one-way communication, as the arrows indicate. Reviewing a large number of network experiments, Shaw indicates that differences in group performances and participant satisfaction are primarily found between the centralized (for example, Wheel) and the decentralized networks (for

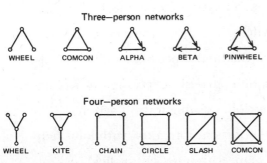

Fig. 15.2. Communication networks of three or four persons as used in experiments on group dynamics. (After Shaw, 1964.)

example, Comcon, Circle). The effect of network on group problem solving is indicated to interact, however, with the complexity of the assigned problem.

Observational category systems

Where a face-to-face interchange takes place among the experimental subjects, the common research practice is to use trained observers to note the various facets of their behavior. These observers cannot be expected to obtain a verbatim record of all discussion. In some cases, tape recording may be employed for this purpose. The observers' task is, rather, to get a record of how the interactions among group members proceed during the session. The specific content of any interchanges of ideas is usually not noted, but attention is directed instead to the nature of the interactions. To accomplish this, the trained observers employ a system of interaction categories which has been prepared to cover most of the aspects of group dynamics.

A set of interaction categories developed by Bales (1950) will acquaint us with some of the features of a systematic observational approach to group dynamics. The trained observers classify every interaction which they note into one of these categories:

1. *Shows solidarity,* raises other's status, gives help, reward.
2. *Shows tension release,* jokes, laughs, shows satisfaction.
3. *Agrees,* shows passive acceptance, understands, concurs, complies.
4. *Gives suggestion,* direction, implying autonomy for other.
5. *Gives opinion,* evaluation, analysis, expresses feeling, wish.
6. *Gives orientation,* information, repeats, clarifies, confirms.
7. *Asks for orientation,* information, repetition, confirmation.
8. *Asks for opinion,* evaluation, analysis, expression of feeling.
9. *Asks for suggestion,* direction, possible ways of action.
10. *Disagrees,* shows passive rejection, formality, withholds help.
11. *Shows tension,* asks for help, withdraws out of field.
12. *Shows antagonism,* deflates other's status, defends or asserts self.

Careful perusal of this list should convince you that an observer would require extensive training and practice before hoping to employ these categories in a reliable fashion. The observations are not oriented toward the content of the group's discussion but toward the social interaction processes which comprise that discussion. Frequency tallies of the different interactions which take place, perhaps taken separately for different time periods, can reveal the quality of the dynamics exhibited by a group and by its individual members. Some groups may be strongly task-oriented and impersonal in their interactions, requiring an observer to make frequent use of Categories 4 through 9. Another group might evidence considerable negative emotionality, causing Categories 10 through 12 to be employed frequently. One individual might be seen in the frequency tallies as one who repeatedly asked questions, Categories 7 through 9, whereas a different person often showed reactions of a positive emotional tone, Categories 1 through 3. The use of the Bales system may be facilitated by the use of a time-marked recording tape as described by Shaw (1966, p. 628) together with other systems for categorizing interaction. Various approaches to observational and recording systems have also been discussed by Steiner (1954).

Ratings

As a substitute or supplement for tallying the occurrence of various interactions, observers of a group may be required to rate the group on certain dimensions. This psychological scaling technique may be directed at the behavior of individuals as well as at the group's functioning. Dimensions of the group that might be rated include morale and degree of task orientation. Aspects of individual participation that might be scaled are amount of leadership exerted and intensity of interest exhibited. Observers' ratings of such a social-psychological trait as group morale can represent a facet of group dynamics that might not be readily apparent in tape-recorded group conversation or even in frequency counts of different interactions of group members. Of course, all the precautions concerning the use of ratings that we discussed in Chapter 6 apply to their employment in group dynamics research. Raters require especially intensive training and practice since they must rate so many aspects of a complex situation that changes moment by moment.

The selection of numerous dimensions to be rated does not mean that interactions between group members need be conceptualized in as complex a fashion as appearances might dictate. Carter (1955) reviewed a number of empirical studies in which the intercorrelations of ratings on various dimensions of individual behavior were examined. Using techniques of factor analysis it was found that about three factors could generally account for an individual's participation in the group session. The factor names which Carter assigned to these three aspects of a person's social behavior are *Individual Prominence*, the tendency to stand out from the group, *Group Goal Facilitation*, the tendency to promote group progress with the assigned task, and *Group Sociability*, a friendly interpersonal relationship to other group members.

Discussion and Decision-Making

A very general question in group dynamics is how small groups operate in carrying out an assigned task as compared with the way the same assignment is handled by individuals, often the same individuals who comprise the experimental groups. Situations requiring decision-making represent favored research tasks for comparing individual decisions with group consensus. Dilemmas where the alternative decisions involved different levels of risk have been posed for subjects in a number of studies. One repeated finding has been that small groups engaged in discussion tend to arrive at collective decisions that are more risky than the average decision earlier favored by the individuals involved. This finding in the group dynamics of decision-making in the face of stated risks has been termed the *risky shift*. In reviewing reported research, Davis (1969, pp. 60–70) points out that the risky shift has not always been observed. With some types of dilemmas presented for consideration, a group consensus has shown a *cautious shift* in a conservative direction. Further, where the risky shift has been observed, different explanations have been offered to account for it. The hypotheses, which are not logical alternatives, have required more experimentation to try to discern the mechanisms that are operating as group members interact. Our illustrative studies will be drawn from separate points in the series of investigations into the group dynamics of discussion with consequent decision-making where risk is involved.

The diffusion-of-responsibility hypothesis

Wallach, Kogan, and Bem (1964) had observed the risky shift in subjects' group consensus in earlier research when they had posed dilemmas for fictional persons in brief narratives. They interpreted their finding as due to the fact that in a group discussion to select a course of recommended action there is a *diffusion of responsibility* for the choice. That is, responsibility is shared by the several group members and this allows each person to accede to a riskier choice than he would make alone if solely responsible. In the previous work only hypothetical risks had been involved. In the 1964 experiment we are to review, real risks involving monetary gain or loss were incorporated in the decision tasks which were posed for the individuals and then for the same subjects performing as a group of three. While expecting the group decision-making to show greater risk-taking, as before, the investigators felt that sharing responsibility for monetary risk that could actually help or hurt the participants would lead to a conservative effect in group consensus. They designed their study to test these two expectations separately and in combination.

The task repeatedly presented to subjects was to choose a difficulty level at which they would face multiple-choice questions taken from old College Board examinations. The risk levels indicated to subjects were based on past administrations of the test. The risk entailed in choosing at a higher difficulty level—before seeing the actual question—was balanced against a greater monetary payoff for more difficult questions. Thus, subjects faced a set of real dilemmas affecting the stipend each would receive. For example, a difficulty level ranging from "10 percent failed" up to "90 percent failed" could be selected with the corresponding reward for a right answer scaled from 17 cents for a low-risk item to $1.50 for the highest risk. After some practice at the task, subjects made 5 choices with their risk levels faced as individuals and then 5 more as group members (except for Condition 1, Control, which continued the individual performance). In the 4 experimental conditions numbered 2 through 5, group decision-making and responsibility for the gain or loss were varied systematically. All 5 conditions are described below. They were administered to groups of 3 college students in each experimental session, men and women students in separate groups so that sex of subject could also be considered as a variable in the study.

Condition 1. Control

The 3 subjects run at any time worked on Sets 6–10 as individuals, just as they and all other subjects had done for Sets 1–5 in establishing baseline data on risk-taking for this task.

Condition 2. Personal Responsibility—Group Decision

All 3 subjects comprising a group had to arrive at a consensus risk or difficulty level for each question topic of Sets 6–10. It was indicated that each individual would then assume personal responsibility for his own monetary gain or loss as he faced the examination questions.

Condition 3. Group Responsibility—Individual Decision

With each individual first choosing his own risk level for the topics, it was indicated that the group as a whole would benefit or lose depending on the question-answering of one subject selected by chance each time.

Condition 4. Group Responsibility—Group Decision—Chance Designation of Responsible Member

A group consensus had to be reached as to the risk or difficulty level to be attempted in Sets 6–10. It was understood that gain or loss would be equal for all members. As in Condition 3, a spinner was used for a chance selection of the person to face the test question in each category.

Condition 5. Group Responsibility—Group Decision—Group Designation of Responsible Member

This treatment was the same as Condition 4 except that each group discussed which member would attempt each category of question in the series.

Since we are not here considering the several content categories for the test questions, we shall examine only the overall shift index, summarized as a mean percent of shift in risk level for each condition when Sets 6–10 were compared with the baseline data of Sets 1–5. The results for male subjects are shown in Table 15.2 with positive values indicating a risky shift toward higher difficulty levels of test item selected.

The shift index of 2.4 in the Control Condition shows that subjects working individually tended to take greater risk as they encountered the second set of 6 items. Condition 2 shows a significantly greater risk level, confirming the investigators' earlier finding that group decision-making involves a risky shift. For Condition 3 a cautious or conservative shift had been expected. Table 15.2 shows that it was indeed found, the shift actually being negative and significantly below the control baseline. The

Table 15.2 Mean Percent Shift in Risk Taking for Male Subjects in Each Condition (After Wallach, Kogan, and Bem, 1964)

Condition	Mean Percent Shift
1. Control	+ 2.4
2. Personal responsibility; group decision	+ 5.6
3. Group responsibility; individual decision	− 1.6
4. Group responsibility; group decision; chance designation	+ 9.4
5. Group responsibility; group decision; group designation	+ 12.5

experimenters were particularly interested in Conditions 4 and 5 which combined the group responsibility and the group decision-making. As separate conditions these showed opposite effects. Would they neutralize each other? The tabled means show clearly that they did not. With group discussion taking place, group responsibility or sharing in outcome seemed to take on a different meaning. It yielded its conservative influence to the effect of group decision-making with a sizeable risky shift being evident for both Conditions 4 and 5. The authors of the report feel that the group discussions led to greater diffusion of responsibility and consequently to an increased risk-taking.

It may be recalled that the data of Table 15.2 covered only the groups comprised of male college students. The women's data showed only that Condition 5 showed a greater risky shift than the other conditions by a significant amount. The investigators attributed the general lack of effect in the female subjects to their lesser concern with the monetary reward aspect of their participation. The report relates this to similar findings in research on motivation.

Familiarization and group discussion

As we have already noted, the diffusion-of-responsibility hypothesis is just one explanation for the risky shift observed when groups discuss risk-taking decisions to arrive at a consensus. Flanders and Thistlethwaite

(1967) experimentally examined another way of explaining how group discussion may lead to a risky shift. Building upon research and analysis by Bateson (1966) they noted that he had found that familiarization through additional study of dilemmas posed for decision had led individual subjects to increase their risk-taking in proposing a course of action. Bateson had indicated that a risky shift might occur after group discussion since this would allow for greater comprehension of the dilemmas being pondered. Comprehension might stem from either group discussion or individual familiarization, his findings had indicated. The research by Flanders and Thistlethwaite which we shall review included a condition in which both familiarization and group discussion were experienced as well as examining these occurrences separately. Before we consider their research design, however, we need to look at samples of the dilemmas posed for subjects by the hypothetical situations that require a risk-taking judgment from them.

Below are given the first 2 of 12 situations devised by Kogan and Wallach and presented in Appendix E of their book (1964) together with Instructions. Five of the situations were used by Bateson and all were used by Flanders and Thistlethwaite in providing the decision-making task for their subjects.

Choice Dilemmas Procedure*

Opinion Questionnaire II

Instructions. On the following pages, you will find a series of situations that are likely to occur in everyday life. The central person in each situation is faced with a choice between two alternative courses of action, which we might call *X* and *Y*. Alternative *X* is more desirable and attractive than alternative *Y*, but the probability of attaining or achieving *X* is less than that of attaining or achieving *Y*.

For each situation on the following pages, you will be asked to indicate the minimum odds of success you would demand before recommending that the more attractive or desirable alternative, *X*, be chosen.

Read each situation carefully before giving your judgment. Try to place yourself in the position of the central person in each of the situations. There are twelve situations in all. Please do not omit any of them.

1. Mr. A, an electrical engineer, who is married and has one child, has been working for a large electronics corporation since graduating from college five years ago. He is assured of a lifetime job with a modest, though adequate, salary, and liberal pension benefits upon retirement. On the other hand, it is very unlikely that his salary will increase much before he retires. While attending a convention, Mr. A is offered a job with a small, newly founded company which has a highly uncertain future. The new job would pay more to start and would offer the possibility of a share in the ownership if the company survived the competition of the larger firms.

Imagine that you are advising Mr. A. Listed below are several probabilities or odds of the new company's proving financially sound.

Please check the *lowest* probability that you would consider acceptable to make it worthwhile for Mr. A to take the new job.

_____ The chances are 1 in 10 that the company will prove financially sound.

_____ The chances are 3 in 10 that the company will prove financially sound.

_____ The chances are 5 in 10 that the company will prove financially sound.

_____ The chances are 7 in 10 that the company will prove financially sound.

_____ The chances are 9 in 10 that the company will prove financially sound.

_____ Place a check here if you think Mr. A should *not* take the new job no matter what the probabilities.

2. Mr. B, a 45-year-old accountant, has recently been informed by his physician that he has developed a severe heart ailment. The disease would be sufficiently serious to force Mr. B to change many of his strongest life habits—reducing his work load, drastically changing his

diet, giving up favorite leisure-time pursuits. The physician suggests that a delicate medical operation could be attempted which, if successful, would completely relieve the heart condition. But its success could not be assured, and in fact, the operation might prove fatal.

Imagine that you are advising Mr. B. Listed below are several probabilities or odds that the operation will prove successful.

Please check the *lowest* probability that you would consider acceptable for the operation to be performed.

_____ Place a check here if you think Mr. B should *not* have the operation no matter what the probabilities.

_____ The chances are 9 in 10 that the operation will be a success.

_____ The chances are 7 in 10 that the operation will be a success.

_____ The chances are 5 in 10 that the operation will be a success.

_____ The chances are 3 in 10 that the operation will be a success.

_____ The chances are 1 in 10 that the operation will be a success.

The task posed in these dilemmas calls for decision-making by the experimental subject with a certain degree of risk attached, the greatest risk (lowest probability of success) that he is willing to accept in recommending alternative X. These same situations may be considered by small groups of subjects as they work toward a consensus decision. The 12 situations were used by Flanders and Thistlethwaite to pretest and to posttest their subjects. Between these tests of risk taking, different subjects were given one of the 4 following treatments, all procedures being made plausible by suitable instructions.

Condition *F*. Familiarization Only

Subjects were asked between the two tests to familiarize themselves more thoroughly with all of the choice dilemmas.

Condition *D*. Discussion Only

In groups of 3, subjects entered into discussion of each situation and arrived at a consensus decision.

Condition *FD*. Familiarization and Discussion

The treatment of these subjects combined those of Conditions *F* and *D*, administered consecutively.

Condition *N*. Neither

Subjects were given no study period or group discussion. After some intervening personality test items the second choice dilemmas testing was given.

Sixty groups with 3 male undergraduates in each reported to the laboratory for this study. The testing with the choice dilemmas was done individually. The group discussions occurred in 15 groups under Condition *D* and 15 under Condition *FD*. Each group's risk score was the arithmetic sum of its members' scores. These individual scores were the "chances in 10" checked for each situation and summed over the 12 dilemmas. A score of 10 was assigned if a subject advised against Alternative *X* no matter what the probabilities. Note that lower scores for an individual or group represent a higher risk since they represent a lesser chance for a favorable outcome. Thus, a downward change in mean score from pretest to posttest represents a risky shift. As Table 15.3 indicates, the experimenters found a risky shift for groups under Conditions *F, D,* and *FD,* but no significant change in risk under Condition *N*.

The measured shifts under Conditions *F, D,* and *FD* were statistically significant but not significantly different from each other. All were

Table 15.3 Shifts in Risk Taking by 15 Groups Under Each Condition (After Flanders and Thistlethwaite, 1967)

Condition	Mean Pretest Score	Mean Posttest Score	Mean Shift*
F	216.3	202.4	− 13.9
D	209.7	200.1	− 9.6
FD	220.3	209.6	− 10.7
N	218.1	219.6	+ 1.5

*Negative values indicate an increase in riskiness, that is, a risky shift.

greater of course than the nonsignificant shift (of opposite sign) found for Condition N. These findings tend to support Bateson's interpretation that greater comprehension of the dilemmas underlies the risky shift seen in posttest responses. This comprehension may be gained in group discussion as seen in the result for condition D. It may also occur without group consultation through individual familiarization as found under condition F. Further, when both familiarization and discussion occur, Condition FD, the effect is not significantly different from Conditions F or D alone. The impact on decision-making seen in the risky shift appears to come from increased comprehension, an individual cognitive process. While group discussion may foster this process, it is not a necessary condition for it. Thus, Flanders and Thistlethwaite argue, the risky shift is not itself the exclusive result of group dynamics as claimed earlier in the diffusion-of-responsibility hypothesis.

Problem Solving

While arriving at a consensus in a decision-making situation is a form of problem solving, there are numerous studies of small-group dynamics which pose more structured problems for solution. We treated the topic of assigned task earlier. Now we shall deal with two studies which examined very different aspects of group functioning—how leadership emerges as group members interact and how the amount of communication among group members affects the solving of a problem. These illustrative experiments are among a vast number of laboratory experiments which require subjects to cooperate in arriving at a solution to a problem posed by research psychologists.

Leadership through competence and conformity

What factors influence the emergence of leadership when a small group of persons interact in solving a problem? Earlier research had shown that the task competence he displayed was one contributor to an individual's acceptance as a leader. This principle was incorporated in a model of emerging leadership formulated by Hollander (1960) together with another mechanism of group dynamics. Hollander felt that conformity to the group's agreed-upon procedures would also contribute to a group member's influence, particularly in early stages of interaction. In later phases of group problem solving, an especially competent member might deviate from acceptable ways of interacting yet still be perceived as a leader. The experiment we are reviewing was creatively designed to test this effect of nonconforming behavior by a competent group member in different phases of group interaction. The central technique of the study was having a confederate serve as an especially competent group member whose conformity or nonconformity was subtly varied as he interacted with different groups of experimental subjects.

Twelve groups of male undergraduates served as the subjects in five-man groups given a problem to solve over a course of 15 trials. The individuals were kept separated from one another as they reported for their research participation. They communicated over microphones and loudspeakers of an electronic network. Only different numbers, for example, "This is Station 2," were used as they identified themselves in dealing with the problems and their procedural rules. The problem to be solved on each trial was for the group to choose one row of the matrix presented in Table 15.4 so as to try for maximum gain when the experi-

Table 15.4 Matrix of Values Used for the Group Problem-Solving Task (After Hollander, 1960)

Row Desig- nations	Column Designations						
	Green	Red	Blue	Yellow	Brown	Orange	Black
Able	−1	−12	+5	−1	−2	+15	−4
Baker	+10	−1	−2	−7	+4	−3	−1
Charlie	−5	+5	−3	+3	−11	−1	+12
Dog	+5	−7	+10	−2	−5	+1	−2
Easy	−4	−1	−1	+1	+13	−10	+2
Fox	−6	+15	−5	−1	−3	−1	+1
George	−1	−1	−2	+10	+4	−2	−8

menter subsequently announced the column which was in effect for that trial. The monetary reward to be shared by group members depended on the points they accumulated over the 15 trials. The confederate, participating at Station 4 or 5, was successful in suggesting the row yielding a high payoff on all but 4 trials (Trials 2, 3, 6, and 12). His comments suggested that he was competently "cracking" the complex system which the experimenter had suggested to be governing the row and column designations on the successive trials. A major indicant of acceptance of this group member as a leader was the number of trials—out of each block of 5—on which his suggested row designation was adopted as the group's problem solution for the trial.

With his evident and increasing competence assured by prearrangement, the key variable in the experiment was the confederate's nonconforming behavior displayed in different time zones of the group's interaction: initial group discussion period on procedures, Trials 1–5, Trials 6–10, or Trials 11–15. Six patterns of his nonconforming behavior (violating agreed-upon procedural rules or suggesting alternative procedures) were used with different groups of subjects. These included a control condition of no nonconformity, noncomformity throughout the experiment, and nonconformity over different blocks of trials: 1–5, 1–10, 6–15, and 11–15. It had been postulated by Hollander that early nonconformity of this group member would reduce his acceptance while late nonconformity would actually enhance his perception as very influential in combination with his demonstrated competence.

The major behavioral test of the hypothesis was established as the mean number of trials in each block for which the different groups chose the row suggested by the confederate as their solution to the problem. These means are arranged in Table 15.5 according to the confederate's behavior during that block of trials and the period immediately preceding it. Based on his demonstrated competence, the confederate's accept-

Table 15.5 Mean Number of Trials on Which a Group Accepted Confederate's Recommended Solution (After Hollander, 1960)

Confederate's Previous Conformity	Time Zone 1 (Trials 1–5)		Time Zone II (Trials 6–10)		Time Zone III (Trials 11–15)	
	Noncon-forming	Con-forming	Noncon-forming	Con-forming	Noncon-forming	Con-forming
WITH procedural nonconformity in immediate past zone	1.67	—	3.25	3.00	4.00	5.00
WITHOUT procedural nonconformity in immediate past zone	—	2.00	5.00	3.75	5.00	4.75

ance as leader clearly increased from the earlier to the later blocks of trials. Statistical analysis also showed a significant effect of the *preceding* period of behavior. If it had been nonconforming, a subject's influence was reduced. However, this prior nonconformity was less hampering to emerging leadership as demonstrated competence continued.

In addition to his obvious impact on group problem solution, the confederate was found to be overwhelmingly seen as principal contributor to group success when rankings were solicited in a postexperimental assessment. He was ranked first by 44 of 48 subjects in "contribution to group activity" and "influence over the group's decisions." Although he was singled out as expected because of the special roles he played, the confederate was manifestly accepted as an authentic group member by the experimental subjects according to Hollander's report of the study. This is attributable to the careful planning and execution of the experiment.

Amount of communication

A general hypothesis that communication among group members facilitates group problem solving was the starting point of the next experiment we shall consider. To test their hypothesis, which appeared consonant with earlier findings by other investigators, McConville and Hemphill (1966) created 3 different conditions encouraging or restraining communication among group members.

No Communication. These 10 groups were shown how to convey their individual solutions of the group problem to the experimenter after each trial. However, group members were not permitted to communicate with each other.

Limited Communication. Members of these 10 groups prepared their solutions for the experimenter, as directed, and sent copies of these brief memoranda to the other 3 group members after each trial.

Free Communication. Members of these 10 groups were allowed to send any written message to any or all of the 3 other subjects after each trial, with a 10-word limit on message length.

Thirty groups of 4 subjects each were comprised of recruits from women's organizations. Their ages ranged from 20 to 60 years. Most were college graduates. When 4 subjects appeared for participation they were ushered into separate booths and requested not to talk during the experiment. In front of each subject was an electrical plugboard containing 25 squares. Each square in the 5 x 5 matrix contained a phone jack and a neon light. When an active plug was inserted into any jack, the corresponding neon light was illuminated on all 4 boards, a subject's own and those of her 3 fellow participants. Each subject had 3 color-coded marker plugs to keep track of the moves of the other group members as they sought to cooperate in solving the problem by inserting an active plug in a designated goal square, *E-1*. A move by any subject, taken in turn, had to be a square adjacent to one already occupied by a fellow player. A certain pattern of moves—5 at the minimum—would solve the problem. Designations on the squares, from *A-1* to *E-5*, permitted subjects to keep track of the moves and to communicate their proposed solutions to the experimenter and, where permitted, to each other after each trial. The experimenter allowed up to 7 moves per trial and gave each group 16 trials unless it earlier solved the problem on 4 successive errorless trials. Since some groups reached this criterion while others did not, a common index of problem solving used in analysis of results was the trial number on which the last error was made. This ranged from 2 to 16 in different groups.

The test of the hypothesis was the trend in group means for the last error trial. It had been expected that the best score (lowest mean) would be made under the condition of Free Communication. No Communication had been anticipated as yielding the poorest score (highest mean). In point of fact, the investigators were surprised to find a reversal in the trend of the three means, as follows: No Communication, 5.4; Limited Communication, 9.9; Free Communication, 8.5. The unexpected trend in group means was found statistically significant through analysis of variance. Faced with their finding, McConville and Hemphill studied the messages sent by group members under the different conditions to try to account for the outcome. The Free Communication groups were found to have sent very few messages which contained problem-oriented proposals for solutions. For the other conditions subjects had been instructed how to communicate their proposed solutions to the experimenter. In sharing these messages with each other some Limited Communication groups appeared to have generated confusion. Having to read each other's solutions created some distraction, the investigators noted. Free from this distraction of receiving messages, often of dubious utility, the No Communication groups proceeded to devote their time to problem analysis and hence eliminated errors earlier. The unexpected experimental outcome emphasizes the dangers in formulating a very general hypothesis on the basis of limited early findings. The type of problem and the type of communication is seen as very crucial in any laboratory study of group problem solving.

Summary

From the complexities of the psychological processes occurring as people meet in groups, research workers abstract certain independent variables and aspects of behavior for special study. Their investigations may sometimes seek principles that can be applied in improving group functioning, or they may be aimed at studying laws of social interaction as a basic contribution to behavior science.

Social processes have been studied by field observation and by sociometry. Another method that has been employed in numerous studies is the group dynamics technique of giving a problem or discussion topic to a group of subjects whose interactions are then carefully observed, perhaps rated. An experimental approach to audience persuasion is made by measuring opinion before and after presenting a persuasive communication to a large group of subjects.

When we investigate the modification of opinion, or overt behavior, through persuasion, we may utilize independent variables from one of three aspects of the situation: communicator, communication, or audience. We are dealing with a research topic of undeniable complexity, and one which will not permit too much simplification. It appears that we need to use many interrelated studies, instead of single decisive experiments, to delineate the social processes which are operative. Proper employment of opinion-measuring techniques is another necessity for success in studying persuasion. Besides the complexities of experimental procedure in this realm of research, we face the need for rigor in the design of our experiments. We must be certain that any observed opinion change is validly attributable to the persuasive communication. Our review of studies illustrated the effects of communicator credibility and amount of opinion change sought; communicator-audience similarity; sex of the communicator; language and logic in the message; level of fear arousal; and forewarning the audience of a persuasive effort.

In group dynamics research, certain aspects of the small-group situation have been singled out for repeated exploration. Size of group, communication net, and assigned task are important ways of introducing independent variables that can serve to reveal some of the intricacies of social processes. The behavior of groups and of the individuals comprising them may be measured by various techniques. Frequency tallies of different interactions are guided by observational categories used by trained observers. Such observers may also rate the behavior of the group and its members.

Our discussion of group dynamics research was augmented by reviewing illustrative experiments. We saw how investigators have studied groups as they engaged in decision-making and problem solving. In group decision-making, our sample of studies was directed at probing the dynamics of how a group shifts to a riskier alternative than they take as individuals. With regard to group problem solving, we reviewed research on the role of the leader as affected by his competence and his conformity to group rules; we also saw that subjects in one experiment seemed unable to take advantage of their opportunities for open communication.

References

Aronson, E., Turner, J. A., & Carlsmith, J. M. Communicator credibility and communication discrepancy as determinants of opinion change. *Journal of Abnormal and Social Psychology*, 1963, **67**, 31–36.

Bales, R. F. *Interaction process analysis: A method for the study of small groups*. Cambridge, Mass.: Addison-Wesley, 1950.

Bateson, N. Familiarization, group discussion, and risk-taking. *Journal of Experimental Social Psychology*, 1966, **2**, 119–129.

Carter, L. F. Recording and evaluating the performance of individuals as members of small groups. In A. P. Hare, E. F. Borgatta, & R. F. Bales (Eds.), *Small groups*. New York: Knopf, 1955. Pp. 492–497.

Davis, J. H. *Group performance*. Reading, Mass.: Addison-Wesley, 1969.

DeLamater, J., McClintock, C. G., & Becker, G. Conceptual orientations of contemporary small group theory. *Psychological Bulletin*, 1965, **64**, 402–412.

Flanders, J. P., & Thistlethwaite, D. L. Effects of familiarization and group discussion upon risk taking. *Journal of Personality and Social Psychology*, 1967, **5**, 91–97.

Freedman, J. L., & Sears, D. O. Warning, distraction, and resistance to influence. *Journal of Personality and Social Psychology*, 1965, **1**, 262–266.

Hare, A. P. *Handbook of small group research*. New York: The Free Press, 1962.

Hollander, E. P. Competence and conformity in the acceptance of influence. *Journal of Abnormal and Social Psychology*, 1960, **61**, 365–369.

Hollander, E. P., & Julian, J. W. Contemporary trends in the analysis of leadership processes. *Psychological Bulletin*, 1969, **71**, 387–397.

Kanouse, D. E., & Abelson, R. P. Language variables affecting the persuasiveness of simple communications. *Journal of Personality and Social Psychology*, 1967, **7**, 158–163.

Kiesler, C. A., & Kiesler, S. B. Role of forewarning in persuasive communications. *Journal of Abnormal and Social Psychology*, 1964, **68**, 547–549.

Kogan, N., & Wallach, M. A. *Risk taking: A study in cognition and personality.* New York: Holt, Rinehart and Winston, 1964.

Leventhal, H., & Singer, R. P. Affect arousal and positioning of recommendations in persuasive communications. *Journal of Personality and Social Psychology*, 1966, **4**, 137–146.

Lott, A. J., & Lott, B. E. Group cohesiveness as interpersonal attraction: A review of relationships with antecedent and consequent variables. *Psychological Bulletin*, 1965, **64**, 259–309.

McConville, C. B., & Hemphill, J. K. Some effects of communication restraints on problem-solving behavior. *Journal of Social Psychology*, 1966, **69**, 265–276.

Mills, J., & Jellison, J. M. Effect on opinion change of similarity between the communicator and the audience he addressed. *Journal of Personality and Social Psychology*, 1968, **9**, 153–156.

Morrissette, J. O., Pearson, W. H., & Switzer, S. A. A mathematically defined task for the study of group performance. *Human Relations*, 1965, **18**, 187–192.

Roby, T. R., & Lanzetta, J. T. Considerations in the analysis of group tasks. *Psychological Bulletin*, 1958, **55**, 88–101.

Sawyer, J., & Friedell, M. F. The Interaction Screen: An operational model for experimentation on interpersonal behavior. *Behavioral Science*, 1965, **10**, 446–460.

Shaw, M. E. Communication networks. In L. Berkowitz (Ed.), *Advances in experimental social psychology*. Vol. 1. New York: Academic Press, 1964. Pp. 111–147.

Shaw, M. E. Social psychology and group processes. In J. B. Sidowski (Ed.), *Experimental methods and instrumentation in psychology*. New York: McGraw-Hill, 1966. Pp. 607–643.

Shaw, M. E., & Wright, J. M. *Scales for the measurement of attitudes.* New York: McGraw-Hill, 1967.

Steiner, I. D. Group dynamics. *Annual review of psychology*, 1964, 15, 421–446.

Vinacke, W. E. Variables in experimental games: Toward a field theory. *Psychological Bulletin*, 1969, 71, 293–318.

Wallach, M. A., Kogan, N., & Bem, D. J. Diffusion of responsibility and level of risk taking in groups. *Journal of Abnormal and Social Psychology*, 1964, 68, 263–274.

Whittaker, J. O., & Meade, R. D. Sex of the communicator as a variable in source credibility. *Journal of Social Psychology*, 1967, 72, 27–34.

Whyte, W. F. Observational field-work methods. In M. Jahoda, M. Deutsch, & S. W. Cook (Eds.), *Research methods in social relations*. New York: Dryden, 1951. Pp. 493–513.

Appendix

Col. 1	Col. 2	Col. 3	Col. 4	Col. 5	Col. 6	Col. 7	Col. 8
3831	7167	1540	1532	6617	1845	3162	0210
6019	4242	1818	4978	8200	7326	5442	7766
6653	7210	0718	2183	0737	4603	2094	1964
8861	5020	6590	5990	3425	9298	5973	9614
9221	6305	6091	8875	6693	8017	8953	5477
2809	9700	8832	0248	3593	4686	9645	3899
1207	0100	3553	8260	7332	7402	9152	5419
6012	3752	2974	7321	5964	7095	2855	6123
0300	0773	5128	0694	3572	5517	3689	7220
1382	2179	5685	9705	9919	1739	0356	7173
0678	7663	4425	6295	4158	6769	7253	8106
8966	0561	9341	8686	8866	2168	7951	9721
6293	3420	9752	9656	7191	1127	7783	2596
9097	7558	1814	0782	0310	7310	5951	8147
3362	3045	6361	4024	1875	4124	7396	3985
5594	1248	2685	1039	0129	5047	6267	0440
6495	8204	9251	1947	9485	3027	9946	7792
9378	0894	7233	2355	1278	8667	5810	8869

*Examples of some uses of a table of random numbers in experimentation are given at the end of this table, beginning on p. 582.

Col. 1	Col. 2	Col. 3	Col. 4	Col. 5	Col. 6	Col. 7	Col. 8
2977	4490	0680	8022	4378	9543	4594	8392
2865	7746	1213	0398	9902	4953	2261	8117
3068	6737	5434	9715	8026	9282	6952	1883
3678	2265	5271	4540	2646	1744	2684	4956
0766	8278	9597	0742	9682	8007	7836	2771
2666	3174	0706	6225	4595	2273	0802	9402
3379	3349	9239	2803	8626	8569	6600	9683
7228	8029	3633	6199	9030	1279	2611	3805
4367	2881	3996	8337	7933	6385	5902	1664
1014	9964	1346	4856	1524	1919	7355	4737
6316	4356	7927	6709	1375	0356	8855	3632
2302	6392	5023	8515	1197	9182	4952	1897
7439	5567	1156	9241	0438	0607	1962	0717
1930	7128	6098	6033	5132	5350	1216	0518
4598	6415	1523	4012	8179	9934	8863	8375
2835	5888	8616	7542	5875	2859	6805	4079
4377	5153	9930	0902	8208	6501	9593	1397
3725	7202	6551	7458	4740	8234	4914	0878
7868	7546	5714	9450	6603	3709	7328	2835
2168	2879	8000	8755	5496	3532	5173	4289
1366	5878	6631	3799	2607	0769	8119	7064
7840	6116	6088	5362	7583	6246	9297	9178
1208	7567	2984	1555	5633	2676	8668	9281
5492	1044	2380	1283	4244	2667	5864	5325
1049	9457	3807	8877	6857	6915	6852	2399
7334	8324	6028	6356	2771	1686	1840	3035
5907	6128	9673	4251	0986	3668	1215	2385
3405	6830	2171	9447	4347	6948	2083	0697
1785	4670	1154	2567	8965	3903	4669	4275
6180	3600	8393	5019	1457	2970	9582	1658
4614	8527	8738	5658	4017	0815	0851	7215
6465	6832	7586	3595	9421	9498	8576	4256
0573	7976	3362	1807	2929	0540	8721	3133
7672	3912	8047	0966	6692	4444	7690	8525
9182	1221	2215	0590	4784	5374	7429	5422
2118	5264	7144	8413	4137	6178	8670	4120
6478	5077	0991	3657	9242	5710	2758	0574
3386	1570	5143	4332	2599	4330	4999	8978
2053	4196	1585	4340	1955	6312	7903	8253
0483	3044	4609	4046	4614	4566	7906	0892
3825	9228	2706	8574	0959	6456	7232	5838
3426	9307	7283	9370	5441	9659	6478	1734

Col. 1	Col. 2	Col. 3	Col. 4	Col. 5	Col. 6	Col. 7	Col. 8
8365	9252	5198	2453	7514	5498	7105	0549
7915	3351	8381	2137	9695	0358	5163	1556
7521	7744	2379	2325	3585	9370	4879	6545
1262	0960	5816	3485	8498	5860	5188	3178
9110	8181	0097	3823	6955	1123	6794	5076
9979	5039	0025	8060	2668	0157	5578	0243
2312	2169	5977	8067	2782	7690	4146	6110
3960	1468	3399	4940	3088	7546	1170	6054
5227	6451	4868	0977	5735	0359	7805	8250
2599	3800	9245	6545	6181	7300	2348	4378
9583	3746	4175	0143	3279	0809	7367	2923
8740	4326	1105	0498	3910	2074	3623	9890
6541	2753	2423	4282	2195	1471	0852	6604
1237	2419	4572	3829	1274	9378	2393	4028
7397	4135	8132	3143	3638	0515	1133	9975
9105	3396	9469	0966	6128	3808	7073	7779
3348	5436	1171	5853	2392	7643	2011	0538
7792	4714	5799	1211	0409	5036	7879	6173
7523	0348	5237	2533	0635	2382	5092	3497
2674	2435	5979	7697	3260	2939	2511	7318
6825	3660	2688	9560	1329	4268	2532	5024
0639	6884	8337	5308	2054	3454	8745	1877
2467	2505	4916	1683	0034	7758	4458	9918
9513	2949	9337	7234	8458	3329	9691	4278
9116	6846	0205	1158	6112	9916	0723	3769
4012	3863	4817	6294	7865	1672	0137	6557
7698	0651	9756	1816	1154	6708	2522	8296
7158	8463	6406	0779	1185	7660	3065	8941
8412	5905	5612	7028	2545	2392	8434	1551
3134	3962	3147	9631	2881	3091	4678	4465
5840	1940	0754	0457	9533	0108	4523	8441
3237	4236	5504	3282	2838	5002	6614	2463
1990	9392	4943	9505	4925	8313	3108	7681
6724	8147	1557	1342	3352	4421	3707	2445
6521	8766	0654	2300	1696	0145	3257	3496
1888	6629	5385	8725	7185	6826	2279	5200
5567	1138	7139	8157	4906	2872	8842	0890
4511	3021	7370	0264	2690	6187	9110	0941
2188	3642	8905	8172	3930	0152	6931	4340
4086	8745	0988	4815	6192	9608	8686	7459
6817	9456	9157	3036	4769	9362	0074	0837
2914	8776	4833	3214	7643	4345	3304	6137
9122	4766	1599	5271	2257	8502	9560	2833

Col. 1	Col. 2	Col. 3	Col. 4	Col. 5	Col. 6	Col. 7	Col. 8
3558	1472	7664	7256	7181	0038	2257	2503
1928	8097	3520	2187	5124	7295	2525	1891
8032	1390	6606	7195	2724	7239	3888	5582
1846	9648	8699	9716	7752	9886	6299	9129
8691	5849	1005	6629	1632	1463	9288	8600
1884	3228	6397	1733	9543	9868	3611	4828
8211	8273	3941	1484	2627	8257	8493	6354
4070	3899	3121	6736	0668	0782	1398	7729
4463	5758	3905	1545	4699	4338	1235	9547
9961	4716	1687	2448	0815	3022	1220	4055
0420	8921	1593	4599	3401	7209	7877	6001
7927	6608	5190	9268	8431	0324	6619	6159
4007	1367	5975	8972	6629	1259	7204	6556
9515	5611	3025	2016	9209	0290	6236	7360
6670	0458	2062	7235	6818	7619	8698	0110
7485	8847	7234	9278	9453	4900	9119	9216
9177	4212	3238	2358	1109	9441	7591	3901

Examples Demonstrating How the Table of Random Numbers May Be Used for Different Purposes in Psychological Research

Example 1. To assign available subjects randomly to treatment groups.

List subjects in any arbitrary way—alphabetically, for instance—and then assign each one a number selected in sequence from any page and column of the Table of Random Numbers—for example, p. 579, Col. 6.

Name	Number	Odd or Even
Adams	1845	Odd
Baker	7326	Even
Cooper	4603	Odd
Davis	9298	Even
Edwards	8017	Odd
Flynn	4686	Even

By flipping a coin, or using some other random method, determine arbitrarily if odd or even numbers are to correspond to the experimental treatment—the other to the control. If, say, even numbers refer to the experimental condition, then Baker, Davis, and Flynn are assigned in our example to this group, the others to the control group.

Of course it is necessary only to use the final digit of the tabled numbers to determine odd or even. Further, if three even numbers should occur for Adams, Baker, and Cooper (as would happen if Col. 3 on the same page had been used), then they comprise one group and Davis, Edwards, and Flynn consequently form the other. Note also that subjects might be given their numbers from a selected column of the table in sequence as they report to participate. When the number of subjects needed in one group is reached, the other group gets the last few subjects required to complete it. Their placement in this group is still determined by chance through the nature of the random series used to assign the earlier-appearing subjects.

If three groups were to be randomly constituted, we might let final digits 1, 2, 3 mean Group *A*, for example. Digits 4, 5, 6 would mean Group *B*, and 7, 8, 9 would mean Group *C*. (This correspondence of digits to groups would ideally be determined randomly in a separate step.) A final digit of 0 would simply be skipped when digits were assigned to the list of names.

Example 2. To put a group of verbal stimulus items in a random order or sequence for presentation to subjects.

List stimuli (for example, the nine High Frequency Words of Category 1 in Table 9.8, p. 323) in alphabetical order and then assign each one a number taken in sequence from any chosen page and column (for example, p. 581, Col. 2, starting about halfway down).

Alphabetized Words	Random Number	Indicated Rank Order (High to Low)
cabin	4714	3
canal	0348	9
decay	2435	8
final	3660	5
honey	6884	1
motor	2505	7
naked	2949	6
robin	6846	2
sugar	3863	4

Using the rank order of magnitude of the assigned random numbers we get a sequence of presentation for the nine words: honey, robin, cabin, sugar, final, naked, motor, decay, canal. Note that we might have decided to use only two-digit numbers, just part of a four-digit column, to achieve our purpose.

There are many different ways to use such a table to accomplish any random grouping or sequencing that is needed. A general rule to follow is to take the numbers from the table in sequence and assign them to the list of subjects or stimuli (or whatever). If, instead, you number the items first and then search the table to see which comes first, second, etc., you may find the task to be unduly time-consuming.

Example 3. To construct a stimulus on a random basis, often with some specified limitations.

(a) Suppose we see how the lower geometric stimulus form of Figure 7.6C on p. 243 was randomly generated. The definitional constraint was that it was to be an eight-unit vertical bar graph with each bar to be one to eight units in height. It was decided to use the first entries of Col. 4 on p. 580—last digits only. The values dictated by this column were 2, 8, 5, 2, 5, 3, 7, 6. These were used, from left to right, in constructing the stimulus form. Digits 0 and 9 were skipped since they were ruled out by the definition of the figure being designed.

(*b*) Single digits and two-digit numbers from a random numbers table were used in generating the CVCVC paralogs of Category 5 in Table 9.8, p. 323. In sequentially forming each paralog by working down a column of random numbers, the experimenter was guided by the set of correspondences tabulated on page 585.

As a specific problem, consider generating a paralog by using the final one or two digits of the first five entries of Col. 1 of p. 580. The needed numbers, in sequence corresponding to the desired CVCVC format, are $77 - 5 - 68 - 8 - 66$. Using the tabulation for consonants and vowels we find that this sequence generates the paralog *wukig*. A limitation which has sometimes been applied is that no consonant or vowel may be repeated within a single paralog.

Finally, note that in these examples the numbers generally used were the first entries at the top of particular columns of the table of random numbers. Obviously a set of random numbers might be selected from any starting point in the table, working systematically in any direction. Beginning at the top of a column is simply a convenience that does not violate the requirement for randomness. Possible difficulty might

*Consonants						Vowels		
b = 11	28	45	62	79		a = 1	6
c = 12	29	46	63	80		e = 2	7
d = 13	30	47	64	81		i = 3	8
f = 14	31	48	65	82		o = 4	9
g = 15	32	49	66	83		u = 5	0
h = 16	33	50	67	84			
k = 17	34	51	68	85			
l = 18	35	52	69	86			
m = 19	36	53	70	87			
n = 20	37	54	71	88			
p = 21	38	55	72	89			
r = 22	39	56	73	90			
s = 23	40	57	74	91			
t = 24	41	58	75	92			
v = 25	42	59	76	93			
w = 26	43	60	77	94			
y = 27	44	61	78	95			

*Consonants j, q, x, and z had been ruled out for Category 5.

arise only if the same column were repeatedly used for a similar purpose in an experiment; this might introduce replication which would not be desirable.

Name Index

Botwinick, J., 357, 387
Bourne, L. E., Jr., 81, 86, 480, 482, 502
Bousfield, W. A., 311, 316, 317, 350, 407,
    409–412, 428, 436
Bower, G. H., 61, 393, 418–419, 436
Boynton, R. M., 81, 86, 218, 226, 236, 262,
    264
Briggs, G. E., 122, 167
Brotsky, S. J., 308, 350
Brown, D. R., 77, 86, 159, 167, 243, 262
Brown, S. C., 340, 350
Brown, W. S., 90, 115
Bruce, D. R., 412–414, 436
Buchwald, A. M., 524–526, 534
Bunsen, R. W. E., 223

Campbell, D. T., 41, 64
Campbell, R. A., 277, 296
Carlsmlth, J. M., 543–546, 576
Carter, L. F., 562, 576
Case, B., 174, 205
Chapanis, A., 20, 32, 215, 262
Chase, A. M., 217, 263
Chatterjea, R. G., 159, 166
Clark, H. H., 477, 502
Clark, K. E., 92, 115
Clarke, F. R., 81, 86, 138, 166
Cofer, C. N., 316–319, 351, 412–414, 436
Cohen, B. H., 315–316, 350, 412, 427, 436
Cohen, J. C., 340, 351
Conrad, R., 419–420
Cook, S. W., 578
Coombs, C. H., 169, 171, 194, 204
Cornsweet, T. N., 122, 166
Corso, J. F., 287, 297
Cox, D. L., 346, 351
Cox, S. J., 510–511, 535
Cramer, P., 300, 316–317, 350
Creelman, C. D., 144, 160, 166, 171, 204
Cronbach, L. J., 22, 23, 32, 252, 262, 331,
    350
Crowley, M. E., 448, 470

Dallenbach, K. M., 123, 166
Dallett, K. M., 452, 470
David, H. A., 193, 204

Davis, G. A., 63, 474, 499–501, 502
Davis, J. A., 562, 576
Dawes, R. M., 59, 64
Dean, S. J., 466–467, 470
DeCroce, C. G., 195, 477
DeLamater, J., 538, 576
Delprato, D. J., 69, 86
Denny, J. P., 22, 33, 60, 252–254, 263
Deutsch, M., 578
Diamond, A. L., 161, 166
DiLollo, V., 160, 168
Dinnerstein, D., 135–137, 166
Dodge, R., 241
Dodson, J. D., 515
Dominowski, R. L., 36, 75, 83, 86,
    495–496, 502
Dukes, W. F., 22, 32, 338–340, 350
Duncan, C. P., 307, 350
Duncker, K., 481, 502

Ebbinghaus, H., 337, 352, 389–390, 437
Ebenholtz, S. M., 337, 350
Edwards, A. L., 174, 204
Edwards, W., 146, 167
Egan, J. P., 81, 86, 138, 166
Egeth, H., 258, 262
Ekman, G., 152, 166, 172, 173, 196–197, 204
Ekstrand, B. R., 36, 83, 341, 350, 353,
    495–496, 502
Eliot, T. S., 544–545
Ellis, H. C., 441, 470
Epstein, S., 508–509, 534
Epstein, W., 337, 350, 433–434, 436
Eriksen, C. W., 243–244, 263

Faust, W. L., 476, 502
Fechner, G. T., 145–146, 168
Feldman, A. S., 276, 297
Fell, J. C., 421–424, 437
Fiske, D. W., 172, 204
Fitts, P. M., 243–244, 262, 356, 359–361,
    362, 382–385, 387
Flanders, J. P., 565–570, 576
Fleishman, E. A., 356, 387
Foss, D. J., 346–347, 351
Foster, H., 448, 470

Sears, D. O., 555–556, 576
Sedgewick, C. H. W., 311, 350, 407, 436
Segal, E. M., 414–415, 437
Segal, S. J., 312–315, 353
Sekuler, R. W., 243–244, 263
Sewall, S. T., 144, 168, 276, 297
Shafer, W., 236, 262
Shapiro, S. S., 308, 353
Shaw, M. E., 81, 87, 543, 559–561, 577
Shea, M., 453–456, 471
Sherman, M. F., 424, 437
Shiffrin, R. M., 392–394, 437
Shuell, T. J., 407–410, 437
Sidowski, J. B., 73, 81, 82, 85–87, 162,
    262, 296, 353, 354, 502, 507
Siegmann, P. J., 94, 115
Silver, M. J., 72, 85
Silverstein, A., 19, 33
Simon, H. A., 20, 33
Simon, J. R., 358, 387
Simpson, C. K., 520–522, 535
Singer, R. P., 551–553, 577
Slamecka, N. J., 337, 353, 459–461, 471,
    482, 503
Slawson, A. W., 276, 297
Slovic, P., 497–499, 503
Small, A. M., Jr., 277, 296
Smith, M. J., 81, 87
Snider, J. G., 322, 353
Spence, J. T., 436–437, 509, 535
Spence, K. W., 436–437, 509, 535
Spielberger, C. D., 22, 33, 60, 252–254, 263,
    535
Spreen, O., 329, 353
Springston, F., 61, 418–419, 436
Stark, K., 84, 402–404, 437
Steiner, G. A., 5, 32
Steiner, I. D., 561, 577
Steinfeld, G. J., 241, 264
Sternheim, C. E., 226, 264
Stevens, J. C., 154, 168
Stevens, S. S., 146–155, 164, 167, 168, 263,
    275, 276, 297, 350
Stevenson, H. W., 70, 87
Sticht, T. G., 293–294, 296
Storms, L. H., 464–466, 471

Strand, B. Z., 317, 351
Suci, G. J., 322, 352
Suedfeld, P., 514–516, 535
Swets, J. A., 138, 144, 167, 168, 276, 297
Switzer, S. A., 558, 577

Tannenbaum, P. H., 322, 352
Tanner, W. P., Jr., 144, 168
Taylor, J. D., 316, 318, 353
Taylor, R. W., 281–282, 297
Teichner, W. H., 368, 388
Thayer, R. E., 510–511, 535
Thistlethwaite, D. L., 565–570, 576
Thorndike, E. L., 253, 264, 318, 324–325,
    329, 341, 344, 353
Thurlow, W. R., 84, 282–283, 297
Thurstone, L. L., 167, 168, 193, 204, 205
Torgerson, W. S., 171, 197–199, 205
Traub, J. F., 90, 115
Treisman, M., 144, 168
Tresselt, M. E., 159, 168, 475, 503
Tulving, E., 254–258, 264, 332, 353,
    415–416, 425–427, 438
Turner, J. A., 543–546, 576
Turvey, M. T., 424, 437
Tyler, F. B., 25, 33

Ulehla, Z. J., 160, 167
Underwood, B. J., 316, 318–319, 325, 329,
    341, 353, 354, 393, 400–402, 410–411,
    436, 438, 489–490, 503

Vale, C. A., 23, 33
Vale, J. R., 23, 33
Vanderplas, J. M., 242–243, 264, 300, 354
Vernon, J., 514–516, 535
Vinacke, W. E., 558, 578
Vitz, P. C., 516–518, 535
Voss, J. F., 337, 354

Walker, E. L., 25, 33, 519–521, 535
Wallach, M. A., 562–568, 577
Watts, T. R., 144, 168
Waugh, N. C., 394, 438
Weber, E. H., 126, 145–146
Wechsler, D., 13

Subject Index

C scale values, 189–190

Card sorting, 364

Category labels, and free recall, 414–415

Category scaling, 155–160, 184–185; *see also* Rating

Cathode ray oscilloscope, 274

Check list, as rating method, 173, 180, 510–511

Children, as subjects, 130, 368, 529–533

Choice Dilemmas Procedure, example, 566–568

Chromatic vision, *see* Color vision

Clustering, in word association, 305–306, 311–312; *see* Free recall

Color vision, chromatic and achromatic colors, 225–226
    experimental methods, 226–234
    fundamentals, 224–225, 234–239
    mixture techniques, 232–234
    stimulus specifications, 226–234

Color wheel, 233–234

Color zones, 235–236

Combination tones, 278

Communication, in science, 82–92; *see also* Group dynamics; Persuasive
    communication; and Speech perception

Communicator, credibility of, 543–546
    sex of, 548

Communicator-audience similarity, 546–547

Comparative judgment, law of, 193–194

Concept identification, example of task in, 474–475
    materials used in, 479–480
    methods of study in, 480, 482
    sample research in, 482–492

Concreteness, of verbal materials, 329, 344–348

Conformity, and leadership, 570–573

Constant error, in illusion, 129–130; *see also* Error

Constant stimuli, method of, 123–125

Constant stimulus differences, 135–137

Contrast, as anchoring effect, 157–158
    in vision, 234–235

Coordinating linkages, in theory, 13

Counterbalancing, 58–59

cps, see Herz

Criterion, in signal detection, 138–144

Cross-modality matching, 154–155

"Crucial" experiments, 28

Cueing, of STM retrieval, 431–434

CVCs and CCCs, as verbal items, 325–329
    in STM, 429–431

CVCVCs, as verbal items, 318, 322–324

Cycles per second, *see* Herz

Subject Index   **597**

Kent-Rosanoff stimulus word list, 300–301
Kinesthesis, 355
Knowledge of results (KR), in concept identification, 482–488, 490–492
    and perceptual-motor memory, 404–406
    in positioning reaction, 359–361, 370–371

Landolt ring, 223–224
Latency, as response index, 83
    of response, *see* Reaction time
Lateralization, in audition, 279–283
Law of comparative judgment, 193–194
Law of effect, *see* Reinforcement
Laws, behavior, 4–10
Leadership, illustrative experiment, 570–573
Learning, perceptual-motor, 368–377, 381–384
    in psychological scaling, 202
    in psychophysics, 162–163
    with response probability as index, 374–377, 529–533
    see also Memory; Transfer; and Verbal learning
Light energy, 210–211
Limen, *see* Threshold
Limits, method of, 119–123, 131–135, 252–258, 291–292
Linguistic parameters, of verbal learning, 346–348
Literature search and retrieval, 92–95
Localization, in audition, 279–283
Long-term memory (LTM), definition, 391–393
    methods, 394–398
    sample studies, 398–406
    see also Memory
Loudness, 274–277
Luminance, experimental control, 220–221
    and luminous activity, 210–211

m, *see* Meaningfulness
Magnitude estimation, 146–147, 150–155, 160
Masking, auditory, 283–287
    visual, 218–220
Massed trials, 372–374
Matched group design, 50, 57–58
Matching groups, study of transfer, 443–444
Maze tasks, 364–365, 374–377
Meaning, 320–322
Meaningfulness (*m*), 99–104, 322–327, 329, 344, 456–458
Measures of behavior, 81–84
Mediation, in STM, 429–431
    in verbal transfer, 464–467

Rating, administrative procedures, 181–186
    data treatments, 181–185
    judgmental tendencies, 175–176
    precautions, 185
    in psychological scaling, 176–186
    in signal detection, 144
    see also Category scaling
Rating scales, aims and approaches, 177–181
    graphic, 179–180
    numerical, 177–179, 185–186
    special, 180–181
    verbal, 177–179, 185–186
Ratio of repetition (RR), 408–409
Ratio of scaling, 146–154, 159–161, 200–201
Reaction time (RT), choice, 358, 377–380, 382–385
    definitions, 357–358
    findings, 357–358, 359–361, 377–380, 382–385
    in word association, 305, 311–312
Reactive inhibition, *see* Fatigue; Massed trials
Reasoning, and syllogism types, 492–494
    tasks, 477, 480
    see also Problem solving
Recall, as measure of memory, 395–396
Receiver operating characteristic (ROC), 141–144
Recognition, as measure of memory, 396, 398
Reductionism, 18–19
Reference sound pressure level, 273
References, form of, 106–107, 110–111
Reinforcement, and motivation, 506, 524–533
    through self-reward, 529–533
    token, 526–527
    verbal, 524–526
    vicarious, 527–529
Relearning, as measure of memory, 396
Repetitive responses, 360–363
Report of research, preparing of, 95–113
    sample, 99–104
Representative experiments, 27–28
Reproduction, method of, 127–131
Research, basic and applied, 76
    introduction, 20–30
    opportunities, 30
    past, as guide, 53–54
    practicality, 44
    and societal needs, 25–26
    and theory, 20–21
    types of, 27–30
Research philosophy, of Ebbinghaus, 389–390